1994

This book, the English translation of *La Culture des apparences* by Daniel Roche, is a study of dress in France in the seventeenth and eighteenth centuries.

Roche discusses general approaches to the history of dress, locates the subject within current French historiography and uses a large sample of inventories to explore the differences between the various social classes in the amount they spent on clothes and the kind of clothes they wore. It is his belief that the choice of clothes, the trade in clothes and the perception of the function of clothing tells us more about the values of a society than the study of any other single commodity; clothes have different uses according to who is wearing them, and in the period under discussion several discrete markets in clothing had already emerged.

Roche's essential argument is that there was a 'clothing revolution' in the later eighteenth century as all sections of the population became caught up in the world of fashion and fast-moving consumption. This was an age of sumptuous fashion gravures and of a new press for ladies of leisure which provided their readers with a stimulating mixture of fashion and public affairs. He demonstrates that this was a period of revolutionary change in the ways in which Parisians thought of dress, for men as well as for women. There was a new concern for decency and respectability as well as a desire to impress.

Taken as a whole, this book is easily the most thorough and wide-ranging study of clothing and its social meaning that has been written to date.

*Past and Present Publications*

# *The culture of clothing*

For a list of titles in Past and Present Publications, see end of book.

# The culture of clothing

*Dress and fashion in the 'ancien régime'*

DANIEL ROCHE

*translated by* JEAN BIRRELL

CAMBRIDGE
UNIVERSITY PRESS

Published by the Press Syndicate of the University of Cambridge
The Pitt Building, Trumpington Street, Cambridge CB2 1RP
40 West 20th Street, New York, NY 10011–4211, USA
10 Stamford Road, Oakleigh, Melbourne 3166, Australia
and Editions de la Maison des Sciences de l'Homme
54 Boulevard Raspail, 75270 Paris Cedex 06

Originally published in French as *La Culture des apparences*
by Librairie Arthème Fayard 1989
and © Librairie Arthème Fayard

First published in England by Editions de la Maison des Sciences de l'Homme and
Cambridge University Press 1994 as *The culture of clothing: dress and fashion in the
'ancien régime'*

English translation © Maison des Sciences de l'Homme and Cambridge University
Press 1994

Printed in Great Britain at the University Press, Cambridge

*Library of Congress cataloguing in publication data*

Roche, Daniel.
    [Culture des apparences. English]
    The culture of clothing: dress and fashion in the ancien régime/
Daniel Roche; translated by Jean Birrell.
        p.        cm. – (Past and present publications)
    Includes bibliographical references.
    ISBN 0 521 41119 X
    1. Costume – France – History – 17th century. 2. Costume – France – History
– 18th century. I. Title.
GT857.R6313    1994        93–29656 CIP
391'.00944 – dc20

ISBN 0 521 41119 X hardback
ISBN 2 7351 0567 9 hardback (France only)

# Contents

# *Plates*

# Tables

# Part 1

## Towards a history of clothing

So you try to best the other 'shoemakers' by building strange
contraptions in your basement?

Walter M. Miller, *A Canticle for Leibowitz*

# 1. *Clothing or costume?*

And they knew that they were naked

Genesis, 3:7

Whilst the last decades of the twentieth century have seen the appearance of museums of fashion, a phenomenon by definition short-lived, historians have yet to think how to write about something other than these sumptuous and insubstantial phantoms. In the history of human appearances, they have always taken pride of place, since, without knowing it, they serve to display power: the ostentatious demonstration of a frivolity seen as the natural expression of an art of living, inaccessible to the majority, becomes the mark of supreme distinction. It is an elusive state, in which the extravagance, the folly and the market and symbolic value of the objects mock ordinary ways and plebeian or vulgar habits. In the world of industrialised consumption, the last refuge of elegance is to wear designer jeans. Fashion actively motivates those who care about appearances; frivolous and volatile, it has always stimulated trade and incarnated change. For the West, it has been a 'mistress of civilisation'.[1]

Let us leave aside, for the moment, this particular history, though without dismissing it entirely; it is not completely trivial, since it is a way of understanding, even regretting, the passage of time. 'Fashion', wrote André Suarès, 'is the best of all farces, where no-one laughs, since everyone takes part' – or almost everyone. There are, perhaps, too many absentees – the less well off, the real poor. To include them, with their costume and clothes, and their bodies, different though gradually transformed

---

[1] F. Braudel, *Civilisation matérielle et capitalisme*, vol. I, *Les Structures du quotidien* (Paris, 1967), pp. 270–5, translated by Sian Reynolds as *Civilisation and Capitalism*, vol. I, *The Structures of Everyday Life* (London, 1981).

3

by 'the shaping of appearances', we need a different type of history.[2]

As in the eighteenth century, let us speak of 'clothes', the word best suited to a social and cultural history of appearances at a time when practices, like social status, were in turmoil. The *Encyclopédie* understood by the word 'everything which serves to cover the body, decorate it, or protect it from harm from the atmosphere'. It preferred the term to *costume*, a word of Italian origin, too ambiguous in its double meaning of custom and dress or way of dressing. Thanks in particular to the use of inventories after death, urban social history has perceived the importance of clothing, less perhaps in patrimonies than in life-styles and human relations. The logic of clothing offers a way of understanding and a means of studying the social transformations taking place within urban melting-pots. From this perspective, the history of material culture and the history of social behaviour are directly linked, as Fernand Braudel has shown.

It is a history less anecdotal than it might appear. It poses all the problems, those of raw materials, of the processes and structures of production, of costs and benefits, of cultural constants and variations in time and space. Clothing, changing at will, everywhere both reveals and conceals social position. One understands how the author of the *Structures du quotidien* found in its history a means of distinguishing the stable societies of the East, conservative in their customs, where change only occurred thanks to major political upheavals, from the unstable societies of the West, variously impelled by the 'follies of fashion'. But an East of calm and stability existed within the turbulent West: 'Our villagers are rather Turkish with regard to fashion', observed Jean-Baptiste Say. The clothes of peasant societies and of the poor, mostly rural in origin, change little, which is not the same as not at all. The aristocratic and urban worlds of the modern period, without wholly abandoning their attachment to the distinctive external signs characteristic of strongly hierarchical societies, were caught up in the wind of change by fashions which innovated and distinguished.

We are today able to carry this theme forward. We should recognise the originality of the approach of Braudel as compared with the immobilism of the traditional history of costume. The

---

[2] P. Perrot, *Le Travail des apparences ou les transformations du corps féminin, XVIIIe–XIXe siècles* (Paris, 1984).

latter's chief landmarks are Quicherat,[3] Racinet,[4] and Boucher,[5] and most work published prior to 1933 is to be found in the massive *Bibliographie générale du costume et de la mode* of René Colas. We can here observe how an object of historical study is constituted. Reading such works, one discovers both backwardness and difficulties. A few recent examples apart, it is a history which has not yet discovered how to respond to the questions which professionals and amateurs have been asking for fifty years.[6]

I believe that a new problematic of the history of clothing is a way of penetrating to the heart of social history. It is another way of posing the essential question: what should be produced? With its train of attendant questions: what should be consumed, what distributed? It is also a good way of trying to observe how the different ideological models which co-exist and compete to regulate behaviour and habits interact in the reality one hopes to attain.

From the seventeenth century, especially after the great movement of religious reflection following the Catholic and Protestant Reformations, clothing was at the centre of debates about wealth and poverty, excess and necessity, superfluity and sufficiency, luxury and adequacy. In the Christian moral vision, both Catholic and Protestant, it served as a means to measure how manners adapted to ethical requirements. For economists who emphasised utility and the motor of consumption, it was still, a century later, the customary example of the human production sought after in order to improve society and life.[7] The history of clothing tells us much about civilisations; it reveals their codes.

In the French society of the *ancien régime*, we thus find two simultaneous discourses. One was of the stationary economy, in

---

[3] J. Quicherat, *Histoire du costume français depuis les temps les plus reculés jusqu'à la fin du XVIIIe siècle* (Paris, 1879).

[4] A. Racinet, *Le Costume historique avec cinq cents planches chromolithographiques* (Paris, 1875–88).

[5] F. Boucher, *Histoire du costume en Occident, de l'Antiquité à nos jours* (Paris, 1967, 2nd edn 1985).

[6] In particular, Y. Deslandres, *Le Costume image de l'homme* (Paris, 1976); F. Piponnier, *Costume et vie sociale, la Cour d'Anjou, XIVe–XVe siècles* (Paris, 1970); P. Perrot, *Les Dessus et les dessous de la bourgeoisie* (Paris, 1981).

[7] I would particularly like to thank here J.-C. Perrot. For examples of texts, see J.-G. de Villethierry, *La Vie des riches et des pauvres ou les obligations de ceux qui possèdent les biens de la terre ou qui vivent de la pauvreté, prouvé par l'Ecriture* (Paris, 1710); Boisguilbert, *Oeuvres* (Paris, 1966); A. Morizet, *L'Apologie du luxe et le mondain de Voltaire* (Paris, 1909).

which everyone had their place and ought to consume according to their rank, where clothing revealed status. Since Erasmus, this had been the basis of the rhetoric of the *civilités*, or manuals of 'good manners',[8] very different from etiquette, where everything concerning clothes characterised, both morally and socially, a type of conduct, that of civil decency. Clothing was 'the body's body, and from [it] one may infer the state of a man's character'.[9] If, in the more worldly texts on this theme which proliferated in the eighteenth century (from whose titles the word *civilité* had often disappeared), the manners taught were those of the gentleman rather than the universal Erasmian Christian, dress still revealed 'the harmony of the inner and the outer man';[10] everyone should regulate their conduct according to the norms appropriate to their occupation or class. A fundamental tension was thus gradually created within baroque and classical society, which saw appearance and reality opposed in social life.[11] It needed all the modesty of a La Salle to return to the Erasmian tradition and rediscover in clothing the proof of moral health, now reconciled with respect for social rank. 'Negligence in dress is a sign of neglect of God's presence, or of insufficient respect for Him; it also reveals a lack of respect for one's own body, which should be honoured as the animate temple of the Holy Spirit, and the tabernacle where Jesus Christ is good enough often to repose.'[12]

In contrast, the practitioners and interpreters of fashion exalted the desire of the privileged, true or false, to distinguish themselves from lesser mortals. Clothes became weapons in the battle of appearances. They were employed to erect a barrier, to stave off the pressure of imitators and followers who must be kept at a distance, and who always lagged behind in some nuance in the choice of colour or way of tying a ribbon or cravat. In a world ruled by the conventions of fashion, innumerable signs thus helped

---

[8] R. Chartier, 'La civilité entre distinction et divulgation', in *Historische Lexicon der Politish Sozialen Grundbegriffe in Frankreich von Ancien Régime zur Revolution, 1680–1820* (Munich, 1986).

[9] Erasmus, *De civilitate morum puerilium* (pp. 269ff. of translation by B. McGregor in *Collected Works*, volume xxv).

[10] A. de Courtin, *Nouveau Traité de la civilité qui se pratique en France parmi les honnêtes gens* (Paris, 1671), p. 29.

[11] Chartier, 'La civilité', p. 13.

[12] J.-B. de La Salle, *Les Règles de la bienséance et de la civilité chrétienne* (Rheims, 1703), pp. 61–2.

everyone to find their way. But the spectre of the confusion and usurpation of values was then raised. For this, towns proved increasingly fertile ground. In his *Tableau de Paris*, Louis Sébastien Mercier devoted himself to tracing the signs of these shifts and displacements, whose driving forces were imitation and social mobility and whose result was a society less easy to read and a more complex hierarchy of values. Fashion existed in a niche between mimetism and protectionism.

We should remember that a whole economy and a whole society were dependent on it – manufacturers and merchants, the development of new patterns and fabrics, the new shapes and arrangements which were both cause and consequence of sartorial competitiveness. We see here how the real and the imaginary are imbricated in the history of clothing. On both levels, which must be compared without creating false opposites, since reality is a factor in the imagined, and the imagined contributes to reality, we must try to link dialectically ideas and manners, practices and images. This is our first difficulty.

A second quickly emerges when we look at the specific sources for the history of clothing. We need to spend some time on these, since the critical spirit dear to the historian cannot but help to convey how the subject of this research has been constructed. For convenience, we can employ five documentary categories: the clothes themselves, the textiles, pictorial sources (which will be discussed at some length), the sources for family, commercial and social history, and the philological sources.[13]

## CLOTHES AS DOCUMENTS: FROM ARCHIVES TO ICONOGRAPHY

As an original and direct source, we must look at old clothes. How can we appreciate the effects evoked or described in the written sources without trying to see them in the flesh? But two questions are posed by every collection of costume and museum of fashion: what is preserved, and what can be preserved?

Old fabrics are rare and fragile, and though specialists can work wonders in the way of restoration, clothes from before the end of the seventeenth century are rarely on display. Further, it is essentially

[13] Deslandres, *Le Costume*, pp. 19–35, is the best introduction to the documentary problems.

outer garments which have been preserved. Linen is extremely rare in museums. Yvonne Deslandres is proud of her collection of forty shirts from the eighteenth century, whilst her colleagues in the Victoria and Albert Museum have only one! What we find is fine linen, usually recovered from châteaux, which tells us little about the normal practice of re-use and alteration characteristic of societies of scarcity and peasant life. In a word, direct historical access is socially biased, consisting mainly of aristocratic dress and fine garments, with very few ordinary clothes. They remain, for all that, fundamental, 'since the information they provide cannot be found in any document'.[14] They make it possible to flesh out the dry bones of the archival sources, to discuss shapes, the use of fabrics, the decoration, the variety of cut, the use of embroidery and buttons. They reveal the gap between image and reality. Above all, by a visual education, they teach the distance and the difference between the clothes of the past and our own.

The study of fabrics is inseparable from that of surviving clothes and suffers from the same limitations. Moths love wool, and their centuries of feasting have spared little of the vast quantities of cloth woven, cut and made up in the modern period; whereas silks, cottons, linens and canvas resist better, which gives a festive, or a rural, or a summery air to the collections on display. For a deeper understanding, a knowledge of textiles and all the materials of dress is indispensable, since we need constantly to compare the fabric and the garment whose approximate date and social trajectory is known.

Statistics for the economic history of cloth manufacture, the wool trade, the spread of cottons, the rise of silks or the stability of linen are not unduly hard to find. But economic historians deal more with production and manufacture than with trade. Huge areas remain untouched – the processing of fabrics, consumption and markets, the relationship between the market and family consumption. The direct study of fabrics and materials raises questions about social habits of use, seasonal variations and levels of production. Further, it is important to compare illustrations and surviving fabrics. The original material sheds new light on artistic representations, whilst the pictures sometimes make it possible to identify fabrics or analyse their cut and the techniques of home manufacture.

---

[14]  Ibid., p. 24.

The value of Marie Risselin-Steenebrugen's study of the lace in Flemish portraits of the sixteenth and seventeenth centuries becomes apparent.[15] The taste for white linen was a characteristic of the patriciate of the Low Countries. In the paintings, it suggests the wealth of fields of blue flax in spring flower, the skill of workers, the dexterity of lace-makers and the domestic accomplishments of good wives. A series of well-dated portraits makes it possible to trace in detail the evolution of the lace and embroidered white linen which, in a variety of forms – ruffs, collars, sleeves, coifs and the trimming of aprons and caps – gradually became a principal motif of the artists. Impeccably executed, delicate and transparent, exploiting the contrast between the stiff shapes, sober costume and black clothes and the dazzling white linen, skillfully worked in Flemish needlepoint, the paintings testify, through the evolving styles, to the triumph of a controlled luxury. Between the modest fragment of lovingly preserved lace and the striking decorative forms in the paintings of clothes, a suggestive exchange is initiated. The means of perceiving the difference between image and practice, the fabrics make it possible to question a subtle language.[16]

PAINTINGS AND ENGRAVINGS OF CLOTHES

With pictorial sources we are on more familiar ground. Sculpture, paintings, drawings, engravings, even money and seals, appear to be a convenient substitute for the clothes we have lost. They portray them both worn and dated. But here, too, there is a problem of bias, since pictures of the great are more accessible than those of the poor, though the latter exist. At a deeper level, the conventions and the significations of the image mean that the work of art is a far-from-simple document. This specificity has to be taken into account in the same way as the literarity of fiction. The clothing portrayed had a role to play within the perspective of a dramatisation of gesture and body; it was sometimes used to support an idea which can only be understood by external reference. The peasant or citizen clothing in genre paintings, from Le Nain to

[15] M. Risselin-Steenebrugen, 'La Dentelle dans les portraits en Flandres du XVIe et XVIIe siècles', in *Actes du 1er Congrès international d'histoire du costume*, Venice, 1952 (Paris, 1955).
[16] P. Hugues, *Le Langage des tissus, textiles, arts, langage* (Paris, 1982).

Chardin or from Greuze to Boilly, was intended to convey a realism which is opposite and symmetrical to the idealisation found elsewhere. Much remains to be done in this field if we are to progress from exemplary illustration to a more systematic, perhaps even a quantitative, approach. This is beyond the scope of our study. However, it suggests a twofold approach – the study of shapes and that of colours.

Every element in paintings, tapestries and sculpture can be revealing. The 4,000 *ex votos* collected by Bernard Cousin call into question the stability of the rural and bourgeois clothing of ancient Provence.[17] This is one way, amongst others,[18] of approaching the problem of regional dress. This theme, always counterposed to a national history identified with the history of elites, valorises immemorial age and immobility. The folklorists of the nineteenth century, to some degree fabricating provincial traditions, emphasised the beautiful exceptions at the expense of the norm. The history of Arlesian costume is a case in point. The study of the little pictures offered to Provençal churches makes plain that everyday costume was less exceptional and elaborate and, above all, that it was not immune to history. Influenced not so much by fashion as by the major changes in male and female dress, it exhibits few regional characteristics, except at Arles itself. The *ex votos* show the social nuances of appearance in the way items and accessories are deployed, and in revealing signs – the man's hat whose shape was a criterion of distinction, the woman's apron whose presence or absence had connotations of labour.[19] Paintings also allow us to study the history of colour in clothes.

'Cloth and colour make the man of honour.' In paintings we can study the use of dyestuffs, the evolution of techniques, the relationship to shapes and circumstances of use and symbolic functions. Together with the lessons of heraldry and religious and love poetry, the colours of the painted clothes offer a new key to understanding. First, colour was one of the principal elements of 'court civilisation', an obligatory reference conveyed in numerous texts beginning with the tradition of Renaissance Italy and the translation of Castiglione's *Courtier*, immortalised in an unforgettable portrait by

[17] B. Cousin, *Le Miracle et le quotidien, les ex-voto provençaux image d'une société* (Paris, 1983).
[18] See the works of Nicole Pellegrin.
[19] Cousin, *Le Miracle et le quotidien*, pp. 214–21.

Raphael. 'Colour makes it possible to attract people's attention just as a magnet attracts iron filings', said Ariosto. Colour was also a way of interpreting the social theatre. It indicated function, situation and rank. The judge drawing up an instrument outside the lawcourts or in ordinary session might wear a black gown; pronouncing judgement, he donned the solemn gown of red. From regimental uniforms to the habits of fraternity penitents, past society offers many variations on the theme of colour; it might be forbidden or imposed by sumptuary laws, or dictated by convention, status and role in time: the colours of marriage and mourning, or of the scaffold and ceremony.

Past society attached more importance than our own to colour and adornment in both ordinary and extraordinary life. But the values of the eye were not reserved only to the rich and the powerful; by complex channels, such as the redistribution of the clothes of masters, they reached the lower classes. Thanks to painting, they form a chapter in the history of sensibility and perceptions.

COLLECTIONS OF COSTUME

Among pictorial sources, engravings and prints deserve special mention. They were much more plentiful than books and, of course, than paintings and sculpture. Loose pictures are recorded in more than 50 per cent of eighteenth-century Parisian inventories. They were a basic instrument in the wide diffusion of norms, patterns, processes and styles. The support suggests both utility and dreams. Thus was born the 'fashion plate'. Its diffusion was accelerated by the ability of the printer–editors of the Renaissance to devise and reproduce these collections or *recueils de costumes* (note the double meaning – costume and custom – of the title). Jacqueline Tuffal has counted more than 200 for Europe as a whole for the period 1520–1610.[20] Their rate of production in France from the sixteenth to the eighteenth centuries can be traced in part thanks to Colas' bibliography, though it omits innumerable pamphlets and brochures printed in every European centre. Minimum figures for published books are given on p. 12.

---

[20] J. Tuffal, 'Les Recueils de costumes gravés au XVIe siècle', in *Actes du 1er Congrès international d'histoire du costume*.

*Books on clothes published in French
from the sixteenth to the eighteenth
centuries*

| Date | Number published | % |
|------|------------------|---|
| Before 1600 | 6 | 5 |
| 1600–49 | 16 | 11 |
| 1650–99 | 10 | 6 |
| 1700–49 | 19 | 12 |
| 1750–99 | 98 | 66 |

On the basis of the titles alone, we can identify different categories of text, distinguished by format, size and function. A more detailed study remains to be done, but the figures illustrate well enough for France their increasing popularity and increased production. The figures for new editions would show this even more clearly.

Before 1600, we need to add a profitable output in Latin inspired by several models: Lazarus Baïf, Bertellius (*Omnium gentium habitus*, Venice, 1563) and Abraham Bruyn, whose treatise of 1576 ran to over ten editions. To these scholarly *De re vestiaris* were added further works published in every western language. It amounted, in fact, to an international debate, extending to England, Germany, Italy and the Low Countries. Its success was probably a direct consequence of the many levels at which these books could be read: in order to learn about, copy and re-invent original models, for pleasure or for instruction. The genre was both an aspect of the humanism of curiosity and part of the effort to classify creatures and things found in other spheres, whose political significance has still to be explained.

Costume and its diverse representations thus took their place in the gallery of marvels of nature and prodigies of human creation. In 1562, the little volume of François Desprez, *Recueil de la diversité des habits qui sont à présent en usage tant es pays d'Europe, Asie, Afrique*, included 120 engravings accompanied by quatrains.[21] Among them were portraits of *The President, The Italian Woman, The Citizen of Paris, The Citizenness of Paris, The Old Citizen, The*

---

[21] N. Pellegrin, 'A propos des classifications et des représentations des costumes régionaux français', in *Vers une anthropologie du vêtement*, Colloque, Musée de l'Homme (Paris, 1983).

*Knight of the Order* and *The Gentleman*, but also *The Englishwoman*, *The Woman of Picardy*, *Mourning*, *The Woman of Lyons*, *The Seafaring Monk*, *The Standing Monkey*, *The Cyclops*, *The Spanish Monk* and so on. Here, in his library, the person of enquiring mind discovered a strangeness and an exoticism in which dress was one element amongst others to mark and ponder. It reflected the variousness of things and human diversity.[22] It is not unreasonable to see the birth of modern states as encouraging a desire to describe and find a way of organising the world theatre. In the diversity of divine creation, in the infinite variety of habits and manners, in the multiplicity of ranks, professions and adhesions, national stereotypes identified by dress were a way of identifying oneself:

> This is what an Englishwoman wears
> See how her square cap is lined with furs
> She is still easy to recognise
> Though we can hardly see into it, so great is its size.

This brief description resembles the stereotyped descriptions of customs and costumes which can be read in travellers' tales. They created an impression and established a difference, but they also revealed what was expected. In the open book of the world, these collections allowed a reading of society whose truth is to be sought less in terms of an illusory and always fleeting reality than in the exploitation of wonder and the creation of a discourse on otherness.[23] The history of clothing was not far off.[24]

Between the seventeenth and the eighteenth centuries, one can detect two phases in the rate of production of books on costume, along with a change of tone and a reorganisation of the genre. Up to 1750, output was modest, with a new title every ten years or so. Their readership was probably limited, consisting of aristocrats of enquiring mind, high-ranking professionals and artists in search of models. At the end of the seventeenth century, a change is visible, as French fashions triumphed and loose pictures and fashion plates became increasingly numerous, copied by the almanacs, widely circulated and pirated. Both general and specialised collections were produced in greater numbers. With Sébastien Leclerc, the

---

[22] P. Falguière, 'Collections encyclopédiques à l'âge maniériste', *Milieux* (1984).

[23] F. Hartog, *Le Miroir d'Hérodote* (Paris, 1980).

[24] J.-L. Nevinson, 'L'Origine de la gravure de mode', in *Actes du 1er Congrès international d'histoire du costume*.

Bonnards, Bérain, Lepautre and Gravelot, engravings of dress often verge on great art. They were one of the signs of French hegemony in Europe.

After 1750, collections of French costume proliferated; 66 per cent of known titles were published after that date and distributed throughout Europe and the world. This explosion suggests a major change in their readership, confirmed by the number of new editions. Far from stopping in 1789, it continued throughout the revolutionary period, expanding further after 1800. As in the previous period, before the crisis of the *ancien régime*, the editors turned their hands to everything: illustrated treatises, booklets of clothed figures, collections of fashion, history books, specialised series. The almanacs exemplify this evolution; in small format, accessible to all, they disseminated the new practices and encouraged dreams of elegance. For example, the *Etrennes chantantes*, edited by Desmos in 1780 in decimo-octavo format, consisted of twenty-four plates with couplets which were intended to be sung and which evoked the tastes of the day, 'enhanced by the most elegant new hairstyles and the clothes now most worn'. The *Cris de Paris*, some sets of which were engraved by the best artists, including Boucher, Bouchardon, Cochin and Poisson, were part of this vogue, inspired by the intense desire to portray the clothes of rich and poor.[25] We will return to the simultaneous explosion of the fashion press characterised by a proliferation of titles, their ephemeral nature and their directly cosmopolitan dimension.[26]

The collections of engravings made in the century of the Enlightenment confirm the persistence of a civilisation of images never wholly dethroned by language or words. Their study, from the double perspective of a history of books and a history of the civilisation of manners, remains to be undertaken. *La Gallerie des modes*[27] of Mme Lebeau, probably the finest of all these collections, has never been studied in detail. However, with its 436 plates, published in albums of from three to six leaves, it is the prototype of the exemplary labour of an editorial team assembled by the

[25] V. Milliot, 'Les Cris de Paris, XVIe–XVIIIe siècles', mémoire de DEA, Paris 1 (1985).

[26] C. Rimbault, 'La Presse féminine de langue française au XVIIIe siècle', thèse de 3e cycle, EHESS, Paris (1981).

[27] Paris, 1778–88. See F. Tetart-Vittu, 'La Gallerie des modes et le costume français', *Nouvelles de l'estampe*, 9 (1907), pp. 16–20.

increasingly rapid dynamic of changing fashion. Renowned engravers such as Bacquoy, Duhamel and Dupin collaborated to make the plates from the drawings of famous artists who included Leclerc, Desrais, Martin, Saint-Aubin and the great-nephew of Watteau. From 1778 to 1788, the publication of Mme Lebeau was a major undertaking for the bookseller-printers Dupin and Rapilly, of the rue Saint-Jacques. Connoisseurs and professionals found in them every type of hairstyle and dress. The plates portrayed a range of social situations (*The Little Master in a Hat, The Governess*), some high-class exoticism (gowns *à la circassienne*, even *à l'australienne*), and the political endorsement familiar from contemporary publications (*The King, The Queen, The Royal Family*). The modernity of the collection is undeniable. It was a milestone in the perception of the evolution of habits.

The *Monuments du costume* of Rétif de La Bretonne are better known.[28] For the historian of clothes they have a double interest: they show the importance of fashion to the pre-Revolutionary book trade, both French and international, thus how the media contributes to the shaping of tastes and manners; and they raise questions about the best method of approach to the relationship between clothes and customs, image and text.

Between 1774 and 1793, some fifteen editions, consisting of successive additions, partial re-uses and modifications to the order of the text and the pictures, of a complexity which defies comment in the absence of a definitive study, testify to the interest of Parisian booksellers and the foreign counterfeiters of Neuwied and Neuchâtel. Many well-known specialists and engravers were employed, including Freundenberg of Berne and Moreau le Jeune after 1776. Gradually, the tone and the orientation of the work changed. It was originally a de-luxe album portraying the practices, furnishings and clothes in vogue in high society. The announcement of the 1777 edition is quite specific: 'We have tried to show celebrated personages as well as the clothes and furniture in fashion during the course of the years 1775 and 1776.' It was thus a catalogue useful for its scope and precision to those working in the

---

[28] P. Testud, *Rétif de La Bretonne et la création littéraire* (Paris/Geneva, 1977); Lacroix, *Bibliographie des oeuvres de Rétif de La Bretonne* (Paris, 1875); J. Riveschild, *Rétif de La Bretonne, témoignages, jugements, bibliographie* (Paris, 1949); C. Bertrand, *Les Monuments du costume de Rétif de La Bretonne, XVIIIe siècle* (1983).

luxury trades: genre painters, cabinet-makers, tailors, hairdressers, fashion merchants, linen-drapers and dressmakers. The editor expressed this purpose clearly as 'presenting the forms which have recently been given to all the furniture and ornaments we use, materials, trimmings'. But its role changed, and the simple history of costume became the history of manners since 'a story [the caption] accompanies the subject of each picture to portray the history of manners in parallel with the annals of fashion'. Rétif was probably involved in the 1786 Neuwied edition, whose text is also attributed to the prince de Ligne; then in 1789, the year of publication, also at Neuwied, of the *Monuments du costume physique et moral*. This was a large folio volume containing twenty prints and some thirty pages of text. Behind the new direction taken by the publication was a curious amateur editor, Eberts, a banker and a man of taste and the theatre, a witness to the thirst for knowledge of a class of cultivated dilettantes.

C. Bertrand, who has made a careful study of the way in which pictures and text were re-employed, has shown how Rétif used the fashion plate to illustrate his general reflection on contemporary manners, so that the *Monuments du costume* cannot be understood without reference to this ideological charge. As they change from worldly illustration to teaching about habits, the pictures change their titles – *The Opera* becomes *The Goodbyes* – and their order subverts the worldly interpretation. Overall, it tends to erect a monument to the glory of a certain image of woman and her social role. From marriage to motherhood, it is also an image of an aristocratic life which was moral in spite of profane temptations and the vanity of the age. The women's clothing only makes sense in the context of customs and moralising reflections, despite the voyeurism and eroticism which inspired Rétif. The themes of the stories in the *Monuments du costume* are those of all his work, found also in the *Famille vertueuse, Les Contemporaines* and, later, in the *Année des dames nationales*. A rereading of this whole fictional, printed oeuvre suggests the presentation of types of behaviour, the importance of social markers, unease at the confusion of ranks and the definition of a vision revealing norms and habits in ways of dressing. It is at the same time a repertoire of ways of acting, an education in manners, a catalogue of symbolic practices and a reflection of Rétif's social seductions and obsessions.

The historian is equally interested in the audience for such works. For the most part, they were expensive and luxurious publications, and it is hardly surprising to find that they appealed to a wealthy and privileged readership. The first series of the *Monuments* cost 36 *livres*, and subsequent editions in the region of 50 *livres*, that is, equivalent to between forty and sixty days' work. But beyond the world of the amateur and the elegant, one can discern a wider circulation amongst professionals of fashion, journalists, men of taste, even the servants in great households. In 1788, the editor of the *Magasin des modes françaises et anglaises* refused to send extra copies to his subscribers because 'it is not fair that if shop assistants, porters and servants make off with copies we should have to supply them twice'. This lengthy foray into the pictorial sources has the value of showing how social representations have a constitutive role in matters of dress.

CLOTHES IN LITERATURE AND THE ARCHIVES

The other sources can be discussed more briefly. There is abundant material in the various documents familiar to social, family and economic historians. The archives of merchants and manufacturers await systematic study. This backwardness, due in part to the difficulty of reconstructing the equivalent of true business archives in an age of proto-industrialisation, is unfortunate. For certain trades – tailors, dressmakers and second-hand clothes dealers – the Parisian notaries' registers yield only limited information about their economy, but make possible a preliminary reconstitution of their activities; when compared with records of bankruptcies, in spite of a certain bias, they throw light on the world of production and trade.

The immensity of the task to be accomplished is sufficient explanation for the limited nature of this study. Above all, it only makes sense within the perspective of a study of social consumption. This can be examined in family papers. The inventory after death, to which we will return, provides a tool of debatable but, when all is said and done, reasonably high, value.[29] We have used over

---

[29] For the notarial sources, see *Les Actes notariés, source de l'histoire sociale, XVIe-XIXe siècles* (Strasburg, 1979); D. Roche, *Le Peuple de Paris* (Paris, 1981), translated by Marie Evans in association with Gwynne Lewis as *The People of Paris* (Leamington Spa, 1987).

1,000 of them for Paris, 500 for the end of the seventeenth century, 500 for the eve of the Revolution,[30] on which some general conclusions can be based. They need to be supplemented, as far as possible, by family record and account books, invoices and sometimes correspondence. Inasmuch as 1,000 inventories represent a sufficient statistical base, we are able to draw up an inventory (though one difficult to qualify by age) of the possessions and principal consumption of the whole population of eighteenth-century Paris. We can make a preliminary survey of the use and care of clothes, especially among the well-off. As always, this type of source is less informative for the majority of the population; nor does it help us to proceed from a functional reading to a symbolic interpretation. The essence of the ownership of things risks eluding the history of the lower classes. At all events, we can discern its features only through mediations which have a coherence which needs to be interrogated.

Lastly, we can draw on the by-no-means negligible printed and philological sources. It is essential to consult dictionaries; reading them throws light on lost forms and ancient practices. Clothing occupies such an important place in the *Encyclopédie* of Diderot and d'Alembert that it demands special consideration.[31] The same is true of fiction, where major novelists and mediocre writers alike could use reality and appearance as the theme of intrigues. Marivaux and Rétif deserve special mention. For this, we have to accept the meaning delivered by the texts, since, like the artist, the novelist provides information about ways of life because he places objects in a context, so conferring on them a different truth from

---

[30] See the following mémoires de maîtrise, all Paris 1 unless otherwise stated: F. Ardelier, 'Essai d'anthropologie urbaine au XVIIIe siècle, les domestiques parisiens d'après les inventaires après décès', Paris 7 (1977); R. Arnette, 'Les Classes inférieures parisiennes au XVIIIe siècle', Paris 7 (1977); I. Levêque, 'Les Vêtements de la bourgeoisie parisienne marchande et rentière au début du XVIIIe siècle, 1695–1715' (1980); P. Maillard, 'Contributions à l'histoire du costume dans la noblesse parisienne à la fin du XVIIIe' (1979); B. Merz, 'Le Costume des bourgeois parisiens de professions libérales' (1983); P. Moreau, 'Le Vêtement dans le monde de la boutique et de l'artisanat parisien, 1780–1790' (1980); D. Kalifa, 'Le Costume dans la petite bourgeoisie artisanale et marchande parisienne, 1695–1715' (1980); C. Peneau, 'Le Costume dans la noblesse parisienne au début du XVIIe siècle' (1982); S. Rouyre, 'Le Costume dans la bourgeoisie des professions libérales parisiennes, 1700–1715' (1983).

[31] D. Pierre, 'Le Système du vêtement dans le *Dictionnaire raisonné des Arts et Métiers*', mémoire de maîtrise, Paris 1 (1983).

that discovered by the deciphering of archives. As Nicole Pellegrin has shown, fiction achieves authentic effects both by the truth of the descriptions and by their location within a story which has a logic which reveals forms of reasoning and structures of the imagination of an age.[32] In the amicable quarrel over the use of texts between literary scholars and historians, this median position must be retained. Certainly, the works never coincide with the gaze directed at the world and at things, in a reality now gone for ever, by the characters put into writing or onto the stage. The writers speak in their place. The relationship to reality is central to the fictional characters, but they also make possible a reading of social values and practices in the very codes which organise the fictions and are part of the communication of the age. For the historian of society and culture, it is less a matter of achieving an illustrative metatext on the basis of the original text of the novels, or of assembling from between them the *realia*, than of understanding the signifying elements of the story and their logic. Thus reality interrogates fiction.[33]

An initial analysis, in which Nicole Pellegrin's study of the *Francion* complements my own study of several texts used in my *Peuple de Paris*, brings out the importance accorded in novels to the function of social markers, whose nature may relate to class, nationality, occupation or age. Past society was in part dependent on this clarity of adhesion, and its stability was realised in the transparency of appearance. But novels also reveal the role of the imagination and the ways in which an identity can disguise itself. In the *Francion*, in its way an expression of the norms of classical society, the conduct of intrigue through the donning of a succession of outfits reveals the desire to make appearance and reality coincide, hence to condemn usurpations of social status. In the novels of the eighteenth century, where the desire to denounce the town and its temptations influenced both the very greatest writers, such as Marivaux, and writers of the second rank, the phenomena of the transmission, acquisition and imitation of sartorial acts and practices, ends up, against expectations, by acquiring a positive value.

[32] N. Pellegrin, 'L'Etre et le paraître au XVIIe siècle: les apparences vestimentaires dans *l'Histoire comique de Francion* de Charles Sorel', in *La France d'Ancien Régime, études réunies en l'honneur de Pierre Goubert* (Toulouse, 1984).

[33] G. Benrekassa, *Fables de la personne, pour une histoire de la subjectivité* (Paris, 1985).

Study of the novel brings out the need for an apprenticeship, as the characters acquire their new identity through sartorial metamorphoses. It also emphasises the importance of dress in amorous intrigues, how it always fed desire and played a part in seduction. Lastly, it gradually came to confer a more positive value on the confusion of ranks which accompanied the borrowing of clothes. The fictional imagination probably reflects the moral and social imperatives of habits which were sometimes contested. Whether to restore everyone to his costume or to accept the disguises which corresponded to new types of conduct was a dilemma which opposed two principles of society: that of the holistic and unequal world, of families, guilds and states; that of individuals regulating their conduct by personal rather than collective imperatives. In revealing this gulf, literary texts are invaluable, since they allow us to see the social and economic strategies which generate the new behaviour from the outside, if not the inside, of the works. The motives expressed pass for real even though it is difficult, except by comparison with other archives, to perceive their results in reality.

So the history of clothes has its sources; they are abundant, though difficult to master from one single approach. It remains to define the problematic and the limits. First, a reading of the traditional historiography of costume and fashion, and a discussion of the different models proposed by anthropology and psychoanalysis, may throw light on certain issues and choices. It is never without interest to reflect on the different ways of writing the history of one subject. The next stage is dictated by the logic which has emerged from our analysis of the sources; the study of clothing consumption makes it possible to establish the hierarchy of appearances through the economic dimension and social distribution, not forgetting that Karl Marx wrote, more than a century ago: 'production is at the same time also consumption, consumption is directly also production'.[34]

It is, therefore, in a sense, on the history of the logics of mediation that we need to shed light. To this end, we can proceed from the modalities of consumption to a discussion of the Parisian system of manufacture and distribution, and a study of manufactur-

---

[34] K. Marx, *Critique of Political Economy*, translated from the 2nd German edn (Calcutta, 1904), pp. 276–7.

ers, vendors and their customers.[35] Lastly, our attempt to discern, between the real and the imaginary, the social role of appearances, from the stationary to the consumer economy, requires that we study other modes of presentation and other logics which reveal social existence. We will look at the novel, at utopias, at the *Encyclopédie*, at the medical discourse and the press.

This book is the result of a collective endeavour. It hopes to contribute to a broad definition of cultural history by giving due weight to the major factors of material civilisation. It has been possible only because this aim has been understood by a group of students, pupils and friends. Such an enterprise makes it possible to accept the imperatives of serial history while retaining unity of presentation and thus dialogue with other types of enquiry. I would like first to thank all those whose mémoires de maîtrise are quoted in notes 30 and 35; also G. Benrekassa, Y.-M. Bercé, J. Bouvet, C. Jouhaud, S. Juratic, M. Manson, V. Milliot, P. Minard, J. Nagle, J. Nicolas, L. Perimi, R. Pasta, P. Perrot, C. Rimbault and M. Sonnet, also N. Pellegrin, C. Reinharez, C. Ungerer and M. Veret; also Franco Angiolini, Angela Groppi, Roger and Anne-Marie Chartier, Luigi Greco, Dominique and Marie-Madeleine Julia, Jacques and Mona Ozouf, Jean-Claude and Michelle Perrot, Jacques and Michelle Revel and Stuart and Anna Woolf. Anne Leclerc and Walter Barberis were responsible for launching the

---

[35] See the following mémoires de maîtrise, all Paris 1 unless otherwise stated: M. Amable, 'Le Vol de vêtement à Paris au XVIIIe siècle' (1981); C. Alric, 'La Consommation vestimentaire de la noblesse provinciale d'après les livres de raison' (1982); M. Cophornic, 'Recherches sur les monuments du costume au XVIIIe siècle' (1984); D. Badiou, 'Les Couturières parisiennes au XVIIIe siècle' (1981); M. C. Desmangeot, 'La Système du vêtement dans *Les Contemporaines*' (1981); B. Dusart, 'La Consommation vestimentaire d'une famille de la noblesse au XVIIIe siècle: les Schomberg' (1981); D. Dutruel, 'Les Revendeuses à Paris dans la seconde moitié du XVIIIe siècle' (1975); M. Franck, 'L'Uniforme des armées de la Révolution' (1981); A. Joffre, 'Le Vêtement à Limoges et dans ses environs d'après les inventaires après décès, 1740–1840', Limoges (1980); F. Lacombe, 'Les Tailleurs d'habits à Paris, 1700–1789' (1985); S. Levu, 'Le Journal de la mode et du goût, 1700–1793' (1983); A. Michel, 'Les Représenta-tions vestimentaires à travers les utopies modernes' (1982); B. Roux Oriel, 'Maîtresses marchandes lingères, maîtresses couturières, ouvrières en linge aux alentours de 1751', Paris 7 (1980); L. Pérez, 'Le Vêtement dans les logiques médicales à la fin du XVIIIe siècle et au début du XIXe siècles' (1982); F. Piwnica, 'Les Fripiers parisiens au XVIIIe siècle' (1985); C. Rimbault, 'Le Corps à travers les manuels de civilité, XVIe–XIXe siècle', Paris 7 (1977).

enterprise and I would like to thank them for reading an early draft; Eric Vigne and Agnès Fontaine have been editors in the true sense of the word and also friends, and to them also, I owe thanks. I wish also to express my gratitude to Bonie Bonis, whose aid has never failed, even against time.

# 2. *The Quicherat effect and after*

Nous commentons depuis des années le langage de notre
culture de ce point où nous avons attendu en vain, pendant
les siècles, la décision de la parole.

Michel Foucault, *Naissance de la clinique*

There are few histories of daily life or civilisation which fail to
devote at least some space to the history of costume and clothes. It
is a staging post, a way of picturesquely evoking upper-class
extravagance or dreary peasant life. But, with few exceptions, in
repeated stereotypes, it is rare to find any attempt to integrate
questions of the social function and economic implications of dress
into ordinary economic activity. Otherwise, it is a highly specialised
activity, in which historians of costume – for the most part curators
of museums of costume – address each other, preoccupied with the
essential tasks of conservation and promotion, a situation hardly
conducive to a break with the traditional problematic. As so often,
change has come from outside, from ethnography and the history
of literature. But to understand this recent development, we need
to examine how this historiographic tradition functioned and how
it has been challenged: in sum, the 'Quicherat effect' – after the
most famous author in the field since the nineteenth century – and
departures from it.

The first historical interest in clothing dates back to the seventeenth and eighteenth centuries, when three traditions converged:
that of the great collections, which conveyed an impression of the
diversity of clothing;[1] that of detailed studies of the dress of the
Ancients and the Moderns, in part bound up with the academic

---

[1] That of Bertellius, *Omnium fere gentium nostrae etatis habitus* (Venice, 1563); see
also under Amman, Bruyn, Broissard and Vecellio in R. Colas, *Bibliographie
générale du costume et de la mode* (Paris, 1933).

tradition of historical painting and its instruction;[2] and that of
works devoted to provincial and regional costume.[3] These galleries
of local costume, whose appearance is linked to the first essays in
proto-ethnography, involved scholars, travellers and provincial
academicians. The birth of the history of dress owed much to the
romantic revival of interest in the past. From Alsace to Auvergne,
from Artois to Provence, amateurs recorded the distinctive features
of their region and its folklore. Jules Quicherat was a turning-point
in these already ancient traditions.

### THE ORIGINS OF THE *MAGASIN PITTORESQUE*

Quicherat, author of a Latin dictionary familiar to generations of
schoolboys, a member of the editorial team assembled by Hachette
and a director of the Ecole des Chartes, brought together under the
title *Histoire du costume en France*[4] a series of articles published
between 1849 and 1865 in the *Magasin pittoresque*, a revue with a
large circulation. He had three principal aims: to be of assistance to
artists, to affirm the role of pictures and to open up new vistas in
the history of manners. He was primarily aiming, therefore, at
painters, sculptors and engravers, and setting out to provide them
with 'a general idea of the costume of each period', useful to their
art not so much by its historical realism as by its faithfulness to the
conditions and customs of the academic tradition. He took pains
to indicate works which artists might consult and he published
many illustrations. The emphasis on illustration and the deliberate
abundance of engravings testify to the progress of technical innovations in typography and to the aesthetic refinement found among
the great editors of the age, which Viollet-le-Duc used to good
effect in his works of popularisation. The many reproductions
'represent things remote from our customs, which it was less easy
to make understood by description'. Lastly, the book had a historical dimension, 'Needing to deal only with one small aspect of
History, I have spoken of events only when they were indispensable,
and as my subject required ... as for my excursions into the

---

[2] For example, Baïf's *De re vestiaria*, or Leclerc, *Divers Habillements des Anciens
grecs et romains* (Paris, several edns. between 1680 and 1706); Vighe's *Le Vade-
mecum du peintre ou recueil de costumes* (1844) is more explicit.

[3] Cf. *Costumes des differents départements de l'Empire français* (Paris, 1815).

[4] *Histoire du costume en France depuis les temps les plus reculés jusqu'à la fin du
XVIIIe siècle* (Paris, 1879).

domain of facts relating to manners, industry and commerce, no justification is needed. Everyone will recognise that they are essential to the history of costume.'

So Quicherat was conscious of an original approach, the definition of a field of research where customs and costumes were linked, which must have derived from an unstated fidelity to the basic tradition of the history of manners. In the late eighteenth century, Legrand d'Aussy, in his *Histoire de la vie privée des Français*, and Desmeunier, in *L'Esprit des usages des peuples*, had oriented the concept of manners in a quasi-ethnological direction, since 'manners convey history because they replace institutions' and because they make it possible to define the identity of a society, a country or a region through their customs, costumes and life-styles.[5] Though Legrand d'Aussy and Desmeunier never fully completed their programme, they helped to create the ethnology of appearances and of our habits, by revealing our own exoticism. 'We know', wrote Desmeunier, 'that the most refined countries in Europe have customs which would surprise us were we to discover them in America or amongst the negroes.' In Book 9 of *L'Esprit des usages*, devoted to adornment and beauty, in his critique of collectors and travellers, Desmeunier observed that 'when it comes to manners and customs', there were no longer any general laws. This may help to explain both the failure of the history of manners in the nineteenth century (it survived in the shadow of academic societies and in the work of provincial amateurs and essayists) and its increasing rigidity. From Quicherat to Magendie, perhaps even to Norbert Elias, there is a continuity in the use of the notion of manners, since its principal and political role relates the private, the social and the public. The dialogue between laws and manners dear to Montesquieu has perhaps never wholly been broken off despite different conceptions of history and the irruption of different perceptions of social reality.[6]

Half way through the nineteenth century, at all events, it still underlay the work of Quicherat. His book progressed in clearly signposted stages, first by epochs (primitive times and the Celtic period in chapter 1; the Gallo-Roman period in chapter 2),

[5] A. Burguière, 'L'anthropologie historique', in *La Nouvelle Histoire*, ed. J. Le Goff (Paris, 1978), pp. 37–61.
[6] G. Benrekassa, *La Notion de moeurs* (forthcoming).

then by reigns (chapter 10 onwards). His periodisation was based essentially on the political context, identified with the accession and power of the monarch, as if the historian of manners was unable to free himself from the dominant narrative method of writing history, and as if public life alone could serve as the context for changes to innumerable private acts. Thus manners and costume unfold from Charles VI to Louis XII, from Francis I to Louis XVI. There are a few detours en route: chapter 14 devoted to lawyers and the peasantry, revealing the author's unease at finding continuity rather than change; chapters 26 and 27 discussing military dress under Louis XIV and Louis XV; the last chapter devoted to the revolutionary rupture. In general, this has continued until very recently to be the structure of all histories of costume. Two flexible but sufficiently directive features probably explain Quicherat's success: a diversified textuality, which reveals his assumptions and dictates his principal choices; his attachment to the chronological analysis of an illusory understanding of formal changes.

## QUICHERAT'S LIMITATIONS

Thoroughly modern, Quicherat used all the documents which were available, but he never questioned the extent to which they reflected reality and only half suspected their major biases. On the one hand, he could not but overestimate the importance of the aristocratic dress and fashion portrayed by the press and engravings. On the other, his presentation of a formal history, dealing with both the whole (the costume) and with detail (the decoration), was dependent on an external interpretation designed to explain constant and trivial change. The emphasis is on explanation by the accidental: the royal mistresses imposed modifications which, by natural imitation rather than social and political choice, were copied by the aristocratic world. But the history of noble dress is inextricably linked to its role as a means to demonstrate distinction, within a system of expenditure organised by the display of 'court society'.[7] Noble rivalries were expressed through different modes of dress, clothes and appearances then calling into question an

---

[7] N. Elias, *La Société de Cour* (Paris, edn of 1985, with an introduction by R. Chartier), translated by E. Jephcott as *Court Society* (Oxford, 1983).

obligation for social representation in the sphere of public civilisation. From this perspective, questions arise regarding the economy of appearances – which economists have approached through the question of luxury and the need for it – but also regarding the meaning of ostentatious expenditure in a society which emphasised the obligation to spend one's income, since to save was always, in a sense, to sin; one has to take account of the importance of redistribution through gifts, and superfluity – hence luxury – was legitimate when it affirmed a level of consumption dictated by rank. The royal mistresses were only one element of variety and variation in the social landscape of a court world which was regulated by more fundamental imperatives.

Quicherat and his followers were hardly any happier when they turned to the mercantilist economy to explain certain changes in the value of clothes, fabrics and adornments. Certainly, the sumptuary laws are an important element in the history of manners.[8] But it takes more than a recapitulation of edicts and texts to explain what was at issue; nor is it at all clear that the measures so constantly reiterated but difficult to control were ever applied or more than partially effective. At the very least, proof is awaited and the significance of the phenomenon remains a matter for debate. From the economic standpoint, it is easy to see the sumptuary laws as signs of a stagnant economy, protectionist and mercantilist. The preambles of the edicts were clear: it was necessary to limit the flow of cash caused by purchases from abroad which were the consequence of the mechanisms of ostentatious consumption. Des Essarts spelled this out in his *Dictionnaire de police*:[9]

> But as everything loses value and prestige in proportion as it becomes abundant and common, clothes of pure silk no longer satisfied the amateurs of luxury, who added gold, silver, pearls and precious stones ... excessive luxury ruined families and so distinguished gold and silver that it was noticed at the Mint. These were the considerations which caused the King to seek a remedy.

And, over and above this first consideration, so many problems remain unresolved: the relation to the monetary conjuncture, the problem of an unusually restricted consumer market, the

---

[8]　H. Aragon, *Les Lois somptuaires* (Paris, 1921).
[9]　Seven vols. (Paris, 1786–8).

implications for trade, manufacture and credit, the effectiveness of the measures taken, and for whom, and at what point (one has only to think of the prohibition on prints, which are nevertheless found in every inventory). In sum, the economy of the sumptuary laws remains to be written.

We are hardly further forward when we examine their other dimension: their logic as an instrument of social and political cohesion.[10] It was God who was offended by the affront to modesty, the superfluity and the licence constituted by the expenditure they were attempting to control, and which threatened not only God, but the whole world order. Consumption should not be 'by each according to their means', but by each according to their rank. The sumptuary laws were one form of expression of the Christian political economy, where consumption should accord to a hierarchy of orders and conditions, and social mobility was limited and denounced. Clothing, like the eighteenth-century town, was an ideal scapegoat for the confusion of social situations. This was a fundamental aspect of past society, which persisted even when social rules and behaviour had changed. Proof is to be found in the *Costume français représentant les différents états du royaume avec les habillements propres à chaque état accompagné de réflexions critiques et morales* engraved in Paris in 1776 by Dupin. From *The Seigneur of the Court* to *The Poor of Each Sex*, 'in the torn clothes usual in their degraded condition', the reader runs the gamut of appearances, and finds observations on characteristics of colour, care and physical aspects; black was appropriate to magistrates, stoutness to wealth, thinness to poverty. It needed the Revolution for the rules of dress according to official rank to be superseded by rules based on function and freedom. Dignity of costume might, as Lamartine observed, enhance the dignity of functions. In public life, every option was now open, from neatness to neglect.

Quicherat also constructed a narrative history of shapes and details. An analysis of chapters 23 and 24 reveals the exaggeration and contrivances he employed in order to endow each period with a specific dominant style, illusory since everyone knows that society is constantly making new out of old. From the boyhood to the

---

[10] See the remarks of Jean Nagle and M. Fogel in *Modèle d'Etat et modèle social de dépense.* CNRS Colloque, Fontevrault, 1984 (Paris, 1987).

apogee of Louis XIV, sequence follows sequence, emphasising the aristocratic liberties of the 'lions of fashion' such as Montauron and Candale, the arbitrary reign of tastes which decreed the cravat, or the knee revealed by the boot, or a lavish profusion of linen or ribbons, the attempts by vulgar ministers to control the proliferation of braid and the proclamation by the court of a model of male and female dress. Suddenly, in 1660, the young king took charge of fashion like everything else, and the series of similar changes now proved the success of a dominant impulse, in brief, the triumph of absolutism. Its progress signalled by a variety of indicators, the chronological succession of the micro-events of fashion, never located within a longer timescale, produces a capricious history, almost indifferent to actual period, though not without a certain charm. Its logic is that of politics, though nothing is more difficult to establish than the relationship between the political and changes to clothes, if, that is, the normative relationships and the relation to the economic, the social and the religious – the culture as a whole – are ignored. It is by no means easy to interpret these superficial changes, but the mechanisms of court society were important in them. It was less the authoritarian psychology of the young king which promoted them than the increasingly rapid consumption of forms consequent upon the fierce rivalry for distinction, which called for ever more elaborate changes.

It remains the case that specific rhythms and variations influence what appear to be the simplest alterations in appearance. They have their logic, as can be seen in a history which might at first sight appear as unhistorical as could be, that of how hair can or cannot be worn. The beard, the moustache, body hair and head hair are unlikely actors on the social scene. It is well known that long hair went with shaven faces up to the beginning of the sixteenth century, when the relationship was reversed. Under Francis I, the beard of président Olivier scandalised the Parlement of Paris, in which he could sit only if he shaved. The church, too, opposed beards, irrespective of custom. It waged war on episcopal beards, which were mocked by beardless young canons. However, in cathedrals as at court, the beard gradually came to equate with old age, with being out of date and out of fashion; the 'greybeards' were foreigners in their own country. 'Seeing them, one was tempted to think that they came from a far-off land', said a contemporary of Louis XIII. By the reign of Louis XIV, anarchic and feudal beards had disappeared from faces; most important of all, between 1630 and 1680, the wig added another dimension, whilst also creating an industry demanding skill, time and flour. What, at first sight, could be more trivial? But on closer inspection, we find a way of understanding the confrontation in the classical period between progress and stagnation, when the changes linked to surface mobility reached the stationary and silent majority. On the surface, the issue was clear; the treasury needed wigs, as it today needs the motor car, since their industrious craft was efficient and profitable, though to measure this accurately would require a proper history of French wig-makers. However, the more hidden social issues are no less interesting and merit our attention.

## WIGS AND THE CHURCH, COSTUME AND CUSTOM

Let us consider the case of Jean-Baptiste Thiers, curé of Champrond and Vibraque, scourge of superstitious practices and author of the admirable *Histoire des perruques où l'on fait voir leur origine, leur usage, leur forme, leurs abus et l'irrégularité de celles des ecclésiastiques.*[11] For this doctor of theology, the debate was comparable to that which inspired the attack on popular and religious superstition; it was a question of exposing whatever departed from an established rule, sometimes even unwittingly and in good faith. Here the bewigged clergy, there dubious religious practices, were a way of indicating the gap between the imposed norm, that of the reformed and transformed church, and custom, through their social vicissitudes, hence of affirming the existence of a catholic and universal law. 'So many ecclesiastics today wear a wig that there is every reason to believe that they are persuaded, at least for the most part, that this strange ornament is not wholly forbidden to them, and that it is not inherently unfitting to the seemliness of their profession. It is to rescue them from their error that I have undertaken this work.'

Thus, in a detail of the history of appearances, we see emerge the whole problem of doctrinal truth and religious discipline, essential to the reform of the clergy in the classical period through a standardisation of practices and customs. In a discourse of definition and classification, based on the enumeration of authorities,

[11]  Paris, 1736.

Jean-Baptiste Thiers put wigs on trial. A recent fashion of the worldly, a protection affected by those with diseased scalps or red hair, they had appeared on ecclesiastical heads ever since the abbé de La Rivière, late bishop of Langres, had seen fit to wear one. He traced their diffusion through successive spheres of eminence, whose articulation is described in unusual detail. Elderly prelates, susceptible to cold and thinning on top, adopted the new practice; they were imitated by a few canons, in the first place those of the turbulent chapter of Rouen around 1676, semi-prebendaries, chaplains and under-choristers followed suit, first in the major churches, then in smaller collegials; next, the new fashion reached the curés, in town and country, who 'prided themselves on their propriety'; curates and unbeneficed priests copied these good shepherds; finally, even regulars were infected. By the end of the seventeenth century, the whole Gallican church was bewigged, contaminated by an error contrary to true doctrine. On this basis, and he was not joking, the anti-wig warrior of Beauce proceeded to demonstrate that the church had always condemned false hair; St Paul provided proof when he recommended praying bare-headed in church, and the Protestants were wrong to believe that his teaching was only local when it was certainly universal.

The religious history recounted here is, of course, one of a laxity whose origins were traced back by Thiers to the reign of Louis XIV: the church had tolerated birettas, mitres, almuces, cowls, capes, hoods, coifs, amices, doctoral caps and calottes. It had been wrong and the result was the scandal of wigs. Neither tradition nor respect for hierarchy nor the rigours of winter nor the chill emanating from sacred vaults found favour in the eyes of Jean-Baptiste Thiers. No artifice in the way of hair escaped his censure, whether curls, dyed hair or false pieces, and from hair to wigs was but a short step, not forgetting the canonical provisions concerning clerical tonsures in which the Council of Trent had not failed to show interest.

We see here the church in action. In an unceasing battle, clothes – and wigs – should testify to the desire for reform, and what was forbidden, with the aid of numerous authorised texts, was a conception of the cleric. For the reformed clergy, the priest, the principal intermediary between the church and the Christian people, should play his role with the blessing of nature and eschew artifice. To this end, he sacrificed some of his hair when he received the tonsure, essential badge of the ecclesiastical condition. He must be taught to fear the seductions of appearance; the wigs so widely worn paved the way for more serious moral errors. They needed a lot of care, which wasted time, and their wearers were in no position to reproach the faithful for their luxurious clothes, their strange ornaments and their exaggerated curls. The wig was contrary to the 'modesty' of a reformed church. Tradition, furthermore, justified its censure, since it was a practice which contradicted the educational principles of the Christian political economy: 'What impression can be made on the minds of the faithful by an ecclesiastic who practises the opposite of what he preaches?' Under an apparently trivial guise, lastly, a relationship with the sacred was expressed. The courtly model and the economy of fashion exposed traditional society to dubious developments, no longer subject to the wishes of the church. To understand these contradictions might be one aim of a history of clothing which would break away from the still omnipresent Quicherat tradition.

It is, most of all, another way of reflecting on temporality and, in particular, on the relationship between two timescales, two tempos of consumption and two chronologies of development, whose emergence in a sense polarised the transformation of the clothing habits of French society after the end of the Middle Ages. The rise of the modern state, its policy of display, already visible at the Field of the Cloth of Gold, the phenomenon of the royal court and the triumph of a consumer ethos[12] introduced into society the values of competition and extravagance as a means to distinction. From then on, the rapid progress of fashion shaped the culture of appearances. New relationships were established between the values of clothing and its wearer. Fashion, 'this way of making things live', according to Furetière, 'which changes according to time and place', gradually infected the social body, and it was its universal action which exercised preachers and moralists, economists and administrators. Before the end of the eighteenth century, before the appearance of fashion magazines, texts and pictures conveyed a motive or a pretext more than a theme or a subject. Fashion is the starting-point for a discussion revealing the significations which make it possible to understand the organising principles of society.

[12] Elias, *La Société de Cour*, pp. 47–60.

Clothing gives rise to the notion of a universal rule, extending its sway indefinitely, whilst fashion reveals the justification for a traditional society with stable hierarchies. To accept this idea is another way of breaking with Quicherat.[13]

The history of clothing can be approached from two principal standpoints: that of the function of clothing and that of changes in sensibility. Dress is a basic need, but a utilitarian approach 'condemns [us] to remain on the surface of the manifest discourse'[14] and confines us to a narrative and descriptive history which makes no attempt to understand what it is that determines, at a profound level, forms, behaviour and their evolution. One cannot therefore avoid a discussion of the complex symbolism of appearances. Clothing, sign of adhesion, of solidarity, of hierarchy, of exclusion, is one of the codes for reading society. But it also signposts the progress of utility and inutility, of market value and use value. In practice, its functions are interdependent, and the *ancien régime* remains a crucial moment for measuring the variability or invariability of sartorial signs. The Revolution, as Quicherat correctly observed, registered the triumph of the principle of diversity over that of hierarchy: 'There was no longer any way of distinguishing the classes by their clothes.'

At the same time, we need to see how clothing helps to constitute the values of sensibility and mobilises the senses. Fabric and how it is arranged, its fullness and its tightness, its signs and its patterns, speak a direct and perceptive body language, of which Patrice Hugues has made himself the historian.[15] For a history of the clothing culture of the modern period, we need to trace the evolution of colours, contacts and the status of fabrics. How appearances were reshaped will be revealed by a topology of the body, by changes to what could and could not be seen, by redefinitions of modesty and immodesty and the lessons of hygiene which challenged the values of the clean and the dirty. Clothes shape the body and the body plays on clothes; they are means of socialisation which have their rite of passage. Between stability and mobility, clothes discover fashion, which appears in the field of the social

[13] L. Godard de Donville, *Signification de la mode sous Louis XIII* (Aix-en-Provence, 1978).
[14] P. Perrot, *Les Dessus et les dessous de la bourgeoisie, une histoire du vêtement au XIXe siècle* (Paris, 1981), pp. 13–29.
[15] Hugues, *Le langage des tissus*, pp. 12–25.

contradictions when there is a possibility of desiring what others desire.[16]

Two contributions have been essential to this new orientation: that of the anthropologists and psychoanalysts, particularly the latter, not least Flügel in 1930;[17] and that of the few historians who have ventured onto the margins of the literature and the economy of manners.[18]

## THE PSYCHOANALYTIC AND ANTHROPOLOGICAL PERSPECTIVE

There is no escape, in the twentieth century, from the detour made necessary by the popularisation of Freudian ideas; clothing, language of the body and of desires, involves so many contradictory impulses and expresses so many needs through a variety of codes that it plays a major role in the constitution of identity. The difficulty with the psychoanalytic interpretation lies in its deliberately transcultural and ahistorical character, which is perhaps no more of an obstacle to the study of clothes than to any reading of a phenomenon with a complex language. The problem is to reconstitute a clothing system, that is the specific way in which social groups dress at a given moment, which takes account of the way in which the items are put together, with its play on inner and outer garments, the relations of exclusion or of tolerance between these elements, and their dynamic; the latter is linked to the life of each item, during which it might temporarily or definitively change its function or even its significance. In the historical documentation, these three elements are rarely found together. Pictorial sources reveal the second and third relationship in a static form, but the first only partially. Inventories of wardrobes give us an accumulation of items, shapes and occasionally patterns, but do not tell how things were used in real life. We must therefore resign ourselves to

[16] Perrot, *Les Dessus*, p. 45.

[17] For the contribution of anthropology, see *Ethnologie générale*, Encyclopédie de la Pléiade, under the direction of J. Poirier; Y. Laporte, ed., *Vêtement et société* (Paris, 1985); *L'Ethnographie* (1984); J. Flügel, *The Psychology of Clothes* (New York, 1930); also E. Luccioni-Lemoine, *La Robe, essai psychanalytique sur le vêtement* (Paris, 1983); J.-T. Maertens, *Dans la peau des autres, essai d'anthropologie des inscriptions vestimentaires* (Paris, 1978); S. Freud, *Trois Essais sur la théorie de la sexualité* (Paris); S. Kofman, *Le Respect des femmes* (Paris, 1982).

[18] Godard de Donville, *Signification de la mode*; Perrot, *Les Dessus*.

partial reconstructions which have some difficulty in attaining the status of the anthropological or psychological analyses which provide an indispensable perspective to our look back in time. They are organised round three principal themes: clothing seen as a response to first causes, protection, decoration and modesty; assessing the categories of sartorial differentiation; measuring the power of the impulse of fashion.

First causes have a history over and above their appearance of universality and timelessness. A systematic study of proverbs, many of which refer to clothes,[19] would no doubt prove this by revealing the dual tendency in sartorial social relations: judging by appearances and bearing; distrusting them since they are by their nature deceptive. In a holistic society, the first imperative is inescapable, but the second is also present. Both, in any case, recognise the social function of a *vestème* in which a person encloses and invents himself, the clothes, even the mask, both concealing and revealing a quantity of information about the person and the personage. In the last analysis, clothes may well respond to constant imperatives, whose anteriorities and priorities the historian is less prepared to discuss than the anthropologist or the psychoanalyst – always rather in search of Columbus' egg; this is more important from a theoretical point of view than to a medium-term historical analysis. What matters is to bring out specific relationships rather than oppositions which often change meaning.

Ornament, an element in the demographic, social and sexual differentiation of appearances, attracts attention and fortifies self-esteem, in fact distinguishes, but differently according to motives and impulses. Modesty varies from one culture to another; for the historian of traditional European societies it has a particular importance in the history of the manufacture and transmission of conventions. In the civilisation of 'good manners', its purpose conflicted with that of ornament; after Erasmus, one was supposed to avoid attracting attention rather than the other way round. Thus the opposition of first causes makes it possible to discuss the changeability of frontiers, prohibitions and conduct and to identify the original features of past clothing practices.

Adornment is particularly powerful as an expression of sexual

[19] F. Loux and P. Richard, *Sagesse du corps, la santé et la maladie dans les proverbes français* (Paris, 1978), pp. 24–30, 105–8, 266–72.

motivation; it serves to provoke desire. For the psychoanalyst, it is a happy hunting-ground in the search for phallic symbols, when fashion holds out the prospect of fruitful symbolic readings.[20] Historians are still unable to explain what lay behind the change from the Rabelaisian cod-piece to the sansculotte trousers, from flamboyant exhibition to deceptive disappearance. The old ladies of the court, returned from exile, were in no doubt: with trousers, you no longer knew what men were thinking! But the ornamental also contributes to the demonstration of distinction, the confirmation of rank and the affirmation of wealth, which at once ranks it with fashion and the ephemeral. Differences emerge between clothes defined by their relation to a past and those which reject it, between clothes characterised by resemblance and those which deny it. In one single eighteenth-century aristocratic wardrobe, they might well co-exist. What matters is that the ornamental is inseparable from an extension of the bodily self and belongs to the history of appearances;[21] and that it is ordered in taxonomies which are complex, precise, conventional, corporeal and plastic (make-up, the wig, the revealed corset),[22] or external, in the organisation of dressing itself. Thus the gown, a garment shared by both sexes until the seventeenth century, later often symbolises a masculine social conflict. The ornamental takes precedence over the functional and plays on dimensions (padding, false pieces) and direction, so that the allure of the clothes determines that of their wearer.

The role of modesty is easier to understand, since here clothing reveals more or less clearly the moral and religious constraints. For psychoanalysts, it implies the existence of a first tendency which it is required to repress, whereas historians assert that there are periods when the negative impulses triumph and others when they are in retreat. Their role is to help trace the historical changes to the frontiers of the sexual and social impropriety operating within ethical or matrimonial strategies. What can, or should, be revealed, and when and how far? In classical civilisation, the separation of the bodily and spiritual imperatives encourages a change of attitude towards care of the body, a specific definition of the clean and the

[20]  Flügel, *Psychology of Clothes.*
[21]  Perrot, *Le Travail des apparences.*
[22]  G. Vigarello, *Le Corps redressé* (Paris, 1978).

dirty,[23] but it also entails a transfer of investment from the body to the clothes and ornament. The change can be traced in the discourse of preachers and in religious instruction – where the norm is both effect and without effect, through the medical logics,[24] and finally in the manuals of 'good manners', which express in popular form the common code of behaviour: between modesty and excess, everyone finds his way. What is crucial is that the frontiers are blurred and can change their meaning; this is the problem for a history of female underclothing, or of the ornamental or sexual significance of the male leg, from tight breeches to trousers, via loose breeches and the false stuffed calves resorted to by poorly equipped gentlemen, the general baron Marbot among them.[25]

There remains protection, a basic function, and essential to the establishment of a compromise between different, and often highly ambivalent, attitudes. Cold and self-defence were no doubt of prime importance in the past,[26] though other concerns operated both in the real (armour) and the imaginary (the decorative amulet) spheres. The discourse on the protection of the body often justified a range of rationalisations, for example, those of medical doctors. Between the seventeenth and the twentieth centuries, conceptions of the harmful or beneficial properties of air on the exposed body have expressed an evolution of modesty as much as a hygienic necessity. What is important is to grasp the possibilities inherent in the social evolution of first motives and perhaps to adopt a cautious attitude with regard to sexual symbolism. A pre-Freudian reading of modesty is also necessary to understand the role of clothes in desire and reproduction, between controlling norms and individual liberty.

Consequently, the reading of sartorial differentiation reveals a history of individual, sexual and social acquisitions. We know that clothing sublimates the exhibitionist tendency, but above all that it is one of the many ways in which the body is shaped and controlled, even to individualisation and recognition by the local or family group. Rites and symbols mark every stage in education in dress,

[23] G. Vigarello, *Le propre et le sale* (Paris, 1984), translated by Jean Birrell as *Concepts of Cleanliness* (Cambridge, 1988); Rimbault, *La Presse féminine*.

[24] Pérez, 'Le vêtement dans les logiques médicales'; N. Pellegrin, 'L'uniforme de la santé. Les médecins et la réforme du costume au XVIIIe siècle', *XVIIIe Siècle* (1987).

[25] Marbot, *Mémoires*, 2 vols. (Paris, 1982).

[26] R. Delort, *Le commerce des fourrures en Occident à la fin du Moyen Age* (Rome, 1980).

from swaddling clothes to the first breeches, in a gradual progression away from nature and animality towards culture and humanity. In the acquisition of sartorial knowledge and wisdom, a world order was transmitted, in which the central notion was that of 'modesty' and 'moderation'. It taught the virtues of control, of order, of the adaptation of the individual to his rank, age, status and sex. The history of children's clothes in all social classes needs to be taken up where it was left off by Philippe Ariès, less knowledgeable about popular and peasant milieus than the urban classes and the aristocracy.[27]

All these issues have consequences for consumption and luxury, but probably none more than sexual differentiation. For many centuries, the two sexes were equal in the pursuit of refinement and decoration. From the Renaissance to the Enlightenment, men in refined milieus dressed both extravagantly and elaborately. But the eighteenth century saw the beginnings of a major historical rupture: the masculine renunciation of decoration, even of elegance, in favour of an austere appearance. An important difference between the sexes emerged: men rely on their clothes for their attraction, women on decoration and exposure, the one reinforcing the other – both physical and sartorial attractions. This contrast was reflected in the condemnation by the church of female wantonness in dress, always the occasion for displaying the body, and an issue in the control of female sexuality by men.[28]

The 'great renunciation', to use Flügel's expression, was a surrender in the war of the sexes over appearance, in which two influences can be detected.[29] First, we see the gradual rupture of the old social order, the simpler clothes of men expressing social change by an affirmation of equality. At the same time, there was a transfer of the motors of distinction from the sphere of the court to public space and the arena of production. Clothes now registered new adherences to new social codes. The place and the role of women in society changed. The age-old inequality of the sexes further increased, and men gained in real power what they lost in the realm of appearances. For the psychoanalytic historian, it is primarily a matter of social power; with regard to real power, the question remains open.

[27] C. Reinharez, 'Habillement et civilité', *Ethnographie* (1984), usefully complements P. Ariès, *L'Enfant et la vie familiale* (Paris, 1960).

[28] Flügel, *Psychology of Clothes*.

[29] Perrot, *Les Dessus*.

A final element of differentiation was the distinction of rank and status. Before the sixteenth century, the link between social distinction and sartorial difference was constantly affirmed. Between the sixteenth and the eighteenth centuries, things grew more complicated: first, as a result of the development of intermediate groups, a feature of the growing complexity of urban civilisation and the spread of the phenomena of distinctive imitation; second, because migration from the country to the town, and probably also to some extent a real upward and downward social mobility, accentuated movement. We need to distinguish locales and tempos; for the former, the court, of course, but also the church, where hierarchical signs were fiercely maintained, the *parlements*, the army, where uniform was a factor for cohesion and discipline, the town, the parish, age groups and festive and social clubs; for the latter, the rates of acquisition and transmission, varying according to place, sex, age and social class. Mention of these themes leads inevitably to a question too simple to be truly problematic, at any rate, one to which there is no single answer: was there really a sartorial *ancien régime*? The existence of sumptuary laws, the classic descriptions of the processional society of orders, the disputes about rank and etiquette, all point to the answer yes.

Distinction through ornament was fundamental to the society of orders at the time of its formation. It was apparent in the disputes over prerogatives which divided the world of officials when they imposed themselves on the monarchy in the late sixteenth and the seventeenth centuries. It declined in importance when the monarchy was more confident of its strength, more distanced from its external pomp, and when court society became the focus for ceremonial, as Jean Nagle has shown. When, at the beginning of the seventeenth century, it was said that one should dress 'in one's own guise', what was meant was according to one's condition. The sumptuary laws were there to prevent anyone from straying too far; a magistrate dressed like a nobleman contravened the norms, he disguised himself, he dressed wrongly; Parlement regularly fulminated against this at the end of the sixteenth century. Each order had its badge: the clergy had the tonsure, the nobility had the sword, the *robe* had its gowns, long for the law, short for finance.

Within the magistrature, there were three hierarchies of distinction: those of form, those of fabric and those of colour. Magistrates wore a long gown over a soutane; notaries, *procureurs* and *commissaires* wore a shorter gown over a tunic; sergeants wore a casaque. Sergeants, *petite robe* and *grande robe* could not be confused. Material provided a further means of distinction; the authors of the sumptuary laws dreamed of a clearly visible hierarchy of textiles. This was most evident in judicial ceremonial. In the Chamber of Accounts, the *présidents* alone enjoyed lustrous silk velvet, the *maîtres* and the king's men wore brilliant satins, the *correcteurs* were in damask, whilst the commissioners of audit and the *greffiers* made do with more modest taffetas. Lastly, there was colour, fundamental in a society still influenced by the glamour of heraldic pomp and the unique power of the visual. Magistrates had the right to wear gowns of scarlet lined with flecked ermine, the scarlet recalling the imperial magistrature, the ermine symbolising nobility and integrity. All wore the square cap or *mortier*. In the king's council, the chancellor dressed in a long gown of crimson velvet and the counsellors in long gowns of violet, the controllers and intendants of finance wore short gowns of the same colour, as did the secretaries of state, but they had the right to a long mantle; secretaries and *greffiers* wore short black gowns, and the ushers wore habits.

The sumptuary order was thus apparent at the very heart of the kingdom, but it was gradually eroded, to be concentrated in the ceremonial of public, judicial and political life. The social eloquence of costume retained its power to act on the imagination of the justiciable, the tax-payer and the subject; elsewhere, it lost ground, tending to merge with other manifestations of power, the ostentation of wealth or the brilliance and majesty of uniforms. In the eighteenth century, the chancellor d'Aguesseau thought that the more magistrates distanced themselves from external pomp, the more they would gain in respect; form had prevailed over matter, and idea over form.[30]

But there were many factors at work producing obscurity and confusion. The domestic servants of the aristocracy are a case in point. In theory, through their livery in the colours of the house, they affirmed the power of their masters, but in practice they exploited their reflected glory to behave insolently and provocatively, whilst also acquiring the clothing habits of their masters and

---

[30] J. Nagle, 'Les fonctionnaires au XVIIe siècle', in *Histoire générale des fonctionnaires français*, vol. II (Paris, 1989).

transmitting them to others, in town and country. The exchange of clothes between master and servant in the course of amorous intrigues or at festivities became a stock situation of novels and the theatre.

Flügel and the psychoanalysts of costume did not duck the problem of the forces for change. From a perspective at once static and dynamic, they sought its causes and consequences. They proposed a classification based on both history and differences in social organisation. In it, two opposite poles orient behaviour and choice: 'fixed' dress and 'modish' dress. The first is characterised by its lack of change over time, its symbolic value lying in its perenniality. In contrast, it varies greatly in space through national, regional, local and even village and family rivalries. It also changes significantly within the social hierarchy since it is almost invariably linked to a professional group, of occupation or status. 'Modish' dress, on the other hand, changes quickly over time, but little in space, and spreads throughout a given cultural area according to the ease of communication. This is the model which has characterised European culture, where fashion has been more than elsewhere a factor for differentiation and innovation.

To these two clothing types correspond different psychological and social natures. Fixed dress derives from a desire for temporal permanency, the supremacy of the group over the individual, the impulse towards uniformity. It is often perceived in a real or mythical relation to the past, inspired by traditions which are deep rooted in locality or group, for example, regimental customs. Innovation is usually resented and is effected by the addition of new elements, from the bottom up, which do not threaten the equilibrium of the whole and are compatible with rivalry in the sphere of ornament.[31] Modish dress corresponds to the values of change, novelty and an obsolescence which requires that it be discarded if a detail suddenly falls out of fashion. Its social flexibility abolishes distinctions by uniting through imitation the 'happy few'. Whilst traditional dress valorises adhesion and cohesion, innovation supposes diversity and the free choice of equal individuals. Fashion, that goddess of appearances, becomes by its caprices the principal motor for changes which are denounced by its detractors and praised by its partisans.

---

[31] D. Pop-Campeanu, *Se vêtir, quand, comment, pourquoi?* (Fribourg, 1985).

HOW TO BE IN FORMER FASHION

In this analysis, the historian has to avoid two pitfalls. The first is to assume that everything moves at the same pace, and that a single factor explains everything. It is a fundamental principle of socio-cultural history to accept the co-existence of different time-scales, hence models. The second pitfall is to believe that social groups or sectors can escape the phenomena of distinctive competition, hence conflicts over appearances. Fashion can affect the most traditional of societies and the most fixed of costumes. No people has been immune, as Leroi-Gourhan showed in 1945: 'Just as with us, the loin-cloth rises or falls from the ankles to the knees, red is in fashion for a while, belts are worn wider or narrower and nose-rings are sometimes more seductive in bone than in polished wood, sometimes more classical or eccentric if they are short or long.'[32] Fashion reached the rural societies of *ancien régime* France, and extended to accessories as well as essentials. It is therefore not uniquely modern, even if modernity has erected it into a god; it affects everything, not only clothes. The analysis of Flügel and the psychoanalysts emphasises rivalries where, in the sartorial effects of fashion, the sexual elements are the least immediately visible and the social elements the most easily legible. Whatever finery and ornament are currently in fashion serve both as social markers and sexual bait.

If the clothing system is fixed by fairly strict norms, fashion can influence quality and accessories, within restricted groups. If, on the other hand, society permits a degree of mobility, the distinctive signs are in danger. The process of imitation begins to operate and threatens a massive dilution, if not the abolition, of differences, unless the privileged and threatened milieus defend their positions and, more or less overtly, the symbols of their superiority. First, prohibition and then renunciation speed up the adoption of new forms and soon of an infinite variety of detail and nuance. Historically, the problematic of the history of fashion is read first in terms of the civilising process, as Tarde,[33] Elias and Bourdieu have shown, each in their own way.[34] The court and then the modern

---

[32] A. Leroi-Gourhan, *Milieu et Technique* (Paris, revised edn 1978).

[33] Gabriel Tarde, *Les Lois de l'imitation*, ed. Raymond Bourdon-Slatkine (1979, facsimile reproduction of Paris, 1895 edn).

[34] P. Bourdieu, *La Distinction* (Paris, 1979).

state have unquestionably been the decisive instruments in establishing a civilisation of fashion and drawing the whole of society, from princely and aristocratic circles to various urban groups and the peasantry, into an increased consumption, in which fashion is ultimately confounded; to be fashionable is the ultimate in unfashionability. The history of dress may aspire to emancipate itself from fashion's influence, but can never manage wholly to escape. Perhaps, in so doing, it would only be following fashion!

To progress, we perhaps need to adopt a more ambitious approach in order to be able to draw together all the elements of this profound history of sensibility, which form both a juxtaposition of contradictory judgements and a system, since on the basis of one it is possible to conceive the whole; as from the relationship between needs and prohibitions traced through objects which are less important than what they symbolise; or as in work, food and ways of living and dressing, past society is torn between desire and rejection, prohibition and permission. Clothes always signify more than they appear to, like the words of a language which needs to be translated and explained. A reading of anthropologists and psychoanalysts is highly suggestive for the history of clothing practices, but too often confined within the framework of an analysis of dress presented as traditional and explicable in terms of basic functions. But clothing can never wholly be explained by custom or by a rather cursory sexual symbolism. The major difficulty is to grasp within the same movement stability and change in appearance; to this end, a historical reading is possible, particularly for the *ancien régime*, where the dress of holistic societies confronts that of the egalitarian worlds of the future.

# 3. History, fashion and clothing systems from the seventeenth to the nineteenth centuries

New fashions, if they are to be successful, must be in accordance with certain ideals current at the time they are launched.

J. C. Flügel, *The Psychology of Clothes*

We cannot escape fashion, so let us make the best of it. Between the seventeenth and the eighteenth centuries, this major phenomenon received a new impetus leading to its diffusion beyond France, which now set the tone for Europe. One of the most important, though most neglected, factors in this development was economic: the existence of a luxury clothing industry, concentrated in Paris, with a tradition, customers and much at stake. To survive, it must maintain the flow of new clothes, to expand, it must increase the frequency with which they were replaced. On this basis, we may wonder how old was the exchange function of fashion,[1] and its nature as in a sense equivalent to the market.

The increase in the speed with which practices and habits changed was contemporary with the explosion of the political economy, of which there are many signs. After 1750, in parallel with the proliferation of economic books and journals and of collections of fashion,[2] economists began to reflect on sartorial luxury and on the role of the consumption, vehicle of wealth creation, of ordinary clothes. In 1770, Bonnaud published an article on 'the degradation of the human species through the demeaning use of whalebone' in the *Journal de l'agriculture*; in 1779, Gauthier, curé of Savigny, brought out his *Traité contre l'amour des parures et le luxe des habits*, 220 pages of fulmination; in 1780, Saint-Vallier wrote a *Discours sur les*

---

[1] J. Baudrillard, *Le Système des objets* (Paris, 1968); *L'Echange symbolique et la mort* (Paris, 1976).

[2] J.-C. Perrot, 'L'Economie politique et ses livres', in *Histoire de l'édition française*, vol. II (Paris, 1984), pp. 240–59; Rimbault, 'La Presse féminine'.

*modes.* These are only three of many such works. They repeat the customary critique of sartorial luxury, and in particular of the excesses of female fashion, in the name of the Christian political economy, but they link it both to harmful effects on morals and civilisation and to the transmission of knowledge through teaching: education was the order of the day. Lastly, like the great texts in praise of wealth,[3] they rediscover the classic alternative; either it was ruinous and a cause of depopulation, or it was made useful to society. Fashion can then be decoded like the market; it, too, was a model of circulation, but it no longer even needed a tangible general equivalent such as gold or money. It was an exchange system of differences and, as with human interchange in general, fashion precedes or announces the economic. At the end of the *ancien régime*, at all events, profound modifications to sensibility,[4] a speeding-up in the circulation of persons and things and the proliferation of means of communication prepared the ground for the rupture.

## DRESS AND / OR COSTUME

The historical study of clothes relates two levels of reality, that of dressing (*habillement*), which Roland Barthes identifies with speech in the Saussurian linguistic system,[5] an individual act by which the individual adapts to himself what is proposed by the group, and that of costume or clothing (*vêtement*), seen from a sociological or historical standpoint as an element within a system which is formal, normative and sanctioned by society. Our reading of Flügel has shown how the primitive facts of protection, decoration and modesty only become clothing facts when they are recognised by different social groups, and form part of cultural wholes defined by links and codes. To understand these rules and sequences, both the power of their constraints and the extent of their derogations, remains the aim of this history. It is therefore less a question of recording the facts, images and features of manners – which others

---

[3] Voltaire, *Le Mondain*, ed. A. Morise.

[4] A. Corbin, *Le Miasme et la jonquille* (Paris, 1982), translated by M. Kochan as *The Foul and the Fragrant* (1986); Roche, *Peuple de Paris*.

[5] R. Barthès, 'Histoire et Sociologie du vêtement', *Annales: ESC* (1957), pp. 430–41 and *Le Système de la mode* (Paris, 1967), translated by Matthew Ward and Richard Howard as *The Fashion System* (London, 1985).

have done, and much better, Quicherat to the fore – than of understanding the normative articulations where social significations and practices are revealed.

Fashion exists at the intersection of the fact of dressing, which an individual can launch and generalise within the clothing system where it becomes common property, and the fact of clothing generalised in a manner of dressing and reproduced on the collective scale, for example, in *haute couture*. Change can be understood within this relationship, the signification of the clothing increasing as we move from personal act to common gesture. The relationship between the clothed individual and the society which proposes the code of dress can be measured against the major changes affecting the clothing system and by comparison with the possibilities of diffusion and reception. From the seventeenth to the eighteenth centuries, a high degree of artificiality and decorative exuberance in dress was required of upper-class men and women. A quarter of a century before the Revolution, the philosophic critique denounced the general excesses of fashion and aristocratic consumption in the name of nature; it ended up by imposing the artificiality of the natural, which was far from cheap. At the same time, the sartorial social function of the sexes, now subject to different ethics, even different rhythms, diverged, in a redistribution of the male and female roles between the private and the public.

Two examples will illustrate the spirit and purpose of my analysis: first, a discussion of the notion of fashion at a period when it provoked the reflection of moralists, even though the theme of fashionable clothes is to some extent anachronistic, since the seventeenth century, unlike the nineteenth and twentieth centuries, had no exemplary corpus, written or pictorial, to record it;[6] second, a discussion of how the clothing system functioned in the nineteenth century,[7] a period when both anonymity and the individual were promoted, thus bringing into play two, to some extent contradictory, animating principles: the quest for a distinctive appearance and that for uniformity and conformity. This tension between difference and a collective identity still inspires our choice of clothes, as a glance at any university lecture theatre or television programme will show. My study covers the period from the first

[6] Godard de Donville, *Signification de la mode, passim*, but especially pp. 11–12.
[7] Perrot, *Les Dessus*, pp. 8–9.

criticism of the social phenomenon of fashion to its undisputed victory, though the meanings of dress had partly changed, that is, from the classical age to the Enlightenment.

In the reigns of Louis XIII and Louis XIV, the notion of fashion had two meanings: on the one hand, custom, styles of life, ways of doing things, a conformism of practices; on the other, whatever changed according to time and place. There were fashionable objects, places and habits. The notion did not apply only to ornament and clothes, but to every means of expression: 'fashion concerns and transforms the whole man'.[8] Thus clothing has to be located within a vast ensemble with shifting frontiers, encompassing the conflicts and aspirations of the age. In his *La Mode*, published in 1642, Grenaille warned his readers that nothing was more polymorphic: 'I offer a general description of our century'; and when, at the same time, his friend Fitelieu published his *Contre Mode*, he maintained that 'the whole world is affected by fashion'.

If fashion is a fairyland of codes, prudence requires that we avoid risk of dilution and confine ourselves to the analysis of writers who drew directly on fashion in support of their theme. The choice is all the more necessary in that there is no specialised literature, and the subject can occur in every type of text. Accordingly, we need to note a double bias; we find not a desire to inform about fashion, but variations on a theme, the discussion being fundamentally moral and anthropological; few books fail, on close analysis, to lead back to human beings and society, or to serve as pretexts for satirising people and the times. Fashion operates in three principal ways: first, through imitation, bringing out the different social *habitus* of the court, the town and the people; second, through the conventions in vogue, fashion reveals human nature through fickleness and artifice, love and its stratagems; finally, the sought-after styles confront the affirmations of the manuals of good manners, instrument of the education of respectable people, ruled and constrained by custom, good sense and the proprieties. It is another way of reading past society than that of the Christian political economy.

To contemporaries of Louis XIII, a fashionable appearance was a specific feature of the national character.

---

[8]  R. Konig, *Sociologie de la mode* (Paris, 1969).

> The French, who have made their name redoubtable
> Everywhere in the world which is habitable
> Come to submit to my command
> To do whatever I demand

said the *Discours nouveau sur la mode* in 1613,[9] proclaiming the universality of fashion's tyranny, the need to submit to its laws and the significance of such a submission as a community's means of recognition. Authors who studied the manners of nations, like d'Avity[10] and Sorel,[11] saw it as a factor for the cohesion of peoples and states. Those who failed to observe its dictates became figures of fun and risked exclusion as obsolete or eccentric. But, at the same time, the mechanisms of recognition were those of the social powers. It was the king who set the fashion, who caused beards to be shaved, or hair to grow longer or shorter; he gave the lead. The court followed suit, as did the rest of France, which took the court as its model, as Montaigne observed: 'Fashion doubtless lies in the encounter between the tastes of the French and the authority of those whom the French admire.'[12] The nobles who incarnated the quintessence of the national spirit promoted an egalitarian policy when they laid down and sanctioned the models of social esteem. Peace in Paris, after the conflicts of the previous reigns, and the emergence of a new type of courtier who formed himself in the antechambers of the Louvre, created the court fashion which proved unifying for all.

But, at the same time, fashion was a way in which to affirm individuality. This can be seen in the attribution and baptism of much-copied inventions such as the shoes *à la Pompignan* and the hair *en cadenette* of M. de Cadenet, brother of Luynes. Creative originality could inspire imitation without loss of basic unity.

Fashion was thus first a point of equilibrium between the collective and the individual, a way of marking the social hierarchy, both fixed and mobile. As sartorial distinctions flourished, the fantasy of some and the conformity of others triggered defensive action on

---

[9] *Variétés historiques et littéraires*, ed. Fournier (Paris, 1855–6), 10 vols., vol. III, pp. 241–63; Godard de Donville, *Signification de la mode*, pp. 20–33.
[10] *Le Théâtre de l'univers, ou abrégé du monde* (Paris, 1646).
[11] *La Science universelle du vêtement* (Paris, 1641), vol. I, p. 194.
[12] Montaigne, *Essais* (Paris, edn 1950), p. 308; Godard de Donville, *Signification de la mode*, p. 32.

the part of the institutions (the church) or groups (the bourgeoisie) left behind. Fashion thus reveals social relations and the way they evolve. The longevity of a practice appears always to relate to the obstacles it encounters which oppose its successful diffusion. 'The way in which our laws try to regulate the foolish and vain expenses of the table and dress is self-defeating ... [since it serves to] increase in everyone the desire to adopt them', wrote Montaigne.[13] The denunciations of the moralists and the sumptuary laws aimed at the same target, the luxury economy which, by encouraging ostentation, slowed down, whilst constantly provoking and prolonging, the imitation which was not pure determinism.

FASHION AND THE SUMPTUARY LAWS

Fogel has demonstrated the imbrication of the social and the political in the genesis of royal legislation directed against 'luxury expenditure'.[14] The eighteen decrees passed between 1485 and 1660 reveal, with regard to clothes and ornament, both an economic policy and a defence of noble appearance. The preamble to the decree of 1514 explicitly identifies title and clothes: 'Prohibiting absolutely categorically all persons, commoners, non-nobles ... from assuming the title of nobility either in their style or *in their clothes*' (my italics). For nearly two centuries, the monarchy struggled to restrict silks to the nobility, to define a hierarchy of colours and prohibit gold and silver in fabrics and ornament, in sum, to limit the merging of conditions. When monetarist justifications prevailed at the beginning of the seventeenth century, the sumptuary laws conveyed the impression of a nation where the extravagance of consumers was diverting precious metal away from useful circuits and state coffers. The policing of expenditure now affected every subject. Nobles and commoners were alike in the sartorial excess which provoked state action. So just as fashion affirmed the primacy of the nobility, the monarchy stole some of it away in order to confine it to the supreme enclave of social distinction, the court. The legislation echoed the treatises; the sumptuary laws attacked the mechanisms which registered social mimesis. How far they were

[13] Godard de Donville, *Signification de la mode*, pp. 35–40.
[14] *Modèle d'Etat et modèle social de dépenses, Les lois somptuaires en France de 1485 à 1660*, CNRS Colloque, *Prélevement et redistribution dans la genèse de l'Etat moderne*, Fontevrault, 1984 (Paris, 1987).

applied is of less importance to our theme than their contribution to defining the image of a model of reserved expenditure.

Court practices gradually took shape. The lordly life-style required by proximity to the king, the sumptuous existence of a society on display, the ostentation of the equipages paraded at every turn, in brief, the spectacle which the high nobility offered to all somewhat changed its meaning. The demonstration of a political and social power as yet still shared, a spectacle seen, dreamed of and imagined by the man in the street and the readers of the pamphlets which made the splendour of the court known to ever wider circles and inspired imitation throughout the kingdom, it had two consequences. First, it provoked a redoubling of the condemnations of luxury by all those who denounced its wastefulness and the perversity it entailed. Puget de La Serre expressed a commonplace of preaching: 'Everyone is at pains to appear that which he is not and no-one endeavours to be seen as he is. A man acts the prince with his clothes alone, I mean without possessing the merit, the title or the income, and in his borrowed finery seeks mirrors everywhere in which to make love to himself.'[15] The vanity of appearances and the narcissism of fashion made the world into a theatre and the position of the moralists who denounced spiritual hypocrisy complemented the Tridentine affirmation of the Christian economy. But at the same time, the spectacle, like the prohibitions, sparked off a further wave of innovations and counterfeits. 'The court look' gave a common measure to the standardisation of the language of appearances by the condemnation of the ostentatious luxury of the parvenus and the exaggerated appearance of the intriguers. The refinement of some contributed to the social decline of others, and satirical works also emphasised the contrast between the costume of the courtier and that of the bourgeois, model of tradition, conformity and respect for the imperatives of religious and social morality.

These two trends, standardisation and transformation, prepared the way for a major rupture of the modern period: the door was thrown open to the confusion of ranks: 'an uncontrollable development, whose very nature defies analysis' had begun.[16] However, to

---

[15] *L'Entretien des bons esprits sur les vanités du monde* (Lyons, 1631), p. 157; Godard de Donville, *Signification de la mode*, pp. 111–12.

[16] Ibid., p. 76.

see the respect expected for the sumptuary laws as a novelty is to ignore the conservatism of royal legislation and its consistency over two centuries; the rupture began elsewhere. Further, to accept that the changing reality of the turn of the sixteenth and seventeenth centuries caused the explosion of satirical writings denouncing the vain prohibitions and the toppling of hierarchies is also to accept the very basis of the conservative discourse, that is the myth of a past golden age and the existence of a perennial bourgeois ethos, hostile to upheaval and believing in the established order. The unease provoked in the urban population by the growth of fashion cannot be perceived only by the analysis of texts about which many questions remain unanswered (how influential in moral production, by whom, for whom?); to understand how fashion functioned and its rejection, between court and town, we must study the concrete content of practices.

Lastly, these books and pamphlets cannot be separated from a larger body of material primarily inspired by Catholic and Protestant theologians attempting to define the new and amended norms of an ascetic and devout appearance. Behind the bourgeois, there lay concealed a moral problem, crucial for the reformed churches, that of the use of wealth in a system of social inequality,[17] or, to use the expression of Jean-Claude Perrot, of the 'transformation of luxury into charity'. This vision was more important than that of the conservative bourgeoisie in the criticism of the fashions which destabilised the stationary economy and the holistic society. Good manners were associated not only with the evolution of types of appearance which revealed social relations, but with a profound conception of the connections between being and seeming. The texts emphasise the theatrical character of life, and an exaggerated baroque world, fascinated by movement, with a taste for metamorphoses, a love of inversions and transmutations, of everything which explains the victory of complex literary forms – analogy, hyperbole, anamorphosis – as shown by the analyses of Jean Rousset.[18] Fashion and fantasy became the very expression of the contrasted being of the age, signs of instability and artifice. To ponder them was to rediscover the question of the meaning of man

---

[17] See J.-C. Perrot, seminaire de 3e cycle, 'Economie – Population – Subsistance', unpublished, University of Paris, EHESS (1984–5).
[18] Circé and le Paon, *La Littérature de l'âge baroque en France* (Paris, 1954).

and the universe, the relationship to a God who cannot be either unstable or artificial. The two aspects throw light on the baroque anthropology of appearances.

## FASHION AS A PRINCIPLE FOR READING THE WORLD

Instability is everywhere; it is of the essence of things whose destiny is to change. Fashion becomes a principle for a social and moral reading which makes no distinction between dress and the whole condition of man. Grenaille spelled this out in the title of his book: *La Mode ou caractères de la religion, de la vie, de la conversation, de la solitude, du compliment, des habits et du style du temps.*[19] This is a typical, even a banal, feature of all the descriptions of manners, a commonplace of preachers of every hue, who exaggerate one element – instability – in order to equate the variations of the individual with those of the universe. Changes in appearance reveal the universal laws of the human heart and make it possible to understand human behaviour, linked to change and to novelty. Grenaille's project constitutes a veritable anamorphosis, because he makes the profound meaning of the phenomena of falsification, oddity and inconstancy converge: 'Everything partakes of everything as much as of itself.'[20] The sartorial microcosm incarnates the world macrocosm. Fashion is a relay station between people and things, between the immutable and the unstable, the expression less of human liberty than of man's downfall. 'Even curiosity, by which we justify the freedom of our fashions, is simply a specious fault, since it is an ingenious trick to torment us rather than a remedy for our ills.'[21] The myth of original nakedness lay behind the passion for knowledge, and the critics of fashion joined their voices to the choir of anti-worldly alarmists. Every change provoked condemnation of unstable practices which reeked of artifice.

At the same time, Fitelieu de Rodolphe et de Montour published *La Contre Mode,*[22] which 'condemns without appeal a power seen, in the strict sense of the words, as alienating and demonic'.[23] Fashion, whose vicissitudes reveal irrationality, teaches the 'folly of

[19]  Paris, 1646.
[20]  Godard de Donville, *Signification de la mode,* pp. 119–69.
[21]  Grenaille, *La Mode,* pp. 126–7.
[22]  Paris, 1642.
[23]  Godard de Donville, *Signification de la mode,* p. 152.

our souls'. Its principle of inconstancy contaminates the whole world, and its diversity challenges even the unity of religion Castigating the worldly, Fitelieu called on them to convert, to abjure those false gods, Circe and fashion, to reject disguises and masks. He denounced the illusion and artifice, contrary to nature, entailed by the conventional modification of appearances, a corruption of natural ends. The body, in all its elements, considered according to the ancient typology of the senses, was revealed as wholly corrupt. The functions intended by God are diverted from their purpose, 'civil society is interrupted'. To renounce fashion is to rediscover the liberty of God's creatures, to choose nature, to reject the world. We find here a rigorist Christian meditation, aiming at moral reform. However, it co-existed with other forms of expression more in touch with urban realities, which tried to define a middle way between the requirements of religious morality and those of civil life. The wisdom of custom prevailed over the precepts of rigour.

Amongst the conciliators, Grenaille appears alongside Pierre de Marbeuf, Du Laurens, Faret, Renaudot, La Mothe Le Vayer and Sorel, the abbé Du Bosq and the Aix-en-Provence lawyer Figuière.[24] This tendency corresponded to the social and geographical expansion of fashion, beyond court circles, beyond the nobility, from the capital to the furthest provinces, as a consequence of the development of the citizen society,[25] which was then discovering a new equilibrium and where the civilisation of 'good manners' and decency flourished. A first model reduced fashion to a collection of customs, mainly sartorial and quotidian; a second utilised it more precisely to provide a new definition of social commerce.

Correct practices constituted a *savoir-vivre* to which the wise should submit:

> Custom is master . . .
> He who fails respect to give
> Shows he knows not how to live

---

[24] *Le Misogyne*, in M. Allem, *Anthologie poétique française, XVIIe* (Paris, 1965), vol. I, p. 344; *Satyres* (Paris, 1633); *Conférences du Bureau d'adresse* (1633, 1644, Lyons, 1656); *L'Honnête Homme* (Paris, 1630); *Opuscules et petits traités* (Paris, 1643); *La Bibliothèque française* (Paris, 1667); *L'Honnête Femme* (Paris, 1626); *La Vertu à la mode* (Aix, 1641). These works form the documentary basis for the last two chapters of Godard de Donville, *Signification de la mode*, pp. 170–204.
[25] R. Chartier, *Histoire de la France urbaine* (Paris, 1981), vol. III.

> The roses always appear in spring
> You have to fall in.[26]

This line of thought rejected the systematic censure of contemporary manners and extended the potential public for noble manners to the town, as the lectures at the *bureau d'adresse* opened by Théophraste Renaudot reveal. This adapted an academic model for the general public, and for nine years experts debated every possible and conceivable subject, from science to rhetoric, from literature to manners.[27] A debate on make-up held in 1636 shows how the reception of fashion and artifice in these circles was totally unlike that depicted in the diatribes of Fitelieu. Respectable people shunned extremes and defined a middle way acceptable to 'the great' as well as to the bourgeoisie. They obeyed the laws of moderation. In his *Honnête homme ou l'art de plaire à la Cour*, published in 1630, Faret assimilated these ideas into the bourgeois and curial reorientation of the model of good manners. This bourgeois of modest origins, barely ennobled by a post as king's secretary, portrayed the court as the summit of the hierarchies, the scene of triumphs where, to be recognised, you now had to know the rules. In the new civility, fashion became not

> [the peculiarity] of some scatter-brains among the young people of the Court, who ... either engulf half their bodies in great boots, or plunge up to their armpits in petticoat breeches, or completely conceal their faces under hat brims as wide as Italian parasols. I mean that fashion which, once sanctioned by the most admired among great and honest men, serves as a law for the rest.[28]

'Good manners' defined the rules for a wise and modest appearance, transmitted by the imitation of distinction. It is a famous detour in the evolution of a genre which materialised the customary habits of clothing behaviour, not without distrust for novelty and extravagance. The fantastic was still condemned, but the reasonable became civil.[29]

---

[26] 'La Moustache des filous arrachés', in Fournier, ed., *Variétés historiques*, vol. II, pp. 152–3.

[27] H. M. Solomon, *Public Welfare, Science and Propaganda in Seventeenth Century France, the Innovations of T. Renaudot* (Princeton, 1972), pp. 60–99.

[28] Faret, *L'Honnête homme*, pp. 179–80.

[29] La Mothe Le Vayer, *Opuscules et petits traités* (Paris, 1643), pp. 208–59.

From this first use of the word and the themes which accompanied it, we pass imperceptibly to the hypothesis of fashion as a principle of social *savoir-faire* and a means to general social stability. To accept the manners of the age, above all with regard to dress, became an inherent faculty of sociability. In the moral and religious polemic, it was the beginning of a disengagement 'with regard to the possible conflicts between religion and custom'. The doctrine of fashionable virtue, which underpins the notion of 'good manners', helps to relativise religion within the sphere of the proprieties. In the face of this retreat, certain authors in the Christian humanist tradition went beyond the opposition between fashion and devotion. Du Bosq devoted a chapter of his *Honnête femme* to persuading Christians away from extravagant clothes and ornaments, advising moderation in all things. In Du Bosq, submission to custom and rank reconciled the conservative tendency of an unequal and Christian society with a concern for appearances acceptable in moderation in the honest man.

## CAN ONE SPEAK OF A SARTORIAL *ANCIEN RÉGIME*?

Between the reign of Henri IV and the accession of Louis XIV, fashion is fundamental to any account of the development of the sartorial *ancien régime*. Moving force behind diversity in appearances, it was portrayed by preachers, moralists and even economists as a cause of wastefulness and confusion, which was why a whole rigorist tendency attempted to limit its effects. Sermons delivered the same message as the sumptuary laws; clothing consumption should be governed by one principle: to each according to his rank. Clothing was thus at the centre of the debate about civilisation in which the societies of the baroque age were torn between libertarianism and rigour, between instability and artifice and fidelity to a Christianised nature. However, social change, the flowering of urban civility and the increase in court consumption encouraged the search for an accommodation. Manuals of good manners accepted the need to respect practices, the treatises advised submission in moderation to custom. Everyone should appear what he was, but might also appear what he aspired to be.

This basic tension explains the ambiguity of the concept of a sartorial *ancien régime*, and the difficulty of an attempt to understand its evolution and the transition to another system. From this starting-point, the triumph of differences is measured by the progress of singularities and individuality detached from rank. It coincides with major technical and economic changes, which reached their apogee in the second half of the nineteenth century. A general embourgeoisement of appearances led to a glorification of fashion and hostility to the levelling of the upper classes. New norms of elegance and behaviour were imposed on everyone. The age of the proprieties began with an increase in the speed with which models were diffused and a renewal of the conventions. Paris became the centre of a vast trade, now world wide, in luxury clothes. Philippe Perrot has traced this development through the works of great authors, including Balzac, who was the first to introduce fashion into literature, and lesser writers, composite readings where words and objects correspond. Painting, drawings and engravings offer a vivid gallery of diverse personages in which the fashion picture sets the tone and caricature forces the pace. The rising and ultimately triumphant bourgeoisie dominated the social landscape of clothing and dress.

My project postulates the existence of a sartorial *ancien régime* with three principal characteristics: inertia and immobility, especially among the lower classes and in the countryside; a coincidence of costume and social position; a desire for control, which imposed sumptuary laws on the authorities and norms of etiquette and conformity to custom on everyone. We have seen how these principles were, by the seventeenth century, to some extent diluted by the growth of the urban economy and of fashion and the subsequent confusion of ranks, which only increased in the eighteenth century. We also know that the sumptuary laws promoted the growth of fashion in France by mobilising the inventiveness of her artisans and by giving to the court the motor role in sartorial distinctions. Lastly, it seems that we can no longer see eighteenth-century society as dominated by an aristocracy in its death-throes, threatened by the bourgeoisie and losing its social legitimacy.[30] Norbert Elias and Philippe Perrot, who take this view, are not altogether justified in speaking of the 'stationary revenues'[31] of the nobility. The noble economy was not on its last legs, and the social conse-

---

[30] Perrot, *Les Dessus*, p. 35.
[31] Elias, *La Civilisation de cour*, pp. 44–5, quoted in Perrot, *Les Dessus*, p. 48.

quences of its supremacy did not have quite the effects they attribute to them. Either the aristocratic model speeded up the circulation of signs, causing the ancient clothing code to collapse and the arbitrary reign of fashion to prevail; or a different bourgeois model challenged the imitation of noble habits and imposed a different style of consumption as a way of distinguishing itself from the upper classes, in the name of an egalitarian ideology, which could easily accommodate a variety of appearances. A study of texts and archives to show the interaction and even the co-existence of these two aspirations remains to be attempted.[32]

It is in any case clear that the critique of fashion was part of the double tradition of the conservative opposition to luxury (which was not confined to the bourgeoisie, the church more prominent than the state, since the inspectors of manufactures encouraged production, hence consumption) and the bourgeois critique in the name of the values of the thrift and austerity necessary to the accumulation of capital.[33] The legitimacy of consumption had progressed since the seventeenth century, since it was profoundly linked to the development of the circulation of money and the exaltation of trade. 'All this wealth consists only of consumption', wrote Boisguilbert in a pamphlet of 1707; clothes and the clothing industry drew strength from the notion that the spending of wealth was one of the keys to economic development, even if the money of the poor was more fruitful since it had a greater impact on production. The ideological emblems and the imbrication of the ancient and modern moralising discourse should not blind us to the reality of the change. Fashion acted as the symbolic stake in the battle of appearances in a society in which the distribution and diffusion of wealth was changing, permitting a greater or lesser social mobility. It was an issue for the nobility as well as the bourgeoisie, for the elites as well as those who had not yet arrived.

---

[32] The text by the abbé Coyer used by Perrot to show the increasing criticism of the imitators of aristocratic fashion in fact repeats an ancient tradition, and should be seen in this light.

[33] For what follows, I draw heavily on the seminar I led jointly with J.-C. Perrot in 1985–6; I would like to thank him in particular for his assistance with the economic interpretation of consumption.

However, the ancient sartorial system lost its legality in the Year II, with the revolutionary measures which proclaimed freedom of action: 'No-one may constrain any citizen or citizenness to dress in a particular manner, on pain of being regarded as suspect and so treated, and prosecuted as a disturber of the public peace; everyone is free to wear whatever garment or whatever outfit of their sex they please.' Though not without an element of unreality (who, for many decades, had constrained whom to wear what in the realm of clothes?), this text marked a major break.

It is visible in the transformation which reversed or modified the habits of men and women at the beginning of the nineteenth century. In the case of men, a complete change of direction began with the adoption of trousers and coat, a certain tidiness and stiffness, an austerity of shape, fabric and colour. Black triumphed. A colourless male society now presented itself in a dress which was *comme il faut*, proclaiming its attachment to notions of decency, correctness, effort, prudence and gravity. The soberly dressed bourgeoisie manifested the virtues appropriate to capital and to work. But at the same time, discreet signs created the necessary social distance, signalling the notion of a refined abnegation: the false collar, the shirt-front, the cravat knotted in a particular way demonstrated inequality within an apparent equality. Quality remained a refuge.

While no-one would dispute this, one would like to know more about the scale and social nuances of such a major development. Austerity, asceticism and stiffness in clothes have their history. Powerful models, those of reform and Puritanism, imposed their rigour on fashion. For a century, a strict style and sober colours conferred a symbolic sartorial colour on the whole of anti-Absolutist Europe, from Flanders to Geneva, from Prussia to England. To the polychrome magnificence of the Catholic aristocracies, displayed in the dazzling gold and silk of processions and festivals, contrasted the voluntary and quasi-republican effacement of the men of the reformed ethic. The desire for political discussion coincided with the sense of thrift, a hostility to extravagance and the free choice of individual conscience and appearance.

In the absence of more detailed studies, prudence requires that we regard this picture, almost too neat to be true, only as a hypothesis. At the dawn of modern Europe, it explains choices which did not become wholly normative until the nineteenth century. But satire at the expense of bourgeois attire had long existed.[34] It lampooned the new rich who flaunted their surplus wealth and aspired to compete with the excesses of the nobility, and it criticised the bad taste in clothes of the middle classes, so casting doubt on the continuity of a bourgeois tradition of discreet and sober good taste. The moralising critique remained faithful to the principle that 'everyone should remain in his estate and each estate ought to dress appropriately'. In fact, the conflicts reveal the instability of the models and the difficulty of incorporating mobility and contestation into social and cultural history.

Satire, like preaching, is valuable in revealing the frontiers of practice by recording incursions and raids of transgression. But so much remains obscure. One example, that of the French *parlementaires* of the eighteenth century, may prove revealing.[35] In the great families of the *robe*, the eldest son, who would inherit office, was expected to dress accordingly; he was doomed to black and grey, and it was inappropriate for him to get himself up like a gentleman, as did his brothers who became *hommes d'épée*. 'To see the majority of our young magistrates, you would think they were ashamed of their profession. Some affect such an air of informality and rakishness that they might easily be taken for pages. Others flaunt their finery and reeking with scent give the vapours to our little mistresses.'[36] This was a general attack on a type of behaviour, on the pretext of the young magistrates who feared nothing so much as to appear what they were.

The texts reveal a double tendency. Within the magistracy there existed a sartorial tradition whose badge remains today the gown. In the seventeenth and eighteenth centuries, it was expressed in many ways and strengthened by family tradition; as chancellor d'Aguesseau remarked, 'the future magistrate ought to be accustomed at an early age to bear the yoke of virtue'. Jansenism and the habits acquired in colleges such as Juilly had for more than a century confirmed these requirements. But at the same time,

[34] J.-V. Alter, *L'Esprit antibourgeois sous l'Ancien Régime* (Geneva, 1970), pp. 70–1, 106–8.

[35] F. Bluche, *Les Parlementaires parisiens au XVIIIe siècle* (Paris, 1960), pp. 307–599.

[36] P.-A. Molyuos-Saint-Cyr, *Tableau du siècle* (Paris, 1759), p. 35.

political and worldly considerations intervened, and the young legal eagles competed in sexual and civil rivalry with the dandies and little marquisses of the court and the town, with all who wore a sword. The clash of the contradictory principles of the *cedant arma togae* and the court can be seen in the famous scene recorded by Barbier, a Parisian *avocat*: when the counsellor Carré de Montgeron, dressed in black with large band and short mantle, handed his work on the agitators to Louis XV,[37] 'everyone wondered who this legal personage was, such flat bands were hardly worn at Court'. On either side of an unwritten boundary, we see what mattered and the convergence of intolerances.

In the fulminations of the procurator general Joly de Fleury, we see the frontiers of these subtle and ingenious ploys shifting. There were three ways in which an elegant magistrate might dress. He might assemble a legal outfit all in black, severe, the gown closed, but giving himself the air of a 'little master of the Palais' – flowing wig, bands tied like a cravat, cassock undone to the fourth button, train borne by a valet and arms akimbo indicated the young magistrate who was non-conformist within conformism. Or he could ruin himself with coloured clothes, though it was scandalous to be seen in colours outside the holidays; this young magistrate mocked the norms but shocked his milieu and the world. Lastly, he could spend large sums on clothes which were black and grey but sumptuous and costly, with elaborate detail; the young magistrate seduced by luxury respected his estate but ruined himself in sartorial follies.

These divisions within the intermediate milieus – culturally, this was the principle characteristic of the *robe* – disappeared after 1789, when, for the last time, in the procession of the Holy Sacrament, the cortège of deputies to Versailles displayed their sartorial differences, proclaimed as if for a final confrontation: the sober costume of the Third Estate, the gaudy plumage of the nobility, the black and purple soutanes of the clergy. The picture is both too beautiful and too well known to be ignored, but it was only a symbol, at a moment of change, in a world which was moving towards diversity of clothing, the confrontation of claims and the ultimate victory of a bourgeois dress as remote from aristocratic costume as from the plebeian *carmagnole* jacket.[38] The

[37]  Barbier, *Mémoires*, vol. III, p. 89.
[38]  Perrot, *Les Dessus*, pp. 57–8.

nineteenth century saw the triumph of uniformity and the political and moral rejection of the values of colour.

For women,[39] in contrast, the history of this period of social transition was one of continuity. There were no changes to the cut, fabrics, colours or regular cycle of fashion and elegance of female clothes. Change came elsewhere, in their ideological and moral significations, if not in practices: 'What does a man look like beside his wife? He, black, plain, dull, smelling of cigars. She, pink, elegant, sparkling, her rice powder wafting all around her the perfume of ambergris. Does he not look like his own cook in his Sunday best?'[40] This observation by Nestor Roqueplan in the middle of the nineteenth century marks the culmination of a profound trend within the prosperous classes, whose importance lay essentially in the new significance of the contrasting appearance of the sexes. For a society where the values of thrift and profit were fundamental, the demonstration of conspicuous consumption was good publicity. The woman was the shop-window of the man; in fabricating an exaggeratedly feminine appearance, she proclaimed her second rank in the social and familial order. It was the triumph of an illusion. The function of the new sartorial norms was to force bodies to be what they were not and souls – this convenient dualism will be forgiven – to confirm the social values of giving, of hereditary phantasms, of duties sublimated in a respected and respectable appearance. New frontiers of modesty and ribaldry accompanied this shift.

The spread of the men's clothing and imitation of the elaborate women's dress well beyond the confines of the bourgeoisie did not entail a real process of sartorial democratisation.[41] The new consumption did not standardise appearances, but it profoundly altered their significance and relationship between the sexes and social groups, creating new inequalities and new hierarchies. A quick glance at clothes was no longer enough to gauge their meaning since so much depended on nuance and detail. There was a proliferation of secondary significations which culminated in the refinement

[39] Ibid., pp. 63–4.
[40] *Parisine* (Paris, 1869), p. 43, in Perrot, *Les Dessus*, p. 63.
[41] I leave aside here the economic dimension of the transformations of the nineteenth century, characterised by the collapse of the old supply system, the rise of ready-made and the triumph of the big store, for which see Perrot, *Les Dessus*, pp. 69–154.

of tact and habits. Male dress had to acquire an extra dimension, imposed by numerous signs visible to the informed eye. With Swann, Proust would dictate the archetype. The dress of the woman who was *comme il faut*, meanwhile, became extremely complex since it had to fulfil many functions, dictated by the hour, the social situation or circumstances. Practices had to conform to norms which were made universally available by dozens of books.

The reign of propriety was firmly established. It imposed rules designed to mark the hour and social distance. It emphasised the slips which disqualified or qualified attitudes, and which were principally revealed in respect for sartorial propriety, the pursuit of a deliberate simplicity and the proclamation of the canonical ideal of a demanding correctness. Every lapse relegated its perpetrator to the purgatory of vulgarity.

This visible construction of conduct and dress was underpinned by a new relationship to the body. The outer and the unmentionable underneath were united in an obsessive pursuit of decency and modesty. This was the beginning of the cult of underwear, the secret exaltation of the corset, the mystique of the tortured body, epitomising the image of the unproductive woman, pure display, pure consumption, whilst silence temporarily reigned on the subject of sexuality. A new and totally irrational economy of manners asserted the omnipotence of the bourgeoisie against both the dirty, teeming, immoral world of the propertyless and the glittering and beribboned nobility of the *ancien régime*.

Such a reading is valuable both for what it reveals and for the questions it raises. Unchallengeable from a pure Weberian perspective, it requires verification on two fronts. On the one hand, was there really a sartorial *ancien régime*, and what were its rules and practices? On the other, can one pass from representations to practices, and discover the tempos of the expansion and renewal of new social codes? In the transition from the traditional order (designed to emphasise differences and exclude all popular pretensions) to the contemporary order (which tries to efface, though it only multiplies, differences), the historian of modern culture can find confirmation of the ambiguity of signs, as well as of fashion and decency. This follows from the readability of ordinary practices in societies even more different from our own than the bourgeois society of the nineteenth century. I hope to throw light on these questions by proceeding first to a discussion of Parisian clothing consumption, a chance to look at possessions, hierarchies and customs in action; second, to an attempt to reconstruct the social and commercial itineraries of clothes, from maker to owner; lastly, to an attempt to see how, between the reality and the representation of appearances, change constantly occurs. Overall, I hope, through a material study, to discover the historical specificity in the modern period of the culture of appearances.

# Part 2

# The economy of wardrobes

L'art de se vêtir, dont l'origine est de toute antiquité, est
certainement un des plus essentiels au genre humain; aussi en
est-on pleinement convaincu: c'est pourquoi en essayant de le
décrire ici, il serait superflu de commencer par s'étendre sur
son utilité et ses avantages; on dira seulement que le but des
Nations a d'abord été de dérober à la vue l'entière nudité, et
en même temps de garantir le corps des attaques de l'air; et
que de la necessité de se couvrir, on est parvenu à la grâce du
vêtement sous des formes différents, à la distinction des
Peuples, et parmi chacun, à celles des différents états et
conditions, ce qui a donné lieu à la parure et à la
magnificence.

F. A. Garsault, *L'Art du tailleur*

# 4. Towards an understanding of the Parisian clothing system

Consumption is the sole end and purpose of all production,
and the interest of the producer ought to be attended to only so
far as it may be necessary for promoting that of the consumer.
Adam Smith, *The Wealth of Nations*

Some 20,000,000 French people under Louis XIV, and nearly 28,000,000 under Louis XVI, rather more women and girls than men and boys, got dressed every morning and undressed every night; which gives some idea of just how many shirts, camisoles, skirts and gowns, pantaloons and breeches, stockings, shoes and clogs were in circulation. No economic historian, however, has studied this active market, spontaneously renewing and expanding, which raises all the problems of the confrontation between the stationary state and the nascent age of urban consumption. Only the large-scale cloth industry – so called though it consisted of a multitude of small workshops with just a few big enterprises – appears to have interested the experts. Its regulation, the length of pieces of cloth, the code of the clothiers, the repression of fraud, the intervention of the Colbertist State, the condition of the factories and the number of entrepreneurs, the scale of activities of cloth manufacturers from Languedoc to the Beauvaisis, of linen weavers from Normandy to the Dauphiné, of silk-workers from Lyons to Tours and of hosiers from Troyes to Nîmes, have all, at one time or another, engaged the attention of historians.

However, between production and consumption lies a vast gulf, a terrain barely touched on by numerous studies of trade, left, for the most part, to the anecdotal approach of historians of everyday life.[1] The social history of the *ancien régime* should now turn its

---

[1] F. Braudel and E. Labrousse, *Histoire économique et sociale de la France*, vol. II, *Des derniers temps de l'âge seigneurial aux préludes de l'âge industriel, 1660–1789* (Paris, 1970), pp. 217–67, 515–40.

attention to what lay behind the labours of manufacturers and merchants, that is, the ordinary acts of millions of consumers, since the study of consumption means the study of income, and thus an understanding of practices and the way they change. It is, then, to attempt to reintroduce people and their bodies, exchange and sociability, into our reading of the past.

## PARIS AND ITS CLOTHES

Paris is our chosen field of research, though hardly because the economy of its consumption or its production is best known.[2] On the contrary, the backwardness in this sphere of the capital's history needs little emphasis, the size and scale of the task having seemingly discouraged or aborted all attempts. But in Paris we can approach the problems of customs and uses through the extremes and the margins. In the confrontation of dire poverty and absolute luxury we may see our way to the truth of things and beings. The cultural patrimony of the Parisians of the past was in part composed of their various ways of dressing and their complex balancing of possibilities and desires, and like their houses and furniture, of the multifarious crafts and their diverse products, of the artists and arts, of the writers and their works. In the sector of the Parisian working world devoted to the protection, decoration and even the modesty of the body, the manufacture of clothes was also the manufacture of cultural signs. The first town of the kingdom is the best place to follow the battle of appearances, to observe both how change came about and how archaic forms were preserved. Between the seventeenth and eighteenth centuries, Paris was the laboratory and the workshop of many different styles of life, for rich and poor alike.

We should not embark on a reconstruction of the clothing practices of Parisian society without some prior warnings. The size of the population poses the first problem. Paris cannot really be compared with any other French town; Lyons and Rouen lagged well behind, with about 100,000 inhabitants. To find anything

---

[2] For the current state of research, see the *Nouvelle Histoire de Paris*, being prepared under the direction of M. Fleury. See also M. Reinhart, *La Révolution, 1789–99* (Paris, 1971); J. Chagniot, *Paris au XVIIIe siècle* (Paris, 1989). For the seventeenth century, see J.-P. Babelon and R. Pillorget, *Nouvelle Histoire de Paris* (1986 and 1987).

analogous, we have to go outside France, to Naples or London. Between 2.5 and 3 or 4 per cent of the population of France between 1700 and 1789 constitutes, nevertheless, a privileged market. However, neither the volume, the mobility nor the demographic and social categories of the Parisian population can be established with precision; the sources are lacking and historians disagree about orders of magnitude, about estimates, even about guesses. For 1680 to 1700, the best estimates are of a population of between 400,000 and 500,000; Vaubun exaggerated when he counted nearly 700,000. By 1750, Paris almost certainly approached 600,000 inhabitants; on the eve of the Revolution, it certainly exceeded 700,000, perhaps even 750,000. The historian, like the royal administration, cannot keep track of either the massive Parisian population or the documents they produced, which were in proportion. This simple fact does not rule out an approach based on sampling, though it puts its value in perspective. In other words, instead of changing the answers to the questions customarily posed of the Parisian archives, we should rather change the questions. In a word, we should accept that Paris was at the centre of a cyclone of disparate and varied consumption, which is what matters.

What immediately catches the eye of anyone negotiating the streets and squares of the twentieth-century metropolis, that is, the motley and mixed crowd of tourists and workers – the latter, in terms of cultural distance, often from further afield than the former – must already have characterised Paris between the classical age and the Enlightenment. 'I doubt whether there can exist anywhere on earth a more terrible fate than to be poor in Paris, to be for ever at the centre of every pleasure, but never able to enjoy one' remarked, in 1750, an English traveller;[3] a keen observer of social reality, he was conscious that when extreme poverty exists side by side with extreme wealth, frustration and want, as much as actual possession, characterise the relationship to objects. Further, we should remember that the economy of consumption and the organisation of distribution and trade today allow a highly complex game of substitutions, which depends on making people believe that the false can be more real than the real, that nylon fur and

[3] *Letter on the French Nation by a Sicilian Gentleman Residing in Paris* (London, 1749), p. 42.

plastic are more 'in' than real fur and natural leather. A rather mischievous study of mail-order catalogues over several decades would show how this is achieved, and for an increasingly large clientele. It means that contrasts in appearance are to some extent concealed.

The very mixed nature of the population and the complexity of circulation and trade only add to our difficulties. The history of dress must take this dimension into account. The town was in a constant state of flux: movement of people, confusion of things, changes in timescales, which differed according to social and cultural milieus. The unemployed, tramps, beggars, seasonal migrants, integrated migrants, settled bourgeois, notables, suburbanites and countrypeople, travellers, provincials and exotic strangers were all exposed to the shop-window effect produced by the commerce of the capital. The confrontation of the clothing hierarchies, the increase in emulation and the obsession of the well-off with fashion were here more visible than anywhere else in France or Europe, in the extreme contrasts of the street spectacle, from ostentatious wealth to poverty.

FROM THE NOTARIAL INVENTORY TO AN INVENTORY OF
CLOTHES

The sources for a study of scales of consumption are few. The inventory after death alone makes such an approach feasible, despite the biases which unfortunately limit its value.[4] For each social category of the Parisian population, it makes it possible to assemble economic and anthropological facts, to calculate wealth, to obtain some idea of the relative proportions of the different types of investment made within families, and at the same time to compile a reasonably complete description of people's possessions.[5] In brief, it constitutes a bank of direct material facts, thanks to which we can establish a basic lexicon of the facts of daily life. However, the inventory after death poses three principal problems, discussed in every study which has used this exceptional source: it corresponds to a specific point in the fortunes of the persons

[4] B. Vogler, *Les Actes notariés, source de l'histoire sociale, XVIe–XIXe siècles* (Strasburg, 1979).
[5] Roche, *Peuple de Paris*, pp. 59–65.

Table 1 *Age of wardrobes calculated on the basis of recorded dates of marriage*

|  | 1685–1715 | | 1780–89 | |
| --- | --- | --- | --- | --- |
|  | Men | Women | Men | Women |
| Nobilities | 38 | 53 | 53 | 52 |
| Wage-earners | 40 | 45 | 38 | 40 |
| Domestics | 42 | 47 | 45 | 49 |
| Artisans and shopkeepers | 43 | 53 | 43 | 52 |
| Office-holders and professions | 40 | 50 | 51 | 53 |

concerned; its social representativeness is debatable; there are always gaps in notarial valuations which are particularly unfortunate for a history of clothing.

The first of these problems casts doubt on the demographic value of the society which the historian can reconstruct on the basis of inventories. With regard to clothes, age is a variable of consumption which cannot be ignored, even in old societies. Of the sample 1,000 documents used, three-quarters were drawn up after some ten to fifteen years of family life. Given that the average age of marriage, in Paris as elsewhere, was between twenty-five and thirty, the wardrobes that we can reconstitute belonged for the most part to people in their forties or fifties, the most common ages falling into the thirty-five to forty, forty-five and fifty-five brackets. The upper limit of the sample average is that of the average Parisian life expectancy; it was, of course, often exceeded.

Table 1 makes it possible to trace slight differences between the end of the seventeenth and the end of the eighteenth centuries, according to sex and social status. The average ages calculated here lack rigour, but give an idea of the principal variables existing within the reconstituted population. The age at death was higher for women in all social categories despite the high mortality of Parisian mothers. The ages of both men and women were higher in the inventories compiled in the 1780s than in those of the early eighteenth century. One anomaly should be noted: the very low average age of male deaths within the nobility between 1700 and 1715; it may be due to an exceptionally high mortality in the military population at that period or, more likely, to the rather unsatisfactory nature of a calculation based on a sample of a hundred documents. The Parisian clothing reconstituted on the basis of these notarial inventories was therefore that of a stable population, which might be distorted by age in two principal ways: either it exaggerated the difficulties associated with illness, poverty and failure or, on the contrary, it emphasised success achieved before death.

A document which registers age characteristics probably gives a partly false idea of the scale of wealth and, in particular, of the distribution of clothes. But it is less important to reconstruct an unknowable hierarchy than to measure change. Given that the source distorts, what matters is to measure change not in relation to an unattainable external reality but within a relation of the same nature, located within a similar time-scale. In comparing two batches of 500 inventories from around 1700 and around 1789, we may be criticised for lack of exhaustiveness, but we avoid dispersion. However, we lose the possibility of tracing changes in the composition of wardrobes as they occur between 1700 and 1790. But historians of costume believe that clothing did not change fundamentally before the 1770s;[6] in which case, we are in a position to confirm the new clothing habits. Lastly, we have to accept that, for a large part of the population, the formal changes were less important than others which were both more informal, since revealing individualised consumption, and more material, since reflecting major changes in cloth manufacture and its commercialisation. The comparison makes it possible, at all events, to question the social displacements of these variables. This is to tackle the problem of the social representativeness of the source and, in another way, that of the history of eighteenth-century Parisian society.

The inventory after death also reflects a specific situation deriving from its juridical function: it was a way of protecting minors, heirs and even creditors confident of their rights. This explains the document's poor social representativeness: less than 10 per cent of inventories in relation to deaths in Paris in the 1730s, 14 per cent in the 1780s, that is, perhaps between 2,000 and 3,000 documents each year. Further, they include more deeds concerning the

[6] A. Ribeiro, *Dress in Eighteenth Century Europe, 1715–1789* (London, 1984), pp. 140–62; Deslandres, *Le Costume*, pp. 126–38.

property-owning rich than the poor and propertyless wage-earners. The inventory, a device of the wealthy, was expensive. The few documents relating to the less well-off show that a notary had to be given on average between 15 and 20 *livres* around 1700, and between 30 and 40 *livres* around 1780, that is, at both periods, more than twenty days' work; some inventories drawn up for the nobility cost thousands of *livres*. So we find mostly inventories of those who could pay and, less often, of those who had to, for example, on remarriage, when, even among the poor, it was necessary to protect the rights of the heirs of the first marriage. To avoid increasing the distortion, we can assemble a social sample of a hundred acts by categories; other problems then arise, but the importance of the questions posed and the sheer number of acts involved makes it possible, nevertheless, to proceed.[7]

## INVENTORIES OR WARDROBES?

A thousand inventories, no small number, collected over five years, do not describe a thousand wardrobes. Table 2 emphasises this characteristic feature of the role of clothes within the family economy: in any social category, clothes might at any time be given away, resold, lent or re-used. In a word, they are not always to be found where they might be expected. Further, fewer male than female wardrobes are described, though the imbalance is less on the eve of the Revolution.[8] The greater frequency of inventories of clothes may reflect a general increase in consumption or a change in attitudes to re-use. In any case, there are more valuations and, in certain social groups, fewer absences: among wage-earners, masters and merchants, office-holders, members of the liberal professions

[7] For comparison, see J. Sentou, *Fortunes et groupes sociaux à Toulouse sous la Révolution* (Toulouse, 1969); R. Lick, 'Les Intérêts domestiques dans la seconde moitié du XVIIIe siècle', *Annales de Normandie* (1970), pp. 293–302; R. Mousnier, *La Stratification sociale parisienne au XVIIe et XVIIIe siècles* (Paris, 1976); M. Carden, *Lyon et les Lyonnais au XVIIIe siècle* (Paris, 1970); M. Baulant, 'Niveaux de vie des paysans autour de Meaux en 1700 et 1750', *Annales: ESC* (1975), pp. 505–18; H. Burstin, *Le Faubourg Saint-Marcel à l'époque révolutionnaire, structure économique et composition sociale* (Paris, 1983); Joffre, 'Le Vêtement à Limoges'.

[8] Joffre ('Le Vêtement à Limoges', pp. 22–4) finds a reverse dimorphism: 9% of the 130 female inventories analysed ignored clothes, compared with 5% of the 402 male inventories. The proportion of inventories from which clothes are absent is higher in Paris than in the provinces, 30–40% compared with 7%, evidence of differences in consumption.

Table 2 *Number of wardrobes reconstituted on the basis of a thousand inventories*

| | 1700 | | 1789 | |
|---|---|---|---|---|
| | Men | Women | Men | Women |
| Nobilities | 46 | 56 | 56 | 55 |
| Wage-earners | 40 | 56 | 65 | 78 |
| Domestics | 60 | 75 | 70 | 76 |
| Artisans and shopkeepers | 55 | 85 | 80 | 84 |
| Office-holders, professions | 62 | 77 | 81 | 61 |
| Total | 263 | 349 | 352 | 354 |
| Overall total | 612 (60%) | | 706 (70%) | |

and men of talents. This may also reflect an increase in the use of the document; at all events, it is an indication of the interest taken in the value of wardrobes, which suggests a more important and general change, probably varying according to social milieu.

The social classification employed in table 2 needs to be justified. Our sample excludes the abject poor, the homeless and vagabonds. For beggars, the true poor, shamefaced or marginalised, the sources provide little information, though they exist, more often for the provinces than for Paris.[9] The absence of the clothing of the poor establishes a first frontier. Chief amongst other absent categories are the clergy. Their case is doubly interesting: first, both male and female ecclesiastical clothing constitutes a museum of ancient practices; the habit of the Daughters of Charity, a seventeenth-century congregation, was still, in the twentieth century, the female dress of the time of the young Louis XIV; monks' robes take us even further back in time. Second, church circles are interesting because they reveal significant changes, for example, the adoption of the soutane as a means of moral reform in the seventeenth century;

---

[9] C. Roman, 'Mendiants et vagabonds à Paris d'après les archives des commissaires de police, 1700–1784', thèse de 3e cycle, EHESS (1981), provides information about the meagre possessions of the poor on the basis of reports of arrests; another source would be the lists drawn up on entry to hospitals, for example, *L'Inventaire général de tous les meubles et effets appartenant aux pauvres détenus à l'hôpital de Marseille, insensés, 1764–1784*, H XIII 3, to which M. Bernos has kindly drawn my attention.

hence Louis XIV was astonished when he saw M. Bourdoise wearing this new garment. Ecclesiastical dress rarely changed but revealed a concern for comfort. Lastly, priestly vestments, interesting to historians of old fabrics and of impressive splendour, allow us to compare the liturgical rules with the customs dictated by the degrees of the ecclesiastical hierarchy: white was reserved for popes, red for cardinals, sacerdotal colours varied according to the calendar and the garments retained a symbolic significance. Conspicuous through their position at the summit of the hierarchy of orders, the clergy hardly appear in ordinary inventories. For a study of change, they are to some extent marginal.

SOCIAL CATEGORIES AND THE HIERARCHY OF CONSUMPTION

Our information has been arranged according to five main categories of the Parisian population on the basis of socio-professional criteria, and with no claim to exhaustivity. An obvious homogeneity unites those within each group, the nobilities despite the diversity of their occupations and wealth, and the various groups of commoners. This identity, juridical, functional and even matrimonial, since endogamy was the rule, serves to describe if not to justify the representativeness of the groups analysed in relation to the population as a whole; it also raises an important issue concerning the role and meaning of a method based on quantification in a socio-cultural study.

The Parisian nobilities of the seventeenth and eighteenth centuries are now well known, though some aspects remain obscure and we lack a general study.[10] Dukes and peers, *parlementaires*, financiers of the seventeenth century, farmers-general of the eighteenth, royal counsellors of state, members of sovereign courts, counsellors at the Châtelet, military men of Parisian origin or temporarily resident attest to the diversity of the milieu. All these noble groups have been the subject of major studies which can tell the reader only what they set out to tell. Inspired by the growth of social

[10] But see F. Bluche, *Les Magistrats du Parlement de Paris au XVIIIe siècle, 1715–1771* (Paris, 1960); Y. Durand, *Les Fermiers généraux au XVIIIe siècle* (Paris, 1971); J.-P. Labatut, *Les Ducs et Pairs aux XVIIe et XVIIIe siècles* (Paris, 1972); M. Antoine, *Le Conseil d'Etat du Roi* (Paris, 1977); P. Rosset, *Les Conseillers au Châtelet* (Paris, 1972); D. Dessert, *Les Financiers de Louis XIV* (Paris, 1984); J. Chagniot, *L'Armée à Paris au XVIIIe siècle* (Paris, 1984).

history in the 1950s, concerned to confirm a relationship between the role of status and that of class and oriented by the analysis of functions fundamental to the state, politics, justice and finance, they have greatly added to our knowledge of economic life and socio-political activity; however, they have not attempted to define a cultural anthropology, and with regard to consumption, intellectual and material, they have not gone beyond generalisations, on the plane of noble luxury or the wealth of libraries, to address the economy of daily life or the culture of consumption. Despite the heterogeneity of their methods, they keep to the chief characteristics and context of a way of life.

THE NOBILITIES

Within Parisian society, the nobility was in a minority: 3 per cent of marriage contracts in 1749–50, 2 per cent of the population of the Marais at the same period, probably little more on the eve of the Revolution. It is a difficult minority to grasp, since it was dispersed throughout the town. Further, its most eminent members were torn between Paris and Versailles; the worldly life of the capital attracted them in the last years of the reign of Louis XIV, whilst the political and social necessity of life at court was interrupted during the Regency, increased under Louis XV and was then contested if not reduced under Louis XVI. It was a minority which played a role out of all proportion to its numerical importance. It staffed the judicial and administrative institutions, controlled the municipal administration, dominated the cultural institutions and still retained a role in the running of the parishes. The nobles participated in the whole range of Parisian activities and contributed to the economic life of the capital throughout the century. Their way of life favoured the development of a range of activities, and their ostentatious consumption remained a model for the whole of the urban population and the rest of the kingdom. They were an extremely mobile group; the provincial nobility were attracted temporarily or permanently to Paris, the Parisian nobility made seasonal or longer visits to their provincial estates, nearby or remote. Military men came to Paris in the course of their duties or to spend their retirement. Families were often dispersed, and it is easier to speak of the nobility in Paris than the nobility of Paris. If all ages, sexes and groups are lumped together, it represented perhaps some 15,000 to 20,000 persons. Tocqueville thought that there were 6,000 nobles in the whole of Paris; in 1789 the noble electors, mostly heads of families, numbered 4,000.[11]

The nobility was as diverse in its administrative and political functions, and in its social landscapes and life-styles, as it was in its origins. Between *robe* and army, court and town, the ennobled and the old lineages, there existed a whole range of distinguishing criteria and connections. Their economic heterogeneity, and perhaps also their many different opportunities for enrichment, were no doubt factors.[12] There were too many differences between the multimillionaires found among the princely families, the mere millionaires who had grown rich in the Farm or finance, the lawyers of solid wealth and the impecunious soldiers and office-holders for the total identity of the group to be accepted without question.

Still, wherever one looks, expenditure, consumption and life-style were a unifying factor. The farmers-general appear as pundits of luxury; the aristocracy engaged in many different forms of investment; the administrative and judicial *robe* were no different. If we take an equal number of representatives of the *robe* and the aristocracy, including men of the court and men of the sword, we can observe the mechanisms of distinction and diversification in clothing practices. Further, we have included only the nobility resident in Paris to achieve an essentially Parisian analysis, most of them from the two main focuses of noble life, the Marais and the faubourg Saint-Germain, and, at the end of the century, the central *hôtels* of the district round the Palais Royal and the Place Vendôme. The group is valid only in order to illustrate the contrast between social categories described by Louis Sébastien Mercier: 'I confess also that it is almost impossible to be happy in Paris because the pleasures of the proud are too visible to the poor.'

[11] A. de Tocqueville, *L'Ancien Régime et la Révolution*, 2 vols. (Paris, 1953), vol. I, p. 192.
[12] D. Roche, 'La Noblesse du Marais au XVIIIe siècle, Recherche sur la noblesse parisienne', *Actes du 80e Congrès des Sociétés savantes* (Paris, 1982), pp. 541–78.

Let us now turn to the people of Paris, that is, those who, at the top, were in contact with the society of masters and merchants, craftsmen and shopkeepers, separated by wages and dependence but similar in habits and life-styles; at the bottom, they came close to the world of misery and marginality, the beggars and the rabble who escape the notarial documents.[13] A precise definition of the lower classes is impossible; the Parisian working class was not orderly, it escaped the statutory classifications, consisting of a cascade of 'estates' which was not homogeneous, since it mixed value judgements and social position. As far as one can tell from the scanty documentation, the tax-paying working classes – that is, excluding the large floating population – represented at least three-quarters of the population. An analysis of marriage contracts for the year 1749, which underestimates the lower levels but includes more than 60 per cent of Parisian marriages, attributes to them 85 per cent of contributions below 15,000 *livres*, that is, more than half of the newly-weds.[14]

Domestic servants, journeymen, home workers, manual labourers, casual labourers, small street traders and people of uncertain status constituted the lower level of Parisian society. They appear in all the essays in social taxonomy attempted by moral observers, Mercier, Rétif de La Bretonne and the authors of medical topographies, all anxious to distinguish a healthy people, integrated by work, from the unruly and dangerous populace.[15] The people discussed here fall essentially into two categories: domestic servants, original model of the urban wage-earner of the modern period, an unstable and shifting group, interesting both for its diversity and cultural complexity and for its role as intermediary between social groups and between town and country;[16] and wage-earners and the more menial workers, also a heterogeneous group, and prominent

---

[13] Roche, *Peuple de Paris*, pp. 53–9; J. Kaplow, *Les Noms des rois les pauvres de Paris à la veille de la Révolution* (Paris, 1974), pp. 59–119; A. Farge, *Vivre dans la rue* (Paris, 1979).

[14] A. Daumard and F. Furet, *Structures sociales à Paris au XVIIIe siècle* (Paris, 1967).

[15] Roche, *Peuple de Paris*, pp. 54–6.

[16] Compare the analysis in my *Peuple de Paris* and in J.-P. Gutton, *Domestiques et serviteurs dans la France de l'Ancien Régime* (Paris, 1981), with those of S. C.

in the multitude of reports characteristic of the preindustrial urban economy.

To rank this working world can only be an arbitrary exercise, since the social and economic realities are obscure and escape rigid classification. However, the contemporary consensus put at the top the worker, the journeyman of the corporations, whose idiom, in part shared with the language of the masters, found its specificity in *compagnonnage*;[17] he was clearly distinguished from the unorganised wage-earners, paid by the job or the day, all influenced by the corporate and regulated model.[18] They are adequately represented in the samples both for the beginning and the end of the century, by sector, wealth and geographical distribution.[19] The journal of Jacques Louis Ménétra has given them a less passive image, even suggested a complex capacity for cultural appropriation.[20]

SHOP AND WORKSHOP

Masters and merchants occupied a fundamental position in the urban social hierarchy. They include an astonishingly wide range of commercial and industrial occupations which are collectively designated by the expression 'arts and crafts' (*arts et métiers*), and whose members were called *gens de métiers*.[21] The capitation tax, analysed by Expilly for mid-century, puts their number at some 35,000, that is, with their families, probably more than 100,000 inhabitants. Craftsmen and shopkeepers have never been studied as

Maza, *Servants and Masters in Eighteenth Century France* (Princeton, 1983) and C. Fairchilds, *Domestic Enemies, Servants and their Masters in Old Regime France* (Baltimore/London, 1984); J. Sabatier, *Figaro et son maître* (Paris, 1984).

[17] W. H. Sewell, *Gens de métier et révolutions, le langage du travail de l'Ancien Régime à 1848* (Paris, 1983), pp. 7–94.

[18] S. Kaplan, 'Réflexion sur la police du monde du travail, 1700–1815', *Revue historique* (1979), pp. 17–77; Burstin, *Le Faubourg Saint-Marcel*, pp. 325–32.

[19] The figures are as follows: Lower classes: guild workers 1695–1715 forty-four, 1775–89 fifty-five; casual labourers thirty-one and twenty-eight; men of the crafts without status twenty-five and seventeenth; building twenty-six and twenty-two; transport thirty-one and thirteenth; clothing, crafts forty-three and sixty-five; geographical distribution: Right Bank sixty-eight and seventy-three; Cité, Left Bank thirty-two and twenty-seven. Domestics: direction 1695–1715 twenty-nine, 1775–89 fifteenth; personal service twenty and twenty; subordinate fifty-one and sixty-five; geographical distribution: Right Bank sixty-six and sixty; Left Bank thirty-four and forty-four.

[20] Ed. D. Roche, *Journal de ma Vie* (Paris, 1982), translated by Arthur Goldhammer as *Journal of My Life* (New York, 1986).

[21] Sewell, *Gens de métier et révolutions*, pp. 40–1.

a group, which would be difficult given the lack of homogeneity of a milieu which included the great merchant, Mercier, a member of the Six Companies, involved in international trade, and the modest pin-maker with a purely local clientele, the small retail trader and the prosperous merchant at ease within the guild system, the clothier controlling many workshops and the shop master who worked alongside his family. But the group has an overall coherence, based both on the juridical status enjoyed by masters and officers of the corporations and on their economic and social role: an army of small, medium and large masters of the old style engaged in manufacture and sales.

The notarial acts also reveal the deviations from the status rules, one profession giving rise to different titles at comparable levels of activity and wealth: Jean Lafaille was called a 'merchant baker' whilst Claude Estienne Renault was called a 'master baker'.[22] The Paris of the *ancien régime* was riddled with incoherences, and the disparate levels of wealth could only add to the infractions to the rules and juridical definitions which were tolerated. A reasonable representation from each sector, reflecting the diversity of the Parisian mercantile and industrial economy, including the principal trades, suggests we may have a valid picture of this population, though without claiming to reflect its every nuance.[23] There was clearly a wealth frontier within the milieu of masters and merchants: 40 per cent contributed over 5,000 *livres* on marriage; the comparable figure for wage-earners was 5 per cent. Scattered throughout the town, though strongly concentrated in the old central quarters, between the port and the market, between the rue Saint-Honoré, 'Mecca of the luxury trade', and the faubourg Saint-Antoine, these many trades and traders both sustained the reputation of Paris and shared in its prosperity. In many other spheres than that of clothing, it was they who ensured that 'by its fashions, the town is mistress of the world'.

The skills and the appearance of these masters and merchants

---

[22] Daumard and Furet, *Structures sociales à Paris*, p. 27; 582 masters and merchants, that is, 25% of the population of the marriage contracts; Moreau, 'Le Vêtement', p. 3.

[23] The figures for 100 masters and artisans are as follows: 1695–1715 clothes thirty, food twenty-eight, wood and building thirteenth, miscellaneous twenty-nine; 1780–92 clothes thirty-seven, food twenty, wood and building seventeenth, miscellaneous twenty-six.

upheld a mode of privileged perfection which was both constitutive of old society and responsive to the changing times in which they lived. Their intermediate position made them the indispensable agents between the people and the great, between the moral economy and profit.

## THE USEFUL AND THE TALENTED

Amongst office-holders and men of talents the homogeneity was socio-cultural rather than economic. This group was one element in the vast tertiary sector – administrative, judicial and intellectual – attracted to Paris by its function as the capital and by increasing centralisation. All those united by intellectual labour, whether middling or high bourgeoisie, shared a social identity. They were the 'mass of busy and virtuous men, corrupted neither by wealth nor poverty' who were called the bourgeoisie by patriotic periodicals and pamphlets after 1789.[24] They included all sorts of lawyers, *avocats*, *procureurs*, notaries, *huissiers*, *greffiers*, the medical and scholarly professions, 'intellectuals' and salary-earners; our sample emphasises the lawyers, though without neglecting the rest. They all had in common an earlier period of study, so that their position was based less on their economic role than on the accumulation, production and transfer of symbolic values. They were divided by the hierarchy of the different bodies to which they belonged – the bar, the faculty, the academies – as well as by their varying degrees of success and prosperity, which once again emerges in an analysis of marriage portions in 1749: more than 60 per cent married with at least 10,000 *livres*. This was not inconsiderable wealth for commoners, and was sufficient to allow an important position in Parisian society. Men of property with an honourable and secure position, they would be ready to play an active role when the time was ripe, but, in the seventeenth and eighteenth centuries, they were important in the diffusion of the manners and ideas characteristic of intermediate societies.[25]

At the end of our presentation of the witnesses called to testify

[24] Reinhart, *La Révolution*, pp. 41–3.
[25] The figures are as follows: *avocats*, *procureurs* 1685–1715 seventy-nine, 1780–9 seventy-six; officers, lawyers, doctors, surgeons twenty-one and twenty-four; geographical distribution: Right Bank fifty-five and fifty-three; Left Bank, Cité forty-five and forty-seven.

Table 3 *Population and society in eighteenth-century Paris*

|  | Married in 1749: 2,165 contracts (%) | Married in 1750: 800 contracts (%) | % in relation to the population | Number of inventories in eighteenth century |
| --- | --- | --- | --- | --- |
| Nobilities | 3 | 5 | 3.5 | 200 |
| Wage-earners | 23 | 27 | 12 | 200 |
| Domestics | 16 | 17 | 15 | 200 |
| Artisans and shopkeepers | 25 | 32 | 15 | 200 |
| Office-holders, professions | 8 | 11 | 7 | 200 |
| Total of sample | 75 | 92 | 52.5 | 1,000 |
| Miscellaneous | 25 | 8 | 47.5 (of whom 30% = indigents) | |

to Parisian behaviour, we should confess to some regrets: the need to assemble a sufficient volume of evidence manageable within the limits imposed by material circumstances – one can always dream of large teams assembling ideal archives; and the need to rely on sampling, which is inevitably distorting. On the borders of the crafts, the professions and the social groups, there are serious absences which are unavoidable: the secondary roles, employees, shop assistants of every sort merit a study in their own right; the *rentiers*, the Parisian bourgeois, the idle living off prudent invest-ments or in retirement would constitute a well-placed observatory on the confines of the leisured and the active classes; the wholesale merchants and bankers, hybrid creatures of profit and business, on the margins of the traditional Parisian economy, but important for the future, offer potentially fruitful ground for comparing practices.[26]

We have had to to leave aside these milieus, for lack of means if not of intellectual ambition. Our picture will lose in diversity, but perhaps gain in coherence. Table 3 summarises the statistical results of the samples and their projection in relation to the total popula-tion of Paris. It shows that we can reasonably claim to discuss between two-thirds and three-quarters of the population of the

[26] Reinhart, *La Révolution*, p. 42.

city. At the close of a collective labour and the assembly of a thousand acts, it is as much as could be hoped.

This modest statistical sample, of the order of a contemporary pre-election opinion poll, is valuable because of the composition of the groups to be compared and because it makes possible, for the first time, a description of how Parisians dressed in the past. However, before proceeding, we need to refer to the current debate about the validity of a method which proceeds by a prior social assignment to the reconstitution of a cultural territory.[27] Is this historical approach in effect reductionist? The question, like every methodological question, has several meanings. Either it identifies the process of statistical description with a way of classifying objects – or ideas – according to the social position of whoever holds or produces them; in which case, there is reductionism, since to assign a sociological determination is not to take account of a function which can only be understood by a more systematic explanation within a totality. Or it supposes the reification of manners, within the hypothesis of the possibility of reconstructing the unequal distributions of the objects to be counted. The use or the appropriation of an object, as of any cultural product, goes beyond a study of distribution, which cannot explain actual manners. The modalities of the practices and tastes are in effect more real, that is, more distinctive, than are either in themselves.

The social history of material culture, in proceeding to these descriptions, stops short of the congeries of explanations which, in their capacity to explain everything, are sometimes revealed as reductive to their level. The point of quantitative methods is first to try to measure the variations and inequalities of distribution. It is still the only means at our disposal in this domain, which makes possible diverse interpretations of social functioning.[28] It is no less valuable for the past than for today as a means of evaluating the role in social differentiation of different accesses to the fields of production and consumption. The notion of field, effective in the system of contemporary objects, is equally valuable as a means of

[27] Bourdieu, *La Distinction*; R. Chartier, 'Histoire intellectuelle et histoire des mentalités; Trajectoires et questions', *Revue de synthèse* (1983), pp. 277–309; R. Darnton, *Le Grand Massacre des chats* (Paris, 1985), pp. 239–45 (first published as *The Great Cat Massacre and Other Episodes in French Cultural History*, New York, 1984).
[28] M. Halbwachs, *Classes sociales et morphologie* (Paris, 1972), pp. 329–48.

registering the diverse social issues of the past. After description, the historian is thrown back on the mediation of practices, hence to readings informed by the economic, social and cultural interpretation of the society he studies.

In the sphere of clothes, the effect of social habits of acquisition is never so marked as in the most ordinary choices. It is a cultural heritage which changes slowly under the influence of many factors. We have seen that clothes attested to adherences and how, in the past even more than today, they served to construct social identities. We also know how they assisted the transmission of social values: for example, the value of aristocratic extravagance, multiplied by the presence of household servants, essential to an understanding of the gift economy; or the value of the moral, scholarly or political competence; or the value of the minimal civilisation which could be shown by respect for the rules of good manners. In the flamboyancy of noble finery, in the colour of the livery worn by lackeys, whose number and magnificence enhanced the splendour of their master and his house, in the red gown of judges in session and the black gown of professors and judicial officers, in the way in which the poor, charity-school children and the sons and daughters of the working class were able to present themselves, even to exploit the rules of presentation, we learn how social relations are objectified. Nevertheless, only the prior study of distribution can make it possible to understand how practices are articulated through possessions. The history of sensibilities cannot avoid a history of social discriminations.

The inventory after death enables us to compare wealth and so to measure the importance of clothes within a patrimony. It makes it possible to describe items owned and thus consider the mode of social existence of common clothes. Through the mediation of a notary, who has his own sociological and psychological particularities, through a text with its own internal coherences, we can perceive the diversity of Parisian behaviour. The difficulty remains to proceed from this reading of functional appropriations, dictated by custom, to a more anthropological and symbolic reading. It is almost impossible to reconstitute for the whole of the population the specific strategies of acquisition of societies of scarcity. It is far from easy to discover what were the simplest of acts such as upkeep, essential to changing manners. It is almost impossible to estimate the roles of being and having which, in all communities, constitute the essence of the possession of things. Clothing is at the centre of numerous social, familial and amorous comedies, expression of numerous symbolic actions. Clothing practices involve redistribution and thrift, pleasure and desire. We will return to these in due course. We must first make the best use we can of the inventory.

# 5. The hierarchy of appearances in Paris from Louis XIV to Louis XVI

Paris était une ville où on jugeait par l'apparence, il n'y a
point de pays au monde où il soit plus facile d'en imposer.

Casanova, *Mémoires*

A reconstitution of the hierarchy of Parisian appearances is hampered by gaps in the sources. However, these very gaps can throw light on certain features of the old clothing system.[1] Let us look first at the problem of private property. When the notary, and the historian after him, try to assess the place of clothing within a family's wealth, they have to allow for the personal possessions of each spouse which, by virtue of clauses in the marriage contract, were excluded from the community of goods. So all or part of a wardrobe can disappear, though the clothes may be described without being valued. Historians of the provinces are luckier, sometimes finding details of marriage trousseaus,[2] which is extremely rare in Paris where the deed of marriage was content to give only a rough description and valuation of each partner's clothes.[3] All our figures should accordingly be regarded as minimum, rock-bottom estimates.

## THE INVENTORIES AND THE EVIDENCE OF CIRCULATION

The prices recorded by the notaries were in general *avant la crue*, so above the real price that the goods might reach if sent for auction.[4]

---

[1] B. Vogler, ed., *Les Actes notariés, source de l'histoire sociale, XVIe–XIXe siècles* (Strasburg, 1979).

[2] T. Larroque, 'Le linge de maison dans les trousseaux du pays d'Orthe', *Ethnologie française* (1986).

[3] Daumard and Furet, *Structures sociales à Paris*, pp. 7–11.

[4] I have so far been unable to find the records of auctions in the Parisian archives. In the provinces, this type of source has rarely been discovered and used since only a small proportion of inventories gave rise to a judicial liquidation and sale.

This does not invalidate our sample since our purpose is not a history of clothing prices, which would not be without interest, but a study of the evolution of similar values between the reigns of Louis XIV and Louis XVI. To go further would require other tools, the creation of a complex price index, taking account of quality and a comparison of the new (not impossible on the basis of invoices)[5] and the used (through notarial inventories). It is not the market value of the clothes which concerns us, but changes to it and, as far as possible, comparison with the other elements which combine with clothes to form a system, such as jewelry and accessories. These are often equally or even more effective social markers.

There are other potentially damaging omissions. Fraud probably affected clothes less than other elements in the patrimony such as gold, cash and jewels. It is, at all events, quite impossible to evaluate and less important than the many other opportunities for clothes to disappear, evidence of their complex role in the everyday economy of the city.[6] It is possible that, at least at the lowest social levels, the total absence of clothes from a notarial inventory might simply indicate extreme poverty. The true poor quitted this earthly life with just one outfit and one pair of shoes, and were buried with all their belongings. The subsequent descriptions of their clothes bring out two characteristic features; they wore rags and tatters, patched remnants acquired in the second-hand market; they wore everything they possessed, according to both the reports prepared at the morgue[7] and the statements made by the *maréchaussée* when vagabonds were arrested on the roads of the Ile-de-France.[8]

More often, the effects of the surviving spouse were regarded as personal possessions and escaped division between heirs. This is probably the chief reason for the disappearance of between 10 and

[5] See chapter 8 below.
[6] The situation was not very different in provincial towns: Joffre, 'Le vêtement à Limoges (8 per cent of inventories fail to mention clothes); B. Garnot, 'Classes populaires urbaines au XVIIIe siècle, l'exemple de Chartres', unpublished thèse pour le doctorat ès lettres, Rennes (1985), 3 vols., vol. II, pp. 524–43.
[7] R. Cobb, *Death in Paris* (London, 1978), pp. 21–4, 73–86; Roche, *Peuple de Paris*, pp. 190–7.
[8] M. Chrétien, 'La Population marginale dans les environs de Paris à la veille de la Révolution' mémoire de maîtrise, Paris 1 (1985), pp. 134–40 (of 278 people arrested in 1780, only 28 possessed a change of clothes).

15 per cent of both male and female wardrobes. It would not be impossible to track them down at the time of their owner's death some years later, but only after a labour quite disproportionate to the results, and without any guarantee of success given the problems of using notarial archives. In most cases, there is a logical explanation for the absence of clothes: *post-mortem* division between children, temporary absence or sale for the benefit of the community.

'The said widow declares that the clothes and linen of the said deceased have been partly employed for the use of the said children and partly sold, and the money received employed to provide prayers to God for the said deceased.'[9] Painstakingly recorded by the notary, the declaration made by the wife of master Pierre Richandeau, a ribbon-weaver, shows that the resale and re-use of clothes was not confined to the lower classes and that the two often went together – it was a way families coped with bad patches. The widow of Jean-Baptiste Thierry, *avocat* at the Paris Parlement, declared that 'there were no black clothes; it was because she had used them for mourning clothes for her son and the said Chantrelle, her servant'.[10] Here, re-use was necessary to provide family and servants with mourning. It was a common practice, as the popular song shows: 'When my granpa dies I'll get his old breeches, when my granpa dies I'll get his cloth breeches.' The handing down of clothes from grandfather to children and grand-children was perhaps in part an expression of the transfer of authority and redistribution of roles from one generation to the next, especially in the country, though also in towns. The practice survives today, with a strong affective and symbolic charge, when we keep a few items in our wardrobe after someone's death, less for their practical value than to remind us of their wearer, and to keep faith. In past society, scarcity made a necessity of such acts of re-use.[11]

Hospitals, the poor, the indigent and the friends and relations mentioned in testamentary bequests were the principal beneficiaries of ordinary redistribution. 'As for the clothes of the said deceased,

[9] Arch. nat., Minut. central, LXIX, 185 (1701).
[10] Arch. nat., Minut. central, XII, 654 (1776).
[11] Arch. nat., Minut. central, IV, 336 (1707) (Inventory after death of Adrien Vollée, merchant butcher).

the said widow Poulain [wife of a merchant baker] declared that as her husband had died in the hospital of La Charité, his clothes had remained there and an old pair of leather breeches which she had given to a pauper.'[12] Charitable gifts of clothes are attested at all levels of society. They were part of the gift economy, and probably by no means unimportant, both in their direct financial and their indirect cultural consequences; whether by resale or charitable distribution, the clothes of one group were made available to another. The widow Pichois reported that her husband, an *avocat*, when he left for the Hôtel-Dieu, took with him his surplus linen and clothes, which had remained there 'as usual'.[13] The 'as usual' is suggestive as to scale when we remember that hospital mortality probably accounted for a quarter of all deaths in Paris. Even if not all of them had anything to leave, a good number must have contributed both to the precarious equilibrium of hospital finances and to the social circulation of clothes and linen.[14]

When they signal absences, inventories may reveal other practices. Brief annotations sometimes show the surviving spouse recovering clothes left with a laundress or dry-cleaner. The inventory of master Guillaume Bertrand, a metal-founder and gilder of the rue de la Verrerie, is a case in point: 'There follows the list of the linen which is at the wash, two sheets, one man's shirt, one woman's shirt, a pile of serviettes, two woollen caps, a bundle of dish-cloths and two coloured handkerchiefs.'[15] A ray of light is shed on how clothes were cared for and on the evolution of manners, but such references are rare. However, the practice of selling the clothes of the deceased to defray the various costs associated with their illness and death or otherwise contribute to the family's expenses seems to have been common. Jean Bridault, another *avocat*, widower of Anne Rouillet, told his notary 'that in view of his modest wealth and the length of the illness of the said deceased sieur Bridault, he had been obliged to sell most of his furniture, part of his own wardrobe and that of his dead wife, and their jewels and silver, and that there remained at the Mont-de-Piété two silk gowns for the

[12] Arch. nat., Minut. central, XXVIII, 89 (1707).
[13] Arch. nat., Minut. central, XVIII, 820 (1781).
[14] D. Roche, 'Paris capitale des pauvres', *Working paper*, Institut européen de Florence (Florence, 1986).
[15] Arch. nat., Minut. central, CI (1717, 1789).

sum of 39 *livres*.[16] We see again a widespread practice. In sum, the size of the gaps corresponds to the poverty of the family – temporary in some cases, permanent in others – which led to the redistribution and circulation of items by gift, alms and resale.

The large number of inventories studied means we can probably ignore this problem. We may therefore proceed from the patrimony to its composition, from evaluating the place of clothes and linen in wealth, which reveals the social topography of appearances, to the composition of the wardrobes which express in daily life the hierarchy of appearances and its constituent elements. The picture which emerges is somewhat confused by age characteristics and absences. The lists of clothes reconstituted from inventories are not wholly dissimilar to the lists of objects recovered by stratigraphic archaeology. Reading the layers makes it possible to calculate indexes which we must try to test. A low index usually reveals a limited diffusion, but may also indicate that a threshold of consumption had long been passed. An accumulation of items may induce imprecision in the writer, this being particularly widespread in the upper ranks of society and wealth. If we need to take account of values, it is therefore essential to look carefully at the items and the elements which make up the wardrobes. When compared with total wealth, clothes allow us to appreciate not only different social practices, but how they are confused by the very fact that they are the result of a perpetual accommodation between individual and collective modes of appropriation. Styles of life, of which family groups are the relay stations, are expressed in appearances. Clothes are therefore a good way of perceiving the process by which socio-cultural personalities are produced, between the practices which constitute the principal types of social existence and those of the ordinary economy. They define the field of the ordinary in the interaction of consumption and need.[17] In the eighteenth-century town, clothes contributed to the awareness of changing manners whose anthropological and moral significance was widely debated by contemporaries, from Louis Sébastien Mercier to Rétif de La Bretonne, from Legrand d'Aussy to Desmeunier.[18]

---

[16]  Arch. nat., Minut. central, XVIII, 880 (1789).
[17]  J.-M. Barbier, *Le Quotidien et son économie* (Paris, 1981), pp. 125–6.
[18]  Benrekassa, *La Notion de moeurs.*

## THE SCRAMBLING OF SARTORIAL SIGNS

In this great cultural transformation, two trends can be discerned. The hierarchy of the signs of social differentiation was tending to disappear from professional and public life. At the same time, there was a shift in the significations of appearances to emphasise social personalities in other ways, and operate differently on social space. What then was the role of ways of dressing in the definition of the private sphere and the constitution of public space? Its emergence, characteristic in the political domain, for example, of the modernity of the second half of the eighteenth century, unquestionably transformed the world of appearances. In an unequal society, the hierarchy of representations ought to coincide with the social hierarchy; it even structured it. This was the traditional argument of the critics of fashion and the luxury of the new rich, since the former spread confusion and the latter usurped appearances, which were reduced to a sham.[19] If the noble was primarily what he represented, and the bourgeois what he produced, the former ought above all to seem and the second to be. When there was confusion, public opinion was up in arms.

A rereading of the *Bourgeois gentilhomme* may help us here. Molière's play was in a long tradition of satire at the expense of the ambitious bourgeois, evidence of the permanence of urban social tensions, exacerbated by the increased role of the court, to which we know the dramatist to have been close. It joins other presentations of the ridiculous, provincials and parvenus, as in *Georges Dandin* and *Monsieur de Pourceaugnac*. From this double perspective, Molière was an acute observer of the taboos of appearance which structure the forms of private life. M. Jourdain is a bourgeois who banks on the effect of a change of behaviour. Early in the play, he surprises his music master and dancing master by appearing in his nightcap and dressing-gown because he wants them to observe his transformation: 'Today', he declares, 'I am to be dressed like people of quality.' He shows off his silk stockings, his tight breeches of red velvet and green velvet jacket, his undress for morning wear, and his wrapper of printed calico, and adds to the

[19] J. Habermas, *L'Espace public, archéologie de la publicité comme dimension constitutive de la société bourgeoise* (French translation, Paris, 1978), pp. 24–5.

impact of the external signs of his social transformation by parading his lackeys, for whose magnificent liveries he seeks praise and admiration.

The figure of M. Jourdain provokes the laughter of social correction and sustains the comic development of the play with several lessons. The first is to demonstrate, in the comic register, the links between learning the manners of a gentleman and ways of dressing. The different instructors, dancing master, music master, fencing master and philosophy master, despite their quarrels, teach that in the life of people of quality everything is connected, that gesture and culture are one. It eventually falls to the master tailor to make a profound revelation. It is he who best expresses how changing one's condition means changing one's clothes. But it doesn't work, because the bourgeois cannot manage his new skin which keeps splitting open, and traditional society, in the name of the 'good sense' which M. Jourdain ought to personify, denounces his extravagant excess. Molière ranges himself on the side of the holist society and the Christian political economy: ranks confused, manners in disarray, lackeys aggravating the baleful consequences of disorder. In the last third of the seventeenth century, the play illustrates a theme which reappears a century later in the denunciations of moral observers and sermons. The disastrous consequences of social change set the scene for urban habits. The tailor robs his customers, his suit is of stolen cloth, the apprentices ridicule a gentleman, a master is mocked by his maidservant, a stupid husband has no authority in the eyes of his wife, a father has lost prestige in his own family. Nothing happens as it ought and society no longer functions as it should when appearances can no longer be trusted. The play's finale further ridicules the inappropriately dressed bourgeois, and the costume of the Mamamouchi, under the mask of a fake exoticism, finally establishes his character.

M. Jourdain, that famous figure of anti-bourgeois mythology, personifies the issues in the battle of appearances in past society. He was intended, though in vain, to serve as a warning to all the disrespecters of class at a time when, with the assistance of absolutism, the scale of social values was hardening. More particularly, the play has been read as a demonstration of the hostility of its author and the cliques who supported him towards Colbert, incarnation of the bourgeois *en route* for ennoblement, from the Rheims cloth industry to controller-general of finances.[20] For everyone, in any case, the play initiated a debate on social imitation: it was not safe for anyone to assume the clothes of public personages or of the masters of display.

## THE PRIVATE CLOTHING ECONOMY AT THE BEGINNING OF THE EIGHTEENTH CENTURY

Let us now test this thesis by measuring the role of clothes in Parisian society through a study of different attitudes to dress. Tables 4 and 5 summarise the results for *c.* 1700 and *c.* 1789. Moveable wealth has been chosen as the standard of comparison. A study of landed fortunes runs into serious difficulties when it comes to measuring the wealth of the landed and is pointless in the case of the majority who are without.[21] Its adoption as a criterion would also only have hugely increased the differences of wealth. Further, we have to accept the possibility of establishing a relationship, in spite of the different monetary milieus studied, since we pass, between the end of the seventeenth and the last quarter of the eighteenth centuries, from a period of turbulence to one of stability, and we have to take account of the general rise in prices. Similarly, we have to accept, despite the risks, that one can argue on the basis of nominal averages.

To understand the changes, and how they were composed, since we cannot calculate a price index of everyday consumption as is done today, we can express the values obtained in the price of a product with a decisive social value, that of a *setier* of wheat (about 300 litres) sold in the Paris market serving as reference.[22] Within moveable wealth, we have distinguished between *bien d'usage*, objects in everyday use including clothes and linen, and *bien d'échange* or savings, such as investments, rents, debts and cash.

Jewels, which have a role in the system of appearances and whose value is by comparison instructive, deserve separate treatment; they were also a way of accumulating capital, or, among the less well-off, a reserve against a rainy day or sudden crisis. In the jewels of the rich and the modest treasures of the poor, the roles of

[20] J. Marion, 'Le Bourgeois gentilhomme', *Revue d'histoire littéraire de la France* (1938).

[21] Roche, *Peuple de Paris*, pp. 75–9, 80–3.

[22] Arch. nat., Minut. central, XXVI, 253 (1711).

Table 4 *Value of wardrobes and linen in 1700*

| | Total moveable wealth (in *livres*) | Goods in everyday use (in *livres*) | Clothing and linen (average value in *livres*) | % of total moveable wealth | % of goods in everyday use | % of linen[b] |
|---|---|---|---|---|---|---|
| Nobilities | 62,000 | 13,500 | 1,800 | 2·9 | 13 | 20 |
| Wage-earners | 776 | 308 | 42 | 5·4 | 12·9 | 35 |
| Domestics | 4,200 | 550 | 115 | 2 | 20 | 51 |
| Artisans and shopkeepers | 4,100 | 1,190 | 344 | 8·4 | 28 | 25 |
| Office-holders, commoners and professions | 27,000 | 2,500 | 148 | 0·5 | 6 | 25 |
| Total[a] | 98,076 | 18,048 | 2,449 | 2·9 | 15·7 | 31·2 |

[a] Calculated from 100 inventories per category
[b] Average calculated from 'complete' reconstituted wardrobes

Table 5 *Value of wardrobes and linen in 1789*

| | Total moveable wealth (in *livres*) | Goods in everyday use (in *livres*) | Clothing and linen (average value in *livres*) | % of total moveable wealth | % of goods in everyday use | % of linen[b] |
|---|---|---|---|---|---|---|
| Nobilities | 500,000 | 112,000 | 6,000 | 1·2 | 5·3 | 27 |
| Wage-earners | 1,776 | 442 | 115 | 7·5 | 30 | 35 |
| Domestics | 8,251 | 990 | 293 | 3·5 | 29·6 | 40 |
| Artisans and shopkeepers | 8,457 | 2,036 | 587 | 6·9 | 28·8 | 27 |
| Office-holders, commoners and professions | 87,500 | 8,699 | 694 | 0·7 | 7·9 | 29 |
| Total[a] | 605,984 | 124,167 | 7,689 | 1·2 | 6 | 31·6 |

[a] Calculated from 100 inventories per category
[b] Average calculated from 'complete' reconstituted wardrobes

appearance and investment were closely intertwined. They can throw light on social differences of behaviour. The evidence suggests that in Parisian society from the seventeenth to the eighteenth centuries, wealth standardised consumption habits vertically, whilst poverty and need made other choices converge, more powerfully perhaps than activities. Over the long term, the contrasts make it possible to measure the social displacements of practices.

In the Paris of 1700, at all levels of wealth, relatively little was spent on clothes and linen; less than 1 per cent among office-holders and the professions, just over 8 per cent among artisans and shopkeepers, a global average of 2.9 per cent, a figure which, though it conceals the variations, is not entirely without value, since it is calculated from 500 inheritances. Clothing was clearly not a prime form of investment of private wealth, as a comparison with the indexes calculated for moveable wealth and goods in everyday use makes plain. In both cases, the hierarchy is almost the same, though it becomes more marked during the course of the century. At one end of the scale, the nobility owned clothes and linen worth 1,800 *livres* on average in nominal value; at the other, wage-earners, independent and organised, owned clothes and linen worth on average 27 *livres*, 15 *livres* for clothes alone. Had they sold their clothes, the former would have been able to buy 15,000 *livres* of corn with the proceeds, the latter less than 400 *livres*.

In both nominal and 'real' value, a commonplace of social descriptions of Paris leaps to the eye: opulence and poverty rubbed shoulders and provoked each other. If the average Parisian noble decided to exchange his clothes for grain without resort to the *boulangerie*, he would have enough to provide at least fifty people with a kilo of bread a day for a year. A Parisian worker who sold his clothes would be able to feed himself for less than three months. Yet the Parisian nobility invested less than 3 per cent of its moveable capital in clothes, excluding jewels. If these are included, the figure rises by between 2 and 3 per cent, which exceeds 15 per cent of a typical patrimony, clear evidence of the immense importance of appearances in the circles where wealth, power and culture were concentrated.

## THE SARTORIAL SPLENDOUR OF THE NOBILITY

At the time of Louis XIV, noble dress had two characteristic features. First, the two nobilities, the sword and the *robe*, spent similarly on clothes. Second, sexual dimorphism was strongly marked; the value of the women's wardrobes was twice that of the men's. However, in both cases, two qualifications are needed: the most expensive clothes were found in the wardrobes of the military and administrative nobility, in particular among the families which frequented the court. There was a hierarchy of manners and wardrobes determined by both wealth and social role. The duc and duchesse d'Aumont owned clothes worth over 5,000 *livres*, though their jewelry was worth less than 200 *livres* (the heirs must have divided it between them); the clothes of the duchesse de Nevers were worth nearly 2,000 *livres*, the jewels again having apparently disappeared.[23] With wardrobes worth 2,000 or 3,000 *livres*, certain great lawyers, counsellors of state like Gérard Le Camus,[24] or a *président à mortier* of *parlement* like M. de Longueil,[25] easily rivalled these representatives of courtly circles.

If we break down the value of the wardrobes (see tables 4 and 5), we observe a normal spread of expenditure: 90 per cent were valued at less than 1,000 *livres* and only 50 per cent at less than 500 *livres*. For the majority, the average value lay between 300 and 1,000 *livres*, and a quarter of the nobles spent little more on their clothes than a prosperous shopkeeper or a well-off merchant mercer. It is a small number of very large fortunes which suggest, even magnify, the role of display and luxury and the increase in the ostentatious expenditure of court circles. Yet we do not see here the effect of the exceptionally high expenditure on clothes of the French or European princes. Some never wore the same outfit twice, and it is hardly surprising that, in time, public opinion was affronted. On the eve of the Revolution, with a yearly allowance of over 120,000 *livres*, Marie-Antoinette had some forty official or semi-official outfits, without counting her many less formal clothes.[26]

At the time of Louis XIV, only the nobilities who enjoyed royal pensions and gifts could sustain an equivalent level of consumption, like the princes of the blood, Orléans, Condé, Conti and the legitimised children, and like the dukes and peers.[27] At the end of the seventeenth century, over 50 per cent of the Parisian nobility

[23] Arch. nat., Minut. central, XXXI, 56 (1715).
[24] Arch. nat., Minut. central, XCVI, 213 (1710).
[25] Arch. nat., Minut. central, XXVI, 295 (1715).
[26] Ribeiro, *Dress in Eighteenth Century Europe*, pp. 58–9.
[27] J. -P. Labatut, *Les Ducs et pairs* (Paris, 1972), p. 300.

had fortunes exceeding 50,000 *livres*, barely 20 per cent had 100,000 *livres*: their attitude to clothes was fairly similar, their expenditure high but relatively limited. With less than 800 *livres*, Louise de Mesme, duchesse de Vivonne, spent little more than the widow of Nicolas de La Mothe, a simple king's counsellor, whose wardrobe was valued at 700 *livres*.[28] At a very modest level of fortune, that is 10,000 or 5,000 *livres* of moveable assets, it is by no means uncommon to find a quarter of the inheritance in the form of clothes; this was the case with Louis Milen de Gunely, cavalry captain, and with Marie Le Vassor, widow of Louis Ancelin, lord of Gournay, controller-general of the queen's household.[29] The number of individuals seeking or constrained to simplicity was small. When we remember that most of these inventories were drawn up at what was an advanced age for the period, we see that they reflect a tendency to accumulate and conserve more than competitive strategies; the latter were more characteristic of the young, though also required of the several hundred courtly families.

The indexes and the nominal and 'real' values fully confirm the existence of ostentatious noble expenditure, but they give the lie to the habitual exaggerations impressed on preachers and moralists, and those historians who have swallowed them whole, by the excesses of the tiny group close to the Sun King and his imitators.

## THE BASIC CLOTHING OF ORDINARY PEOPLE

The chests and wardrobes of that sector of the lower class which was stabilised and integrated by marriage and work held clothes worth considerably less: one hundred inventories listed clothes and linen worth altogether 2,700 *livres*, that is an average of 27 *livres* per household, or 32 *livres* if we include only the complete wardrobes reconstituted for the beginning of the eighteenth century. Clothes were relatively unimportant within inherited moveable goods: 5 per cent, or barely 3 per cent if we take into account the meagre property owned by the lower classes. However, they were by no means negligible as a proportion of goods in everyday use: 8 per cent, evidence of the diversity of consumer behaviour. Among

[28] Arch. nat., Minut. central, XXXIII, 414 (1709); IX, 574 (1709).
[29] Arch. nat., Minut. central, LIV, 703 (1710); XCIV, 132 (1709).

inheritances below 500 *livres* (two-thirds of Parisian wage-earners died with a capital of less), clothes represented 7 per cent of moveable wealth, and linen – above 3,000 *livres* of patrimony, that is 5 per cent of examples – represented less than 1 per cent. In the most comfortable homes, clothes, old and new, under and outer, were proportionately less important than in the poorest. One understands how poor families threatened by illness, unemployment or the death of one partner could resort to their clothes as a temporary expedient. Clothing, even more than amongst the Parisian nobility, is an effective sign of the economic hierarchy and its expression in the social representations which are more easily measured against the mobilisation of use values.

Also, sartorial sexual dimorphism was much less marked; male and female wardrobes were close in value, alike in their mediocrity, with the former worth very slightly more. In the case of twenty wardrobes where we know precise costs, the average value of the men's wardrobes was 17 *livres*, that of the women's wardrobes 15 *livres*. The average value of the female wardrobes exceeded that of the male wardrobes in eight cases; the opposite was true in twelve cases.

Both the guild workers and the more or less regulated workers attracted by the town and its trade spent overall sixty times less on their linen and clothes than the military or legal nobility. Two worlds existed side by side: one where fashion and accumulation were all, as La Bruyère noted and explained in a chapter entitled 'Of fashion' in his *Caractères*, the other where necessity ruled, and the typical family needed all its resources for survival, with nothing left over for the good life: '[The people] have a sound base and nothing outside, [the great] have nothing but outsides and surfaces', concluded the moralist.[30] To the historian of material culture, such low figures suggest a limited capacity to replace clothes, the near impossibility of responding to the changing seasons, and a certain marginalisation in the hygienic practices dependent on linen. The poor feared winter and welcomed warm weather, when the vagaries of the climate were generally kinder to all.

---

[30] J. de La Bruyère, *Les Caractères* (Paris, 1690), 5th edn. 'De la Mode et des Grands'.

DOMESTIC SERVANTS: ON THE BORDERS OF CLOTHING
CULTURES

By the reign of Louis XIV, Parisian domestic servants had, for the most part, already crossed this threshold of need. Preachers and moralists had long denounced the excessive luxury of servants' clothes,[31] and throughout the eighteenth century satirists and polemicists continued to denounce behaviour so conducive to the usurpation of rank.

Our inventories allow us to make sense of representations and conventions. The global value of the wardrobes exceeded 5,000 *livres*, that is, an average of rather over 50 *livres* per household, not including linen, which was almost double the total for wage-earners. The principal characteristic of the urban servant class, as compared with the working and labouring classes as a whole, was its visibility. Domestic servants were in general better dressed. A minority wore livery and bore distinctive marks whose social function played an important symbolic role, both affirming the rank and wealth of the masters and contributing to an ambivalence in the behaviour of servants, depersonalised but enjoying an added social value.

Servants' clothes were modern and interesting in another way: the complete wardrobe of a waiting-maid or a chambermaid was worth double that of a manservant or an ordinary lackey. This must be in imitation of the sexual dimorphism already observed higher up the social scale, though less pronounced when expressed in nominal value: 34 *livres* for a male wardrobe, 61 *livres* for a female one. The degree of interest shown by families and individuals in their appearance emerges more clearly as a proportion of their expenditure: around 1700 it represented 2 per cent of their moveable possessions and 20 per cent of goods in everyday use; for those with wealth amounting to over 3,000 *livres*, the figures are 0.2 per cent and 14 per cent; for those with less than 500 *livres*, 1.8 per cent and 6 per cent. In other words, the richest servants modelled their behaviour on their masters, whilst poorer servants, thanks to a higher standard of living by the end of the seventeenth century, still had more clothes than the poor in general. Maidservants, chambermaids, skilled cooks, companions and housekeepers in general, but

---

[31] Sabatier, *Figaro et son maître*, pp. 47–60; Fairchilds, *Domestic Enemies*, pp. 31–8; Maza, *Servants and Masters in Eighteenth Century France,* pp. *25–6, 119–23.*

especially in the great houses, had opted for a certain frivolity; their menfriends and husbands were rather less affected unless they were employed in the upper levels of service, as *maîtres d'hôtel*, personal valets or chefs. The inventories reveal their collective role as cultural intermediaries.[32]

It was not the livery which was crucial. Liveries belonged to the masters. They were among the panoply of external signs of rank; they helped to standardise a disparate population for ease of identification and, in addition, at the turn of the seventeenth century, bolstered competing aristocratic vanities. Originally confined to the royal family and the very greatest noble houses, livery had spread to all privileged houses, which vied with each other in the ostentation of the dress outfits in which they kitted out their porters, lackeys, coachmen, postillions, sedan-chair bearers, *valets de chambre*, in sum, their men, especially those whose jobs took them into both private and public space. The proliferation of splendid and costly liveries, cut from rich fabrics, embellished with braid, ribbons and expensive buttons, in choice and brilliant colours, became part of the street spectacle.

This fashion, by encouraging and increasing extravagance, attracted the attention of the authorities, who attempted to control it.[33] In 1717, a royal edict limited the number of liveried servants and confined distinguishing marks to the colour of the braid and ribbons; in 1724, an ordinance prohibited liveried servants from wearing gold or silver on their clothes, especially their waistcoats and breeches, silk stockings decorated with gold or silver pieces, or velvet, on pain of confiscation of the garments, a fine for the masters and prison for the servants. Like all sumptuary laws, these ordinances were issued in vain. The costly liveries sported by insufferably brazen or insolent domestic servants might guarantee them impunity, or mobilise a hostile crowd. They threatened the social order by their excessive cost, prejudicial to family fortunes, and by concealing the true social position of employers and servants. The legislation tried to control what it could not prevent by imposing a livery which was pared down but identifiable, and by

---

[32] D. Roche, *Les Domestiques parisiens comme intermédiaires culturels au XVIIIe siècle, Les Intermédiaires culturels* (Aix, 1982).

[33] Sabatier, *Figaro et son maître*, pp. 50–4; Maza, *Servants and Masters in Eighteenth Century France*, pp. 121–3.

forbidding excessive ornamentation. The history of servants' liveries was part of the history of the sumptuary expenditure of the Parisian nobility and highlights the importance of social markers in an unequal society.[34]

In 1789, the Constituent Assembly, seeing liveries as an expression of the servile status of servants, abolished them. But the conflict between the visibility necessary to control domestic servants and the rejection of signs of inequality could only be resolved, in the nineteenth and twentieth centuries, by the substitution of a new code. The vertical rules which in traditional society imposed sumptuous and colourful liveries, which rendered personal differences invisible in the eyes of the masters, and the social power of the masters visible in the eyes of the world, were succeeded by the horizontal norm of discretion in the dress of domestic servants, which should be unobtrusive and sober, both like and unlike that of their masters, expressive both of deference and distance. The real difference and the role of domestic servants as intermediaries at the end of the seventeenth century was less a matter of livery than of many acts integrated into relationships of subordination. Before the ubiquity of wage labour had standardised the position of domestic servants, gifts in kind, old clothes among them, were part of their remuneration, along with food and lodgings. The contract of hire sometimes provided for servants to be given items of clothing, lengths of material or even a bonus so that they could change their old clothes for a festival or a funeral.

It is clear from Parisian wills that employers frequently bequeathed clothes or linen to their manservants and maidservants.[35] François Grimod of Beauregard left his two lackeys 'all [his] nightshirts without embroidery, also [his] daytime shirts without embroidery, all [his] corsets, nightcaps, stockings of every sort, new and old, all [his] coats, waistcoats, breeches, dressing-gowns, collars, shaving linen and handkerchiefs except for the set of gold buttons on one coat, and to each one a dozen of the least handsome and fine of [his] fine embroidered shirts'. Though exceptional items such as court dress, suits and outfits belonging to the king, cloth of gold and silver, precious lace and costly jewels and ornaments were

---

[34] Maza, *Servants and Masters in Eighteenth Century France*, pp. 316–25.
[35] Sabatier, *Figaro et son maître*, pp. 26–7, 267–70; Fairchilds, *Domestic Enemies*, pp. 54–5, 96–7.

sometimes excluded from bequests, and though valets and chamber-maids were usually given clothes which were worn or outmoded, the gifts of masters and the scrounging of servants still made for an active trade and circulation. It was profitable and advantageous, and it was an effective agent for cultural change through its influence on behaviour and manners. It was a factor for cohesion within the urban population and an element in the moral and social ambiguity of the servant class. 'Monkeys of their masters', was how one time-honoured expression rather brutally put it. The servant was his master's standard-bearer through the clothes he wore, and through which he both espoused the dominant models and aspirations and instructed the common people in different life-styles. He might be envied or denounced, and writers did both in good measure; by mimesis or osmosis, the servant was an agent for a profound social and cultural change. Sartorial socialisation was both the sign and the consequence of this role, which probably dated back to very early in the modern period. Further, it affected the whole social body since servants linked town and country, and refined and inferior milieus. In Paris, at least, they were everywhere and might learn lessons from every social category.

### THE MODEST DRESS OF THE BOURGEOISIE

Among the bourgeoisie of office and talents, wardrobes were worth three times as much as those of domestic servants, and five times as much as those of wage-earners. Overall, they represented only 0.5 per cent of moveable wealth, so little because the moveable wealth of this group was inflated by the presence of items rare amongst the working class, such as office and rents; however, they represented 13 per cent of goods in everyday use, that is, a significant element in their ordinary expenditure, if not on the lavish scale of the nobility. Some twenty families had wardrobes worth over 300 *livres*, whilst a quarter of them had wardrobes worth less than 50 *livres*. It is amongst middling fortunes, those with moveable goods worth between 3,000 and 4,000 *livres*, that we find instances of high clothing consumption, but the Parisian world of officers, *avocats*, the liberal professions and even intellectuals did not, on the whole, go to extremes in their clothing, and accumulation was relatively rare. Exceptionally, Elisabeth Lecamus,[36] and her husband, a rich *avocat* whose patrimony was valued at 7,000 *livres*, had together spent 1,154 *livres* on clothes and linen, that is, 16 per cent of their fortune; this was an almost aristocratic level of sartorial consumption. In contrast, Louise Delafresnay, widow of a surgeon, left clothes worth rather less than 80 *livres*,[37] Jean Trochet, *procureur* at the Châtelet, had clothes valued at 90 *livres*,[38] and François Raimond, notary, and his wife together had clothes worth 300 *livres*.[39] Inequality between these male and female bourgeois wardrobes was general. In the Lecamus household, it was one-third for the husband, two-thirds for the wife; in the majority of cases, men spent half as much as women on their appearance, though not all wives could indulge in fine clothes, especially if they had several children.

It is fairly rare, more so among doctors than lawyers, as Françoise Lehoux observed,[40] to find references to the doctoral robes or formal suits reserved for judicial or university ceremonies, whose cost sometimes raised the otherwise low valuations of male clothes. They might remain in faculty wardrobes, or figure in bequests, so not appear in the inventories;[41] it was not, in any case, obligatory to purchase them, as acts could be witnessed in a black suit and doctoral cap. Overall, the *petite robe* of the time of Louis XIV was distinguished by its sartorial moderation and its utilitarian air rather than by its concern for decorum. If its members spent only moderately and shunned ostentation, this was probably in part an economic choice – it was a milieu which counted its pennies – but probably also the expression of a religious and moral attitude. This was the group that provided many of those who witnessed or participated in the religious reformation of the century, including Jansenism. It preferred essentials to accessories and comfort to fashion, in an edifying fidelity to principles which ensured spiritual and cultural cohesion.

We come finally to artisans and shopkeepers. Economic independ-

---

[36] Arch. nat., Minut, central, XXIII, 383 (1700).
[37] Arch. nat., Minut, central, CI, 123 (1708).
[38] Arch. nat., Minut, central, CIX, 399 (1710).
[39] Arch. nat., Minut, central, CI, 138 (1715).
[40] F. Lehoux, *Le Cadre de vie des médecins parisiens au XVIIe siècle* (Paris, 1976), p. 246.
[41] Lehoux, *Cadre de vie des médecins parisiens*, p. 241.

ence, and the ownership by two-thirds of our sample of a shop or workshop, sharply differentiated these shopkeepers and manufacturers from the world of unorganised street traders, often living on the edge of poverty; they were equally remote from the wealthy merchants at the peaks of business and commercial success. They formed a coherent group, their wealth modest, many of them notables in their own street or quarter, often officers in their corporation (a position sometimes decided by age), some successful, some stagnating; they were an intermediate class.

They spent a considerable amount on clothes: 344 *livres* on average, twelve times more than wage-earners, twice as much as non-noble office-holders. Their wardrobes ranged in value from 10 to 1,000 *livres*, but two thresholds are visible. A third of their wardrobes were worth between 100 and 300 *livres*, that is, were substantial, though not lavish. Below 100 *livres*, the wardrobe of one spouse has disappeared in a quarter of cases so we can assume undervaluation; in the dozen cases above 300 *livres*, the clothes were many, varied and choice. This small and middling urban bourgeoisie spent lavishly on its clothes; 8 per cent of moveable possessions, 28 per cent of goods in everyday use, the highest proportion of any Parisian group. The fact is all the more significant in that fewer than half (45 per cent) of the craftsmen and shopkeepers devoted more than 20 per cent of their moveable wealth to clothes. The two indexes together reveal a trend towards sartorial refinement which was again more pronounced among women than men. The intermediate milieus, worth between 5,000 and 10,000 *livres*, were unquestionably the most affected. Above 10,000 *livres*, clothes became less important proportionately. The most abundant clothes, and often the most expensive and luxurious, were found in the wardrobes of the middling groups, as is shown by the figures on p. 105; they were the models for their category.

It appears that it was neither the richest nor the poorest within this group who in a sense defined the norm of clothing consumption, but rather the middling categories, with no discernible difference between craftsmen and merchants. At one end of the scale, Antoine Bourgoing, master saddler and coach-builder, though he owned moveable wealth valued at almost 3,000 *livres*, left his heirs a wardrobe worth only 8 *livres*. In contrast, Gilles Oudry, a

Value of the wardrobes of artisans and shopkeepers *c.* 1700

| | | | | |
|---|---|---|---|---|
| 0–50 *livres* | 26 | | 100–300 *livres* | 37 |
| 50–100 *livres* | 27 | | > 311 *livres* | 10 |
| | | 100 wardrobes | | |
| *Patrimonies of less than 500* livres | | | | |
| 0–50 *livres* | 15 | | > 800 *livres* | 3 |
| 50–100 *livres* | 8 | | | |
| | | 26 wardrobes | | |
| *Patrimonies of above 10,000* livres | | | | |
| 0–50 *livres* | 3 | | > 100 *livres* | 5 |
| 50–100 *livres* | 4 | | | |
| | | 12 wardrobes | | |

merchant brazier, worth more than 10,000 *livres*, spent more than 1,100 *livres* on his clothes.[42]

The richest had no wish to succumb to the folly of emulating a higher consumption model, whilst the poorest were in no position to do so, Appearances were, however, a fundamental element in the divisions within Parisian artisanal and shopkeeping society. Those scenting success appreciated the prestige bestowed by a good appearance and devoted a substantial part of their income to this end; those who were already successful had less need of it, whilst those still on the bottom rungs of the ladder, the poorest, without being excluded, lacked the wherewithal. A concern with costume seems to have typified those groups and individuals who were most ambitious and most determined to achieve integration via wealth. This was the result, perhaps, of the shop-window effect in trade or a craft, where a prosperous appearance was necessary for credit; the proprieties and conventions of the shop-keeping bourgeoisie and the discreet elegance of the women no doubt also contributed; for the men, lastly, it was probably to some extent a hangover from the habits acquired before marriage in the economic and sexual rivalry of their years as apprentices.

To find evidence of the distinctiveness of the small shopkeepers and craftsmen we need to look at other indicators, such as jewels, silverware, fine furniture and books; these, together with dress, brought the small and middling Parisian bourgeoisie closer to the models of aristocratic and bourgeois success. If craftsmen spent money on clothes, it was as much from a desire for social distinction

[42] Arch. nat., Minut, central, II, 12 (1700); XXVIII, 104 (1710).

as from a taste for elegance or respect for the imperatives of fashion. Stylish costume was concentrated amongst the more ambitious.[43]

## AT THE END OF THE SEVENTEENTH CENTURY: THREE SARTORIAL SENSIBILITIES

In Parisian society in the reign of Louis XIV, clothes and linen were of relatively small value, though in no social group were they negligible. In relation to the potential consumer market, they were important if we can extrapolate the whole on the basis of our sample. The 450,000 or 500,000 inhabitants of the capital had between them accumulated clothes worth many tens of thousands of *livres*. At the top, a tiny fraction of the population – the nobility and the richest members of the third estate, heterogeneous groups but the holders of real power – was caught up in the cycle of ostentatious expenditure; clothing was a sign which could entail excess and extravagance along with the other elements of luxury; it was a symbol in the social parade of ranks and conditions. It is significant that, in this world of appearances, the dress of domestic servants was designed as a further demonstration of the omnipotence of their masters. Through their clothes, servants were introduced to habits of consumption which they, in their turn, passed on to other sectors of the population. Bars, dancehalls, theatres, festivals and fairs were the most obvious locales for such transfers, but the home and the family were just as, if not more, important. At the bottom, those who had crossed the threshold of simple need, wage-earners stabilised by employment and integrated by marriage, whose activities brought them into close contact with the small bosses of workshops and shops, were already poised to achieve a minimal elegance. Ordinary popular consumption gave clothing a motor role in the economy. Between these two groups, artisans and shopkeepers revealed their own characteristic attitudes and a range of types of behaviour; the bourgeoisie of office and rents also made specific choices which revealed a preference for the utilitarian and the necessary over decorum.

Different sartorial sensibilities existed within these bourgeoisies,

---

[43] Kalifa, 'Le Costume dans la petite bourgeoisie', pp. 39–40.

since the most costly and abundant clothes were not automatically found where there was the greatest wealth. Three types of *habitus* are visible. In the first, possession of clothes was reduced to the utilitarian: one had such clothes as were necessary and satisfied the conventions of the milieu, adapted to religious, social or economic requirements. For the very poor, the choice of clothes was a matter of necessity and the motive of protection operated most strongly. In the second, great importance was attached to sartorial refinement as an indicator of social distinction. Concern with appearances and their effect was primarily a feature of the intermediate groups in the merchant, craft and liberal bourgeoisie, that is, those who constituted the essential social backbone of urban life, neither poor nor rich, but comfortably off and aspiring for betterment. Their basic attitude accorded with the religious and moral rules of the civilisation of good manners. Thirdly, there were the individuals and micro-milieus open to change. The values of imitation and the influence of fashion handed down from on high dictated a specific aesthetic. For the richest, it might entail the primitive accumulation of a considerable clothing capital.

These three sensibilities existed independently of economic factors. The Parisian clothing system consisted less of a strict superposition of strata corresponding to economic and social levels than of a constant interweaving of choices and behaviour operating among rich and less rich alike. The scale of the phenomenon acquired a collective value with an accumulation which was the result of a large number of individual choices. Clothing was a mirror to men's and women's lives. The latter played a dynamic and motor role in every milieu, except perhaps amongst wage-earners, where the equality of necessity prevailed, and amongst the wealthiest of the aristocracy, where men, 'obliged to assert their prestige and rank by sumptuary expenditure, symbol of social status',[44] spent as much as their partners on clothes; courtiers and intimates of the king were impelled by the logic of etiquette into sartorial overconsumption, integral element in the aristocratic ethos, fundamentally different from that of the professional bourgeois classes. Among the latter, it was women who were the prime movers in the transformation of sensibilities.

Thus, at the dawn of the Enlightenment, the Parisian clothing

---

[44] Elias, *La Société de Cour*, pp. 54–5.

system obeyed three logics: that of the society of status and rank, that of the controlled rationality of bourgeois economic choices, and that of necessity for the poor. None of these logics coincided exactly with one social stratum, but spread across all groups in ways which had their own reasons and constraints, intersecting within the town.

## THE VALUE OF CLOTHING ON THE EVE OF THE REVOLUTION

By the end of the *ancien régime*, everything had changed (see tables 5, 6 and 7). For all social groups except the merchant and craft bourgeoisie, wardrobes had increased in value much more rapidly than goods in everyday use, and for all, without exception, more than the average increase in moveable wealth. In nominal or real value, the picture is the same, though the increase is rather smaller when calculated in *sétiers* of corn than in cash. Everyone now owned more, luxury goods were more widely diffused and every social and intimate expression of appearances had acquired great importance. The intermediate categories, domestic servants, the richer wage-earners and the prosperous bourgeoisie, led the field, with an average rate of growth exceeding 250 per cent. But if more or less everybody had gained, the gulfs had grown wider and been relocated within the social topography. The birth of a consumer society in the last quarter of the eighteenth century was based on a series of transformations and reclassifications of sensibilities and of social *habitus*.

## THE ADVANCES MADE BY ORDINARY PEOPLE

At the bottom of the social pyramid, there had been a profound transformation.[45] The global value of lower-class wardrobes now exceeded 8,500 *livres*, that is an average per family of 85 *livres*, 115 *livres* if linen is included, a rate of increase of 215 per cent in nominal value compared with the beginning of the century, 148 per cent in real value. At the same time, clothing had risen from 5 to 7.5 per cent of patrimonies, and the increase within goods in everyday use was nearly fourfold, Clothing was now an important element in the budgets of the less well-off, but one which reveals even more

---

[45]    Roche, *Peuple de Paris*, chapter 6 (I summarise here the main conclusions).

Table 6 *Nominal and real value of wardrobes and linen (1700–89)*

| | *c.* 1700 | | *c.* 1789 | |
|---|---|---|---|---|
| | Nominal value (in *livres*) | Value in corn (in *sétiers*)[a] | Nominal value (in *livres*) | Value in corn (in *sétiers*)[b] |
| Nobilities | 1,800 | 97·6 | 6,000 | 254·0 |
| Wage-earners | 42 | 1·4 | 115 | 3·6 |
| Domestics | 115 | 2·9 | 293 | 12·4 |
| Artisans and shopkeepers | 344 | 18·5 | 587 | 24·8 |
| Office-holders, commoners and the professions | 148 | 7·9 | 694 | 29·2 |
| Total | 2,449 | 128·3 | 7,689 | 324·0 |

[a] Calculated on the basis of the decennial average price in the Paris market, 1695–1704; one *sétier* of corn = 18·6 *livres*
[b] Calculated on the basis of the decennial average price in the Paris market, 1780–9; one *sétier* of corn = 23·6 *livres*

Table 7 *Increase in value of wardrobes (1700–89)[a]*

| | Increase in moveable wealth (%) | Increase in goods in everyday use (%) | Increase in wardrobes (%) | Increase in real value[b] (%) |
|---|---|---|---|---|
| Nobilities | 700 | 730 | 233 | 163 |
| Wage-earners | 129 | 44 | 215 | 148 |
| Domestics | 96 | 80 | 436 | 321 |
| Artisans and shopkeepers | 106 | 71 | 70 | 35 |
| Office-holders, commoners and the professions | 224 | 248 | 369 | 272 |

[a] Calculated on the basis of the figures given in tables 4–6
[b] Calculated on the basis of the decennial average price of a *sétier* of corn in the Paris market, 1635–1765, 18·6 *livres* and 1780–9, 23·6 *livres*

clearly than before the differences in wealth, hence the balance which was, or was not, struck between individual needs, possibilities and choices; clothes were more important for everyone, but especially for the poorest. For those whose wealth was assessed at less than 500 *livres*, the proportion of clothes rose from 7.5 per cent in 1700 to 16 per cent in 1789; for those with wealth assessed at above 3,000 *livres*, the equivalent figures were 0.6 per cent and 1.6 per cent.

This striking increase was primarily based on purchases by women. Men's wardrobes were worth on average 36 *livres*, those of women 92 *livres*, that is for the former a twofold increase, for the latter, sixfold. The Parisian 'woman of the people' had adopted the general model of clothing consumption, and sexual dimorphism was now everywhere the rule. It sometimes took an extreme form: Jean Bertos, a cook-shop employee who died in 1784, left clothes worth 38 *livres*, whilst his widow had a wardrobe worth 346 *livres*;[46] the wife of Julien Patel, employed by an ice-cream maker, had clothes worth 214 *livres*, whereas those of her husband were worth only 60 *livres*.[47] To understand these differences in behaviour, we would need to be able to trace the sartorial life of a couple. It is clear that women entered the married state better provided with clothes and linen than men, and the gap was likely to widen as long as the family avoided misfortune and surmounted the hazards of 'the fragile life'.[48] Women tended not only to keep clothes but to acquire new ones. The integrated working class had entered the consumption cycle. This was a fundamental silent revolution, as important in its way as the spread of literacy. The search for greater comfort was initially characteristic of women, the desire to look better a feature of both sexes.

We probably observe here the consequences of a general wave of imitation, in which domestic servants had been prominent since the beginning of the century. During the reign of Louis XVI, the value of the latter's wardrobes together exceeded 29,000 *livres*, that is, a record increase of 436 per cent. This was double the increase among the lower classes in general and between three and four times more than the average increase in all the inventories put together. These changes are indicative of two attitudes which were characteristic of the Parisian servant class: the accumulation of clothes on a temporary basis, and a continued very pronounced sexual dimorphism. More than elsewhere, clothes circulated within the servant class by means of gifts, scrounging and the acquisitive-

---

[46] Arch. nat., Minut. central, CXI, 362 (1784).
[47] Arch. nat., Minut. central, CV, 1368 (1782).
[48] A. Farge, *La Vie fragile, violence, pouvoirs et solidarités à Paris au XVIIIe siècle* (Paris, 1986).

ness which was easily satisfied by the appropriation, voluntary or involuntary, of articles from their employers' wardrobes.[49] In 1700, servants devoted 10 per cent of their ordinary expenditure to their wardrobes; in 1780 it was 30 per cent. We see the results of a surge of emulation, remarked on by all observers, in which the wearing of ever more luxurious liveries symbolised a breakdown of order in the world of customary consumption. The contrast between male and female behaviour visible by the end of the seventeenth century persisted: 88 *livres* on average for a masculine wardrobe, 151 *livres* for a feminine one, but the former had grown as fast as the latter (rates of 257 and 246 per cent). This testifies to the improved standard of living of the servant class as compared with other wage-earners.[50]

However, the change was more marked amongst the richest, where sexual dimorphism had diminished: *maîtres d'hôtel*, butlers and chefs spent as much as their wives (the average value of the wardrobes of those possessing over 3,000 *livres* was 225 *livres* for men, 230 *livres* for women). After the example of their masters, their clothes were varied, numerous, embellished and ornamented. Down amongst coachmen, porters, grooms and simple lackeys, the women's wardrobes had changed much more than the men's. We see the effects of the greater or lesser proximity of servants to their masters, at the end of a trend traced back by Rétif de La Bretonne and Mercier to the seventies, when working-class women and domestic servants had begun to aspire to 'good taste' and pay attention to their dress, and when the clothes-conscious had begun to hanker after fashionable *robes d'agrément*.[51] What had once been confined to the narrow circle of the high aristocracy or the very rich bourgeoisie had become a general phenomenon, hence the social scrambling of conditions and ranks.[52] Valets and masters, maidservants and mistresses were confused in the urban theatre, as they had long been in theatrical convention.[53]

[49] Sabatier, *Figaro et son maître*, pp. 269–70.
[50] Roche, *Peuple de Paris*, pp. 75–94.
[51] L.-S. Mercier, *Tableaux de Paris* (Amsterdam), 12 vols., vol. X, pp. 190–1; Rétif de La Bretonne, *Les Nuits de Paris* (Paris, 1788), 7 vols., pp. 2493–4, 2521–2.
[52] Sabatier, *Figaro et son maître*, pp. 52–4.
[53] J. Emelina, *Les Valets et les servantes dans le théâtre comique en France de 1610 à 1700* (Grenoble, 1975); M. Ribaric-Demers, *Le Valet et la soubrette, de Molière à la Révolution* (Paris, 1971).

THE SARTORIAL SUPERFLUITY OF THE PRE-REVOLUTIONARY
NOBILITY

On the eve of the Revolution, the Parisian nobilities were no more homogeneous than in the time of Louis XIV: 7 per cent of moveable patrimonies exceeded a thousand *livres*, 80 per cent exceeded 500,000 *livres*. The increase – 700 per cent – in less than a century is considerable, probably the result of the concentration in Paris of those nobles attracted by service to the state or life at court; it was swelled by the presence of a few huge fortunes, those of Argouges, d'Aguesseau, Boulongne, Ormesson, Saron and Soubise. As a proportion of expenditure, clothes (6,000 *livres* on average; never less than 100 *livres*) were less important: 1.2 per cent of moveable capital (2.9 per cent in 1700), 5.3 per cent of goods in everyday use (13 per cent in 1700). Nevertheless, attitudes to clothes were very similar, expenditure not increasing systematically in line with the level of wealth. The growth in the value of noble wardrobes, nominally 233 per cent, in real terms 163 per cent, reveals a new situation: a ceiling of consumption, sometimes of prodigality, had been reached, which it was difficult to exceed. Men and women continued to spend equally, lawyers and *hommes d'épée* had very similar attitudes, though in the families of *parlementaires* the women's wardrobes were often worth more than men's. It was thanks to a shift in female behaviour that the standardisation of the *habitus* had been able to succeed within the nobility.[54] The majority of noble families spent a hundred times more than working-class families on clothes and linen, and barely ten times more than bourgeois households, which corresponds to the general integration of appearances.

Attitudes to clothing within the Parisian nobility were highly standardised. They stimulated trade and fashion. They set the tone for other social groups, setting in motion a range of imitative mechanisms which were adopted according to means. Fashion had been commercialised, in Paris as in London.[55] Criticism of sartorial excess could now desert the moral and economic high ground to

---

[54] Bluche (*Les Magistrats du Parlement de Paris*) only really discusses male behaviour.

[55] N. McKendrick, J. Brewer and J. H. Plumb, *The Birth of a Consumer Society* (London, 1982), pp. 34–100. This remarkable study makes possible many comparisons between Paris and London.

become a political argument, principally through an attack on the sumptuary expenditure of courtiers. Mme Campan tells how women of the high nobility hastened to copy the frivolous behaviour of Marie-Antoinette. 'The expenditure of the young ladies was thereby hugely increased, mothers and husbands murmured, some silly young women contracted debts, there were angry family scenes, many couples quarrelled or were estranged, and people said that the Queen would be the ruin of French women.'[56] This little vignette is a useful reminder of the way female behaviour was perceived, even though, among the aristocracy of Versailles, the two sexes spent almost identically on their appearance.[57] It records the reaction of public opinion to the phenomenon of conspicuous court consumption and catches the reality of a particular milieu and age-group. The economic consequences for the luxury trade and its real political repercussions remain to be established.

## THE MODEST PROGRESS OF THE BOURGEOISIE UP TO 1789

Costly and onerous accumulation on this scale was, of course, confined to the Parisian nobility. Among the commercial and craft bourgeoisie, average spending on clothes reached 587 *livres*. Compared with the beginning of the century, this was the social category which had made least progress; a simple doubling of moveable fortunes, a 71 per cent increase in goods in everyday use, only 70 per cent for clothes, or barely 35 per cent expressed in grain. However, the value of wardrobes was maintained with a threshold around 200 *livres*: 47 per cent of wardrobes were below. Clothes and linen were by no means unimportant to industrious shopkeepers and craftsmen, but the group as a whole seems rather to have maintained than increased its expenditure on clothes. It had been influenced by the clothing revolution at an early date, and around 1700 every indicator ranked it close behind the nobility. This busy

---

[56] *Mémoires sur la vie privée de la reine Marie-Antoinette* (Paris), p. 72; see also Mme de Genlis, *Dictionnaire critique et raisonné de la Cour des usages* (Paris, 1818).

[57] It would be useful to be able to trace expenditure throughout life, since it is clear that the trousseaus of young married women from the nobility could comprise a large part of their dowries. In 1787, the trousseau of the marquise de La Tour du Pin cost her family 45,000 *livres*, whilst the fiancée of the baron de Montmorency had a portion of 25,000 *livres*. See also Ribeiro, *Dress in Eighteenth Century Europe*, pp. 56–7.

and productive milieu still needed to maintain its position in the urban hierarchy of appearances, and towards 1789 it maintained its consumption, but no more.

There are two possible explanations: the upward mobility of the most enterprising and the luckiest, social hybrids who escape our sample; or the economic development of the crafts was perhaps not alike for all, so the analysis may conceal a range of fates which may one day be clearer. It comes as no surprise that sexual dimorphism and a similarity of behaviour was maintained whatever the level of wealth. Differences appeared elsewhere, for example in the accumulation of jewels, cash or commercial assets. In a milieu which saw emerge, between 1790 and 1793, the characteristic features of the sansculotte mentality, a mass of small and middling bourgeois already, on the eve of the Revolution, spent perhaps relatively slightly less than their grandfathers and great-grandfathers in the age of the Sun King. However, they spent six times more on their clothes than did the journeymen and salaried workers with whom they were in daily contact in the workshop or at the counter, and who shared their lives and even, in essence, their culture. Jacques-Louis Ménétra, who moved from one social level to the other during the course of his life, neatly illustrates the contrasts in behaviour, at least for bachelors and married men.[58] Before his marriage, whilst making his tour of France, he paid little attention to his appearance, replacing his few worldly possessions as and when need or opportunity arose; however, he was perfectly capable of making himself presentable, and once established, and a little older, he assumed the dress of a Parisian bourgeois, taking pains with his appearance. Dress was probably to a degree a motor of trade and its necessary confidence, but this did not demand ostentation, rather the reverse.

Among the bourgeoisie of office and talent, the changes were more marked. The increase in value of their wardrobes is spectacular since, with domestic servants, theirs is the category with the highest rate of increase between 1700 and 1789; 369 per cent, 272 per cent in terms of grain. However, the importance of clothes within moveable wealth was unchanged: 0.5 per cent in 1700, 0.7 per cent in 1789; as a proportion of everyday goods, it had even declined, falling from 13 to 8 per cent. This points to a sartorial

[58]    Ménétra, *Journal de ma vie*.

moderation which to some extent unified a group diverse in its activities and wealth; 19 per cent disposed of less than 1,000 *livres*, and were thus not very far distant from the lower classes, whilst 21 per cent had more than 10,000 *livres*. Amongst the richest, the value of clothes was higher; large sums were spent on linen and clothing of high quality, and they had many and costly accessories, but their wardrobes were still relatively unimportant in their inheritances; the opposite is the case with those at the bottom of the scale of wealth. The clothes, linen and jewelry of Jean-Baptiste Munirel, an unmarried *avocat*,[59] represented just under 90 per cent of the meagre goods valued by the notary at 300 *livres*; in contrast, those of François Guillaume Trousseau, also an *avocat* in *parlement*,[60] came to over 4,000 *livres*, that is, more than 10 per cent of the total. Sexual dimorphism was maintained, the average complete female wardrobe being worth 739 *livres*, that of men, 320 *livres*.[61] The poor representation of the different professions makes it impossible to distinguish any variations in their behaviour. However, in the case of the two best represented groups, *avocats* and doctors, no significant differences are discernible. The Parisian bourgeoisie of the liberal professions were active in the clothing revolution of the eighteenth century, especially the women, the rich spending as much on their appearance as the nobility. In the social spectacle, they actively contributed to the confusion of the visible hierarchies.

At the conclusion of this initial survey, it is abundantly clear that the study of clothes cannot be content with a uniquely economic analysis; a comparison of the figures and the qualitative descriptions of the contents of wardrobes will tell us more about the connections between social groups and their appearance. In 1789, at all levels of Parisian society, clothes were of limited, though far from negligible, importance within moveable patrimonies; their importance was greater among wage-earners and in commercial and craft circles, less among the nobility and the bourgeoisie; as a general rule, it was in inverse proportion to the increase in prosperity, since a certain ceiling seems soon to have been reached and wealth appears not to be an adequate criterion for an understanding

[59] Arch. nat., Minut. central, LXXIII, 991 (1778).
[60] Arch. nat., Minut. central, LXXIII, 968 (1775).
[61] Merz, *Le Costume des bourgeois parisiens*, pp. 26–32. 72% of men's wardrobes were worth less than 400 *livres*, 52% between 100 and 500 *livres*; for women, 24% were worth less than 400 *livres*, 12% over 1,000 *livres*.

of clothing habits.[62] If we look only at goods in everyday use and the hierarchised distribution of wardrobes, these two attitudes, which combine necessity and choice, are confirmed. In spite of the gulf between bourgeoisie and nobility, a certain unity existed within the two milieus in which culture, power and wealth were concentrated, and it played a motor role in accelerating consumption. The rest of the population followed suit.

Everybody spent more on improving their appearance, though the distance between richest and poorest sharply increased. The unification of the *habitus* gradually affected the whole population, since innumerable intermediaries – the better-off among the poor, bachelors out to seduce, servants, insolent or compliant, and women from every social category – spread the new choices and the long-term or immediate effects of fashion, in general and specifically. The fact that a late eighteenth-century wife spent twice as much as her husband, except perhaps among the nobility, is a fact of major social and anthropological importance, since it was a general attitude and not a class phenomenon. She was already the shop-window of the man, but perhaps even more an effective transmitter of cultural education. The shaping of appearances which transformed the female body between the seventeenth and the eighteenth centuries had its implications for the conduct and looks of men.[63] The trends of the nineteenth century and sexual differentiation in clothing had begun in towns well before the political and social revolution of 1789.[64]

Two problems remain: the first is to estimate the real role of Paris, its priority within both a kingdom of peasants and the urban network; we will return to this after examining the characteristic features of Parisian wardrobes. The second is to observe the composition of the wardrobes accumulated, in order to understand the connections between means and needs and between individual desires and actual possibilities which structure family economies. It is unfortunate in this regard that we have so little information about children's clothes,[65] still in their infancy, so a novel element

---

[62] Maillard, 'Contributions à l'histoire du costume', p. 66.

[63] Perrot, *Le Travail des apparences*, pp. 61–8.

[64] Perrot, *Les Dessus*.

[65] They are absent in 90% of cases, all the more surprising when the children are young; otherwise the age or independence of the heirs may be the explanation. We will return to the few exceptions.

within the clothing system. To understand them better would need other sources and another study. Meanwhile, it is clear that they created a new frontier between rich and poor:[66] the children of the rich were dressed like children, the rest like miniature adults.

---

[66] N. Pellegrin, 'Les manières d'habiller les enfants sous l'Ancien Régime' (forthcoming); Ariès, *L'enfant et la vie familiale*.

# 6. *The contents of wardrobes from the classical age to the Revolution*

Dans ces lieux d'un concours général, où les femmes se
rassemblent pour montrer une belle étoffe et pour recueillir le
fruit de leur toilette . . . on se joint ensemble pour se rassurer
sur le théâtre.

La Bruyère, *Les Caractères* (*de la Ville*)

An analysis of wardrobes in economic terms alone cannot explain
the clothing system of a period. Acquisition, even at the highest
and costliest levels, always reaches a ceiling. What is important is
to understand strategies of purchase and of use and wear. Here,
both social and personal imperatives operate, existentially. Whatever the milieu, codes for interpreting the dress of others structure
the reality of the social spectacle, and impose a grammar of
recognition in daily relations, ordinary and extraordinary.[1] Some
milieus are more skilful than others in manipulating distinctive
signs, some age groups are more extreme in their use of sartorial
signifiers. Yves Delaporte has shown how ethnological analysis can
reconstitute a veritable language of sartorial behaviour by effectively deciphering the signified and the signifiers of the code.[2] This
semiology should attract the historian since it alone can really take
account of this complex activity, which develops over time, but at
different speeds according to place (Paris, large towns, small towns,
the countryside), social milieu, sex, matrimonial status and age.

Though a degree of sartorial autonomy exists, we may still ask
what clothes communicate, whether in relation to the group or the
world-view specific to each community, or to other people within a
private or public relationship, or whether based on the social

---

[1] E. Goffman, *The Presentation of the Self in Everyday Life* (New York, 1959).
[2] Y. Delaporte, 'Le Signe vestimentaire', unpublished typescript (Paris, 1978). (I
would like to thank Claudine Reinharez for drawing my attention to this important text.)

division of time organised according to the changing seasons, the calendar of religious or civic festivals or the routines of daily life. Anthropological studies carried out from this perspective emphasise four classes of principal significations – age and sex, social status, rites of passage and events, seasons – which may be combined in various permutations. The concrete sartorial system is revealed through the perception of those associations which refer back to the interpretation of the world of clothed individuals inasmuch as it can be reconstructed by the observer.

Historians have still to come to terms with relational anthropology. On the one hand, they cannot observe directly the communities they study, cannot get at the life of the significant associations, which they can know only through texts, discourses and images, which reveal the norms of conduct, good manners and polite behaviour and the aesthetic or dramatic conventions. Further, since the eighteenth century, the hypertrophy of the sign of fashion has provoked the retreat – or silence – of other signs.[3] The history of costume is then reduced, as we have seen, to that of a succession of fashions. On the other, the richest and most usable document for gaining access to the collective, the inventory, provides only stocks; how they were used at different times or in different circumstances is never immediately visible. It needs little more than an apron for Sylvia, in *Les Jeux de l'amour et du hasard*, to become a credible Lisette,[4] but not all the aprons found in Parisian wardrobes served as theatrical disguises. The circuits of clothing consumption are complex, and in an unequal, past society, where scarcity remained fundamental, a Parisian observatory understates both the perenniality of meanings and the longevity, re-use and slow replacement of things.[5]

To begin to get round this problem, historians of material culture can propose a social picture of types of consumption. The risk is then the opposite of that run by the historian of forms: not so much a picture of ordinary dress as an accumulation of component parts, which do not in themselves reveal their logic; we need to look elsewhere to discover the functional dress of everyday or

[3] Delaporte, 'Le Signe vestimentaire', pp. 3–4.
[4] Sabatier, *Figaro et son maître*, p. 268.
[5] N. Pellegrin, *L'Habillement rural en Poitou d'après les inventaires après décès. Evolution et éclatement du monde rurale, France-Québec, XVIIIe–XXe s.*, Colloque de Rochefort (Paris, 1986), pp. 475–85.

festive clothes, in their own right or as expression of a culture. Iconography, as we have already noted, provides helpful information, which ought some day to be collected and studied systematically, by establishing typical images.[6] Meanwhile, the wealth of information in Parisian inventories gives us a good snapshot of possessions. It allows an initial understanding of social consumption through the perception of constants and changes, to quantity and quality; it provides a convincing picture of the results of the strategies of appearance and structures of sensibility which embody clothing intentions, enabling symbolic relationships to be expressed. It is an initial reading of the urban clothing system which combines economic hierarchies and the evolution of shapes and garments, textiles and colours. Unfortunately, it is a picture dominated by the polysemy of habits, even if clothing retains its discriminatory character at the lower social levels and abandons it higher up, where to discover the distinctive nuances, other signs must be found.

WOMEN'S CLOTHES IN THE AGE OF LOUIS XIV

Our analysis of wardrobes reveals a population which was essentially homogeneous in its practices. Since the basic elements of clothing were everywhere the same, social differentiation was a matter of quality and quantity, and of the contrast between the necessary and the superfluous. Both men and women in different social milieus shared common habits which transcended social frontiers. Tables 8 and 9, both calculated from 100 inventories, summarise the principal evidence for both sexes around 1700.

The female wardrobe was based on five principal items which were common to all social categories and widely found: skirt and petticoat, mantua (or mantle), apron and stiff bodice (*corps de robe*). The absence of a particular item was not necessarily a sign of poverty, but might result from the vagaries of inheritance, adding to the difficulties of interpreting the information in the inventories; these difficulties are compounded by the variety and the confusion

---

[6] For an attempt with regard to children's clothes in the Middle Ages, see D. Alexandre-Bidon and M. Closson, *L'Enfant à l'ombre des cathédrales* (Paris, 1985); also D. Alexandre-Bidon, 'Le Vêtement de la prime enfance au Moyen Age', *Ethnologie française* (1986).

Table 8 *Composition of female wardrobes* c. *1700*

|  | Nobilities | Domestics | Wage-earners | Artisans and shopkeepers | Office-holders and professions |
|---|---|---|---|---|---|
| Skirt, petticoat | 100 | 100 | 89 | 89 | 93 |
| Gown | 16 | — | — | 2 | 5 |
| Mantua (*manteau*) | 91 | 90 | 87 | 90 | 93 |
| Apron | 46 | 65 | 57 | 70 | 31 |
| Waistcoat (*veste*) | 3 | — | — | — | — |
| Palatine | 12 | — | — | — | 6 |
| Bodice (*corps*) | 53 | 45 | 41 | 50 | 38 |
| Shoes | 16 | 25 | 19 | 20 | 16 |

Table 9 *Composition of male wardrobes* c. *1700*

|  | Nobilities | Domestics | Wage-earners | Artisans and shopkeepers | Office-holders and professions |
|---|---|---|---|---|---|
| Coat (*justaucorps*) | 94 | 89 | 95 | 100 | 85 |
| Waistcoat (*veste*) | 94 | 75 | 65 | 90 | 80 |
| Breeches | 89 | 90 | 80 | 92 | 85 |
| Mantle | 59 | 20 | 27 | 46 | 63 |
| Casaque (usually doublet) | 30 | — | — | 5 | 24 |
| Hat | 67 | 50 | 57 | 65 | 66 |
| Shoes | 35 | 21 | 35 | 32 | 53 |

of the terms used to describe female dress.[7] The garments were put together very much as they had been in the sixteenth century: the basic element was the skirt, gathered into pleats and attached at the hips, worn over one or more petticoats,[8] the number varying according to means or season. The Parisian inventories did not strictly differentiate these garments. They were worn with a *manteau*, a word which might mean another skirt, long and full and worn tucked up or, more often, 'an outer garment worn in summer

---

[7] Ribeiro, *Dress in Eighteenth Century Europe*, p. 32; de Marle, *The Vocabulary of the Female*. Waffen und Kostum Kunde (1975).

[8] Deslandres, *Le Costume*, pp. 122–38; M. Leloir, *Histoire du costume*, vols. VIII–XII (Paris, 1933–49).

for ornament and in winter for protection against the cold and rain' (as defined by Furetière, an accurate observer in such matters, freely plundered by the lexicographers of the eighteenth century). The word was also sometimes used for a sort of dressing-gown worn over the stiff bodice. It is impossible to distinguish between the different types of *manteau*, whose cost ranged from 3 to 50 *livres*, but was usually not more than 20 *livres*. This character-istic garment, originally perhaps tailored like a kimono and worn mostly indoors, was in the process of being transformed and generalised, losing its informal character to acquire a more elabor-ate appearance and assume a protective role closer to that with which we are familiar,[9] that is, the sleeved mantle, usually lined with warm material, even fur. It was essentially a garment of the rich.

Sartorial differences, that is, differences in female social appear-ance, showed primarily in three items which are unevenly recorded: the apron, the bodice and the gown. Aprons were found in every wardrobe, though they were more common among the lower classes and the bourgeoisie of workshops and shops. The figures reveal a frontier in their use: for some, they were primarily a working garment, for others, a useful and ornamental accessory. The ladies of the Parisian nobility might possess half a dozen aprons in fancy linen, broadcloth or more often in silk trimmed with lace. Among women of the merchant class and the bourgeoisie, the majority (80 per cent) of aprons were of canvas or home-spun linen. Those of domestic servants were almost equally divided between the utilitarian and decorative types. For working women, it was a normal accessory, of poorer quality, in white linen, only a few of the better-off being able to afford a more elegant apron in serge or trimmed taffeta. It was a garment whose significance varied accord-ing to milieu and circumstances, here adding a final touch of luxury to a generally rather modest dress, there an air of modesty and simplicity to a more expensive outfit.

The stiff bodice (*corps de robe* or simply *corps*), or external corset (here the terminology of the notaries is particularly vague), was not found everywhere. Worn with a skirt, a chemise or less often a corsage, it established a hierarchy of feminine shapes. An outer garment, it covered the upper part of the body and waist and

[9]  Ribeiro, *Dress in Eighteenth Century Europe*, pp. 35, 41.

was hooked or laced, in front or behind; if front fastening, it was combined with the stomacher, which covered the lower part of the bust. It also served to keep the bust rigid since it was often stiffened with whale-bone or layers of cloth. It thus helped to support the figure but should not be confused with the corset or stays, an undergarment, stiff and designed to correct the body, found with the linen. Here, too, the turn of the seventeenth and eighteenth centuries was a period of change, stays replacing bodices.

The presence or absence of this garment in its various forms reveals two styles of appearance. For the nobility (51 per cent of wardrobes), it was constricting and valorised the norms of stiffness and self-control, defining a social position.[10] Aristocratic stays were inseparably linked to court display and training in correct posture. Whereas the lower classes preferred greater flexibility and spent a minimim of 2 or a maximum of 7 *livres* on the purchase of bodices or stays (41 per cent). We see here not so much a contrast in means as the diffusion of a cultural model,[11] that of the uprightness copied from the Spanish and Italian courts, which reshaped aristocratic silhouettes and conferred on posture a 'proud, imposing, theatrical form, manifesting the qualities of a soul and the virtues of a state'.[12] Court society imposed its aesthetic of erectness, which was also a way of mastering the passions and emphasising the defences indispensable to a female nature seen as fragile. The bodies of lower-class women, in contrast, were bent by hardship and toil,[13] or enjoyed a freedom unconstricted by etiquette. The debate about the shackles of corsets which marked the second half of the century was an aspect of the great contemporary polemic about nature and culture, social control and permissiveness.

In addition to these almost universally present garments, there are a few essential articles which appear only occasionally, and serve as social markers, classifying according to economic means. Gowns are rare. Only among the high aristocracy was this garment,

---

[10] Ibid., pp. 40, 118–19.

[11] Perrot, *Le Travail des apparences*, pp. 72–3; G. Vigarello, *Le Corps redressé* (Paris, 1978), pp. 49–76; F. Libron and H. Clouzot, *Le Corset dans l'art et les moeurs du XIIIe au XXe* (1933).

[12] Perrot, *Le Travail des apparences*, p. 72.

[13] Ibid., p. 73.

still new and costly, at all common: gowns were valued at between 20 and 100 *livres*, a skirt at between 5 to 40 *livres*, a corsage or a chemise at between one and 5 *livres*. The gown which is so prominent in histories of the costume of this period was in practice rare and select, whether open (a corsage and skirt revealing the petticoat), closed,[14] or, less common, in the latest fashion, that is, loose and floating, less heavy than was traditional at court, but as it appears in the iconography of festivals and in the drawings and paintings of Watteau or de Troy. The duchesse de Nevers owned eight gowns in different fabrics (silk, damask and velvet), six *habits complets* (the term reserved by notaries for the combination of mantua, skirt and petticoat), eight skirts, two petticoats, a dozen linen stays and two quilted bodices, the whole valued at a total of 950 *livres*, that is, equivalent to sixty lower-class female wardrobes.[15] The widow of Maître Crignon, a merchant with assets valued at 20,000 *livres*, had only four skirts, a 'shabby gown with a striped skirt of satin trimmed at the bottom with a silver fringe', two mantuas and three 'suits'; hers was a wardrobe already showing the influence of fashion and, at about 100 *livres*, the costliest bourgeois wardrobe.[16] Around 1700, the Parisian female silhouette was formally fairly standardised, overwhelmingly dominated by the flexible shape preferred by the lower classes.[17]

Social diversity, already apparent in a slight trend towards the stiff manners of the nobility, was revealed by the quantity and the quality of fabrics and linens. Quantity was a direct reflection of financial means or the individual love of finery which could to a degree be combined with thrift. Labouring woman owned on average two or three petticoats and as many skirts, a mantua and two or three aprons; a not exceptionally frivolous servant might have four or five petticoats, twice as many aprons and skirts and at least two mantuas. Among the women of the craft and commercial bourgeoisie, where the shop-window effect begins to operate, 52 per cent had at least two mantuas, and a third more than four; whilst a quarter had only one skirt, a third had more than ten;

[14] Ribeiro, *Dress in Eighteenth Century Europe*, pp. 32–7; Deslandres, *Le Costume*, pp. 130–1.
[15] Arch. nat., Minut. central, XXXI, 188 (1702).
[16] Arch. nat., Minut. central, XI, 429 (1715).
[17] Roche, *Peuple de Paris*, pp. 171–2.

three-quarters of the female shopkeepers had more than two petticoats and as many aprons. The wives of the *procureurs, avocats*
and doctors, the female bourgeoisie of Paris, mostly had more than
three petticoats and two mantuas, a quarter had three skirts, whilst
only five inventories mentioned gowns. It is among the nobilities
that we find clothing in large quantities: 10 per cent of the
inventories mention only one mantua, but the majority record at
least four; two-thirds noted three petticoats, three-quarters more
than three skirts. Charlotte de Melson, widow of André Gérard
Lecamus, counsellor of state,[18] owned twenty-two skirts, sixteen
petticoats and a dozen fine aprons, We see the requirements of
different sociabilities and the capacity to change weekly or daily.

The absence of shoes is puzzling; they are least common in noble
inventories – only 16 per cent – and most common in those of
domestic servants – 26 per cent. Either the best pairs are
absent, or an article still expensive and fragile had been exchanged
or, even more likely, vanished. Shoes had become common and the
guilds of the Parisian shoemakers and cobblers who made and
repaired them prospered. By the end of the seventeenth century,
the urban shoe had largely replaced the rural clog.[19] The lists of
gold, silver, steel and tin buckles, almost always included with the
jewelry, provide further proof. They adorned shoes made of cloth –
silk, velvet or felt – or leather. They were a frequent gift to servants.
But the shoe remained a potent token in worldly and amorous
intrigue, even a catalyst of eroticism: Cinderella's slipper and the
shoe of Marivaux's Marianne are reminders of such ploys among
court circles and the rich. We should not forget that the
seventeenth-century shoe was not like our own; it was symmetrical,
with no proper left or right foot, pointed, and bad for the feet;
equipped since the Renaissance with a heel which changed height
according to fashion, it helped to define the gait of people who
rarely walked.[20] For the rest of the population, it was more or less
well suited to more plebeian and economical habits.

The social hierarchy was also expressed in the quality of garments, and even more in the way in which fashion was followed or

[18] Arch. nat., Minut. central, LXIX, 189 (1702).
[19] According to Joffre ('Le Vêtement à Limoges', pp. 48–57), this was the case in
Limoges by 1750.
[20] Perrot, *Le Travail des apparences*, pp. 70–3; P. Lacroix, *Histoire de la chaussure*
(Paris, 1862).

set. A comparison of the recorded fabrics and colours reveals two types of conduct (see tables 10 and 11). At the top of society, the nobilities dressed their wives in silk, mixed fabrics or, more rarely, in woollen cloth. Linen was common for summer skirts and petticoats. Wool was reserved for winter clothes made of warm and solid materials, good quality broadcloths or luxury serges. Damask, brocade, taffeta, satin, cloth of gold and silver alone or combined as decoration were used for dress clothes.[21] Despite the prohibitions against them – further proof of the ineffectiveness of mercantilist sumptuary control – the light cottons, 'indiennes' and muslins were found in noble wardrobes. By the reign of Louis XIV the use of silks and cottons for clothes had become general among the privileged. It was they who kept the looms of the factories of Lyons and Tours at work, and for them that Parisian merchants imported fabrics from Italy, Persia and India. The dazzling deployment of colour and the magnificent embroidery of flowers and foliage still impresses in paintings in which specialists can identify *gros de Tours* or the plushes and velvets of Lyons.[22] Two skills combined to create these effects: that of the weavers and manufacturers, and that of the designers for the manufactories, such as Jean Revel of Lyons in the 1730s.[23]

Elsewhere, solid fabrics predominated, a smaller vocabulary sufficed to describe them and variety was confined to a few rich shopkeepers or bourgeois women. Heavy materials remained in the majority, but the presence of silks and cottons in many inventories points to imitation of aristocratic practices. Silks and indiennes, satins and moires, and a variety of decoration, often the only sign of a love of finery, appear among the rich, and distinguish the refined and the stylish. We may draw a first conclusion: among the population at large and in the street spectacle, the quality of fabrics and their finish was all-important and, by nuances imperceptible to the vulgar or the newly arrived, set the standards to be aspired to. Second, dark colours – blacks, greys and browns – were everywhere

---

[21] Ribeiro, *Dress in Eighteenth Century Europe*, pp. 38–9.

[22] Hugues, *Le Langage des tissus*, pp. 25–50.

[23] The rich vocabulary of fabrics in the inventories is of great interest. It included both ordinary fabrics – wool, silk, damask, cotton, etc., and specialised products – 'Holland' or 'Marseilles' linen, *ras de Saint-Maur*, gros de Tours, tabby, not to speak of novelties such as 'tree bark' and 'speculation'. Much work remains to be done to discover how these various fabrics were employed.

Table 10 *Fabrics* c. *1700 (percentages calculated for both sexes)*

|  | Nobilities | Domestics | Wage-earners | Artisans and shopkeepers | Office-holders and professions |
|---|---|---|---|---|---|
| Linens | 46 | 16 | 14 | 42 | 37 |
| Wool | 8 | 60 | 58 | 23 | 22 |
| Silk | 17 | 9 | 9 | 13 | 17 |
| Cotton | 7 | 7 | 7 | 8 | 3 |
| Miscellaneous | 22 | 8 | 12 | 14 | 21 |
| Total | 100 | 100 | 100 | 100 | 100 |

Table 11 *Colours and patterns* c. *1700 (percentages calculated for both sexes)*

|  | Nobilities | Domestics | Wage-earners | Artisans and shopkeepers | Office-holders and professions |
|---|---|---|---|---|---|
| Blacks | 33 | 29 | 33 | 28 | 44 |
| Greys | 5 | 20 | 10 | 16 | 13 |
| Browns | 27 | 23 | 18 | 14 | 10 |
| Whites | 21 | 6 | 9 | 12 | 14 |
| Reds, yellows, blues | 8 | 13 | 12 | 9 | 8 |
| Miscellaneous | 6 | 9 | 18 | 21 | 11 |
| Total | 100 | 100 | 100 | 100 | 100 |
| Stripes | 48 | 75 | 88 | 6 | 63 |
| Flowers | 10 | 12 | 6 | 20 | 24 |
| Various checks | 42 | 13 | 6 | 4 | 13 |

predominant, though women's clothes were more brightly coloured than men's in every social category. Dazzling reds and yellows, more subdued violets and purples, colder blues and greens, every example of the dyers' art, accounted for no more than fifteen per cent of the attire of noble women, but were more often chosen by the other categories. The overall colour scheme was sombre, though not to the total exclusion of colour.

We find a curious contradiction: among the nobilities, their imitators and the rich in general, the predominant fabrics were supple, elaborate and striking, if often sombre, and fashion dictated an imposing and controlled shape. This was probably more true of public than of private life, where things were more relaxed. Amongst the working classes, colours were restrained, less often vivid, more often dark; stiff fabrics of poor quality, difficult to wash or dye, deprived women of some of the flexibility conferred by their way of life and work. The better-off with social aspirations prided themselves on their striking and elaborate attire and no doubt on the care with which they dressed. Iconography only rarely shows the clothing of the poor and sometimes exaggerates, as with Le Nain, whilst evidence for the rich is plentiful. It confirms the homogeneity of a female sartorial style faithful to norms which were already old, a basic structure on which a range of social choices in quantity and quality could be displayed, hence the greater or lesser revolution in sensibility linked to tactile and optical capacity, the taste for variations and combinations, in sum, already, to fashion.

The fabrics of women's clothes were lighter and more diversified than those of men, as well as being more colourful; among the nobility, woollen fabrics accounted for less than 6 per cent in female wardrobes, over a quarter in those of men; silks and cottons were more important for all, but more so for women. Among wage-earners, broadcloths accounted for 76 per cent of male wardrobes, 42 per cent for their wives and the unmarried, where silks rose to 16 per cent, cottons to 11 per cent. A similar dimorphism existed in the other social categories, but in most cases it was characteristic of the better-off,[24] Lastly, we should not forget that at least two-thirds of the Parisian population consisted of recent arrivals, mostly of rural origin. These immigrants arrived with their own clothing practices, which were gradually transformed in the melting-pot of Paris. The servants of plays and novels, for whom a change of dress was almost ritual, symbolised this metamorphosis, news of which eventually filtered down to the villages. By the end of the reign of Louis XIV, consumerism was under way, with women to the fore. The variety of the sartorial scene can no longer be appreciated by a simple description of the main formal lines

---

[24] A more refined analysis, comparing shapes with fabrics and colours, would be valuable. See Levêque, 'Les Vêtements de la bourgeoisie parisienne'. pp. 48–50.

characteristic of the upper classes, whose style was now copied throughout Europe.

## THE COSTUME OF PARISIAN MEN AROUND 1700

During the reigns of Louis XIV and Louis XV, men's clothing slowly changed. The figures for the distribution of the principal garments reveal a homogeneity comparable to that for women. The full suit (*habit complet*), with its three component parts of coat (*justaucorps*), skirted waistcoat (*veste*) and breeches, was in every wardrobe. In male appearance, too, differentiation was a matter of quantity and quality, in sum, of the capacity to select an elegant combination, vary the cut and the colour, indulge personal inclination and be always in fashion. By now, the whole male population integrated by work or residence, or enrolled in the guilds and corporations, wore shoes and hats. It was therefore the way clothes were worn or individual sensibility revealed by the choice of items that differentiated.

Amongst wage-earners, a simple costume, solid, made to last and withstand the rigours of work and weather, gave everyone a certain stiff and severe uniformity and a sobriety of aspect; it can be seen in the dress of the man of the people painted by Watteau in the corner of *L'Enseigne de Gersaint*.[25] The majority of the male population consisted not of barefoot tramps in rags and tatters but of people of a relatively dignified bearing. They had little opportunity to vary their clothes or adapt to the seasons.[26] For them, clothing was a necessary expense, but one easier to control than food or lodgings, which posed the family with the problem of care and replacement.

The better-off, especially domestic servants, possessed clothes in moderate abundance – three or four breeches, three or four waistcoats, a winter mantle, a beaver or caudebec. A few who were rich, with more than 3,000 *livres* of moveable capital, aspired to a certain elegance; unmarried journeymen, *maîtres d'hôtel* and personal valets followed fashion, but at a distance and in details and accessories more than in their everyday clothes. They were beginning to dress up for the cheap and cheerful dance-halls, where they assumed the airs of *petits maîtres* to impress the girls.

---

[25] Roche, *Peuple de Paris*, pp. 169–75.
[26] The rarity of the mantle (27%) is one sign of this.

Among the nobility, who rubbed shoulders with and were observed by the common people, clothing changed rapidly, not so much in essentials as in the way it adapted to the requirements of aristocratic sociability. The number of garments increased: 25 per cent of complete wardrobes contained more than six examples of the items comprising the suit of the well-dressed man. The silhouette, elongated by the high, conical wigs, was imposing, slender, following the body. Its effect was heightened by the predominantly sober colours, and the gold and silver buttons and trimming round pockets and cuffs.[27] The decoration accounted for a large part of the cost of these suits made from costly broadcloths or heavy silks; a fifth were of damask or brocade.

The presence of items rare in other milieus shows how noblemen adapted to the changing seasons and to old and new habits. They alone retained outmoded doublets, casaques and petticoat breeches (rhinegraves). The marquis de La Valette, Louis Félix Nogaret, kept his suits 'in the old colours', his rhinegraves of grey brocade, his doublets of yellow satin and even his old-style breeches.[28] The chevalier de La Barre, Jean-Baptiste Lefebvre, commander of Saint-Lazare and *prévôt*, left his heirs a wardrobe worth less than 1,000 *livres*.[29] It included five full suits, one coat and two odd waistcoats of lighter fabrics; in his cabinet, he had three mantles, one of barragon, one of cloth of scarlet trimmed with gold, one of purple velvet with a gold border, worn to grace the ceremonies of the knights of the order. Here was a man able to vary his outfits, alternate his waistcoats of cinnamon broadcloth and his coats of pink pinchina, match his breeches of purple velvet or cloth of scarlet with either and, on great occasions, choose between a waistcoat of green damask with green flowers lined with purple satin and an under-waistcoat of white, purple and green satin with a gold border. We see in him an example of the ostentatious elegance of the court.

The men of the law were not to be outdone by the men of the sword. Messire Nicolas Esmery, ordinary counsellor to the *Cour des aides*, had four coats, four breeches and six waistcoats, two mantles, one casaque and, unusually, three legal gowns (hats and

---

[27] Ribeiro, *Dress in Eighteenth Century Europe*, pp. 20–5.
[28] Arch. nat., Minut. central, CV, 947 (1695).
[29] Arch. nat., Minut. central, XXVI, 256 (1711).

shoes were missing from this inventory which exceeded 500 *livres*). He liked good-quality broadcloths, glossy-wool calamancos and pinchina, a heavy cloth made in Provence and Champagne; his waistcoats were of rateen or of wool or silk velvet. His chosen colours ranged from black to musk, his greys were elegant, his cinnamon choice, and some of his fabrics were trimmed with gold and silver. All were enhanced by embroidery and trimmings. Gentlemen were more likely than others to possess garments of leather, indoor gowns and a profusion of additional items such as jackets or the first redingotes, recorded before 1715. The ordinary inventory shows no sign of the exotic or fantastic touches noted by travellers and observers of the court. The noble appearance remained unchanged till the dawn of the nineteenth century, though fashion dictated variations in details, which dandies throughout Europe hastened to copy.[30]

The suit worn by craftsmen and shopkeepers was formally no different; it comprised the same elements, and matching sets were found in a quarter of their wardrobes. Some capacity to change emerges, even if it involved non-matching garments; the majority of inventories record more than two daytime outfits. The coat that could be changed was what chiefly distinguished the employer from the wage-earner, who had few interchangeable items. In any case,[31] they were solid and comfortable garments: 95 per cent were in broadcloth, serge or camlet. As many as 50 per cent of merchants and clothiers already had more than two waistcoats and two breeches; a few rich men had six or seven. The average number of waistcoats was even higher than that of coats – one to two – as they were easily changed. New, their cost varied enormously (from 15 to 30 *livres*), but second-hand and valued by the notary they were worth between 2 and 24 *livres*, according to condition, and coats between 5 and 60 *livres*. Rich merchants prided themselves on their waistcoats; Nicolas Basin, a mercer, had four, 'one of *ras de Saint-Maur* [silk], one of striped linen, one with facings, of green damask with silver flowers, and the fourth of coffee-coloured broadcloth'.[32] The other items were less common, and the mantles expensive (46 per cent, and never more than one). As a general

---

[30] Deslandres, *La Costume*, pp. 126–7.
[31] Kalifa, 'Le Costume dans la petite bourgeoisie', pp. 45–7.
[32] Arch. nat., Minut. central, LXIX, 163 (1697).

rule, the men of the merchant and working bourgeoisie dressed more soberly and with less decorum than women; they preferred solidity and richness to frivolity, broadcloths to silks, and inclined towards the stiff and rather stilted silhouette of the upper classes. A love of finery was indulged in facings, a means by which one could proclaim one's rank and create an impression in spite of sumptuary prohibitions; they showed who had money.[33] Nevertheless, more sober and not in general particularly stylish, the dress of the men of workshops and shops revealed social gulfs and disparities in wealth less than that of the women, which already showed the influence of fashion.

Non-noble lawyers and other members of the professional middle class were hardly more innovative. They remained loyal to the three-piece suit which was found in 95 per cent of their wardrobes (the rate closest to that achieved by the nobility). Only a quarter of their wardrobes held more than two; additional assorted breeches, waistcoats and coats, valued separately, made it possible for them to ring the changes. The majority of these garments (91 per cent) were made of sombre broadcloths, black or grey, but the fabrics and colours of the waistcoats and coats were more varied, some were of linen or silk, and musk, ecru, red, pearl grey and cinnamon had appeared. The waistcoat was often adorned with facings of richer cloth which were glimpsed through the opening of the coat and at the wrists. Some garments had buttons, braids and fringes of gold and silver. A few of the richer men and the occasional dandy indulged their fancies. François Dullou, *procureur* to *parlement*, though worth 7,000 *livres*, devoted barely 100 *livres* to the clothes which were valued at his death, but he had more than five different waistcoats, two complete suits and two odd breeches.[34] Pierre Denis, a surgeon, owned clothes worth some 200 *livres*, including one full suit, eight waistcoats, four coats and three odd breeches, though his meagre possessions were in all worth less than 500 *livres*.[35] This group as a whole had a greater capacity to change than did the craftsmen, a concern for decorum revealed by the presence in a third of their wardrobes of the black legal gowns which are missing from the inventories of the office-

[33] Levêque, 'Les Vêtements de la bourgeoisie parisienne', pp. 58–63.
[34] Arch. nat., Minut. central, XVIII, 424 (1703).
[35] Arch. nat., Minut. central, CIX, 413 (1713).

holding nobility,[36] and a certain taste for variety and fantasy. It was a social category where mantles were common (63 per cent), along with equivalent items such as roquelaures, Brandenburgs and the perhaps more outmoded casaque. The richest, as elsewhere, had all of these, and the equation of clothes and wealth, though imperfect, was fairly marked. The bourgeois of the Parisian *robe* were soberly dressed, whilst their more clothes-conscious wives were the cause of no little distress to the royal economists and financiers, devotees of the sumptuary laws.[37]

A popular picture of a fashionable bourgeois woman in despair after the terrible edict which prohibited gilt, striking a mortal blow to all such ornament, was captioned: *A grieving wife, but a happy husband.*[38] Guérard's engraving brought together many ingredients of the bourgeois sartorial scene: the affectation of the good lady's outfit, the incorporation of fashion into amorous intrigue, the husband who held the family purse-strings and, lastly, the familiarity of the knowing servingmaid, who, all got up in her own finery, drew the final moral:

> Said Fanchon, her maid
> Why make such a fuss?
> A well-known inn can still trade
> Without a sign or a bush.

It is hardly Molière, but the satire aims at the same target; a sartorial order existed, and must be protected against the first onslaught of a system of consumption whose pace was accelerating thanks to the nobility, the wealthy and the emulation of their inferiors.

From top to bottom of Parisian society, at the turn of the seventeenth and eighteenth centuries, the population dressed according to the same formal rules. Degrees of wealth and poverty determined the extent to which male and female wardrobes were diversified. Moderation and parsimony still characterised the clothing consumption of the majority, who preferred the solid and the durable, broadcloths and sombre colours. Women were the most

---

[36] Most *avocats* and *procureurs* owned this professional costume (52 per cent), but not doctors. The ordinary legal gowns could be kept for a long time as they hardly dated; they were usually of tammy or broadcloth.

[37] Rouyre, 'Le Costume dans la bourgeoisie des professions libérales', pp. 19–22.

[38] Gravure de Gérard, reproduced in the folder of illustrations, document no. 11.

active agents of such variety as existed; moralists and agents of the fisc notwithstanding, it was through them that the influence of fashion was disseminated,[39] though signs of it were still rare in inventories outside the nobility.[40] For the majority, it remained a world of permanence and limited change. Novelty was confined to an active minority, for which we might risk the estimate, on the basis of our notarial sample, of at most between 10 and 20 per cent of the integrated population, probably more women than men. This reflects a world where, between luxury and necessity, Paris was beginning to show signs of the major transformation which would characterise the century to come.

## THE TRANSFORMATION OF MEN'S CLOTHES

On the eve of the Revolution, the Parisian clothing system retained its essential homogeneity. Tables 12 to 15 record the principal changes, and show an overall increase in the numbers of garments owned. This was a development common to both sexes, based on a wider range of possessions following changes to both the principal items and accessories. The different strata of Parisian society embarked simultaneously on both a quantitative and a qualitative progress.

In the case of male wardrobes, the figures record both a formal diminution and an aggravation of social differences, the frivolity and freedom of the twenty years preceding the political explosion effectively emphasising rank and fortune. The suit, with its usual components, was now almost universal; the *justaucorps* had disappeared, the sleeveless waistcoat or gilet had replaced it, worn with the *veste*. It was these items which revealed the frontier between the stylish and wealthy and the rest of the population, though a lighter,

---

[39] The inventory is not a particularly helpful document for tracing the way forms changed in line with changing tastes. There are occasional revealing descriptions; for example, the marquis de La Valette had an old-fashioned wardrobe which included rhinegrave, breeches and doublets (Arch. nat., Minut. central, CV, 947).

[40] Levêque, 'Les Vêtements de la bourgeoisie parisienne', pp. 94–5. The author correctly observes that it is easier to trace the progress of accessories; for example, the Steinkirk (1692) appeared in an inventory in 1700, evidence not so much that it had not previously been adopted by the Parisian bourgeoisie, but of its slow but ultimately successful diffusion; they were later to be found in all wardrobes worth more than 500 *livres*.

Table 12 *Composition of male wardrobes* c. 1789

|  | Nobilities | Domestics | Wage-earners | Artisans and shopkeepers | Professions |
|---|---|---|---|---|---|
| *Veste* | 100 | 90 | 86 | 91 | 100 |
| Breeches | 100 | 95 | 89 | 86 | 100 |
| Gilet | 100 | 47 | 51 | 56 | 30 |
| *Habit* | 100 | 100 | 84 | 83 | 72 |
| Mantle | 51 | 30 | 3 | 10 | 55 |
| Redingote | 71 | 45 | 41 | 45 | 53 |
| Frock, surtout, etc. | 90 | 80 | 54 | 48 | 73 |
| Shoes | 100 | 81 | 73 | 66 | 85 |
| Hat | 100 | 68 | 80 | 76 | 81 |

Table 13 *Composition of female wardrobes* c. 1789

|  | Nobilities | Domestics | Wage-earners | Artisans and shopkeepers | Professions |
|---|---|---|---|---|---|
| Skirt, petticoat | 100 | 95 | 94 | 100 | 100 |
| 'Suit' | 18 | — | — | — | — |
| Gown | 100 | 100 | 53 | 90 | 100 |
| *Manteau* | 44 | 5 | — | — | — |
| Redingote | 5 | — | — | — | 4 |
| Pelisse | 2 | 11 | — | 19 | 39 |
| Mantelet | 55 | 85 | 58 | 82 | 85 |
| Apron | 100 | 62 | 88 | 55 | 39 |
| Shoes | 76 | 60 | 56 | 66 | 68 |
| Stays | 81 | 60 | 50 | 66 | 65 |

slimmer and in a way less sculptural silhouette than that of the classical period was common to all. The smaller wigs contributed. Clothing had been touched by rococo, but it was the capacity to rotate one's garments more rapidly and endlessly ring the changes which differentiated. Further, the Parisian wardrobe was enriched by new items: the redingote, the frock (*frac* or *fraque*) – 'a sort of light *justaucorps*' – and the more common surtout, which tailors cut from supple materials. These are the first indications of an overall improvement in standards.

In the wardrobes of the nobility, the average number of the principal garments reached eighty, and more than half held between ten and thirty items; this was in a sense the social floor of maximum accumulation. Certain fashionable grandees, such as the duc de Nivernais, M. de Boulongne, the comte de Damas, M. de Guibert, the marquis de Castelnau and the prince de Soubise, accumulated garments by the hundred, and such men often spent more on clothes than did women. There was little to differentiate the *robe* and the sword, though the latter provided most of the tiny group of *élégants*, wealthy and close to the court. The diversity of fabrics and the multiplicity of colours almost lives up to the image conveyed by painters and travellers. The well-dressed man wore magnificent silks (38 per cent of references to type of cloth), though without renouncing the costly broadcloths which were used for his mantles, redingotes and winter waistcoats (*vestes*); cottons accounted for a quarter of the references, luxury cloths of gold and silver for less than 1 per cent. Brilliant and glowing colours characterised the aristocracy of court and town, where fabrics dyed in reds and pinks, blues, yellows and greens predominated, associated with floral patterns and embroidery, stripes and zig-zags; but 42 per cent of the colours were still sombre and low key.

The noble male wardrobe thus now combined elegance and sober discretion with a costlier brilliance. This to some extent qualifies the impression conveyed by painters, which has generally been accepted by historians of costume; we have to accept a range of practices, and a distinction between the festive and the everyday, the private and the public. The parade of colour by the leaders of fashion could not be maintained on a daily basis, even by the wealthiest. They fired the imagination and set standards to which the stylish adhered as best they could, sometimes to their ruin, depending on their age and need to keep up appearances. A significant proportion of clothes made from black fabrics (25 per cent) shows that, in certain circumstances, the noble elite had already adopted this basic feature of the clothes of the future.

Amongst wage-earners and domestic servants, the changes were more marked; for every two items previously inventoried, there were now five or six.[41] Wardrobes containing between four and ten principal garments were the norm. Ordinary people were better dressed and, above all, better protected; mantles and capotes were no longer rare, and were accompanied by redingotes, frocks and surtouts. Hats, black three-cornered or grey felt, were on every

---

[41] Roche, *Peuple de Paris*, pp. 174–8.

head, shoes on every foot; most servants owned two pairs. As among the privileged, the accumulation of clothes which made it possible to change was what established the main distinctions; the downwards diffusion of new tastes is everywhere apparent.

The textile revolution had made itself felt in the wardrobes of wage-earners; silks and cottons were gaining ground and helped to slim down the silhouette, People were more lightly clad, but what they gained in diversity they perhaps lost in solidity, so that it was necessary to buy more and fight against wear and tear. The inventories register the effects of the secular development of the manufactories and the speculations of the 'modern' entrepreneurs, in sum, of a production already dependent on mass consumption and replacement.[42] The same development was responsible for the decline of dark colours – blacks, greys and browns – though they still accounted for two-thirds of the colours used; however, whites, blues, yellows, reds, pinks, plum and innumerable variations were fighting a winning battle against the sombre hues common a century earlier. Above all, the third quarter of the century saw the triumph in this sector, too, of stripes and checks, the inventories confirming both the advice of the *Cabinet des modes* and the observation of Louis Sébastien Mercier: 'The King's zebra has become the model for the fashion of the day; all materials are striped; coats and waistcoats resemble the skin of the handsome onager, men of all ages are in stripes from top to toe.'[43] Working-class men had succumbed to fashion.

This new masculine consumption testifies to the wide conversion to a seductive diversity, even though uniformity remained more characteristic of most items of clothing. A desire for self-expression and a sense of the pleasure provided to the eye became general, in what amounted to a veritable transformation of sensibilities. The utilitarian and the solid co-existed with the trivial and the pleasing; rich servants, frequenters of the great and well-off journeymen shared a capacity to consume which was directly linked to their capacity to imitate, stimulated by their daily contact within urban society.

Artisans, shopkeepers, small employers and rich bourgeois

---

[42] Braudel and Labrousse, *Histoire économique et sociale*, vol. II, pp. 227–50, 514–27, 543–53.
[43] Mercier, *Tableaux de Paris*, vol. XI, pp. 191–2.

Table 14 *Fabrics and textiles* c. *1789 (percentages)*

|  | Nobilities | Domestics | Wage-earners | Artisans and shopkeepers | Professions |
|---|---|---|---|---|---|
| Linens | 17 | 8 | 12 | 12 | 13 |
| Wool | 18 | 26 | 33 | 23 | 23 |
| Cotton | 25 | 40 | 38 | 39 | 20 |
| Silk | 38 | 12 | 15 | 21 | 31 |
| Miscellaneous (mixed) | 2 | 14 | 2 | 5 | 13 |
| Total | 100 | 100 | 100 | 100 | 100 |

Table 15 *Colours and patterns* c. *1789 (percentages)*

|  | Nobilities | Domestic | Wage-earners | Artisans and shopkeepers | Professions |
|---|---|---|---|---|---|
| Blacks | 23 | 13 | 12 | 32 | 37 |
| Browns | 7 | 4 | 6 | 9 | 13 |
| Greys | 12 | 17 | 21 | 23 | 11 |
| Whites | 19 | 28 | 32 | 17 | 28 |
| Reds | 11 | 13 | 13 | 6 | 6 |
| Various: yellows, greens, blues | 28 | 25 | 16 | 13 | 5 |
| Stripes | 67 | 60 | 66 | 44 | 75 |
| Flowered | 27 | 25 | 18 | 36 | 20 |
| Miscellaneous | 6 | 15 | 14 | 20 | 5 |

remained conservative in their clothes in the face of the progressive ideals then being proclaimed. They continued to prefer standard colour combinations, dark colours and a comfortable solidity.[44] They all owned between fifteen and twenty principal garments, and a few of the wealthier aspired to elegance, affected by the fever of accumulation and spending. Antoine Denoyelle, a master eating-house keeper of the rue Dauphine, who had 30,000 *livres* of moveable assets, owned thirteen *habits*, fifteen *vestes*, seventeen

[44] Moreau, 'Le Vêtement', pp. 77–88. For 1,523 garments, and 1,160 mentions of fabrics: wool 57%, cotton 26%, silk 16.5%; 874 indications of colour, black 33%, grey 23%, white 17%, red 17%, in other words predominantly dark. A further indication is the absence of patterns and the predominance of plain.

breeches, a dozen assorted gilets, a redingote, a frock and, of course, all the accessories; his wardrobe was worthy of a *petit maître* though it cost only 500 *livres*.[45] However, as in the time of Louis XIV, a love of fine clothes and elegance did not coincide totally with wealth. The inventories of a handful of the wealthiest lack any mention of those items which reveal a taste for the new habits; for example, redingotes were found in 45 per cent of wardrobes, and in 16 per cent they were in addition to surtouts, but in only three such cases were the owners amongst the richest, with assets worth more than 10,000 *livres*.

These working and commercial milieus were the only ones within the lower classes where we find trousers. Philippe Ariès believed trousers to be a sign of collective craft identity, like the worker's overall of the nineteenth century.[46] This is something of a problem for the history of material culture.[47] The Revolution established trousers as the symbolic garment of the sansculottes of 1793, but they are rarely found in the inventories; three for every eighty breeches among wage-earners, in only 5 per cent of the wardrobes of artisans and shopkeepers, concentrated among wine merchants. We know from the study of pictorial sources that it was not until the 1820s that breeches ceased to be worn other than at official ceremonies or in the offices of the faubourg Saint-Germain.[48] We know also that trousers were the working clothes of sailors, rivermen, ostlers and a few lesser street traders; they are worn by the corn seller and the Turpin operative in Leblond's drawings for the 1775 *Cris de Paris*, and by Scaramouche on the fairground stage, in sum, three trousers to twenty-four breeches. Trousers were not a rural garment, to judge by inventories from Poitou and Brie.[49] The fragility and cost of thread stockings would alone justify the substitution, but there is no evidence either way. They may have been sold or buried, though this seems unlikely in the case of a utilitarian article which could easily be re-used. Perhaps notaries regarded them as beneath their notice, but this, too, seems unlikely,

[45] Arch. nat., Minut. central, CXXIX, 302 (1790).
[46] Ariès, *L'Enfant et la vie familiale*.
[47] M. Pertué, in AHRF (1983), dismisses this problem as futile, perhaps because he cannot see (from the viewpoint of a legal historian?) the connection between politics and culture.
[48] Deslandres, *Le Costume*, p. 180.
[49] See also *Cabinet des Estampes*, *Métiers* for the true cries of Paris; also the work of N. Pellegrin and M. Baulant.

since they they were by no means cheap, worth several *livres* according to condition. In sum, the trousers of workers and fair-ground artists would enjoy their hour of triumph over aristocratic breeches, but when and how remains to be established.[50]

First, they are proof that an upwards diffusion of clothing is possible; the aristocratic children put into trousers by their govern-esses were effective intermediaries. But so, too, were soldiers, since from 1780 the Hussar regiments wore narrow trousers with their boots. Prior to 1789, manners and fashion remained faithful to breeches and together limited the diffusion of trousers. They were an informal garment, worn for leisure, in the country, on horseback. They were still worn by piece-workers and suburbanites. For a few months, when patriotism took a hand in fashion, they were a discriminating sign of political norms, a development to which we will return. Before the Revolution, trousers were more characteristic of certain journeymen than their masters, whilst among the upper classes they testified to a taste for social exoticism. For the inter-mediate bourgeoisie, they were not so much distinctive as a compo-nent of an outfit which was respectable and comfortable. They had adopted them by the beginning of the century and been imitated by their employees in shops and workshops, especially after 1775. In the world of work and the guilds, a tiny, better-off and fashion-conscious minority indulged in imitative spending, for the most part unmarried womanisers or successful bourgeois who had es-caped the discipline of the family.[51]

The clothes of lawyers and the professions experienced a similar transformation but with its own specific features. They were all well-provided; most had between two and six coats (*habits-vestes*) with additional gilets; frocks, redingotes and surtouts were fairly common. François Guillaume Trousseau, *avocat* in Parlement, had three redingotes, four surtouts, a frock and two complete suits,

---

[50] Regarding the drawing by H. Bunbury, *An Englishman in Paris* (1767) reproduced in Ribeiro, *Dress in Eighteenth Century Europe*, p. 93, there is no justification for identifying the man in clogs and trousers as a peasant. He could be a worker, a sailor or a groom, contemplating the street spectacle, where the clothes are exaggerated by the artist. We see a frivolous wig-maker, an elegant nobleman in his cabriolet, his servant in a pelisse, an imposing monk, a child dressed like a miniature adult and, in the centre, the English traveller, firmly buckled into his mantle and leaning on his cane, French lightness and eccentricity versus British comfort? See also pp. 162, 175.

[51] Arch. nat., Minut. central, LXXIII, 968 (1775).

plus several *vestes* and gilets. The specific concern of this group to refine its everyday appearance shows in their choice of colours for coat and breeches: 66 per cent were matching, so conformism and modernism were reconciled. The liberal professions remained faithful to the black suit, to stout and undating broadcloth, but were a little more adventurous in their choice of waistcoats of silk and cotton and assorted gilets. They were not immune to fashion, but theirs was the category, after the nobility, most attached to dark colours, more so than the artisanate of shop and workshop[52] whatever the temptations of a colourful appearance.

A rather facile class symbolism, read retrospectively on the basis of the etiquette imposed on the deputies of the Third Estate for the opening session of the Estates General, has been used to explain the traditionalism of this group. In a period when the great were frivolous and lesser men had achieved a degree of liberation, it reveals an attachment to the serious, even a distrust of too rapid a confusion of ranks and conditions which meant that a great lord could no longer be distinguished from a tipsy lackey. This was an attitude easily reconciled with the temporary gaiety demanded by private or public festivities. Since the clothing of the inventories is neither wholly that of daily life nor wholly that of the collective imagination, it offers a mixed and tenuous indication of lost realities. The suit in black, colour of mourning, which freed its wearer from fashion and signified a modest competence, was also the sign of a quiet confidence. Combined with other signs, it affirmed the virtue and morality of a class whose political future was as yet wholly unknown.

## THE METAMORPHOSIS OF WOMEN

The principal change affecting Parisian women was the spread of the gown. Derived from the old court gown, the *robe à la française* and *robe volante* or sack, it was now worn over skirts or petticoats of varying degrees of stiffness, depending on the size of the bodice or the hoops (we might add that notaries almost never record this accessory, common since the seventeenth century). The female

---

[52] Merz, 'Le Costume des bourgeois parisiens', pp. 39–59; of 1,421 mentions of fabrics: wool 44%, silk 25%, cotton 17%, linens 14%; of 1,478 indications of colour: black 52% (20% more than among craftsmen), grey 12%, brown 7%.

silhouette had been standardised: gowns were now everywhere, though less common in working-class wardrobes (only a 53 per cent index of presence). This is explained by their continuing high price,[53] and perhaps also by the fact that they were less comfortable to wear than the traditional outfit of working women, that is, the separate skirt and bodice, even the caraco or casaquin.[54] As a general rule, garments specific to particular occasions or seasons were less widespread than amongst men. Redingotes were rare among noblewomen and the female members of non-noble legal families; warm pelisses and light mantles were sporadically found. However, the almost universal presence of the mantelet restored a certain uniformity to the female population. The apron had retained its social ubiquity; it had progressed at the two extremes and retreated in the intermediate categories. While it had everywhere retained its utilitarian dimension, its decorative role had developed among the nobility and domestic servants, where it sometimes matched the gown or skirt.

The philosophical and medical reshaping of the female nature thus had its echoes in the notarial documents. Dress was freer and less restrictive compared with the old formal, aristocratic style. The norm was more natural, and aristocratic women adopted a more popular air whilst working-class women indulged in a little aristocratic fantasy.[55] This greater independence disturbed the defenders of sexual dimorphism, who feared that men were growing effeminate, thanks to an excessive love of finery, and women becoming too masculine by so much borrowing from men.[56] However that may be, stays, ranked with the linen by the valuers, gained ground at the expense of boned bodices. Unpretentious and lighter gowns revealed more natural and less constricted figures. In sum, here too things had gone awry and the sartorial order had become confused. The social gulfs did not disappear; the rich amassed clothes and indulged their taste for the finery decreed by fashion, now liberated from the constraints of the sumptuary laws, on a scale well beyond the means of the poor and the only moderately well-off.

Indeed, the two principal characteristics of the wardrobe of the

---

[53] Mostly between 40 *livres* (at least a month's work) and 300 *livres*. Court gowns cost much more.

[54] Ribeiro, *Dress in Eighteenth Century Europe*, pp. 98–114, 149–60.

[55] Perrot, *Le Travail des apparences*, pp. 75–86; Deslandres, *Le Costume*, pp. 137–9.

[56] Perrot, *Le Travail des apparences*, p. 86, 'a woman's clothes should have a sex'.

noblewoman were now abundance and fashionableness. On average, it contained fifty-five garments, which meant that noblewomen, like noblemen, could change more frequently and dress appropriately for festivities and for the season. Most of them owned between twenty and forty garments – in this they were better off than the men – including some twenty gowns, as many petticoats, and ten or so additional items: déshabillés to be worn indoors, mantelets, mantles, 'amazons' (riding habits), redingotes, surtouts, caracos, casaquins, jackets and shawls. The princesse de Talmont had 186 outer garments, the vicomtesse de Tavannes had 150 and Madame d'Hérouville had 130; they were typical of the big spenders at court. The marquise de Clermont-Tonnerre, from the same milieu, was less ostentatious: six suits, fourteen gowns, fourteen petticoats, one déshabillé and one casaquin.[57] All these women were rich enough to replace their wardrobes as and when fashion decreed.

The valuers had to expand their vocabulary. New terms appeared: the 'polonaise' and the 'lévite' launched by Marie-Antoinette during her pregnancy in 1778, gowns *à l'anglaise*, *à la turque* and *à l'italienne*, the chemise gown *à la Reine* popularised by Vigée Lebrun's portrait of 1783. These costly collections, presided over by chambermaids and, regardless of the age of their wearer, always in the latest fashion, were above all varied and elaborate. More than 150 types of trimming are recorded, with names like 'lamentation', 'indiscreet', 'impervious', 'of great repute' and 'frustrated desire'; women's magazines and fashion handbooks explained how they should be used. Colours were equally exotic, every one represented, but in shades impenetrable to the uninitiated or the historian of today: 'queen's hair', 'king's eyes', 'bull's blood', 'Paris mud' or 'goose shit'. These few expressions from the pen of one notary, unlikely to have been an expert in such matters, suffice to evoke a consuming passion, a triumphant battle against greyness, the definitive victory of light fabrics. The dream and the reality, sometimes confused, had toppled the theatre of aristocratic appearances, though at great cost. The passion for the natural and the simple was more expensive than ever. The range of possible significances of women's dress expanded enormously, between economic necessity and the imperatives of fashion. To make sense of it, the gazettes and the *Monuments du costume* must be read.

---

[57] Maillard, 'Contributions à l'histoire du costume', pp. 51–115.

Similar changes are apparent among lower-class women, who copied the more complex tastes and practices first adopted by domestic servants.[58] Their wardrobes were diversified; the skirt and the petticoat remained the basic items, but the gown, almost non-existent at the end of the seventeenth century, was now found, sometimes several at a time, in the wardrobes of a majority of wage-earners (53 per cent) and all domestic servants. This was a specifically Parisian phenomenon; in contemporary Limoges, 82 per cent of inventories fail to mention the gown, and even in the period 1800–40 they were still barely as common as they had been in Paris in 1780.[59] In Chartres, it was still a rich woman's garment, and the skirt–petticoat combination remained the norm.[60] The better-off wage-earners and most servants, like their mistresses, owned mantelets, casaquins, caracos and mantles.

Women, too, now normally wore shoes. Greater comfort in walking was a major achievement of the century of the Enlightenment. Less precious than those of the rich, working-class shoes had more rounded toes and flat heels (though the stylish and the rich affected high heels), and were made of leather, goatskin or cloth. They were still fastened by buckles, but strings, ancestors of the later laces, appeared in a few inventories. Mercier, watching the crowds of labourers, stonemasons and carpenters returning to their suburban homes, observed that these workers, many of them recent immigrants, could be recognised by their footprints, because the plaster from their shoes whitened the pavements. New shoes cost between 3 and 10 *livres* a pair. Boots were confined to the rich, but Parisians of both sexes could now change their shoes, and they provided employment for the 4,000 masters of the shoemakers' guilds. This was, it should be stressed, a major advance which helped to alter the way people walked, lighten their labour and speed up the spectacle and activity of the street. It was a victory over the fragile life.

However, for women, even more than for men, utility and solidity were not everything, but went with a concern for effect, and a liking for the new shapes, colours and patterns.[61] Most

[58] Roche, *Peuple de Paris*, pp. 176–7.
[59] Joffre, 'Le Vêtement à Limoges', pp. 149–51.
[60] Garnot, 'Classes populaires urbaines', vol. II, pp. 536–7.
[61] The chief figures for fabrics are as follows: wage-earners: wool 60% men, 6% women; cotton 20% and 57%; linen 1.5% and 16%; silk 4.5% and 20%;

important of all were the lighter fabrics; fewer broadcloths and woollens, more cottons and even silks. Lower-class women were much better dressed, and women servants better dressed still; they could enjoy supple satins, soft taffetas, cheerful prints and exotic siamoises, Persians and nankeens. They, too, adopted the new shades; less than a quarter of their outer garments were in blacks, greys or browns; blues, yellows, greens and above all innumerable soft and subdued shades competed with white, ecru and the reds. The eye of the Parisian woman grew more discriminating, her perceptions matured, the street scene lost its harsh contrasts, the signs of social recognition grew less clear, everything changed with the seasons and with fashion, now endlessly discussed on staircases and doorsteps, announced by the elegant and worldly, gradually copied, reproduced and reworked. The evolution of patterns was similar to that noted in aristocratic inventories,[62] and the wardrobe of the average working-class woman was no longer distinguishable from that of a domestic servant except perhaps by a slightly lesser abundance or fineness of detail. Even differences in wealth were less apparent, though without disappearing altogether. The cultural gap was maintained by the capacity to make a better choice from a wider range of products, colours and qualities. The Enlightenment brought all the colours of the rainbow within reach of ordinary people.

Among women of the rentier and bourgeois class, there was an even more pronounced tendency to a real, if still limited, accumulation and diversification. The gown, a useful indicator, was ubiquitous, and two-thirds of the inventories recorded more than five. Madame Trousseau, wife of the *avocat* François Guillaume, whose wardrobe we have already described, owned eighteen, together with seventeen matching skirts and petticoats, two déshabillés, two polonaises, fourteen other skirts, a further dozen petticoats, six caracos, a redingote, nine mantelets, one pelisse, and, a rarity at

miscellaneous 14% and 1%. Domestics: wool 54% men, 11% women; cotton 21% and 59%; linen 10% and 7%; silk 12% and 19%; miscellaneous 3% and 4%. For colours, the figures are: wage-earners: browns 7% men, 5% women; blacks 21% and 7%; greys 30% and 12%; reds 6% and 20%; whites 12% and 23%; yellows, blues, greens 17% and 26%; miscellaneous 7% and 7%. Domestics: browns 5% men, 3% women; blacks 15% and 8%; greys 25% and 11%; reds 4% and 22%; whites 11% and 24%; yellows, blues, greens 22% and 28%; miscellaneous 18% and 4%.

[62] 60% of stripes were combined with checks or floral patterns.

that period, a fourreau gown. She is a good example of the way in which women of the liberal professions had acquired luxurious wardrobes and succumbed to fashion. Informal garments, fantasy and exoticism appeared only amongst the very richest, that is above 15,000 *livres*. At this level, we find lévites (8 per cent), chemise gowns, gowns *à l'enfant* and *à la créole*, redingote gowns and all the new styles being elaborated by modest and elegant dressmakers. Almost all female wardrobes in legal circles contained one or two fashionable items. It is hardly necessary to add that they also had the new textiles and were beginning to adopt the new colours.[63] The only sign of the persistence of the old clothing system was a continued indifference to season. Cold was still combatted by extra layers, and warmth, more easily, by fewer. Unlike their husbands, the women of the high bourgeoisie of office and the liberal professions clearly hankered after aristocratic elegance.

This was not the case among the women of workshops and shops. They had accumulated fewer clothes; compared with the ten items found in legal wardrobes, only six were found amongst the crafts and trade, where the range was from two to a dozen. Wealth was more accurately reflected in dress; where there was only one suit, gown and matching skirt, the inventory never exceeded 1,000 *livres*; among the better-off, the sky was the limit. The wife of Nicolas Bouillon, a brewer, had 150 items in her wardrobe, including a dozen gowns, fifteen *habits*, twenty-four skirts, eight mantelets, eight aprons, a capote, a muff and four pairs of shoes.[64] This was a lavish wardrobe, suggestive of great wealth but untouched by fashion. However, fashion was apparent in this milieu in the choice of fabrics, where silks predominated, which was not the case with the men.[65] The same is true of colours, which followed the general

---

[63] Fabrics: wool 44% men, 2% women; cotton 17% and 23%; silk 25% and 37%; linen and other 14% and 38%. Colours: blacks 52% men, 22% women; greys 12% and 6.5%; browns 7% and 5%; reds 4.5% and 8.5%; blues, yellows and greens 6.5% and 10.5%; miscellaneous 2% and 4%; whites 16% and 43.5%. There was a correlation between lighter garments and brighter colours (more than sixty shades).

[64] Arch. nat., Minut. central, IV, 800 (1784). The family fortune amounted to 55,800 *livres*.

[65] Fabrics: wool 53% men, 4% women; silk 16% and 64%; cotton 26% and 26%; miscellaneous 5% and 6%.

trend, though not to the total exclusion of dark shades.[66] They were an intermediate category, less caught up than others in the fashion system, less so than servants or the better-off wage-earners. A concern with appearance was more closely than elsewhere related to resources. The novelties were rare and, except at the top, it appears that clothes were replaced only slowly. The shop-window effect visible at the beginning of the century had not, as one might have expected, resulted in the pursuit of greater comfort, and a desire for greater simplicity was more marked than concern for fashion. However, their clothes were rather more diversified than those of their menfolk.[67]

Between the end of the seventeenth and the last quarter of the eighteenth centuries, the Parisian clothing system experienced great change. Every social category was caught up in the acceleration of the rate of change and replacement, made possible by the accumulation of basic items, whilst the greater range of garments made possible seasonal variations. An enhanced tactile and ocular sensibility went with the choice of less coarse textiles and the vogue for lighter fabrics made by skilful entrepreneurs or imported by successful merchants. A point of rare perfection was achieved by the end of the century. The alternation of essential items and even more of accessories gave expression to the taste for spectacle and festivity. The silhouette had changed; it was less dignified, more flexible, influenced by English and exotic manners. All observers commented on the confusion of manners; the man of fashion borrowed from the man of the people who, in his turn, imitated the *petits maîtres*. The more solemn and pessimistic saw these exchanges as potentially catastrophic and certainly calamitous, 'since in ceasing to respect the public, one forgets all nuances in society'.[68]

However, these nuances were alive and well, dictated by rank, fortune and education. Though the signs were more difficult to read, the differences were perceptible in a greater or lesser capacity to respond to fashion and absorb the effects of the global clothing

---

[66] Colours: blacks 32.4% men, 6.7% women; browns 9.8% and 13.9%; greys 23.1% and 4.8%; whites 17.4% and 24.6%; reds 6.1% and 17.7%; blues, greens and yellows 7.5% and 29.5%; miscellaneous 3.7% and 2.8%.

[67] Moreau, 'Le Vêtement dans le monde de la boutique', pp. 112–16.

[68] Ribeiro, *Dress in Eighteenth Century Europe*, p. 17, quoting J.-A. de Ségur, *Les femmes, leur condition et leur influence dans la vie sociale*, 3 vols. (Paris, 1803), vol. III, p. 7.

revolution. For the majority, shapes evolved less rapidly than details and colours. This was because the manufacture of clothing had not yet broken through the basic technical barriers, in spite of the progress of ready-made and the growth of the socially standard-ising second-hand trade. Sexual dimorphism was emphasised by the pioneering and bold behaviour of women, as compared with the more conservative behaviour, and even resistance to innovation, of men, who are, as everybody knows, more sensitive to the cold. Clothes changed more rapidly in Paris than in the provinces. The consumption of fashions had begun. A first revolution was com-plete. A study of hairstyles and trimmings would only confirm this.

### THE REVOLUTION IN APPEARANCES OR THE APPEARANCES OF THE REVOLUTION

The great political Revolution did not so much transform practices as accelerate certain changes. This has been shown for the people of Paris by both Richard Cobb and myself.[69] Political events at first checked the progress of fashion,[70] but it soon recovered: 'Everything followed the Revolution and experienced the general unease.'[71] The traditional centres of influence, the court and foreign models, gave way before philosophic and patriotic imperatives. Shapes did not change, but details, accessories and ways of wearing clothes quickly responded to the new order. Colours and patterns became national; the return to nature, antique austerity and Roman virtues imposed a certain restraint on the exaggerated outfits of the past. The nation's clothes were purged of costly ornament, 'luxury went out, but is now within reach of all citizens, since it resides in the comfort, propriety and elegance of forms', said *Le Cabinet des modes*.

New attitudes were shown by the adoption of certain clothes. Military dress, of the National Guard or the volunteers, became fashionable and was adapted to the habits of citizen soldiers. It was not within everyone's reach since it cost, with equipment, 80 *livres*: Ménétra was amongst those who could not resist.[72] Equality made

---

[69] Roche, *Peuple de Paris*, pp. 191–7; R. Cobb, *Death in Paris*, pp. 22–3, 70–86.
[70] N.-H. Courtine, 'Etude du costume masculin populaire à Paris, 1789–1794', DES, Paris 1 (1961), pp. 56–9.
[71] *Le Cabinet des modes*, 21 September 1790.
[72] Ménétra, *Journal*, pp. 331–3.

it advisable for bourgeois and aristocratic men to wear twill trousers and working-men's coats. Liberty dictated casual styles and the affectation of working-class simplicity to women. In a few months, or a few years, a large part of the population grew accustomed to changes imposed less by need than by external imperatives, serving to define the place of man within the body politic. Costume was definitively brought within the domain of the public, and the sense of festivity and the role of uniforms made it a terrain favourable to the deployment of the symbols dear to the revolutionary imagination.[73]

When, after 1791, the social and political crises followed even faster, sartorial initiatives echoed events. A new and outrageous outfit served to rally the sansculottes, who made it a profession of revolutionary faith, a way of clearly signalling vigilant patriotism.[74] It was the dress of the true patriot which was painted by Sergent for the salon of 1793 and is visible in the watercolours of Lesueur and the engravings of Berthault. The actor of the *opéra-comique*, Chenard, was immortalised by Boilly in trousers, carmagnole, red woollen cap and greatcoat of grey-green broadcloth. Chaumette added clogs, and the revolutionary women, with Rose Lacombe and Théroigne de Méricourt, dressed *à la jolie sans-culotte*. The counter-revolutionaries spoke of the 'trouser brigade' (*pantalon-nades*) and 'Punch and Judy sansculottes'. The popular societies dreamed of imposing a national costume, alike for all. Artists and politicians constructed a utopia propitious to the disappearance of divisive obstacles and the triumph of transparency. No-one dreamed that sartorial excess or disguise concealed as much as it revealed. A sartorial reaction set in after Thermidor when dandies and *jeunesse dorée* proudly flaunted their refined appearance in the face of the slovenliness of the hard-line sansculottes. The revolutionary clothing culture had had its day and survived only in symbolic secondary details.

[73] M. Ozouf, *La Fête révolutionnaire* (Paris, 1976); J.-P. Bertaud, *La Vie quotidienne pendant la Révolution française* (Paris, 1982); M. Pellegrin, *Les Vêtements de la liberté, abécédaire des pratiques vestimentaires de 1780 à 1800* (Aix, 1989).

[74] These politics of surveillance have never been studied. I am grateful to J. Guilhaumou for several references: *Chronique de Paris*, 29 July 1793, account of the Commune: 'Hébert informed the Conseil that there was a new plot ... mistrust those men who wear checked clothes; even those young men who wear tight breeches; have no doubt, this costume is a sign of subversion'; *Correspondance politique de Paris*, 30 July 1793, p. 3; *Courrier universel*, 24 August 1793.

A whole history remains to be written along these broad lines. The Revolution accelerated a double trend which had already begun. It inclined the population towards a greater simplicity without stopping the formal evolution already under way, so working towards a general standardisation; at the same time, clothing took on a clearer significance. It spoke for whoever wore it and became a symbol of political dignity. The Revolution could not destroy sartorial barriers and clearly revealed the profound link which, by a permanent circulation, united the social classes in one system perpetuated beyond the politico-social rupture. A study of what lay beneath the surface will lead us to similar conclusions.

# 7. *The invention of linen*

Si les habits sont nets et, surtout si on a du linge blanc, il
n'importe que l'on soit magnifiquement vêtu.

Antoine Courtin, *De la civilité*

Every society can be decoded by what it reveals, but read even
better by what it conceals. Outer garments express an ethos of
display, increasingly, according to Rousseau, at the expense of
utility:

Fancy dictates [clothing], pride rules; it serves to distinguish
wealth and rank. It is an abuse which cries out for reform; it
would accord with the spirit of the regeneration of France to
return costume to its original purpose and to egalitarian ways.[1]

This was the aim of the revolutionaries who aspired to liberty,
equality and transparency. They may not, like some sixteenth-century millenarians, have envisaged a return to a basic and even more
egalitarian nudity,[2] but they knew that no movement of clothing
reform could be restricted to the surface. Their ideas had slowly
matured with the philosophical and medical ideas of the century of
Enlightenment, by reference to nature and the new hygiene, and
they accepted that everything was connected, the surface and
beneath, body and soul. 'In the moral as in the physical world,
liberty is the mother of energy, prudery is the mother of weakness',
wrote Doctor Venel.[3] The whole body was at issue, and with it
cleanliness and linen as social signs of reference and norms of
behaviour. The seventeenth and eighteenth centuries saw the

---

[1] 'Considération sur les avantages de changer le costume français par la société
populaire et républicaine des Arts', *La Décade philosophique littéraire et politique*, 10 Floréal, Year II, pp. 60–2.

[2] For the millenarists, see W. Fraemger, *Le Royaume millénaire de Jérôme Bosch*
(Paris, 1966).

[3] J.-A. Venel, *Essai sur la santé et sur l'éducation médicale des filles destinées au
mariage* (Yverdon, 1776), pp. 108–9.

shaping and diffusion of modes of conduct and codes of action linked to the invention of linen.[4]

THE BIRTH OF LINEN

Linen, it might be thought, has always existed, but the history of words and that of things do not always precisely coincide, though they throw light on each other. In the thirteenth century, when the word 'linen' from being an adjective became a noun, the use of linen was in the process of becoming universal. Barely a century later, around 1393, the *Ménagier de Paris* reveals how important the care and deployment of linen had already become within the domestic economy of the rich Parisian bourgeoisie. The history of linen could then begin, embarking on its slow progress towards the time when it would be taken for granted. A cultural system was established though the codes which would explain it most clearly were not yet visible, the material bases being first in place. Linen was present in the chests and coffers of townspeople and peasants, but it was not yet discussed, though 'everything was in position for it to serve a conception of cleanliness, for example, by being regularly changed'.[5] Medieval inventories – such as those for urban and rural Burgundy studied by F. Piponnier,[6] or the accounts of rich families from Paris and the provinces – list in varying degrees of detail clothes worn next to the body, usually made from finer fabrics than outer garments. In contrast to the usual accumulations of household linen – sheets, shrouds, table covers, embroidered cloths, napkins and *touailles* (towels and napkins in one) – body linen was rare, though not unknown even among the poor. Care of the body did not yet involve the need to change, to meet some vague conception of cleanliness, and the outer clothes still monopolised attention; in them was subsumed the whole body. The shirt was universal but had not yet attracted the attention or reflection of specialists in therapeutics or fashion.[7] As habits

---

[4] For an interdisciplinary survey, see *Ethnologie française* (1986), a special number under the direction of M. Verlet and D. Roche; see also Perrot, *Le Travail des apparences* and Vigarello, *Concepts of Cleanliness.*

[5] Vigarello, *Concepts of Cleanliness*, pp. 49–50.

[6] F. Piponnier, 'Avant l'armoire linge, linge de maison et linge de corps au Moyen Age, d'après les inventaires après décès bourguignons', *Ethnologie française* (1986).

[7] Vigarello, *Concepts of Cleanliness*, pp. 51–3.

changed at the turn of the fifteenth and sixteenth centuries, the social possibilities of play on what was concealed and what revealed had yet to be discovered. Linen contributed to the creation of this imperceptible frontier between the private and the public, where the body was a complex terrain, and the family still the principal place where basic lessons were learned. The acquisition of linen and its use, perhaps even more for children than for adults, reveal the cultural values which underpinned the system, through modes of use and upkeep, in the pedagogies of the clothed and the unclothed, the clean and the dirty.

It might be useful to begin by tracing the progress from the old to the new vocabulary. In the seventeenth and eighteenth centuries, people spoke of 'great' and 'small' linen (*gros linge* and *menu linge*), the domestic lexicon both uniting and separating bed and household linen and underwear. The definitions were firmly rooted in the concrete. According to Furetière:

> Linen (*linge*) is first the cloth (*toile*) put to use, suitable for the household and the person. Table linen is usually decorated or damask, sheets are of solid and plain linen, shirts are of fine and soft linen. The word comes from *lin* (flax), from which 'great' linen is made. We call 'great' linen that which is put to wash, which is sent to the laundry for 'great' linen, such as sheets, napkins, cloths and shirts. We call 'small' or 'fine' linen the bands, cuffs, cravats and handkerchiefs which are sent to the starchers to be soaped. It is said that someone is in plain linen when there is no lace, that there is beautiful linen when it is trimmed with lace and fancy stitching. It is also said that a person is 'handsome under the linen' (*belle sous le linge*), that is from the breast to the knees. It is proverbially said of someone that they are 'curious in dirty linen' ['curious' then meaning both indiscreet and curious].

The linen draper (*linger*) dealt in both linen (*linge*) and underwear (*lingerie*). The descriptions in this late seventeenth-century dictionary, repeated, usually in abbreviated form, by later dictionaries, were expanded by the *Encyclopédie*: linen was used 'in general of all linen cloth put to use. There is table linen, fine linen, great linen, day linen and night linen.'

The familiar vocabulary records an increasingly wide range of uses, casting doubt on daily changing by 1750, but remaining basically faithful to the original technical definition, since one was referred to the article '*toile*', which was economic and technological; it elaborated on *linger*, *lingère* and *lingerie* in their commercial aspects – 'one makes lingerie like one makes jewelry' – and from the perspective of upkeep, *lingerie* meaning both body linen and the place designed to store, prepare and care for it.

This brief lexicographical digression brings out the three themes which dominate any discussion of linen: appearance and its economy, hygiene, the role of the erotic and play on the body. It is clear that in the past, as still today, if in other ways, linen helped to define the frontiers between what should be worn in public and what in private. It was both an issue in and a test of distinction since personal linen was caught up in the whirlwind of fashion. It was also a sign of the life-styles legitimised by court civilisation and disseminated by the manuals of good manners. Thin or coarse, heavy or fine, in dress or household use, linen was an effective marker in social topographies. This was universally recognised, and inseparable from the social and moral identity of the common manners. It was one of the roles of educative manuals to teach the correct use of linen in dress and one of the functions of the family and the little schools to teach what was and was not done in this sphere.[8]

Linen was one of the materialisations by which customary rules of conduct were diffused, The situation was not wholly the same for girls and boys, since the symbolic burden of linen was not wholly comparable or read in the same way for both sexes.[9] For all, through its intermediate position and its proximity to the body, which made it a sort of second skin, linen underwear acquired a carnal value which was emphasised by the rituals of socialisation.[10] It was one of the ways by which children won their autonomy and passed from an incomplete and animal state to a social existence, hence the importance of children's clothes such as the cap and swaddling clothes or bands, hence the power of rites of transfer, such as making the first garment of childhood from the father's shirt.[11] In all the symbolic acts on which traditional beliefs con-

---

[8]  C. Reinharez, 'Habillement et civilité', *Ethnographie* (1984).

[9]  Y. Verdier, *Façons de dire, façons de faire* (Paris, 1979).

[10]  F. Loux and P. Richard, *Sagesse du corps* (Paris, 1978); F. Loux, *Le Corps, pratiques et savoirs populaires dans la société traditionnelle* (Paris, 1979); *Le jeune Enfant et son corps dans la médicine traditionnelle* (Paris, 1978).

[11]  It is the first significant act in the socialisation of children; the father removes his

ferred efficacy, the recourse against misfortune or sickness, or for future assurance, was grafted onto the concrete act: the linen of the father warms and transmits, it proclaims the gift of life; the shirt which has been dipped into miraculous springs or touched a holy body, such as that of the Black Virgin of Chartres,[12] transforms everyday trivial objects into instruments of sacrality and fecundity. This is why the linen visible on the margins of appearances has so many meanings; it is why girls in past society had their special apprenticeship in the management of linen, in needlework, in making garments and in their repair.

The particular contact at puberty with the onset of menstruation produced yet another awareness.[13] Old texts referring to this are rare, but sufficiently numerous to link, in legend, magic and reality, linen and the blood taboo, linen and the presence of sex or death. The attention which both country and urban girls lavished on their trousseaus was an expression of these values.[14] They were revealed in all sorts of amorous, festive or social strategies, but also by the fact of accumulation, which stuffed wardrobes full of household and personal linen far beyond what would ever be needed; it was regarded as a prestigious possession, treasured by rich and poor alike, exhibited on the wedding day, never sold. In sum, the discovery of linen cannot be read only in terms of changes associated with cleanliness, central though this may be to clothing practices.

THE CLEAN AND THE DIRTY

In a history of linen, habits of hygiene have a crucial role.[15] Cleanliness has not always assumed washing, and the triumph of body linen after the sixteenth century generalised a specific corporeal dimension unknown to the Middle Ages. A new epidemiology

own shirt and wraps it round the new-born baby, so making the baby's natural body into a cultural body.
[12] See J. Gélis, *L'Arbre et le fruit* (Paris, 1984).
[13] Verdier, *Façons de dire*, pp. 170–85; N. Pellegrin, 'Chemises et chiffons, le vieux et le neuf en Poitou, aux XVIIIe et XIXe siècles', *Ethnologie française* (1986). Little is known about this aspect of feminine linen, essential for a history of the body and sexuality; might the 'packets of small bad linen' recorded in women's chests by notarial inventories be sanitary towels?
[14] We need a historical geography of the customs and social role of young married girls' trousseaus.
[15] Vigarello, *Concepts of Cleanliness*, pp. 41–69.

focused attention on linen. Plague, which did not finally disappear from France until 1720, triggered off recurring obsessions with and attacks on the linen which was accused of transmitting the miasmas of the disease and which could well encourage rats and fleas, true carriers of plague.[16] The persistence of the vermin lodged in clothing, which proliferated when it was infrequently changed, did not inevitably lead to a demand for bodily cleanliness.[17] It expressed the corruption of humours which secreted lice, mites and scabies, against which one fought with purges, bleeding, emetics, even dietary regimes.[18] The rarity of linen encouraged skin diseases, which the medical observers of the seventeenth and eighteenth centuries saw retreat, but which the wars of the twentieth century have caused to reappear, among soldiers and civilians. The old criteria of cleanliness did not demand an attack on these invisible ills, preferring to concentrate on the visible and require the cleanliness only of those parts of the body which were seen, especially the face and hands. The spread of linen, especially shirts, paved the way for the introduction of the more systematic bodily cleanliness of changing.[19] Here, too, it was in childhood that the rules of cleanliness and correctness were learned. What was specific to the society of the *ancien régime*, and survived despite political ruptures into the nineteenth century, was its frontier between the clean and the dirty, the healthy and the unhealthy, a boundary which did not always coincide with that of the definers of hygienic and moral norms.

There remains play on the body and the relationships which developed between linen and the erotic. The connection is obvious in the sphere of literature, even in gallant iconography. Here, the gaze, our own and that of contemporaries, lingers on the transgressive value which might or might not be accorded to the frontiers between the visible and the invisible, the revealed and the concealed, the dressed and the undressed. In the past, one did not lightly take off one's clothes, even in painting, and the frontiers of modesty were crossed even less easily in ordinary life. A certain reserve persisted in an age when the libertinage of spirit and manners went

[16] J.-N. Biraben, *Les Hommes et la peste en France et dans les pays méditerranéens* (Paris, 1976), vol. II.

[17] *Le Ménagier de Paris* (Paris, 1846), vol. I, pp. 172–3.

[18] G. de Chauliac, *La Grande Chirurgie, XIVe siècle*, ed. Lyon (1592), pp. 470–1.

[19] Vigarello, *Concepts of Cleanliness*, pp. 49, 58–66.

well with litotes. Not everyone shared the imagination of the divine marquis, whose amassed and undressed bodies acquired, at the end of the day, the pure virtues of abstraction. For most people, the major contrast was between daytime and night, hence the emphasis placed, both by gallant tradition and by prurient surveillance (such as lodging-house regulations), on retiring in the half-dark and the toilet of early morning. The ambiguity of those times of day, and their private practices, easily inflamed the imagination, which must be combatted or sublimated in art.

Here too, a tradition of ribaldry and the conformism of prudery wage the same devalorising war, emphasising the recurrence of themes and representations specific to each period and within a long continuum of appearances and acts, associating linen and the erotic; thus history is excluded from a domain which is neither trivial nor vulgar. But the close connection between clothing habits and the mute functions of life should not constrain us to silence. By breaking it, the history of material culture linked to that of sensibilities will benefit, and a study of the consumption of linen in Paris, taking account of economic trends, social appropriations and symbolic roles grafted onto concrete functions, will aid our understanding.

THE WEALTH OF LINEN

In the eighth book of his *Confessions*, Jean-Jacques Rousseau gives a concrete demonstration of the role of linen in the economy of daily life in the mid-eighteenth century:

In spite of the severity of my reform [he had just chosen independence and the life of a writer, abandoning white stockings and gilded finery], I did not extend it at first to my linen, which was good in quality and quantity, being the remains of my Venice outfit, of which I was particularly fond. I had attached such importance to its cleanliness that it had become a matter of luxury and a continuous source of expense to me. Someone did me the favour of delivering me from this servitude. On Christmas Eve, while Thérèse and Madame Le Vasseur were at Vespers and I was at a concert of sacred music, the door of a garret where all our linen was spread out after a recent wash was forced open, and everything was stolen, including forty-two very fine linen shirts of mine, which made the principal part of my stock . . .

this incident cured me of my taste for fine linen, and I have only worn the most common kind since, which is more in keeping with the rest of my dress.[20]

The story nicely demonstrates the importance of fine linen for a man who wished to hold on to his position and make his way in the world. We see also how a change of status might entail a change of habits and the choice of poorer quality. We see the importance of appearances on the social frontiers, and how the ordinary necessities of laundering and upkeep were performed. Lastly, we see theft confirmed as an important element in the distribution and circulation of clothes within towns.[21] For Rousseau, as for many other Parisians, rich, less rich or frankly poor, the possession, care and cost of linen constituted a good indicator of social usages and, above all, of how the practices of groups and individuals commonly combined reality and representation.[22] Fine linen was a necessity if you wanted to appear other than what you were. The two issues ostensibly at stake in the incident described by Rousseau were cleanliness and luxury. He abandoned the latter the better to condemn it in the name of equality, but remained faithful to the former despite his personal sartorial revolution, which was not altogether typical of his century.[23] Paris and most urban societies mixed both requirements in their social and economic dynamics. Rousseau's reform was perhaps in any case a gesture made possible only by incipient success and a modest abundance, and motivated by a rare determination to break with men of letters, in their own way 'monkeys of the rich and the great'. We have already observed how sartorial snobbery could result in a costly simplicity. For ordinary people, for the majority

---

[20] J.-J. Rousseau, *Les Confessions. Oeuvres complètes* (Paris, 1959), vol. I, p. 364 (pp. 339–40 of Penguin edition of 1953).

[21] A. Longnon, 'Un vol commis au préjudice de Jean-Jacques Rousseau, le 25 décembre 1751', *Bulletin de la Société d'histoire de Paris* (1877), pp. 29–32. Rousseau said he had lost forty shirts, but the formal complaint mentioned only twenty-two – fine, trimmed with sleeve-ruffles, plain, embroidered, scalloped and mostly marked with the letter R on the right collar, also 'four kerchiefs of which three are white and blue and one blue, fourteen collars with four buttonholes and nine nightcaps'. We will return to the subject of clothing theft in chapter 12.

[22] Rousseau, *Oeuvres complètes*, vol. I, pp. 1192–1205; B. M. Neuchâtel, MS. 7840, ff. 4, 11–12, 76–8.

[23] B. Mely, *Jean-Jacques Rousseau, un intellectuel en rupture* (Paris, 1985).

of the urban population, the conquest of linen marked a decisive transformation of behaviour.[24]

On the basis of our thousand wardrobes, we can calculate, if not the precise ratio of the value of the linen owned, at least a general estimate. The figures below are based on a limited number of examples, when the gaps seemed relatively few and the descriptions complete: according to category, between two-thirds and a half of our wardrobes. We cannot fully appreciate the differences between the sexes because of the imprecision of the notarial lists, which may reflect both the similarity of male and female underwear and the practice of storing it together. However, the household and personal linen of men and women was slightly more clearly differentiated in the wardrobes of the rich than the poor, and by the 1780s than in 1700. Both social distinction and changing manners seem to have increased the sexual dimorphism of nomenclature. This, as with clothing in general, seems to reflect a crucial moment of change, when people were acquiring a wider range of clothing and beginning to demand greater refinement. The greater precision is evidence of a greater interest, just as the absences and approximations reveal the complexities of actual use.

## THE LINEN THAT DISTINGUISHED

In 1700, at all levels of Parisian wealth, linen was relatively unimportant, even less so than the clothes with which it was ranked by the valuers (see tables sixteen and seventeen on pp. 164 and 165). At the top, the nobility devoted on average 20 per cent of their clothing capital to household and personal linen, that is some 360 *livres*, almost a year's wages for a day labourer, making no allowance for workless days or holidays. The imprecision of the sources makes it difficult to refine this observation, but those who owned many clothes did not necessarily own much linen and, conversely, those who showed least interest in clothes might have large numbers of undergarments. The chevalier de La Barre, whose wardrobe was worth more than 1,000 *livres tournois*, owned linen worth less than 30 *écus*: this was a rather lower-than-average clothes/linen ratio, but it would easily have bought several horses or kept a

---

[24] Roche, *Peuple de Paris*, pp, 176–7; McKendrick, Brewer and Plumb, *Birth of a Consumer Society*, pp. 34–100.

Parisian skilled worker for six months.[25] Jean-Baptiste François de Molesan, lord of Besmaur, a *Maître de camp* in the cavalry, possessed clothes worth 2,000 *livres* – enough to buy a comfortable small farm – a third of which consisted of linen of good quality.[26] The duchesse de Nevers owned clothes valued at 350 *livres* at her death, half of which consisted of her smalls and her shirts;[27] this would have bought 42 *sétiers* of corn in the Paris market or fed several ordinary people for several months. At the time of Louis XIV, the Parisian nobility spent forty times more on linen than the integrated workers in the guilds.

Among the lower classes, the average wardrobe worth 42 *livres* contained linen worth 15 *livres*, enough to buy three-quarters of a *sétier* of wheat. It was unimportant absolutely, but significant as a proportion of their meagre patrimonies, and more so lower down the scale of wealth. Nicolas Cordier, a journeyman cooper, shared with his wife a modest fortune of 200 *livres*: their linen was worth 50 *livres*. So also was that of the Poiret family, whose possessions were worth 8,500 *livres*.[28] What is of most interest to us is that linen was found everywhere and was occasionally abundant. It was something that most people now had.

Of the groups intermediate between nobility and people, artisans and shopkeepers – who had acquired more clothes in general – also had more linen; it accounted for a quarter of their wardrobes, on average 86 *livres*, that is more than 2 per cent of their moveable patrimonies, though it varied according to wealth and individual preference. Large accumulations of linen begin to appear at the intermediate levels, where between 200 and 300 *livres* were devoted to appearances. The Oudry family – he was a merchant brazier – was rich, with a total fortune of 9,550 *livres*, including moveables to the value of 4,511 *livres*; their wardrobe was worth more than 1,100 *livres* (32 per cent of their moveable wealth), but the linen came to less than a quarter.[29] The master butcher Adrien Vollé and his wife had moveable wealth worth 2,116 *livres* and a total fortune of 15,000 *livres*, but their clothes and linen were worth only some 74 *livres* (3.5 per cent), which can hardly

[25] Arch. nat., Minut. central, XXVI, 256 (1711).
[26] Arch. nat., Minut. central, LXXV, 410 (1697).
[27] Arch. nat., Minut. central, XXXI, 56 (1715).
[28] Roche, *Peuple de Paris*, pp. 175ff.
[29] Arch. nat., Minut. central, XXVIII, 104 (1710).

have covered more than the bare necessities.[30] In contrast, François Martin, master vinegar-maker, devoted 209 *livres* to linen and clothes for his family, which represents 12 per cent of a moveable fortune of 1,825 *livres*; Martin was a successful man, worth more than 8,600 *livres*. Among artisans and shopkeepers, a greater use of linen went with wealth and a concern for appearances.[31]

Among the bourgeoisie of the liberal professions, expenditure on linen rose to a quarter of the value of wardrobes, which rarely accounted for more than 1 per cent of moveable wealth. This was a consequence of their preference for certain specific investments – in particular offices and rents – and their attachment to the necessary to the exclusion of the superfluous. In their linen as in their outer garments, lawyers affected an air of rather diffident correctness. They had what was required, but were more concerned with utility than with an ostentatious decorum. The *procureur* in *parlement*, Pierre Leroux, was very comfortably off with a fortune in moveable goods of 10,000 *livres* of which clothes and household linen accounted for less than 250 *livres*, that is 2.5 per cent. Meanwhile, he kept the tidy sum of 3,000 *livres* in ready cash in a coffer; if he was something of a miser, his wife was hardly a paragon of elegance though, with more than 200 *livres*, neither would go short.[32] A few elderly lawyers had only such linen as was necessary to preserve the decency expected in their milieu; such a one was Noël Lammeau, also a *procureur*, who lavished on his linen barely more than 10 *livres* in a wardrobe valued altogether at 30 *livres*.

This bourgeoisie of talents, rents and office avoided extravagance, though they had grown accustomed to linen. In contrast, domestic servants quickly became lavish users of linen. Their expenditure was on average four times greater than that of wage-earners. With 8.4 per cent of their moveable wealth invested in their wardrobes, they headed the ranks of clothes consumers, and linen was of prime importance, accounting for 51 per cent of the value of the wardrobes reconstituted. Their behaviour clearly reveals their fascination with the clothes of their employers and of the wealthy. Here, too, they were effective intermediaries.[33]

---

[30] Arch. nat., Minut. central, IV, 336 (1707).
[31] Arch. nat., Minut. central, IV, 339 (1707).
[32] Arch. nat., Minut. central, CIX, 395 (1709).
[33] Roche, *Peuple de Paris*, p. 175.

By the end of the *ancien régime*, the picture had changed. Spending on linen had increased in line with spending on clothes in general. Domestic servants still led the field. Clothes accounted for 3.5 per cent of their movable possessions, that is 293 *livres*, of which linen accounted for 117 *livres*, that is, 40 per cent, though this was ten points less than in 1700. The position of linen was similar in noble and bourgeois wardrobes, but rose to 35 per cent amongst wage-earners, not a particularly large increase. The 40 per cent reached by servants alone shows that they had maintained their taste for linen, but that other purchases now vied with it. In sum, everybody had progressed a little, and attitudes had become more homogeneous, as is revealed by the figures for linen as a proportion of goods in everyday use: nobility and bourgeoisie office-holders spent less than 3 per cent on their underwear, wage-earners, domestic servants, artisans and shopkeepers, between 10.5 and 71 per cent.

Linen had become more important among the mass of the population, in all the categories from which the Parisian sans-culottes were recruited. Elsewhere, its consumption was stable; it was much greater in the case of outer garments, which was part of a double change. The first was associated with the cycle of fashion, in the short term more influential towards the top than the bottom of society; the second seems to indicate the beginning of the revolution in behaviour associated with hygiene, the use of water and the life-styles of the urban elites. The gulfs had increased; whilst in 1700 the nobility spent 360 *livres* on linen and wage-earners 15 *livres*, in the reign of Louis XVI, the linen of the nobility was worth more than 1,600 *livres*, that of the workers only 48 *livres*: the ratio had changed from 24 to 200! In the circles influenced by the new norms of good manners and cleanliness, the accumulation of linen, a feature of the old practices stabilised in the seventeenth century, had only grown in parallel with the return of water to towns and the rise of the new pedagogies of washing, to which we will return.[34] Linen still accounted for one-third of the Parisian patrimonies studied, but it had increased less than other goods in everyday use and than clothing in general. The greater hardship of a larger number and the relative impoverishment of a sector

---

[34] Perrot, *Le Travail des apparences*, pp. 13ff.; Vigarello, *Concepts of Cleanliness*, pp. 93ff.

among the wage-earners on the eve of the Revolution did not prevent habits from changing, and limited gains were part of a general transformation of sensibilities.[35] Sectarianism would impose choices of a political nature; slovenliness, the red bonnet, a grubby shirt, wrinkled stockings and contempt for the refined linen of the aristocracy became, for a while, the essential passports to the militant life.

Such gestures conceal more profound transformations and the general advent of a different society, in which consumption was firmly entrenched and obsolescence more important than scarcity. The revolution in manners,[36] in which linen was a way of classifying and distinguishing, and which was analysed, lauded or deplored by contemporaries after 1750–60, owed much to the cumulative process by which needs were standardised and different responses adopted to satisfy them. As with outer clothing, it was one aspect of the separation of public and private space and of the role of distinction in the social field.

## FEMALE UNDERWEAR FROM LOUIS XIV TO LOUIS XVI

An analysis of the different types of linen throws light on its role in the world of appearances. Sexual dimorphism and socio-economic level affected underclothes just as they did outer clothes (see tables 16 and 17). Let us look first at women; at the end of the seventeenth century, all the indicators concur that women in every social category had no more underwear than men, which was not the case with outer garments. Female underclothes also cost little more than men's. Six or seven articles were ubiquitous: the petticoat, on the frontier of the visible and the invisible, utilitarian, since several of them provided protection against the cold and, when trimmed, revealed a taste for luxury; the shirt, often sexually undifferentiated, but varying in the elegance of its trimming and decoration; headwear, infinitely adaptable, with its own considerable vocabulary and of amazing variety, from the simple old-style coif to the fashionable beribboned caps;[37] stockings, thread or silk; and the

---

[35] Roche, *Peuple de Paris*, pp. 66–95; A. Soboul, *Les Sans-culottes parisiens en l'An II* (Paris, 1958), pp. 433–57, 649–81.

[36] A. Chabrit, *Le Compatriote ou du luxe dans la Limagne* (Paris, 1779), p. 20.

[37] A. Franklin, *La Vie privée d'autrefois, les magasins de nouveautés*, 4 vols. (Paris, 1894–8), vol. I, pp. 289–90.

Table 16 *Male linen c. 1700 (percentage presence in wardrobes)*

|  | Shirts | Trimmings | Stockings | Drawers | Indoor and night-clothes | Handkerchiefs |
|---|---|---|---|---|---|---|
| Nobilities | 53 | 65 | 66 | 20 | 45 | 60 |
| Wage-earners | 87 | 15 | 47 | 17 | 22 | — |
| Domestics | 100 | 30 | 50 | 20 | 25 | 27 |
| Artisans and shopkeepers | 98 | 50 | 56 | 18 | 32 | 43 |
| Office-holders and professions | 88 | 56 | 68 | 32 | 43 | 56 |

Table 17 *Female linen c. 1700 (percentage presence in wardrobes)*

| | Petticoats | Shirts | Trimmings | Stockings | Head-wear | Drawers | Night-clothes | Stays |
|---|---|---|---|---|---|---|---|---|
| Nobilities | 90 | 76 | 74 | 62 | 50 | 3·5 | 25 | 14 |
| Wage-earners | 53 | 78 | 46 | 39 | 79 | — | 5 | 41 |
| Domestics | 60 | 75 | 60 | 46 | 75 | 1·6 | 25 | 25 |
| Artisans and shopkeepers | 80 | 91 | 87 | 30 | 57 | 12 | 30 | 22 |
| Office-holders and professions | 75 | 73 | 56 | 38 | 54 | 1·6 | 59 | 38 |

Table 18 *Female linen c. 1789 (percentage presence in wardrobes)*

| | Petticoats | Shirts | Trimmings | Stockings | Head-wear | Drawers | Night-clothes | Stays |
|---|---|---|---|---|---|---|---|---|
| Nobilities | 100 | 100 | 100 | 100 | 90 | 7·2 | 50 | 81 |
| Wage-earners | 94 | 93 | 30 | 87 | 96 | — | 19 | 50 |
| Domestics | 95 | 100 | 64 | 90 | 84 | 2·6 | 57 | 60 |
| Artisans and shopkeepers | 100 | 100 | 41 | 97 | 100 | — | 76 | 66 |
| Office-holders and professions | 100 | 100 | 56 | 100 | 100 | 6·6 | 90 | 65 |

Table 19 *Male linen c. 1789 (percentage presence in wardrobes)*

| | Shirts | Trimmings | Stockings | Drawers | Indoor and night-clothes | Handkerchiefs |
|---|---|---|---|---|---|---|
| Nobilities | 100 | 80 | 100 | 46 | 57 | 100 |
| Wage-earners | 96 | 63 | 80 | 4 | 33 | 12 |
| Domestics | 100 | 92 | 74 | 12 | 28 | 53 |
| Artisans and shopkeepers | 97 | 58 | 91 | 6·2 | 16 | 37 |
| Office-holders and professions | 100 | 95 | 97 | 22 | 100 | 83 |

panoply of indoor and night clothes. Stays, like the petticoat worn sometimes outside and sometimes inside, complete the list. These articles were found at all social levels, evidence of the definitive conquest of linen, but their quantity and quality, even their elegance and grace, reveal a range of attitudes, in particular to changing. Modernity consisted of the capacity to rotate garments more frequently, which raised new problems with regard to storage and, even more, upkeep and laundry.

The range of prices shows how wide was the range of qualities.[38] A pair of stockings cost between 1 and 15 *livres* according to fineness of weave and decoration, a shirt from 18 *sols* to over 30 *livres*, stays from 1 to 7 *livres*, dressing-gowns from 2 to 20 *livres*.

Table 18 shows that lower-class women had fewest garments, except for shirts and stays: two or three petticoats, one or two stays, a dozen or so shirts, an average of five or six mob-caps, caps and fichus per inventory, and only one or two pairs of stockings. This was the situation of the majority of women; except for the poor, virtuous or not, they had what was necessary, but only a tiny minority had more. A working woman or a mother of a family could change her shirt every day of the week and, with five in reserve, twice a day on occasion. But she had to be much more economical with her stockings, which she could wash only every two days. Long skirts gave women some protection against the mud and dirt of the streets, to which men were exposed, and men owned more stockings than the women.

By the reign of Louis XVI, all the garments were more widely found and in larger numbers: five or six petticoats, two or three stays (which fashion had liberated from the iron cage of whalebone and steel strips), between six and twelve pairs of stockings, but only half a dozen shirts. This last figure is particularly interesting; though the average had fallen, the general index of diffusion had risen from 78 to 93 per cent; further, the decline of the average was accompanied by an increase among the richest, who were better provided than in the time of Louis XIV. In other words, the use of shirts had become almost universal and the better-off had adopted the habits already common among the elites of a century earlier. Working-class women owned a wider range of linen thanks to the

---

[38] Levêque, 'Les Vêtements de la bourgeoisie', pp. 27–9.

appearance of new articles such as the caraco jacket and the déshabillé; their underclothes were of better quality, and fine linens more widely found. However, linen trimmings and decorations were no more numerous. In sum, the accumulation of linen made it possible to change and was designed to achieve greater comfort rather than a more elegant appearance. A few rich women, touched by the grace of the hygienists, were beginning to recoil from strong smells, and alter their ways, requiring greater cleanliness.[39] Among the mass of the population, where water was scarce, linen retained the role it had acquired at the end of the sixteenth century, that is, as a substitute for washing the skin.[40]

In sum, it was white linen which conferred respectability, that is, truly differentiated, and its frequent renewal allowed an appearance which conformed to polite norms. This was the case with the linen of the aristocracy, and it was being imitated by other women, from the bourgeoisie to domestic servants, by the beginning of the century. The range of garments was everywhere the same, and the principal linen items general by 1700. What varied was quantity and quality, what mattered was diversity and the capacity to change frequently, thus to proclaim one's cleanliness to the world. In the time of Louis XIV, noblewomen had, on average, a dozen shirts. This was hardly more than amongst ordinary people, but we should remember both that the presence of servants made it easier to look after shirts and wash them frequently and that bequests of shirts were common, which helped to bring down the average. By 1789, the inventories record some two dozen shirts for the less well-off, fifty to sixty for the middling groups and hundreds for the rich. The norm which had triumphed by the seventeenth century had become increasingly powerful with the passage of time and with the increasing taste for the informal and the values of intimacy, both family and personal.[41] Further, the quality of underwear had generally improved; homespun linen had been replaced by the fine linen of Holland and France, by lawns and muslins, occasionally

---

[39] Corbin, *Le Miasme*; Perrot, *Le Travail des apparences*, pp. 16–25.

[40] Roche, *Peuple de Paris*, pp. 158–60.

[41] Ariès, *L'Enfant et la vie familiale*; P. Ariès, G. Duby and R. Chartier, eds., *Histoire de la vie privée*, 5 vols. (Paris, 1985–8), translated by Arthur Goldhammer as *A History of Private Life* (Cambridge, Mass./London, 1987– ), vol. III, *De la Renaissance aux Lumières*; P. Goubert and D. Roche, *Les Français et l'Ancien Régime* (Paris, 1984), vol. II.

by silk. Decoration and trimmings had proliferated and become even more elaborate; lace adorned collars and cuffs; gathered and pleated sleeve ruffles, ribbons and scallops everywhere proclaimed the demands of elegance and fashion,

White linen was an essential criterion for the pupils turned out by Saint-Cyr; Mme de Maintenon had enjoined the mistresses to ensure this in their own case, before seeing that the young daughters of the nobility did likewise: 'I assure you that nothing would be so unseemly as to see you all well dressed and well turned out in white linen, while they were all dirty and negligent.'[42] The very success of this institution, which recruited from well beyond the impoverished nobility, contributed to the dissemination of the principles, the means and the sphere of influence of the norms of clean, white linen, testimony to the cleanliness and whiteness of bodies and souls. By 1780, a court trousseau might comprise thousands of items and cost more than 25,000 *livres*, a figure well beyond the aspirations of a woman of the bourgeoisie. The wardrobes distributed on the occasion of the birth of the duc de Bourgogne, in 1751, to 600 deserving young couples 'from the artisanate, workers, or others whom the insufficiency of their fortune or of the product of their labour renders unable to provide for their establishment',[43] did not include shirts for the young women; they received a dowry of 300 *livres*, a gown and petticoat of a mixed cloth of silk, thread and cotton, a mob-cap, a neckerchief, a pair of muslin cuffs and a pair of woollen stockings. We see an increased consumption of clothes, but a still limited consumption of linen. The absence may mean that everyone had crossed the threshold of ownership: you did not give what you expected would already be owned. However that may be, the threshold had been crossed by 1780: the bundles of clothing belonging to Rétif de La Bretonne's fleeing poor clerk and orphan girl each contained six shirts.[44]

---

[42] Madame de Maintenon, *Education morale, choix de lettres* (Paris, 1884), p. 154; D. Picco, 'Les Demoiselles de Saint-Cyr', mémoire de maîtrise, Paris 1 (1980); D. Roche, 'Education et société dans la France du XVIIIe siècle, l'exemple de la maison royale de Saint-Cyr', *Cahiers d'histoire* (1978).

[43] H. Vanier, *La Vie populaire en France* (Paris, 1965), pp. 187–8.

[44] Rétif de La Bretonne, *Les Nuits*, p. 163, lists the contents of the bundles of the two fleeing lovers; six men's shirts, collars, stockings, a cotton cap and two white breeches in one, six women's shirts, some stockings, some round and very clean caps, a few ribbons, two lawn aprons, two silk skirts, two casaquins, two pairs of pockets in the other (not forgetting what they had on).

Among shopkeepers and the crafts, the tradition of thrift allowed for the acquisition of the essentials: one or two petticoats, usually simple, between one and three pairs of stockings, mostly of wool, and more than six shirts in three-quarters of the wardrobes, more than a dozen in a good third. Louise Chouraud, widow of a merchant baker, owned thirty shirts, though she and her husband had a wardrobe valued at only 206 *livres*.[45] The shop-window effect which we have noted in the case of outer clothes applied equally here with regard to trimmings: 87 per cent, the highest figure, higher even than for the nobility. Collars of muslin, breast pieces, sleeve ruffles and *engageantes* of several layers and different lengths, gathered at the wrist or pleated (present in 80 per cent of wardrobes), show the importance attached to the visible aids to invisible cleanliness in a social milieu where display was confined by custom to work in the shop. Head-dresses were equally numerous and varied: most common was the coif, very often of black taffeta; the fichu was rare (in 7 per cent of inventories), mob-caps were common, and the richest followed fashion, if at a distance.[46] This was the situation in 1700.

By the time of Louis XVI, both quantity and quality had increased. Women shopkeepers had attained worldly elegance and refinement in fabric and colour. They had camisoles of siamoises and indiennes, shirts of fine linen and cotton, light stays of quilted linen, night gowns, peignoirs and déshabillés *à la Reine*. Whereas at the time of Louis XIV they had owned an average of three pairs of stockings, they now had nine or ten pairs, a third of them silk.

In sum, there had here been a general advance, and whatever pretty shopkeepers revealed increasingly excited interest in what they concealed: their linen had increased in value as a proportion of their wardrobes. This was noted by both Rétif and Mercier; it encouraged trade and attracted shoppers. We can see it as a form of publicity appropriate to ancient street life, since shops impinged far more on communal space than is the case today. It was part of a general trend towards the acquisition of better-quality goods.

---

[45] Arch. nat., Minut. central, XXVIII, 103 (1709).
[46] Arch. nat., Minut. central, LXIX, 163 (1696). Marie-Madeleine Caillot, wife of a merchant mercer, had 'two ribbons used as fontanges, one with gold flowers on a blue background, the other bean colour with gold stripes'.

THE STIFF BODICE REJECTED, FLEXIBLE STAYS PREFERRED

Among the wives of *procureurs*, *avocats*, doctors and surgeons, we see an analogous increase in comfort and quantity. To begin with, a hint of austerity rather than economy can be detected in the indexes of diffusion: all were lower than for the nobility or the working women of the bourgeoisie. The average inventory comprised three or four petticoats, almost invariably five or six pairs of stockings of wool, thread or cotton, ten or so shirts, not always trimmed, various head-dresses, a few stays and a few indoor and night clothes. A handful of the richer women evinced all the signs of a serious interest in their appearance, in the form of sleeve ruffles, *engageantes*, lace collars, cravats and fontanges.[47] However, by the eve of the Revolution, the bourgeoisie of office had joined the consumers, albeit with a certain reserve: theirs was the least marked increase in the value of wardrobes, Further, the irregular incidence of success and failure accelerated or delayed the crossing of the invisible barrier separating necessity from superfluity. They had more of everything, but especially so at over 5,000 *livres* of moveable wealth. They now all had more than twenty shirts, a dozen petticoats and a dozen pairs of stockings, but only the wealthiest had a variety of qualities of fabric, colours and trimmings.[48] As many as thirty-three different types of linen for shirts are recorded, and a dozen types of head-dress, from the cap *à l'heureux destin* to the coif *à la jeanette*; peignoirs, night gowns, bedjackets and other camisoles for night wear appeared in three-quarters of the inventories, always more of them among the richest. The rejection of the stiff bodice, here as elsewhere, assured the success of flexible stays, which some forty women had acquired in dimity, fustian, linen, cambric or, less often, siamoise. A rich and enlightened fringe among the bourgeoisie of the *ancien régime* had everything necessary to elegance, whilst the rest held back, remaining loyal to the rather archaic style of the old Parisian gown.

[47] One single case, Anne Elisabeth Lecamus, wife of an *avocat*. Arch. nat., Minut. central, XXIII, 383 (1701).

[48] Merz, 'Le Costume des bourgeois parisiens', pp. 73–99. A hundred inventories record 543 pairs of sleeve ruffles and 186 trimmings (*garnitures*), in linens (a third), silks (a quarter) or lace, and described in a way which testifies to the imagination of the modistes: the trimmings might be flat, *à la bouchère*, *au bonhomme*, mignonettes, have one, two or three layers, be frayed or mounted on linen.

Mercier would make this one of his significant contrasts when he described the Marais and the faubourg Saint-Germain. It was another sign of the link between economic, social and cultural situation and choice in matters of appearance.

We see this again in the case of domestic servants. A mobile group, constantly changing and being replaced, in contact with all social classes, female servants did not all behave alike. By the beginning of the century, a minority in the service of the aristocracy copied, at their own level, the manners of their superiors, but the average and often high indexes of consumption show that the majority had already significantly diverged from ordinary habits. It was a question of quantity: shirts were counted in dozens, as were stockings, and four, five, even six petticoats were the norm. The possibilities varied greatly according to matrimonial status (the unmarried being at an advantage) and nature of work: chambermaids made free with the fine linen in the chests of their mistresses, whilst the maid of a small shopkeeper had to be content with more rustic finery.[49] By 1780, they were all in possession of a wider range of linen articles, whilst the essentials had become general. Their petticoats and shirts were now trimmed with inexpensive trifles, bits of ribbon and elegant little pieces of lace. Coifs were more numerous but caps and fancy head-dresses had also proliferated. Two-thirds of the inventories listed stays of the new lighter type, and there was a wider range of fabrics, even of patterns. Further, every female servant now had at least a dozen pairs of stockings, mostly white, less often grey or black, occasionally flesh-coloured, plum-coloured, striped or sprigged; a good third were of silk. Domestic servants had clearly participated in the general cultural change, and they had certainly contributed to the diffusion throughout the working class, and beyond the towns, of a more refined sensibility, greater cleanliness and simple visual pleasures.[50]

---

[49] Roche, *Peuple de Paris*, pp. 176–8.

[50] The books by Maza (*Servants and Masters*), Fairchilds (*Domestic Enemies*) and Sabatier (*Figaro et son maître*) analyse clothing only as a specific social sign by posing the classic problem of the degree of identification and imitation. None of the three shows any interest in the impact on values of the intimacy imposed by the constant proximity – day and night, at the toilet – which was the norm, especially in great houses; sexual norms interest them only when transgressed, for example, the rape or debauch of servantmaids, never in connection with new habits or new sensibilities which might be acquired.

BETWEEN THE VISIBLE AND THE INVISIBLE: MALE
UNDERWEAR IN THE EIGHTEENTH CENTURY

Men's wardrobes held fewer of both the principal and the accessory
linen items. Two articles were universal; the shirt and stockings.
Night-clothes and handkerchiefs, often difficult to attribute to one
or other sex, were less common. As with women, the trend was
above all towards more of the principal items and a wider range of
accessories and styles. In 1700, working men owned little, though
shirts were widely found (in 85 per cent of wardrobes), six
each on average, so it was already possible to change fairly frequently in accord with the dictates of cleanliness. A few rich
journeymen had better-stocked wardrobes. The low index of diffusion for stockings (47 per cent) makes it plain that by no
means everybody enjoyed this comfort, though the high average
(of six pairs) shows that the smarter men could change fairly
frequently as long as they replenished their stocks reasonably
regularly. Archaic touches persisted; shirts tended to be plain,
fabrics were coarse and rustic, woven from rough flax or coarse
country hemp. They had mostly acquired the essentials, which
suggests a body of poor who made do with very little. Male
domestics were not very different, and did not play the same
intermediary role as female servants. Only a handful of *maîtres
d'hôtel* and *valets de chambre*, going some way to imitate their
masters, were both better protected and better dressed. For the
rest, the minimum sufficed; they all owned shirts and stockings,
though not enough to enable them to change frequently for reasons
of either hygiene or style. The special stamp of service was more
apparent in outer than in inner clothes.[51]

Shopkeepers, artisans, *avocats, huissiers, procureurs*, doctors and
surgeons were also more homogeneous in their behaviour than
were their wives. Certain features were common to all categories of
the urban male bourgeoisie, namely a controlled plenty, a decency
without superfluity. Among the men of the liberal professions,
stockings and shirts were universal, and a good third of their
wardrobes held more than ten dozen, of good quality, though
rarely trimmed. Lace, embroidered kerchiefs, dazzling white cuffs
and fine linens proclaimed the success of a few talented *avocats*

---

[51] Roche, *Peuple de Paris*, p. 177.

and rich doctors who were members of the faculty. This had probably been generally the case for more than fifty years.[52] Artisans and shopkeepers prized above all solidity and the necessary; all their inventories included shirts (on average, six) and 68 per cent mentioned stockings (on average, two or three pairs). Decoration, trimmings and the quality of garments or fabrics were of little interest to half this group, and only a good third had acquired trimmed, gathered and pleated wristbands or ruffles of two, three or even four layers. The same individuals showed signs of interest in private and night-time comfort – mantles for night wear, dressing-gowns, nightcaps and coifs. These indoor garments were found in comparable numbers among lawyers and doctors. Both groups had achieved a higher degree of comfort and preferred solidity and utility to decorum. The Parisian bourgeoisie had adopted the new norms of cleanliness through linen before the end of the seventeenth century, but only the better-off among them had internalised the values of display. A majority of the population had not yet been seduced by fine fabrics, replaceable pieces and a profusion of white spilling out over their outer clothing; they still dressed with a certain austerity, which might be dictated by necessity or lack of means, but also by a conscious rejection of the marks of a morally dubious refinement.

Paradoxically, the indexes are not high among the male nobility, which is perhaps indicative less of absence than of a more rapid dispersal prior to the inventory. However, they possessed the largest average number of items: fifty. We see the originality of the Parisian nobilities of the last years of the reign of Louis XIV, before the return of the court to Paris under the Regency had revived the economic and social influence of aristocratic fashions. The refinement visible in their outer clothes seems not to have extended to their inner clothes. The visible was all-important, though not necessarily related to the display of the hidden which was more marked among women. Whilst linen had emerged onto the surface, and become highly symbolic and strongly distinctive, it was not yet universal, even among the nobility.[53] What

---

[52] Lehoux, *Cadre de vie des médecins parisiens*, pp. 96–8.

[53] Vigarello, *Concepts of Cleanliness*, pp. 69–77. Noble inventories reveal great variety: 1 to 5 shirts 9.5%; 6 to 10 26.5%; 10 to 20 28.5%; 20 to 50 34.5%; over 50 5%. A quarter would have been unable to change daily; over a third had twenty-one shirts, so could change three times a day with regular washing. Only

distinguished the man of quality was the ability to change his shirt
and stockings frequently and, in the case of the very rich alone,
observe the laws of gallantry, imitate the lions of the court, even
aspire to the embroidery and lace of the king and the princes, who
squandered annually the equivalent of respectable patrimonies to
pay for their sumptuous furbelows.[54] Cleanliness had changed its
meaning and now indicated distinction, but outer clothes remained
both more valuable and more numerous than inner clothes. Finery,
the art of display and the creation of an illusion were permitted to
the elites of rank, fortune and culture, but in practice, sexual
dimorphism, the economic hierarchy and culture impeded the downwards diffusion of norms and codes.

On the eve of the Revolution, the return of the high nobility to
Paris, increased wealth after a century of rising landed rents and
the lucrative growth of the linen trade made themselves felt in the
refinement of male, as well as female, wardrobes. The pursuit of
distinction is apparent in the general rise in the indexes of consumption. The number of every item, except drawers and indoor clothes,
was close to the optimum. Linen must have been accumulated on a
large scale, since it is unlikely that redistribution had ceased: shirts
by the dozen, even dozens of dozens, pairs of stockings by the
dozen, over forty on average, casaquins, camisoles, peignoirs, déshabillés, night mantles, nightcaps, also toilet and shaving linen, new
arrivals on the scene and sign of the greater cleanliness of the
upper classes thanks to the wider availability of water; there is
every indication of progress, greater comfort, a certain hygiene,
based partly on linen and partly on washing, and the affirmation
of wealth. In some cases, this verged on profligacy.[55] The men
often had more linen than the women.

Among the rest of the population, the rise in all the indexes

a quarter of the shirts were trimmed, but most were of white linen, *toile de lin*,
Holland or half-Holland. All were white, except for a few which were 'yellow'.
The mercantile and office-holding bourgeoisie owned shirts as follows: 1 to 5 30–
33%; 6 to 10 50–36%; 10 to 20 20–29%; more than 20 2%. Perhaps the norm was
possession of a dozen shirts at the time of marriage, after which the rich replaced
their stock, whilst the poor gradually wore them out. See Kalifa, 'Le Costume
dans la petite bourgeoisie' p. 53.

[54] Franklin, *La Vie privée d'autrefois*, vol. IV, pp. 126–30; F. A. Garsault, *Descriptions des arts et métiers, l'art de la lingère* (Paris, 1780).

[55] For the nobility, the figures are: shirts: men 82, women 57; average total number
of items; men 283, women 223; pairs of sleeve ruffles: men 37, women 20. The
woman's shirt could easily be replaced by the camisole.

between 1700 and 1780 was analogous, and the increase sometimes more rapid since starting from a lower base. The figures for *avocats* and doctors were comparable, but at a lower level: twenty-six shirts on average, ten pairs of stockings, ten or so ornaments and trimmings. Greater refinement was achieved by means of softer fabrics and the indoor clothes which enjoyed a huge success in this milieu, and which it is tempting to relate to the requirements of intellectual labour. For all these men of talents, whose dress was sober, linen was kept for best, sometimes for a conscious ostentation, if we remember their attachment to the sober and severe outfits made into the symbol of the triumphant black-suited bourgeoisie.[56] They had assimilated the common good manners and the art of revealing the invisible by the appeal of the visible. Tradesmen and craftsmen, too, had copied the big spenders. The honest shopkeeper and the respectable artisan changed their shirts more than was necessary, owning fifteen on average. They had adopted sleeve ruffles and stylish trimmings. They were seduced by frivolity and were sufficiently rich, inventive and cultivated to take a greater interest in visual effects, 'to change the order of the colours, the material, the shapes of the costume and thus the order of the social categories'.[57]

At the bottom of the ladder, among workers, journeymen and domestic servants, things had also changed. The latter, like their wives, imitated their masters, if from afar, the former copied their employers; they had succumbed to the temptations of the urban market. Stockings were on every foot (people owned on average six pairs), shirts on every back (six or seven on average), but the increase was not particularly marked compared with 1700. A few collars and cuffs were found in two-thirds of their inventories. The difference between the two groups showed less in their habits, which were increasingly standardised, than in quantities. Those in service could change their shirts more frequently (they owned twenty-five on average), and indoor clothes, nightcaps, turbans and dressing-gowns added to the comfort of the better-off. The less well-off, too, had acquired the taste for linen and comfort. Parisians

[56] Braudel, *Civilisation matérielle*, p. 242. The figures for the artisanate are: 1–5 shirts 10%; 6–10 15%; 10–20 50%; 20–30 25%; stockings 11.48 pairs; sleeve ruffles 33 pairs. The figures for the non-noble *robe* are: 1–5 shirts 5%; 6–10 15%; 10–20 45%; 20–30 35%; stockings 10.92 pairs; sleeve ruffles 35 pairs.

[57] Perrot, *Les Dessus*, pp. 32–83.

had learned to blow their noses politely: the index of consumption of the handkerchief had risen from 0.39 to 0.57. People may still have used their fingers to blow their noses, or used their handkerchiefs as purses, but they had embarked on the road towards correct behaviour as prescribed in the manuals.

PARIS LEARNS TO BLOW ITS NOSE

Between 1700 and 1789, linen in a sense changed its role and importance in Paris. Never totally invisible, for men and for women, it originally marked the hierarchy of appearances according to how remote one was from respect for the distinctive cleanliness which had been proved by fine, white linen since the sixteenth century.[58] It was the sign of a system of cleanliness based on the rejection of water, at a period which saw the human body as porous, wide open, dangerously exposed to attack by water-borne miasmas, when the valorisation of appearances was satisfied by a hygiene more peripheral than profound. Emphasising the privileges of the visible, it ordered all the elements of etiquette into a system: white linen, clean clothes, clean hands and face, powdered wigs, plenty of perfume, even an excess of make-up and cosmetics.[59] Immaculate white linen to some extent freshened the body since it cleansed it of sweat when the shirt was changed: 'Linen washed without the use of water, but, at the same time, it displayed.'[60] Expressing a hygiene different from our own, conforming to the moral style of 'good manners', suited to the technological capacity of an age when water was scarce, the invention of linen marked the apogee of an aristocratic civilisation in which appearances were all important.

The historian of material culture does more than simply refine this picture; he reveals the gap which existed between, on the one hand, the norm prescribed by the practices of the elite, elaborated in the discourse of the privileged, generalised by preaching and teaching, by portraits, the arts and the manuals of teachers and doctors and, on the other, the social materiality of practices. Refined linen was initially the preserve of a narrow circle, which, in

---

[58] R. Chartier, 'Histoire d'eau à travers les siècles', *Libération*, 6 March 1985.
[59] Perrot, *Le Travail des apparences*. pp. 45–60.
[60] Vigarello, *Concepts of Cleanliness*, p. 71.

the reign of Louis XIV, expanded a little, attracting first the rich, women of fashion, the integrated and the comfortably off, in a word, the converts to the civilisation of manners.[61] The majority of the rural and urban population was at first excluded from this magic circle of distinguished appearance. It remained confined within the restricted medieval hygiene of clean hands and face, which only really reached the intimate on rare occasions.

The eighteenth century saw the true discovery of linen, since it was then that its use became general. The widespread adoption of these norms was at first urban, with Paris in the lead. The provinces lagged behind, though not by much. At Chartres between 1700 and 1720, the masters and journeymen of the crafts were as well provided with shirts as were Parisians; only the peasants of the outlying districts trailed behind.[62] Women played the same role as in Paris, demonstrating a more developed visual and tactile sense than men. At Limoges in mid-century, the use of linen was comparable: 83 per cent of inventories mention shirts, a dozen on average, though two-thirds of households had fewer than ten. By 1830, the proportions were reversed.[63] Round Meaux, the rural inventories of the eighteenth century record similar numbers, and even before 1665 70 per cent had more than five shirts, though a third had none. After 1750, shirts were ubiquitous and 45 per cent of wardrobes contained more than twenty.[64] The gap between Paris and the provinces was maintained in two ways: first, the quality remained traditionally and overwhelmingly more rustic, *toiles de brin* and shirts of coarse canvas were more numerous than fine linens and shirts;[65] second, the opportunity to observe the privileged was more limited, more confined to notables of whatever type and to special occasions. The rural clothing system was still based on the prolonged use of garments, their re-use and constant mending by women.[66] The obsolescence of linen had conquered the capital, leaving the true poor behind.

[61] N. Elias, *The Civilising Process, State Formation and Civilisation* (London, 1982); *La Civilisation des moeurs* (Paris, 1973); *La Société de Cour* (Paris, 1985).

[62] Garnot, 'Classes populaires urbaines', vol. I, pp. 525–42.

[63] Joffre, 'Le Vêtement à Limoges', pp. 69–75.

[64] M. Baulant and S. Vari, 'Du fil à l'armoire, production et consommation du linge à Meaux', *Ethnologie française* (1986), pp. 3–7.

[65] This is why the value of linen did not rise between 1700 and 1789 in the Chartres inventories although the number of articles increased.

[66] Pellegrin, *L'Habillement rural en Poitou*, pp. 475–85.

One conclusion is clear: the rules of sartorial conduct spread slowly at a time when economic and technological possibilities combined to restrict their diffusion. In Paris, cleanliness through linen, triumphant at court and in town at the time of Louis XIV, was only widely accessible a century later. The general imitation of aristocratic luxury had its pioneers, namely the intermediaries, the daughters and wives of shopkeepers and women of the world. The bourgeoisies of the *ancien régime* and the traditional producers also paid more attention to what could not be seen: their costume was austere, their linen refined, and they combined a sense of thrift and a concern for appearances. But the trend was inspired less by a specific class affirmation – that of the rising bourgeoisie – than by the civilising process which, in the long term, internalised all the bodily constraints, disciplined society from top to bottom and transformed the manners of all.[67] In this sphere, bourgeois values relayed the norms of the holist society, and the privileges of the visible gradually made way for other imperatives.[68]

The country followed the town, to a greater or lesser extent, more or less rapidly, and it was not until the middle of the nineteenth century that the linen revolution was complete. In 1846, Michelet wrote in *Le Peuple*: 'Little remarked on, but important; a revolution in cleanliness, an improvement experienced by poor households; body linen, bed-linen, table linen, curtains, were all owned by whole classes for the first time in human history.'[69] Poverty now had to show itself to be clean, since slovenly dress increasingly revealed moral perversion. Learning to wash, the end of scarce water,[70] and the hygienists' values of vigour and the bodily forces did not end the tyranny of the aesthetic and the ethic of the visible; in a way, it still rules over western societies and reality, today as in the past, sometimes wrongfoots the reader of normative texts and images.

[67]  Elias, *La Civilisation des moeurs*, pp. 90–120.
[68]  Vigarello, *Concepts of Cleanliness*, pp. 131–55, 192–214, 228–9.
[69]  J. Michelet, *Le Peuple* (Paris, 1846), pp. 80–1.
[70]  Roche, 'L'intellectuel au travail', *Annales: ESC* (1982), pp. 465–80; Perrot, *Le Travail des apparences*, pp. 108–39.

1789: THE POLITICAL CONFRONTATION AND LINEN

Events can suddenly reveal such oppositions: Robespierre, tacit representative of the established and integrated bourgeoisie, fussy about his appearance, his wig powdered and his linen white, confident of his distinction in the midst of the turbulent assembly; Marat, boorishly unkempt, receiving in a dirty shirt, open at the neck, red Madras on his head, his hair greasy, bare-legged, a 'friend of the people'; Danton, exaggeratedly affected, as infatuated with fine clothes as with fine living, mixing *nouveau-riche* airs, lace and fancy sleeves with plebeian neglect, the disparities in his clothing corresponding to deeper attitudes. We now know where victory lay but we should not forget that the popular days of the Year II were unquestionably an exceptional and extreme moment in history, the affirmation of a policy which drew some of its power from the provocative defence of necessary existential liberties in behaviour: a violent and precarious passion to be different. We need to listen to the denunciations of the bourgeoisie and of the 'reactionaries', in the face of mob rule (that is, the shouting populace), and we need to read the perceptive remarks of foreign travellers fascinated by the theatricality of the sartorial posturing of the sansculottes.[71] The untidiness and slovenliness visible in all the pictures of the disturbances, which no doubt deliberately exaggerated ordinary features, might conceal opportunism, but were not only the behaviour of fanatics or the manners of a suburban rabble. At a crucial moment, they were authentically challenging values, because they expressed a culture for a different liberty – whose characteristics we have attempted to describe elsewhere.[72] In the face of the rich, dirty linen, unwashed bodies, uncombed hair, black wigs and red bonnets proclaimed the counter-values of the 'fragile life' of the common people, in an idiom which was not that of the prescribers of norms.[73] Their liberty was compatible with a sensual pleasure in colours and fabrics, even a temporary reappropriation of effects drawn from elsewhere.[74] This is a by no

[71] Mercier, *Nouveau tableaux de Paris* (Paris, 1798); Hélena Maria Williams, *Lettres écrites de France sur l'époque de la terreur* (London, 1795); Quicherat, *Histoire de costume français*, pp. 620–45.

[72] Roche, *Peuple de Paris*, pp. 278–87; A. Farge, *La Vie fragile* (Paris, 1985).

[73] H. Burstin, *I Sanculotti: un dossier da raprire. Passato e Presente* (1986), pp. 13, 52; M. Vovelle, *Les Mentalités révolutionnaires* (Paris, 1985).

[74] Cobb, *Death in Paris*, pp. 78–81.

means negligible qualification, given that, ever since, the first concern of an authentic revolutionary has been to present a correct, orderly, even uniform appearance. For a whole generation, in a different sartorial conformism, the boiler suit of China proclaimed the virtues of revolution.

Under these assaults from the cultural depths, certain practices remained unaffected, almost totally ignored by the sartorial revolution. True underwear, the invisible linen which enjoyed a special relationship to the body and eroticism, did not triumph; knickers and drawers were rare, even in aristocratic wardrobes.[75] There was nothing, other perhaps than the comfort of a few chilly individuals fearful of draughts, to make them required wearing, not even the needs of the hunt for cavaliers and Amazons, or for modesty when dancing became, with the Camargo, more demonstrative. The moralists feared that their improbable vogue revealed a surge of immorality propitious to immodesty as much as to coquetry. Confessors were unshocked by an absence which we, with our norms, tend to see as contrary to decency. The *Bijoux indiscrets* and light novels, engravings, Fragonard's *Les Hasards heureux de l'escarpolette*, not to speak of Mlle Lambercier's behind bared to the king of Sardinia in the *Confessions* of Rousseau,[76] all confirm the inventories and vice versa.[77] A conception of the body and of sexual relations is revealed by this convenient absence. Under the petticoat, fresh air; under the breeches, weapon at the ready: Jacques-Louis Ménétra bears witness on behalf of the urban population. The rarity of underclothes, the infrequency of intimate washing and the gradual victory of water among the rich alone are all in line with the absent and hidden body; it was also, in exalted milieus, the guarantee of an unimpeded libertinage, another difference from our own culture.

In Paris, actresses apart, women wore no underclothes,[78] and no-one was shocked. They were at the mercy of tumbles or gusts of wind. Rousseau, Casanova and the sansculottes who patriotically

---

[75] See tables 16–18. For a history of undergarments, P. Dufay, *Le Pantalon féminin* (Paris, 1905); Romi, *Histoire pittoresque du pantalon féminin* (Paris, 1979); also Perrot, *Le Travail des apparences*, pp. 74–6.

[76] Rousseau, *Oeuvres complètes*, *Les Confessions*, p. 21 (pp. 31–2 of Penguin edition).

[77] J. Laurent, *Le Nu vêtu et dévêtu* (Paris, 1979), pp. 118–19.

[78] Mercier, *Nouveaux tableaux de Paris*, vol. VI, pp. 18–19.

whipped aristocratic backsides reveal what was the norm. A different custom could only become general as part of a major change to bodily relations and relations to the elementary functions, which would happen in the nineteenth century.[79] This transformation of manners was prepared by the slow accumulation of linen in the century of the Enlightenment, and rather more by a new conception of the family and the medicalisation of the social body – another labour of culture on nature – than by the juridical and political rupture which allowed expression to liberating experiences. For this, however, there had to be a change of sensibility, a new acuteness, a stronger requirement of the perceptions; first the eye, excited and instructed by many centuries of need, then, or simultaneously, the sense of smell. This upheaval, which is still with us, called everything into question, from the system of acquisition to replacement, from upkeep to laundry, from the transmission of norms to modes of appropriation. Louis Sébastien Mercier jokingly saluted the Parisian firstfruits: 'Horror of linen is the badge of the Parisian. It appears to be because it is constantly being torn and they fear the laundresses' beetle and brush.'[80]

[79] Corbin, *Le Miasme*.
[80] Mercier, *Nouveaux tableaux de Paris*, vol. V, p. 117.

# 8. *The triumph of appearances: nobilities and clothes*

> ... supplient humblement les dames et damoiselles qui ont l'honneur de paraître à la Cour, disant qu'encore de tout temps, il ait été pratiqué et que partout le monde il soit en usage que la Cour des princes souverains est le lieu principal où doit éclater leur magnificence ... et il soit véritable que la plus nécessaire pompe de la Cour consiste en l'ornement et en la propreté des dames qui en composent la plus brillante partie.
>
> Plainte des dames de la Cour contre les marchandes ou bourgeoises de Paris

Many reasons combine to make the clothing practices of the nobilities of the *ancien régime* of interest to social and cultural history. The first is in origin sociological. To the extent that the second order of the holist society retained its pre-eminence, we now know that it played a motor role in the economy, above all in urban commerce.[1] These privileged persons, with their growing incomes from landed rent,[2] were a stimulus to building, trade and circulation as they engaged in the prestige expenditure dictated by their need to retain and display their rank. In Paris, Lyons and Marseilles, in administrative and cultural capitals, in Brittany and Provence,[3] in large and small centres, they nowhere appear, as has for too long been claimed, as representatives of a declining class. They contributed to intellectual life, they were involved in circles and lodges, they debated in salons and academies, in Paris and the provinces; these citizen nobles were in the first rank of a new

[1] E. Le Roy-Ladurie, ed., *Histoire de la France urbaine*, vol. II (Paris, 1981).

[2] H. Luthy, *La Banque protestante en France*, 2 vols. (Paris, 1959).

[3] M. Cubells, *La Provence des Lumières, les parlementaires aixois au XVIIIe siècle* (Paris, 1984); J. Meyer, *La Noblesse bretonne*, 2 vols. (Paris, 1966); D. Roche, *Le Siècle des Lumières en province, Académies et académiciens provinciaux*, 2 vols. (Paris, 1978).

sociability, which, in civil society, succeeded in reconciling egalitarian principles and the unequal conditions which were the basis of the old order.[4]

From this perspective, a major frontier seems to have separated the urban nobilities, caught up in the rapid expansion of trade and consumption, from the country gentlemen, village squires, sometime soldiers in the royal army, who remained to a degree apart.[5] The noble appearance was now no longer protected by insistence on sartorial privileges. The century of the Enlightenment in practice abandoned sumptuary laws. The last were promulgated at the end of the seventeenth century and, as we have seen, their effect on consumption has never been assessed; their purpose at that time was, in any case, more economic and above all protectionist than socially repressive.[6]

## NOBLE DRESS: A SOCIAL SIGN

The dress of the nobility thus takes its place within a luxury economy on which it had considerable impact, on manufacture on the one hand, on commercialisation on the other, through the imitation it inspired and through the changes dictated by fashion, of which it was the principal client. This was the beginning of a major trend which, through many intermediaries, in particular domestic servants, affected every social milieu, and in which economic determinants and aspirations, the purchasing power of individuals and the ploys of presenting an appearance all played a part.[7] We perhaps need at this point to re-read and, in all modesty, rewrite a little, Norbert Elias. The conspicuous consumption which permitted social differentiation in the external aspects of life was an instrument of group self-affirmation in the constant competition for rank and prestige. Expenditure on clothes corresponded less to actual economic possibilities than to the desire to be different.[8] But rather than the financiers spurring on the great lords, it was more that, for the bourgeois gentleman, the quest for distinction began

[4] M. Agulhon, *Pénitents et francs-maçons* (Paris, 1965).
[5] J. Meyer, 'Un problème mal posé, la noblesse pauvre au XVIIIe siècle', *Revue d'histoire moderne et contemporaine* (1971).
[6] Deslandres, *Le Costume*, pp. 175–8.
[7] Roche, *Peuple de Paris*, pp. 164–201.
[8] Elias, *La Société de Cour*, pp. 44–5, 55–7.

by acquiring a noble appearance. Further, though the price of raw materials and hence expenditure constantly grew, so did landed rents and, above all, for the privileged of the privileged with access to the royal redistribution of fiscal revenues, resources of every sort.[9] On the one hand, the values of economy – and petit-bourgeois thrift – hinder our understanding of the crucial role of ostentatious expenditure; on the other, we know too little about the consequences of the organised competition of court society, that is, the extent of failure or success, ruin or prosperity, among the ruling strata.[10] The percentage of each is unknown, and royal favour could save anyone from the abyss.[11]

Clothing therefore gives us a way of observing the mechanisms of court society in action; it was a way of demonstrating rank and acquiring prestige. It was an essential element in the representations and the realities of a system which was stoked up or damped down by the monarch himself, or by his entourage, the queen, the royal family, the favourites, the mistresses, the princes or the grandees, and through which the king induced his subjects to think as he wished. From Louis XIV to Louis XVI, from brilliant favourites to the frivolous young Queen Marie-Antoinette, the models, incitements and degrees of proximity – that is, of the speed of access and response to the imperatives of change – created tensions and disequilibriums at the very heart of the dominant circles. Appearances proclaimed the conflicts, and the pamphleteers were not mistaken when they gave to the frivolities of courtiers and king an unwonted political echo.

The ills of France began with the deficit, and the queen, who lost huge sums at faro, lavished money on clothes, jewels and extravagances.[12] Thèveneau de Morande illustrated this nicely when he attacked the ministry of Rose Bertin, the favourite fashion

[9] F. Bluche, *La Vie quotidienne de la noblesse française au XVIIIe siècle* (Paris, 1973); G. Chaussinand-Nogaret, *La Noblesse au XVIIIe siècle, de la féodalité aux Lumières* (Paris, 1976); J. Meyer, *Noblesses et pouvoirs dans l'Europe d'Ancien Régime* (Paris, 1974).

[10] For a Parisian example, D. Roche, 'La noblesse du Marais au milieu du XVIIIe siècle', in *Actes du 86e Congrès des Sociétés savantes*, Montpellier, 1961 (Paris, 1962), pp. 545–78, also 'La fortune et les revenus des princes de Condé à l'aube du XVIIIe siècle', *Revue d'histoire moderne et contemporaine* (1967), pp. 143–216.

[11] Elias, *La Société de Cour*, pp. 57–8.

[12] 'Liste civile et les têtes à prix des personnes soldées par cette liste' (Paris, 1792), p. 20 (pamphlets, B. N., Lb 39–10911).

merchant of Marie-Antoinette; the bizarre ideas and concoctions of this modiste entailed very high expenditure which '[the queen] was unable to conceal and which the king monitored and criticised with all the vehemence of a good husband, miserly with his income, and by no means enamoured of seeing it spent on gauzes, tulles and feathers'.[13] The critique of the excesses of luxury, aggravated by the distinctive imitation of court and town, shows how a model of sartorial behaviour which reproduced cultural differences and destabilised the dominant social model made the outfits of the queen and the nobility into a political issue which would persist throughout the Revolution. It is by no means certain, however, that the powerful images inspired by the political battle accurately portray the reality of noble consumption; they exaggerated and reduced them to stereotypes of extravagance. We can try to view it from a different angle, and from within, as a manifestation of the cultural practice of appearances, taking account of the various imperatives which organised and limited the possibilities of consumption, when these proclaimed a sort of feigned victory but when social power was affected by a major transformation.

A second reason for observing how the clothing habits of the nobilities functioned, on the material as much as on the social psychological plane, is the need to understand a general acceleration. Fashion ceased to be the prerogative of rank or birth alone.[14] In the second half of the eighteenth century, a specialised press, read by both men and women, written by female journalists disguised as men and male writers concealed under female names, developed and spread from the capital.[15] From 1700 to 1800, some fifty French periodicals transmitted everywhere, directly or indirectly, the imperatives of Parisian good form, and proclaimed the clothing crafts and trades, the appeal of an attractive appearance, rules for the care of the body and ephemeral codes of beauty, in sum the principles and examples, the discourse and illustrations, of a new philosophy of taste.

The first readers of *Le Cabinet des modes*, *Le Journal des dames* and *Les Amusements de la toilette*, the aristocracy of court and

[13] E. Langlade, *La Marchande de mode de Marie-Antoinette, Rose Bertin*, pp. 170–1; H. Fleischmann, *Les Pamphlets libertins contre Marie-Antoinette* (Paris, 1908), pp. 41–61.

[14] Perrot, *Les Dessus*, pp. 34–6.

[15] Rimbault, 'La Presse féminine': see below, chapter 16.

town, played a role in proportion to their means and psychological resources; but also and increasingly, so did an urban clientele, provincial for the most part, noble and bourgeois, obliged by its rank to 'work at the means to please'.[16] Through these journals, elegant citizens of both sexes breathed the air of Paris and found a subject for their worldly conversations. The good taste of articles and outfits circulated together in the milieus where the need for a distinctive appearance was real, and they everywhere suggested new social needs.[17] To test the actual consequences of the discourse of fashion should form part of the study of noble consumption. Such an approach would address the increasingly visible link at the heart of cultural change between intellectual innovation and material practices.[18]

We will not unduly labour a third reason for the study of noble consumption: the abundance of the sources. The nobilities are privileged in the exceptional preservation of their archives, and the difficulty here lies less in compensating for documentary shortfalls, as is the case with the common people, than in devising ways of coping with a sea of information. Noble inventories are counted in thousands, and in most provincial archives it is possible to compare them with other sources such as family record and account books. We have seen what the inventory after death, reconstituted for several hundred Parisian families, can tell us about the values invested in appearances, the contents of wardrobes and how they changed.[19] It is more difficult to use family papers; their multiplicity, their richness and their profusion impose choices, but they give our information and our answers greater precision. Family accounts and papers enable us to observe the constituent elements of a wardrobe over several years, and thus reconstruct rates of replacement, and go some way to discovering the influence of fashion on individuals, once new clothes were bought more often than was necessary simply to compensate for wear and tear.[20] It is also possible to establish expenditure on clothing on a daily and an

---

[16]  *Le Magasin des modes*, 20 May 1787, pp. 145–6.

[17]  Bourdieu, *La Distinction*, pp. 60–75.

[18]  M. Spufford, *The Great Reclothing of Rural England, Petty Chapmen and their Wares in the 17th Century* (London, 1984), pp. 33–43, 107–20.

[19]  See chapters 6 and 7 above; also D. Roche, 'Noblesses urbaines et vêtements dans la France du XVIIIe siècle', *Ethnographie* (1984), pp. 323–31.

[20]  Barthes, *Le Système de la Mode*.

annual basis. Further, we can see the role of habits and constraints in the organisation and evolution of a family's consumption of clothing.

The accounts pose specific problems. Family cartularies almost always provide three types of usable documents, which are more or less well represented: books and registers of account; invoices and bills of suppliers of clothes, shoes, accessories, even their upkeep; family correspondence or that relating to the administration of property which may refer to purchases, concrete problems or circumstances of use. The whole puzzle could be pieced together for a large number of families, but necessity has restricted us to the study of only a few cases, which seem to be reasonably typical of many consumption profiles: with the Montesquiou-Fezensac we see the ostentation and magnificence of court circles;[21] with the Schomberg we have a model of the model noble family;[22] with the Boudon de Saint-Amans and the Boyer,[23] we see the manners of the provincial nobility, specifically between Agen and Albi, far from Paris, directly and at ground level.[24] With these case studies, whose representativeness I need hardly justify, I hope to illustrate a certain way of describing an ensemble of cultural acts, and offer an introduction to a system of global interpretation in which the index speaks for the norm.

Despite the chronological gaps – the accounts for certain years are missing – and the documentary absences, attested or not, since one is never absolutely sure of having assembled all the receipts or all the accounts, this noble quartet reveals itself from every point of view as highly typical of the ways in which privileged persons dressed. The principal difficulty in these reconstitutions lies in the immensely detailed labour necessary to put them together, to make possible a critical comparison of the elements which compose the

[21] BHVP, unclassified MS. Papiers Montesquiou-Fezensac; Dusart, 'La Consommation vestimentaire d'une famille.'

[22] Arch. dép., Versailles, E 3106–3164; J. Préjean, 'Une famille noble dans le seconde moitié du XVIIIe siècle, le baron et la baronne de Schomberg', thèse de 3e cycle, Paris 1 (1974); Dusart, 'La consommation vestimentaire d'une famille', pp. 4–15.

[23] Arch. dép., Tarn, E 144, livres de raison de la comtesse de Boyer; B.N., Na 6541, 6542, 6580, livres de raison de la famille Boudon de Saint-Amans; Alric, 'La Consommation vestimentaire de la noblesse provinciale'.

[24] For comparison, for levels of fortune and expenditure: Bluche, *La Vie quotidienne*, pp. 173–229; Chaussinand-Nogaret, *Le Noblesse au XVIIIe siècle*, pp. 75–92.

whole. The documentation is varied, but its use requires prudence and patience. To assess the true role of clothing expenditure, it is necessary to put together the whole family budget, analyse a balance-sheet of receipts and expenses, study different categories of consumption over several years and attribute belongings to each individual, parents, children, friends of the family or servants.

The information first allows us to reassemble wardrobes, establish the nature and number of garments and, as with inventories, list the fabrics and colours and count the linen and accessories. In some cases, for example with the Schomberg, wardrobe lists and inventories of linen show the degree of interest taken in the care of garments and give greater precision to the description of the whole.[25] We can then reconstitute the system of clothing expenditure and trace its evolution. We can calculate each person's share in the family consumption. The bills of suppliers and the registers together give concrete form to the clothing economy beyond the domestic circle, and its organisation into crafts – tailors, dressmakers, linen merchants, mercers, embroiderers, hatters, bootmakers, shoemakers – as well as to the fluctuations resulting from changes in the family's activities, the enlargement or contraction of its social field of action.

Books of private expenses also enable us to assess the cost of upkeep and perceive the ways in which repairs, home manufacture, cleaning and laundry were organised. The relationship between the market and the system of family consumption is here very characteristic of clothing behaviour. In the ordinary life of the nobility, as no doubt elsewhere, the organisation and control of purchases raises the question of the distribution of the male and female roles, the principles of action instilled by education,[26] the reliance on servants, greater here than elsewhere, and the actors' independence from or community with economic attitudes; cultural manners and anthropological behaviour are revealed in the record of everyday actions and series of accounts.

Last but not least, the documentation makes it possible to answer questions as to when and how frequently clothes were

---

[25] Arch. dép., Versailles, E 3129–38.

[26] Roche, 'Education et Société dans la France du XVIIIe siècle', pp. 3–24; M. Sonnet, 'L'Education et filles à Paris au XVIIIe siècle', thèse de 3e cycle, EHESS (1983), MS.; *L'Education des filles au temps des Lumières* (Paris, 1987).

replaced. We thus follow the constraints and appeals of fashion and etiquette, since during a life, and over successive years, months and seasons, these influences were not constant. Fluctuations of greater or lesser extent and seasonal rhythms operated at the mercy of necessity (children grew up, servants left, military campaigns dragged on, removing the father from the family, expenses at court varied) or of the fantasy which could only operate within constraints. Financial imperatives and personal choices dictated habits and traced the frontiers of dependence recognisable *vis-à-vis* social and moral codes, fashion and manners. The study of correspondence adds confirmatory evidence. We can re-read the noble way of life in Paris and the provinces from the observatory of clothing and the four noble profiles outlined below.

## THE MONTESQUIOU AND THE SCHOMBERG: THE COURT, EVEN THE TOWN

The Montesquiou-Fezensac belonged to the highest echelons of the nobility. In their way of life and their character, they were typical courtiers. Anne Pierre, first baron d'Armagnac, was about forty years old when his earliest surviving invoices begin. Connected to the greatest Gascon families, that of the lords of Artagnan being particularly illustrious, the marquis de Montesquiou was a soldier. In 1780, he was a *maréchal de camp*. He lived at Versailles and in Paris, dividing his time between the court, the town and the army. At the Revolution, he was elected a deputy to the Estates General and a lieutenant general. He died in 1798. His son, Elisabeth Pierre, comte de Montesquiou, died in 1834. Born in 1764, he, too, pursued a military career, but rose to fame only under the Empire when he became a *grand chambellan* and a senator. He probably owes some of his posthumous renown to the celebrity of his wife, Louise Charlotte Le Tellier de Courtanvaux, better known as 'Maman Quiou' and governess to the king of Rome. In their son, Eugène Rodrigue, the two inheritances came together.

We are therefore able to observe a family group spanning three generations, whose illustrious careers at court, on the battlefield and in the diplomatic and political world placed them among the elite of the kingdom. Their existence was that of the habitués of Versailles and Trianon. Anne Pierre de Montesquiou was close to the royal family since he was Ménin to the royal children of

France. His different biographies emphasise the antiquity of his ancestry and his tendency to parade it (he claimed to be descended from Clovis), his flexible and sycophantic character, his love of intrigue and his pretensions to the role of worldly wit.[27] First equerry to the king's brother, the count of Provence, from 1771, an office which passed to his son Elisabeth Pierre in 1781, his wealth and his interest required and allowed an ostentatious and magnificent style of life. With an annual income of over 75,000 *livres* in 1789, the Montesquiou spent in proportion and in accord with the rules of display. Belonging to the two or three hundred families who dominated from on high the rest of the French nobility and the whole of society, they were amongst the masters and slaves of the high life.

In spite of their proximity, the social profile of the Schomberg was altogether different. The family was illustrious, having come to France to seek its fortune in the footsteps of distant cousins who had been marshals of France in the sixteenth century, but it had entered service only two generations previously and achieved neither the renown nor the wealth of the illustrious lineages. They may be ranked among those excellent families – of whom there were perhaps 3,000 in the whole of the kingdom – whose resources did not exceed 50,000 *livres*. In the provinces, such an income allowed a luxurious life-style; in Paris, and especially at court, it did not permit extravagance. At the height of their fortunes, their registers of account record an income of between 25,000 and 30,000 *livres* a year. At the time of his marriage, the baron de Schomberg, Jean Ferdinand, was receiving barely 4,000 *écus* and on his retirement, in 1789, he could count on some 20,000 *livres*.[28] Disappointed in his hopes of an inheritance, Jean Ferdinand received nothing from his Saxon rights, and his marriage to an heiress provided with a comfortable dowry, but of no special nobility, only just enabled him to maintain a rank for which his modest pay as a soldier (he was a brigadier in the cavalry) was inadequate. It was Anne Charlotte Duperrier-Dumouriez who appears to have played the principal role in the management and life-

---

[27] Duc de Montesquiou-Fezensac, *Histoire de la maison de Montesquiou* (Paris, 1847); B. Montesquiou (de), *Le Marquis de Montesquiou*, mémoire d'histoire (Paris, 1900). I would like to thank Bernard de Brye and the Montesquiou family for drawing my attention to this text.

[28] Préjean, 'Une famille noble', pp. 110–48.

style she supported. Sister of the future general Dumouriez, soberly brought up, she seems to have been a cultivated woman, calm and of simple tastes. Two children, Xavier Marie César and Cécile, were born of this union, concluded in 1767, and lived with their parents until they were fifteen. The son then entered the army, the daughter, after a brief spell with the Ursulines, died of a sudden illness.

Here we can follow one family's attitude to clothes over two generations, during less than twenty years. The Schomberg lived both in Paris and at their château of Corbeville, at Orsay, appearing at Versailles and at court only when service and need made attendance urgent – 'those closest to the source of honours are more likely to get what they ask', wrote the baron. It was a family more typical than tends to be thought, united, and at the opposite pole from the extravagant habits of the profligates and courtiers. The military career of the father, the moral and educational principles of the baronne (reading her correspondence is a reminder of the continuing influence of Fénelon),[29] accommodated as best they could to the imperatives of the worldly life and attendance at court. The Schomberg and their children longed to live *à l'anglaise*, that is, to spin, sew, read, hunt and dream in the country, with their dogs and horses.[30] Except for journeys and campaigns, they separated with reluctance. Their ideal was to frequent the great and the king only 'as long as necessary' in order not to be forgotten and to serve the state.[31] The analysis of their expenditure on clothes reveals decisions dictated by function, social position, fluctuating budgetary possibilities, personality and character.

In sum, differing degrees of integration into court society meant different internalisations – visible in the case of the Montesquiou – of its code. Accounts and correspondence are better than inventories in revealing levels of significance beyond the functional as dictated by custom. They introduce us to something other than inherited habits, and allow us to question the lived social and symbolic values which combine with economic constraints and the collective norms to guide the play of individuality and of desire.

---

[29] Roche, 'Education et Société dans la France du XVIIIe siècle'; Dusart, 'La Consommation vestimentaire d'une famille', pp. 39–41.

[30] Arch. dép., Versailles, E 3151; Préjean, 'Une famille noble', pp. 104–5.

[31] Préjean, 'Une famille noble', p. 207.

## THE PROVINCIAL NOBILITY

To descend one stage to reach the ranks of the provincial nobility is possible by choosing an example from among several thousand available family record books. To differing degrees, they contain three principal types of contents: the accounts of the administration of property in which appear income, expenses and debts; domestic accounts consisting of a daily record of miscellaneous information concerning the house, the household and everyday life; lastly, fragments of family or personal chronicles giving information about civil life, the social life of the family, even occasional historical events in which they participated, and also autobiographical information, which makes the family record book the bare bones of a life story;[32] which is to say that there are as many books as there are authors.

Such books were commonly kept among both the urban and rural nobility of the provinces, indicative of a certain culture, and they record festivities as well as work and the daily round, though irregularly and often idiosyncratically. This is the case in the Agenais, with the archives left by the Boudon de Saint-Amans, and at Albi with those kept by the Boyer family.[33] Their use, which poses the same problems and enables the same questions to be asked as the archives of the great families, makes possible a concrete and often revealing vision of daily concerns. Precious for the reconstitution of clothing consumption over two or three generations, these books make it possible to establish rates of purchase, choices and influences.

Different pictures emerge. The registers of the Saint-Amans begin in the seventeenth century. We will read them as they were kept by Paul Robert de Saint-Amans, a priest, guardian of the property of nephews who were minors, orphan son of a father from the lesser nobility, half rural and half urban, well connected to the good families of the Agenais, a cavalry officer and retired consul and mayor of the town. His heir did not continue the registers, but this was done by his younger brother, François III de Saint-Amans, who opened what was to be the last of the family's

---

[32] D. Roche, 'Noblesse et vêtements au XVIIIe siècle', *Ethnographie* (1984), pp. 323–31; P. de Gouberville, *Journal*, ed. E. de Beaurepaire (Rouen, Paris, 1882); M. Foisil, *Le Sire de Gouberville* (Paris, 1981).

[33] Alric, 'La Consommation vestimentaire de la noblesse provinciale', pp. 5–13.

account books. It is the fullest and probably the most original, in the care with which it was compiled, its regularity, the abundance of the information assembled and the piquant details which its author liked to include.[34] On his death, in 1761, his widow, a Mlle de Raymond, whose fortune and quality had helped to strengthen the social position of the Boudon, took up the pen in her turn. The series ceased in 1773 when the heir to the name, Jean Florimond, left for the West Indies. On his return, after his marriage, he added a few entries, as did his son.[35]

The document concerns three generations whose income grew from a few thousand *livres* at the time of Louis XIV to more than 10,000 *livres* by 1771. This was a comfortable income, quite large for the provinces, which put the Saint-Amans among the upper ranks of the land-owning nobility, who enjoyed the profits from their farms, and a few rents and pensions acquired through service. It did not rank them among the favoured few such as the Montesquiou, but it allowed them to live comfortably. They belonged to provincial high society, its way of life dominated by its concern to preserve its patrimony, with its own ways, preoccupied with its interests and local influence. A period in the army gave them polished manners and opened up horizons which were soon closed but never forgotten.

The Boyer family operated on a different scale. It left only one family record and account book, evidence for two generations;[36] that of its compiler, the comtesse de Boyer, and her husband, colonel of the regiment of La Fére, and that of their only daughter, Charlotte, sent to boarding-school at the age of eight. Kept over ten years, from 1779 to 1789, but regularly, the register reveals once again the importance of those women who managed noble fortunes in the absence of husbands pursuing their military careers far away. Though from a family of financiers, Antoine François de Boyer was primarily a soldier. He climbed every rung of the ladder

---

[34] B. N., MS, NAF, 6580, ff. 9–10; Alric, 'La Consommation vestimentaire de la noblesse provinciale', pp. 35–8.

[35] Jean Florimond, a sub-lieutenant, married in 1773 Mlle de Guillen, by whom he had two children: Jean Casimir (1785–1873), a cavalry officer, and Pierre-Honoré (1774–1858); he was a person of some importance, an academician and friend of Lacépède, in fact an exemplary provincial scholar. See M. Chaudruc de Grazanne, *Notice sur la vie et les ouvrages de Boudon de Saint-Amans* (Agen, 1832).

[36] Arch. dép., Tarn, E 144.

between the Seven Years War and the Revolution, emigrated, then died in Paris in 1805. Moving from garrison to garrison, he barely appears in the family register; he had no lands of his own to manage and his wife entrusted hers to an intendant. This was an example of a recently ennobled family, only three or four generations separating the proud colonel from his notary and shoemaker ancestors. In the Albigeois of the eighteenth century, they were a little on the margins, though they lived on a grand scale, with an income of between 15,000 and 20,000 *livres* a year. Their style of life oriented them towards the world, and Paris, and made them susceptible to the new fashions and influences.

At the close of the *ancien régime*, these four families, Montesquiou, Schomberg, Saint-Amans and Boyer, illustrate the diversity of the nobility. One bond – military service – united them; status and its privileges, money and its possibilities, divided them. Between Paris and the provinces, they enable us to assess the principal features of the formation, renewal, upkeep and management of clothing capital.

## PARISIAN NOBLE OPULENCE

The details of the wardrobes of masters, mistresses and their servants paint the sartorial landscape of the seriously rich.[37] Between 1772 and 1788, the marquis de Montesquiou bought thirty-five full suits, fifteen non-matching suits, four frocks, forty-six waistcoats (*vestes*), seventeen gilets and ninety-six breeches, that is, new breeches every two months and a new suit practically every three months. He could change whenever he wished. Between 1780 and 1787, his son, the baron de Montesquiou, added fifty-three breeches, twenty-six waistcoats and twenty-five gilets to his wardrobe. Fancy waistcoats were all the rage amongst the smart young men about the court, as was the suit, which was often bought incomplete (thirty-two in seven years, of which only fourteen were complete). The difference between the generations showed in the ways in which the common forms were used to produce different effects. The baron de Schomberg, who frequented the court less, ordered from his tailors between 1759 and 1787, that is, in just under thirty years, thirty-seven full suits, forty-four breeches, forty-

---

[37]    Dusart, 'La Consommation vestimentaire d'une famille', pp. 52–68, 69.

two waistcoats, sixteen incomplete suits, ten frocks and just five gilets. He replaced his clothes less often, but could still vary his outfits at will. In 1770, when Ferdinand de Schomberg was authorised to follow the royal hunt, he bought himself two suits, one of grey broadcloth, one of blue. The Montesquiou, father and son, bought two suits every year. In 1787, the marquis de Montesquiou owned a dozen of the suits customarily worn for hunting and visiting royal châteaux.[38] He was a knight of the Saint-Esprit, and had three full suits and three great embroidered black mantles made for his reception.

Uniform was important for all three men, since they all pursued a military career and frequented the court. Schomberg had four full uniforms made in thirty years, each one corresponding to a promotion, including one at Cassel in 1755. Anne Pierre de Montesquiou bought twice as many in ten years, but he had been promoted *maréchal de camp* four times more quickly. These were wardrobes adapted to specific circumstances, and revealing their owners' desire to follow fashion in both essentials and accessories. For the baron de Schomberg, the principal imperative was to steer a course between what he had to have and what he could do without. He ordered a dozen redingotes – a garment which had become common – but six were described as uniform. Anne Pierre and Elisabeth Pierre Montesquiou, who did not count their pennies, bought two or three times that number over a similar period, whilst their wardrobes were full of the comfortable garments and indoor clothes which were essential to the man of fashion at court: 'chenilles', déshabillés and dressing-gowns, even pantaloons. These were a mark of refinement; the marquis de Montesquiou had four, M. de Schomberg one only.

These clothes were made from a wide range of high-quality cloths (there were thirty different types of material in the Schomberg wardrobe, and a similar number in that of the Montesquiou); the difference lay in the cost and the capacity to respond to the changing seasons, the regular routines of everyday life and court festivities. Comfortable woollen cloths dominated the wardrobe of Ferdinand de Schomberg: fabrics of silk, trimmed with gold and

---

[38] At Choisy, the suits were of green broadcloth with gold braid, at Bellevue of purple and gold, then plum and gold; at Brunoy, with the comte de Provence, and at Maupertuis, they were different again. See G. Duplessis, *Costumes historiques*, 2 vols. (Paris, 1877), vol. II, pp. 102–20.

silver were prominent in those of the Montesquiou. The two elegant courtiers bought mainly luxury fabrics, printed linens, cashmeres, indiennes, nankeens and silks from Lyons, whereas the baron preferred coarser materials such as barracan and velour.[39] Refinement was what mattered to the former, utility and diversity to the latter.

The range of colours reflects the same imperatives. Ferdinand de Schomberg liked greys and blacks but had a taste for fine fabrics, patterned and floral embroideries, glossy shimmering velvets and unusual and vivid colours. His fashionable garments, his frocks and déshabillés, were of yellowy-green, puce, carmelite and pigeon. The opposite was true of the Montesquiou; they chose a wider range of colours, in accord with the prevailing taste, and though black dominated quantitatively,[40] it was usually matched with other colours, and above all, as with M. de Schomberg, with two essential elements of aristocratic male costume: gold and silver embroidery, which might represent 80 per cent of the value of a garment, and sets of buttons of elaborate shape – diamonds, spirals, stars – and infinite variety.

There was a similar disparity in their linen. It was sparse in the case of Ferdinand de Schomberg, who bought only thirty shirts in thirty years, and whose wife saw that the fabrics were solid and well cared for. It was abundant in the case of the Montesquiou, who bought stockings by the dozen, trimmings by the gross and fine linen kerchiefs and ruffles ten at a time.[41] A sign of the times was that all three men wore drawers; according to their laundry lists, M. de Schomberg changed his once a week, M. de Mon-

---

[39] According to Dusart, 'La Consommation vestimentaire d'une famille' (pp. 206–9), the fabrics in their wardrobes were as follows: woollens: Montesquiou 177, Schomberg 80; silks: 192 and 58; miscellaneous and cotton: 79 and 37; totals 448 and 175.

[40] The colours were as follows: blacks: Montesquiou 93, Schomberg 30; greys 19 and 32; browns 26 and 6; whites 34 and 6; reds 37 and 12; yellows, blues and greens 35 and 34; miscellaneous 5 and 10; patterned 19 and 6; stripes 36 and 10; total: Montesquiou 304, Schomberg 146.

[41] Between 1759 and 1775, M. de Schomberg bought seventy pairs of ruffles; then, having finally ceased to frequent the court, he bought no more. They were mostly of muslin or cambric, white, very occasionally black, and were worth about 10 *livres*: he had five or six dress sleeve ruffles of Valenciennes or Malines lace for wearing at court, which were worth nearly 200 *livres*. The Montesquiou never counted such items, but the number was not huge since fashions changed and, at the end of the 1780s, the sleeve ruffle was less common as a decoration to men's shirts, once the sleeves had shrunk.

tesquiou every day or every two days. In the case of hats, shoes, boots and gloves, we find a similar abundance and extravagance on the part of the courtiers, comfort combined with economy on the part of the soldier.[42]

The same was true of the wardrobes of their wives.[43] Gowns headed the list of garments owned by the baronne de Schomberg: an inventory drawn up in 1770 recorded twenty, five *grand habits de Cour* (formal court gowns), one amazon (a riding habit) and two déshabillés. Up to 1775, she remained faithful to the *robe à la française* and the sumptuous *grand robe de Cour*. Later, she increasingly bought lighter garments and adopted the fashionable simplicity popularised by the queen: polonaises, lévites and caracos appearing in her wardrobe. Mme de Montesquiou, insofar as one can judge from the scattered bills which survive, owned more clothes but was hardly more elegant. In both cases, we can see the victory of a refined modesty which did not preclude variety of fabric and diversity of colour. In both wardrobes, taffetas and satins predominated. The former, which came mostly from Italy, Florence and England, were mainly black, white and pink; the satins were French and more varied in colour, ranging from white to English blue, from plum to puce. The light fabrics, cottons, Persians, indiennes, 'Turks', 'Pekins' and 'musulmanes' were used for summer clothes. For court dress, both the forty-year-old baronne and the twenty-year-old baronne bought and had made up faille or *gros de Tours*, *gros de Naples*, poult-de-soie, silken fabric woven with gold and silver. Both clearly reflected the tension in female appearance on the eve of the Revolution. Between etiquette and liberty, between courtly fantasy and constraint, they obeyed the dictates of fashion; their wardrobes differed less than those of their spouses thanks to a streak of frivolity which, by and large (the traditional distribution of tasks within the household contributing), allowed character to be expressed, if it did not give free rein to caprice or imagination. Both at Versailles and in Paris, innovation,

---

[42] The baron de Schomberg had twenty hats, as did the baron de Montesquiou; the most expensive hats were uniform. The Schomberg had forty-five pairs of shoes, the Montesquiou 108, that is, respectively, two and ten pairs a year, not including hunting or uniform campaign boots.

[43] The sources are the same, but purchases are recorded in less detail; those of fabrics have more often been preserved than those of garments, perhaps a sign of home manufacture.

change and originality were more feminine than masculine.

The same was true of the linen of Mme de Schomberg. She listed it in mid summer: some forty varieties, ranging from the shift to stockings of silk and cotton, are recorded for three years (1767, 1769 and 1771). This was a typical wardrobe for a young married woman from the aristocracy where the family shunned costly extravagance.[44] Every known linen article was represented: night-shirts (twenty-two), day shirts (twenty-four), peignoirs and déshabillés (six), underskirts (eighteen), mantles for night wear, mante-lets, toilettes, furbelows, caps, fichus, coifs, cuffs, pockets and aprons. The baronne could change her shift twice a day, with a wash every ten days; she had thirteen pairs of stockings, so could change them every day, with a similar frequency of washing. The three inventories reveal the stability of the wardrobe: an optimum had been reached, but including a greater range of qualities, depend-ing on the nature of the fabric and the trimming, rustic fustian or modest cotton on the one hand, muslins with petit-point embroi-dery and fine lawns of dazzling white on the other. We see the triumph of the visible: neither knickers nor drawers appear in these meticulous inventories, except for one pair, to be worn with the amazon for the royal hunt.

We can calculate a modest replacement rate: two or three pairs of stockings a year, four or five fichus, three caps. Mme de Schomberg, meticulous and prudent, took great care of her linen, for ever drawing up inventories and lists ('list of linen to take to Paris this winter 1767', 'list of my night linen', 'list of linen in Paris 12 December 1772').[45] Mme de Montesquiou could afford to be more lavish. The bills from her suppliers, fashion merchants and linen-drapers, suggest both greater abundance and a higher level of luxury, and replacement on a daily and monthly basis. The trim-mings alone on the gowns of Mlle de Montmirail, once she was baronne de Montesquiou, cost more than the linen of the baronne de Schomberg. Similarly, the former had 172 pairs of shoes made for her between 1782 and 1788, that is, twenty-nine pairs a year, which she could match to her outfits.[46] In contrast, the baronne de Schomberg thriftily made do with a few dozen pairs. Give or take

[44] Arch. dép., Versailles, E 3129; Dusart, 'La Consommation vestimentaire d'une famille', pp. 75–8.
[45] Arch. dép., Versailles, E 3132; registre relié, in-12, 58.
[46] BHVP, Papiers Montesquiou, vol. I, f. 79.

such differences, we see the size of the consumer market opened up by noble clothing practices; one understands better the anger of the critics of luxury, 'this superfluity of expenses, prejudicial to reproduction', to quote Mirabeau, the '*ami des hommes*'; all the more so in that the extravagance of the parents rubbed off on their children and servants.

Some fifteen years apart, the wardrobes and linen of the young men – Xavier de Schomberg, born in 1770, and Eugène de Montesquiou, born in 1785 – were very similar. They passed from baby clothes to sailor suits,[47] then to the suits and uniforms of the young adolescent by the same stages: at two or three years of age, the dress was abandoned in favour of trousers *à la marinière* and camisole (earlier than Ariès thought);[48] at around eighteen, young aristocrats assumed the adult dress with a military air which announced their preparation for a soldier's career. Children's clothes were thus not confined to the bourgeoisie, but found also among the nobility, in the variety allowed by their wealth. Eugène was better provided than Xavier with both outer and inner clothes.[49] He was more of a child dressed as a man, since he had his first formal silk suit (*habit à la française*) when he was only three. Cécile de Schomberg, like all little girls of her class, wore the fourreau and stiff bodice (*corps de robe*) at a very early age. Like her brother, she graduated almost without transition to the dress of an adult woman; she had her first polonaise at nine, and her first déshabillé at seven. Her wardrobe and her linen were on a smaller scale than her mother's; both her and her brother's clothes were replaced as required by the normal process of growth. Children were introduced very early to the culture of appearances.

This culture was also transmitted to domestics. We have already

---

[47] Arch. dép., Versailles, E 3132 has a rare description of a layette: 2 cotton shirts, 6 cotton bedjackets, 3 cotton camisoles, 9 draw-sheets, 4 bandages for the abdomen (*bandes de ventre*), 4 caps of quilted cotton trimmed with lace, 6 pelvis bands (*tours de bassin*) of fustian, 7 pieces of breast linen (*linges de sein*), 41 hot cloths, 2 pairs of tight sleeves, 1 pair of small cuffs and two half-sheets, and nursing linen, 6 swaddling cloths (*langes*) of fustian, 4 'of Dreux', 2 of flannel, 1 of quilted satin, 2 *tours de lange* trimmed with muslin, 2 woollen brassières, 3 caps, 12 shirts *à brassière*, a complete set of muslin *du Sud*, bib, bonnet, *tour de bonnet*, cap, sleeves and fichus cut on the bias, 1 baby's cap, 1 *tour* of embroidered linen, 1 of *lange* like 2 fichus, 6 *tours de bonnet*, 6 bandages, 42 nappies, 6 caps, 6 bibs, 6 shirts, 2 *thérèses*.

[48] Ariès, *L'Enfant et la vie familiale*, pp. 85–6 of 1974 ed.

[49] Dusart, 'La Consommation vestimentaire d'une famille,' p. 88.

observed how in their dress and their personal habits they set the tone.[50] Here, we are able to spell out how their masters contributed to the transformation of their habits. An inventory drawn up in 1788 and the registers kept by the baronne de Schomberg give some idea of the nature and number of the clothes of a servant body of average size, namely, between two and five persons, at most eight, depending on the year: fourteen frocks, twenty-six full suits, sixty-six *vestes*, thirteen of them for morning, fifty-three breeches, fifteen redingotes, one gilet, two pantaloons and two roquelaures. The suits, frocks, waistcoats and breeches between them probably represent some twenty full liveries, plus additional waistcoats and breeches, the redingote being habitual. All these suits were made from broadcloth or, less often, from drill or ratteen, serge or camlet. The cut was that of the suits of the masters; what distinguished them, other than the quality of the fabrics, was the braid: silver in the case of the Schomberg, gold in the case of the Montesquiou; the colours were restricted to green, grey and red. Only the *valets de chambre* used their master's money to give free rein to their imagination; the valet of Anne Pierre de Montesquiou sported a coat of carmelite, breeches of black satin and buttons of gold. The suit of the servant taught a double lesson: that of adherence to an elite and that of respect for the hierarchies.

### BETWEEN ALBI AND AGEN, DIVERSITY IN THE PROVINCES

With regard to clothes, these two Parisian noble families were in tune with their times. What distinguished them was less the chronological difference – the Schomberg were older, the Montesquiou younger – than the qualitative and quantitive choices which resulted from their different habits and means; an examination of their expenditure will shed further light on this. Meanwhile, in the Agenais and the Albigeois, we observe analogous contrasts and evolution.

Paul Robert de Saint-Amans was a cleric who kept careful accounts. He had inherited clothes from his brother and bought what more he needed.[51] In 1749, his wardrobe contained two or three suits, five or six waistcoats and a similar number of breeches,

[50]  See chapters 6 and 7.
[51]  B. N., M. S. NAF, 6542, ff. 28–57.

a mere ten shirts, with collars and cuffs to go with them, six pairs of stockings and two soutanes. The latter apart, this was the wardrobe of a Parisian *petit bourgeois* of the period, and the clothing culture of the Agen priest was distinguished only by the abundance of his accessories, kerchiefs, wigs, sleeve ruffles and headgear. This man of the church was by no means austere; he used jasmine perfume, which he bought by the packet; he powdered and combed his own wigs, shaved closely and trimmed his clothes generously with 'silver pieces and thread', 'sprigs' and 'little buttons'. His income allowed him to replace his clothes regularly, if not particularly frequently: one pair of shoes a year, one suit every two years, a dozen shirts every six years. Otherwise, he was far removed from the ostentatious consumption of the Parisian nobility. Fashion mattered to him less than custom and comfort; he owned gloves, a heavy mantle to brave the icy winds of January and a muff. He impresses as thrifty yet anxious to dress correctly, and this guided his management of the wardrobe of his nephew, François III.[52]

The clothes of the heir to the Saint-Amans were entered in the accounts from a very early stage, but nothing in their description or value – that of the best-quality cloth – distinguished them from the clothes of his uncle. From infancy to adolescence, the young nobleman exchanged one coat for another (broadcloth for winter, linen for summer) and holey breeches and worn-out waistcoats for new. He had several shirts of linen and hemp, and an adequate number – five or six pairs – of stockings of thread and wool. As with his guardian, it all breathed solidity and ease. There was more broadcloth than silk, more ordinary linen than lawn. Elegance and refinement were achieved only by a range of waistcoats made from more luxurious embroidered silks (the material was very often bought to be made up by the local tailor). Breeches of tammy from Le Mans, a skull-cap from Paris, a beaver from Ireland and assorted trimmings extended the horizons of Agen fashion far beyond rustic caddis and druggets, horn buttons and country homespun linens.

Let us leap a generation. With Madame de Raymond,[53] in 1761, following the death of François III, the family consisted of four

---

[52] Alric, 'La Consommation vestimentaire de la noblesse provinciale', pp. 71–2.
[53] B. N., M. S. N A F, 6580, ff. 29–79.

persons: the mother, a woman of attractive personality, Jean Florimond, the eldest son, and two younger sons, Michel and Florimond. Few purchases recorded in the Sant-Amans family record
book were on behalf of its compiler: gowns, shoes, gloves, mittens,
fabrics, ribbons, buttons, thread, head-dresses, mourning coifs and
dressed wigs. This provincial wardrobe suggests discretion and was
indistinguishable in its items, materials and colours from the majority of female wardrobes of the period. A widow, responsible for the
education of her three children, busy with the administration of her
estates, Mme de Sant-Amans knew the value of things, and that a
shilling bought more in Agen than in Paris. Her register paid more
attention to the clothing of her sons.

For the eldest, who left for the Antilles in 1766, she made up a
trunk which she filled with essentials, following it with a chest of
linen three years later. The young sub-lieutenant was equipped
with two suits (to which should be added the uniform he wore),
three breeches, three waistcoats and four gilets. His linen was
slightly more abundant; thirty-eight shirts would make it easy to
change, twenty-five collars, twenty-five pairs of stockings, thirteen
pairs of half-hose – an original feature since they were not common
– thirty-six kerchiefs, fourteen nightcaps and, as luxury and refinement required, six pairs of drawers. Jean Florimond could not
pretend to the refined elegance of an Elisabeth Pierre de
Montesquiou-Fezensac, a dandy blooming in the Parisian sun, but
he had what was necessary and, for his time, more. His shirts were
fine, his stockings 'fairly fine', the fabrics solid and hard-wearing.
An air of utility prevailed, which must have been common to many
families of old extraction, modest income and a comfortable but
not extravagant life-style. Florimond's two brothers paid the price
for this outfit since they, at this period, had to be content with less
than half as much. When the lieutenant married Mlle de Guillen in
1773, Mme de Raymond equipped her whole household with new
clothes: a suit for each boy, three waistcoats each for Jean Florimond and Michel, two for the youngest, three breeches for Jean
Florimond and Florimond, four for Michel, fifteen shirts for the
eldest, seven for the middle boy, nine for the youngest, two pairs of
shoes each and various accessories: neckerchiefs, peignoirs and
wigs for the eldest, but not the others.

The typical consumption pattern of an average noble family is
here revealed; a moderate replacement rate; a suit had to last

several years and might then pass to a younger brother or the servants. The real luxury was the abundant linen, which the provinces had copied from Paris. A change of clothes according to season was obtained with the minimum of effort, linen replacing broadcloth for the coat or waistcoat. Lastly, there were hints of refinement in the drawers, the elegant redingote, the muslin collars and the decorative buttons. The marriage of the eldest son was the occasion for a sartorial feast for all. The chevalier de Guillen, brother-in-law of Jean Florimond, spent some 2,600 *livres* on clothes brought from Paris; the gown of white taffeta and lace head-dress of the young bride cost less than 300 *livres*, but more than the value of the young officer's wardrobe on his departure. Such were the clothes and customs of a middling noble family.

A practical outlook, the need to spend on the heir for the good of the family name, utilitarianism and thrift, a partial self-sufficiency, economical and careful attitudes were all features which distanced them from the reserved ostentation of the Schomberg or the courtly extravagance of the Montesquiou. The fashions of the capital were not ignored, but their influence was limited, felt in accessories more than essentials, and at the major festivals of life rather than in normal times. Lastly, on the chessboard of provincial elegance, men and women did not always occupy the same positions. Age, the situation of the family, births, deaths and fluctuating financial circumstances all helped to determine appearances.

Mme de Boyer had the education and the principles to enable her to keep an exemplary record book. It is a blessing for the historian in spite of the rather random nature of the annotations.[54] It is all there, for the ten years between 1779 and 1789, except for a brief interruption caused by a journey to Normandy; 3,600 days of daily accounts which record outfits and accessories. Since M. de Boyer was with his regiment for much of the year, his wardrobe is incomplete. He bought in Albi only what he was short of or could carry easily. However, when the revolutionary committee searched his chests in 1792, they exposed a wardrobe of Parisian scale and quality: seven full suits, winter, summer and uniform, of broadcloth, silk and linen; waistcoats for morning and afternoon; gilets, redingotes and frocks, not to mention fashionable pantaloons.[55]

---

[54] Arch. dép., Tarn, E 144, 80 folios are used in this book.
[55] Arch. dép., Tarn, Q 491 (8 December 1792).

We will not go into detail; suffice to say that he had outer and inner clothes in profusion, and the register of accounts shows how frequently he might change and the variety of his purchases. The shirts, cravats, sleeve ruffles, under-sleeve ruffles and kerchiefs were those of an *élégant*. The fabrics and colours, chosen with care, were of superior quality, and silk was common both for visible and concealed garments. M. de Boyer, when in Albi, must have been the arbiter of elegance.

In the case of his wife, the register reveals a true passion for clothes; she, too, had what was necessary and plenty more – gowns of every fabric and colour, caracos and *pets en l'air*, stays, petticoats, déshabillés, cottons, dozens of pairs of stockings. After 1785, she wore a redingote and cravat. Her hats must have provoked the curiosity of the citizens of Albi, her hairstyles emulated the extravagant erections concocted in Paris by Rose Bertin. She was a woman at the height of fashion. Her clothes were cut and sewn from a variety of fabrics, which she usually bought by the ell (that is, in lengths of just under 1.2 metres). They included taffetas, satins, velvets, silks, indiennes, lawns, cambrics, quantities of gauze and muslin suitable for light gowns and chemise-gowns, less often fustians – from which she made petticoats – or homespun linens, which had many uses. Her daughter Charlotte echoed her mother's sartorial habits, with similar garments and materials. Meticulously recording the provenance of the fabrics in her wardrobe, Mme de Boyer traced, in the depths of the Albigeois, an imaginary geography based on exotic textiles: the taffeta came from England, sometimes from the Indies, the velvet was from Utrecht, the gauze from Italy, one silk from Florence, another from (the rather closer) Ganges. Her book reveals a sensibility to fabrics and their perceptive virtuality: 'Monsieur's silk' was *de fantaisie*; she refers to 'four ugly thread stockings made for me at Montauban'; she described the gauze as 'in fashion'. It is evident that the countess took pleasure in listing the colours, and her wardrobe included every shade, black for hats, head-dresses and aprons, white for sleeve ruffles, shirts and coifs, black together with white for stays, fichus and a few gowns, and a host of other shades. Her daily entries record greens for the material of gowns and coats, reds and blues, crimsons, plum, sea-green, 'English' green, 'dragon' green, all the costly products of the dyers' art (black and white fabrics being cheaper than coloured).

However, she replaced her clothes far less frequently than was the case in Paris: two gowns a year for the comtesse, one for her daughter – this is a minimum since the quantities of material bought may have allowed for additional items to be made; the shirts must have been home-made, since they do not appear in the accounts; she bought at least two pairs of stockings a year, and four or five pairs of shoes, plus clogs. Certain items circulated less rapidly: two aprons in ten years, one pelisse every five years, one muff in the decade and two or three pairs of sleeve ruffles a year. This was abundance, but not excess, since income was crucial, and social demands and personal preferences both influenced the way in which money was spent.

## WHAT THE SCHOMBERG SPENT ON CLOTHES

The careful accounts kept by the Schomberg family provide a model for comparison between the inventory of a wardrobe and the dynamic evolution of ordinary and luxury expenditure.[56] We will as far as possible compare them with the other examples, in order to bring out the different elements in the social system of consumption.

Between 1756 and 1767, M. de Schomberg, a bachelor soldier, spent an average of 1,200 *livres* a year, but very unevenly from one year to the next: 500 *livres* in 1756, nothing in 1757 (when he was in the army), 3,000 *livres* in 1763. The fluctuations reflect his way of life; when after 1761, Ferdinand de Schomberg settled in one place, or when towards 1766 he was preparing for marriage, his spending on clothes increased and stabilised. Overall, it consumed the whole of his pay, which was 1,200, then 1,800, *livres* a year. For his other expenses, he had to draw on the family rents. From 1768 to 1788, we can trace the gaps between payments made and debts contracted, except for one year, 1779, when the Schomberg family was in Corsica, where the baron was in command at Corte with the grade of *maréchal de camp*; it looks as if they then reduced this category of expenditure to what was strictly necessary, the bills from suppliers not reappearing until 1780.[57] In the period 1768–79, the family spent an average of 2,800 *livres* a year on clothes, the

[56] Dusart, 'La Consommation vestimentaire d'une famille', pp. 100–45.
[57] Arch. dép., Versailles, E 3138, E 3142, f. 25, letter of 12 April 1780.

actual sum being as much as five times higher in some years than others; the variation from one year to the next was principally a function of the volume of debt tolerated by the suppliers; in 1770 the Schomberg owed 2,580 *livres* for clothes bought during the year. The baronne succeeded in balancing income and outgoings after 1775. From 1780 to the Revolution, purchases were restricted to between 1,000 and 1,500 *livres* a year. Their whole life-style was simplified after the baron's retirement in 1783 and a reduction of a good third in their income (it was 20,000 *livres* in 1789). The Schomberg did not run up debts through borrowing, but they saved hardly at all.

The annual expenditure of each person on clothes can be seen in table 20 (calculated by Benoît Dusart).[58] A hierarchy within the family is visible: at the head comes the baronne with 40 per cent of total expenditure, though unevenly (77 per cent in 1771, 1 per cent in 1783); the baron came next with a third of purchases, then the servants (on average seven or eight persons) whose liveries swallowed up 6,565 *livres*, and lastly the children and the communal expenses.[59] The variations from year to year in every case are immediately noticeable, suggesting that decisions were suited to needs and occasions. The expenses of the children were more regular than those of their parents and they probably benefited from much of the communal expenditure. The baron and the baronne spent far more, and their expenses were correlated. The peaks of the baron's consumption curve came when he cleared the decks and settled his accumulated tailors' bills, roughly every two or three years. After 1780, he was the highest spender, whilst his wife's expenses fell steadily.

Before 1779, accounts were settled at spectacular intervals; this fundamental feature of the aristocratic way of life, also typical of the Montesquiou, was built into the consumption system. Customers and suppliers saw things very differently; for the latter, the aim was to reduce the gap between the advance made and payment; for the former, the economic logic was the opposite. This fragile equilibrium depended on the extent and the manner in which the debts of a network of customers were settled, otherwise

---

[58] Table 1, see Dusart, 'La Consommation vestimentaire d'une famille,' pp. 108–12.

[59] The general expenses include purchases of thread, linen and costs of upkeep. The nature and designation of the articles are quite adequate for calculating the individual expenses.

Table 20 *The clothing consumption of the members of the Schomberg family*

| Year | Baron | | Baronne | | Domestics | | Children | | Communal | | Total |
|---|---|---|---|---|---|---|---|---|---|---|---|
| | In *livres* | % | In *livres* | % | In *livres* | % | In *livres* | % | In *livres* | % | |
| 1768 | 757 | 52·8 | 367 | 25·6 | 79 | 5·5 | 154 | 10·7 | 78 | 5·4 | 1,435 |
| 1769 | 450 | 47·0 | 232 | 24·2 | 95 | 9·9 | 98 | 10·2 | 83 | 8·7 | 958 |
| 1770 | 3,128 | 68·4 | 261 | 5·7 | 1,034 | 22·6 | 108 | 2·4 | 41 | 0·9 | 4,572 |
| 1771 | 630 | 15·8 | 3,084 | 77·4 | 69 | 1·7 | 71 | 1·8 | 133 | 3·3 | 3,987 |
| 1772 | 538 | 23·7 | 1,156 | 50·9 | 163 | 7·2 | 68 | 3·0 | 347 | 15·3 | 2,272 |
| 1773 | 1,654 | 32·7 | 2,252 | 44·5 | 936 | 18·5 | 140 | 2·8 | 77 | 1·5 | 5,059 |
| 1774 | 740 | 23·3 | 2,195 | 69·1 | 102 | 3·2 | 35 | 1·1 | 107 | 3·4 | 3,179 |
| 1775 | 1,225 | 35·6 | 1,305 | 38·0 | 239 | 7 | 258 | 7·5 | 411 | 12·0 | 3,438 |
| 1776 | 166 | 7·0 | 1,288 | 54·6 | 169 | 7·2 | 439 | 18·6 | 298 | 12·6 | 2,360 |
| 1777 | 665 | 27·9 | 858 | 36·0 | 522 | 21·9 | 121 | 5·1 | 218 | 9·1 | 2,384 |
| 1778 | 16 | 1·7 | 80 | 8·4 | 516 | 54·4 | 337 | 35·5 | 0 | 0·0 | 949 |
| 1780 | 1,040 | 19 | 3,106 | 56·6 | 737 | 13·4 | 349 | 6·4 | 256 | 4·7 | 5,488 |
| 1781 | 280 | 26·1 | 396 | 36·8 | 113 | 10·5 | 197 | 18·3 | 89 | 8·3 | 1,075 |
| 1782 | 516 | 25·1 | 356 | 17·3 | 651 | 31·7 | 283 | 13·8 | 247 | 12·0 | 2,053 |
| 1783 | 573 | 73·6 | 9 | 1·2 | 56 | 7·2 | 7 | 0·9 | 134 | 17·2 | 779 |
| 1784 | 668 | 80·4 | 35 | 4·2 | 0 | 0·0 | 0 | 0·0 | 128 | 15·4 | 831 |
| 1785 | 33 | 5·7 | 36 | 6·3 | 427 | 74·3 | 51 | 8·9 | 28 | 4·9 | 575 |
| 1786 | 239 | 35·6 | 96 | 14·4 | 252 | 37·5 | 0 | 0·0 | 84 | 12·5 | 672 |
| 1787 | 760 | 73·4 | 10 | 1·0 | 109 | 10·5 | 0 | 0·0 | 157 | 15·2 | 1,036 |
| 1788 | 500 | 48·6 | 109 | 10·6 | 296 | 28·8 | 0 | 0·0 | 124 | 12·0 | 1,029 |
| Total | 14,578 | | 17,232 | | 6,565 | | 2,716 | | 3,040 | | 44,131 |

failure threatened. After 1780, the Schomberg's expenditure stabilised, settling at a lower level than the decennial maximum of 5,488
*livres* for 1779–80. Their spending on clothes lost its irregular
character, the urgency associated with the service and honours of
the court had less impact on their habits and projects. Purchases
were more even and more evenly divided, with a three- or four-
yearly rhythm. The extravagance of distinction was economically
and socially dictated by life at court and, to a lesser degree, by the
display essential to an active life in Paris.

The contribution of each supplier to their express is shown in
table 21.[60] Two principal types of supplier account for four-fifths
of the budget: the bills of the bespoke tailor and dressmaker, and
those for fabrics; the latter were more numerous after the marriage,
when the baronne de Schomberg needed to draw on more suppliers
to meet the increased needs of the family and their servants. Her
highest expenditure on clothes coincided with the largest number of
accounts from clothiers, a sign of much home dressmaking, whilst
the highest annual expenditure on the part of the baron coincided
with the biggest bills from his tailor. The role of the dressmaker *vis-
à-vis* women was not entirely analogous to that of the tailor for
men. This emerged in discussion between husband and wife. 'Have
yourself made a reasonable spring outfit and, I beg you, delay the
bill from your tailor until I know how I stand with him', wrote the
baronne in 1770,[61] and in 1777: 'I have this morning received your
bonus which amounts to 2,940 and a few *livres*. I have sent for your
embroiderer who is coming and summoned Verdet [the Schomberg's
tailor] for tomorrow morning. I will see what I can pay for the two
articles.'[62] The tailor exploited their difficulties to cheat and increase his bills. The Schomberg severed relations with him, and by
resorting to several suppliers partly broke out of the circle of debt
accumulated with one alone. Similarly, by reducing her purchases
of fabrics, Madame de Schomberg adapted her needs to necessity;
she used up remnants and had her old clothes altered, but for court,
expense was unavoidable: 'It is an outfit for life, and even for my
daughter after me, since embroidery never goes out of fashion',[63]
she commented after buying her last court dress.

[60]  Dusart, 'La Consommation vestimentaire d'une famille', pp. 121–3.
[61]  Arch. dép., Versailles, E 3144, 1 April 1777.
[62]  Arch. dép., Versailles, E 3146, 27 September 1777.
[63]  Arch. dép., Versailles, E 3146, 13 July 1780.

Table 21 *Contribution of each supplier in the expenditure on clothes of the baron de Schomberg and his family (in livres)*

| Year | Tailoring | Dressmaking | Cloth | Linen | Fashion | Braid | Hats | Shoes | Total |
|---|---|---|---|---|---|---|---|---|---|
| 1756 | 439 | — | — | 75 | — | — | — | — | 514 |
| 1758 | 43 | — | — | 113 | — | — | — | — | 156 |
| 1759 | 63 | — | 185 | 55 | — | 112 | — | — | 415 |
| 1761 | 900 | — | — | — | — | — | — | — | 900 |
| 1762 | 526 | — | 233 | 30 | — | 765 | 65 | — | 1,619 |
| 1763 | 826 | — | 343 | 410 | — | 1,138 | 94 | 53 | 2,864 |
| 1764 | 174 | — | 416 | 408 | — | 727 | 30 | 30 | 1,785 |
| 1765 | 176 | — | — | 243 | — | 92 | — | — | 511 |
| 1766 | 115 | — | 292 | 112 | — | — | 33 | — | 552 |
| Total | 3,262 | | 1,469 | 1,446 | | 2,834 | 222 | 83 | 9,316 |
| % | 35 | | 15·8 | 15·5 | | 30·4 | 2·4 | 0·9 | 100 |
| 1769 | 115 | — | — | — | — | — | — | — | 115 |
| 1770 | 584 | — | 516 | — | — | — | 45 | — | 1,145 |
| 1771 | 800 | 192 | 1,800 | — | 268 | — | 86 | — | 3,146 |
| 1772 | 1,851 | — | 559 | 28 | 247 | — | 15 | — | 2,700 |
| 1773 | 1,210 | — | 919 | 195 | 197 | 553 | 37 | 18 | 3,129 |
| 1774 | 1,387 | 93 | 1,425 | 23 | 867 | — | 12 | — | 3,807 |
| 1775 | 355 | 196 | 975 | 69 | 366 | 117 | 29 | — | 2,107 |
| 1776 | 128 | 23 | 575 | 53 | 61 | — | — | — | 840 |
| 1777 | 495 | 81 | 256 | 45 | 93 | 15 | — | 39 | 1,024 |
| 1778 | 935 | 130 | 252 | 8 | — | — | — | 60 | 1,385 |
| 1780 | 910 | 97 | 1,612 | 207 | 181 | — | 45 | — | 3,052 |
| 1781 | 300 | — | 160 | 38 | — | — | — | — | 498 |
| 1782 | 1,024 | 119 | 889 | — | — | 42 | — | 24 | 2,098 |
| 1783 | 422 | — | 44 | 88 | — | 68 | — | 5 | 627 |
| 1784 | 165 | — | 354 | 17 | 21 | 45 | — | 12 | 614 |
| 1785 | 448 | — | — | 131 | 24 | — | 12 | — | 615 |
| 1786 | 469 | 79 | — | 5 | — | — | — | — | 553 |
| 1787 | 856 | — | — | — | — | — | — | 8 | 864 |
| 1788 | 507 | 46 | 15 | — | 117 | — | 11 | — | 696 |
| Total | 12,961 | 1,056 | 10,351 | 907 | 2,442 | 840 | 292 | 166 | 29,015 |
| % | 44·7 | 3·6 | 35·7 | 3·1 | 8·4 | 2·9 | 1·0 | 0·6 | 100 |

Linen merchants, fashion merchants and suppliers of braid, shoes and hats accounted for less than 16 per cent of their expenditure. This avoidance of extravagance is an indication of the resolutely reasonable character of these costs, even if they were occasionally obliged to spend more than expected; for example, in 1773, for a complete headdress, for which 702 *livres* (the patrimony of several workers) had to be paid to a modiste. The embroiderers and braidmakers who supplied the gold and silver accessories which, though expensive, were essential to anyone wishing to proclaim his rank, presented large bills, sometimes attached to those of the tailors. Shoemakers, bootmakers and hatters made up the rest, but none on a very large scale; the Schomberg were not big spenders in any of these spheres.

If we return to the registers of expenses and revenues, and add the bills paid and receipts, we can calculate the proportion spent on clothes for the period 1768–1780–1781. It varied, from 600 and 700 *livres* in 1768 and 1769 (that is 11 and 6 per cent of expenditure) to 3,845 and 2,430 *livres* in 1774 and 1776 (that is 22 and 21 per cent). The annual average was around 14 per cent of the total budget. Clothing was certainly the most expensive item bought since, being both durable and obsolete, it needed to be constantly replaced for two separate reasons: because of wear and tear, and because of the functioning of the social language, part fashion, part stability. The logic of the clothing costs incurred by an aristocratic family was dictated by the equilibrium it aimed to achieve between these two imperatives. In the last analysis, it was a matter of its social position within noble society.

The Montesquiou chose to err on the side of extravagance. This trait, already noted with regard to the contents of their wardrobes, is confirmed by an analysis of the bills from their suppliers. The baron spent on average, for himself, his wife and his son, some 2,500 *livres* a year from 1780 to 1791. Table 22 shows that he was in debt to his suppliers and had to appeal to his father, the marquis, to satisfy his creditors. In 1791 and 1792, for clothes and to settle his family's debts, the head of the family spent 18,000 *livres*, of which 9,000 *livres* went to tailors and 6,000 *livres* to fashion merchants. Unlike his son, he paid his bills regularly; no more than three months ever elapsed between the submission of a bill and its payment. The younger generation spent without counting the cost; overall, though for fewer persons, as much as the Schomberg (2,800 *livres* a year around 1780), and more than their

Table 22   *The Montesquiou's expenditure 1780–93 (in* livres)

| Year | Consumption | Payment | Gap | Cumulatively |
|------|-------------|---------|------|--------------|
| 1780 | 1,315 | 1,315 | | — |
| 1781 | 2,504 | 155 | − 2,349 | − 2,349 |
| 1782 | 5,452 | 1,370 | − 4,082 | − 6,431 |
| 1783 | 3,910 | 1,291 | − 2,619 | − 9,050 |
| 1784 | 4,492 | 1,033 | − 3,459 | − 12,509 |
| 1785 | 2,790 | 7,187 | + 4,397 | − 8,112 |
| 1786 | 2,787 | 1,625 | − 1,162 | − 9,274 |
| 1787 | 4,081 | 4,167 | + 86 | − 9,188 |
| 1788 | 440 | 791 | + 351 | − 8,837 |
| 1789 | 300 | 1,336 | + 1,036 | − 7,801 |
| 1790 | 814 | 226 | − 588 | − 8,389 |
| 1791 | 1,014 | 716 | − 298 | − 8,687 |
| 1792 | — | 1,467 | + 1,467 | − 7,220 |
| 1793 | — | 101 | + 101 | − 7,119 |

income. The older generation spent but kept count, and assumed responsibility for the extravagances of the young. Closer to the source of the revenues lavishly distributed by the monarchy,[64] they were all equally engaged in the pursuit of distinction and the competitiveness in the splendour of outfits and linen which developed between the seventeenth and eighteenth centuries as a consequence of the mechanisms of court society.

The ostentatious spending of the Versailles and Paris aristocracy deserves one day to be re-examined as a whole, within the context of the total cost entailed by the canons of etiquette and fashion and in relation to resources. For the moment, it can be said that it is misleading to reduce noble behaviour to the model of those caught up in the whirlwind of luxury expenditure like the Montesquiou, the Saulx-Tavannes and the Polignac. The clothing habits of the Schomberg reveal the differences inherent to the whole second order.

### PROVINCIAL CLOTHING BUDGETS

These differences have a faint echo in the provinces, where big spenders were fewer, but where the relativity of things displaced the frontiers of rivalry. The Saint-Amans consumed relatively little,

---

[64] Dusart, 'La Consommation vestimentaire d'une famille', pp. 109–10.

and their expenditure was regular, without the peaks and troughs inseparable from a Parisian life-style.[65] On the other hand, the record book of the comtesse de Boyer reveals higher expenses and a greater irregularity.[66] The abbé Paul Robert de Saint-Amans spent less on himself than on his nephew; he usually paid his suppliers in cash, except when a delay in receiving income from his farms or an unexpected difficulty obliged him to make an advance and settle the bill later. Mme de Raymond usually paid in cash, and the healthy situation of the family finances enabled her to pay promptly for the clothes acquired for the marriage of her eldest son. Mme de Boyer represents a mid-point between Parisian habits and provincial rigour. Paul Robert de Saint-Amans devoted some 12 per cent of his budget to clothes for himself, his nephew and the servants when he had charge of the small fortune of his nephew, 14 per cent when reduced to his own resources, that is 162 *livres* per year before 1743, and 78 *livres* after. We have noted that this level of expenditure was enough for only a limited amount of replacement and ruled out flights of fancy. Mme de Raymond, in easier circumstances, with 2,300 *livres* to spend between 1760 and 1775, devoted on average 120 *livres* to her family's wardrobe. In the year of Jean Florimond's marriage, the household budget came to nearly 5,500 *livres*, 62 per cent of which went to tailors, drapers and modistes in Paris or Agen. The Saint-Amans family indulged in an uncharacteristic bout of luxury spending, proof of the importance of festive occasions in stimulating and increasing an expenditure which was usually moderate and regular. Mme de Boyer, who normally spent twice as much a month as Mme de Raymond (1,250 *livres*), devoted 5 per cent of her expenditure to dress, that is, as much as the Saint-Amans in proportion, but six times more in cash, that is, 682 *livres* a year.

How were these family budgets organised, and according to what principles? This is a chapter which remains to be written in the history of the economy of everyday, or a history of consumption. What rules, or what body of knowledge, governed these choices? The evidence suggests that the provincial noble economy demonstrates the diversity of family economies, both in differences

[65] Alric, 'La Consommation vestimentaire de la noblesse provinciale', pp. 101–3, 106–12, 143–4, 148–9.

[66] Alric, 'La Consommation vestimentaire de la noblesse provinciale', pp. 149–52.

in income and possibilities, and in reactions to them, the latter no doubt determined by the status of the family and the way in which individual conduct responded to economic and social situation.[67] In the last analysis, we need to seek answers in a comparative history, in social and regional space, comparing town and country. When we look at the triumph of appearances as promoted by the nobility, we begin to see the production of social personalities, whose acts and choices are explicable in relation to the economy as a whole, but also in the autonomous sphere of the domestic and family economy. We then perceive the importance of the study of the various ways in which social agents acted on the management of the daily economy, and especially on women. Education and the transmission of individual family models are unquestionably one of the keys to an understanding of consumption. It is they which reveal, or fail to reveal, the factors for regularity, stability, equilibrium or acceleration. Education constitutes the identity of the consumer, in particular, the school for girls.[68]

## WHAT ORDINARY PEOPLE SPENT ON CLOTHES

It will be useful to conclude this chapter devoted to the privileged with a comparison. A brief survey of lower-class spending on clothes will show the common features and emphasise both the autonomy of the sphere of consumption and the enormous differences according to social status. We know little about the household economy of ordinary people, and nothing about that of the bourgeoisie, since budgets of both are rare, and difficult to reconstitute. The poor have rarely left family record books, whilst the well-off have bequeathed many that remain largely unread. The majority of both urban and rural wage-earners found their whole income was swallowed up by the essentials of food and lodging. We have discussed elsewhere how the Parisian economy considerably influenced the evolution of standards of living, though, principally from lack of sources, we are unable to measure this precisely.[69] We have, therefore, to be content with general estimates, which it is difficult to relate to reality.

[67] J.-M. Barbier, *Le Quotidien et son économie* (Paris, 1981), pp. 161–9.
[68] M. Sonnet, *L'Education des filles au temps des Lumières* (Paris, 1987).
[69] Roche, *Peuple de Paris*, pp. 85–125.

Michel Morineau has collected them, from Vauban to La-voisier.[70] During the reign of Louis XIV, Vauban, the soldier economist, calculated what remained to a weaver or a workman once he had bought the daily bread for his family, which he reckoned at four persons. Out of 150 *livres* a year (in 1740, the four Boudon spent ten times as much), he allowed 60 *livres* for the baker and the butcher (mostly the former), and assumed 40 *livres* as the annual rent for a single room. The 50 *livres* which remained had to pay for heat, light and, in Vauban's words, 'the purchase of some household goods, if only a few earthenware pots; clothes and linen'. In sum, if the family ate its fill and had a roof over its head, little was left for clothing. The marshal, a pessimist but an acute observer, saw in the district of Vézelay 'people in such poor condition that they had little strength. To which it must be added that what they suffer by way of nakedness contributes greatly, three-quarters of them being clad, winter and summer, only in half-rotted and torn materials and shod with clogs in which their feet are bare all year round.'[71] This was the lowest level of clothing consumption, and only the extremes of urban poverty offer a comparable picture.

The modern commentator can be slightly more optimistic; with one wage, the family of the working man of the eighteenth century had no surplus, but they had what was necessary. Only long hours of toil and the labour of women and children made it possible to acquire a few commodities. The unmarried and childless households were slightly better off, with only themselves to consider. This was one step in the direction of style, and it is often in their inventories that we find indications of a greater consumption of clothing. On occasion, if work was regular and prices fairly stable, they might envisage the transition from essentials to extras, both being relative to resources as much as to needs. But scarcity and the need to make new out of old was everywhere the general rule.[72]

We see the advantages, both in Paris and the provinces, enjoyed by domestics. In service, they benefited at every turn; lodged, fed and partly clothed, they could further extend their wardrobes with the cast-offs of their masters, either received as gifts or bought

[70] Goubert and Roche, *Les Français et l'Ancien Régime*, vol. I, pp. 73–5.
[71] *Mémoire sur la nécessité de diminuer les fêtes*, Paris, 1763.
[72] N. Pellegrin, 'Chemises et chiffons', pp. 183–294.

cheaply from the *maître d'hôtel* or the valets and chambermaids responsible for the wardrobes. In Paris, as in the provinces, especially after 1740, when the movement of prices was favourable, they benefited from the enhanced resources of their masters. In the budget of the abbé Paul Robert de Saint-Amans, they accounted for 8 per cent (169 *livres* between four servants), more than he spent annually on clothes, from which they also benefited.[73] Nor were they behind in their economic and material situation. In the years prior to the Revolution, things changed and our information is fuller. The budgets calculated for the Aunis peasant, the Abbeville weaver and the Lyons silk-worker are the best we have on which to base our picture of the sartorial possibilities of ordinary people. The unmarried peasant from Aunis, who earned 183 *livres* a year in 1765 – according to the calculations of the academicians of La Rochelle – devoted 66 per cent of his income to food and 18 per cent to household expenses, including taxes, leaving 16 per cent for clothes.[74] In cloth-manufacturing Abbeville, a family of working weavers (father, mother and two children) had between 7 and 8 *livres* a working week between them (probably 370 *livres* a year); they spent between 4 and 5 *livres* a week on food, including on what the compiler of this meagre budget calls the 'good things of life' – cheese, eggs and fruit; they had to pay a further 12 *sous* for rent (30 *livres* per year) plus some 16 *sous* on heat and light.[75] Between 1764 and 1787, wages were unchanged; they would therefore usually have almost 20 per cent for clothes and everything else, that is, 75 *livres* (18 *livres* each), when a pair of new shoes cost between 4 and 6 *livres*, a shirt cost 10 *livres*, a full suit and a gown about 30 or 40 *livres* – average prices in Paris, where cheapness co-existed with high prices for good quality.

With the Lyons silk-weaver,[76] we are on the border between the upper working class and the bottom levels of the urban bourgeoisie; in 1785, his family disposed of some 2,000 *livres* a year (as much as the Boudon at Agen in 1740), 50 per cent of which went on food, less than 15 per cent (300 *livres*) remaining for the wardrobe. The

---

[73] Alric, 'La Consommation vestimentaire de la noblesse provinciale', pp. 146–7.

[74] *Mémoire sur la nécessité ce diminuer les fêtes.*

[75] M. Morineau, 'Budgets populaires en France', *Revue d'Histoire Economique et Sociale*, nos. 2–3 (1972), pp. 230–51.

[76] Ibid., pp. 471–9; M. Garden, *Lyon et les Lyonnais au XVIIIe siècle* (Paris, 1970), pp. 232–53.

independence of the master silk-weaver was precarious and in crisis years he was little better off than the workers. Overall, the amount spent on clothes by the less well-off was very different from that of noble families, and the disparities in what each had available were very great: 138 *livres* in the case of the artisan, 24 *livres* in the case of the unmarried worker and 10 *livres* for the married workman. All else being equal, most of them could devote between 10 and 15 per cent of their income to their appearance, by dint of hard labour. The married Parisian journeyman, with two wages, could take pains with his own appearance and that of his wife, according to the number of children they had to care for. A master craftsman such as Jacques-Louis Ménétra was in a rather better position and could achieve his own level of elegance.[77] Domestic servants were always in a privileged position.

It is interesting to note which garments were being replaced, and how frequently. The silk-worker had a suit worth 80 *livres*, changed every eight years; for work, he wore a matelotte and breeches, replaced every three years, and costing some 30 *livres*; his hat, replaced at a similar interval, cost say 12 *livres*; lastly, two pairs of shoes and a thorough repair cost a further dozen *livres*. This micro-bourgeoisie was tending towards a greater variety and capacity to change: different clothes for work and holidays, shoes rather than clogs, and better-quality material and cut. The silk-worker spent 50 *livres* a year, his wife spent just over 80. The dimorphism noted in the wardrobes of ordinary people was thus the result both of accumulating and of more frequently replacing clothes. The silk-worker's wife changed her gown and her petticoat every three years, also her casaquins, stays and mantelets; like her husband, she was used to two linen shirts a year, two pairs of stockings, two neckerchiefs, two pairs of pockets, two aprons, two pairs of shoes plus a pair of galoshes, a round cap for work, a coif for night and one for going out. In order to justify increases in tariff, a clothing budget of 138 *livres* was calculated. At the same time, the wardrobe of the Parisian wage-earner valued on his death and at its second-hand price came to 133 *livres*. Such an accumulation of clothes raises the question of the economy, market and resale system which made it possible for the town to satisfy higher norms at lower cost.

[77] Ménétra, *Journal de ma vie*.

In the country, the rural worker described by the academicians of La Rochelle acquired every two years: four shirts at 48 *sols*, one collar at 1 *livre*, two kerchiefs at 10 *sols*, two pairs of stockings at 30 *sols*, six pairs of gaiters at 16 *sols*, an ordinary hat at 2 *livres*, a woollen winter cap at 1 *livre*, a suit of *tiretain* which would cost 22 *livres* new, but second-hand from an old-clothes dealer only 12 *livres*. He also needed clogs, eight pairs of willow-wood and six pairs of strong wood, that is, 4 *livres*, and his laundry cost 5 *livres*. In sum, everything included, from head to foot, every year, he needed to spend, or save, a good 30 *livres* at least: most of his clothes were replaced only slowly, the clogs once a year, the rest every two years. The threshold of sartorial aspirations thus varied enormously from the top to the bottom of society, but the huge differences – 30 *livres* a year for a rural worker, 130–140 *livres* for an urban craftsman, several hundred *livres* for a family of urban gentlemen, several thousand *livres* in a household of not outstandingly zealous courtiers, and many thousands of *livres* regularly in the prodigal aristocracy – should not be expressed in a simplified interpretation of the language of clothes.

Thrift and a shortage of clothes were the rule amongst the peasantry, and there were considerable variations from one region to another;[78] where circumstances were favourable, among the better-off categories, consumption was growing. In towns, the improvement was apparent by the seventeenth century. The poor cloth and few clothes of the peasant and the town dweller did not necessarily imply a cultural underdevelopment of appearances. Coarse fabrics and straitened circumstances were compatible with subtle ploys; accessories, colour and the spread of cheerful prints made it possible to vary outfits, display preferences, even follow the fashions which set village elegance on the road to emulation and increased consumption. In Paris, and no doubt in most large towns, the major turning-point came in the second half of the eighteenth century. This was an international trend, also visible in London.[79]

However, clothing, in its diversity, established a common language shared by rich and poor.[80] It was an object of desire as

[78] N. Pellegrin and J. Peret, 'Meubles et vêtements dans les inventaires après décès poitevins au XVIIIe siècle', in *L'Habillement rural en Poitou*, pp. 469–73.

[79] McKendrick, Brewer and Plumb, *Birth of a Consumer Society*, pp. 34–96.

[80] Hugues, *Le Langage des tissus*, pp. 345–6.

much as a necessity, and new demands of hygiene and public socialising imposed higher standards. It helped to transform societies. Without paradox, it can be argued that the sartorial revolution of the age of Enlightenment had a role in the cultural origins of the Revolution. Certainly, the greater gulfs apparent in towns and the country contributed. But above all, in the spectacular, even provocative, demonstration of the triumph of noble appearances, there was a sort of incitement to change, an appeal less to an unrealistic imitation than to the affirmation of a new capacity for change, a new entitlement, a sharing of means of expression by the exchange of the signs transmitted by clothes and fabrics, which were all the more comprehensible in that their language was common to all.

In this transformation of age-old behaviour, the role of women was crucial; knowledgeable about textiles and arbiters of fashion, they had the advantage over men. However, for both sexes, personal identity was nourished by the lessons of clothing consumption, which was never reduced to the purely functional. The nobility, by its ever-increasing extravagance, and the people, by their acquisition of a new capacity for change, moved in the same direction, that is, towards the advent of a new society where the value system would be based less on the durability and scarcity of things than on their obsolescence. Marcel Mauss could write: 'It was not in production properly speaking that society found its impetus . . . luxury was the great mover.'[81]

---

[81]    *Manuel d'ethnographie* (Paris, 1947).

# 9. *The discipline of appearances: the prestige of uniform*

Il est d'ailleurs très agréable que la guerre se fasse
honnêtement, tout le monde y gagne pour le détail.

The maréchal de Belle-Isle to the comte de Clermont,
7 May 1758

A work by the Flemish painter, Pieter Meulener, *The Battle of Nördlingen* [*1634*], *at the start of the combat,* now in the National Museum of Stockholm, provides a splendid and powerful picture of armies without uniform. In fact, nothing could be more uniform, yet no-one is mistaken in the general tumult. Formed into a compact column, the mass of pikemen, preceded by a thick line of musketeers, await the battle, weapons at their feet. Men and equipment form a sombre mass of grey and brown, in which the dress of the soldiers is that of ordinary men, from which it is distinguished only by details – the weapons, the cloak thrown over the shoulder, the hat pulled down over the eye. Two officers are at the head of the troop, one wearing a blue coat over grey breeches, the other, on horseback, in a red coat and a cuirass, sign of command. These splashes of colour apart, the painting portrays a world made resoundingly uniform by action and function, but with no special features of dress. The dominant monochrome tone is that of a predominantly peasant civil society, the grisaille of rustic clothes the colours of earth and the seasons. The soldier still dressed how he could and not as he should, since military society was still feeling its way between instability and permanence, between war and peace.

A century and a half later, from the reign of Louis XV to the Empire, battle paintings present a very different picture to the attentive observer. From Parrocel to Casanova the younger, from Lejeune to the baron Gros, never does military dress offer less variety once uniform has become standard, nor ever show such contrasts between arms and units. Polychrome ruled in military painting, whose specialists learned to portray the movement of the masses and the individuals engaged in gentlemanly combat or in the confrontations of the revolutionary and imperial struggle. Painting exaggerated, but only in accord with the trends which had shaped military society. The history of uniform thus deserves our attention since it is at the heart of the encounter between appearances and social discipline. It deserves better than what it is and what it has been: a passion for the perennially youthful amateurs of lead soldiers, an antiquarian taste for the secret admirers of Detaille and Raffet, an obsession for those nostalgic for the taxonomies visible in 'uniformology'; these works remain, for all that, an indispensable base for any more general discussion.[1]

Uniform is of recent origin. Both the word and the thing are less than three centuries old in the sense of a military costume defined by orders and decrees, and the prehistory of the initiatives which worked in a confused way to impose uniformity on soldiers in arms remains to be written. There is no doubt that the Thirty Years War, so vividly portrayed by Jacques Callot, constituted a decisive step. It involved a longer and larger-scale mobilisation of men, who were maintained permanently on fixed terms: it took them from the north to the south of Europe; it confronted them over and beyond opposing religions and nations, and this major civil and religious war between Europeans probably made remedies against confusion essential.[2] It is at this point that military historians note the general adoption, even the beginning of a systematisation, of distinctive signs.[3] The freedom which reigned in soldiers' dress began to give way before initiatives to differentiate sides and units.

In France, until the decisive and definitive intervention of the *louis-quatorzien* state, the history of military costume was that both of civilian clothes and of a specific, internal response to the requirements of war. Subject to the general influences, it responded to fashion, especially in the case of the officers and their imitators,

---

[1] See, for example, the *Cahiers de la Sabretache*; the large (26,000) print-run of *Uniformes, les archives de l'histoire* is evidence of the size of the amateur readership.

[2] G. Parker, *The Thirty Years' War* (London, 1986).

[3] H. Lehre, *Uniforme, Etude historique* (Paris, 1930); H. Boutmy de Bavelaer, *L'Uniforme français de Louvois à nos jours* (Paris, no date).

who vied with each other in elegance when means permitted or circumstances, such as the proximity of the king or the great, required. The Condé staff office collected the lions of perfection and ornament. But at the same time, military costume changed little, in line with the slow rhythms of the development of rural and urban dress, from one generation to the next. For most soldiers, their dress was always the same. Changes were functional, took place on the margins and responded to tactical concerns. It was a matter of distinguishing oneself from the enemy, preventing unfortunate confusions in battle, avoiding mistakes.[4] The appropriate measures thus became general: a large sash of variegated colours tied at the waist so one could find one's own side, clothes of a uniform colour, standardised headgear, various distinctive signs on the hat and the coat. After 1670, at least in our current state of knowledge, the initiatives of colonels and captains passed from the scale of the company and regiment to that of the army as a whole; Louvois was the great reorganiser between 1662 and 1691.[5] At this point, fashion and immediate necessity were superseded by another mechanism: a drive towards collective regulation, which was a part of absolutism and of the response of classical society to the general crisis of conscience and manners.

My aim is not so much to trace every step in the evolution of the orders and decrees emanating from the royal military administration from the seventeenth century to the Revolution as to attempt to understand the complex issues concealed in the spread of uniform for a social and cultural history of appearances. Beyond the technical perspectives, a reading of the transformation of the dress of French soldiers reveals new types of behaviour, inspired by the mechanisms of both utility and distinctive symbolism. One can understand why uniform so preoccupied the military philosophers.[6] Triumphing between the reigns of Louis XIV, warrior king, and Louis XVI, pacific monarch, the subject after 1791 of crucial debates between military and civilians, which revealed the future

---

[4] M. Pétard, 'Un bilan: L'évolution de l'uniforme d'infanterie, 1670–1812', *Uniformes*, 61 (1981), pp. 29–34; Pétard's remarkable studies of uniform (ibid., vols. 19–61, 1974–81) constitute an invaluable descriptive base for the uniform revolution of the seventeenth and eighteenth centuries.

[5] C. Rousset, *Histoire de Louvois*, 4 vols. (Paris, n.d.); L. André, *Michel Le Tellier et l'organisation de l'armée monarchique* (Paris, 1906); A. Corvisier, *Louvois* (Paris, 1982).

[6] E.-G. Léonard, *L'Armée et ses problèmes au XVIIIe siècle* (Paris, 1958).

cleavages between the nation and its army,[7] the costume of the soldier became a major social sign, discriminatory and effective. Easily recognisable both to those who wore it and those who did not, it served to cement the unity of the military world. Fixed in the hierarchy of its detail over and above the variations imposed by changes to regulations, 'it subjected minds to the costume and not to the man', as Vigny, who understood such matters, so well expressed it in his *Servitudes et grandeurs militaires*. Lastly, it wholly identified the person with the social personage suggested by the costume.

Parade-ground and battle between them gave birth to the prestige of uniform, which, paradoxically, only acquired its full force in the egalitarian society of the nineteenth century. When most civilians of consequence adopted the strict and sober costume of the triumphant bourgeoisie, the military remained the only males to exploit the impact of coloured and ornamented clothes.[8] In the holist society of the *ancien régime*, the identification of role and person was in an early stage which it would be premature to assume had already reached its nineteenth-century form. The birth of uniform has to be understood in the context of the application of rules, slow and difficult, since always subject to material imperatives, of a range of customs to which the historian has few witnesses, and of the new dialogue between military and civil society.

THE IMPOSITION OF UNIFORM

Dorival le Cadet, author of the article 'Clothing' in the *Encyclopédie méthodique*, identified the principal problem for the study of uniforms, ancient and modern. 'Military clothing, equipment and arms', he said, 'these three words collectively express the various items which serve to clothe, equip and arm the cavalry, hussars, dragoons and soldiers.'[9] Uniform is recognised as only one element in a complex system, whose evolution may depend on that of

---

[7] J.-P. Bertaud, *La Révolution armée, les soldats citoyens et la Révolution française* (Paris, 1979); S. E. Scott, *The Response of the Royal Army to the French Revolution, the Role and the Development of the Line Army 1787–1793* (Oxford, 1978).

[8] Deslandres, *Le Costume*, pp. 209–17.

[9] 'Art militaire' in *Encyclopédie méthodique*, 4 vols. (Paris, 1784–97), vol. III (Paris, 1787), pp. 3–20.

military society, itself part of global society, or on changes to its specific components – clothes, weapons and all the accessories which are indispensable to the soldier's life (cartridge-pouches, shoulder-belts, bandoliers, sword-belts, knapsacks). The transformation of one element in the system may entail, or permit, the alteration and adaptation of the system as a whole.

The birth of uniform in the seventeenth century should thus be seen as part of the social transformation of armies, when princes, to reduce their dependence on the feudal nobility, increasingly resorted to cash or wages (*solde*) to pay conscripted troops or mercenaries. The word 'soldier' still preserves the memory of this phase of social evolution.[10] Large and ever-increasing numbers of soldiers, recruited from the lower classes, now faced each other on the battlefield. Changes in tactics and weaponry accompanied and influenced these profound modifications, which involved the developing relations between the civil and the military, and between the army and the state, at a time when these words had yet to acquire their modern meaning. If the army became more military, and the nation less warlike, the difference between soldiers and civilians was not yet as pronounced as it has since become.[11] As André Corvisier has noted, the use of the word 'civil' as opposed to 'military' is late. The dictionaries of the Academy and of Trévoux in 1771 knew the word only in its traditional meaning of 'what concerns citizens'. Military service was still a civil service.[12] War was the continuation of diplomacy, its administration, largely created by Le Tellier and Louvois in the second half of the seventeenth century, was originally staffed by civilians, generals from the *robe*; military society remained very open at the beginning of the eighteenth century.

The imposition of uniform coincided with many fundamental changes to *ancien regime* society: the consolidation of the absolute monarchy, the development of a standing army, the generalisation of firearms for the infantry and the birth of the modern artillery, the beginning of the separation between military and civil society. Uniform was one of the elements in the transition to court society, when 'in the balance of tensions between the warrior nobility and

[10] Elias, *La Société de cour*, pp. 164–8.
[11] A. Corvisier, *L'Armée française de la fin du XVIIe siècle au ministère de Choiseul*, 2 vols. (Paris, 1964), vol. I, pp. 129–43.
[12] Ibid., p. 140.

the ruling princes, the weight shifts in the latter's favour in the military sphere too',[13] when in the social equilibrium, new relations were established between nobility and king, between bourgeoisie and monarch, when the prestige of arms began to fade in the mental horizon of elites and people.

No-one today can say with any precision how this happened on the ground, at company or regimental level. However, the existence of a preparatory phase between 1660 and 1670 is clear.[14] Louvois then supported the initiative of those commanding officers, particularly of foreign origin, who had adopted a special outfit for their regiment. In 1671, when Louvois reviewed the German soldiers of Fustenberg's regiment at Dunkirk, all wore a blue uniform with a yellow lining. Progress was slower amongst the French troops since the war office seems not to have decided its policy as regards the administration of the clothing departments. An order of 5 December 1666 provided for a deduction of thirty *sols* a month from the pay of the cavalry and footsoldiers, so creating the *système de la masse*, to be used to acquire fabrics and objects, stockings and shoes; however, its administration varied considerably, either devolved to the officers themselves or the responsibility of a commissariat entrusted to entrepreneurs or *régisseurs* under the control of royal officers.

These institutional details are necessary if we are to trace the progress of the uniform revolution; change was slow, though more rapid at some points than others. Military campaigns caused wear and tear and accustomed men to replacement, though this was to some extent thwarted by the different practices of different units and the persistent contradiction between the desire for unity and uniformity on the part of the central authority and staff office, and the localising tendencies, linked to circumstances and means, of the colonels and captains who were responsible for and owned regiments and companies. We see this in the letter sent by Louvois to the intendant of the armies in Piedmont on 12 September 1680: 'His majesty does not disapprove of the economy of preserving the new clothes and making the old last as long as possible, but only on condition that neither their clothes nor their hats are bad

[13]  Elias, *La Société de cour*, p. 168.
[14]  Boutmy de Bavelaer, *L'Uniforme française*, pp. 10–14; Lehr, *L'Uniforme*, pp. 8–14; Dr Leinhart and R. Humbert, *L'Uniformes de l'armée française depuis 1690 jusqu'à nos jours*, 4 vols. (Leipzig, 1897–1902), vol. III, *L'Infanterie*, pp. 1–6.

enough to shock foreigners who might pass through the towns.[15]
The ordinances in which uniforms were described and regulated in
every detail were one thing, the reality of everyday, where the
application of the texts constantly came up against practical necessities, was another; the uniform of peacetime was one thing, that of
war another. The study of uniforms has too often confused the
two.

Louis XIV was nicknamed 'king of reviews' because he took
such a close interest in the appearance of his soldiers. However, he
did not impose definitive solutions as regards the administration of
military clothing either in general or in particular, and it was,
throughout the eighteenth century, repeatedly changed. This is
reflected in the debate which took place in the pages of the
*Encyclopédie méthodique* of 1785,[16] where the partisans of different
systems confronted each other. They condemned the entrepreneurs
who grew rich on the backs of soldiers, but were divided as to the
*régie* defended by a general officer, the regimental administration
supported by a colonel and the initiative of company officers
pleaded by a captain.

Up to the end of the *ancien régime*, two basic tensions affected
the move to put troops into uniform, hence the generalised discipline of appearances. From Versailles and the centre came ordinances and decrees designed to spread the principles of regularity
and fix replacement rates – which were crucial – in time of peace.
The monarchy specified how funds were to be employed, and
imposed the notion of a fixed term of use, essential given the
economic scale of the problem;[17] it supervised measures to
strengthen control of quality and markets, it intervened in exceptional circumstances to mobilise entrepreneurs and it imposed
deductions from pay in order to achieve a balance between income
and expenditure.

On the periphery, there was persistent resistance. In particular,
it seems that the captains responsible for clothing, directly or

---

[15] Boutmy de Bavelaer, *L'Uniforme française*, p. 12.

[16] *Encyclopédie méthodique*, pp. 16–19.

[17] There is no good history of the administration and supply system of the royal
army; the biographies of Louvois discuss them primarily from their subject's
standpoint; the sketches of engineer-general Bernardin ('Origines et formations
du service de l'habillement', *Revue historique de l'armée* (1968), pp. 159–70 and
of the intendant-general Léger (ibid. (1960), pp. 147–72) are inadequate and far
too general.

indirectly in the case of a *régie*, blocked reform. They refused it first on their own behalf, rejecting uniform as a rustic and egalitarian principle. It had to be forced on them. They rejected it also out of incomprehension and incompetence. As the general officer writing in the *Encyclopédie méthodique* pointed out, military men were not as a rule very enlightened, they lacked an economic or administrative training, confused *régie* and private enterprise or, for reasons of economy, made the uniforms of their troops last as long as was humanly possible:

> As a result, they were universally threadbare and covered in stains, bits and rags; eight or ten days before the inspection, they hastily refurbished the old clothes and handed out a few new; as soon as the inspector had gone, they retrieved the latter and let the former relapse into the most deplorable condition. In order to save on clothes, some captains allowed their soldiers to wear non-uniform waistcoats and breeches; they even often sent them on leave in civilian dress.

Discernible in this text are the imperatives of and responses to the imposition of uniform on soldiers. On the eve of the Revolution, the troop units managed their funds and the localising and aristocratic impulses had been defeated: an equipment depot functioned from 1787, a directory of clothing was responsible for controlling supplies and centralising the regimental orders. The decisive step had been taken by the end of the first quarter of the eighteenth century; between the wars of the end of the reign of Louis XIV, which promoted unification, and the peace of the Regency and Louis XV, officers and soldiers alike were all measured for uniform. Looking at the soldier of the years 1710–20 in contemporary paintings, stripped of ribbons and feathers, uniformly clad, waist belted, rifle on shoulder, we already see a modern fighting man, equipped to be for ever on the move, bearing the firearms which now dominated battles and displaying the imprint of discipline.[18]

## THE DISCIPLINE OF UNIFORM

The word 'discipline' encompasses several realities which together constitute the essence of the soldier. The need to shape minds and bodies finds in uniform a valuable aid: it is a training, an element

---

[18] Quicherat, *Histoire du costume français*, p. 549.

in the education of controlled individual power. The fundamental purpose behind the standardisation of military dress is less the necessary tactical aim of making troops recognisable in action than the formation and training of bodies for combat.[19] It is an instrument in a process designed to shape the physique and the bearing of a combative individual, whose autonomy conditions his docility and whose obedience transforms individual strength into collective power. Uniform is at the heart of the military logic which has been developed in modern times, that of the *ultima ratio*, when war is a necessary continuation of politics. Uniform constructs the fighting man for mortal combat. It imposes control, a source of efficiency in battle and means to social power. Uniform, along with the congeries of military disciplinary procedures, should not be seen only in terms of docility and repression, or ideological instrumentality. It creates through education, realises a personage and affirms a political project by demonstrating omnipotence.

The debate about the army which developed after 1760 reveals the political consequences of the discipline of uniform on two levels: that of the policy which involved the reconciliation of the army and society in the person of the citizen soldier – the army is a school for citizenship where dress demonstrates obedience and efficiency; that of the medical and pedagogic discourse of the body perceived as the seat of forces whose training should increase resistance – to which uniform contributes by shaping actions and habits. Uniform is central to a utopian and voluntarist vision of the social which reconciles the conflict between automatic docility 'and the concrete economy of the individual liberty in which the autonomy of each constitutes the measure of his obedience'. It impregnates the whole of society.

In his *Essai général de tactique*, Guibert may at first appear an opponent of uniform. He contrasts the useful manoeuvres and drill necessary to develop the physical strength of the soldier with the futility and time-wasting of the minutely detailed and ridiculous rules of discipline and upkeep. 'An outfit has been created which means [soldiers] have to spend three hours a day on their appearance, which turns them into wig-makers, polishers and varnishers, everything but, in a word, men of war.' However, in point of fact,

---

[19] A. Ehrenberg, *Le Corps militaire, politique et pédagogie en démocratie* (Paris, 1983), pp. 8–9, 15–53.

uniform was a crucial element in the new tactics: 'It is the excesses of uniform which I attack and not the uniform itself. Up to a point, it is necessary. It is a proof of discipline. It contributes to the soldier's health. It raises him above ordinary people. It puts him into the class of well off and happy citizens.'[20] The discourse of the military philosopher, given concrete form in a series of decrees and orders which, between 1776 and 1788, transformed the physiognomy and habits of the royal army, reveals the principles which underlie uniform.

At a time when the art of war and the traditional institutions of the army required a more scientific training and a more permanent mobilisation, hence a more restrictive service for officers and men,[21] the dress of the French soldier responded to a number of different requirements. Some were functional, others derived from a vision of the erect body and a training in posture, yet others revealed an image of the military ethos. The uniform of the cavalryman and the footsoldier must first be alternately warm and cool. In time of war, the soldier might find himself in central Germany or in central Italy; the nights were often cold when the days were blazing hot. It had to protect him, his provisions and his spares from rain; the replacement of the canvas bag by the knapsack on a strap, then, after 1767, the calfskin bag lined with canvas which would hold all his kit, followed from this concern for better protection and increased mobility.[22] Above all, the soldier's dress had to be tailored in such a way that the different parts would not all get wet at the same time; it had to serve as a blanket when under canvas or bivouacking. It had to be easy to look after, simple to repair, light in weight and convenient to put on and take off.[23] It is immediately apparent how far these ideal requirements diverged from reality. The maréchal de Saxe, M. de Bohan,[24] and other reformers all demonstrated how the dress of French soldiers in the second half of the eighteenth century was expensive and unsuitable, inconvenient and inefficient. It required a lot of cloth, it was badly designed

[20] Comte de Guibert, *Ecrits militaires, 1772–1790* (Paris, 1977), pp. 107–8.

[21] Guibert, *Ecrits militaires*, preface by Général Menard, pp. 33–4.

[22] J. Margerand, *Armement et équipement de l'infanterie française du XVIe au XXe siècle* (Paris, 1930).

[23] *Encyclopédie méthodique*, vol. III, pp. 9–11.

[24] F. P. L. baron de Bohan, *Examen critique du militaire français ou des principes qui doivent déterminer sa constitution, sa discipline, son instruction*, 2 vols. (Paris, 1789), vol. II, pp. 90–115.

for drill, it failed to protect from rain and cold, causing sickness which was prejudicial to the army. Those officers anxious for change continued until the Revolution to propose alterations to the lines adopted and modified by the duc de Choiseul in 1767 and the comte de Saint-Germain in 1776. But uniform hardly changed until the Empire, a point to which we will return.

Similarly, the dress of the footsoldier and the cavalryman should be cut so as not to impede men when drilling, marching or fighting. 'Any clothing which can reduce the flexibility of the joints or interrupt the circulation of the blood is harmful to health or at least causes great suffering to the wearer.'[25] It ought to be simple, and every useless fold or superfluous button should be banished; we see here the gulf between the ideal of the theoreticians and the reality of the barracks and the military tailors, where the decorative fought a constant battle with the utilitarian, and the desire to cut a fine figure was sometimes transformed into a passion to be different, hence the misuse of collars, lapels, buttons and trimmings.[26]

Colombier, in his *La Médecine des gens de guerre*, published in 1774, emphasised the need for a costume which allowed freedom of movement and posture; care must be taken not to constrict the body within the clothes; the uniform should be more flexible, more rational and heed the laws of anatomy, a point also made by M. de Bohan.[27] It became fundamental to achieving an erect and disciplined posture, since it was part of a system designed to render the dispositions of the tactical units more manageable.[28] The posture to which military costume bears witness reveals an individual labour on the body and the acquisition of the rigorous and collective principles of order. It was part of a new delineation of public space, it established distances, a code of human and social relations, and was all the more persuasive in that it developed an aesthetic. As the editor of the *Encyclopédie méthodique* so nicely put it:

[Uniform] should detract nothing from the beauty of form of its wearer. The Frenchman is proud of the gifts of nature; care should be taken not to extinguish this vanity especially among soldiers. It is often what makes a good-looking man into 'a bit of

[25] *Encyclopédie méthodique*, vol. III, p. 10.
[26] Pétard, 'Un bilan', p. 34.
[27] de Bohan, *Examen critique*, vol. II, p. 95.
[28] Vigarello, *Le Corps redressé*, pp. 113–24.

a lad'. This expression indicates in the language of the barrack-room a man who possesses many excellent soldierly qualities.[29] Uniform perfectly incarnates the ethos of a military society which was formed in contradictions and crisis,[30] which is why it had to be basically different from civilian dress. 'The military costume will thus be less subject to the caprices of fashion, it will create and foster the military spirit. If this observation is true, it is important, especially for a nation where the defenders of their country form a class apart.'[31]

## THE CENTRALITY OF UNIFORM TO THE CONSTITUTION OF THE MILITARY

In the last quarter of the eighteenth century, the clothing of soldiers became a subject of prime importance. All the reformers believed that though a poorly clad army might be able to defeat troops who were better dressed, 'it is probable that during the course of a long war, the power which has given its soldiers the better military costume will enjoy great advantages over its enemy, whilst the latter will see its soldiers enter hospital in large numbers, remain there for long periods, and emerge weak and listless, only to return, never to leave'.[32] This highlights an essential role of uniform in past society and explains why it was fundamental to army medicine: it was a vehicle of collective hygiene.

The discipline of appearances was thus one link in the chain of elements constituting the military. If not carried to the extremes denounced by the comte de Guibert, it inculcated habits of cleanliness. These served to strengthen motivation and pride in bearing, making it possible to break unruly spirits, but also generalising hygienic habits effective against sicknesses such as mange which could be transmitted by insects. This entailed a large consumption of soap. To keep one's clothes up to the required standard (not easy when the uniform and its leather straps remained for the most part of a white particularly liable to show the dirt), to polish the buttons and the leather, to bring a shine to brass buckles, in sum, to perform all those acts which, if carried to extremes, can breed disaffection or transform the soldier into a mere

[29] *Encyclopédie méthodique*, vol. III, p. 10.
[30] Corvisier, *L'Armée française*, vol. I, pp. 138–43.
[31] *Encyclopédie méthodique*, vol. III, pp. 8–9.
[32] Ibid., vol. III, pp. 8–9.

show-piece, could, in moderation, contribute not only to tactical success but also to a profound transformation of manners in general.

Lastly, the army was the only collective space where, paradoxically, female roles could, for a while and to a degree, permute with male roles. In battle and on campaign, the soldier cooked, washed his linen, did his mending and made shift for himself. The *vivandière* was only an auxiliary, supplier of essential objects: soap, needles, thread, leather paste, spirits, fancies. The formation of modern armies was inimical to auxiliaries, unintegrated, undisciplined and difficult to control. They did not disappear all at once or all together; large armies on campaign were followed by a more or less tolerated train of parasites and prostitutes, but also of families. Here, too, the whole history of military reality needs to be reviewed. The discipline of the eighteenth century, the recruiting depots, the barracks and the improved services all contributed to this routine separation of the civil from the military, the masculine from the feminine. The Revolutionary and Imperial wars undoubtedly helped to accelerate these profound transformations by compulsory military service and by the length and remoteness of their campaigns.

The decree of 1 October 1786 lists the kit which together with the uniform transformed the civilian into a new man.[33] The uniform was in principle of good quality and, above all, replaced according to a fixed timetable: every three years for the waistcoats and coats, every year for the breeches, every two years for the hats; with it went three shirts, two collars of white dimity, two breeches, two pairs of shoes, three pairs of gaiters, two pairs of stockings, two kerchiefs, one collar buckle, one pair of shoe buckles, two pairs of garter buckles, a powder sack and its puff, a hair comb, a tooth-comb, a clothes brush, two shoe brushes, a brush for brass, another small brush (*pinceau*), a thimble, a corkscrew, a wad-hook, a pricker, a screw-driver, thread, needles, some old cloth and old linen. The detail may be forgiven in view of the importance of an inventory which specifies objects and explains actions in a way rarely found elsewhere. Their significance for the transformation of habits is fundamental; the uniform shaped a different person, its upkeep encouraged an acculturation which might simultaneously

---

[33] Leinhart and Humbert, *Les Uniformes de l'armée française*, vol. III, pp. 475–6, p. 60, note 1; see also vol. II, p. 139 for the cavalry.

be required by the apprenticeship in elementary culture, and the army was on the way to the great sartorial revolution which is an unknown aspect of the Enlightenment.

## FROM THE MARKET IN RECRUITS TO THE MARKET IN EQUIPMENT

It is by no means easy to measure the impact of this major transformation on civilian life. This is in part because the royal army did not rely on compulsory conscription, but recruited volunteers, in principle freely. It therefore seems likely that the effects of imposing uniform were initially confined to one age group with its own strongly marked social and psychological characteristics. The failure of attempts to transform the militias into quasi-compulsory military service by the drawing of lots, and resistance and insubordination eventually made it necessary to rely on volunteers – 'hardly corresponding to military requirements, but demanded by public opinion'.[34] The falling-off of recruitment of the seigneurial type after 1750 tended in the same direction. The market in recruits thus followed the fluctuating prestige of arms within society; it varied as a function of economic factors which, according to time and place, or the employment and material situation of families, might increase demand; it changed as a function of circumstances, the immediacy or remoteness of danger, the raising or damping down of the community's defensive reflexes, in brief of supply and demand, and just as irregular. By and large, the army attracted not so much the discontented and the disinherited as individuals who were susceptible to different ties than those which bound people together within the traditional community: foreigners, Protestants, orphans, the born comrades and good pals, all found in it a niche. The attraction and prestige which the military life could exercise for the majority of the population were therefore of a different order to the psychological and intellectual motives of the crisis of the army for the philosopher elites. The military ethos which to a degree united men and their officers drew some of its strength from this, when the efforts of the government, by means of barracks, stronger discipline and the uniform which symbolised belonging and

---

[34] Corvisier, *L'Armée française*, vol. I, p. 231; J. Chagniot, *Paris et l'armée au XVIIIe siècle, étude politique et sociale* (Paris, 1985), pp. 355–8.

revealed a personality, were helping to distance the civilian from the soldier and consolidate the peculiar character of military society.[35]

We still need to allow for the importance of the army in eighteenth-century society, and take account on the one hand of its renewal rates and the development of recruitment, and on the other of the social and geographical mobility created by army life.

Uniform played a by no means negligible role in attracting recruits; its appeal might be superficial but was often decisive in the decision to enlist, because it symbolised power; it helped to differentiate arms and units in accord with the hierarchy which had the cavalry at the top and the infantry militias at the bottom. It – that is, clothes, linen, shoes and food – played a major role in the bounties offered by the recruiters, especially in the case of the cavalry. Recruiting posters are one demonstration of this.[36] Recruiting sergeants were well aware of its impact, beginning with their own.[37] Mazenat, sergeant in the French Guards, made his concern plain in a letter of 3 May 1784 to his captain, M. de Roussy, who operated in Languedoc. He asked for a new uniform 'given that the one I have is very shabby. I have worn it for six years' and that it had previously been worn 'for a long time' by the sergeant director at the hospital. 'It needs', he went on, 'something dazzling to make the young men envious' and he begged, among other things, for a new hat with 'a larger than normal brim'. It was 1786 before sergeant Mazenat got what he wanted and his spontaneous complaint makes plain both the distance between real life and theory and the powerful appeal of military dress. It may not have been what ultimately decided someone to enlist, but it contributed, so preparing the way for the social diffusion of a type of behaviour.

Once the wars of Louis XIV's reign were over, eighteenth-century France was a country largely spared fighting, despite its involvement in numerous conflicts which devoured men and equipment.[38] Consequently, the French view of uniform was bound up with the primarily peaceful presence of the army, and its practices were spread by the large number of men who had become accustomed to them and propagated them by example, either immediately or later, after leaving the army. For example, on their absolute

[35] Corvisier, *L'Armée française*, vol. I, p. 143.
[36] Roche, *Peuple de Paris*, pp. 233–4.
[37] Corvisier, *L'Armée française*, vol. I, pp. 181–3.
[38] Ibid., pp. 73ff.

discharge, after six years of service, they could take away with them some or all of their clothes and linen.[39] Direct contacts with the population were also important; they were more frequent, thanks to increased numbers, than in the seventeenth century and closer, since the army was less feared and lived in the midst of the civilian population. Lodging with local inhabitants was the norm, and barracks made only slow progress, though it was more rapid for the units of the Royal Household and in Paris, where proximity to people of all social classes remained close.[40] The various routines of military life, the entries, departures, revues, concerts, manoeuvres, drills and inspections, were an integral part of city life, demonstrating to one and all the appeal of uniform. This existence in the midst of the urban population created a familiarity in which both reciprocal goodwill and conflicts entailed exposure to military life.

This gained further publicity from commercial and mercantile contacts, since the army drew on both the Parisian and national market for the maintenance and replacement of uniform. Every winter a certain number of regiments from provincial garrisons sent officers to Paris to order cloth, uniforms, shoes and accoutrements, and do business with the clothiers of the parish of Saint-Germain-l'Auxerrois and the rue Saint-Honoré.[41] A whole market, whose economic and social significance remains to be studied, was supported by the army. Merchants and soldiers preferred to make purchases over a very wide area, from Languedoc to Berry for broadcloth, from Normandy to the Beauvaisis for lightweight fabrics. Provincial manufacturers took their revenge on the merchants of Paris after 1715, in spite of the expertise which made the latter first choice for goods of high quality and the outfits of officers. Everywhere, looms clattered and tailors, shoemakers and hatters laboured on behalf of the military.

They were responding to a growing demand.[42] Here, too, we should mistrust the theoretical figures, since actual numbers varied greatly, according to the need to replace the retired, the deserters, the dead or the missing, whilst the recruiting system, which devolved on the captains, produced very different results from one

---

[39] *Encyclopédie méthodique*, vol. III, p. 5; see also Corvisier, *L'Armée française*, vol. I, pp. 297, 302.

[40] Chagniot, *Paris et l'armée*, pp. 421–89.

[41] Ibid., pp. 266–77.

[42] Lienhart and Humbert, *Les Uniformes de l'armée française*, vol. III, p. 6.

unit to another.[43] It is accepted that between 1726 and 1760, to maintain regiments at full strength, it was necessary to recruit about 20,000 men a year, that is, provide 20,000 outfits. On the basis of the official specification for the uniform of a footsoldier (a theoretical calculation, since both new recruits and old soldiers could be put into used uniforms), this represents a huge potential market: 30,000 metres of Lodève broadcloth for the coats; 3,000 metres of coloured cloth for the facings; more than 100,000 metres of serge of Aumale for the linings; nearly 65,000 metres of knitted fabric or a further 90,000 metres of grey caddis, according to the practice of the unit, for the waistcoats and breeches. To which should be added the shirts, the linen drawers which acted as linings for the otherwise unlined breeches, the shoes, the stockings and the other minor bits and pieces of the soldier's kit. The enormous size of the market in military supplies in peacetime, further increased by the inevitable need for replacements, is apparent. If the French army consisted of an average of 160,000 men in the period 1720–50, it still amounts in theory to more than 50,000 coats and waistcoats (changed every three years), plus 160,000 breeches (replaced in theory every year), that is, 75,000 metres of broadcloth of Lodève and more than 250,000 metres of serge. So several thousand *livres* were spent every year on the *force de frappe* of uniform; the coats of recruits and draftees alone caused the captains responsible to spend perhaps 525,000 *livres* on Lodève broadcloth in 1747, that is, the equivalent of half a million days' pay of a good Parisian worker.[44] The economic stakes were far from negligible for manufacturers and merchants, and we see how wide was the diffusion of the practices transmitted by enlisted men.

In time of war, men were replaced at a faster rate; André Corvisier has ventured the figure of 35,000 men a year as replacements, to which should be added the extraordinary levies and additions demanded by war: during the War of Spanish Succession, between 1700 and 1713, probably more than 50,000 men a year; during the Seven Years War, nearly 40,000. In sum, between 1700 and 1762 the army added more than two million soldiers, and between 1763 and 1786 probably more than 500,000. We may

[43] The figures are in Corvisier, *L'Armée française*, vol. I, pp. 152–5, 175–200.
[44] The price of an ell of Lodève broadcloth is in G. d'Avenel, *Histoire économique de la propriété, des salaires* (n.d., n.p.), vol. III, p. 613.

assume that the publicity of uniform directly affected, in an average year, slightly more than one man in twenty: 200,000 soldiers for 3,800,000 adults of between sixteen and forty years old, of an age to bear arms. If the militias and the periodic wartime levies are added, it might be as high as one in ten.

The permanent body of old soldiers who had learned new habits of cleanliness, dress and presentation was thus considerable, if not of equal importance in all provinces or social milieus. Eastern France always provided more recruits for all branches than the Midi or the west, and the century saw a further specialisation of recruitment in the frontier provinces. The economy, the existence of ancient military traditions (as in Normandy, country of cavalry-men, or in Béarn), the more or less strong survival of ties between men, established a frontier between two Frances: in the north and east the appeal of uniform was strong, in the south and west it was less so, even though southern France provided so many non-commissioned officers. Until compulsory military service, the prestige of the military uniform still divided France.

The same was true socially. The military muster-rolls have enabled Corvisier to demonstrate this in some detail. Most striking is the increase in importance of the lower social groups: 78 per cent of recruits in 1716, 85 per cent in 1763; military service had been abandoned to the poorest sectors of the rural and urban population. Uniform and the practices associated with it thus descended step by step within the social body as a whole, their spread benefiting from the 'melting-pot effect' characteristic of the army. This tended to diminish regional differences; it drew country dwellers out of their isolation; it mingled natives of the newly acquired provinces, such as Roussillon, Alsace and Lorraine, and men from the old French regions; townsmen rubbed shoulders with countrymen, native French with foreigners. In 1716, men of village origin comprised two-thirds of the army, a higher proportion in the cavalry (72 per cent) than the infantry (60 per cent); in 1763, the figures had hardly changed; up to the Revolution, the proportion of townsmen slightly decreased, that of countrymen increased.

The innovation of uniform thus primarily affected villagers, in general less influenced by the clothing revolution, but it was proportionately more important among townsmen, who comprised less than 20 per cent of the population but between 30 and 40 per cent of the army. The notables and townspeople retained a motor role in the spread of habits associated with uniform, since they provided rather more under officers and officers than the other social categories. Though the great majority of soldiers came from economically and socially modest backgrounds, they benefited most from the multifarious effects of military institutions. Their contribution was ultimately positive after a period of service which averaged about three years, that is, roughly the time it took to wear out a full outfit. The listings of old soldiers show that the army also promoted geographical mobility: a third of the former villagers were attracted by town life on their retirement, so helping to generalise further the new clothing practices; another third moved, so spreading the new practices throughout the kingdom. When the phenomenon was accompanied by social promotion, however slight, the impact was only enhanced. Old soldiers were men who, whatever their rank, constituted nuclei of model behaviour, whose positive aspects should be remembered as much as the negative.

## TOWARDS A HISTORY OF TYPES OF UNIFORM

Uniform, by influencing character, created men perhaps more susceptible to change, with the aspiration to uniformity and capacity to adapt which mark the cultural intermediary. The evolution of minds cannot be separated from that of actions.

In spite of the evident flaws in the military institution, manners were shaped by regimental practices. These are fundamental; one can envisage a global reconstitution, in the form of a case study, of all the elements which help to standardise men, on the basis of the study of one single unit, taking in the variety and uniformity of its recruitment, the characteristics of its command and the diversity of its acculturing practices, adapted to place, movements, material means and circumstances. One would surely discover the two principles which underlie the use of uniform: to separate, in order to inculcate the military ethos and instil a sense of hierarchy; to unite, so as to demonstrate a common adherence, encourage *esprit de corps* and promote harmony between the specialised arms.

In other words, there is nothing less uniform than the uniform which reflects both the desire for distinction and that for conformity; they are apparent in the changes which can be traced in the orders and decrees specifying variations in shape and colour, and the diversity of the military signs which respect the move towards greater efficiency; their mechanisms are perhaps more difficult to understand for minds accustomed to greater rationality and simplicity, acquired, let us remember, only after an evolution of barely two or three centuries. To discuss the details of changing lapels, facings, folds or buttons would require a technical analysis beyond our competence. We will confine ourselves to a few main lines which reveal the fundamental cultural phenomena, entering into detail only to the extent that it is necessary to emphasise, or contradict, the general trends. These, lastly, need to be compared to what we know of real life.

Formally, unity was achieved very early in intention and practice. The main texts fixing the cut of the coat and the nature and deployment of the other items appeared between 1690 and 1747. Innovation is to be sought in the fancy of theoreticians who multiplied the number of buttons or strained ingenuity to find different ways of carrying cartridges.[45] For fifty years, the soldiers, corporals and anspessades of the infantry wore a roomy broadcloth coat, the long *justaucorps*, very similar to civilian dress. Waistcoats (*vestes*) and breeches were uniformly of jersey or caddis; the waistcoat was double-breasted and cut shorter than the coat, the breeches stopped just below the knee. The drawings of Watteau accurately portray the general appearance of the trooper, his clothes straight and conforming to the new disciplinary correctness, but at the same time his coat flexible and ample, his wide-brimmed hat already becoming three-cornered by the beginning of the century, gaiters concealing his stockings.

The *justaucorps* played a major role in the soldier's existence. Its pockets were invaluable for holding small items; its wide facings and collar could be turned up to give maximum protection against bad weather; it was thick enough to serve as a blanket at night. Individualistic military tailors were able to add features specific to each unit to this basic garment, a different cut of lapel or number of buttons or even fullness of pleat. Such initiatives might be incorporated into ordinances and so generalised, especially if they contributed to the desired simplification and standardisation. The cavalryman was not to be outdone; better dressed than the

[45] Pétard, 'Un bilan', pp. 29–34; and his 'Le fusilier au début de la guerre de succession d'Autriche', *Uniformes*, 55 (1980), pp. 25–31; also 'L'homme de 1776, le fusilier ou le réformisme au pouvoir', *Uniformes*, 58 (1980), pp. 26–30.

footsoldier, especially in the elite units of the Royal Household, he benefited in the fifty or so regiments of light cavalry from the spread of the *justaucorps*, and the standardisation of coats (*habits-vestes*) and breeches made from sheepskin or heavy cloth. Their distinctive characteristic was the rigid boot. No special features marked the appearance of the developing technical arms and the artillery and the pioneer engineers were not distinguished from the ordinary fusilier or cavalryman. Throughout the reigns of Louis XIV and Louis XV, a unified uniform existed, even if it did not wholly conform to our canons of interchangeability and retained original select features, desirable because they actively promoted *esprit de corps*.

With the duc de Choiseul, things were no longer left to chance and the army embarked on a new phase. In the aftermath of the defeats of the Seven Years War, the soldier benefited from a greater solicitude which was part of an intensification of the ethos of a military society at once torn apart and strengthened by these difficulties. The great order of 25 February 1767, the decree of 2 September 1775, the order promulgated by the comte de Saint-Germain on 31 May 1776 and that of 1 October 1786 took uniform to the state in which it would remain throughout the Revolutionary period and the Empire. The footsoldier acquired a coat which was closer fitting, with a small upright collar, the lateral pleats stitched, and a larger number of buttons, emphasising the narrow, even clinging, nature of the uniform. At a time when experts dreamed of generalising Prussian-type discipline, not without provoking numerous conflicts, hotly debated topics ranged from whether disciplinary correction should be administered with the flat of the sword to whether distinctive marks on the facings should be generalised, or whether soldiers' hair should be cropped. The theoreticians of uniform succeeded in imposing a rigid outfit which lasted for nearly half a century. The coat was narrow and could no longer be fastened right to the bottom; it thus lost its functionalism in favour of its corrective and disciplinary virtues. The sleeves, also narrower, were split above a smaller and tighter facing, and buttoned with a flap. Frederick II thought that these buttons were intended to prevent the soldier from wiping his nose on his sleeve; in fact, they had a utilitarian and also a corrective role: they held the flap which protected the cloth from wear and dirt, and with the rest of the buttons (twenty or thirty on the coat, a dozen on the gilet or surtout), they added greatly to the soldier's task of maintenance.

The aesthetic gained ground, but functionalism persisted. It explains the triumph of the *habit-veste*, whose elongated tails freed the soldier's thighs when it was open but covered them completely in front when closed. The skirted waistcoat (*veste*) disappeared, to be replaced by the gilet; the breeches were worn with a wide belt of jersey which supported the stomach and indicates a degree of concern for comfort. Lastly, the fusilier was provided with a mantle or redingote, like the cavalryman (who also got an *habit-veste*). This was an important innovation, the result of a desire for comfort, but restricted for reasons of economy. The distribution of capotes ceased in 1779, to resume in 1792, and only a few units had in practice received the new uniform prescribed in 1776 by the comte de Saint-Germain. The army of 1789, then, was clothed according to the dispositions of 1775–6; it was the coat *à la française* of the footsoldier and cavalryman which predominated on the battlefields of the American War and the Revolutionary wars in Europe. A compromise between reform and tradition determined the appearance of the citizen soldier.

The almost complete standardisation was from this point of view a mirror of obedience and efficiency. In the minds of the experts it was part of an increasingly exacting preoccupation with appearance, encompassing both attire and figure, which was expected to be ever more handsome and harmonious. Uniform is a subject in itself in the anthropology of military appearances. For example, to standardise figures, the *justaucorps* were made in only three sizes – large, medium and small; the control of manufacture universalised the unifying and corrective principles to create a discipline of military elegance.

The trend to diversity and distinction is both better known and more complex. The sense of hierarchy required the application of strict rules governing clothes. Throughout the century, the dress of the officers was in principle the same as that of the soldier, except that the materials were of higher quality and the insignia of rank emphasised function: the gorget, 'mark of the actual service of infantry officers', the braid and, at the end of the *ancien régime*, ornate epaulettes for non-commissioned officers and officers from 1759. The permanence of *esprit de corps* fostered a deeper conservatism in the elite units, the Royal Household – where, on parade, the Swiss dressed in the military style of the sixteenth century – and the cavalry, where the dragoons and hussars were always conspicuous even though they did not escape uniform.

The hussars exercise a special fascination for historians of military costume, testifying to the power of exoticism and the survival of archaism.[46] Quicherat noted that in 1870 their uniform was, all else being equal, similar to that of 1770, and that the names of the items which comprised it were unchanged: plumed shako with pennant, pelisse of broadcloth lined with sheepskin, dolman, woollen stole worn as a belt, long Hungarian-style breeches like pantaloons, big leather boots, suppler than those of the other units, green coat and red breeches from 1776. With their long hair in cadenettes, their ear-rings and their long moustaches, they caught the imagination. We see this in the *Mémoires* of the young Marbot,[47] when he describes the flashy and ruffianly airs adopted by old under officers such as sergeant Pertelay the elder, defender of the traditions of the Bercheny hussars: 'A jolly fellow, very well turned out, it is true, but his shako over his ear, his sabre trailing, his face flushed and bisected by an immense scar, moustaches half a foot long and so stiffly waxed that they disappeared into his ears, two thick plaits of hair braided at the temples, emerging from his shako, and, all in all, what an air!'[48]

## DISTINCTIONS AND COLOUR IN UNIFORM

Swashbuckling attitudes and camp and barracks life had as much if not more effect than theory on uniform.[49] However, in the taxonomy of military colours, theory ruled. Orders and regulations struggled to reconcile the principles of general uniformity and distinctive variety, which operated more or less strongly according to the hierarchy of arms and the determination of the government to standardise, which constantly ran up against regimental resistance and financial difficulties.[50]

The standardisation of colours was largely successful in the case

---

[46] Quicherat, *Histoire du costume français*, pp. 589–92.

[47] 4 vols. (Paris, 1924), vol. I, pp. 50–4. Marbot, too young to have a moustache, was equipped by the older Pertelay with two tusks of black wax: 'I didn't wince, I was a hussar!'

[48] *Mémoires*, vol. I, p. 50.

[49] Examples are to be found in soldiers' memoirs, rare before 1792, more common after; see Bertaud, *La Révolution armée*, p. 352.

[50] The technical details come from Lienhart and Humbert, *Les Uniformes de l'armée française*, vol. I, *Maison du Roi et état-major*; vol. II, *Cavalerie*; vol. III, *Infanterie*; vol. IV, *Artillerie, Génie*.

of the infantry. In 1720, out of some hundred line regiments, four-fifths wore white or grey-white coats, though less than half had breeches and waistcoats of these colours; thirty years earlier, in 1690, some sixty units had worn a white coat and thirty a grey-white *justaucorps*. In 1757, again on the basis of the 113 regiments listed by Lienhard and Humbert, 80 per cent had grey-white coats, breeches and waistcoats. The French infantry was 'all in grey' until the Revolution. There were two sets of exceptions: first were the foreign regiments; the Swiss and the Irish wore a madder-red coat and the Germans wore blue, which was an essential element in their distinctiveness within military society and the national solidarity of their recruitment. Second were the units placed directly under the view and protection of the monarch: the French Guards wore royal blue; the Royal Artillery and Royal Bombardiers had changed from clear grey to royal blue; the officers of the fortifications engineers, who had originally worn red, adopted blue in 1758; the war commissioners and the army intendants abandoned iron grey for blue. In general, in 1786, the learned arms retained in the general review the colours of the guards regiments.

The adoption of grey-white, magnificently portrayed in the tapestry of *L'Histoire du Roi consacrée au siège de Tournai* (27 June 1667),[51] raises questions about the history of sensibilities and that of colours. It is difficult to explain an army so prone to show the dirt unless, over and above the technical reasons explaining the choice – which was by no means confined to the French army – there were no other decisive factors; these were emphasised in the crisis of 1792.

The grey-white of the royal troops – a few cavalry regiments had a coat of grey stitched with blue – can be explained by the fact that it was the colour which best met a balance of tactical requirements, economic necessity and the technical possibilities of the cloth market and the dyeing industry.[52] Undressed broadcloth or serge was a stronger fabric; it included less poor-quality wool, whose presence was easily spotted; 'there was a difference of a quarter in price and an eighth in strength' compared with fabrics dyed other colours; repairs were less visible and patches soon merged into a

[51]  *Gli Arazzi del Re Sole* (Florence, 1982), plates 9–10, pp. 72–3.
[52]  *Encyclopédie méthodique*, vol. III, pp. 13–14.

1 *Jeunes filles éduquées par des religieuses*

2 *Louis XIV devant la grotte de Thétis*

*Edit
Contre
le luxe*

*reue à la
bourse du
mari jusqu'a
nouuelle mode*

Aparis chez Guerard Graveur rue S.ᵗ Jacques a la reyne du clerge proche S.ᵗ yues. C.P.R.

## La Coquette Bourgeoise desolée.

Edit fatal qui deffend les dorures     Bon vous cryés il semble qu'on vous tüe
Tu est le coup mortel à tous mes agrements     Dit aussy tost sa servante Fanchon
Ne pouuant plus briller par les parures     Allez allez tauerne bien cognüe
C'en est fait dit iris ie n'auré plus d'amants     Se peut passer d'enseigne et de bouchon

3 *La coquette bourgeoise désolée*

4 *L'art du Tailleur* (male), Garsault

5 *L'art du Tailleur* (female), Garsault

6 a and b *Mme Seriziat*

7 *Une femme de condition fouettée pour avoir craché sur le portrait de M. de Necker*

8 *La toilette*

9 Tailleur d'habits

10 *Démolition des maisons du Pont Notre-Dame*

background of white-tending-to-grey; lastly, it was the colour least penetrated by the rays of the sun. There remained the problem of keeping it clean. The author of the *Encyclopédie méthodique* understood this; he realised that a white uniform showed the dirt more than a blue one, but he knew that grey-white was 'yellowish . . . not particularly white' and that it could easily be restored to the necessary degree of whiteness and cleanliness by applying bran or 'bluish clay' [*terre de Troyes*]'; removing the stains this way did not remove the colour. The value of the exercise from the disciplinary point of view is easily apparent; the contributor to the *Encyclopédie méthodique* also pointed to this when he bemoaned 'the colonels who were fanatical about appearance'.

Cheaper, more resistant and reasonably easy to look after, white satisfied the commissariat; it was perhaps conspicuous, but this suited contemporary tactics since, tending to yellow or ash grey once it had been worn, it merged with the majority of objects found in the countryside. The brightness of the white was not as dangerous as was sometimes claimed, since it faded however carefully it was looked after, and its unifying and symbolic value remained, in the last analysis, the prime justification for its choice and its generalisation. It was a moral reason: 'The French have long seen the colour white as the national colour; why change this colour?' As regards colour, the history of uniform is fertile ground since it reveals the imbrication of material imperatives and social codes, that is, the cultural role of colours, including their ambivalence.[53] White, symbol of justice and eternity, proclaimed the authority of the monarchy through its ensigns and uniforms. The white army was that of the sovereign. Come the Revolution, white would indicate the ambiguity of the enemies of the nation. For the military ethos, at all events, the uniformity of royal white was a factor for cohesion and, for the author of the *Encyclopédie méthodique*, it 'would be advisable to give it to the whole French army'.

For diversity still flourished. It operated in an obvious way to affirm the pre-eminence of the cavalry, more conservative, more elitist, more diversified than the infantry; and it distinguished foreign troops. The *Détail militaire* shows this sumptuous polychrome, the cavalry of the guards are in blue, the gendarmes in

---

[53]  M. Pastoureau, 'L'Uomo e il colore', *Storia e dossier*, 3 (Rome, 1987).

red, the musketeers in red with casaque of regulation blue; the coat of their mounts varied according to the tradition of the company – bay, chestnut, grey or black. In 1690, of the forty-two mounted regiments analysed by Lienhard and Humbert, thirty-seven were in grey-white, Conti and Maître de Camp retaining a red mantle. Colonel General, Fitz-James, Noailles and La Reine were in red, Du Roi in blue. In 1761, thirty units had changed to blue for the *habit-veste*, their mantles remaining grey; in 1786, of some forty mounted regiments, twenty-four had royal-blue coats, blue waistcoats, white leather breeches and mantles of white broadcloth stiched with blue; the Royal German, the carabineers – the 'big brothers' – and the Royal Household were dressed in red, Berry in white, Nassau in orange, Artois, Orléans and Du Roi in blue. Uniformity was greater, but still incomplete, the French cavalryman remaining more loyal to polychrome than the footsoldier.[54]

Men on foot and men on horseback thus benefited unequally from attachment to tradition or the defence of old prerogatives. The military administration imposed uniformity but also tolerated the diversity necessary to distinguish units. This took concrete form in the colour of facings, collars and linings, each regiment having its distinctive colours which might be combined with the arrangement of the buttons, the colour of the braids for the facings or the hat-brim. Reading the stream of orders published over the century makes the historian dizzy. In 1690, out of the hundred infantry regiments, eleven wore facings of white, nine of grey-white, forty-six of red, thirty-nine of blue; collars and linings ranged from black (three) to yellow (four), violet and green and more or less matched. After 1756, the number of colours was reduced and the majority of regiments had facings and braids, collars and linings of grey-white and white, red and blue. Buttons were now numbered and sometimes bore an original stamp. With the exception of the royal regiments, those of the princes and Colonel General, they were classed in sixes in order of age and distinguished by a colour assigned to the class, which the first

---

[54] In 1786–9, classed in order of age like the infantry, the six regiments had red lapels and facings, three auroras, six yellows and jonquils, six camels, two whites. All the coats were of blue cloth. The trappings – saddle cloth, portmanteau – varied accordingly. Things were simpler than in 1762, though hardly more than in 1690; various units, carabineers, dragoons, light horse, chasseurs and hussars, increased the diversity.

regiment of each division always wore on the lapels and facings, the second on the lapels, the third on the facings. Thus the Second of each regiment of the Provence infantry (the First Picardy was all in white) had lapels and facings of sky blue; the Third Piedmont had blue lapels and white facings; the Fourth Blaisois had blue facings and white lapels. The foreign regiments, Swiss and Grisons, Irish, Germans and the Royal Italian, each had their own colours. The order of 1779 which specified this hierarchy was confirmed in 1786 with only slight modifications; the regiments were divided in series of twelve colours emphasised by the distinctive border of the same colouring, which became general after the ministry of Saint-Germain.

The discipline involved in learning to read such a code is obvious. It evokes a visual sensibility different from our own, at a time when the forces for uniformity were struggling to achieve simplification. The Revolution would see two major but temporary changes to the taxonomy of colours: the unification of the arms and the general numbering, evidence of the transition to another type of code. In 1806, the distinctive colours reappeared, as the military empire rediscovered the controlled fantasy of the monarchy, which undoubtedly contributed to the harmonisation of the warlike spirit.

Had it ever disappeared? In the absence of research into the realities of supply and replacement, it is open to doubt. The uniform army, yesterday as today, was made up of temporary arrangements in which theoretical rationality and the logic of making do always co-existed. Between peacetime parades and the vicissitudes of campaigns, the many imponderables of real life complicate the history of military appearances.

WAR: UNIFORM PUT TO THE TEST

War put uniform to the test, its functionality and its resistance to the hazards of time, wear and unsuitability. Broadcloths withstood but colours faded in the absence of dyes firm enough to withstand the rigours of the climate, dirt of every kind and the stains left by soil, fire, blood, sweat, urine, sunshine and even the ultra-violet rays of the moon.[55] A general discoloration was soon apparent,

[55] P. Dervaux, 'Les draps militaires aux XVIIe et XVIIIe siècles, leur teinture, leur détérioration', *Cahiers de la Sabretache*, new series, 46 (1949), p. 25; F.-C. Laukhard, *Un Espion sous la Terreur* (Paris, 1987), pp. 55–70.

and uniforms took on a nondescript hue, the blues turning green, the greens rapidly fading, the reds surviving but duller, grey-white becoming yellowish and washed out. Bad weather made the army uniform much more effectively than regulations, and it is a near-miracle that the dyers' skill guaranteed even temporarily the colours of military fabrics.

So we should distrust those painters of battles who forget about discoloration and dirt. 'The legendary Prussian cleanliness has long passed into the realms of myth', wrote Frederic Christian Laukhard in his *Souvenirs* after Valmy,

> but you should have seen Messieurs the Prussians, officers and simple soldiers, normally so highly polished, at Haus [a village in Champagne]. A thick layer of dirt covered breeches and tunics, already soiled by smoke and soot; their gaiters were caked with mud, their shoes were in tatters, to the point where many soldiers had to tie them on with osiers; their tunics bore traces of the red, white or yellow clay which had stuck to them; their hats had lost all shape and sagged miserably like nightcaps, and their unkempt beards gave the soldiers the air of veritable savages.

The chalk-white Prussian army was foundering in disorder and dirt, badges of defeat; after a few months of fighting, can we still speak of the regulation uniform?

The care devoted by the military administration to imposing uniformity by standardising colours and outfits, to allow a rapid, if not immediate, response to losses, might suggest that we can. Both military decrees and eye-witness reports attest to this unflagging effort. Let us choose as an example of the former the *Règlement concernant le service intérieur, la police et la discipline des troupes à cheval* of 24 June 1792, which applied the law of 15 September 1791, and which I quote in the edition of 1809, proof of the persistence of the practices it decribes.[56] For the latter, I refer to the ineffable Captain Coignet, whose recollections are here highly pertinent.[57]

The clauses concerning the internal regulation of the cavalry reveal first the omnipresence of uniform. In the barrack-rooms, portmanteau and mantle had to be placed above each man's bed,

---

[56]   Paris, 1809 (*Règlement*).
[57]   Ed. Jean Mistler, *Les Carnets* (Paris, 1968).

his clothes and gear put away at the bed head.[58] The daily routines were accompanied by changes of outfit: stable gear consisting of clogs or old shoes, trousers and gilets, especially for the dirty jobs of mucking out and feeding; grooming gear, worn for an hour every morning and three-quarters of an hour every afternoon.[59] The officers in charge of the barrack-rooms saw that the men kept their clothes in good order and dressed correctly for whatever duty they had to perform: guard, exercises, parade, Sunday mass. Every month, the captains had to make a general inspection of gear and update the cavalrymen's handbook – copies of the checklists were attached to the decree. The unit commander made a similar inspection every three months. The regulations were read after the visits, and posted so that no-one could remain unaware of them. Lastly, the details of the uniform were meticulously listed for both officers and men.[60]

The clauses keep to the order of the old schemas of anthropological description, progressing from head to foot. Officers and cavalry wore their hair tied in a queue, but cut shorter at the front. They wore hats, the front corner placed over the left eyebrow, 'uncovered to the width of half a thumb'. The uniform collar was of black silk for officers, black cloth for men; it must cover the collar of the shirt. Summer and winter outfits were distinguished; both must conform to the rules and customs of the regiment. Officers wore boots, as did mounted cavalrymen, those on foot wore shoes and gaiters.

On paper, uniform worked. In real life, it varied according to means and discipline.[61] The latter emphasised everything to do with keeping clothes and linen clean: stains were to be got rid of, but the uniform could not be washed; everything had to be done dry, with soap, small amounts of water left to dry on stains, stones for scraping and bran to clean white fabrics. Buttons and buckles were treated with whiting, wood button-sticks protecting the cloth of coats and waistcoats. Elbow-grease made the brass shine and remained the magic ingredient. In 1789, the *Règlement intérieur* reflected all the changes and showed how the army adapted to new notions of cleanliness and hygiene, uniformity and aesthetics. Its

[58] *Règlement*, pp. 12, 54, 56.
[59] Ibid., pp. 20–1, 31.
[60] Ibid., pp. 52–61.
[61] Ibid., pp. 58–62.

principal guarantee was, in the end, the individual responsibility encouraged by the regular deductions for the ordinary expenses of upkeep and gear, and the extraordinary levies authorised to make good damage and deterioration.

The handbooks made it possible to rationalise, and were no doubt easier to observe in the garrison than on campaign.[62] Some figures for the *masse* give an idea of the individually small but cumulatively considerable budgets, and hence expenditure. The budget calculated by the anonymous author of the *Considérations sur l'état actuel du soldat français* in 1772 survives. He was a reformer in the style of Guibert, who painted a gloomy picture the better to plead his cause. Nevertheless, he revealed the many advantages soldiers enjoyed in comparison with the majority of the population: food, necessities, clothes and lodgings all guaranteed. Even if the military life was for many 'barely above that of the poorest of country people', as Guibert claimed, the soldier escaped the hazards of the common lot and enjoyed additional advantages. The fusilier with 73 *livres* a year deducted for food and nearly 46 *livres* for his upkeep ended up 16 *livres* short, since he received less than 102 *livres* a year. But the army saw to the replacement of his clothing and the rest of his expenses and the soldier found numerous opportunities to increase his income: replacement guard duty, work inside the garrison or elsewhere.[63] It was on campaign that he suffered most and had to resort to the expedients of plunder and pillage.

As a general rule, the soldier was entitled to a more generous clothing budget than that of the labourer or artisan: two pairs of shoes each year, resoled twice, three shirts every two years, one pair of gaiters, several collars, a nightcap, three pairs of stockings, three pocket handkerchiefs; new shoe and clothes brushes, combs, powder and leather bag (every four years), brooms for the barrackroom, thread, needles, soap, hair ribbons, oil, wax polish and whiting cost him less than 2 *livres* a year. He spent annually 3 *livres*

---

[62] In 1914, the handbooks of my father, an under-officer then officer in the 10th Chasseurs, testify to this difference, the specifications for his troop changing completely before and after hostilities, during operations and rest periods. The uniform and equipment of men and horses similarly changed.

[63] H.-J. de Butet, colonel, 'La dépense du soldat en 1772', in *Actes du quatre-vingt-dixième Congrès national des sociétés savantes*, Nice, 1965 (Paris, 1966), Modern and Contemporary History Section, vol. I, pp. 141–8 (an analysis of the anonymous manuscript Ya, 1791 in the Archives de la Guerre).

18 *sols* on his laundry and 1 *livre* 16 *sols* on his barber. Overall, clothes, hygiene and cleanliness consumed three-quarters of his annual income; this was the exact opposite of the typical budget of the majority of the population, in which food and lodgings were always the largest items. The army thus drew a sector of the population into the consumer revolution.[64]

It is likely that war contributed by encouraging wastefulness and gift, archaic economic forms which survived despite the moralisation of conduct and progress of rationalisation. This dimension is visible in the ostentatious expenditure of the officers and elite troops, the cost of their equipages, the high quality and rarity of their horses and equipment. This is a chapter in the history of noble luxury which remains to be written; for the reforming *philosophes*, it was a page which had to be turned to bring greater asceticism to the nation's military. War plunged most people into an economy of risk and instability. The soldier lived for the moment, and survived thanks to resourcefulness and pilfering.

Jean Roch Coignet has left us an imperishable and racy account, in which we can follow all the century's military theories and their application in real life. A little shepherd-boy, for many years covered with vermin and barefoot,[65] he received a preliminary education with some great Brie landowners enriched by the Revolution and army supply.[66] A born horseman, he was a footsoldier, taken on in 1799, when he was already twenty-three years old. For fifteen years, from the line to the Guards, from the ranks to staff office, he traversed Europe, accumulating experiences. Retired on half-pay, faithful to the lure of the army and its life-style (he was unable, whatever the cost, to do without a horse), he compiled his *Mémoires*, redolent of the soldier's existence and ethos, full of glimpses of the life of bivouacs, marches, garrisons and battle.

For the soldier on campaign, what mattered most was a full belly, which could usually be achieved by guile if the commissariat failed. Next came his feet, hence his shoes. Those supplied soon fell to pieces; they had to be patched up and it was a great comfort to set out in new shoes.[67] If an item of uniform was lacking, it could easily be replaced from the dead or wounded or an enemy prisoner;

[64] See also chapter 7.
[65] *Les Carnets*, pp. 24–5.
[66] Ibid., pp. 47–71.
[67] Ibid., pp. 86, 115.

you often had to resign yourself to marching in whatever you could lay your hands on.[68] When water penetrated his uniform, the trooper had to be stoical and hold his head high under a sodden hat which drooped to his shoulders.[69] If the weather got worse, they stole cloth for their trousers, as from the Polish peasants on the eve of Eylau.

Linen was a perennial problem, since soldiers washed rarely but changed their shirts often, in line with the times. Failure to find a clean shirt and stockings after a long march or in a poor garrison meant an infestation of vermin.[70] When a young conscript, Coignet lost a uniform when he tried to boil his waistcoat and jersey breeches, which were swarming with fleas and lice: 'What a disaster, only the lining was left, the jersey had dissolved like paper, there I was stark naked, with nothing in my bag to change into; my pals came to my rescue.'[71] One can imagine how soldiers washed their linen in free moments, and sought out the shirts hidden by peasants, even cloth from which the regimental tailors made replacements. The desire to rid himself of vermin made the soldier a wily marauder.[72] The good turn-out and efficiency of the armies of the *ancien régime* and of the Empire were based on linen and shoes.

Peacetime brought a concern for elegance. The Guards in which Coignet served had inherited the prestigious traditions of the elite units. They were models in their uniform and their cleanliness; every grenadier was an arbiter of military elegance, even if this meant improving on nature: Coignet, endowed with spindly legs, wore three pairs of stockings and false calves.[73] Revues and inspections promoted discipline and inculcated habits.[74] General Dorsenne lifted the grenadiers' gilets to see if their shirts were white, inspected their feet to see if they were clean and their nails cut, riffled through their trunks in search of dirty linen and made the veterans parade before the surgeon-major in nothing but their shirts once a fortnight to reveal the sick and the syphilitic. The Guards set an example and, if need be, stripped down in the open

---

[68]  Ibid., pp. 91, 107.
[69]  Ibid., p. 142.
[70]  Ibid., pp. 115, 185–6, 187.
[71]  Ibid., p. 108.
[72]  Ibid., pp. 185, 189.
[73]  Ibid., pp. 236–8.
[74]  Ibid., pp. 164, 191, 199, 206, 256.

to wash before setting out.[75] When, before Metz, they opened their bags to get out their full dress, 'the wind blew their shirts in the air, and the coast was soon clear: women shrieked with terror at seeing the handsomest men in France stark naked'. They were a laboratory of hygienic experiences, in line with the related models of the medicine and the military discipline of the *ancien régime*. In the recollections of this old soldier, military life was polarised round two ways of behaving, symbolised by life on the march and life in quarters: in the former, you had to struggle against nature and circumstances to keep clean; in the latter, the review and the officers combined to inculcate clean habits. At the end of his life, proud of his ceremonial uniform, possessor of forty shirts,[76] Coignet was proof of the effectiveness of an education as well as revealing its limitations. It is with this triumph of discipline surviving the rupture of the Revolution that we will end our analysis.

On the eve of 1789, the French soldier had been rehabilitated in public opinion after a period of crisis and questioning. The republic of letters had accepted military philosophers and beneficial soldiers.[77] The problems derived partly from the economic situation,[78] relations between men, mostly commoners, and officers, largely noble in certain units, were difficult after the disciplinary reforms applied by the 'fanatical colonels'.[79] We should beware of generalisation since military society was traversed by many currents, and the spirit of professional cohesion co-existed with factors promoting animosity, tension and strife.[80] Uniform probably contributed more to the former than to the latter; it served to reveal military society in its entirety to civil society, it symbolised royal authority and it enhanced the glory of the soldiers, the honour of the regiment and the solidarity of the units. It was a sign of equality within inequality.

---

[75] Ibid., p. 217.
[76] Ibid., p. 411.
[77] Chagniot, *Paris et l'armée*, pp. 611–31.
[78] A. Babeau (*La Vie militaire sous l'Ancien Régime*, 2 vols. (Paris, 1891), vol. I, pp. 110–12) doubts the economic difficulties: 'Never has the soldier been better looked after than he is today.' We await a definitive study.
[79] Bertaud, *La Révolution armée*, pp. 35–8.
[80] See, for example, J. Aman, *Les Officiers bleus dans la marine française au XVIIIe siècle* (Geneva, 1974). Naval uniforms deserve a study to themselves.

## UNIFORM AND THE REVOLUTION

The crisis of society did not spare the army, and in the atmosphere
of the years 1789–92 the question of uniform took on a special
significance[81] The dress of the royal troops changed its meaning;
recognised symbol of power, sign of obedience to a contested and
shaken order, it was rejected or travestied. During the revolt at
Nancy, the officers of *Mestre de Camp Général de Cavalerie*
'found men disguised in all sorts of ways, soldiers, musicians who,
by their reciprocal disguise, had made themselves unrecognisable'.[82]
In many units, the soldiers protested by tearing off their buttons
and unpicking the facings in distinctive colours. The rise of national
and patriotic spirit was accompanied by rejection of the old signs
of loyalty and allegiance. It rapidly found another model in the
uniform of the National Guards, where each citizen owned his own
outfit: royal-blue coat, white lining, scarlet trimmings, collars and
piping, white waistcoat and breeches, scarlet facings. From
14 October 1791 this was the costume of all Frenchmen able to serve,
the uniform of the volunteers. The national colours triumphed over
royal white, the soldier thereby demonstrating his definitive reinteg-
ration into the nation. In general and in detail, uniforms promulgated, in France then in Europe, the new civic ideal. The buttons
with regimental numbers were now stamped with political slogans:
in September 1790, the stamp was 'The Law, the King' for all; in
December, it was 'The Nation, the Law, the King'; on 4 October
1792, the Convention imposed the legend 'République française',
with a fasces surmounted by a cap of liberty.[83] For uniform, the
Revolution was primarily a revolution of emblems; uniform became
a 'rallying cry against the enemies of liberty ... the national
colours will do more, they will remind soldiers that they have a
country'.[84] The clothing of volunteers was made the subject of a
civic education and if the regulation outfits were lacking, the
committed made do with other signs. 'They wore little objects

---

[81]  M. Franck, 'L'Uniforme des armées de la Révolution, aspects idéologiques et
pratiques', mémoire de maîtrise, Paris 1 (1981).

[82]  Archives de la Guerre, A4/65A; Franck, 'L'Uniforme des armées', pp. 12–14.

[83]  Archives de la Guerre, A D VI 53.

[84]  H. Lachouque, *Aux armes citoyens, les soldats de la Révolution* (Paris, 1969),
p. 73, speech of the deputy for Tours Menou, 30 June 1791.

which alluded to liberty and equality.'[85] The appeal of the military lost ground to civilian fashions.[86]

The issue of amalgamation, that is, the fusion of the old and new units into a national army, very soon came up against the question of uniform. The law of 21 and 23 February 1793 specified that it should be the same for the whole of the infantry and in the national colours. The technical reorganisation of the army required the patriotic fusion of the 'blue bottles' and the 'white arses', to use the language of those who confronted each other in the name of *esprit de corps*. The new universal uniform became the guarantee of new relations between army and country, but it did not – far from it – do away with the particularism of soldiers; this soon reappeared, with the victories and the Year IV, which adapted to the new equality. It was wholly political.

The new attitude provoked a general debate about the functionalism of the uniform, and its critics denounced its unsuitability, tight clothes in the Prussian style and poor quality. Hoche collected the basic arguments in his *Mémoire* of the Year V on the *Réorganisation de nos armées*.[87] We may well ask why no fundamental reform of the cut was achieved and why the distinctive details were retained. The cost and the difficulties of organising the supply system perhaps explain this failure less than the power of the uniform itself. Certainly, reform fell victim to the slowness and indecision of the Convention, which had better things to do, but it was above all technical imperatives which prevented the total unification and perfect egalitarianism of units and contingents.[88] The principle of distinction between the arms, regiments and grades would prevail when the central government eventually managed to grapple with penury and confusion. The military ethos tended in this direction, as we are told by Marbot,[89] and Gouvion-Saint-Cyr,[90] defenders of the privileges of the cavalry and the artillery. The Convention member Calon, twelve Ventôse Year II, rapporteur of the uniform project, soon relapsed into indecision. The signs of

[85] Franck, 'L'Uniforme des armées', pp. 21–3; B. N., Oa. 10 SC, mémoire anonyme, p. 9.
[86] See *Journal de la mode* 1971; D. Roche, 'Révolution de vêtement et vêtement dans la Révolution', *Imago* (1987).
[87] B. N., 8° LF, 159, 1318, edn Paris 1910.
[88] Franck, 'L'Uniforme des armées', pp. 25–51.
[89] *Mémoires*, p. 57.
[90] Quoted by Lachouque, *Aux armes citoyens*, pp. 340–1.

despotism disappeared from military uniforms, but the distinctive privileges survived, in contradiction to the ideal of the amalgamated citizen army. The real army felt its way within and beyond civil society. The prestige of uniform could now definitively be born.

Between the end of the seventeenth and the beginning of the nineteenth centuries, the history of military dress raises all the problems of a history of the culture of appearances. It reveals the material and technological imperatives, it involves the economy, it reflects the medical, even the philosophical, debates and it brings out specific developments. The army put uniform at both ends of a military life which began with voluntary recruitment and ended with retirement; it trained and changed men, inculcating the discipline of the body and of uniform, the hygiene of linen and the conformism of appearance to the new facts of a rational anthropology of the soldier. It produced many models and its success depended as much on real factors – the number of soldiers, the presence of the army – as on collective representations. It created individuality just as it taught the mechanisms of obedience and passive imitation.

This structural ambiguity should not lead us to forget that uniform could serve to tame violence and be a tool of progress. This is why the comte de Guibert, including it among the essential elements of his *Constitutions militaires*, could emphasise its political role. The failure of the Revolution to effect a radical transformation of manners in this respect reveals the strength of a cultural structure.

# Part 3

# Producing, selling and stealing: the distribution of appearances

Il faut d'abord examiner les techniques les plus insignifiantes et les plus simples, et de préférence celles où règne davantage un ordre comme celles des artisans qui tissent des toiles et des tapis, ou celles des femmes qui piquent à l'aiguille ou tricotent des fils.

René Descartes, *Règles pour la direction de l'esprit*

# 10. *From crafts to customers: the Parisian clothing economy*

Voltaire souriait à toutes les créations de luxe.

Louis Sébastien Mercier

Cloth and clothing create a code, as Descartes was aware, since the successive processes, from the production of fabrics to the making of garments, have such far-reaching implications. But fashion and regional variations confuse the social signs. Philosophers since Plato have found in the orderly manufacture of fabrics and in their materiality a model for understanding thought in the face of reality;[1] praise of the weaver and the lace-maker are its symbols. Historians, meanwhile, have traced the fortunes of an exemplary industry and described the economy of production. It is undoubtedly one of the best-known aspects of the history of the industrial development of France, indeed of Europe.[2] Through it, we have begun to rewrite the history of the industrial revolution and discovered the complexity of the proto-industrialisation which disseminated among rural and urban families the textile culture;[3] that is, the technical, economic and social principles of an industry without entrepreneur when the market was organised by the initiative of the merchant. Spinning and weaving generalised the habits, skills and ways of the early modern textile industry. Their expansion in the countryside helped to destroy the power of the urban textile corporations and guilds.

---

[1] F. Dagognet, *Rematérialiser, matières et matérialismes* (Paris, 1985), pp. 101–3.

[2] The classic texts are: G. Martin, *La Grande Industrie sous Louis XIV* (Paris, 1899); E. Levasseur, *Histoire des classes ouvrières et de l'industrie en France avant 1789*, 2 vols. (Paris, 1902); Braudel and Labrousse, *Histoire économique et sociale*, vol. II, *Des derniers temps de l'âge seigneurial aux préludes de l'âge industriel (1660–1789)*; S. Chassagne, *La Manufacture de toiles imprimées de Tournemine-les-Angers* (Paris, 1971).

[3] W. M. Reddy, *The Rise of Market, the Textile Trade and French Society, 1750–1900* (Cambridge and Paris, 1977), has a bibliography of recent works on proto-industrialisation; see also M. Sonenscher, *Work and Wages. Natural Law, Politics and the Eighteenth Century Trade* (Cambridge, 1989).

The development of new technologies led to new social relations, different types of behaviour and even a politics of artisans, journeymen, merchants and industrialists. Between the seventeenth and the eighteenth centuries, the increase in the production of broadcloths and linens, cottons and silks is visible in every graph. New spatial distributions appear on every map recording the creation of new establishments and the dynamism of profits.[4] A growth rate of 1 per cent between 1730 and 1790 seems likely for the broadcloth industry, which retained a leading role, though it was eventually overtaken by the new textiles: printed linens, cottons and silks. During the Enlightenment, the France of broadcloths and linens, the textile kingdom of the west, from Flanders to Brittany, lost ground to Languedoc, the east and the south-east. In brief, the cloth industry was on the move.

It was a process which involved chemists, dyers and engineers. Réaumur dreamed of liberating man from the vegetable and the animal by creating artificial fabric; the production of 'indiennes' promoted improved mechanisation in the printing of fabrics; Hallot, Macquer and Chaptal – whose *Chimie appliqué aux Arts* dates from 1806 – strove to discover new processes and new colours.[5] The urban clothing revolution reflects the successive stages of these transformations, in which a different materiality helped to transform social and cultural relations.

## THE PRODUCTION OF TEXTILES AND TEXTILE CULTURE

To recognise this is to admit the pressure of the consumer market. Throughout France, a greater volume of trade responded to a more diversified internal demand. Only this could stimulate the merchant and the artisan to produce more, cheaper and less undifferentiated fabrics. We have observed in the case of Paris the major developments which encouraged the manufacture of more elaborate textiles. The taste of the public stimulated an industrial production and a commercial élan which then grew through exports. French textiles and French fashions progressed hand in hand.

Though no historical economist or economic historian questions

---

[4] P. Léon, in Braudel and Labrousse, *Histoire économique et sociale*, pp. 217–67, 518–27.
[5] Dagognet, *Rematérialiser*, pp. 132–5.

the increase in demand, none has so far studied the intermediate stages by which a piece of cloth is turned into a garment, or a length of linen into an item of underwear. It is as if the mechanisms of luxury consumption and the increase in popular demand acted without mediation to regulate the market. It is no part of our project to write this history, but it seems necessary to open the dossier the better to understand the modalities of a profound transformation in which the material facts – the production and commercialisation of the raw materials, wool, cotton, linen, natural silk and hemp, and the economic and social factors – the production and commercialisation of yarns and fabrics, accompanied and stimulated needs. Cloth was thus at the interface between two worlds, the old and the new,[6] its manufacture transformed by the application of intellect. Its formidable materiality influenced behaviour and altered sensibilities.

For perhaps the first time in history we see so clearly outlined two systems of production, two economies and two types of consumption.[7] On the one hand, mass manufacture, rapid, dominated by a concern for productivity and profit, strongly influenced by financial and technical imperatives; cottons and printed indiennes were its characteristic products. On the other, high-quality production, dependent on long hours of toil, protected from competition by privilege, sheltered by guild regulation; the traditional textile products typify its stability, security, even routine. The two economic conceptions and the two models of activity were not entirely separate, the two types of conduct and the two outlooks interacting through response and exchange as tastes and needs evolved.

The originality of the innovations of the eighteenth century lies in this ambivalence. It is visible in the work of the inspectors of manufactories, torn between strengthening defences and protecting tradition,[8] and the ideas of economists aware of changes in taste and changes in the market. 'The new conditions', said an inspector in Picardy, 'render the old regulations useless. Everybody knows that when people dress today they intend to replace [their clothes] as soon as their means allow. Trade itself and the sale of these

[6] Ibid., p. 149.
[7] Chassagne, *La Manufacture de toiles imprimées*, pp. 45, 65–9.
[8] Minard, 'Les Inspecteurs des manufactures', mémoire de DEA, Paris 1 (1986); Chassagne, *La Manufacture de toiles imprimées*, pp. 67–8.

fabrics used to proceed only gradually; today things happen more quickly; we need to seek out and attract the consumer throughout the whole of Europe.'[9] 'The people love the novelties', wrote Pradier to the Bureau du Commerce, 'they find them cheap, durable and clean.'[10] To understand these imperatives, we need to examine the crucial contribution of the garment makers and linen merchants to the formation of new material and mental structures. In their way, they helped to disseminate the consumer revolution, when increasing needs coincided with the possibility of increased production.[11] In France as in England, incomes and wages responded, though with both social and geographical disparities.[12]

Paris is central to our project for two principal reasons: in spite of its economic complexity and historiographical lacunae, the capital is ideal for the analysis of the commercialisation of needs and tastes, since it combines all the problems; second, because of the size and nature of its population, we are able to observe in action the imbrication of causalities and the action of supply and demand through their various circuits. Here, producers and consumers, in the commercial relationship, shaped the new manners. The originality of Paris and the town will emerge more clearly after a brief detour into the countryside, in which we will try to piece together a picture of rural production, that is, of a consumption which was in some ways different and also quantitatively predominant.

Urban specificity appears in the old structure of the clothing crafts, dominated by a few key figures: the tailor, practitioner of a male craft, who shaped the style of French costume; various women – mistress artisans, dressmakers, linen-drapers, fashion merchants – whose skills were in a sense common knowledge, but were enhanced by new ways of doing things and new requirements. Lastly, we need to include modes of redistribution which were economically marginal but perhaps socially more significant than

[9] Arch. dép., Somme, C 350, in Levasseur, *Histoire des classes ouvrières*, pp. 575–95.
[10] Arch. nat., F 12196, ff. 334ff, in Chassagne, *La Manufacture de toiles imprimées*, p. 65.
[11] McKendrick, Brewer and Plumb, *Birth of a Consumer Society*, pp. 22–3. For France, we have only the unpublished thesis of B. Lemire, 'The British Cotton Industry and Domestic Market, Trade and Fashion in an Early Industrial Society, 1750–1800', University of Oxford (1984).
[12] E. Labrousse, *Esquisse du mouvement des prix et des revenues en France au XVIIIe siècle*, 2 vols. (Paris, 1933).

the recognised and established occupations. Where old clothes were more common than new, theft and the second-hand trade were crucial means of transmission and transfer, and their role in promoting the new textiles and sensibilities was considerable. Between guild tradition and flexible free crafts, the clothing and linen revolution can be seen in the most diverse social reappropriations.

## IN THE COUNTRY

In the village, cloth was everywhere, at the heart of social and customary relations, in rites of passage and their lessons, in ordinary and working life, still closely intertwined, and in ways of assessing economic hierarchies, behaviour and morals; proverbial wisdom bears witness.[13] Nevertheless, in the absence of any study, it is not easy to know how things actually happened, from the production to the utilisation of fabrics and clothes. The rural domestic life reconstructed by ethnographers, based both on archival study and field work, makes a useful starting-point; valid for the nineteenth century, it remains to be tested for earlier periods.[14] Essentially, we know about village clothing through analysis of the outfits and objects described in notarial documents or, less frequently, by travellers and observers or through study of the transmission of a complex but customary *savoir-faire*. The division of labour within the peasant household and its organisation within the village community are revealed where people produced their own cloth.

In the regions affected by the proto-industrial economy, it is clear that self-sufficiency, more or less complete elsewhere, more or less threatened by the opening up of rural France between the seventeenth and eighteenth centuries, was on the decline.[15] The distribution of raw materials to be spun and woven in the innumerable workshops controlled by clothiers, the production of lengths of fine or coarse broadcloths and the manufacture of serges and linens for distribution in urban markets introduced new practices, disseminated new models and increased the number of occasions on which traditional habits were ousted by new. There were allega-

---

[13] Loux and Richard, *Sagesse du corps*, pp. 24–31, 105–6, 115–28.
[14] Verdier, *Façons de dire*; M.-C. Pingaud, *Paysans de Bourgogne, les gens de Minot* (Paris, 1978); F. Zonabend, *La Mémoire longue* (Paris, 1980).
[15] P. Deyon, 'Aux origines de la Révolution industrielle', *Revue du Nord* (1979).

tions of fraud with regard to quantity and quality and disputes over the remnants – scraps of warp or weft – which had customarily been allowed to rural weavers for their own use or to sell for a tiny profit; they testify to the mixture of economies, that of the household and that of the factory.[16] These remnants, *echets*, *pennes* and *corrompus*, were disputed between workers and employers in both town and village, since they were part of popular consumption. In the second half of the eighteenth century, their widespread recovery by owners preoccupied with increased productivity and profit expressed the decline of the moral economy of the people, in favour of the assertion of relations of ownership and authority; it probably meant changes to rural clothing consumption and a reorganisation of distribution. The change was, of course, slow. In early nineteenth-century Sedan, theft and fraud persisted because the interest of the workers might coincide with that of the clothiers:[17] 'This disorder, one of the worst which could afflict the manufacture of Sedan, would not amount to much if the thieving workers only used their booty to make cloth for their own use, but unfortunately, we know only too well the profound immorality of certain clothiers who do not blush to buy this stuff cheap.'

The relationships between domestic labour and professional input and between the male and female roles were different in the traditional rural clothing economy of the seventeenth and eighteenth centuries from those of the nineteenth.[18] Women were involved in the preparation of hemp and linen yarn in the areas of production, and of woollen thread elsewhere, whilst cotton was still rare. Inventories list both the materials and the tools for producing them, such as spindles of turned wood and distaffs of hazelwood. The work could be done in the fields while watching over beasts or at evening social gatherings. The more efficient but more expensive spinning-wheel was less common, and was primarily an urban tool. It is clear that hemp, frieze, tow and spun wool were found more or less everywhere, even among non-producers.

---

[16] G. Gayot, 'Les entrepreneurs au bon temps des privilèges, la draperie royale de Sedan au XVIIIe siècle', *Revue du Nord* (1985), pp. 413–45, and 'Le Second Empire drapier des Neuflize à Sedan', *Histoire, Economie et Société* (1986), pp. 101–21.

[17] Gayot, 'Le Second Empire', pp. 104–5, report to Chaptal de Scipion-Mourges, 15 Floréal, Year XI.

[18] S. Tardieu, *La Vie domestique dans le Maconnais pré-industriel* (Paris, 1964), pp. 140–62.

From spinning onwards, trade permeated the rural clothing economy. More than is generally realised, peasant clothing depended on merchants for the sale and purchase of raw materials, and even on the barter common between neighbours. Weaving was done by specialists, and every commune had one or two weavers. They made rustic cloth and linens, which varied only according to the materials used and the need for clothes, linen, sheets, table covers, cloths, aprons and bags. Some making-up was done within the family; women knitted stockings, half-hose, gilets and mittens and sewed shirts, table covers and towels. The extent of home production of linen in Brie in the seventeenth and eighteenth centuries can be calculated with some precision; it almost certainly involved some 60 per cent of households.[19] The number was probably fewer in the case of garments, which involved village specialists, tailors, linen-drapers of both sexes and, of course, shoemakers and cobblers. We see already the complexity of the circuit, in which technical expertise, a real circulation of objects and money and contacts between market towns and rural parishes all played a part.

The manufacture of garments was an almost exclusively male activity, while the preparation of linen, in particular the trousseaus of young girls, was mainly women's work. Linen articles were produced at home in huge quantities, to accumulate in the wardrobes of rich peasants, used but also acting as a reserve, and probably acquiring a symbolic role in the affirmation of identity. Production was sometimes greater than consumption; exceptionally, linen might be used to pay for urgent purchases or settle pressing debts. For the most part, the wealthier households kept a textile capital slumbering quietly in their chests. It was not so much hoarding as a demonstration of conformity (in which technical skills played a part) to the shared know-how and principles of a female culture – the femininitude of anthropologists.[20] The feminine dimension of the social could thus very early associate the manufacture, upkeep and laundering of linen with rites of passage, from birth to puberty, from marriage to death. This invested the rural female collectivity with some of its strength, since all was

[19]  Baulant, 'Du fil à l'armoire', pp. 278–80.
[20]  D. Fabre, 'Passeuses aux gués du destin', *Critique* (1980), pp. 1075–99, and *La Vie quotidienne des paysans du Languedoc au XIXe siècle* (Paris, 1973), pp. 327–9.

revealed by needlework or in the wash. 'Stains, fragments and holes cause tongues to wag.'[21] The culture of rural appearances was subtly formed in the meeting of ages and sexes and the efficacy of norms and apprenticeships. We will return to this when we discuss the care of clothing.

Needlework, when done at home, accurately reflected a world in the process of industrialisation and urbanisation.[22] It increased social differences and modified the sartorial relationship between the sexes. Its expansion coincided with the retreat of the spinning of wool, hemp and flax with distaff or spinning-wheel, tasks traditionally reserved to women, but which usually employed raw materials produced on the holding by male members of the household. 'The disappearance of this sexual complementarity within households was contemporary with the retreat of weavers, deprived of domestic yarns and hit by the competition of cheaper materials of industrial origin, which were carried by new means of transport into even the most remote parts.'[23] Everywhere, the concrete acts of the production and use of clothes changed. The promotion of models of family conduct passed in part from the home to the school. This was where girls learnt the needlework they performed at home to make trousseaus, linen and even women's clothes. The transmission of knowledge from mother to daughter did not cease, but now preceded and reinforced that of the school. How to mark linen and knit, and the rudiments of cutting-out and embroidery, were learned at an early age and practised at home, in the evening or in the fields. In teaching how to use needles and pins, mothers, older sisters and schoolmistresses also taught the principles of good housekeeping, the elements of a female morality, in a word, its 'ways of speaking' and 'ways of doing', that is, its culture. The contraction of the world of women's clothes went with an expansion of that of men, which drew on markets and fairs and on shops in market and larger towns; it went with a sharper differentiation of roles within the family and, in a sense, allowed a real emancipation of women, under cover of the continuance, even intensification, of their traditional functions.

We need to proceed by two routes if we are to understand more

---

[21] Fabre, 'Passeuses aux gués du destin', p. 1079.
[22] N. Pellegrin, 'Techniques et productions du vêtement en Poitou, 1880–1950' in *L'Aiguille et le Sabaron* (Poitiers, 1983), pp. 15–20, 28–39.
[23] Pellegrin, 'Techniques et productions du vêtement', p. 28.

clearly this essential transition in the collective rural identity of the modern period, in which, in a sense, girls acquired the clothing ethos and became the makers and managers of wardrobes; on the one hand, that of rural education and the diffusion of urban scholarly models from the seventeenth to the nineteenth centuries; on the other, that of the peddlars who, before the railway revolution, disseminated the basic means of elegance throughout the countryside. With packs crammed full of needles, thimbles, pins, ribbons, lace, pieces of cloth, sewing materials, crochet-hooks and scissors, they travelled far and wide, penetrating even to the most isolated of hamlets.[24] They were the artisans of the transformation of rural appearances, though its success was partly due to an educative model.

By the seventeenth century, urban schools taught girls how to sew.[25] For the charitable institutions, it was an accepted way of giving young girls a professional skill; for the parish schools, it was an essential component in their training; for upper-class boarding schools, it was an introduction to household management, consistent with the religious and social activity of the congregations. For all the educational establishments, it was a powerful element in education, acquired, like learning to read and write, in a codified progression from the easiest and most necessary to the more sophisticated. Though the ultimate objective of this practical education was not the same for all girls, it nevertheless greatly standardised female roles.

The diffusion of this mixture of technical instruction and moral knowledge was both vertical, through imitation within the family or household (mothers, nurses in noble houses and servants all playing a role), and horizontal, through schools for girls, in town and country. This slow evolution allowed the development of the regional costumes which emerged in the eighteenth century, to reach their apogee in the nineteenth. Clothing began to adapt to the routines of daily life and holidays.[26] For work, heavy materials, dark colours and almost unchanging, even archaic, shapes predominated:

---

[24] L. Fontaine, *Le Voyage et la mémoire: colporteurs de l'Oisans au XIXe siècle* (Lyons, 1984); see also M. Spufford, *The Great Reclothing of England* (London, 1984); Chassagne, *La Manufacture de toiles imprimées*, p. 319.

[25] M. Sonnet, *L'Education des filles aux temps des Lumières* (Paris, 1987), pp. 251–61.

[26] *Costume, Coutume* (Paris, 1987), pp. 91–140.

this was the domain of the domestic economy, into which linen introduced luxury and cleanliness. For holidays and journeys, a mixture of fabrics and embroidery were preferred: this was the domain of the market economy and the peddlar, and it progressed more rapidly where communications were easier, contacts with the town more frequent and the rich more numerous. Fashion steadily infiltrated both highlands and lowlands. The revolution of appearances reached the peasantry, men and women alike.

## THE PRODUCTION OF CLOTHES IN PARIS

It is no easy task to study the economic and social processes which made Paris both the most famous centre of clothes manufacture in Europe and the place where the empire of distribution simultaneously shaped both a particular form of commercial capitalism and new aspects of the urban social personality.

The 'Mecca of Fashion' has no proper archives, and those which exist are difficult to use.[27] We are largely dependent on private archives such as notarial documents and bankruptcy papers, which are one-sided and hardly allow an overall picture. We cannot compare them with other sources accessible elsewhere but lacking for Paris, such as tax or census returns which would make it possible to estimate the size of the working population and its various elements. The picture proposed here accordingly has many limitations, which need to be signalled so as to encourage other researchers to follow, wherever possible, the paths opened up. For example, for none of the categories engaged in production or distribution do we have thorough studies to enable us to trace the economico-social circuit from raw material to finished product. Further, we are hardly able to answer fundamental economic questions regarding the division of labour in each branch, from textiles to garments, or the numbers employed or the processes which, between the seventeenth and the nineteenth centuries, transformed the organisation of labour and the size of the labour force, even the status of the people concerned. In Paris, as elsewhere, the professional language of the period is an obstacle to our knowledge and it is difficult to relate the statutes to the real world.

We have to make do with what we have, and perhaps let

---

[27] For what follows, I have greatly benefited from discussions with J.-C. Perrot.

ourselves be guided by the archives of the crafts and contemporary perceptions. I offer simply a preliminary sketch, which owes much to the traditional approach to the socio-professional study of the guilds and corporations. This is a shortcoming which is at present unavoidable, but which needs to be emphasised, since our discipline tries to solve intellectual problems as best it can. The problem here is to discover how the economic and social processes of an urban sector of the old economy contributed to the way people changed.

## PRODUCTION AND CONSUMPTION: THE ECONOMY OF THE BURLESQUES

One approach to the problem is through a literary and descriptive tradition, that of the burlesque or realist *Tableaux de Paris*, onto which were gradually grafted the formulas of the guide and the directory.[28] In the *Paris ridicule* and the *Paris burlesque*, in the *Foire Saint-Germain*, the *Tracas* and the *Cris de Paris*, we can trace the omnipresent itinerary of Parisian clothing. In a literary genre which demanded stock figures consistent with representations of the town,[29] the centrality of the clothes trade serves to evoke a new urbanity and a sociability triumphing in tandem. It contrasts with silence regarding the ordinary, everyday processes of manufacture and distribution.

Within Paris, we find three main focuses of interest: the arcades of the Palais, the cemetery of the Innocents and the street, domain of small traders; they evoke the thriving fashion trade stimulated by the mechanisms of court society, the busy traffic in second-hand clothes and the important role of door-to-door salesmen. The pre-eminence of an economy of distribution organised to meet the luxury requirements of the rich and the everyday needs of the poor is clearly visible by the mid eighteenth century. 'Listen to this merchant: Gentlemen, I've got beautiful Holland, lace, fine bands, fine collars, very fine stockings. Will you take this shirt? Look at these splendid goods! Come, sir, come to me, you'll get a bargain here, I tell

[28] G. Chabaud and J.-P. Monzani, 'Les Guides de Paris aux XVIIe et XVIIIe siècles, images de la ville', mémoire de maîtrise, Paris 1 (1979).

[29] V. Milliot, 'Les Représentations de la ville à travers la littérature de colportage, du milieu du XVIe siècle au milieu du XIXe siècle', mémoire de maîtrise, Paris 1 (1983).

you.'[30] For Berthod as for Colletet, the arcades and their fashion merchants (*marchandes de modes*) were emblematic of the way that people were transformed by the goods which a centralised commercial economy made universally available. 'The Fair was the natural habitat of the stylish', and the gallery of the Palais was, in effect, a permanent fair, replicating the animation and the shopping of the temporary and seasonal Saint-Germain market and Saint-Laurent fair,[31] crucial moments when the mechanisms of exchange and change reached a crescendo. It was not by chance that the theatre, its characters – such as Harlequin – and its costumes also contributed.

At the other end of the spectrum were the street traders.[32] Small merchants, they traversed the city, offering their wares, all the little items which helped care for clothes, enhanced the appearance and so modified manners; *masse tâche* for washing greasy caps, black stone for blacking shoes, Fuller's earth, boot soles, fine needles, feather brushes, old shoes, old clothes, spindles of holly wood, pious pictures, fashion pictures, linen bags and combs. It made for a picturesque street activity whose aesthetic possibilities endeared it to engravers, musicians, poets and draughtsmen; it was a permanent element in distribution from the end of the Middle Ages to the industrial era.[33] It was an aspect of the capital classically portrayed by Louis Sébastien Mercier and an important element in the urban personality of popular Paris.

Between the small street traders and the great merchants of the Palais, the burlesque texts reveal a connecting link in the form of the second-hand clothes trade of Les Halles or the Holy Innocents,[34] and the rue de la Tonnellerie, at the heart of the mercantile town. Whilst the arcades of the Palais can symbolise the economy of the court, the old-clothes trade of Les Halles evokes the commerce of everyday, which helped to topple the hierarchy of appearances and destroy the old inegalitarian conception of existence. As early as 1650, the second-hand clothes trade provided the middling bourgeoisie and the populace with the means to a new but fictitious

[30] Berthod, *La Ville de Paris en vers burlesques*, ed. P. L. Jacob (Paris, 1859), pp. 101–3.

[31] F. Colletet, 'Le Tracas de Paris ou la second partie de la Ville de Paris', ibid., pp. 195–200, 252–4.

[32] 'Les Cris de Paris', ibid., pp. 299–325.

[33] Roche, *Peuple de Paris*; Milliot, 'Les Représentations de la ville'.

[34] C. Lepetit, *La Chronique scandaleuse ou le Paris burlesque*, ed. P. L. Jacob (Paris, 1859), pp. 24–5; Berthod, *Ville de Paris*, pp. 141–50.

distinction. The testimony of Colletet, Scarron and sieur Berthod is biased by their moralising intent, their critical spirit and their unease in the presence of changing manners, but they nevertheless hit the nail on the head; redistribution consigned the social nuances to oblivion. The organisation of the market, the dazzling array of old clothes and the publicising skills of the *fripiers* put one more nail in the coffin of the transparency of urban appearances and contributed to their opacity. The second-hand clothes trade of Les Halles, emblem of the trade, was a thorn in the side of the moral observers, since it was an uncontrollable means to a metamorphosis of social personalities. Its activity was enlivened by the mechanisms of the theatre; it was a world of faking, where old became new, where an obvious fault was extolled as a selling point, in sum, where black was white: 'Is it not surprising? You'd have to be a clown, or a puppet-master, or else a seller of soap, or apprentice to a charlatan, or servant to a quack, to be eccentric enough to buy such rubbish.'[35] As the derisive metaphors accumulate, indicative of the contempt of cultivated people for the showy pleasures of the populace, sieur Berthod incidentally reveals how an economy functioned and how the distribution of activities and their representation were always connected.

## CATEGORIES IN THE CLOTHING TRADE: AN EVALUATION

Let us now attempt a less qualitative observation of the economic categories engaged in the production and trade in clothes. For 1720–40 and 1750–60, we have two guides to their ranking, if not to their real importance or the numbers employed. In the first volume of his *Dictionnaire universel du commerce*,[36] Savary des Bruslons listed the guilds and communities; he elsewhere gave the number of masters, so that we have an indirect means to a rough estimate of the numbers employed in the clothing industry, both in manufacturing and selling. M. de Jèze, in the various editions of his *Etat de la Ville de Paris considérée relativement au nécessaire, à l'utile, à l'agréable et à l'administration*,[37] gives, as well as comple-

[35] Berthod, *Ville de Paris*, p. 147.
[36] J. Savary des Bruslons, *Dictionnaire universel de commerce* (Paris, 1741), 3 vols.
[37] De Jèze, *Etat ou tableau de la Ville de Paris* (Paris, 1760); for the identifications, I have used A. Franklin, *Dictionnaire historique des arts et métiers et professions* (Paris 1906), 2 vols.

mentary information about the crafts, a formula for interpreting the extreme complexity of the Parisian clothing economy. The figures are, of course, only approximations, but they allow an illuminating comparison of sectors, if we allow for a change taking place during the revolutionary and imperial period. Other analyses would be necessary to reveal developments between the seventeenth and eighteenth centuries, probably a phase of equal importance.

As with any socio-economic study of a particular activity, the first problem is to decide on its boundaries. Industrial and economic logic would demand that we trace every stage of production and sale, from the raw materials to articles of clothing. Our sources do not allow such an overall analysis, but we can compare the scale of the textile and clothing sectors. The resulting picture has two principal failings. First, it overestimates the traditional corporate structures and underestimates the new forms of proto-industrial manufacture; Paris was very far from escaping the general trend, which it may well have encouraged. Second, it tells us little about the internal economic mechanisms, capitalist–producer relations, the ebb and flow of products, the differing fortunes of the various sub-branches within the whole. It is too static and too limited. It poses more questions than it answers.

Let us begin by risking three figures: for the number of crafts involved in the clothing trades, textiles included, at the end of the sixteenth century,[38] the end of the seventeenth (using the list of Savary) and the end of the eighteenth, when Turgot set in motion the final stage in the process of guild restructuring, and there was a return from short-lived freedom to control.

In 1586, Paris had more than 120 crafts, either incorporated or regulated but free as far as the police of the Châtelet were concerned. They were divided into five classes, from the 'best' to the 'small', passing through the 'mediocre' and intermediate categories. It is a hierarchy which reflects both the economic importance of their social roles and an evaluation of their prestige; it mixed function and distinction. Textiles and clothes accounted for forty-nine occupations, that is, just over a third.

Between 1690 and 1725,[39] after a period during which the

---

[38] Levasseur, *Histoire des classes ouvrières*, vol. II, p. 591; Franklin, *Dictionnaire historique*, vol. I, pp. 210–13.

[39] Savary, *Dictionnaire universel*, vol. I, pp. 130–6; Franklin, *Dictionnaire historique*, vol. I, pp. 291–2.

corporations were strengthened, Savary listed 126 guilds. There were fewer free crafts – the sector accounted for just under a third, with thirty-eight crafts. There were two reasons for this decline; first, the free crafts were no longer included; second, technical and economic developments had caused the disappearance of certain trades as a result of an amalgamation of tasks, independently of a concentration of enterprises not visible here. As in eighteenth-century Caen,[40] we see in the Paris of Louis XIV a trend towards concentration, which had begun earlier and was more rapid, and which partly reflected a different rationalisation of labour. The tailor alone did what a number of specialist groups – the makers of actons (*hoquetonniers*), doublets (*doubletiers*), tunics (*gipponiers*), pourpoints (*pourpointiers*) and breeches (*chaussetiers*), the ordinary tailors (*de robe*), the sewers (*couturiers*), the menders (*rafreschisseurs*) and even the *fripiers* – had each done separately in the fourteenth and even the sixteenth centuries. It might also reflect a concentration of labour in certain establishments, more economic than geographical, accompanied by a regional and national redeployment of the cloth and clothes manufacture of Paris.

The lace merchants are a case in point.[41] They were simply intermediaries between the rural small family producers and the Parisian creditors and clients who provided the raw materials or sold the lace produced in the Ile-de-France throughout France and Europe. This trade brought together wholesalers and retailers in the rue Saint-Denis, selling a very wide range of goods – linen, braid, ribbons, buttons and lingerie – and they might be merchant mercers, master button and trimmings makers, linen merchants, merchant ribbon-weavers, mistress linen-drapers. There were no guilds of lace merchants, but there were dynasties of specialists who worked with local lace-makers to develop and concentrate production. At the end of the day, sales depended on consumer choice. The example is useful to emphasise that as far as textiles and clothing are concerned, the Parisian economy cannot be understood without looking beyond the walls of the town.

Lastly, in 1776, after the period of freedom, the revived guilds

[40] J.-C. Perrot, *Caen au XVIIIe siècle, Genèse d'une ville moderne*, Paris, 1975, vol. I, pp. 246–326.
[41] E. de Buffévent, *L'Economie dentellière en région parisienne au XVIIe siècle* (Pontoise, 1984).

Table 23 *The clothing economy according to Jèze*

|  | Necessary things | Useful things | Nice things | Total |
|---|---|---|---|---|
| Food | 7 | — | 4 | 11 |
| Clothing | 16 | 8 | 7 | 31 |
| Housing, everyday items | 24 | 18 | 15 | 57 |
| Total | 47 | 26 | 26 | 99 |

consisted of fifty-four crafts.[42] Those with an affinity or similarity had been combined: for example, drapers and mercers, hosiers, furriers and hatters, glovers, purse-makers and girdlers, the tailors and second-hand clothes dealers (*fripiers*) who formed the fortieth class, the dressmakers and *découpeuses* (who made trimmings for gowns) the fifteenth class. Overall, the cloth and clothes trades accounted for about 10 per cent. The amalgamation of activities and enterprises had speeded up; it was stronger in textiles and anything to do with the manufacture of raw materials, from fabrics to buttons, than in the production and sale of clothes.

### THE CLOTHING ECONOMY FROM NECESSITIES TO LUXURIES

It is interesting to compare the figures above with those in the *Etat de Paris*. Jèze classed the guilds and communities of the *arts et métiers* into three categories those which were 'necessary to life', those which were 'useful' and those which produced 'nice things'. This approach presents us with a new view of the town, combining functionalism, utility and sociability. Table 23 summarises the figures for the different sectors of the economy according to these three new categories.

Certain omissions compared with the lists of Savary or the police lieutenant in 1776 can only be explained by a desire to simplify, since archaic or tiny communities have been ignored. The distribution between the necessary, the useful and the agreeable reveals an interesting scale of needs, a way of understanding the relationship between supply and demand in Paris. The producers of necessities were in a majority, further evidence of the importance of consump-

[42] Franklin, *Dictionnaire historique*, vol. I, pp. 292–5.

tion, hence of the impact of the total population; the importance of housing and anything concerning furnishings, building and objects in daily use is also incontrovertible evidence of a commercialisation of needs. Clothing, textiles included – which Jèze lumped together – accounted for a third, but was proportionately more important within the agreeable and the useful categories than within the necessary. We find here weavers, linen-drapers, tailors, button-makers, dressmakers, dyers with fast dyes (*de grand teint*), with 'small' dyes (*de petit teint*) and dyers of silk (three separate guilds which combined in 1776), curriers and tanners, shoemakers and soap-makers, hatters, fullers, cloth shearers, flax-dressers, wool carders and purse-makers. On the grounds of their necessity, Jèze grouped together the basic activities of the trade in and manufacture of clothes, the craftsmen working with various raw materials – principally broadcloths, fabrics and leathers – and a handful of basic occupations in the sector which were involved at various stages during the process of manufacture, or even sale or repair. We will return to tailors, dressmakers and linen-drapers. The shoe-makers, soap-makers and other guilds would equally repay study.

Among the producers and vendors of 'useful' and 'agreeable' things, Jèze lumped together the functional and those catering for the economy of luxury and frivolity. Wig-makers headed a list which included all the crafts working on the trimming and decoration of clothes and bodies: girdlers, embroiderers, pin-makers, the *découpeuses* privileged to cut out taffetas and satins and make seductive beauty-spots, fan-makers, feather-dressers and ribbon-weavers. The number of technical specialisms within the Parisian clothing industry was immense.

The hierarchy of this microcosm was partly economic and social, since the scale of activities, sums of money involved and the extent of the market determined the leaders in the money–merchandise–money chain, partly based on tradition and history, since the age and ethos of a guild gave it a power which was evident in the way it perceived its interests, offensively or defensively, with regard to other crafts. The conflicts reveal how things were changing, whether through secession – the fashion merchants, beneficiaries of the accelerating pace of the fashion revolution, split off from the mercers' guild, or amalgamation – the makers of brass wire buttons and copper buttons combined at the end of the seventeenth century with the makers of trimmings such as cords, laces and shoulder-knots, a union which was the consequence of the crucial shift from buttoning to lacing. Similarly, in 1723, the hosiers combined with the machine knitters of stockings, an alliance of manual and loom workers; the new guild was able to dominate the Parisian stocking market. Such changes are fundamental because they reveal the forms taken by technological innovation and the social initiative of the groups, all the more so since society both wanted to be and saw itself as stable.[43] In the domain of appearances, they located the frontiers where needs and changing tastes connected with commercialisation, causing significant shifts in production.

It is not without interest to note that Jèze remained faithful to the spirit of the old Parisian guild organisation by treating separately, though at the end of his study of the *Arts et Métiers*, the 'trade of the Six Companies',[44] which normally headed the list. This placing and the tone of his article reveal a change of attitude and perhaps emphasise the industrial dynamism of these old crafts. Opening with a eulogy of commercial culture, he recalled the need for young merchants to be educated and emphasised the motor role of trade with regard to the primary and secondary activities of Paris. In the clothing sector, four of the Six Companies played an entrepreneurial role in production and distribution on the scale of the town, the Ile-de-France or the kingdom: the drapers, the hosiers, the furriers and above all the mercers. The Parisian mercers were general merchants and controlled the manufacture of many different articles; they traded in more or less everything at every level, from wholesale to retail. We have noted their involvement in military supply and we will see them, together with the drapers, play an active role in the growth of clothes manufacture and consumption. In 1717, the Parisian merchant drapers handled 59,149 pieces of cloth for the supply of the capital.[45] We should not too readily assume that the purchasing power of Parisians enabled them to consume on average four times more cloth than the rest of the king's subjects, since some of it was destined for the provinces, the army or elsewhere in Europe.[46] But we can note

[43] Perrot, *Caen*, vol. I, pp. 331–6.
[44] De Jèze, *Etat ou tableau*, pp. 234–8.
[45] J. T. Markovitch, 'L'industrie lainière en France au début du XVIIIe siècle', *Revue d'histoire économique et sociale* (1968), pp. 550–70; also Paris, Geneva (1967), pp. 193–5 (analysis of a document in Arch. nat., F$^{12}$ 1562, 1717).
[46] Léon, in Braudel and Labrousse, *Histoire économique et sociale*, pp. 227–9.

both the key role of these merchants and the range of needs which had been commercialised: 24 per cent of broadcloths, 37 per cent of serges and 15 per cent of muslins accounted for three-quarters of what the capital received essentially from Rheims, Amiens, Beauvais, Sedan and Aumale, Picardy and Champagne accounting for 75 per cent of the suppliers. It seems clear that there was growth from the Regency to the Revolution.

This supposes a double process of technical and commercial rationalisation and concentration of manufacture, but Parisian drapers and mercers had perhaps been able to encourage this development, since they benefited from the steady and immediate profits of the urban market. Their diversity allowed the master mercers to adapt readily to economic change.[47] They became increasingly specialised. Six categories are generally assumed for the beginning of the seventeenth century, twenty for the beginning of the eighteenth.[48] The town's trade was undergoing a process of extreme division usually associated with industrial development after Adam Smith: eleven of these categories were involved in the production and sale of clothes. The many lawsuits between the mercers and rival or intermediate communities – tailors, fan-makers, furriers, perfumer-glovers, furbishers, stocking-makers, second-hand clothes dealers, skin-dressers, dyers, gold- and silver-drawers, ribbon-weavers – reveal their ascendancy and their prestige; there were some sixty of them between 1690 and 1775.

Masters of the arcades of the Palais since the seventeenth century, the mercers established themselves at the heart of Les Halles and followed the exodus of the luxury trades westwards; they settled in the rue Saint-Honoré, the rue Saint-Denis, the quartier Saint-Eustache and near the Palais-Royal, to which their lavishly decorated

---

[47] P. Vidal and L. Duru, *Histoire de la corporation des merciers parisiens* (Paris, 1911), pp. 91–3.

[48] Ibid., p. 92: at the end of the sixteenth century, the mercers were grouped into six classes: wholesale merchant mercers; merchant mercers of cloth of gold and silver and silk; merchant mercers of *ostade* and serge; mercer tapestry-makers; haberdashers (*menu mercerie*); mercer jewellers. In the eighteenth century, the community was divided into twenty classes: wholesale merchants; and merchants of cloth and stuffs of gold; gilt; woollen stuffs; jewelry; linens; lace; silk; skins; metals; tapestry; ironmongery; *objets d'art*; velvet bags; ribbons; paper; braziery; waxed cloths; haberdashery; lesser merchants and merchants of knick-knacks. To which should be added before 1770, the fashion merchants and the florist-decorators.

boutiques attracted crowds of shoppers. They exploited the new possibilities for publicity, from newspapers to the prospectus describing their specialities. Together with the drapers,[49] they kept the Parisian market supplied with fine cloth and rich, decorated fabrics as well as the coarser and more rustic broadcloths, the common linens and every kind of yarn. They were the masters in Paris of the trade in silks from Tours, even more from Lyons and to a lesser extent from Italy.[50] They were highly efficient intermediaries between consumption and production, since the clothiers fought over the business of the Parisian merchants; by this means, they relayed the caprices of court society to industry, which transmitted them to a larger body of consumers: in 1780, 100,000 pieces of silk arrived in Paris, three-quarters from Lyons, though some were destined for the provinces or abroad.

The correspondence of the mercer-barber who, between 1750 and 1792, owned one of the biggest shops in Paris, *A la Barbe d'or*, in the rue des Bourdonnais, faubourg Saint-Honoré, shows the variety of activities of the mercers and the social range of their customers. The mercer to some extent dictated their tastes, though he remained very dependent, since he was obliged to give lengthy credit to his wealthy clients.[51] In him, we see the ascendency of distribution over the Parisian clothing economy as a whole.

## THE MASTERS OF APPEARANCES AND THE CLOTHING WORKERS

It is impossible to establish at all accurately the numbers of people engaged in these activities. On the basis of the figures provided by Savary and checked by Franklin, we can first calculate the number of masters in relation to the total of 35,000 to 40,000 holders of masterships in Paris. If we separate out the manufacturing or trading masters engaged in the production and sale of raw materials – fabrics, linens and thread – or of the materials used in the

[49] There is no study of this community. See Savary, *Dictionnaire universel*, vol. II, p. 420. In the eighteenth century, their numbers fluctuated between 190 and 200.

[50] L. Guéneau, 'Les industries et le commerce de la soie et des soieries à Paris à la fin de l'Ancien Régime', *Revue d'histoire moderne et contemporaine* (1924), pp. 280–306, 423–43.

[51] M. Schoeser, 'Letters to Mr. Barber Parisian Silk Merchant, 1755–1797', M.A. Thesis, University of London, Courtauld Institute (1979); Ribeiro, *Dress in Eighteenth Century Europe*, pp. 49–52.

assembly and trimming of clothes – buttons, ribbons, thread, feathers, clasps and pins – we have mainly the cloth trades, though not exclusively, since leather, furs and dyeing were also included. Of course, these crafts worked not only for the clothing sector, but also for housing, transport and a host of other sectors. Overall, they represented fewer than 6,000 persons, on whom depended an unknown number of workers and apprentices. The ratio of wage-earners to employers varied according to the craft, its dynamism, its level of development, its geographical and technical concentration and its specialisation. If we apply the ratio calculated for Lyons, a town dominated by textiles,[52] we would have in Paris between 1.5 and 2 wage-earners per master, that is, nearly 10,000 journeymen and apprentices working in the preliminary stages of the clothing economy, perhaps 20 per cent of the town's masters and probably a higher proportion of workers.

Those directly engaged in the manufacture of clothes and appearances, including wig-makers and hairdressers, amount to some 12,000 masters, to whom should be added those in a handful of free crafts such as the laundresses, criers of old hats and florists, to produce a total of perhaps 15,000 men and women, that is, more than 40 per cent of masters. The number of workers was probably nearly 20,000 persons. Table 24 gives the figures by craft. For a true assessment of the importance of the sector, we need to compare the number of masters and wage-earners with the total working population. From start to finish, the number of craft masters engaged in one way or another in the clothing trade in Paris was of the order of 60 per cent; the figures for Lyons are similar, those for Caen lower.[53]

The calculation of the total number of workers is much less precise. With a minimum of between 20,000 and 25,000 wage-earners, the sector was much less significant within a working population swollen by large numbers of unspecialised workers, day-labourers and irregular and seasonal workers.[54] Here, the traditional crafts are overestimated, but the quite large gap between the proportion of masters engaged in manufacture and those

[52] Garden, *Lyon et les Lyonnais*, pp. 315–37.
[53] Ibid. p. 318: textiles and clothing together came to 71.4 per cent. For Caen, see Perrot, *Caen*, vol. I, pp. 264–9.
[54] The figure for Paris is probably closer to that for Caen than Lyons, but it is not certain that the decline of the sector was comparable between 1750 and 1789.

Table 24 *The number of masters in the clothing trade 1700–25*

| Sale and production of raw materials, semi-finished products and requisites | | Processing and sale of clothes and aids to their care | |
|---|---|---|---|
| Drapers | 190 | Embroiderers, chasuble-makers | 265 |
| Mercers | 2,167 | Girdlers | 43 |
| Furriers | 47 | Hatters | 319 |
| Hosiers | 540 | Shoemakers | 1,820 |
| Needle-makers | 20 | Dressmakers | 1,700 |
| Spinners in gold | 38 | Spurriers | 20 |
| Gold-drawers | 20 | Second-hand clothes dealers | 700 |
| Carders | 22 | Soap makers | 2,000 |
| Pin-makers | 200 | Linen-drapers and weavers | 659 |
| Master last-makers | 20 | Tailors | 1,882 |
| Fullers | 20 | Glover-perfumers | 250 |
| Linen- and flax-dressers | 245 | Barbers, wig-makers and | |
| Skinners | 90 | hairdressers | 2,600 |
| Merchants in cloth of gold and | | Washerwomen | 400 |
| silver | 390 | | |
| Feather-dressers | 24 | | |
| 'Great' and 'small' dyers | 269 | | |
| Linen-weavers | 70 | | |
| Trimmings- and button-makers | 530 | | |
| Ribbon-weavers | 735 | | |
| Total | 5,637 | Total | 12,658 |
| Grand total | 18,295 | | |

involved only in the making-up and sale of clothes and elegant extras is a pointer to the originality of Paris. The capital had a sufficient number of craftsmen and workers, male and female, to respond to the very high local demand, and also to supply a large-scale national and international export market. The logic of economic development was perhaps particularly compatible with the traditional guild structure in a branch which enjoyed two markets, that of the luxury consumption of the elites and that of the ordinary consumpton of the urban and rural populace.

A hierarchy of crafts according to size of labour force clearly has a different significance in the case of textiles than of clothing. In the case of textiles and raw materials, an average of 300 masters per craft already conceals a tendency to concentration which emerges when we remember that the 2,000 or so mercers included great merchants engaged in international trade and small traders selling trumpery objects from their shops. This company, which all observers agreed was richer than the other five members of the Six

Companies put together, typified the inevitable contrast marking the whole of the clothing sector, split between necessity and luxury. It was characteristic of wholesalers and retailers alike, and it is difficult to distinguish one from the other: 'Mercers, dealers in everything, makers of nothing', went the saying.

Nevertheless, of the twenty categories comprising the community, the ten first – wholesale merchants and merchants of broadcloth and cloth of gold, gilt, woollen stuffs, jewels, linen, lace, silks and skins – seem to have traded in everything necessary to the clothes manufacture which was the business of other crafts. Merchants not manufacturers, they exercised over production a role which was indirect but crucial for the economy of taste: they spread it to the furthest limits of the civilised world, and Parisian style was inseparable from the Enlightenment, from Saint Petersburg to Botany Bay.

THE PARISIAN MERCERS

The correspondence of M. Barbier shows how, at this economic level, the wholesaler was also a retailer.[55] He worked with his customers, discussing which fabric would be best for which garment, and kept a pattern book for those not entirely confident in his taste.[56] The clients chose the principal fabric, but the merchant suggested the material for the linings and trimmings. Thus for an aristocratic clientele, the manufacture, cut and decoration, that is, the skill and the flair for sensing what was in fashion, devolved on the cloth merchant rather than on the tailor or dressmaker, whose technical, social and economic status was lower. Some of the more important cloth merchants may well have employed local tailors to advise them on measures or cut out clothes for foreign clients.[57] The economic role of M. Barbier was to relate manufacturers and customers, directly or indirectly, through a network of suppliers and tailors. His correspondence shows that he bought from other merchants and that they might, on occasion, have recourse to him. The superiority of the merchant over the craftsman was a specific feature of the old clothing economy. The relationship between customer, cloth merchant and manufacturer was completely reversed

---

[55] Schoeser, 'Letters to Mr. Barber', pp. 10–15.
[56] Ribeiro, *Dress in Eighteenth Century Europe*, p. 49.
[57] Ibid., pp. 49–50.

in the nineteenth century, a change which probably had its origins in practices designed to cater for a mass market.

The success of the mercers was symbolised by the ambience and animation of their shops, places of resort for chic Parisians. On the eve of the Revolution, fashion favoured that of M. Granchez, the *Petit Dunkerque*, which, according to its publicity, was a 'shop for French and foreign goods with every novelty which the arts produce, sold at reasonable prices, wholesale or retail'.[58] Mercier has left us a typical description of it.[59]

> The *Petit Dunkerque* sparkles with every frivolous jewel that money can buy or folly covet ... The many drawers are packed with countless trifles, where the genie of frivolity has exhausted his shapes and contours. The price is ten times higher than the value of their material ... Our little lords take these small jewels on credit, and distribute them with a nonchalant air. In the first few days of the year, the place is crowded with shoppers; a guard is posted ... We must pay tribute to the master's taste. He inspires and directs the artists, he knows what will please. In making so many trinkets fashionable, he has caused to be made in the capital what previously had to be sought abroad. The jewelry trade has made great progress since he brought to the attention of the public elegant and varied models which had not been made for many a year ... Voltaire, on his last visit to Paris, took great pleasure in the rich shop of this curious house. He smiled on all the creations of luxury.

Mercier had grasped the role of the mercers in the economy of appearances: they were creators, intermediaries, magicians of the social signs, whose trade might encompass the whole world, as their coat of arms and motto proclaimed: *Te toto orbe sequenter* – we will follow you (that is, the sun, zodiacal sign of power and royal allegiance, shown surmounting three equipped vessels, in full sail) all over the world.

As in all the guilds, there were many intermediate situations between the wealthy, established, wholesale merchants and the small retail shopkeepers. The merchants who dealt in small items of mercery and the small mercers sold something of everything, and there were many master artisans who made and retailed the

---

[58] Franklin, *Dictionnaire historique*, vol. II, p. 566.
[59] Mercier, *Tableaux de Paris*, vol. VII, pp. 81–2.

traditional items of modern mercery: shoulder-knots and braces, clasps, needles and pins, thimbles, belts, buckles, buttons, garters, 'which you cannot get properly made unless you get them from Paris', according to Voltaire. Further research is needed to assess the extent of relations of dependence, the nature of the technical liaisons and the levels of success achieved among these artisans in the seventeenth and eighteenth centuries. What is important here is the articulation within one system of a large number of tasks ultimately inspired by the consumers of the capital and by the national, even international, market. The production and sale of the finished or semi-finished products and of the requisites probably occupied more workers and fewer employers than the manufacture and sale of linen clothing.

## DYEING IN PARIS

Before concluding our account of the Revolutionary period, for which the documentation is relatively abundant, let us examine the dyeing industry, which will give us one last insight into the professional and technical imbrication of the old guild system and the new economic attitudes, so revealing the links between structures and change, consumption and its economy.

The Parisian dyeing industry had long been regulated by the general instruction of 18 March 1671, which dealt with the dyeing of wools and woollens of every colour, and with the production of the chemicals and ingredients employed; it was re-issued and completed in the *Règlements concernant les manufactures et la teinture des étoffes*, published in 1723.[60] Dyeing was organised into three technical divisions and three distinct communities: the 'fast dyers' (*teinturiers du grand et du bon teint*), who alone had the right to dye broadcloths and woollens, of whom there were about ten at the end of the eighteenth century; the fifteen or so 'dyers of small dye' (*du petit teint*), who could dye only common fabrics or re-dye fabrics worked on by the fast dyers; the 'dyers of silk, wool and yarn', of whom there were about 240, who differed from the other groups in that they specialised in one fabric and were entitled to dye thread and cottons. One can imagine the complexity of the relations between these three companies and the dependence which

[60] Paris, 1691 and 1723; Savary, *Dictionnaire universel*, vol. II, pp. 425–6.

might develop between the three specialisms with their constant interconnections. The urban authorities strengthened their cohesion by subjecting them to a common policy to restrict the nuisance they caused, and by trying to localise them outside the town, in the faubourg Saint-Marcel or at Chaillot. In vain; the dyers remained masters of the river they polluted. In 1776, the controller-general regrouped them into the forty-second class of the new communities, bringing to an end a rivalry hallowed by tradition and differences of technical origin, and perhaps also facilitating the concentration of tasks by reason of different specialities.

It was these 250 master dyers – who probably employed between 500 and 1,000 journeymen – who supplied finished broadcloths and fabrics to the other communities within the clothing network. A detailed study would be necessary to reveal their contribution to the explosion of colour which characterised the eighteenth century. These busy artisans played a crucial role in the transformation of ways of seeing, and helped to transform the traditional symbolism of colours by greatly increasing the number of shades available and speeding up the changes associated with clothing fashions.

Only the masters *du grand teint* could employ the seventeen secondary colours of scarlet, from red scarlet to slate scarlet; they employed five shades of grey and of green, from grey-brown to beaver grey and from grass-green to sea-green; acquiring a thorough knowledge of a palette of colours, respect for which was an integral part of the guild order, was an important part of their apprenticeship. Their use of these colours prevented confusion with the dyers *du petit teint*, who were entitled to use other colours and other refinements; they produced shades such as 'bitch's belly', 'cinnamon', 'sad friend', 'wholemeal bread', 'musk', 'chestnut' and 'the little Minim'. They could produce cloth in eleven types of grey, ranging from grey-white to flax-grey, via water-grey, mouse-grey, wine-grey and bear-grey. Black was reserved to the fast dye masters, grey-black to the small dye masters. The other dyers used any colour according to their textile speciality. It was the skills of these technicians of colour that made possible the urban spectacle in all its ordinary and extraordinary hues. They responded to the requirements of a consumer market animated by court festivities and mourning, the demands of the mercers and the ingenuity of the dressmakers, in sum to the general conversion to clothes of a less uniform colour.

To supply the town with mourning was no small task, since the whole population was supposed to wear black on the death of kings, queens, princesses or members of the family; etiquette laid down strict rules regarding timing, types and materials. The mourning period for a father or mother was six months, the first three in wool, poplin or *ras de Saint-Maur*, with stockings and gloves of black silk and shoes and buckles of bronze; after three months, black silk was worn. On the death of a grandfather, mourning lasted four-and-a-half months, of a brother or sister three weeks, of a cousin eight days. One can imagine the impact on the clothes and dye trade in a town where several thousand respectable bourgeois and nobles died every year, and where the proximity of the court imposed respect for custom on all who sought distinction. The protests of the dyers and the manufacturers do not tally with the behaviour described by observers and which, according to Mercier,[61] extended to the humblest classes of society; they, for reasons of economy, readily accommodated to permanent mourning: 'These deaths suit everybody, since black clothes go very nicely with mud, bad weather, thrift and a reluctance to devote hours to one's toilet.' Tradition, a way of proclaiming the constant presence of death and a taste for black, sumptuous or ordinary, retreated before the advance of the luxury trades. Royal ordinances from 1716 encouraged this. The clothing trade in its own way reveals the imbrication of economic forces and major cultural changes. Black retreated, colour advanced.

## THE REVOLUTION AND THE CLOTHING ECONOMY

We know that the Revolution deeply affected the luxury trades, which suffered temporarily from emigration and the new patriotic habits. These economic difficulties have their redeeming feature for the historian in that they throw light on the conditions of production and the deep structures, so permitting a better understanding of the traditional organisation of the clothing economy. The *Statistique des ouvriers*, drawn up in 1807 when Paris had 580,600 inhabitants, retained three categories more or less analogous to those of Jèze: workers producing necessities, useful goods and luxuries, all classed by branches of activity.[62] This enables us to

---

[61] Mercier, *Tableaux de Paris*, vol. I, p. 246.
[62] Arch. nat., F 12502; G. Vauthier, 'Les ouvriers de Paris sous l'Empire', *Revue des études napoléoniennes* (1913), pp. 426–51.

Table 25 *Workers with* livrets *in cloth and clothing in 1807*

| Cloth production | | Clothes manufacture | |
|---|---|---|---|
| Spinners | 771 | Tailors | 3,700 |
| Weavers | 959 | Shoe and bootmakers | 7,474 |
| Challoners | 641 | Hatters | 1,912 |
| Dyers | 79 | Dressmakers | 12,000 |
| Printers on linen | 196 | Wig-makers | 2,460 |
| Gauze- and linen-weavers | 623 | Furriers | 47 |
| Ribbon-weavers | 222 | Perfumer-glovers | 420 |
| Hosiers | 1,603 | Embroiderers | 19 |
| | | Fashion merchants | 2,500 |
| | | Miscellaneous | 119 |
| Total | 5,094 | Total | 30,651 |

make an estimate of the labour force which we can, at the risk of simplifying, compare with the figures for licensed workers to get some idea of the relationship of dependence of wage-earners.

The figures in table 25 are based on the figures of the prefect of police. A term-by-term comparison with the figures for the *ancien régime* would require detailed adjustments which the exercise would hardly justify, and which the imprecision of the sources does not for the moment permit. The destructuring of the guild world appears less overall – a total of 44,000 licensed workers (*patentés*) as against 35,000 to 40,000 masters – than in detail, where the disappearance of the companies has meant that of many of the portmanteau categories; thus the wholesale mercers have to be sought amongst the merchants, certain merchant-clothiers among the manufacturers. Further, the prefect of police basically only counted those workers who carried a *livret*, which significantly reduces the figure for the total working population, denuded of its non-specialised members and probably many unregulated wage-earners. This under-registration explains the low figure for cloth – some 5,000 wage-earners – when, as we will see, there were nearly 20,000 in the Revolutionary period, and probably almost as many during the eighteenth century. The female working population is probably similarly underestimated, as is shown by the embarrassment of the inquisitor who refers 'from memory' to wage-earning women only in the crafts where they were particularly numerous.

Table 25 suggests, for a total wage-earning population of the order of 100,000 persons, nearly 36,000 working in the cloth and clothing trades, that is, a good third of the total. The corresponding number of licensed workers is of the order of 20 per cent. Overall, we have something of an underestimate of the level of clothing activity, and its importance at the dawn of the nineteenth century is confirmed.

Globally, cloth production was in decline. The same was true of the service functions and trade; no representative of this sector appears in the list of manufacturers who had taken out a loan in 1806, but they are numerous in the lists of bankruptcies: a hundred merchant mercers and as many drapers.[63] The Parisian clothing economy did not emerge unscathed from the Revolutionary crisis and suffered further during the economic difficulties experienced by the Empire around 1812. The figures produced by the prefect of police's statisticians give a useful order of magnitude for the branches of making-up and repair. They suggest that the trades involved in the production of necessities recovered more quickly under the impulse of urban, even military, demand; the same was true of some of the crafts producing luxury, 'useful' and 'agreeable' goods, in response to the consumer needs of a new Parisian elite. For the rest, especially for those who, during the *ancien régime*, had articulated the trade in luxury goods and in essentials – for example, in mercery, drapery, dyeing or ribbon-weaving – it was necessary to form different concentrations and undertake major conversions, transfers and reorganisations in order to respond to the difficulties and transformations of the structures of production.[64]

Our statistics emphasise the contrast between the skilled crafts which were expanding, especially if producing for export – such as bootmakers, glovers and hatters – and those which were stagnating, where the workers were close to penury and threatened by unemployment. These were the people open to political agitation and dispute. This politico-moralist viewpoint may have significantly biased the figures to the extent that it was necessary – Fouché was a specialist – to demonstrate the threat of sansculottism. Nevertheless, as far as the clothing economy in general is concerned, they

[63] J. Tulard, *Nouvelle Histoire de Paris. Le Consulat et l'Empire*, pp. 415–35 and appendices.
[64] L. Bergeron, *Banquiers, négociants et manufacturiers parisiens* (Paris, 1979).

reveal a world which was already in 1807 very different from what it had been in the eighteenth century. It was certainly more contrasted, more hierarchical and harsher, perhaps divided between manufacturers and employers for whom industry was all and workers who were veritable machines. Probably as many as 150,000 inhabitants, that is, a third of the population of Paris, were dependent on its dynamism or stagnation.

Some fifteen years earlier, between 1791 and 1792, the municipal authorities had counted part of the working population and entrepreneurs in order to estimate the sum necessary to cover the *assignats* corresponding to wages. Discovered by F. Braesch, and argued over ever since, these documents are interesting for two reasons:[65] they provide estimates by sector which are invaluable in the absence of other sources, despite the evident bias of the declarations; they provide information about the organisation of labour, the distribution of the labour force and its geographical concentration.[66] They give us a picture whose value is only relative but which allows reliable comparisons. In the case of textiles and clothing, we have something of an underestimate of a whole disorganised by the crisis: we have statements for only forty-two of the forty-eight sections; the occupational gaps are obvious: 64 wigmakers in 1791, compared with nearly 2,500 in 1807, fewer than 1,000 tailors, including employers and workers, compared with 3,700 workers in 1807, and an estimated 2,800 masters and 5,000 journeymen in 1780! For the categories concerned with requisites and repairing clothes alone, several thousand people are probably missing. Nevertheless, when we remember that the gaps are found more or less everywhere, the fact that the clothing trades comprised, with more than 20,000 out of a total of 75,000 persons listed, between 15 and 20 per cent, reveals the onset of the hard times still in evidence in 1807.

The figures for each section reveal the principal features of the

[65] F. Braesch, 'Essai de statistique de la population ouvrière de Paris vers 1791', *Révolution française* (1912), pp. 289–321; G. Rudé, 'La Population ouvrière parisienne, de 1789 à 1791', *Annales historiques de la Révolution française* (1954), pp. 15–33; I would like to thank A. Groppi, who is about to complete a major study of the 'Braesch papers', for very kindly letting me have the information about the textile sector in the *Correspondance relative aux échanges d'assignats.*

[66] A. Groppi, 'Le travail des femmes à Paris à l'époque de la Révolution française', *Bulletin d'histoire économique et social de la Révolution française*, 1979 (Paris, 1980), pp. 27–46.

Table 26 *Employers and workers in the clothing trades in 1791–2*

| Production and sale of raw materials, semi-finished products and requisites | | | Processing and sale – upkeep and clothes | | |
|---|---|---|---|---|---|
| | Masters | Workers | | Masters | Workers |
| Button- and trimmings-makers | 31 | 772 | Tailors | 96 | 781 |
| | | | Dressmakers | 9 | 57 |
| Hosiers, ribbon-weavers | 71 | 1,669 | Embroiderers | 34 | 1,115 |
| | | | Shoemakers | 75 | 899 |
| Drapers | 6 | 2,012 | Wig-makers | 11 | 53 |
| Mercers | 29 | 2,050 | Linen-drapers, fashion | 12 | 434 |
| Weavers, braid-makers | 73 | 1,447 | Perfumer-glovers | 10 | 253 |
| Linen-weavers | 19 | 324 | Furriers | 10 | 247 |
| Dyers | 12 | 89 | Florists | 20 | 263 |
| Miscellaneous | 31 | } 5,195 | Hatters | 68 | 1,157 |
| Gauze-makers | 25 | | Second-hand clothes dealers | 2 | 15 |
| | | | Miscellaneous | 15 | 197 |
| Total | 297 | 13,558 | Total | 362 | 5,471 |

Total number of employers: 659
Total number of workers: 19,029

geography of the Parisian clothing trades at the time of the Revolution. Whilst the textile workers were scattered, though mainly in the sections in the centre and suburbs, the entrepreneurs were mostly established at the heart of the old mercantile Paris, in the Mauconseil and Les Halles and Innocents and Poissonnière sections; we see, in sum, the triumph of the axis of the rues Saint-Denis, Saint-Antoine and Saint-Honoré. The clothing trades had two peculiarities: the luxury trades, such as the fashion merchants, mercers and glovers, were highly concentrated at the centre of these sections, though they were to be found more or less everywhere; the more common trades, the tailors, the shoemakers and the hatters, were rather more scattered.

Let us look at the list for the Mauconseil section (which was Ménétra's), traversed by the rue Saint-Denis. It had some sixty entrepreneurs; half were in the cloth trade – makers of broadcloths, fabrics, loom-knit stockings and buttons – and half in clothing – tailors, embroiderers and shoemakers; that is, three-quarters of the 1,866 workers in the section and 38 per cent of the employers. This is an example of the predominance of clothing in certain districts. It also reveals the geographical proximity of the establishments, with clothiers, small employers and small shopkeepers, factories, workshops and shops juxtaposed. In the Gravilliers section,[67] clothing and textiles retained this commercial and manufacturing primacy, with more than 50 per cent of both workers and enterprises; the latter included large workshops, like that of the clothier-hatter Boscary, and those making gauze or embroidery, *chez* Bontemps, Darcua and Tichelly, which existed side by side with small tailoring or wig-making workshops and mercers' shops.

In the faubourg Saint-Antoine, the Braesch papers are misleading, since they fail to record all the little workshops known from other sources.[68] Here, clothing and textiles were no longer predominant: fewer than 3,000 persons out of 16,000, but some of the labour force escape every count, in particular women. We see the co-existence of two industrial models; in clothing and adornment, the traditional artisanate, some fifteen enterprises, most of them with fewer than five workers; in cloth manufacture, a similar number of enterprises, but twice the number of workers (431) and an average of twenty-seven workers per employer. With the beginnings of the concentration of workers, the textile and clothing sector was more than others torn between the economic past and future, and between two functions: the small-scale trade and local provision of a population whose needs had increased, and the fashion trade and manufacture which would suffer in the crisis.

The faubourg Saint-Marcel presents a similar picture on the basis of both the Braesch papers and the *cartes de sûreté*.[69] Textiles, clothing and ornamentation employed 2,600 male wage-earners, that is 16 per cent of a total of nearly 15,000 persons; the figure would probably be slightly higher if female workers were included. These trades were not predominant; like the working-class sections of the faubourg Saint-Antoine, it was torn between two poles: the satisfaction of ordinary needs (through workshops and shops scattered all along the axes of circulation and trade, la Mouffe, the rue Saint-Victoire, the rue de Lourcine), and establish-

---

[67] A. Groppi, 'Sur la structure socio-professionelle de la section des Gravilliers', *Annales historique de la Révolution française* (1978), pp. 245–76, and table 4.

[68] R. Monnier, *Le Faubourg Saint-Antoine et les classes laborieuses sous la Révolution et l'Empire* (Paris, 1981).

[69] H. Burstin, *Le Faubourg Saint-Marcel à l'époque révolutionnaire* (Paris, 1983).

ments dedicated to the fashion trades, where petty production, division of labour and the beginnings of concentration and standardisation co-existed. The dispersed small workshops and home work combined with concentration into several large enterprises. In the populous sections of the faubourg Saint-Marcel, the gauze makers and hosiers worked in their own homes for a few clothiers, and as a result would be much affected by the crisis in the silk trades; the challoners, a terminological reconversion of the weavers of woollens and cottons, were more concentrated, with 140 wage-earners per employer. Here, the industrialists employed a labour force concentrated in workshops in Paris and the provinces; they adapted better to the crisis, producing for the army and the hospitals, buying up national property in which to establish new workshops and hiring many workers. It is clear that the masters and clothiers of a particular quarter always employed workers both inside and outside their quarter, imposing a unity on the whole town, which adapted to both the old organisation of labour (stronger in clothing than in textiles) and the new manufacture.

## WOMEN, PRODUCTION AND MAKING CLOTHES

A last, but by no means the least interesting, feature of the clothing economy is clearly revealed by the Revolutionary sources, that is the importance of female labour, a structural feature which was probably responsible for the success of the fashion industry in the eighteenth century. The Braesch papers give ample evidence of the presence of women in the textile and clothing sectors, either as workers or as mistresses of new or previously incorporated enterprises. There were some fifty among the clothing employers, some fifteen in textiles and requisites, and women made up at least a quarter of the workforce in the latter, 12 per cent in the former.

We can discern two basic features. First, certain crafts were predominantly female – dressmaking, the linen trades, fashion and lace – and these were fundamental to the clothing revolution, in which, as we know, women gave a lead. If we consider the textile and clothing economy within the context of a family activity, the productive and animating role of the capital's female shopkeepers and artisans was thus absolutely and cumulatively crucial. Second, discrimination, both in wages and in the way female labour was organised, constituted both the strength and the weakness of the

Parisian clothing crafts; strength, because they were able to draw on a reservoir of particularly flexible workers; weakness, because this increased dependence on a market which was constantly torn between the useful and necessary and the futile, even luxurious, that is, between an abundant consumption for all and the needs of a tiny few.

The Revolutionary crisis highlighted this state of affairs by increasing female unemployment in the luxury trades. This only confirmed an old tendency to regard these occupations as the privileged preserve of Parisian prostitutes.[70] We see here one of the specific effects of the clothing economy which meant lumping together the women whose labour assured its vitality and those whose disorder, proclaimed by their manners and appearance, and a particular type of consumption, was vigorously denounced. Textiles, ordinary clothes and fashion were driven by the same dynamism, that of the consumer revolution and universal mobility.

[70] M. Benabou, *La Prostitution et la police des moeurs au XVIIIe siècle* (Paris, 1986), pp. 274–314. Of the women arrested, 55% declared a trade: 91% were in textiles, clothing or decoration. If there were 40,000 prostitutes in Paris, this represents nearly 18,000 women who had at some stage worked in the clothing economy.

# 11. *From crafts to customers: tailors, dressmakers, linen-drapers and fashion merchants*

Le travail des modes est un art, un art chéri, triumphant.

Louis Sébastien Mercier

A diagrammatic model of the clothing economy between the reigns of Louis XIV and Louis XVI (table 27) reveals both the complexity of its technical and commercial organisation and the central role of certain occupations. Tailors, dressmakers, mistress linen-drapers and fashion merchants occupied a key position between the fragmented world of cloth manufacture and the consumers of clothes and linen; their activities also brought them into constant contact with the many suppliers of the Parisian industry. They were dependent on them for raw materials, for a wide range of requisites and even for secondary activities such as embroidery. The diagram suggests a great variety not only of technical relationships but also of manufacturing and commercial associations. To clothe from top to toe some 500,000 Parisians at the end of the seventeenth century, and some 800,000 on the eve of the Revolution, whilst simultaneously catering for a luxury market, was no small matter; it involved a whole sector of production in the search for wider markets and drew it into the spiral of a new economy fuelled by the commercialisation of fashion.

This was not a specifically Parisian phenomenon, but a historic development of the western economy. It supposes that we no longer automatically assume that the market responds to the supply of production. Interest has now shifted from measuring production and productivity to the study of social behaviour.[1] As Eric Jones has observed, from the point of view of economic analysis, there is no difference between induced income and induced tastes; in each case the demand curve rises when consumption increases.[2] Neverthe-

---

[1] McKendrick, Brewer and Plumb, *Birth of a Consumer Society*, pp. 34–99.
[2] E. L. Jones, 'The Fashion Manipulators, Consumer Tastes and British Industries, 1660–1800', in L. P. Cain and P. J. Uselding, eds., *Business Enterprise and Economic Change* (Ohio, 1973), pp. 198–226.

Table 27 *Organisation and relationships of the principal trade guilds in the Parisian clothing economy of the eighteenth century*

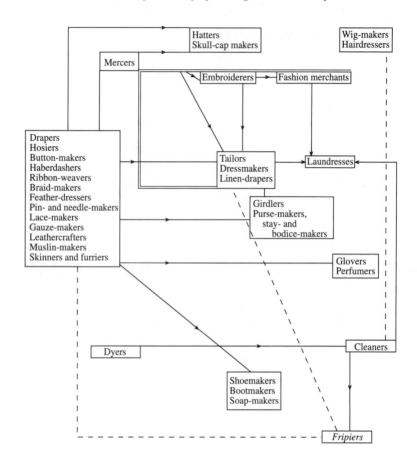

Key
→ Technical and commercial relationships
= Guild relationships
- - - Probable relationships

less, socially, culturally and historically, there is a considerable difference, which we need to understand if changes in taste affect the scale of production, the value of products and the forms they take. How, therefore, did demand affect the supply which it absorbed?

A study of the intermediaries in production, in particular those central figures in the clothing economy, the clothiers and the merchants, will help us to approach for Paris, as others have done for London, an understanding of a key element in our identity: how, in economic competition and struggles for distinction in the constitution of personalities, there emerge the obsolescence of things, the move from necessity to luxury and the accentuation of the simultaneous relativity of knowledge and objects. The crafts of the Parisian clothing industry played a crucial role, the measure of which is the creation of the habits which make a more or less inert society into a changing and freer one.

Three types of analysis intersect in our study: to understand the specific organisation of a professional group, and its originality in a guild world which was being transformed by the development of urban society and economy; to appreciate the social and cultural characteristics of a milieu one of whose principal characteristics was its reliance on the abundant female labour force of the capital; to gain a clearer picture of the practices within the crafts which contributed to the sociability and the economic revival produced by the city. The reader will here recognise the constant aim of this book to link the perspectives of social and cultural history and analysis of the imbrications of social images and reality.

Guild history is garrulous, and still surprisingly weak in conceptualisation after several decades during which the discipline of history has become more precise and demanding. Nevertheless, it has to be our starting-point, since it assembles the socio-economic facts of tradition and change, and the past which unknowingly shapes the future.

Four communities are here of special interest: the tailors, the dressmakers, the linen-drapers and the fashion merchants.[3] The first embodies the male monopoly in the sphere of clothing, a

---

[3] A Franklin, 'Les Magasins de nouveautés', in *Arts et métiers, modes, moeurs, usages des Parisiens, du XIIe au XVIIIe siècle*, 4 vols. (Paris, 1891–8), 1894 vol. and *Dictionnaire historique*; Lacombe, 'Les Tailleurs d'habits;' Badiou, 'Les Couturières parisiennes'; Roux Oriel, 'Maîtresses marchandes lingères'.

legacy from the old medieval and early modern past, which, when the trade guilds were organised, distributed the social roles: to men, the privilege of clothing both sexes; to women, the humbler tasks of sewing, housekeeping and home work. The other three guilds consisted primarily of autonomous women; they were typical of Parisian female labour within the urban pre-industrial world, integrated, yet of low status. In practice, female corporations existed in spite of the customary prohibition on the entry of women to crafts; the latter are frequently to be found associated with their husbands, even fully engaged in the direction of craft or manufacturing establishments; they were often widows. However, they were still second-class citizens; the number of mistresses in the corporations was always lower than that of masters and women's wages always lower than men's, though they made, nevertheless, a substantial contribution to the Parisian family economy. Lastly, the female guilds had a further characteristic: they had to impose themselves, through various vicissitudes, on the male guilds; their offensive and defensive actions in the quest for a professional, social and sexual identity led them to play a role of particular importance: they in part controlled the linen revolution of the seventeenth and eighteenth centuries; with a quickness less common among men, they were able to manipulate fashion and concern for appearances. They were prime movers in the transformation of manners.

1660: THE MONOPOLY OF THE PARISIAN TAILORS

By the seventeenth century, the Parisian tailors enjoyed a solid reputation. It rested on a tradition consolidated in the sixteenth century, when the royal government definitively united all the hitherto scattered crafts which specialised in making both men's and women's clothes. From 1588, they controlled for a century the manufacture of garments.

The community's statutes, elaborated and amended from the thirteenth to the seventeenth centuries, were important both in defining its function and encouraging its cohesion.[4] Guild law, on the familiar pattern of the legal systems of unequal societies, both

---

[4] R. de Lespinasse, *Métiers et corporations de la Ville de Paris*, 3 vols. (Paris, 1879–97), vol. III, pp. 180ff.

separated (it made the craft a distinct and privileged body) and united (it created an identity group inspired by the twin objectives of ensuring survival *vis-à-vis* the outside world and achieving a stronger basic internal homogeneity, in spite of divergences of interest). The dream of former jurists was universal transparency, guarantee of a stable order. The reality of guild law was largely the adaptation of the productive processes to economic and social change, hence the constant humdrum pettifogging which typified guild life.

The tailors did not escape these problems, but their statutes permanently enshrined three principles: they defined a hierarchy responsible for the enforcement of the regulations, and thus for the maintenance of a social egalitarianism despite competition; they prescribed the conditions for the exercise of the craft in accord with the customary social and cultural norms; they established the technical rules, hence the limits to innovation.[5] The Parisian tailors internalised, through all the acts of communal life, the sense of their social activity, as did all members of corporations, who can accordingly appear to economists as the principal obstacles to increased production. The development of a consumer economy inevitably provoked deceit and trickery on the part of those committed to change. This was a cleavage which traversed the whole guild world, from the humblest body, of which the glass-makers are a good example,[6] to the grand Six Companies, as we have observed in the case of the mercers.

The tailors had at their head four officers sworn for two years by all the masters, the former sworn masters and the bachelors.[7] Assisted by sixteen young masters, 'in cap and gown', they visited shops and workshops. Nominated in the presence of the king's procurator at the Châtelet, the sworn tailors incarnated the ideal of government by good fathers of families, an emanation of royal power, a mode of intellectual (they had to be able to read and write 'as much as necessary') and technical primacy, in sum, authority, though temporary and transitory. They supervised the craft, enforced its discipline and assured its cohesion, especially as

---

[5] Perrot, *Caen*, vol. I, pp. 246–8.

[6] Ménétra, *Journal de ma vie*.

[7] See also *Statuts et ordonnances des marchands, maîtres tailleurs d'habits, pourpointiers, chaussetiers de la ville, faubourgs et banlieu de Paris* (Paris, 1763); articles 20–4 of the statutes of 1660.

regards its conditions of exercise. They administered all the clothing crafts: doublet-makers, pourpoint-makers, dressmakers, breeches-makers, makers of padding, corsets and farthingales and tailors of suits.

This concentration into one body, under one moral, administrative and technical authority, corresponded, with the advent of Colbertism, before Colbert, around 1660, to the mercantilist dream of efficiency; it was intended to guarantee the progress of a high-quality industry. To this end, the statutes regulated the conditions of entry to a mastership:[8] ten masters admitted a year, not including the sons of masters; three years of apprenticeship and another three as journeyman; an obligatory masterpiece, for which experience might substitute in the case of boys born into the trade; the widows of masters could continue the business of their husband. Each master could employ a maximum of six journeymen,[9] widows one only; they must not have two shops, evidence both of the beginnings of concentration, compared with the usual regulated division of labour in the Parisian guild world, and of the desire to limit its inegalitarian consequences.

To demonstrate mastery of their trade, the tailors had to be able to sew, cut out and assemble without damage or error (the statutes provided for unlucky customers to be indemnified) in accord with the norms. The masters were then obliged to make 'suits and accoutrements, cloaks (*sayes*) and gendarmes' casaques' to order, which should fit and hang properly, be well trimmed and lined with good fabrics, under pain of confiscation of the garment and a fine of two *écus*[10] (ten days' wages around 1700). Two principles guided the definition of the tailors' activities: the aggregation of the tasks of making-up from fabrics, which was the basis of their monopoly; the definition of a frontier separating made-to-measure using new material and the making-up and alteration of used and old garments, reserved principally to the second-hand clothes dealers (*fripiers*). This was to define two types of consumption and two types of manufacture and sale of garments. At both ends of the process, the surveillance by the jurors and syndics of the two communities was intended to seek out infractions and illegal com-

[8]  Articles 5, 6, 26.
[9]  Articles 22, 11.
[10]  Article 7.

petition. The latter was facilitated by a whole shifting milieu which is difficult to define, consisting of clandestine workers, journeymen tailors from the provinces and not registered in Paris in defiance of the rules, home workers hidden in suburban attics and masters without masterships who had taken refuge in the privileged locales which escaped the guild. In all these marginal zones, shady practices flourished in spite of the detailed regulations, which, for example, forbade a master tailor from living in the same house as a master *fripier* 'given the abuses which happen everyday by acknowledging the clothes and merchandise made by the enterprise of the said old-clothes dealers'.[11]

Similarly, it was strictly forbidden to employ journeymen except in houses with shops or give work to other workers outside the workshops. The statutes here reveal the desire to control the labour force in a town which attracted large numbers of immigrants, and defend the monopoly of the tailors; they came down firmly against the dynamic trends of the consumer economy, which exploited to the full every opportunity offered by the demand for and ambiguities in the manufacture of the ordinary or luxury items which anyone could make.

We see clearly the limits of corporate effectiveness; the search for profit induced anti-community behaviour, encouraged by a rapidly expanding market. In the eighteenth century, the guild's attitude hardened. This enhanced the power of an oligarchy of minor notables who controlled elections and enjoyed the confidence of the police. It hastened the closure of the mastership to others than the sons of employers or those able to find 500 *livres*, the average cost of the letters of mastership, to which were added royal dues, the guild 'pins', the price of the reception banquet, the cost of a shop and its stock of requisites and materials and the capacity to indemnify potential creditors.[12] Marriage and birth were responsible for more tailoring dynasties than the savings of workers or the purchase of letters sold when the king needed money, which obliged the company to run up debts to repurchase them: forty-five by title of the decree of 1738, sixty in 1745, forty more in 1759. Torn between self-interest – selling letters to unqualified masters for 600

[11] Article 14.
[12] Though several factors suggest closure of the mastership, it needs to be confirmed by a study of admissions; see Arch. nat., Y 9334 (register of new masters).

or 700 *livres*, and the rigorous defence of its monopoly – reserving the market in new clothes to the elect if not to the experts, the community sought its role in a productive system which was changing under the pressure of demand.[13]

The list of lawsuits resulting from this tension between the end of the seventeenth century and the Revolution is long: 24 July 1670, defeat of the tailors by the mercers, who could in future sell linens, camisoles, dressing-gowns and waistcoats which had been made by tailors, marked by their jurors, then embellished by the mercers; 25 July 1676, victory of the tailors over the second-hand clothes dealers, who were forbidden once again to sell new clothes, but were permitted to 'have made and sell' all sorts of new clothes for the use of men, women and children 'to the value of eight *livres* the ell' (we see an early example of the two models of circulation and the two sectors of consumption which characterised the clothing economy); 13 March 1727, victory over the dressmakers, who could not work the whalebone necessary to stiffen bodices, a privilege of the tailors; 30 July 1737, a draw with the cappers, who could make and sell caps of broadcloth in competition with the tailors; 18 March 1747, status quo recognised *vis-à-vis* the purse-makers, namely that the tailors had the right to make purses of hair and skull-caps of cloth; 16 May 1740, crushing defeat of the farthingale-maker Mareschal, who claimed to make clothes, though not a tailor; 17 February 1785, renewed conflict with the second-hand clothes dealers in the trial between Quénain, champion of the tailors, and Frémont, challenger on behalf of the *fripiers*. In sum, each time, from the shelter of the Colbertian regulation, the tailors' guild confronted companies or individuals who were attacking the old ways. So many lawsuits reveal the challenge to its central position by the increase in demand and the call for new forms of manufacture and sale. Nevertheless, the relative opening-up of the company through matrimonial alliances and, above all, the adaptability of the individuals most able to take advantage of the new markets, reveal the capacity for guile and appropriation inherent in social practices.

[13] Lacombe, 'Les Tailleurs d'habits', pp. 45–52.

## DRESSMAKERS, LINEN-DRAPERS AND FASHION MERCHANTS

A first and decisive breach in the male monopoly was opened up in 1675, when the royal government recognised the juridical existence of the community of mistress dressmakers. Female dressmakers had, of course, existed before the guild and despite the tailors who, throughout the seventeenth century, waged guerilla war on their rivals by means of seizures, complaints and lawsuits. The women workers without status carried the day against their powerful adversaries, well established, including at court. In fact, the new community met two distinct needs.

First, it recognised the *de facto* existence of female competition in the clothes trade, specialisation in the making-up of clothes and the pressure of the demand from different clienteles. The text of the letters patent is clear on this point; it was hoped to impose order on a clothes trade which was disrupted by the legal shenanigans of the tailors and threatened by the anarchy of clandestine labour:[14]

Many women and girls, having shown us that they have always worked at dressmaking, to clothe young children and persons of their sex, and that this work was their only means to earn an honest living ... the custom has become so widespread among women and girls of all sorts and conditions of going to dressmakers for their skirts, dressing-gowns, bodices and other informal garments, that, notwithstanding the seizures carried out by the sworn tailors and the condemnations pronounced against the dressmakers, they did not cease to work as before; that this severity exposed them to great vexations, but did not stop their trade; so that their formation into a community would not be greatly prejudicial to that of the master tailors, since they have hitherto not worked any less, even though they were without status. Having also considered that it was convenient and appropriate to the decency and modesty of women and girls to allow them to be dressed by persons of their own sex when they judge this to be appropriate.[15]

[14] Arch. nat., H 2120; B. N., coll. Delamare, MS. fr 21799, ff. 122ff; Franklin, *Dictionnaire historique*, pp. 227–8; Badiou, 'Les Couturières parisiennes', pp. 5–8.

[15] Edit de création de maîtrise pour les couturières de la Ville de Paris (30 March 1675), in Lespinasse, *Métiers et corporations*, vol. II, and *Statuts, ordonnances et déclaration du Roi, confirmatives d'iceuyx, pour la communauté des couturières de la Ville, faubourgs et banlieu de Paris* (1707).

Citing disorder, inability to find a legal remedy, the threat to the respectability of women who risked being reduced to unemployment and the demand of a large number of female customers, the statutes of the dressmakers were accorded by the government, in line with the teachings of 'Delamarism' (the police commissioner who best epitomises the attitude of the authorities in labour affairs being Nicolas Delamare, author of the *Traité de Police*). There was also a financial advantage to the government; it made into a community a body which already existed *de facto* and was ready to accept the financial burdens of its new status. The importance of morality in the statutes – the conduct and morals of the female workers, the respectability and modesty of their customers, concerns which suggest new requirements in commercial relations between the sexes – reveals the transformation of manners in a Parisian society which had been subjected to three-quarters of a century of Counter-Reformation pressure.

In the realm of the economy and sociology of clothing, 1675 saw a fundamental shift in social practices. Religious imperatives and socio-political reasons combined to separate the spheres of operation of men and women;[16] they created a consistent female working identity, keeping to the contemporary image of woman as subordinate to man, though complementing him within the family economy, but also split between a limited recognition of their independence and the nascent ideal of woman as the mother of a family, the good housekeeper, the home worker.[17] This split was the second reason for the victory of the dressmakers in the eighteenth century.

Once established, they behaved like any other guild. The community was hierarchical; its sworn mistresses saw that the statutes were applied and supervised the recruitment of apprentices, the hiring and movement of workers and access to the mistress-ship, which cost some 200 *livres*.[18] The mistress dressmakers resisted as

[16] O. Hufton, 'Women in Revolution 1789–1796', *Past and Present*, 53 (1971), pp. 90–108; Groppi, 'Le Travail des femmes', pp. 39–40.

[17] A. Farge, *Le Miroir des femmes, textes de la Bibliothèque bleue* (Paris 1982) and *La Vie fragile*, pp. 123–93.

[18] The price of a dressmaker's mistress-ship varied between 1675 and 1789; it was fixed at 200 *livres* by the royal declaration of 28 April 1693, reached 248 *livres* in 1748, and was reduced by the king to 100 *livres* in 1776. Badiou, 'Les Couturières parisiennes', pp. 63–79.

best they could the interference of the state and repurchased the offices imposed, but accepted its financial control. The guild operated very much like any other Parisian corporation. It regulated the labour of clandestine workers and mistresses without status, by urging them to seek recognition or sew only for employers who were members of the community. The records of the court of the royal procurator at the Châtelet reveal these constant pettifogging and repetitive efforts; distraints, complaints, lawsuits and threats failed to put a stop to the activities of the clandestine workers. The guild of dressmakers condemned with equal vigour failings in internal good order,[19] such as non-payment of apprenticeship dues or membership fees, in fact all the usual issues which were a source of conflict within the guilds.

We should note two features which were to some extent original, and important for the functioning of the clothing system: first, the mistress dressmakers recruited widely. This reflected both the growing needs of the female population and the ready availability of cheap female labour; admissions to the mistress-ship over the century were on average between 100 and 150 a year, and 75 per cent of the new mistresses were former apprentices who had become workers, a situation which continued unchanged after the reforms of 1775.[20]

Second, the community was able greatly to extend its sphere of activities. The new statutes published in 1781 recognised their right to make dominoes for balls and dressing-gowns for men in competition with the master tailors and master second-hand clothes dealers.[21] The dressmakers' offensive had overcome the tailors' defences in the domain of elite consumption; they had won the right to make whalebone hoops before 1730. They were now arguing for greater specificity of genres, whereas before they had benefited from their being lumped together;[22] though not wholly unisex,

[19] Ibid., pp. 80–101.
[20] Arch. nat., Y 9323ff.; Badiou, 'Les Couturières parisiennes', pp. 9–21.
[21] Arch. nat., AD XI, 16, 64; Badiou, 'Les Couturières parisiennes', pp. 132–6.
[22] Like the tailors, the dressmakers could use whalebone for bodices, even gowns. Article one of the statutes of 1675, gave them 'the right to make and sell dressing gowns, skirt, bodices, mantuas, *hongrelines* (trimmed waistcoats), *justaucorps* (waistcoats for women which resembled the male pourpoint), camisoles and all other items of all sorts of fabrics for women and girls', with the exception of the full outer gown, which remained a monopoly of the tailors. The conflict over whalebone in the bodice and skirt showed the impossibility of assigning limits to

dominoes and dressing-gowns were to some extent interchangeable. Above all, the mistress dressmakers attacked the power of the mercers by nibbling away at the privileges of the fashion merchants. In 1781, they were officially entitled to handle trimmings, hitherto reserved to the modistes, testimony to the power acquired by access to a larger and more fashionable clientele. Article IX of the Edict of August 1776 implicitly recognised the dynamism of the corporation when it admitted the possibility of a dressmaker accumulating several mistress-ships, as long as she could take on the necessary financial burden, a clause which applied also to the modistes.[23] The members of the community of mistress dressmakers were key players in the female clothing revolution.

## THE PRODUCTION OF LINEN

The linen-drapers occupied an intermediate position.[24] Mistress and merchant *toilières*, *lingères* and *canevassières en fil*, they were entitled to make and sell 'all sorts of fabrics of flax and hemp, such as batiste, lawn, cambric and Holland, coarse and fine canvas, white and yellow sacking, old and new sheets, of white and yellow yarn, all either wholesale or retail, and lastly in general all sorts of linen items and articles made of linen such as shirts, drawers, bands, half-hose, socks and suchlike'.[25] In fact, they occupied with regard to linen the position held by tailors and dressmakers jointly with regard to outer garments, but their specialisation was far from confined to the 'second skin' of underwear; they also controlled household textiles, sheets, cloths and all household linen, not forgetting ecclesiastical linen. Their role as intermediaries was all the more important in that they were entitled to 'go and send to purchase all sorts of goods in the places where they are made and where they are traded in and sold'.

They were, in fact, female merchants who could boast of a commercial tradition many centuries old, dating back to the appearance of linen goods in medieval towns and villages in the thirteenth

---

the activities of either body. The dressmakers could also make clothes for little boys up to the age of eight, and the tailors for little girls.

[23] Arch. nat., AD XI, 16, 64; Badiou, 'Les Couturières parisiennes', pp. 133–4; *Encyclopédie méthodique*, vol. IX, p. 615.

[24] Franklin, 'Magasins de nouveautés', pp. 119–132.

[25] Savary, *Dictionnaire universel*, pp. 390–1.

and fourteenth centuries.[26] As the use of linen became general, there appeared, in addition to numerous urban and rural technical specialisations, male spindle and shuttle makers, flax merchants and hemp merchants, both male and female tow combers, hemp and linen spinsters, male canvas-makers and women linen merchants who bought, processed and resold the products of thousands of weavers. The linen merchants operated between manufacture and sale, between the provinces and Paris and between women and men; indeed, until the sixteenth century, the two were not distinguished. In 1595, the community included three trades, the female makers and vendors of linen cloth and of canvas and the female linen-drapers properly speaking. The reorganisation put the men with the mercers.[27]

This division and regrouping corresponded to two principal phenomena: first, to the specialisation of activities which tended to define the levels of exercise of the trade, largely though never completely reserving manufacture and the wholesale trade to the members of the third of the Six Companies (a hypothesis which is probable, but remains to be verified). The linen-drapers enjoyed a total monopoly of trade in the Paris linen market, where purchases were forbidden to the mercers, as well as within a radius of twenty leagues (some eighty kilometres) round Paris, from 1681. There was, in effect, both a geographical and an economic division of tasks. Second, the sixteenth- and seventeenth-century statutes strengthened control over the labour and morals of the linen-drapers. It was thus also part of the social moralisation of female labour, a sense of which is conveyed by the practice of well-off Parisians at this period of placing their daughters with linen-drapers to learn household tasks and needlework, along with a respectable appearance.

This phenomenon, which deserves further research, was reflected throughout Europe by the appearance of 'pattern books' to enable both professional and amateur women to produce pieces of knitting, sewing and lace: 400 editions from before 1620 have been counted.[28] This is a measure of a general trend towards the

[26] Piponnier, 'Linge de maison', pp. 239–49.
[27] B.N. MS. FFR, 21–796, p. 4; Lespinasse, *Métiers et corporations*, vol. III; Franklin, 'Magasins de nouveautés', pp. 79–80.
[28] A. Lotz, *Bibliographie der Modelbucher* (Leipzig, 1933); A. Mottola Molfino, 'Nobili sagge e virtuose donne', in *La Famiglia e la vita quotidiana in Europa dal 400 al 600* (Rome, 1986), pp. 277–93.

precision of female roles through 'ways of doing [things]' and specific tasks which were linked to a religious and moral training, and which would be incarnated in the industrious and devout woman. It lasted into the eighteenth century among educationalists, for the nobility at Saint-Cyr with Madame de Maintenon,[29] and for the working classes in the little schools.[30] The corporate language of the linen-drapers, like that of the dressmakers, contributed to the formation of the female identity.

Their statutes reveal similar aims and methods to those of other communities: to defend the quality of manufacture and the monopoly of sale, to impose a hierarchy on and control of the craft and its apprenticeship. This can be seen in the statutes of 1645, constantly reiterated up to the eighteenth century.[31] A more detailed study would no doubt reveal the same offensive and defensive preoccupations as existed in the other communities of the textile and clothing trades. The principal objective remained to keep the merchant mercers who traded in linen in their place, and hang on to the Parisian market for luxury and ordinary linen fabrics and items. This is certainly evident in the request (its result unknown) prepared by the sworn linen-drapers in 1738 to exclude the merchant mercers from the linen market, which the government wished to throw open to them;[32] the linen-drapers wanted to preserve their independence, their right to visit and their own superiority in relation to foreign merchants. Their community waged against the Six Companies a war analogous to that waged by the dressmakers against the merchant tailors. The guild flourished, and was re-established without difficulty in 1776. Its success shows clearly how market forces, the advantage of a plentiful labour force drawn from the female population of Paris and the revolution of a generalised consumption of linen-oriented production between the guild tradition and the new urban capitalism.

---

[29] Roche, 'Education et Société dans la France du XVIIIe siècle'.
[30] Sonnet, *L'Education des filles*, pp. 255–6; M.-A. Jégou, *Les Ursulines du faubourg Saint-Jacques à Paris, 1607–1662* (Paris, 1981).
[31] Franklin, 'Magasins de nouveautés', pp. 119–24; Roux Oriel, 'Maîtresses marchandes lingères', pp. 6–15.
[32] *Mémoires pour les gardes-jurées et anciennes de la communauté des marchandes lingères de la Ville et des faubourgs de Paris* (Paris, 1738); Roux Oriel, 'Maîtresses marchandes lingères', pp. 12–13.

The fashion merchant (*marchande des modes*), who completes our survey of the principal 'appearance trades', probably enjoyed a special position; she was central to the speeding up in clothing consumption; she has benefited from the activities of a few outstanding personalities who have been much studied by the traditional historiography of costume.[33] The modiste incarnated both the frivolous manners of the last days of the *ancien régime* and the new dynamism of a luxury economy based on the professional skills of its artisans and the more rapid change to manners and things. Between the female labour force which made the requisites and the largely, but not entirely, female clientele, the modiste was one more effective agent of changing habits.

This trade, about which we know little, appeared from within the midst of the merchant mercers at the end of the seventeenth century. It is further evidence of the diversification of this rich community, all the more significant in that it reveals the importance accorded by these masters of distribution to anything to do with the toilet. We should not forget that 'toilet' originally meant a little *toile*, or piece of linen; then the pieces of furniture designed to assist the process of preparing an elegant appearance, small chests or tables with their equipment, that is, a container; then the articles they contained – combs, brushes, flasks, trinkets; and only lastly the acts of bodily care. The toilet became a favoured theme of gallant painting. It will be observed that the chain of commercial operations of the mercers was such that it could culminate at any point in the lexical journey of the word 'toilet' from the seventeenth to the eighteenth centuries, from the sale of the pieces of furniture to that of the accessories and knick-knacks seen as essential aids to elegance. The 'modistes' – the word only appeared with its final meaning in nineteenth-century dictionaries – emerged at a point where the needs of court society in this sphere had become more demanding. They were not directly involved in the manufacture of articles, which continued to be made by other bodies of artisans such as the ribbon-weavers, trimmings-makers (*passementiers*), braiders, linen-drapers, dressmakers and tailors, but they embellished them, and it was this further process which developed into a veritable industry.

[33] Comte de Reiset, *Le Livre-journal de Madame Eloffe* (Paris, 1885), 2 vols.; Langlade, *Marchande de mode*.

## A 'MINOR ITEM OF TRADE': FINERY

The fashion merchants existed juridically and commercially in the shadow of the Parisian mercers. Little is known about their early growth in the first half of the eighteenth century. It was not until 1776 that the edict reorganising the guilds made them independent under the title of 'fashion merchants, feather-dressers and florists'. This change records a juridical and probably an economic separation, but perhaps also, and not the least important, a family and sexual rupture. If we are to believe Garsault, who published in 1769 his *L'Art du tailleur*, an invaluable technical survey of the clothing trades, the fashion merchants then belonged to 'no craft guild and worked only in the shadow of their husbands, who, to allow them this faculty, had to be of the mercers guild'.[34] By grouping together several female occupations within the fashion trade, the edict of 1776 reveals the increased independence of women who had attained a very high level of specialisation and qualification, and who directed a large area of manufacture and trade within the clothing sector. The great figures of the milieu before the Revolution, such as Mlle Bertin and Mme Eloffe, testify to this decisive advance.

> It is in itself a minor item of trade and profit ... cause of an unfortunate revolution in domestic manners. The excessive expenditure in which women and even men are accustomed to indulge for constantly changing ornaments and finery, does, by its effects and repercussions, incalculable harm.[35]

The rather moralistic tone of the writer in the *Encyclopédie méthodique* should not mislead; he had perceived something important: the rise of the Parisian luxury trade, and the importance of the consequences of the commercialisation of new needs inspired by the struggle for distinction.

The fashion merchants were at the heart of the clothing economy, and central to the system for the distribution of objects, tastes and manners. They mobilised the energies of thousands of artisans and suppliers to stock their shops with an infinite variety of items –

---

[34] F. A. Garsault, *L'Art du tailleur, contenant le tailleur d'habit d'homme; les culottes de peau; le tailleur de corps de femmes et d'enfants, et la marchande de modes* (Paris, 1769), pp. 54–6.

[35] *Manufactures*, vol. I, pp. 133–5 and *Jurisprudence*, vol. X, pp. 534–6; Franklin, 'Magasins de nouveautés', pp. 235–67.

taffetas, gauzes, feathers, ribbons, lace, braid, clasps, pendants, artificial flowers and laces. They drew on the labour of tailors, dressmakers, stay-makers, hosiers and innumerable workers. Their business was dependent on talent, that of 'making and trimming head-dresses, gowns, petticoats etc., that is, sewing and arranging according to the fashion of the day the embellishments which they and the ladies constantly concoct'.[36] The domain of the modistes was arranging and changing; custom and fancy, taste and caprice inspired their activities and hastened their pace. The art of the fashion merchants, on the eve of the Revolution, was the triumph of artifice.

### THE ACTORS AND THE ACTS OF SARTORIAL CHANGE

Our examination of the four principal communities entrusted with making clothes, linen and fashionable trimmings has brought out the constraints which weighed on the clothing economy. Production was in principle strictly regulated and methods of work, apprenticeship, pay and conditions of employment were clearly defined by statute up to the Revolution; the legislative initiatives of the Constituent Assembly hardly altered this proto-industrial scene.

Real change would come in the middle of the nineteenth century, with the appearance of factories turning out cheaper textiles, workshops producing ready-made clothes and large stores and a network of shops which everywhere replaced the old system of distribution. Till then, the guild economic structure, openly or not, was able to some degree to impose its language and its rules. By the eighteenth century, there were many signs, both on the margins of the corporations and at the heart of the system, that the world of producers was changing. Production and commercialisation stimulated each other in a more active society. We need therefore to adopt another approach in an attempt to see more clearly the cultural originality of the producers or, in other words, to establish how they resemble and how differ from the population of Paris in all its social diversity and in its capacity to receive innovations, whose acceleration might unite as well as divide.

[36] Garsault, *L'Art du tailleur*, p. 54.

## THE SIZE OF THE SECTORS IN THE CLOTHING TRADES

I have already emphasised the importance of knowing the numbers of people employed. My aim here is to establish the size of the principal corporations (only approximately, unfortunately, in the absence of figures), since this is the essential point of departure for the evaluation of a social and economic relationship. Let us distinguish those in possession of the corporate privilege and the various dependants they employed, wage-earners in the corporation or more or less clandestine workers of either sex. There were some 1,900 master tailors in 1720–50; according to the abbé Expilly, this represented one tailor for every 300–400 inhabitants (out of a total population he estimated at around 690,000 persons in 1768); the figure is comparable, all else being equal, to that of taverns, and sufficient to put a tailor's workshop within everyone's reach. Around 1780, Mercier counted 2,800 masters, still approximately one shop per 300 inhabitants; if we compare this figure to that of the male population, we find one workshop for every 150–200 potential customers. Tailors were obviously a prominent feature of the social landscape, able to cater for many social levels of clientele. Made-to-measure clothes were accessible to more people than they are today, for obvious economic reasons: labour was cheaper and it was always possible to negotiate the quality of the material, hence the price, and the value of the trimmings, as still happens today in workshops in Crete or Sicily. The increase in the number of master tailors was roughly in proportion to that of the population as a whole.

The development of the mistress dressmakers was similar. According to Savary, there were 1,700 dressmakers in 1725; the number was more or less the same in 1770, according to Expilly, that is, one for every 400 persons, or for every 200 women and girls. If we look at the registrations of new mistresses admitted to the guild between 1736 and 1770 (some thirty years equating to a generation), we find some 4,850 names, which suggests a considerable increase. The decennial annual average of receptions was 130 before 1760; it rose to 140 before 1770, 152 on the eve of the edicts of Turgot and 156 between 1776 and 1790. There must have been not far short of 4,000 incorporated workshops in 1789, probably one for just under every 200 women; a doubling of workshops had thus been necessary to maintain the ratio established fifty years earlier to the population of women and children. At the beginning of the century, the merchant linen-drapers were half as many with 659 mistresses; the number of receptions on the eve of the Revolution suggests an increase, but smaller than that for the *couseuses* and *découpeuses*; a good thousand, probably, with a different ratio to their clientele.

Tailors and dressmakers supplied made-to-measure clothes to a sizeable proportion of the population. They included a tiny number who sold to an elite clientele of Parisians and foreigners (both Robert Adam and Smollett had outfits made when they were in Paris).[37] The linen-drapers enjoyed the amazing monopoly of supplying all linen textiles. They were not so much clothiers as merchants who encouraged manufacture and supplied a huge public; this being the case, they must have employed a female labour force larger overall than that of the mistress dressmakers. In any case, two social levels of customer are apparent in the figures in the almanacs which selected the shops and workshops which were smarter or belonged to the elites of the trade: some fifty tailors, forty or so linen-drapers, a dozen modistes. Dressmakers were not always listed, an indication of their more dependent (they worked for the modistes) and inferior professional status. The fashion merchants constituted a small elite: some twenty in the *Almanach des arts et métiers* in 1774, roughly the same number in the *Almanach Dauphin* just before the Revolution. We do not at present know their total number.

## THE GEOGRAPHY OF SHOPS AND WORKSHOPS

Tailors, dressmakers and linen-drapers were scattered throughout the town, whereas the modistes were almost exclusively located in the centre. In both the faubourg Saint-Marcel and the faubourg Saint-Antoine, where there was a predominantly working-class clientele, shops making new clothes were thin on the ground, with only one tailor for every 1,000 inhabitants. A detailed study of the addresses provided by the *taxe des pauvres* of 1745 and the almanacs reveals a strong concentration in half-a-dozen parishes on the right bank, and a shift of the guild elites towards the rich districts to the west. Three-quarters of the tailors, mistress dressmakers and linen-drapers lived in the parishes of Saint-Eustache (35 per cent

---

[37] Ribeiro, *Dress in Eighteenth Century Europe*, p. 53.

of the master tailors), Saint-Germain-l'Auxerrois, Saint-Jacques-la-Boucherie, Saint-Merri and, alone on the left bank, Saint-Séverin. The notarial documentation – many hundreds of marriage deeds and inventories after death – confirms this topography, but emphasises the number of establishments in the parishes of Saint-Roch and Saint-Sulpice, or even beyond.

Overall, the sources distort. At all levels, they overestimate the successes and the personalities. They record fairly reliably the relationship to the Parisian economy and the presence at the centre of the city, in the high places of both traditional and new commerce, near to Les Halles, rue de la Ferronnerie, rue Saint-Denis and above all rue Saint-Honoré, rue de Richelieu and rue de la Monnaie, of tailors, linen-drapers and chic modistes such as Mlle Alexandre, Mme Dubois, Mlle Henriot, Mme Prévoteau and, of course, Mme Eloffe and Mlle Bertin.[38] They only partially reveal the small local establishments catering for a different clientele, humbler shops and more rough-and-ready local workshops. They tell us nothing about the spatial relationship between employers and employees.

The total number of employees is impossible to estimate with any certainty. In the case of the tailors, the guild statutes forbade the employment of more than six journeymen per shop; this maximum rate would give us a ceiling of 11,000 journeymen before 1750 and 17,000 in 1789, which seems rather too high. If we accept the abbé Expilly's ratio of 1.7 workers per master – which is also that of Mercier – we reach a ceiling of 3,200 wage-earners at the time of Louis XV, and probably 5,000 under Louis XVI. The number of women employed by dressmakers and linen-drapers was certainly higher; at the same rate, it would be 5,000 in the first half of the century and 9,000 in the second. This is a calculation useful only to emphasise the proximity of all these trades for the Parisian population as a whole.

Lastly, in all three corporations, diversity of status was the rule among the employees, further complicating the picture. To the journeymen and female workers recorded in the guild registers, we have to add the apprentices, the *alloués*, the day labourers, the clandestine workers and the home workers. Such diversity of situation was entirely typical of the dressmakers.[39] An apprentice

[38] Franklin, 'Magasins de nouveautés', pp. 261–2.
[39] Badiou, 'Les Couturières parisiennes', pp. 167–80.

entrusted by her family to a mistress dressmaker might remain with her for at least five years; she might then choose the route which led to a mistress-ship (of the 5,500 mistresses received between 1736 and 1790, 4,112 had made this choice), or she might equally well decide to continue with her employer but without trying to become a mistress, or she might work at home, without joining the corporation, paid by the day, by the year or by piece-work.[40] All these categories co-existed, even cohabited, within the same workshop. Apprentices, workers and *allouées* might live with their employers, or not. A quarter of the journeymen tailors mentioned in the notarial deeds lived with their master. There was thus both a degree of concentration in the centre of the town and some mobility between the quarters and the periphery, sign of the future.

The Braesch papers confirm these features for the early years of the Revolution, as do the judicial sources.[41] First, there existed a handful of workshops with a large number of employees: sixteen out of 100 establishments declared by tailors employed more than six workers, whilst the majority employed fewer than five journeymen. The average number of women employed by dressmakers was six, and the figure for mistress linen-drapers was hardly any higher. However, two linen enterprises employed between them some two hundred persons, men and women, who worked at home; one, in the Grenelle section, was run by a woman, Mme Lefuel. The dressmaking, clothes and linen crafts as a whole were dominated by small workshops and family labour at home, but the way the establishments were organised and the wage-earners distributed was already clearly moving towards integration through commerce, either for a costly and highly specialised product suited to workshops of modest size, or for a diversified and wider consumption based on larger units. In either case, both male and female workers

---

[40] The letters of *allouage* for 1751 show that nine out of ten were fed and lodged without wages; the yearly workers were paid between 60 and 200 *livres*, according to age, terms and capacity and mostly lodged with mistress dressmakers; see, for example, Arch. nat., Minut. central, C XII – 571 – May 1759, papers of Laurence Ducouroy and notes concerning the three workers, Henriette, Aimée and Lucas; Badiou, 'Les Couturières parisiennes', pp. 178–80. Paid by the day, a woman could earn between 10 and 14 *livres* a week.

[41] Groppi, 'Le Travail des femmes'; D. Godineau, 'Les Femmes des milieux populaires Parisiens pendant le Révolution française', thesis, Paris 1 (1986), Aix (1985).

shared a common dependence on a small number of employers, big merchant tailors, mercer linen-drapers, mistress linen-drapers and modistes.

A detailed cartography of their establishments would show that the clothing economy around 1791–2 still combined the beginnings of concentration in the centre, in the fashionable districts preferred by the principal merchant-clothiers, and a continued dispersal throughout the town, from Les Halles to the *faubourgs*. Scattered workshops were probably more important at the two ends of the clothing chain, that is, in the textile sector and the making of caps, broadcloth, silk and gauze, and among the decorative crafts, lace-making and embroidery, where the workers were employed by modistes, ribbon-weavers and braiders. Here, large merchants provided the raw materials for a largely female population of workers through the intermediary of masters or mistresses who put out the work.

Walbecq, a merchant-manufacturer of embroidery in the Gardes-Françaises section, declared in 1790 that he employed 200 women workers whom he 'directed' with six female entrepreneurs 'who had themselves many women workers and who did not work exclusively for him but for anyone who wished to give them work'.[42] Mlle Deshayes, of the Bonnet-Rouge section, is a good example of this; she took orders from several merchants and put out their work to ninety women, impoverished day labourers whom she paid herself and who worked at home. The fashion workers without shops belonged to a wage-earning aristocracy, well paid (450 *livres* a year in 1792), often highly qualified, and working at home or grouped in busy shops. They were often dependent on fashion merchants, clever florists and feather-dressers who could hold their own against their male rivals. In the feather trade, twenty-two clothiers employed between a dozen and twenty workers of both sexes; a third were women, and there were five women workers for every male. At the time of the Terror and the Maximum, this was the category most threatened by the crisis evident since 1790, following the emigration of part of the Parisian nobility and, perhaps even more, the temporary triumph of simplicity in dress.

The motion of the unfortunate Javotte lists the grievances of the

[42] Godineau, 'Les Femmes des milieux populaires', p. 212.

female work-force:[43] 'My mother makes accessories and anything to do with fashion; my sister can make lace and gowns, I can sew and embroider ... The embroiderers are going bankrupt, the fashion merchants are closing their shops, the dressmakers have sacked three-quarters of their workers ... We are dying of hunger.' This text, which amounts to a fierce indictment of the policy of the Constituents, and also a policy decided by men, succinctly summarises the lot of the poor women of Paris: unemployment, sex discrimination in employment and training, fear of prostitution as a last resort. Their situation reveals the structural difficulties in the clothing trades. Men to some extent escaped, thanks to the army and army supply. But the situation in the Year II was not new,[44] as the list of prostitutes arrested between 1765 and 1787 makes plain: dressmakers, linen workers, makers of trimmings for tailors and tailoresses, embroiderers, lace-makers, florists and feather-dressers predominate. These figures from life remind us of characters in fiction: the *Margot la ravaudeuse* of Fougeret de Montbron, the pretty little shop girls of easy virtue in Mercier and the compliant modistes of Rétif convey the impression of an only too easy journey from fashion to prostitution: 'the class of girls in the fashion business is very large and they enjoy in general a bad reputation'.[45]

At the heart of the population, the clothing trades demonstrate a general economic and cultural development. A plentiful labour force, for the most part women, had been set to work to satisfy an increased demand. Socially and professionally, they demonstrated weakness and strength, success and failure. In the eighteenth century, the group as a whole was able to play an original role as intermediaries and interpreters of change and tradition. First, they were a group firmly integrated into the merchant and craft society of Paris, that is, into the essential base of urban activity and culture; next, they formed a very hierarchical society, ranked by function, means and wealth; lastly, they were very homogeneous in the acts and behaviour affected by the material changes.

---

[43] *Motion de la pauvre Javotte, député des pauvres femmes, lesquelles composent le second ordre du royaume depuis l'abolition de ceux du clergé et de la noblesse.* Paris, 1970, B.N., Lb$^{19}$ 3489; Groppi, 'Le Travail des femmes', pp. 34–6.

[44] Benabou, *La Prostitution*, pp. 280–5.

[45] Rétif de La Bretonne, *Les Contemporaines*, quoted in Benabou, *La Prostitution*, p. 285.

## THE HIERARCHY AND THE HOMOGENEITY OF THE CLOTHING CRAFTS

Contracts of apprenticeship and marriage deeds reveal the extent of their integration into the city. Four-fifths of the apprentice tailors came from families with shops and workshops in Paris; three-quarters of them, young married men who mostly married Parisian girls, were themselves Parisians, half being sons of Parisian tailors, masters or sometimes journeymen. When the time came for them to establish themselves professionally, the young master tailors could count on the support of their families, fathers, uncles and cousins who were mostly from the same social background – the Parisian bourgeoisie, merchants, masters and lesser officials.[46] The social background and geographical provenance of the journeymen was quite different: 80 per cent were of provincial origin, and most came from humbler social levels. We see here the degree of their dependence and the closed nature of the guilds.

Among the dressmakers, the notarial documents reveal comparable similarities and differences. The 100 identifiable parents who apprenticed their daughters, mostly aged between fifteen and seventeen, were all Parisians, three-quarters of them living in the same parish as the mistress dressmakers; 38 per cent were masters or merchants in the textile sector, 40 per cent were traders and shopkeepers and bourgeois of Paris, whilst the rest came from the Parisian domestic servant or wage-earning class. The differences appeared when they married. The female workers were often immigrants, as were their husbands, and their parents were of modest status, journeymen, servants, even peasants (though the term is a vague one).[47] The mistress dressmakers lived in Paris and married Parisians: 18 per cent craftsmen in the clothing trades, 42 per cent bourgeois and traders.[48] The large number of domestic servants – 20 per cent – is not without interest, as evidence of a particular professional mode; it was a means of reaching a wide clientele and of initiating a useful circuit involving exchange, repair, sale and manufacture.

Socially, the guild of dressmakers was fairly open – 75 per cent

---

[46] Lacombe, 'Les Tailleurs d'habits', pp. 73–7.
[47] Badiou, 'Les Couturières parisiennes', pp. 20–32.
[48] Ibid. pp. 33–44.

of the mistresses received were not daughters of mistresses – but its recruits still came from a distinctive milieu – 80 per cent of the apprentices and young married women came from the middling bourgeoisie. The merchant linen-drapers were even less open;[49] four-fifths of their apprentices, who cost their parents an average of 400 *livres* a year (the price of a good boarding-school for girls), were the daughters of small bosses in textiles or clothing, from workshops and shops, with a larger number than elsewhere of lesser officials and bourgeois; apprenticeship to a linen-draper had retained some of its educational appeal for the respectable classes of the capital. When the apprentices married, it was to good craftsmen or solid tradesmen in the same mould as their parents. The husbands of the linen workers were less successful and established; three-quarters were wage-earners, of whom 40 per cent were recent arrivals in Paris. Their fathers and mothers, as also their witnesses, were socially more modest than those of their employers. Overall, we find a fairly original pattern, but one which is also characteristic of the matrimonial relations of the merchant and craft categories. At the same time, the divisions in the guilds were directly linked to the socio-professional structure of recruitment.

DIVERSITY OF WEALTH, HOMOGENEITY OF CULTURE

An analysis of levels of wealth reveals similar disparities. Three groups emerge: a peak of occupational success and manufacturing flair; the majority of masters and mistresses, well established but not distinguished; a minority of masters and a majority of workers and journeymen, men and women, married and unmarried, whose wealth or lack of it was on a par with that of the majority of those in the bottom ranks of guild society, who merged into the body of clandestine or semi-concealed workers. Fewer than 15 per cent of the master tailors married wives with dowries of more than 5,000 *livres*, the average being around 2,000 *livres*, whilst 20 per cent had less than 100 *livres*, which was the situation of 13 per cent of all masters and mistresses at time of marriage in 1750.[50] The journeymen married and settled with a capital less than half

[49] Roux Oriel, 'Maîtresses marchandes lingères', pp. 23–6.
[50] Lacombe, 'Les Tailleurs d'habits', pp. 74–5.

this size. The mistress dressmakers were not as well off as the young master tailors; only a third had dowries of more than 2,000 *livres*, three-quarters had less than 1,000 *livres*, though the average was 1,500 *livres*.[51] Their female employees did not have more than 900 *livres*, and four-fifths between 100 and 1,000 *livres*. The merchant linen-drapers were a little better off with nearly 8,000 *livres*.[52]

A similar hierarchy is revealed by inventories after death and bankruptcies. However, fewer than a hundred acts for the three occupations are not enough for a reliable estimate of the degrees of failure or success. On the eve of the Revolution, a Parisian master tailor died leaving on average 3,000 *livres*, whilst a journeyman left three times less. Barely 15 per cent of fortunes in this group exceeded 5,000 *livres*; though these were the big successes,[53] they were far less well off than the average shopkeeper or craftsman.[54] The majority of mistress dressmakers had 300 *écus*; the mistress linen-drapers were better off with twice as much.[55] But in both female guilds, the notarial inventories for wage-earners reveal fortunes of the order of 700 *livres*, which is below the average for the working classes calculated at the end of the eighteenth century. Neither the composition of their inheritances nor their conditions of life distinguished either group from the generality of the ordinary population or the shopkeeping and craft bourgeoisie of Paris.

However, we can detect some signs of features specific to the clothes trades. Tailors and dressmakers rarely had a shop or a workshop; their work was done on the premises of the master, where supplies and the tools of the trade were widely found. A few

---

[51] Badiou, 'Les Courturières parisiennes', pp. 33–5.

[52] Roux Oriel, 'Maîtresses marchandes lingères', pp. 42–3.

[53] Lacombe, 'Les Tailleurs d'habits', pp. 74–6.

[54] The *taxe des pauvres* of 1743 (B.N., MS. Joly de Fleury, 1277–1278–1279) lists 431 tailors, of whom 7 were taxed at more than 13 *sols*. 42 bankrupt master tailors produce 33 with less than 1,000 *livres*, 5 with 5,000–10,000 *livres* and 1 with more than 10,000 *livres*: Jacques Carsenac 'entrepreneur for clothes, Hôtel des Invalides', whose fortune was around 270,000 *livres*, an indication of the importance of army supply. Lacombe, 'Les Tailleurs d'habits', p. 55; also Arch. dép., Paris, D4 B6, 59-3755, 26 July 1776.

[55] Roux Oriel, 'Maîtresses marchandes lingères', pp. 31, 35–7 (Mlle Gruel, merchant linen-draper, had a shop in the rue de la Mégisserie, and was in association with a merchant mercer). Arch. nat., Minut. central, LXXXV, 28 January 1751. Out of ten failures, 7 had assets worth close to or more than 10,000 *livres* (for the debts alone), and liabilities were proportionately higher; the average active debt was 13,170 *livres*, that of liabilities was 21,561 *livres* (pp. 60–3).

rich masters with large clienteles had a house of their own, a shop and frontage on the rue Saint-Denis, rue Saint-Martin or rue Saint-Honoré. The mistress linen-drapers were established around the rue de Saint-Eustache and the richest of them had shops in the rue de la Ferronnerie. For a rent of 500 or 1,500 *livres*, they acquired a house of which they were the principal tenants, with workshops and storerooms on the ground floor. To rise in the hierarchy of distribution or play an active role in the diffusion of fashion, it was necessary for linen-drapers, dressmakers and tailors to engage in exhibition and display, in the publicity of appearances.

At the summit of the garment trades, the rich fashion merchants, like the mercers, had sumptuous and ornate shops where trade was presented as sociability, exchange as the practice of distinctive manners. Though idealised, the pictures in the *Encyclopédie* convey an impression of this transformation. Together with the text, they present a tranquil picture, a eulogy of the industry and of human labour and skills, where the very transparency of the iconography and its pedagogic intention erect a screen between reality and the reader.[56] These engravings also illustrate economic and social functions, and their ranking in the scale of production and distribution; the arts of fashion came at the top.

The workshop of the tailor of suits is a large and airy room, well lit, a big window open to the street reminding us of the importance of light and good lighting to the making of clothes, a visual skill, needing a good eye and a feel for relationships; the surroundings are worthy of the activity. The space is well peopled; we can distinguish the workers – five or six, in accord with the regulations – sitting cross-legged on a bench and wearing surtouts, another journeyman cuts from a pattern at a desk, the apprentice heats an iron at the fire, the master tailor measures a customer. The tailor is well dressed, almost indistinguishable from his client, a good advertisement for his trade. The engraver has not dramatised, but he has constructed a picture which is enlivened by a few carefully placed objects (scissors on the table, lengths of material, partly made suits hanging on the wall) and organised according to the characteristic acts of the trade: the master in the centre, a little behind him the first journeyman cutting, the four workmen busy in full daylight,

[56] J. Proust, 'L'image du peuple au travail dans les planches de l'*Encyclopédie*', in *Images du peuple au XVIIIe siècle* (Paris, 1973), pp. 65–85.

the apprentice to one side, on all fours, testing the warmth of an iron against his cheek, and at the back an unidentified person, client or supplier, surveying the scene, which presents all the principal stages in manufacture, that is, measuring, cutting, sewing, displaying. With no confusion or disorder, the scene illustrates harmony in labour and in relations with a rich, even aristocratic, clientele.[57] Compared with the illustrations of a workshop included in Garsault's *L'Art du tailleur*, the more beautiful and more effective representation of the *Encyclopédie* demonstrates the dignity of a strongly socialised practice: the stylish armchair is there less out of realism than to draw attention to the comfortable conversation inherent to the trade.

The shops of the merchant linen-drapers and modistes present a similar picture of harmony between surroundings and activities. In both cases, we see a feminine space, where shopkeepers, shop-girls and their female customers talk and do business. The shop is presented as if seen from the street; it is a scene of conspicuous calm, the walls covered with shelves laden with fabrics in the case of the linen-draper, pannelled and lined with drawers, a few trinkets on display, in the case of the modiste; in both, buyers and assistants are separated by a counter, on which lie fabrics and fashionable accessories. The linen-drapers are dressed more soberly than their customers, but the fashion merchants are good advertisements for their trade. Simpler in one case, richer in the other, the pictures illustrate the high quality of the luxury trades, their economic promotion, even their social dignity, in defiance of the physiocratic discourse so critical of urban consumption and inegalitarian logics, so unhappy at the changes which induced confusion between social ranks. We are given not so much a realistic representation of the trades as their presentation within a vision of a world transformed by commerce. The workshop of the tailor and the shops of the linen-draper and the modiste were the theatres of the clothing revolution.

Mercier perceived this, but exaggerated it into a picturesque confusion, as befitted his perspective as a moral observer who mixed exchange value and symbolic value as the town demanded. His commerce sexualised the exchange and he perhaps distorts the more conformist habitual reality of the real participants.

The idea of a seraglio springs to the mind of every foreigner who sees for the first time a fashion merchant's shop. There charming pretty faces alongside ugly figures, sitting in line at a counter; they trim the pompoms and baubles which change with the fashion; they are ogled by passers-by. The girls, needle in hand, are forever stealing glances at the street . . . As they pass in front of the shops, an abbé, a soldier and a young senator enter so as to examine the little beauties. The purchases are merely an excuse.[58]

Mercier restores some of its life to the commercial space and reintroduces the needlework which has disappeared from the engravings of the *Encyclopédie*, but, in so doing, he further emphasises the sociability of trade; the feminine space becomes a meeting place of the sexes. The commercial relationship is inseparable from a wider picture, where habits change as consumption increases and manners are transformed, with a profound effect on the material and cultural conduct of the actors, from top to bottom of the social scale.

### THE CLOTHES OF THE CLOTHES TRADES

The inventories show us how seriously the little linen-drapers, the dressmakers on the verge of poverty and the journeymen tailors took their clothes. They were only following the example set by their masters and mistresses, who often spent a sizeable proportion of their modest fortunes on dress: 200 *livres* in the case of one linen worker, 300 *livres* in the case of a dressmaker's assistant, but almost double, that is, 500 *livres*, in the case of a mistress linen-draper, whose jewels might be even more valuable; a mistress dressmaker might own gowns and linen worth between 800 and 1,000 *livres* and a more sober master tailor clothes worth 600 *livres*.[59] In sum, the actors were in the front rank of consumers, and the higher they rose in wealth and success, the more they demonstrated the crucial role played by appearances in the very functioning of the clothing economy.

Further evidence comes with the number of mirrors; everywhere on the increase among Parisians, it seems to rise even more rapidly among the clothing trades, where inventories suggest almost twice as many as among the poor and as many as, sometimes more than, domestic servants. The pictures in the *Encyclopédie* emphasise the contrast

[58] Mercier, *Tableaux de Paris*, vol. VI, pp. 7–8, vol. XI, p. 110.
[59] Roux Oriel, 'Maîtresses marchandes lingères', pp. 83–4; Badiou, 'Les Couturières parisiennes', pp. 229–30; Lacombe, 'Les Tailleurs d'habits', pp. 66–8.

between the coarse clothing of labourers and journeymen engaged in manual labour and the smarter clothes of the tailoring workers, neat and even stylish. Here, the clothes emphasise not so much the differences within one corporation as those between crafts and tasks.[60] Like the reality of the inventory, the logic of the iconographical representations has to be understood in the context of the powerful surge of social imitation and exchange sweeping through the town.

Let us look at three mistress dressmakers at the time of their marriage:[61] Quentine Souply had a wardrobe worth 1,400 *livres* in 1749, Jeanne Vante had clothes worth 768 *livres* in 1751 and those of Anne Marguerite Bécart, who married in 1728, were worth 600 *livres*. Quentine Souply, who contributed 4,000 *livres* in ready cash to the community of goods, is a good illustration of what had become an art of appearances for workers and their mistresses. She had seven gowns, as many as a noblewoman at that date, worth in all 500 *livres*; two were of sprigged satin, two of striped satin, one of silk (*ras de Saint-Maur*) and two of coarser cloth; she had six petticoats of silk, damask, satin and linen, worth a further 400 *livres*; she had five dozen shirts, for day or night-time wear, two casaquins, ten sets of lace or linen trimmings, six dozen mob-caps and nightcaps and four pairs of silk stockings. Linen workers, dressmakers, tailors and modistes had to dress themselves before they could dress others. In addition to this adaptation of appearances, hardly surprising, or at least not hard to understand, we find other cultural signs of the adaptability essential to this milieu.

READING AND WRITING: SIGNS OF ADAPTATION

Chiffons and silks were only part of a wider trend, which extended to books, engravings and pictures and the ability to read and

---

[60] Proust, 'L'image du peuple au travail', p. 81.

[61] Badiou, 'Les Courturières parisiennes', pp. 188–92; Arch. nat., Minut. central, XX, 491, 21 November 1728 (Anne Bécart); I. 439, 11 February 1749 (Quentine Souply); LI, 970, 12 May 1751 (Jeanne Vante); Y 15707, the victims of the accident on 30 May 1770 included three dressmakers. Reine Birard was wearing a gown of indienne with a pink background and a floral pattern, a petticoat of the same material, a little petticoat, a brown apron and white cotton stockings. She had a pair of pockets of dimity, in which were a white handkerchief with red stripes, a wooden box, a snuff-box, a flask with a gold stopper in a holder, a pair of scissors and a steel corkscrew, 5 *livres*, 1 *sol* and 6 *deniers*, a key and some papers. Her inventory came to less than 500 *livres*. Arch. nat., Minut. central, XCVIII, 587, May 1770.

count. One-third of the inventories of dressmakers, slightly fewer among the linen-drapers and a quarter of those of tailors mention books.[62] These modest libraries are evidence of the incontrovertible respectability of the clothing trades, which score high in the lists of Parisian readers.[63] Among the dressmakers and linen-drapers, devotional books predominated. The tailors shared this taste but also enjoyed some lighter reading of a more varied nature, a little history, some literature. It seems likely that what counted was more the act of reading itself, liberating in so many ways and opening up so many possibilities, than the content of the books, in which the notaries showed little interest. Like owning books, owning pictures was a symbol of openness to the world. If here, too, religious subjects predominated (at least 70 per cent of those recorded in a hundred acts), there was a steady increase in the number of domestic scenes, landscapes and moralising illustrations of fables, together with portraits, anonymous or family, historical or political. The originality here lies less in the themes, which are universal, than in the relatively high incidence: between 54 and 70 per cent of the inventories, depending on status, trade and wealth.

We may read in the range of interests indicated by their books and pictures not so much a transformation of religious feeling, in any case improbable, as further evidence of a gradual transformation of habits taking place generally and within the craft and its contacts, evidence of individual choice. A degree of prosperity and comfort, even if confined to a few, led to behaviour split between freedom and respectability. We must see this phenomenon in the context of a general increase in literacy.

The 'modest enlightenment' of basic reading, writing and arithmetic is very apparent in this milieu. The scores for the master tailors and mistress dressmakers and linen-drapers place them in the highest levels in a town where elementary school attendance had been increasing since the seventeenth century: all the men could sign their names, as could between 90 and 100 per cent of the women. The wage-earners of both sexes were slightly less educated, but four-fifths of the journeymen tailors and three-quarters of the dressmaking and linen workers were able to sign their names. The

---

[62] Roux Oriel, 'Maîtresses marchandes lingères', pp. 85–6; Badiou, 'Les Courturières parisiennes', pp. 41–7; Lacombe, Les Tailleurs d'habits', pp. 71–2.
[63] Roche, *Peuple de Paris*, pp. 207–9; M. Marion, *Les Bibliothèques privées, à Paris au milieu du XVIIIe siècle* (Paris, 1975).

clothing sector at all its levels enjoyed the benefits of the better education available in towns than in the countryside, in Paris than in other towns, and in the occupations caught up in the dynamism of luxury and the manufacture of consumption. It was a trade where, more than most, it was necessary to be able to keep accounts, compile registers, draw up bills, read orders and correspondence.

This gave rise to a professional culture, which is visible in documents concerning inheritance and bankruptcy records. The *Livre journal* of Mme Eloffe is only one example among others which demonstrates a basic economic skill learned more in the shop than at school. Kept up to date, lined or 'squared' according to the rhythms of payment, the books are evidence that the rudiments of the *Barême* and the *Parfait Négociant* had been learned. They show the extraordinary dependence on credit which dominated the luxury trades, an extreme example of a general feature of the urban economy, from the humble food trade to big business. It was necessary constantly to watch over transactions and keep track of the credit and debit of clients who were too often unassailable. Payment by instalments and bills receipted after acceptance are evidence of the adaptability of the clothing workers to the imperatives of the commercial economy, whether the luxury trade involving large sums or the everyday consumption based on innumerable small advances and mostly on trust without paperwork. The evidence is better for the top level, which is also that of wealth and success, if not always assured, than for the second level, which has left few traces but was that of the complex mechanisms of indebtedness and credit typical of the mass of the population.

Françoise Leclerc and Mme Eloffe are good examples of practices which we have already noted in connection with noble consumption. The former enjoyed a warrant as 'dressmaker to the queen' from 27 December 1725.[64] This was a super-privilege in a world of privilege, and good publicity in the quest for the aristocratic clientele her records reveal: the comtesse de Mailly, the marquise de La Fare, the princesse de Guémené and others. These noble ladies together owed the dressmaker a total of some 14,000 *livres*. Her business was not in difficulties, but the documents are good evidence of how credit was negotiated. Table 28 shows the scale of the advances and debts of three important clients.

Table 28 *A dressmaker's accounts*

| | Accounts opened | Bills drawn up | Received | | | Remaining |
| | | | 1 | 2 | 3 | |
| --- | --- | --- | --- | --- | --- | --- |
| Comtesse d'Auvrey | 1721 | February 1723 230 *livres* July 1724 265 *livres* | 1723 60 *livres* 1724 60 *livres* | 1723 28 *livres* | 1724 40 *livres* | 307 *livres* |
| Mme de Béthisy, princesse de Montauban | 1735 | September 1735 518 *livres* | 1737 192 livres | 1739 100 *livres* | | 226 *livres* |
| Comtesse de Maurepas | 1728 | September 1737 1,981 *livres* | 1737 467 *livres* | 1738 382 *livres* | 1739 666 *livres* | 466 *livres* |

Between four and five years after a job, two or three years after an invoice was sent, the dressmaker was still owed between a good third and a half of the sums due. For both small jobs – a gown mended, a petticoat altered, and large – the supply of more important garments or lengths of cloth, staggered payments and medium-term credit, one year, three years, sometimes as many as nine years, were the rule. A detailed study of the bankruptcy records and attachments of seals reveal to what extent this example was typical of the profession.

## THE TRIUMPH OF THE MODISTES

With Mme Eloffe, we come to the fashion merchants.[65] Succeeding her aunt, Mme Pompey, she sold all the little articles used for decorating and trimming persons and gowns, head-dresses, fichus, feathers, etc. Her *Livre journal* reveals that she coordinated the labours of many crafts on behalf of her noble clients. She supplied both articles and ideas, and no doubt did particularly well out of creating complete ensembles, witness the triumph of her *grand habits* for presentation at court. That of Mme de Villedeuil for 19 May 1787 cost 2,049 *livres*, equivalent to more than two thousand days' labour. Heading the list of her largely aristocratic clientele came the queen, Mme Victoire, Mme Adelaide and the comtesse d'Artois; between 1787 and 1793, these four were responsible for two-thirds of her turnover: 365,000 *livres*. Some hundred others made up the rest, each spending between two and 10,000 *livres*; below 2,000 *livres*, her loyal customers spent less than 100 *livres* per year. They were mostly from court circles, with a few bourgeois women, a few dressmakers and even a few domestic servants, exceptions in this 'Who's who' of frivolity. It is hardly surprising that her receipts fell dramatically in 1790; they came to 100,000 *livres* a year before the return of the court to Paris, no more than 16,000 after. The Revolution brought to an abrupt halt the rapid increase in luxury consumption associated with the festivities and ceremonies of Versailles.

Mme Eloffe was dependent on her rich clients; after 1789, she prepared her bills more quickly, instead of sending them quarterly or half-yearly, and she probably increased her over-the-counter sales. If the *Livre journal* accurately reflects the evolution of Paris fashions on

[65] De Reiset, *Livre-journal*.

the eve of 1789, it makes it possible to follow changing shapes, choices of fabrics and styles, use of colour and the embellishment which constituted the art of the modiste; it is also good evidence of the commercial relationship at the very highest level of clothing consumption. It shows the dependence on credit and the social link between manners and politics. After 1789, unable to sell court gowns, Mme Eloffe sold cockades by the gross to her aristocratic customers.

Her book also shows the high degree of specialisation then existing within the clothing system, in both decoration and selling.[66] Mme Eloffe had the quasi-privilege of supplying gowns and ornaments to royalty, whilst Mlle Bertin, 'minister of fashion', as she was called once she had won entrée to the queen, had that of caps and their elaborate trimming. A shrewd and skilful businesswoman, she reigned over Parisian head-wear for more than twenty years and her shop, the *Grand Mogol*, at the corner of the quai de Gesvres and the rue Saint-Honoré, was a social centre which combined luxury and elegance. Mlle Bertin concocted the 'extravagances' which were made famous not only by *Le Cabinet de modes* but by songs, caricatures and pamphlets. A syndic of the community in 1776, she lived like her sisters in credit on the state and noble rents. In 1785, the queen, who had that year spent 250,000 *livres* on her wardrobe, owed Mlle Bertin nearly 90,000 *livres* and Mme Eloffe more than 25,000 *livres*. The financial difficulties of the monarchy meant problems for the modistes and unemployment for their women workers. Mlle Bertin sent the queen a last bill for 40,000 *livres* three days before 10 August 1792, the day on which, during the sack of the Tuileries, the people of Paris shared out the royal wardrobe.

THE SUCCESS OF PARIS FASHIONS

The triumph of the fashion merchants reveals the economic and social importance of the clothing system, its strength lying in its intelligence and knowledge, its weakness its reliance on the consumption of court society. It is more difficult to identify the cultural consequences of this phenomenon, which provided work for Paris and stimulated trade throughout Europe. It seems to me that the very presence in Paris of these striking shops, the animation and brilliance they conferred on the humdrum face of the city and

[66] Langlade, *Marchande de mode*.

the attraction of their customers were the beginnings of a basic education. This was continued in the processes of trade and manufacture, which the guild structure restricted but did not entirely inhibit. The producers were themselves part of it and acted, within the population of Paris, as models, to be imitated both in general and in particular; the shop and the workshop, the conviviality of work and family also contributed.

The forces for individualism which disturbed the end of the *ancien régime* accentuated the transformation of manners since, though dreaming of wealth and the end of restrictions, they did not abandon the ideal of the unequal and hierarchical society.[67] Clothing was therefore both an object of social reproduction and a challenge to it. The interchanges, sometimes by obvious but more often by indirect channels, between the two models of production, selling and consumption, between a limited and distinctive diffusion among the privileged and mass distribution among the people, between clothing workers and clothing consumers, were the stuff of this major change; it was perhaps only possible because the art, that is, the ability which consisted of the perspicacity and technical imagination of the workers, had reached its apogee.

French dress had attained a point of equilibrium in form and perfect harmony between elegance of cut and variety of decoration;[68] this explains its pre-eminence throughout Europe and its diffusion from elites to people and from Paris to the provinces. Between the reign of Louis XIV and the Revolution, the formal stability of costume was connected with the resistance of social structures, and the socio-cultural forces which transformed the latter also modified the former. Under the aegis of the Academy of Sciences, the Parisian master tailor, Garsault, erected a triple monument to the glory of the clothing revolution and the triumph of appearances, and revealed its profound mechanisms.

In fewer than ten years, in his *L'Art du perruquier* (1767), *L'Art du tailleur* (1769) and *L'Art de la lingère* (1771), Garsault demonstrated the essential link which harmonised outer and inner clothes, look and form, from top to toe. He offered norms, patterns, practical descriptions, hairstyles and examples of correct dress. He throws light on the evolution of behaviour, since his code made it

[67] Farge, *La Vie fragile*, pp. 151–2.
[68] Y.-E. Broutin, in *Costume, Coutume*, pp. 75–84.

possible to combine stability and adaptability, formal immobility and ease of appropriation, individual, social or even geographical. His costume contained in itself its educative power and its social eloquence: 'The tailor who is able to make with precision, grace and economy the complete French, one might say European, suit, that is to say the coat, waistcoat and breeches, since they are the most complicated, will have little difficulty in making any other type of garment.'[69] The skills of the tailor, the dressmaker and the fashion merchant,[70] in accord with basic principles, made it possible for everyone, men, women and children, to dress correctly and in accord with circumstances, whether for everyday life or for presentation at court. The solidity of the basic structure of dress allowed its makers to add, without major modifications, fashionable details and displays of wealth. Both ornamentation and quality of fabric served to distinguish status and condition, as well as sustaining, through the deployment of embroidery and colour, the complex language of clothing, its transforming power and its incitement to imitate.

Garsault also perceived how the power of the social signs diffused by dress was rooted in necessity and how this permitted propriety and luxury: 'It is the linen-draper who clothes man from the moment of his birth, throughout his life, and even after; it is she who covers tables, beds and altars.'[71] *L'Art de la lingère* reveals what had made possible the generalised invention of linen: the articulation of its consumption round the major events of life, since they demanded the exercise of artistic skills: marriage, which brought together in the trousseau everything needed to set up house (Garsault specified in detail the contents of a model trousseau);[72] birth, the natural consequence of marriage ('now that the bride is pregnant . . . it is time to prepare the layette').[73]

With ecclesiastical linen and shrouds, the products of the linen-draper accompanied man through his every stage. Tailors, dressmakers, merchant linen-drapers and fashion merchants manufactured the spectacle of life itself. Their skills emphasised all the conventions and all the contradictions; they generalised the instability and confusion of the social signs in a world of continuity, even of immobility.

[69] Garsault, *L'Art du tailleur*, p. 7.
[70] Ibid., pp. 54–7.
[71] Garsault, *L'Art de la lingère*, pp. 1–3.
[72] Ibid., pp. 10–11.
[73] Ibid., pp. 29–30.

# 12. *From theft to resale: another aspect of the clothes trade*

Nous avons le plaisir de faire le raccourci d'un inventaire de
cinq cent mille guenillons de vieux morceaux de cotillons . . .
De toutes sortes de couleurs qui sont le butin des voleurs Et
de tous les tireurs de laine qui vont vers la Samaritaine.
                                    Berthod, *Le Paris burlesque*

To begin by suggesting a connection between theft and the second-
hand clothes trade might appear to be to conform to a literary
image and to swallow a police stereotype. There was a Parisian
tradition of policing clothing which emerged and grew along with
the early modern capital, and this attitude, visible in both the daily
activities of the commissioners of the *quartiers* and in the more
juridical treatises of Nicolas Delamare or Nicholas Toussaint des
Essarts, coincides exactly with a literary vein. This, from the
burlesque authors of the baroque age to the moral observers of
pre-Revolutionary times, repeats the same clichés at the expense of
those who bought and sold old clothes. It was a trade which served
to identify the populace and the base instincts of the lower classes.
It appeared in every description of the city and served as a symbol
of its corruption.

For the historian of appearances, the old-clothes trade offers an
opportunity to observe the social imagination in action and study
the connection, assumed and debated by Parisians of the *ancien
régime*, between changing manners, the greater complexity of social
relations, allegedly or in reality less transparent, and the role of the
actors in the sartorial theatre, vendors and consumers. The *Inventaire de la fripperie* (*sic*) drawn up by sieur Berthod for his
'friends from the country' around 1650,[1] described once and for all
the theatrical, even crooked, side of this trade: it created illusions.

---

[1] Berthod, *La Ville de Paris*, pp. 141–50.

Burlesque description saw the many garments made accessible by their low price – mantles, pourpoints, hats, caps, servants' liveries, coats, old fur-lined gowns, collars, camisoles, 'Spanish' pantaloons, greatcoats, petticoats and underskirts, rags and tatters – as 'the epitome of deception'. It was not by chance that the poet saw in the second-hand clothes trade the same moral and social dangers that contemporary theologians attributed to fashion. With others, among them Claude Petit,[2] Scarron and Furetière, he established the enduring myth of the old-clothes man as thief and cheat, but almost obligatory intermediary between the sartorial culture of the rich and that of the poor. The social evil of resale was a necessity: clothes made the man and man made the clothes, what then was the man who wore the clothes of another?

From the seventeenth to the eighteenth centuries, the image of a fraudulent metamorphosis persisted, despite the fact that the *fripiers* formed an honourable community and that the *revendeurs* and *revendeuses* were closely supervised by the Parisian police. Their utility could not be denied, since without them, in the words of Nicolas des Essarts, 'countless poor citizens would be obliged to go without necessities', but the police should 'watch out for the frauds to which this type of clandestine trade lends itself, and it will be observed that they are very careful to prevent these merchant *fripiers* from encouraging theft by purchasing, at rock-bottom prices, articles offered to them by unknown persons'.[3] In sum, the trade had a bad press, for economist merchants such as Savary des Bruslons ('they [the *fripiers*] sell dear to the public what they have bought cheap from the same public')[4] and the encyclopedists ('lost or stolen items are frequently found in their possession, even though the police and the courts treat them with great severity').[5] So we are able to compare ordinary reality and traditional image, whilst at the same time observing how the circuits of clothing

---

[2] Petit (*La Chronique scandaleuse*, pp. 24–5) emphasises the Jewish character of the second-hand clothes trade. In the seventeenth century the *fripiers* were assumed to be Jews, but it is impossible to know if this was really the case; in the eighteenth century, some Jews specialised in *friperie*, but they could not belong to the community.

[3] Nicolas Toussaint des Essarts, *Dictionnaire universel de police*, 7 vols. (Paris, 1786–90), article 'Fripier', vol. III, p. 181.

[4] Savary, *Dictionnaire universel*, vol. II, p. 1396.

[5] *Encyclopédie ou Dictionnaire raisonné des sciences, des arts et des métiers* (Paris, from 1751), articles 'Fripiers' and 'Crieuses des vieux chapeaux'.

distribution and manufacture functioned within Paris. Who bought from whom, and what? Who resold to whom, and what?

However, we should beware of models which are too neat: the shop and stability, honesty and a good class of customer, in the case of the tailor, the dressmaker, the fashion merchant and the linen-draper; the street stall and itineracy, dishonesty and a lower-class clientele, in the case of the *fripier*, the *revendeuse*, the crier of old hats and the *marchande à la toilette*. The two types of trade and consumption overlapped in space and in social activity. At all levels, they were occasions for action and reproduction. Their more elitist or more popular character simply corresponded to the manner in which they encouraged people to change their habits. To study them is to learn more about the changing attitudes and cultural ferment promoted by crafts which operated in a social no-man's land, and whose rise owed more to necessity than to utility or pleasure.

We need to trace the connections between the world of illegality and marginality, of thieves and receivers of clothes, and the world of a disputed and supervised legality, that of the *fripiers* and the *revendeurs*. Their customers frequented one or the other according to means and need; both vendors and purchasers, they were, in fact, the public referred to by Savary. The frontier they crossed varied within the Parisian landscape, that of the reality of sartorial behaviour like that of the mental images which gave them their identity, in line with changes to the relationship of men to things.

## FROM THE HISTORY OF CRIME TO THE HISTORY OF CLOTHES

A history of stealing clothes might at first appear a strange conception, but it can be justified on a number of grounds. It is part of the history of Parisian crime, which throws light on several issues of interest to us; for example, it helps to explain how a sector of the Parisian population which was economically fragile and lived precariously could both survive and participate in the general transformation of sartorial habits.[6] Second, the theft of linen and

---

[6] A. Abiatecci *et al.*, *Crimes et criminalité en France, XVII–XVIIIe siècles*, ed. F. Billacois (Paris, 1971); Benabou, *La Prostitution*, especially the first part; A. Farge, *Le Vol d'aliment à Paris au XVIIIe siècle* (Paris, 1974), also *La Vie fragile*, chapter 2 of part 2.

clothing was sufficiently important within contemporary crime for a study of its motives and methods to be worth while;[7] they tell us, of course, as much about the perceptions of those responsible for its repression – it was an image of society – as about the culprits themselves. The way both changed, however, was part of the clothing revolution.

For the most part, thefts of clothes came under the authority of the Châtelet of Paris, and in particular of the great criminal court, whose archives contain thousands of preliminary investigations and records of trials. However, not all thieves were tried and not all allegations of theft gave rise to trials. We encounter a classic problem for all studies of crime, ancient or modern: the difficulty of estimating at all accurately the gap between the volume of real and that of recorded crime. However, the study of society's attitude towards an offence, through the importance attached to particular types of crime and the zeal with which offenders were pursued, reveals much about the threshold of tolerance they were accorded.

The theft of linen and clothing is thus informative about two, more or less directly linked, facts: the numerical importance of the deeds, and the seriousness of the threat to the social order they were assumed to pose. The relationship between the thieves and society was neither timeless nor definitive, but rather a sort of function of supply and demand. As the consumption of clothing increased, obsolescence ought to have moderated repression, but crime against clothing was also a more or less serious and insidious act of aggression against the rise of property rights. Every shift in the curve of recorded crime registers the tension established between economic interests and those of the images of social representations, the arithmetic of the passions. In sum, the theft of clothes read from the perspective of the economic theory of crime can reveal both mental changes affecting consumption and sociological changes among consumers.[8]

---

[7] For this section, I have drawn on three theses drawn to my attention by François Billacois (to whom my thanks): Pugibet, 'Etude du vol de linge', Quicroix, 'Le Vol de linge' and Bluette Caron, 'La Répression du vol de linge 1760–1765', mémoires de maîtrise, Paris 10 (1970). See also Amable, 'Le vol de vêtement'.

[8] J.-Y. Caro, *La Théorie économique du crime, sociologie du travail* (1981), pp. 122–8.

CLOTHING AS PARADIGM OF SIGNS

The theft of linen and clothing was, like other offences, repressed with increasing vigour by royal justice from the seventeenth century. The general greater severity, symbolised by the major ordinance of 1670, made it subject to a whole strengthened apparatus of prevention and punishment. The thief emerged more or less chastened from a process which began with the complaint, progressed to the interrogation and ended with the sentence and its execution. Clothing theft was dealt with no differently than theft in general, though the circumstances or even more the condition of the persons involved might cause the generally harsh penalties to be lighter or more severe.[9]

The justice of the *ancien régime* did not allow the same opportunities as our own to those presumed guilty. It was sometimes 'more terrible than the crime',[10] but, at the same time, it made its social role quite clear: to guarantee and assure the continuance of an unequal and sacred order against the forces which threatened it. The theft of clothing shows these active both on the margins, between the worlds of ordinary and of criminal life, and in the centre, since they tended, by a wholly perverse consequence of redistribution, to modify the real equilibrium of social relations and, above all, render them more opaque.

To steal linen and clothing was to help to disrupt and destroy the fundamental principle of a holist world which longed for transparency, and to defy the police in their efforts to make the world legible despite the confusion inherent to the hurly-burly of urban life, notably through attempts to organise space and control movement.[11] The scrutiny of clothing was always central to police investigations. The way in which it was worn, or flaunted, its richness or its poverty, were in themselves signs to note and incitements to punish. The guilty, dashing rogues, the exemplary criminals, often indulged their love of finery, swaggering about in

---

[9] M. Foucault, *Surveiller et punir* (Paris, 1975); E. Dutourbet, *La Procédure criminelle au XVIIe siècle* (Paris, 1975); M.-F. Muyart de Vouglans, *Institute au droit criminel* (Paris, 1757), pp. 220ff.; D. Jousse, *Traité de la justice criminelle en France*, 4 vols. (Paris, 1771), vol. II, pp. 275–80.

[10] Mercier, *Tableaux de Paris*, vol. III, p. 173.

[11] Roche, *Peuple de Paris*, pp. 189–91; S. Kaplan, *Provisioning Paris* (Cornell, 1984); Farge, *La Vie fragile*, pp. 162–4.

outfits which proclaimed their daring and were the stuff of legend: Guilleri in grey from head to foot, or the red coat of Mandrin. Songs, stories, pictures and the publications of the Bibliothèque Bleu, all the stock contents of the ubiquitous peddlars' packs, carried tales of these provocative figures the length and breadth of the land.[12]

For the police, clothes were a means of identification, as they were among the population in general.[13] Worn-out clothes bespoke poverty, rich details told of a better-off past or the desire for a distinctive style; colours betrayed status – the blue of hospices, the dirty white of old uniform, all the extraordinary shades which the dyers could produce, but faded in the clothing of the poor. Police and people had different perceptions; ordinary people were spontaneously hostile to black, colour of the church and the law, of foreigners and strangers, of evildoers and spies; the police had a particular fondness for it. Those announcing ruin or death wore black or the special green which was actually a filthy, faded and washed-out black. For everyone, police and policed, clothes told a story, revealed an identity, indeed, the life of their wearers.

## THE OLD-CLOTHES WOMEN, THE PEOPLE AND THE POLICE

The women who traded in old clothes and at the same time acted as informers are a case in point.[14] In the eighteenth century, the Parisian police employed an increasing number of spies and informers, including the women who supplied information to the commissioners and inspectors of the clandestine clothes trade. Just as procuresses and prostitutes played a special role in the policing of morals,[15] so the *revendeuses* helped to identify criminals and arrest thieves trying to dispose of their spoils. They were knowledgeable about places and people; they frequented the Pont-Neuf, 'which was to the town what the heart is to the human body, the centre of movement and circulation', to quote Louis Sébastien Mercier,[16]

---

[12] H.-J. Lusebrink, *Histoires curieuses et véritables de Cartouche et de Mandrin* (Paris, 1984).

[13] Cobb, *Death in Paris*, pp. 80–6.

[14] Dutruel, 'Les Revendeuses', pp. 65–70, 198–209.

[15] Benabou, *La Prostitution*, pp. 169–86.

[16] Mercier, *Tableaux de Paris*, vol. I, chapter 1 'Le Pont-Neuf'; Dutruel, 'Les Revendeuses', p. 200.

the place des Trois-Maries, the pillars of Les Halles and the quai de l'Ecole and the quai de la Mégisserie, and there they procured the arrest of people who came hoping to sell them shirts, casaquins, breeches, coats, cloths, handkerchiefs and tablecovers.

They often worked as a group in liaison with police spies, such as Morel or Gaillard in the 1760s and 1770s.[17] They questioned vendors, noted suspicious details and drew the attention of the police to any passers-by who looked shifty or hesitated or behaved oddly. Anything unusual about an article offered for sale aroused their suspicion. On 7 March 1758, several of them 'saw the here present person selling a whitish waistcoat to a passer-by; as the waistcoat was not his size, they thought it suspicious'.[18] When a water-carrier, Nicolas Nandin, sold some linen shirts which were rather too fine for someone of his station, they alerted an inspector. They were valuable auxiliaries who helped to identify offenders, confirm evidence and point out possible culprits. For the period between 1758 and 1778, Dominique Dutruel has identified some thirty women, all of some maturity and experience, married to men of a similar type, who worked for the police in return for being left in peace and a small cash reward. One such was Marie Thérèse Jobard, wife of a day labourer; having been arrested by Inspector Chenon in 1757 for stealing a table-cloth, she became his informer. Some women managed to get away with acting as spies whilst continuing to deal in stolen goods. They are evidence of the ambivalence of the milieu and the importance of clandestine circuits to the circulation of clothes, in fact of another textile culture.

In pre-industrial society, before the ready availability of cheap fabrics and the mass manufacture of garments, clothing, whilst it had to be functional, also made it possible to present an appearance, that is, to construct an identity which combined the social proprieties and custom, individual appropriation and the desire to be different. Any excessive departure betrayed a misuse of the code and, to the police, both defiance of the proprieties and sartorial conformity were signs of potential guilt. Thus punitive justice reveals the transformation of the customary relationships taking place within the Parisian melting-pot.

[17]  Arch. nat., Y 10200, 7 May 1758; Dutruel, 'Les Revendeuses', pp. 201–2.
[18]  Arch. nat., Y 10200, 7 May 1758, also Y 10264, 10265, Y 11342 (Archives du commissaire Chenon).

Table 29 *Thefts of clothing and linen tried at the Châtelet of Paris in the eighteenth century*

| | 1710–35 | | 1760–9 | | 1770 | | 1775 | |
|---|---|---|---|---|---|---|---|---|
| | Number | % | Number | % | Number | % | Number | % |
| Thefts of linen and clothes | 205 | 28 | 919 | 52 | 120 | 38 | 101 | 37 |
| Other thefts | 280 | 38 | 714 | 40 | 177 | 55 | 156 | 56 |
| Murders and violence | 169 | 23 | 114 | 6 | 20 | 6 | 18 | 6·5 |
| Morals | 79 | 11 | 30 | 2 | 4 | 1 | 1 | 0·5 |
| Total | 733 | — | 1,777 | — | 321 | — | 276 | — |
| Thefts of clothes alone | 69 | 9 | 307 | 17 | 39 | 12 | 37 | 13 |

Table 30 *Thefts of clothes and linen tried at the Châtelet of Paris in the eighteenth century (sampled at intervals of five years)*

| | 1721–41 (of 444 trials) | | 1770–90 (of 1,857 trials) | |
|---|---|---|---|---|
| Thefts of clothes alone | 57 | | 181 | |
| Thefts of clothes and linen | 50 | | 500 | |
| Total | 107 (24%) | | 681 (37%) | |
| Numbers accused | Men 109 | Women 49 | Men 498 | Women 189 |
| Total | 158 | | 687 | |

## THE INCREASE IN CLOTHING THEFT

The scale of clothing theft is shown in tables 29 and 30, which are based on actual trials. Between 1710 and 1735, 205 (28 per cent) of over 700 cases heard by the judges of the Châtelet concerned thefts of linen and clothing. Between 1760 and 1769, over 900 (52 per cent) of some 1,700 trials concerned thefts of clothing and linen. In 1770 and in 1775, such cases still accounted for nearly 40 per cent of the total. A more detailed study of trials between 1721 and 1741 and between 1770 and 1790 shows that the offences primarily concerning clothes, with linen only an accessory, rose from 24 per cent to 37 per cent. There can be no question of the importance of clothing theft within the totality of judicial proceedings; between the reigns of Louis XV and Louis XVI, thefts of foodstuffs amounted to only 10–15 per cent of the total.[19] Clothing crime resulted every year in the appearance before the judges of the great criminal court of between twenty and fifty persons, guilty or innocent. Quantitatively, the offence followed the upward curve which was essentially that of the repression of attacks on property. While it probably reflected a real increase in the number of offences, in line with that of the population of Paris, it is primarily evidence of the new and greater seriousness with which they were viewed by police and judges, that is, by society.

Both the real (a fourfold increase) and the relative (a rate of some 12 per cent above the minimum) increase in the number of trials involving thefts of clothing and linen demonstrate a desire to supervise and punish which was particularly marked in this case because born on privileged territory. Within Parisian crime, the theft of clothes and linen was the most important both absolutely and relatively; given the low value of the sums involved, it occupied a strategically symbolic social position.

## CLOTHING THEFT: THE POOR ROBBING THE POOR

The sociological analysis of the thieves and their victims confirms this picture.[20] The former were people of small means and mostly men, wholly typical of the lower levels of the population: neither marginals nor professional criminals, but occasional offenders. Two-thirds were wage-earners in the crafts or urban services, journeymen in the guilds or less often casual labourers, day labourers, errand-boys or shop-assistants, even clerks and employees. They included many domestic servants: 11 per cent of the total, almost invariably from the lowest levels of service, lackeys, porters or postillions. They included some soldiers (3.5 per cent), but the latter were mostly subject to a special jurisdiction and so escaped the regular judges. Hardly surprisingly, the higher social groups were rare: a few bourgeois, a handful of artisans and merchants, a few tavern-keepers and, more particularly, landlords.

---

[19] Farge, *Le Vol d'aliment*.
[20] Pugibet, *Etude du vol de linge*, pp. 70–80; Quicroix, *Le Vol de linge*, pp. 55–100; Amable, 'Le Vol de vêtement', pp. 52–88, tables 33, 34.

The women were mostly workers: 42 per cent were wage-earners in the textile trades, linen workers, menders, dressmakers, lace or silk workers, employed by tailors or modistes. The social profile of female thieves was similar to that of prostitutes. We may see this as further confirmation of the importance of the textile sector in the economy of Paris and as a sign of its fragility from the point of view of employment; washerwomen (7 per cent) and women who sold old clothes (19 per cent) further increased the representation of specifically female trades, as did a sizeable number of women domestic servants. The other categories were practically negligible.

Though the vast majority of the accused declared a trade or a status, 20 per cent claimed to be unemployed at the time of arrest. This was the real world of consumers: a majority living in the old central Paris (60 per cent), a slightly smaller number from the populous surrounding suburbs, a few from villages on the outskirts. It was also a world of immigrants (75 per cent were provincials newly arrived in Paris) and illiterates (only 30 per cent claimed a basic culture). In sum, we are here at the heart of the process of urban acculturation, on its down side, where unemployment or poverty led to temporary marginalisation or crime. This probably explains the very high proportion of young men (52 per cent of the accused were between sixteen and thirty-five years of age) and the rather high proportion of women who were either young (a quarter were less than twenty-five years old) or old (13 per cent admitted to being over forty-five), most of them unmarried. All these characteristics, which are also those of the small-time Parisian criminal, were rather more pronounced in the case of clothing theft. It may be seen as the emblematic crime of a nascent consumer society, rather like car and motor-bike theft today.

These petty and small-time thieves were an ideal target for the repressive strategies and justifications of police and judges. They paid for a crime which was being viewed differently by the public authorities as the number of immigrants increased; they accounted for just over half under Louis XV and more than three-quarters under Louis XVI, when they also came from further away, and they were poorer, or at any rate more deprived, at the end than at the beginning of the century. Clothing crime reflected the real poverty of a larger number, the greater problems encountered by those attracted by the lights of the city. But it also revealed the general increase in consumption. It was a crime of proximity, since it affected for the most part people of the same social level and took place within the normal surroundings of 'the fragile life'.

The men and women who stole clothing and linen did not on the whole rob the well-off or the rich; they stole first and foremost from the poor.[21] Their victims fell into three principal groups: more than half came from the same categories of wage-earners in the crafts, shops and domestic service; a third were shopkeepers, small bosses, merchants, tavern-keepers and landlords being most often specified; the rest consisted of the rich, the privileged, merchants, well-off bourgeois, ecclesiastics and nobles.[22] If the poor stole mainly from the poor it was because they were opportunists. Most crimes were carried out close to home, in a shared bedroom, in a workshop or shop, at a laundress's street stall, from the counter of a small trader, even from a stall selling old clothes. We should note two significant changes between the beginning and the end of the century: under Louis XVI, the very rich were much more numerous than in the early years of the reign of Louis XV, and, over the same period, the number of bosses, masters in the guilds and employers increased from 25 to 36 per cent.

The theft of clothing was primarily a theft of recuperation. It was perhaps a specific mode of appropriation of consumer items when their circulation was significantly increasing. It was performed without accomplices and usually without planning. However, at the end of the century, signs of change appear, since clothing theft by burglary or house-breaking, with several accomplices, became increasingly common.[23] A few professional thieves were involved, though the man who stole clothing remained, for the most part, a man of the people. Lastly, the behaviour of the victims changed. At the beginning of the century, they were often not wholly unsympathetic and sometimes ready to reach a settlement, whereas in the years preceding the Revolution they showed less pity and were more determined, if not to recover their property, at least to see their aggressor punished.[24]

---

[21] Amable, 'Le Vol de vêtement', pp. 126–9.

[22] Ibid. 'Les Victimes de vol vestimentaire', table 46.

[23] Pugibet, *Etude du vol de linge*, pp. 59–60; Quicroix, *Le Vol de linge*, pp. 90–5; Amable, 'Le Vol de vêtement', pp. 104–15.

[24] Quicroix, *Le Vol de linge*, pp. 56–7; Amable, 'Le Vol de vêtement', pp. 129–56.

On 5 March 1726, Joseph Dutour, boots at the hôtel des Mousquetaires, was surprised with a bundle of clothes under his arm by a fellow employee, a groom, who, not wanting to appear too nosy, let him go. Three days later, there was another theft, and Dutour was again challenged. His victim, M. de Cabre, who had lost a coat of cinnamon broadcloth, a coat of pinchina, a waistcoat of buff-coloured broadcloth trimmed with silver and a uniform hat, showed no particular animus against his aggressor, telling the inquiry that the stolen clothes 'did not amount to much'. The crime had been organised, Dutour having acted with two accomplices, Gabriel Potel, a 25-year-old mason, and Claude Thomas, a labourer, probably at the instigation of their landlord, Balthazar Chartier, innkeeper of the rue de Grenelle; nevertheless, the judges only sentenced him to be whipped and to be confined for three years in the General Hospital (he was only thirteen and a half). His accomplices were treated even more leniently: three months in prison in return for more information.[25] The case shows how a little band of thieves could form, united by their common life, sharing the precariousness of uncertain employment, the lot of many new Parisians. The leniency of the victims, and even of the judges, reveals a certain tolerance.

CLOTHING THEFT: INDICATOR OF INTOLERANCE

After 1770, in contrast, examples abound of angry victims, fiercely determined to track down, denounce and see punished whoever had robbed them. Jean Pierre Manemit, a vigneron who had been robbed by his maidservant, Marie Louise Marais, aged nineteen and a half, a linen sempstress, pursued her as far as Rambouillet, but without success. Then, meeting her by chance on the road, wearing the stolen clothes, Manemit arrested her.[26] She 'fell on her knees and begged him not to ruin her, saying she would return everything she had stolen except for the lace trimming and the apron which she had given to a girlfriend', but he handed her over to the *maréchaussée*. The increase in opportunistic petty crime – Marie Louise Marais had not stayed long with the Manemit

[25] Arch. nat., Y 10034, June 1726; Amable, 'Le Vol de vêtement', pp. 113–14, 129–31.
[26] Arch. nat., Y 10409, 21 April 1780; Amable, 'Le Vol de vêtement', pp. 135–6.

family, before she had robbed them and fled – provoked fear and intolerance. More victims, more anxious to protect their possessions, which might be few or many but were in any case more numerous than in the past, urged greater repression. In the face of this trend, the attitude of the judges was ambivalent. On the one hand, they inflicted harsher corporal punishment for serious offences and organised crime; on the other, they were less harsh, even lenient, towards the generality of petty thieves, and in particular towards domestic servants, who had been pitilessly punished during the reign of the Sun King.

Clothing thefts as they appear in these records reveal fluctuating attitudes to crime and different notions of threshold with regard to security. For the magistrates, the threshold was high and varied according to the condition of the thieves, the victims and the circumstances of the theft; the garments themselves mattered less than the nature of the deed and its motives. For the victims, the threshold was lower and the clothes, by their increasing ubiquity, appear paradoxically to have acquired a higher value. This ambivalence seems to emphasise both the familiarity resulting from increased consumption of clothes, which made the offence banal, and the intolerance of victims who felt their loss more deeply. Their patience exhausted by the frequency of the offences, quick to accuse, they seem more anxious to protect their property, especially at an equal or barely higher social level, than were the rich who were the true entrepreneurs and beneficiaries of clothing accumulation.

The zeal of witnesses indicates a general attitude. Passers-by in the street, customers in shops, fellow-tenants in lodging-houses, work-mates in workshops, the washerwomen at the drying grounds, all were eager to identify petty thieves, even themselves to denounce or apprehend culprits. Such crimes only reached the judges at the end of a complex process in which police surveillance and the internal tensions of a disparate and divided lower class world had played a part.

The theft of clothes was part of the economy of everyday and confirms the importance of a wealth which was particularly symbolic, and sometimes, according to their inventories, almost the only wealth possessed by ordinary people. Precious and scarce among the poor, clothing was increasingly more than a necessity, and something to covet. It was a relatively convenient means of exchange, whose monetary value constantly grew, but also the means to a figurative recuperation of the appearances of another.

For the majority of petty thieves, impelled by poverty, the rewards were far from negligible.[27] Around 1710–20, a stolen shirt would pay a thief's rent for seventeen days; a bundle of clothes and linen worth around 10 *livres* would allow him to placate his landlord for three months. The average value of thefts was of the order of 2 to 3 *livres* during the reigns of Louis XIV and Louis XV, three or four times greater in the reign of Louis XVI. A poor shirt could be sold for 3 or 4 *livres*, the equivalent to four or five days' work, and it could buy a miserable furnished room, at 2 or 3 *sols* a night, for nearly a month. A coat of blue broadcloth sold for 10 *livres* represented some ten days' pay and would support a thief for rather longer. A redingote worth 18 or 20 *livres* represented a fortune to a poor man; it could keep him for a month and, when the opportunity arose, allow him to replace his linen and his wardrobe by exchanging a stolen garment which was too conspicuous for him to wear himself. The seasonal curve of clothing theft rose with the onset of cold weather and for part of the winter, and fell when the weather improved; it reflected both the trends in employment prospects – which diminished in the sectors using largely unskilled labour when frost first struck the river or building sites – and the need for some minimal protection. The season for clothing theft was the season of hardship for the poor.[28]

The increase in clothing consumption made theft an agent of general redistribution and clothing itself a monetary tool. One summer evening in 1785, Louis Maynard, a 29-year-old casual labourer, had a meal and a drink in a tavern; having no cash on him, he offered to pay with some breeches and a gilet.[29] The rate of exchange was exorbitant: clothes worth 20 *livres* for a bill of 7 *sols*. The innkeeper made a profit, the thief was caught. Stolen clothes equally served as security with a landlord or as deposit for a loan with a private person or at the Mont-de-Piété. Clothing cropped up all the time and everywhere within the popular economy. It entered into countless transactions and served many purposes.

[27] Pugibet, *Etude du vol de linge*, pp. 43–4; Amable, 'Le Vol de vêtement', pp. 107–70.
[28] Pugibet, *Etude du vol de linge*, pp. 14–25; Quicroix, *Le Vol de linge*, pp. 60–5.
[29] Arch. nat., Y 10463, 15 June 1785; see also Y 10460, 10412.

It was linen – so easy to snatch – which was most frequently stolen; handkerchiefs, shirts, stockings and collars figured in a third to a half of thefts. Handkerchiefs were nicked in a crowd, shirts and underwear filched from bundles of laundry, or the washing-boats, or the laundresses' stalls, or from wherever they had been left to dry (as Jean-Jacques Rousseau discovered). Further, these items, as well as being easy to steal, had become essential to daily hygiene. When a handkerchief cost between 10 and 20 *sols*, a coarse linen shirt 30 *sols* and a pair of stockings a further 20 *sols*, a little theft made it possible to keep up appearances. In this way, consumption created crooks.

Other clothes were less often stolen. Coats, waistcoats, breeches and petticoats were mentioned in fewer than 20 per cent of cases; gowns and déshabillés, camisoles, mantelets, shoes and hats in fewer than 10 per cent. The police inventories contained a bit of everything: sheets, redingotes, gloves and slippers, trimmings and stays. They reveal the habits of both robbers and robbed, in the predominance of linen and the principal items of clothing in general use. Unusual or particularly luxurious items were not normally stolen as they were dangerous to wear or sell. On the eve of the Revolution, the increase in the use of linen and clothes meant larger and more varied thefts; almost three-quarters of the average wardrobe occurred in most lists of stolen goods, compared with only a third fifty years earlier.

Between 1721 and 1741, the average number of items stolen was 6.9 per incident, whereas between 1770 and 1790 it was 12. The curve of clothing theft thus faithfully reflected the general transformation of habits, just as the items stolen reflected the new shapes, the more varied and lighter fabrics and the new colours. Criminal acts were rooted in ordinary life; they emphasised its social gulfs by contrasting the wardrobes of the poor and the rich, they helped to change it by making clothes circulate more rapidly and by mixing manners through resale.

### THE SECOND-HAND TRADE AND RESALE AS ACCELERATORS OF CONSUMPTION

Whilst stealing clothes can be seen as a specific crime of the age in which needs were commercialised, the second-hand clothes trade, organised within the framework of the incorporated and free crafts, corresponded to an original form of redistribution without which the clothing revolution could not have been so profound. We have seen how the police, economists, jurists, consumers and thieves, not to speak of their victims, connected criminal practices and the resale of clothes in reality and in the mind as necessity and chance. To complete our analysis of the clothing economy, we need to look more carefully at the operation of this original circuit. It was central to a distribution which was partly regulated and partly free, and which developed different techniques for different customers, but to which the requirements of the majority gave a certain homogeneity. It existed on the frontier between the new and the old, between made-to-measure and ready-to-wear. It thus appears to incarnate the virtues and vices of the circulation of objects whose social alchemy was beginning to change the world.[30]

We should not draw too sharp a distinction between the *fripiers*, a recognised and established community, and the *revendeurs*, a free craft. Their status differed, but the two occupations enjoyed similar attention from the police and operated in similar locations, using similar methods. They remained separate until the end of the *ancien régime*, according to the social principle of division according to estate and tradition. The distance between them increased over time; in 1776, the *fripiers* were amalgamated with the tailors, ending a rivalry which had lasted for centuries, a union made inevitable by their increasingly similar roles and practices; the *revendeurs* remained part of the teeming world of crafts outside the corporations, street merchants and stall-holders, specialising in redistribution rather than distribution.

### THE GUILD OF THE *FRIPIERS* AND THE FREEDOM OF RESALE

In 1725 there were some 700 *fripiers*; it was a community 'which occupied a prominent position among the guilds of this town', according to the abbé Expilly.[31] Between them, they had only a fifth as many shops as the 3,500 or so tailors and dressmakers who made new clothes, that is, one point of sale for every thousand Parisians, on a par with the merchant linen-drapers. They were far from quantitatively dominant in the clothes trade, but probably

---

[30] K. Marx, *Capital* (vol. I, p. 137 of French translation by J. Roy).
[31] Abbé Jean-Joseph d'Expilly *Dictionnaire géographique, historique et politique des Gaules et de la France*, 6 vols. (Paris, 1762–70), vol. V.

played a role disproportionate to their actual numbers. From the sixteenth century, the community also included shopkeepers and *brocanteurs* (dealers in second-hand goods), clothes merchants and furniture and tapestry merchants, the latter less numerous than the former.[32]

From 1664, their statutes defined in minute detail activities which were contested by several rival groups, led by the tailors, the joiners and the tapestry-makers.[33] Their main activity was selling, but they had the right to embellish, mend, clean and even, up to a point, make. 'The trade of the merchant *fripiers*', it was specified in article 15:

> consists of the sale of all sorts of merchandise of every possible type and quality; we allow the merchant *fripiers* to buy and sell, barter and exchange all sorts of furniture, clothes, linen, tapestries, fabrics, lace, braid, trimmings, muffs, furs, leather goods, hats, belts, shoulder-belts, swords, spurs, brasses, tins, irons, old feathers in packs and all other types of old and new resold merchandise.[34]

Article 17 protected them from seizures by 'the sworn tailors or others'. Article 25 authorised them to mend, remove stains and grease from, clean, press and embellish all sorts of furniture and clothes; lastly, Article 28 allowed them to make and resell all sorts of remnants of woollen, silk, gold and silver fabrics and Article 22 to make 'all sorts of new clothes on spec, not to measure, coats and mantles, fabrics of wool, hair and silk ... up to the value of ten *livres* the ell'. In sum, the Parisian *fripiers* enjoyed a monopoly of the second-hand trade plus the privilege of cleaning, and they had also acquired a toe-hold in the market in new clothes; they were, before the name, the creators of ready-made and made-to-measure. We can appreciate their economic power at a period of increasing demand, since they were in a position to satisfy a large number of customers by performing a wide range of essential tasks.

The definition of the tasks of the Parisian *fripiers* makes it plain that it was the *revendeuses* who were its principal rivals. *Revendeurs* and *revendeuses* were authorised to buy and sell in the streets

---

[32] Piwnica, 'Les Fripiers parisiens', pp. 8–24.

[33] Arch. nat., A D XI, 26: Lespinasse, *Métiers et corporations*, Statuts et règlements, vol. III, pp. 421ff.

[34] Arch. nat., A D XI, 26; Piwnica, 'Les Fripiers parisiens', pp. 9–11; Arch. nat., Y 9508 (1767–89).

without forming a corporation. After 1767, the police made them into a 'free craft' subject to registration. Some of the registers signed by all the itinerant or stationary merchants who were not in a community have survived. They record 1,263 women and 486 men, the majority of them (800 women and 250 men) engaged in selling old clothes and second-hand linen.[35] These are likely to be minimum figures. Savary claimed that there were between 1,000 and 1,200 criers of old hats, of whom only 200 – barely 20 per cent – appear in the register. The total cannot have been far from 6,000 to 7,000 persons, that is, at least one for every 100 to 150 Parisians. Within the clothing sector, this was one of the trades which was thickest on the ground.

It was, however, a very disparate group. Both dictionaries and the police emphasised a hierarchy in which the ranking was according to specialisation, position in the resale circuit and clients.[36] At the top came the *revendeuses à la toilette* who had the best class of customer, and who bought and sold fabrics, lace, jewels and other items which the rich wished to dispose of, that is, second-hand but never old. It is significant that moral observers and novelists saw them as almost obligatory figures in the link between prostitution and luxury. They bought articles from those in need of ready cash to pay gambling debts, delivered amorous messages, reconciled lovers or served secretly as procuresses. The gallant iconography of the period portrays them busy as both confidantes and merchants at the morning toilets of ladies.[37] At the bottom of the hierarchy came the *revendeuses en vieux*, who sold the same old clothes and articles as the *fripiers*, principally among the lesser bourgeoisie and the mass of the people, along with the *revendeurs* who sold old clothes, small linen goods and old breeches, the *revendeuses* who sold old blonde-lace and ribbons, the *refaçonneuses* and *raccomodeuses* who altered or repaired old clothes, the *dépeceuses* who unpicked garments and lastly the criers of old hats, estimated at over 1,000 by Savary; they were in a majority in a milieu which strikes us as picturesque but which was above all necessary.

---

[35] Dutruel, 'Les Revendeuses', pp. 33–9; Kaplow, *Les Noms des rois*, pp. 88–91.

[36] Savary, *Dictionnaire universel*, articles 'Revendeuses', 'Crieuses de vieux chapeaux' and 'Fripiers'; des Essarts, *Dictionnaire universel de police*, same articles.

[37] Mercier, *Tableaux de Paris*, vol. II, 'Revendeuses', 'Cabinet des estampes', 'Gérard le fils' and 'Dame chiffon la revendeuse en revend au plus fin en fait d'être trompeuse'.

For the men and women *fripiers* they were crucial intermediaries who supplied goods to their shops, but also increasingly dangerous competitors. Resale was primarily a female occupation, which was more a sign of its adaptation to the circumstances of ordinary life and family economy than proof of its ambiguous role in the moral sphere. To understand it, we need to rid ourselves of the pessimistic and reductionist clichés of the *Tableaux de Paris* or *Les Contemporaines*, which express in other ways the suspicions of the police and the disdain of their social superiors. In a world of scarcity, resale was essential; it prevented objects from being lost, ensured their re-use and facilitated the circulation of habits. In the case of clothes, at a time when the rich were consuming ever more, resale allowed the poor to gain some benefit. It is striking evidence of the habits and customs promoted by the greater mixing and mobility of urban life. It was an activity which required more intelligence than is often assumed, an expert knowledge of place, of the relationship of houses and streets, the social status of their residents, their family and economic circumstances.[38] A trade in which psychology played a crucial role, it was intermediary between being and seeming.

This is why the guild of *fripiers* tried so hard to see that it was marginalised, though it was itself subject to the same regulatory zeal on the part of the authorities. Des Essarts, in the articles '*Fripier*' and '*Brocanteur*' in his *Dictionnaire universel de police*, shows that the aim was not so much to restrict sales as to control purchases. Both *fripiers* and *revendeurs* were forbidden to buy clothes from people with infectious diseases or from soldiers; they were forbidden to buy anything from children or apprentices or from domestic or other servants without the permission of their parents or employers, or from vagabonds or strangers.[39] We observe here the desire to discourage the sale of stolen goods, which also explains the obligation to keep a police register in which they had to record 'day by day, immediately and without gaps' the items bought, the price and the name, status and address of the vendors: this proved a valuable tool for the police in their war on clothing theft.[40] Even if these norms were not scrupulously ob-

---

[38] Farge, *Vivre dans la rue*, also *La Vie fragile*.

[39] Des Essarts, *Dictionnaire universel de police*, article 'Brocanteur'; Dutruel, 'Les Revendeuses', pp. 58–64.

[40] Arch. dép., Paris, D5, B6, 13 (1766); Dutruel, 'Les Revendeuses', p. 61.

served, as was clearly the case, they were intended to impose order on a turbulent and suspect milieu. By the same title, they reveal the ubiquity of resale and theft in the clothing economy. It was a growing sector of employment, indispensable to all.

In 1776, when the *fripiers* were amalgamated with the community of tailors, the status of the free *brocanteurs* and *revendeuses* was defined; their activities were restricted to the free purchase and sale, though without display, of all the goods of the second-hand trade, but they were strictly prohibited from handling anything new. In return, they had the right to mend old clothes but only using family labour. To exercise their trade they were required to register with the police and carry a numbered plaque as evidence. For the master tailors and *fripiers*, the monopoly of made-to-measure, ready-made and the renovation 'of any old garments composing' the wardrobe of men, women and children, was definitively guaranteed. This brought to an end a centuries-old battle. The *fripiers* had become indistinguishable from the tailors, and the latter could engage in all the traditional activities of the former.

This regrouping was within the economic logic of the clothing revolution and created, prematurely, a coherent milieu of clothing occupations from which only the dressmakers were absent; the latter could also make new clothes for women, alter and mend, but 'without being able to trade in every sort of gown'.[41] Thus manufacture remained partly divided, but commerce was highly concentrated. Clothing proclaimed the triumph of distribution.

THE *FRIPIERS* IN THE CENTRE, THE *REVENDEURS* DISPERSED

This union also benefited from a spatial reorganisation, which revealed the complementarity of their activities. The shops of the *fripiers* were concentrated in the centre of Paris in the Les Halles quarter, and the community had its office in the rue de la Grande-Friperie, in the parish of Saint-Eustache.[42] The registers of the *taxe des pauvres* for 1743 reveal a high degree of concentration – 75 per cent of the 338 addresses recorded, that is, nearly half the

---

[41] Piwnica, 'Les Fripiers parisiens', pp. 18–23.
[42] Dutruel, 'Les Revendeuses', pp. 126–52; Piwnica, 'Les Fripiers parisiens', pp. 27–30.

corporation – around the church of Saint-Eustache, in the rue de la Grand-Friperie and the rue de la Petite-Friperie and under the pillars of Les Halles; there were a few shops in the adjoining parishes and they were also beginning to appear on the Left Bank, in the parish of Saint-Etienne and Saint-Sulpice. The notarial deeds confirm this topography and add further detail: in 150 acts, 55 per cent of *fripiers* were domiciled in the parish of Saint-Eustache, 12 per cent in the adjacent parish of Saint-Germain-l'Auxerrois and 15 per cent on the Left Bank. No other occupation within the clothing sector was so exclusively central and so highly concentrated at the heart of Parisian distribution.

These were the districts frequented by both customers and observers, from Berthod to Mercier and from Petit to Rétif, drawn by the goods in the shops and the curiosity of the spectacle. The author of the *Tableaux de Paris* painted a familiar picture, if rather biased by his desire to emphasise its low-class and vulgar character and criminal connections:

> There you find a long row of shops belonging to the *fripiers*, who sell old clothes in poorly lit shops where it is difficult to make out stains or colours . . . you see many old outfits hanging from strings and turning in the wind, making a hideous display . . . police spies lie in wait for crooks coming to sell handkerchiefs, napkins and other stolen goods.[43]

The reality was both less sombre and more banal, certainly less deceptive even if the art of deception remained indispensable to the trade. The *fripier* was a shopkeeper who often paid handsomely for a good establishment: 508 *livres* for a shop with a mezzanine storey in the rue de la Grande-Friperie; 350 *livres* a year for a shop in the rue de la Tonnellerie. Beneath the pillars of Les Halles, conditions were more cramped and the dealers shared the limited space available with others, hatters, hosiers, dealers in second-hand goods and tapestry-makers. It was highly desirable to have a pillar on which merchandise could be displayed. Space was expensive and landlords benefited accordingly. An agreement between one landlord and Nicolas Cahouet, *fripier* of the rue and hôtel de la Monnaie, in the parish of Saint-Germain-l'Auxerrois, survives. It describes a shop

---

[43] Mercier, *Tableaux de Paris*, vol. I, 'Escrocs polis', 'Filoux'; vol. II, 'Piliers des Halles'; vol. III 'Regrets'.

with a chimney-piece 'fitted with its plaque', the whole of stout timber-frame construction, a partition separating off a kitchen, an oak ladder up to the loft and a cellar below with a trap-door; the shop was closed 'by seven great grooved oak planks, a wooden bar behind and a great door equipped with a large lock and key'.[44] The agreement reveals both the integration of work and daily life and the need for solidity and security in a trade whose value was constantly increasing.

The inventories describe shops filled to overflowing with the clothes presented to the customers in an organised confusion, with the dearer and better quality garments in the window or at the front. There was always a wooden counter, sometimes a table or two, a few chairs, benches, '*empiloirs*' to hold the clothes, sometimes wardrobes or chests, often mirrors. In sum, we see a functional use of space, where the windows and the display were designed to attract customers, the interior and above all the variety of the merchandise being the means to detain them.

There were major differences between the world of the *revendeurs* and *revendeuses* and that of an established community poised to achieve respectability. First, residence and work were separated. The majority of dealers in second-hand goods and street merchants lived scattered throughout the capital, and no parish was without them: the police register recorded 65 per cent in the town, 35 per cent in the suburbs. Saint-Eustache again had the largest number, but still only 16 per cent; over a quarter were concentrated in the parishes of Saint-Nicolas-des-Champs and Saint-Gervais and Saint-Paul; nearly 10 per cent lived south of the Seine, especially round the place Maubert or on the Ile Notre-Dame near the new market. The cost of renting shops and lodgings and the itinerant character of the trade explain why at least one *revendeur* out of four was obliged to make a longish journey across Paris to reach his or her main areas of activity. The geography of the second-hand clothes trades shows the persistence into the eighteenth century of the old practice of distribution concentrated and centralised in the densely populated parts of the old mercantile Paris, together with a trend towards dispersal which took the small merchants closer to their customers.

---

[44] Arch. nat., Minut. central, XCIV, 255, 9 September 1751; Piwnica, 'Les Fripiers parisiens', pp. 86–91.

Their methods were also different. For the *revendeurs*, selling from door to door was the rule, with occasional attendance at fairs and markets; others erected stalls daily in authorised locations such as the quai de la Ferraille, the quai de l'Ecole, the place des Trois-Maries and at the end of the Pont-Neuf. The latter was always a desirable location thanks to the constant flow of Parisians, provincials, travellers and foreigners. Many simply walked the streets, carrying their stock on their backs – the characteristic posture of the trade. *Revendeurs* and *revendeuses* frequented the public sales at which advantageous contacts might be made. They were past masters at knowing where to be and when, always around when there was something to be bought or sold. This ubiquity, which could easily be mistaken for confusion, and the attendant obstruction, dirt and noise, fascinated observers: 'No, there is no other town in the world where the street criers, men and women, have a sharper or more piercing sound . . . the spoils go to whoever shouts loudest.'[45]

### RICH *FRIPIERS*, POOR *REVENDEURS*

It comes as no surprise that the socio-cultural analysis of those engaged in the second-hand clothes trade reveals both cohesion and diversity. They differed in degrees of success and wealth and in social and geographical recruitment; they were alike in material behaviour and cultural practices, since their business activities united more than divided them.

It is a mistake to see *fripiers* and *brocanteurs* as a commercial underclass on the edge of poverty. Some *revendeuses* were apparently very poor, to the extent of being arrested for begging or theft. The majority certainly lived in very modest circumstances. The bankruptcies and inventories after death of *fripiers* confirm this, but show that success was a real possibility.[46]

Though the figures in table 31 should be treated with caution, they show an average level superior to that of tailors, dressmakers and linen-drapers. The Parisian *fripier* could prosper, and with an average patrimony of 16,000 *livres* he cut a by no means negligible figure among the bourgeoisie of the crafts and trade. The composi-

---

[45] Mercier, *Tableaux de Paris*, vol. II, 'Piliers des Halles', 'Cris de Paris'.
[46] Piwnica, 'Les Fripiers parisiens', pp. 150–65, table 13, p. 149.

Table 31 *Wealth of the* fripiers (%)

|                          | Failures | Inventories | Total |
|--------------------------|----------|-------------|-------|
| Less than 1,000 *livres* | 7        | 6           | 13    |
| 1,001–5,000 *livres*     | 24       | 6           | 30    |
| 5,001–10,000 *livres*    | 9        | 7           | 16    |
| More than 10,000 *livres*| 35       | 6           | 41    |
| Total                    | 75       | 25          | 100   |

tion of the patrimonies confirms this for the majority of masters; they acquired some landed property and rents, but between a third and a half of the fortunes inventoried consisted of accumulated merchandise. Obviously, the burden of debt was higher among the bankrupts than in the notarial inventories; it everywhere underlines the dependence of trade. We can measure the volume of success through marriage contracts; at time of marriage, two-thirds of the couples had less than 2,000 *livres* and only 27 per cent had a capital of above 5,000 *livres*. In the mercantile and craft population as a whole, 13 per cent of the young spouses contributed less than 1,000 *livres* to the community of goods; among the *fripiers*, the figure was 30 per cent. But inheritances and capital of less than 1,000 *livres* represented only 12 per cent of the total, whilst 58 per cent had more than 5,000 *livres*. It was a potentially profitable business which benefited from the general obsession with clothes.

We also find comfortably off, even rich, *revendeurs*. The bankruptcy records suggest that they were men and women who mixed retail and wholesale business, making some very large purchases.[47] Madame Petit, *revendeuse*, owed over 20,000 *livres* to various merchant mercers; Madame Léonard, *courtière* and *revendeuse à la toilette*, owed nearly 30,000 *livres* for 'merchandise supplied', to five creditors, who included one male and one female merchant mercer.[48] She sold a little of everything: Persian carpets, Indian fabrics, satins, gowns, jewels, watches. In sum, these *revendeuses* acted as intermediaries, buying from some merchants and reselling to others.

---

[47] Dutruel, 'Les Revendeuses', pp. 155–64.
[48] Arch. dép., Paris, D5 B6, registre 13.

The *Livre de Police* of Anne Bondet, a merchant *fripier*,[49] shows that she handled substantial sums of money: 3,000 *livres* on 10 October 1769, 1,600 *livres* on 12 October, a total of 7,000 *livres* during the month as a whole. Their high assets and liabilities show several such women to be engaged in wholesale trade; they lent and they borrowed. For some, prosperity had been won on the margins of guild legality, or at any rate was based on their ability to exploit the loopholes in the system and take advantage of the surge of consumerism. For example, Marie-Anne Riffant, *revendeuse à la toilette*, dealt in linens and muslins in illegal competition with the linen-drapers. She redistributed goods and lent money to other money-lenders.[50] Their success is undoubted, even if it was sometimes fragile and uncertain given the fierce competition inherent to the trade, the very high dependence on credit for sales and purchases and perhaps also its susceptibility to any downturns in the circumstances of the mass of their customers, reflected in the volume of transactions.

The business of the *fripiers* was based on analogous conditions. Buying anything from anybody, they took advantage of the difficulties of ordinary people when prices were low, selling anything to anybody; they were very dependent on fluctuations in employment opportunities, which prevented or permitted the purchase of clothes. They probably usually possessed larger capital than most *revendeuses* or *brocanteurs*, and gave them work since they could supply them with clothes and goods more cheaply. Savary understood this: 'It was the *revendeuses* who lived from hand to mouth; and who for meagre profits supplied the *fripiers* with their purchases.' But an analysis of the merchandise inventoried at bankruptcy or after death makes it plain that the *fripiers* did most of their business with the textile sector and those making clothes. Table 32 records the creditors of 56 *fripiers*: there were a further 91 merchants and 37 wholesale merchants whose speciality was not recorded.[51]

Of the sixty-four 'other crafts', half were from the textile and clothing sector; linen-drapers, dressmakers, linen merchants, fash-

[49] Arch. dép., Paris, D4 36, carton 58, 3698.
[50] Arch. nat., Y 10260 (1764); Dutruel, 'Les Revendeuses', p. 158.
[51] Piwnica, 'Les Fripiers parisiens', pp. 36–7, based on 56 bankruptcy dossiers, in which appear 471 clothiers and merchants.

Table 32 *The* fripiers' *customers*

|                   | Number | %      |
| ----------------- | ------ | ------ |
| Mercers           | 113    | 33·0   |
| Drapers           | 43     | 12·5   |
| *Fripiers*        | 41     | 12·0   |
| Silk merchants    | 23     | 6·7    |
| Braid merchants   | 20     | 5·9    |
| Buttoners         | 12     | 3·5    |
| Tapestry weavers  | 11     | 3·2    |
| Tailors           | 10     | 2·9    |
| Hosiers           | 6      | 1·7    |
| Other crafts      | 64     | 18·6   |
| Total             | 343    | 100·00 |

ion merchants, hatters, ribbon-weavers, etc. The number of merchant mercers appears to confirm the role described above. Overall, the centrality of the *fripiers* to the organisation of the clothing economy is plain. The interdependence of *fripiers* and mercers emerges even more clearly from a calculation of the average amount of the debts: 2,736 *livres* in the case of debts to mercers, 2,000 *livres* to drapers, 659 to silk merchants (who were mercers), only 111 *livres* to tailors and 438 to other *fripiers*.

The geography of this trade shows that it was primarily Parisian and, where provincial, concentrated in the cloth-manufacturing areas of northern and central France. The Parisian *fripier* bought and sold fabrics, processed them through the intermediary of clothing workers in the guilds or in the black economy and bought and sold all sorts of clothes. A certain specialisation is visible, which can be made clearer by a more detailed analysis of their stocks.

## FROM TRADE IN EVERYTHING TO TRADE IN NEW AND SECOND-HAND CLOTHES

A majority of *fripiers* sold everything, but principally old or new men's clothes; a minority sold remnants of cloth, whilst a few sold men's, women's and children's clothing.[52] This pattern reflects the

---

[52] Ibid., pp. 43–85.

influence of the guilds; the dressmakers defended their monopoly of the manufacture of women's clothes, whilst the *fripiers*, before joining them, had made extensive inroads into the preserve of the tailors; merchant linen-drapers and merchants of the Six Companies, mercers and drapers to the fore, were far too big fish to be worried by resale. Of twenty-one inventories, only one *fripier* had both men's and women's clothes, though mostly the latter (68 per cent of his stock); three sold exclusively women's clothes and the rest sold mostly men's clothes interspersed with the occasional item of female clothing.

The *fripiers* sold all items of clothing but in different proportions. Jouvenet, whose shop was in the Palais-Royal, sold fashionable coats and large numbers of elegant gilets; thus specialisation might result from the quest for originality or be dictated by the taste of a local clientele. The notaries list every garment found in the Parisian wardrobe. Chief amongst them was the waistcoat (consistently 20 per cent of the items inventoried), then breeches (just under 20 per cent), coats (between 10 and 20 per cent), redingotes (found everywhere but in smaller numbers) and then a variety of items, in particular gilets and frocks. The shop of the *fripier* reflected the trends in fashion: after 1770, the *justaucorps* almost completely disappeared; after 1760, redingotes became common, accounting for nearly 9 per cent of stocks by the years 1768–89. Gilets, which had appeared by 1750, were in one out of three shops by 1768. The frock was universal. The *fripiers* sold everything needed for the enrichment and diversification of Parisian clothing; they invented 'prêt à porter', by selling fashionable items to a wider clientele but with a slight time-lag. They sold whatever Parisians wore. Indoor clothes, pantaloons (only nineteen in Jouvenet's inventory in 1788, 4 per cent of sales), new and second-hand clerical clothing, uniforms (despite prohibitions), children's clothes, clothes for women and young girls and sometimes all the accessories.

There are two indications of the social orientation of their customers. The colours, which can be calculated for a third of the clothes inventoried, were mostly sombre: black, brown, maroon and grey accounted for 75 per cent of those recorded; the garments were usually plain, only occasionally striped or flower-patterned. The second-hand trade allowed Parisians to follow changing tastes, but in a modified form. Utility and convenience ranked higher than trendiness or attractiveness. The commercial strength of the *fripiers* lay in offering something for everybody; known for selling old, or at least nearly new, clothes, they had encroached on the trade in new clothes thanks to making garments 'not to measure and on spec'. It is difficult to tell what was most important overall, as the precise condition of the garments is not always specified in the inventories of shop contents. We know that one *fripier*, sieur Mennet, sold more new clothes (54 per cent) than old; about a third of the stock of Desbords and Cahouet was new; the rest sold mostly old (usually 10 to 15 per cent new). In other words, the *fripiers* remained faithful to their traditional function of redistribution, but a few behaved like both old-style *fripiers* and tailors; shops selling ready-to-wear clothes were the issue of this marriage. Thus sieur Boucher, whose business failed in 1771, owed seventeen cloth merchants some 20,000 *livres*; since he and his assistant could not make up such a quantity of cloth, he put work out to men and women in whose homes were found '1,500 *livres*' worth of diverse merchandise not made either to measure or in the shop'. Only 10 per cent of his stock consisted of clothes clearly described as new.[53]

The Parisian second-hand clothes trade was part and parcel of the thriving trade in clothes; it adapted to the circumstances and social position of its customers, which in turn determined its hierarchy. The stock of M. Menier, rue Saint-Honoré, was that of a luxury boutique, that of M. Chéron, faubourg Saint-Antoine, was more suited to the poor and the less prosperous artisans.

A brief glance at the prices charged in their shops reveals the enterprise and adaptability of the *fripiers*. The range was enormous, evidence of the variety offered to tempt the customer: 17 *sous* for an old waistcoat of shabby cloth, 216 *livres* for a coat of embroidered silk. The price varied with the type and above all the quality of the fabric: breeches of solid and hard-wearing Elbeuf broadcloth cost more than a pair made of ordinary cloth of Vire. The finish, the trim, the lining, the braid or embroidery were also factors and it is hardly possible to give an average price for garments sold second-hand. They sometimes cost more than new. The price might be reached by haggling. Whilst it is accordingly somewhat risky to suggest the average value of a wardrobe bought second-hand,

[53]  Ibid., pp. 59–61.

Table 33 *Price of waistcoats sold by* fripiers

|  | Under 5 *livres* | 6–10 *livres* | 11–20 *livres* | 21 *livres* |
|---|---|---|---|---|
| Broadcloth: new | — | 1 | 9 | 40 |
| Second-hand | 28 | 40 | 28 | 27 |
| Silk: new | — | — | 1 | 9 |
| Second-hand | 41 | 15 | — | — |
| Velvet: new | — | — | — | — |
| Second-hand | — | 2 | 34 | — |
| Linen: new | 57 | — | — | — |
| Second-hand | — | 2 | — | — |

the exercise at least tells us something about the play of supply and demand.[54]

Table 33 shows that to buy a waistcoat of a common material, it was necessary to work on average between ten and twenty days.[55] The difference between new and second-hand prices is very marked, and varied with the fabric. It was cheaper to buy a new summer waistcoat of light linen than a second-hand winter waistcoat of broadcloth. The second-hand trade promoted the practice of changing one's clothes with the season.

The same was true of breeches. A working man would have to labour for between one and two weeks to be able to buy comfortable and reasonably hard-wearing breeches; if he fancied breeches of silk, he would have to work for a month. Poor-quality working trousers cost the equivalent of three days' labour, but trousers more often cost as much as breeches, which may help to explain their relative rarity before the Revolution.

The balancing of taste and means is even more apparent in the range of prices for coats. For a new coat of good-quality broadcloth, it was usually necessary to spend between 50 and 70 *livres*; a reasonable second-hand coat could be bought for between 30 and 40 *livres*, though some exceptional examples cost over 200 *livres*. In sum, a second-hand waistcoat, breeches and coat could be got for 60 *livres*, and a new outfit for less than a hundred, that is, between two and three months' wages for a labourer. It was still expensive to dress with a minimum of elegance and comfort, but the second-

[54]  Ibid., pp. 62–81.
[55]  Ibid., tables 2–4.

Table 34 *Price of breeches sold by* fripiers

|  | Under 5 *livres* | 6–10 *livres* | 11–20 *livres* | 21 *livres* |
|---|---|---|---|---|
| Broadcloth: new | — | 28 | 27 | — |
| Second-hand | 152 | 1 | — | — |
| Velvet: new | — | — | — | — |
| Second-hand | — | 22 | 11 | — |
| Calimanco: new | — | 26 | — | — |
| Second-hand | — | — | — | — |

hand trade made it possible for a working man who earned twenty-five *sols* a day to find a coat suited to his purse with less outlay and expense.[56] The stalls of the *revendeurs* and *revendeuses* also helped. They sold the linen and shirts which were never or hardly ever handled by the *fripiers*. Only the stock of M. Lafontaine inventoried in 1778 contained handkerchiefs, stockings, caps, shirts and nightshirts. Lastly, we should not forget the role played by hire on certain occasions (mourning or festivals) and for certain social categories. Lafontaine noted that he had lost 4,500 *livres* with various 'women of the world' (prostitutes) who had died in prison or hospital, taking with them clothes hired or bought from him. At every level of Parisian society, the second-hand trade accentuated the effects of the changing appearances.[57]

It was by no means only the lower classes who bought second-hand clothes; customers were as socially diverse as the merchandise. An analysis of the debtors noted in bankruptcy records reflects indebtedness rather than actual customers and sales, but the credit of some may partially reflect the acquisitions of others. Table 35 gives a breakdown of 511 debtors owing money to *fripiers*.[58]

In proportion to the total population, the upper classes and the

[56] It would be useful to compare with tailors' prices. In 1768, a tailor accused by the corporation of selling new coats at reduced prices sold his cheapest complete suit for 34 *livres*, that is, four or five times more than the cheapest second-hand coats at 5 *livres*; but the new coats sold by *fripiers* were dearer, all the recorded prices being between 30 and 200 *livres*. See Kaplow, *Les Noms des rois*, p. 88; Piwnica, 'Les Fripiers parisiens', pp. 69–70.

[57] This is confirmed by the contents and shapes of women's wardrobes. The small number of *fripiers* catering for women points to the importance of female domestic labour, the increased role of the dressmakers, incorporated and clandestine, and the preponderance of women *revendeuses*.

[58] Piwnica, 'Les Fripiers parisiens', pp. 36–7, 92–3.

Table 35 *Those owing money to* fripiers

|  | Number | % |
|---|---|---|
| Nobles and clerics | 60 | 12 |
| Soldiers | 28 | 5 |
| Domestic servants | 26 | 5 |
| Crafts and shops | 282 | 56 |
| Office-holders and liberal professions | 63 | 13 |
| Wage-earners and lesser crafts | 52 | 9 |
| Total | 511 | 100 |

world of shop and workshop – which had contracted both commercial and consumer debts – are over-represented; on the other hand, the lower classes are under-represented since the majority of their purchases did not involve credit. Everyone frequented the shops of the *fripiers* and the stalls of the *revendeurs*, as Mercier observed at the fair of the Saint-Esprit, near la Grève: 'The women *fripiers* display everything needed to dress women and children. It is where bourgeoisie, bawds and bargain-hunters buy their caps, gowns, casaquins, cloths, even their shoes.'[59]

On the eve of the Revolution, the system for the redistribution of appearances seems to have found, in Paris, its point of equilibrium. It benefited from the impetus provided by the increased demand for clothing and it made it possible, as *L'Espion turc* had observed at the beginning of the century, to dress some by undressing others.[60] Those engaged in the battle for distinction could change their clothes and vary their appearance at frequent intervals at a modest cost; in the last analysis, the second-hand trade was a promoter of fashion. It allowed the poor to find clothes and replace their wardrobes for very little.

It also helped to improve appearances throughout the whole social body, since it catered both for basic needs and more sophisticated tastes. Its organisation, whether within the guilds or in the free crafts, presented no obstacle. The *fripiers* were clever enough to take advantage of corporate porosity; they invented ready-made, which was taken up by the shrewdest tailors towards the end of the

---

[59] Mercier, *Tableaux de Paris*, vol. II, 'Place de Grève'.
[60] *Letter from a Sicilian* (Paris, 1706), p. 25; Franklin, *Dictionnaire historique*, p. 348.

century. The *affiches et avis* of 4 April 1770 published the advertisement of sieur Dartigalongue, master and merchant tailor, who had

recently established a shop for ready-made new clothes of every type and every size, and in the height of fashion. If those in the shop are not to the taste of persons who wish to have their clothes quickly, he is in a position to satisfy them almost immediately thanks to the large number of workers he employs. He will deliver anywhere cheaply as possible. He will despatch to the provinces and even abroad.

Innovation has here been upwardly diffused, from the most common, if not the most plebeian, practices, as a consequence of the downwards diffusion of new demands in the spheres of clothing and hygiene.

The resale of old clothes also benefited from its extraordinary ubiquity, both geographical – one sector could only function thanks to its extreme spatial mobility – and social, and it was essentially a regulator of the market. The diversity of the social and economic situations of its practitioners certainly contributed. At the lowest level, a majority of male and especially female hawkers ensured that the supply and demand of the majority were brought together. Their domain was the street and they were on the whole indistinguishable from the mass of the population, from which, indeed, they came: they were mostly from the provinces, barely literate in spite of the obligation to keep police books, but they could count and got others to compile their registers; they lived from hand to mouth, as did the mass of wage-earners. The *marchandes à la toilette*, half-procuresses, half-usurers, with an eye to every opportunity, comprised a sort of aristocracy; their clients ranged from humble women workers to noble ladies, perennially short of ready cash; the sign of their tortuous but ultimately successful upward progress was the acquisition of a shop. Their success was rooted in the common culture they shared with the men and women amongst whom they ordinarily moved: of a hundred married *revendeuses*, 94 per cent had married a wage-earner in the guilds, a casual labourer, a domestic servant or an ex-soldier; only 6 per cent had set their sights higher. At this social level, resale was a fact of life.

At a higher level, it had a different social and cultural resonance. The *fripiers* offered useful and attractive articles at a modest price to better-off people who enjoyed a more established situation.

Most *fripiers* lived comfortably, well provided with furniture and linen, clothes and jewels, well-housed, for the most part financially secure. They were literate, able to read, write and do arithmetic. Clever small shopkeepers, they knew the basic commercial rules, which could be learned from the *Tarif des marchands fripiers, tailleurs, tapissiers et autres*, published in Paris by de Roslin in 1734. This contained three types of information which symbolise the basic practices in the manufacture of and trade in clothes: the names and locations of manufacture and the fabrics made, with their dimensions, the ways of 'setting the tariff', that is, the amount of fabric contained in the pieces, the way of using them, which involved a knowledge of measures in all their diversity, basic arithmetic for adding, subtracting, multiplying and dividing the alnages and carrying out the tasks of commercial accounting.

In sum, a successful second-hand clothes dealer had to know some geography and some practical mathematics and he had to know about measures and products. We see once again the constant imbrication of material and cultural change. Certainly, the *fripiers* were not in a majority within the clothing economy – 700 masters as against 6,000 or 7,000 *revendeuses* – but they represented the technical knowledge and professional sensibility of the clothing arts. They directed, registered and disseminated the effects of the massive change in Parisian consumption. It can be argued that they helped to solve a key problem of any economy: by their labour, even by their skill, they assured the producers a sufficient profit to compensate for the disappearance of certain products.[61] It was an activity ideally suited to reconcile mercantilists and physiocrats, since it showed the tertiary sector triumphant but able to contribute to the common good.

> You used to see patrolling the landing in front of the second-hand clothes shops runners who dragged you in in spite of yourself by their gift of the gab. The man up from the country, the Gascon, the foreigner, made the spiral staircase creak as they sought out the shadowy region containing the clothes. There, after trying on twenty different coats in succession, the one they chose, described as Louviers, was in the light of day no more than a threadbare, washed-out cloth, which had been given a

seductively youthful appearance by the mangle. Experience having taught them the misleading nature of the descriptions and the tricks of the menders, the old-clothes man holds his tongue, and lets his shop sign speak on his behalf.[62]

Mercier is once again hardly charitably disposed towards the *fripiers* as a class, but he was a shrewd observer, perceiving abundance made available to a larger number, the circulation of garments between Paris, the provinces and abroad, the exchange of habits between classes and publicity switching from the spoken to the written word. The clothing revolution announced the empire of distribution and contributed to the achievement of the civilisation of manners.

[62] Bibl. de l'Arsenal, MS 15079 2Q, Papiers Mercier, ff. 241–2.

# 13. *Caring for clothes: from propriety to cleanliness*

La seconde partie de la propreté est la netteté qui est d'autant
plus nécessaire qu'elle supplée à la bienséance quand elle
manque.

A. de Courtin, *De la Civilité*, 1671

Two major trends can be simultaneously discerned in the rural
and urban societies of the seventeenth and eighteenth centuries. On
the one hand, the civilisation of manners gradually imposed on
everyone new constraints in the sphere of clothing and bodily
habits; on the other, the consumption of linen and clothes increased
in proportion, and fully materialised the internalisation of the
norms. The one could not happen without the other, though
historians have so far looked mainly at the values which established
the modern frontiers between the clean and the dirty, and their
transmission.[1]

After a long and obscure evolution, the ethnologists and, today,
the historians of the contemporary world discover a complex
situation, to which the increasingly widespread and general use of
linen, rural and urban, and the rise of the new textiles and consequent decline of traditional fabrics and rustic cloths of flax and
hemp have all contributed.[2] The appearance of ostentatious practices which proclaim the honour of the family and the liberation of
individual desires is widely seen as marking the end of a long
period, plurisecular at the very least, when the decline of poverty,
the retreat of famine and shortage and the end of major demographic crises (breaking the Biblical cycle of plague, epidemic,
famine and agrarian catastrophe) made possible a gradual shift
towards other needs. It would therefore be unwise to assume that
the traditional practices of the nineteenth century, which accompa-

[1] Vigarello, *Concepts of Cleanliness*.
[2] A. Corbin, 'Le Grand Siècle du linge', *Ethnologie française* (1986), pp. 299–310.

nied the growing prosperity of the countryside and the triumph of urban bourgeois civilisation, had necessarily existed beforehand.

The principal impediment to discovering and understanding past behaviour and its gradual evolution is in part a matter of documentation. The discourse on care became abundant once the social norms of hygiene and cleanliness had definitively triumphed, even if they had not yet been incorporated into the general *habitus*; the obscurity still surrounding the history of intimate linen in the nineteenth century provides proof.[3] For the earlier period, we have little to go on. The urban notarial inventory, for example, is not very helpful since it usually contains only scrappy entries indicative of the limited interest felt by the valuers in minor everyday objects such as needles, thread, smoothing irons, soap and old cloths. Rural inventories are sometimes more informative, listing a range of utensils and, above all, referring to practices characteristic of a civilisation in which the new had not yet completely supplanted the old, such as the handing down of articles.[4] The way in which clothes were cared for and mended is sometimes revealed, for example, by the presence of sewing materials or more indirectly in descriptions of objects or places.

The need to look after clothes had long been recognised as necessary. This is apparent in the treatises on domestic economy; the *Maisons rustiques*, the *Ménages des champs* and the *Théâtre d'agriculture* codified the relevant skills for mansions and manor houses, that is, for the elite of agrarian society.[5] But we cannot assume that such practices were everywhere the norm. Similarly, the medical discourse, which, under the guise of a new scientificity, linked a proper appearance and proverbial cleanliness, was not always or everywhere applied, and when the doctors succeeded in asserting the necessity of hygiene for the collective good of the people,[6] we find a hotch-potch of values and prejudices, ideas which profoundly affected reality, but whose slow and silent influence on social structures is difficult to discern.[7]

[3] Perrot, *Les Dessus*, p. 80.
[4] Tardieu, *La Vie domestique dans le Mâconnais*, pp. 145–52; Verdier, *Façons de dire*, pp. 108–51, 171–86; Pellegrin, 'Chemises et chiffons', pp. 283–94.
[5] This unknown aspect of the literature of agrarian reform has not been studied. See Barbier, *Le Quotidien*, pp. 15–35.
[6] Corbin, *Le Miasme*; J. Léonard, *La Médecine entre les pouvoirs et les savoirs*, Histoire intellectuelle et politique de la médecine française au XIXe siècle (Paris, 1981)
[7] G. Thuillier, *Pour une histoire du quotidien* (Paris, 1974), pp. 15ff.

## SARTORIAL UPKEEP AND ORDER

In the triumph of cleanliness in the sphere of clothing and linen (the two go together, even if, in the moral discourse, linen was a more powerful symbol), there were many factors at work. The first was the definition of the household as the model of domestic economy and of a general economic conduct.[8] Within the family, the logic of the division of labour made women responsible for the house, hence for everything concerning the production and upkeep of clothes and linen. The sixteenth to the eighteenth centuries saw the construction of a new feminine identity, in which a decline in the juridical and social status of women was accompanied by the promotion of new values which were incorporated into their education as housewives. Bit by bit, this model travelled from the landed aristocracy to the ordinary people, whom it had reached by the end of the nineteenth century.[9]

The strength of the female education transmitted by family and school lay in the affirmation of a dependent status within the family economy, linked to the performance of the ordinary economic tasks. For the ruling classes, the management of a household and the ideal of the housewife were wholly compatible with a concern for social representation: the culture of appearances was one of its keys. Girls must be taught the appropriate appearance for their condition, then to perform those functions which proclaimed the honour of the family, the cleanliness of clothes, the quality of servants' livery, an abundance of linen. Upkeep was first and foremost the expression and confirmation of status.

However, we need to ponder the how and the why of these 'ways of doing' as a function of social situations. The town was here a laboratory for change; the concentration of population increased the material constraints, making it more necessary to go outside the home and the family in order to look after one's clothes. We must try to assess the extent of this trend, which to some degree corresponded to urban social divisions.

As Parisians accumulated more clothes, they were able to change more frequently and according to season. We have seen how the

---

[8] M. Ségalen, *Mari et femme dans la société paysanne* (Paris, 1980); Barbier, *Le Quotidien*, pp. 42–3, 49–54.

[9] M. Perrot, 'La ménagère dans l'espace parisien au XIXe siècle', *Annales de la recherches urbaine* (1980), pp. 15ff.

circulation of new clothes led to the trade in nearly new, second-hand and, frankly, old clothes. At the end of the chain, the rags on the backs of beggars, so picturesque to observers, recorded every stage in the downwards progress of garments, from luxury via respectable poverty to abject misery: the beggar was unclean. The gift of clothes was an imperative of Christian charity – to clothe the naked, and then of the semi-laicised do-gooding of the age of Enlightenment – to keep up appearances in spite of the disorder of the wretched. So the assorted cast-offs of the rich and old clothes which had been cleaned, sterilised and made uniformly drab by repeated hospital washes became the lot of the poor, though some were better altered, repaired or laundered than others. The urban spectacle was slowly constructed on the basis of a gradual acceptance of constraints of a material, spiritual, technical and moral order, the codification of hygiene and the installation of facilities.

## THE IMPOSSIBILITY OF KEEPING CLEAN

We should not forget that old fabrics were not like those of today, and that the methods and processes of cleaning and mending depended not so much on what was needed as on what was physically possible.[10] The vast majority of the clothes of both sexes were made from fabrics which could not be washed, as Jean Roch Coignet discovered during the Italian campaign. Uniform was privileged territory for the confrontation between the discipline of stains and the art of the cleaner. Let us listen to the comte de Vaublanc recalling his time as a young sub-lieutenant after emerging from military college in 1778:

> The hair was pulled back and up behind the head, above the nape of the neck, pulling the skin, to form a large Cadogan, which was then cemented by a mass of grease and powder ... I do not believe that bad taste has ever imagined anything more hideous ... the only way the hair of the officers differed was that pomade substituted for sweat. Added to which, a white coat, on which it was almost impossible to prevent stains, so it had to be sent to the cleaner, who returned it covered with ceruse, which meant that a cavalry officer, whose coat was blue, could only

[10] Ribeiro, *Dress in Eighteenth Century Europe*, pp. 64–5.

approach a footsoldier, all in white, at the risk of getting his coat whitened.[11]

We have here a vivid illustration of the uneasy encounter in the military world between sartorial discipline and the practices dictated by technical considerations. However, the civilian world was no better off. It was a literary commonplace to characterise the populace by their dirt and squalor. The mud and crowding of towns were as responsible as the dirt inseparable from rural labour. It was the achievement of the civilisation of manners to imbue everyone with the idea that dirty clothing indicated a blemished soul, a prejudice so universal that the art of cleaning was stretched to the limits. For the poor, sartorial cleanliness was an uphill struggle. Water was scarce and expensive,[12] fabrics could not withstand repeated washing, colours faded when subjected to the laundry or bad weather. Above all, to be clean, you had to own enough linen and clothes to allow time for them to be cleaned. Every southern traveller and painter recorded the linen put out to dry and the fabrics bleaching in the sun on lines stretched across the streets. A sunny climate was a blessing for the poor, wrote Stendhal; everything was easier, including caring for one's appearance.

The clothes of the rich fared little better. They faded quickly and 'lasted no longer than the life of a flower'.[13] Damaged and much the worse for wear, they descended a degree in the social scale of possessions, passed from one hand to another, ending up in a second-hand clothes shop. The urban *fripiers* were masters of the arts of patching, mending and cleaning, and their accumulated talents made them into instructors in matters of social legerdemain. In Paris, they shared the monopoly of cleaning with the master dyers *du petit teint* who had, as we have seen, the privilege of dyeing common fabrics and re-dyeing fabrics already dyed by the fast-dyers. Cleaning and re-dyeing were subject to the same criticism; they left fabrics more fragile, unable to withstand soap and hot water. One might well ask how the fourteen dyers with small dye – even supposing they employed a large labour force, which

[11] *Mémoires* (Paris, 1883), pp. 70ff.
[12] D. Roche, 'Le temps de l'eau rare', *Annales: ESC* (1984); J.-P. Goubert, *La conquête de l'eau. Analyse historique du rapport à l'eau dans la France contemporaine* (Paris, 1985), translated by Andrew Wilson as *The Conquest of Water, the advent of health in the Industrial Age* (Princeton, 1989).
[13] Marana, *Lettres d'un espion turc* (Paris, 1684), p. 25.

their regulations and technical conditions in any case prohibited – could cater for the needs of between 600,000 and 700,000 Parisians. To remove the stains from an old garment or piece of material, the usual recourse was to one of the 700 *fripiers*; to get the grease off a hat, you went to the hatters who cleaned and dyed their own products, or relied on your servants, or your wife, or even did it yourself, in all cases something of a gamble.

In these circumstances, which underline just how difficult it was to maintain the level of cleanliness required by the distinctive hierarchy and the moral tradition, it is easy to understand why the frontier between the clean and the dirty was primarily located in white linen, which was easier to clean since made from solid fabrics which were rarely dyed. One understands also why the pictorial reading of social class privileged colours which were brilliant and rich or of unusual or sought-after shades. In the rural parishes, the rustics toiling away in their patched rags and tatters, their clothes never entirely free from mud, knew what it cost to try to keep up with the bourgeoisie.

In the country, cleanliness was women's work, whether in manor house or cottage. In town, it was already to some extent a specialised activity. In the country, colour was for long achieved by simple processes, and the colours of nature, white, brown, raw silk or of domestic yarns predominated. The colour of a few clothes – the blue of Indian indigo, the red of madder – was an opening to the outside world. It was difficult to look after, and was probably crucial to maintaining the frontier between working and holiday clothes. In the towns, colour, like cleaning, was a product of the alchemy of the dyers and old-clothes men.[14]

It has long been thought that dry-cleaning was a nineteenth-century invention, and that the only common method previously was to wash whatever could be washed in hot or cold soapy water. However, a study of the procedures employed by cleaners, insofar as they can be deduced from the usual technical dictionaries, makes it plain that the progress of upkeep echoed that of consumption. Complex techniques and processes were already employed in London and Paris, where dry-cleaning cost more than ordinary cleaning. Volatile alkali, various oils, bran for removing the stains

---

[14] A. Mansfield, 'Dyeing and cleaning clothes in the late eighteenth and early nineteenth centuries', *Costume* (1968), pp. 24–9.

from white cloth, alum-stone, *pierre de Troyes*, lemon juice to remove ink stains and the *malle tache* (or *masse tache*)[15] puffed by itinerant cleaners and street criers were amongst the panoply of substances employed by the *fripier*, the dyer and, very likely, the efficient housewife.

Cleaning did not come cheap. In late eighteenth-century London, the price of cleaning a man's gown or coat could reach 10s. 6d., but the cost varied according to the quality of the fabric and the trim: linen and calico were cheaper to clean than silk or cloth of gold or silver. To clean a waistcoat cost 1s. if it was made from an ordinary fabric, 5s. if it was of satin; the price for breeches was at least 9d. Comparable prices in Paris put dry-cleaning beyond the purse of most people, which explains the popularity of family and familiar methods. All this is interesting less in itself than because it emphasises the real contradiction between the requirement to be clean and the cost of cleaning. The role of the second-hand clothes dealers, emphasised by all observers, in the absence of generally available cheaper or more effective methods, was to make possible all the tricks of illusion and reality.

THE NEED TO LOOK AFTER ONESELF: MANNERS AND CLEANLINESS

A study of manuals of *civilités* from the sixteenth to the nineteenth centuries reveals the principles underlying the requirement to look after oneself.[16] C. Reinharez has shown how, from Erasmus to Jean-Baptiste de La Salle, occasional directions materialise the customary rules of sartorial conduct: choices of fabric, colour and ornament, which contain echoes of the sumptuary laws and rules for wearing clothes. It is interesting to note that these authors all emphasise the obligations of cleanliness and order, with slight variations over time, whilst remaining true to the proverbial discourse which propagated the 'wisdom of the body'.[17] These manuals widely diffused the pedagogic discourse in which the civilisation

---

[15] Franklin, *Dictionnaire historique*, article 'Dégraisseur', p. 249.

[16] C. Reinharez, 'L'analyse du chapitre consacré aux habits dans les manuels de civilité: un moyen d'approche du comportement vestimentaire', *Ethnographie, vêtement et société*, 2 (1984); Rimbault, 'Le Corps à travers les manuels de civilité'.

[17] Loux and Richard, *Sagesse du corps*, pp. 24–5, 105–6, 126–7.

of good manners was elaborated; Norbert Elias has made good use of them. They are primarily informative with regard to the increase in civilising requirements, hence the evolution of the social morality of their authors. But, at the same time, their central position within the educational system, where they served as the basis for instruction in the alphabet, in how to read and write and how to behave, in propriety, modesty and decency, reveals how wide was the diffusion of the obligatory norms and ways of behaving. Originally a universal, even an inter-class, text, when Erasmus offered the first model in his *De civilitate morum puerilium*, it adapted to periods and milieus, so that its extraordinarily successful pedagogic formula passed from the aristocratic world of Erasmian humanism to court circles preoccupied with worldly etiquette, and then on to the urban and rural schools where it was haltingly recited by little future citizens and villagers.

*Les Règles de la bienséance et de la civilité*, published in 1703 by Jean-Baptiste de La Salle, was a best-seller, widely distributed in town and country by an army of peddlars; 175 versions have been traced from the eighteenth and nineteenth centuries. Its success was assisted by its shape and size; it served many purposes, was easy to handle and fitted the pocket; it was an ideal acculturing instrument for both elites and people. Perused by the former, its principles appropriated by the latter, the need to look after oneself was learned by all.

## SARTORIAL GOOD MANNERS

Of some hundred texts, almost all devote a chapter to the rules of dress. These usually appeared among the group of duties which 'encompass all the actions of our life, those which concern our body as much as those which relate to the spirit and feelings'. Throughout the corpus, the notion of propriety (*bienséance*) epitomises an attitude which saw clothing as 'the body's body', in the words of Erasmus, and cleanliness as an essential requirement of propriety, which persisted even in the *civilités républicaines*. The metaphors of the mirror and reflection came spontaneously to the minds of their authors, who shared a common acceptance of the notion that the cleanliness of clothing and body revealed the nature of an adult or a child. 'Judging people by their sartorial appearance entailed the obligation to teach and learn the correct way to dress

Table 36 *Hygienic requirements in the* civilités

| Publications (new titles) | Topography of bodily cleanliness | Frequency of attentions |
|---|---|---|
| 1500–19 | Hands, nails, hair | Morning and evening |
| 1520–39 | Face, mouth, teeth, hands | Morning |
| 1540–59 | Hair, mouth, hands, nails | Before and after meals |
| 1560–79 | Eyes, mouth, hair | Morning |
| 1580–99 | Face, hair | Morning |
| 1600–19 | Face, mouth, teeth, hands | Morning |
| 1620–39 | Mouth, teeth, hair | Not specified |
| 1640–59 | Mouth, teeth, head | Not specified |
| 1660–79 | Head, ears, face | Not specified |
| 1680–99 | Head, eyes, teeth, mouth, nails, hair | Not specified |
| 1700–19 | Teeth, hands, hair | Morning and mealtimes |
| 1720–39 | Face, hair, hands, feet | Morning |
| 1740–59 | Only re-editions | |
| 1760–79 | Only re-editions | |
| 1780–99 | Hair, mouth, eyes, hands, feet | Morning |
| 1800–19 | Mouth, eyes, hands, teeth, head, ears, nose, nails, feet | Morning |
| 1820–39 | Mouth, eyes, teeth, head, hands, feet, baths | Morning |

in order to present a just and good image of oneself which corresponded to the real person', in the words of Reinharez. The manuals would transmit the values which daily example and practice would foster, 'since the shortest route to becoming an honest man is to frequent honest men and observe how they behave, since example speaks louder than words', according to the preface of the manual published in Troyes by Oudot in 1649.

The manuals taught a middle way, where everyone could discover what was appropriate to their estate and condition. They recommended modesty in the choice of fabrics, ornaments and colours. For Erasmus, clothes which were 'embroidered and multicoloured' were for 'idiots and apes', and for La Salle, 'clothes which are trimmed are fitting only to people of high status'.

Above all, these obligations, completed by abundant advice about how clothes should be worn, were accompanied by recommendations relating to cleanliness and order. They are inseparable from the conception of the body and the hygiene which triumphed in the sixteenth century. Table 36 summarises the principal contents of the precepts formulated in a hundred editions of manuals of good manners.[18]

For three centuries, cleanliness was essentially peripheral and visible. The head and the hands were the crucial zone, to the exclusion of three-quarters of the body, which was absent, concealed, hidden away within the outer garments. The invisible, the feet and the rest, emerged between the mid eighteenth and the early nineteenth centuries, the bath after 1820. When we remember that the morning toilet and the simple washing of hands before or after meals coincided with a reduced employment of water, we can appreciate the symbolic force of the whiteness of linen and the importance of principles of cleanliness and order with regard to clothing. They were equally influential in the choice of the parts to demonstrate decency, that is essentially the face and hands, and in the formulation of new rules for socially acceptable gestures, which required control of the natural functions: nose-blowing, spitting, farting and defecating were henceforward excluded from the public sphere and restricted to the private. In this regulatory system for instinctual acts, clothes constantly served to express and enunciate the norms. Their care, sign of a conforming appearance, expressed a cleanliness of a different order from that of bodily hygiene, that is, goodness and modesty, the simplicity of the soul.

The paragraph from *Propreté en général* which I reproduce below from the anonymous Blois edition of 1740 is in this regard quite explicit:

> Propriety being a certain fitness of the clothes to the person, it is necessary, if we wish to be proper, to suit our clothes to our form, our condition and our age. The opposite of propriety is the impropriety which consists of an excess of propriety, the vice of those who love themselves too well, or of excessive negligence, the vice of those who are weak, dirty and unclean by nature ... Propriety ... serves as well as anything to convey a person's virtue and soul ... the second aspect of propriety is cleanliness which is all the more necessary in that it makes up for the other when it is lacking: for if your clothes are clean, and especially if your linen is white, there is no need to be richly dressed: you will feel your best, even in poverty. In addition, you should take care to keep your head clean, and your eyes and your teeth, neglect of

---

[18] Rimbault, 'Le Corps à traver les manuels', pp. 75–7.

which taints the mouth and pollutes those to whom we speak, also the hands and even the feet, particularly in summer so as not to disgust those with whom we converse.[19]

Here we have the basic baggage of a social skill in which clothes, their cleanliness and care make sense only as part of a total system in which the code makes it possible to materialise conditions; thus the interior can triumph over the exterior. For three centuries, good manners expressed the necessary unity of external, tangible appearances and the interior and soul, of the represented and the representing. The aesthetic of appearances, in *ancien régime* France and until the transformations of today, could not but be a moral theology. The constantly reiterated formulas, summarising requirements in the matter of the care and repair of clothing, were designed not only to prolong the life of garments in a society where they were still scarce, but concerned the intimate link between man and the world. At the heart of the scholarly and religious education, still inseparable, stable and reiterated unchanged, when the sumptuary laws had been abandoned, the norms of good manners largely survived the disappearance of the social milieu which had both created and imposed them.[20] It was perhaps because they embodied everything which had given power to the normative discourse for which costume was primarily a distinctive sign; its effects are still visible in the popular psychology, according to Arnold Van Gennep, and to historians of the nineteenth-century working class, for whom dress had a crucial symbolic function, 'last vestige of the *ancien régime*'.[21]

The gap between sense and signifier began to widen in towns, beginning with Paris, when the consumption of clothing increased and the commercialisation of needs was materialised by choices which largely defied the rules of good manners. On the eve of the Revolution, the wage-earners, domestic servants and ordinary artisans of Paris were no longer playing according to the old Erasmian rules,[22] or even those of La Salle. Both men and women found a

---

[19] Ibid., pp. 43–5.

[20] C. Reinharez, 'Contraintes et habitudes vestimentaires dans la société française traditionelle', mémoire de DEA, EHESS (1978), pp. 24–31.

[21] A. Van Gennep, *Manuel du folklore contemporaine, bibliographie méthodique*, vol. III (Paris, 1937), also his *Le Folklore* (Paris, 1924), p. 107; Reinharez, 'Contraintes et habitudes vestimentaires', pp. 14–15; M. Perrot, *Les Ouvriers en grève 1871–1890*, 2 vols. (Paris/The Hague, 1974), vol. I, chapter 1.

[22] Roche, *Peuple de Paris*; see also chapters 7 and 8 above.

different social and political identity, in which the link between appearances and conformity was broken. This is the real significance of the much-caricatured episode of Revolutionary sartorial manifestations. In this sphere, the Restoration began early. With the suppression of the Parisian sections, everyone could resume his place, but the language of popular urban clothing retained some of its originality. Ordinary people were indifferent to the fluctuating fashions which excited the various political groups, Directorial, moderate, neo-Jacobin or army partisans, unmoved by the practices promoted by the militants and the experts in sansculottism, which were primarily a middle-class vogue; they dressed according to their own rules. They happily mingled attachment to the past, in part the distinctive heritage of the *civilités*, in part the necessity which put new clothes beyond their reach, and innovations which were an affirmation of individuality and fancy; it was, as Richard Cobb observed, an ultimate victory over the forces of repression.[23]

In the country, in contrast, traditional ideas survived more easily. On the one hand, they had been less eroded by the constant nibbling away of new types of behaviour, and less influenced by politics; on the other, the respect for social hierarchy proclaimed by clothes easily accommodated the transition from the old to the new ruling elites. To be able to place an individual at first glance and establish correct relations with them remained a necessity in the 40,000 parishes which comprised post- as well as pre-Revolutionary rural France. The sartorial code of the *civilités* could be implemented at leisure, first in details or on the periphery, for example, in the head-dress, trimming or colour, then in the whole, to express regional or local characteristics. This produced the folkloric costumes which were firstly modes of representation in the eighteenth century for the prosperous classes. Clothes were essential to the social lexicon of peasant France, expressing the individual's attachment to their costume, and their loyalty and adherence to the group to which they belonged by age, fortune and estate, in sum seemliness and propriety.[24] This, at least, is suggested by an analysis of proverbs.

---

[23] Cobb, *Death in Paris*, pp. 80–1.
[24] Reinharez, 'Contraintes et habitudes vestimentaires', p. 15.

## PROVERBIAL WISDOM AND CLOTHES

The difficulty here is classic: how are we to date a corpus formed over several centuries and by dint of constant interchange between the written and the oral, the scholarly and the popular? The collections made in the nineteenth and twentieth centuries have at least the virtue of constituting a reasonably systematic, if not complete, survey, at the point when traditional habits were starting to disappear.[25] They enable us to study clothing customs seen in their literal as well as their metaphorical sense, since proverbs place man at the centre of the universe, play down social differences and cross geographical frontiers.

For the historian, the point is not so much to discover the stability of an unchanging and immobile world as to recognise the expression of a peasant society which saw itself as unchanging, changes notwithstanding. A more refined historical perspective would perhaps reveal how, between the present and the past, the norms and the representations were constituted. However, it would require other tools and take us far from our purpose; this remains simply to emphasise the encounter between the pedagogic expression – the manual of good manners – of sartorial constraints and the importance attached to the rules for the care and upkeep of clothing in a type of language which remained accessible to all, even in the autumn of traditional society, since sartorial conduct and moral and social conduct were still closely linked.

Clothes occupy a by no means negligible place in the corpus of proverbs collected by F. Loux and P. Richard. Types of clothing and their use – ornament, seasonal variation, everyday practices, propriety and suitability – account for some 600 out of a total of nearly 5,000 formulas, that is, about 12 per cent. Further, the regional origin of the proverbs is extremely diverse, from Gascony to Alsace, from Nice to Flanders. The link between folk wisdom and sartorial wisdom is expressed in three ways: clothes serve to emphasise the necessary harmony between appearance and status; they proclaim acceptance of a universal natural order; they must testify to the manifest equation between morality and propriety. In other words, the proverbial discourse offered fewer recipes than references; it gave less practical advice than ways of finding one's

[25] Loux and Richard, *Sagesse du corps*, pp. 229–60 (appendices).

bearings in the world by means of very concrete formulas, rules for the ordinary life of everyone and everyday, which complemented the other types of instruction provided by the family, the school and the catechism.

Thus sartorial correctness was a matter of propriety. It should emphasise beauty modestly and respect custom: 'New breeches don't go with old doublets.' This is an essential element, as it is in the basic treatises of good manners: to dress correctly meant to respect custom and dress appropriately for one's condition and age, paying due heed to fashion. Costume appears less as a matter of personal taste than of relationships to others, in which stability was more important than change. Proverbs insisted on the link between dress and social status; to be well dressed was an advertisement for the person as well as for the family, the dress was what mattered. 'Dress up a bush, it might be a person; undress it, and it's only a bush.' Clothes should also be moderate, especially in the case of women, convenient and appropriate to one's means: 'He who is not accustomed to wearing drawers hurts himself on the seams.'

Proverbs emphasise the protective function of clothes, which are valued more highly if they protect from heat or cold, rain or sun: 'Woollen clothes mean a healthy skin.' It was better to wear too much than too little, and one should not be in too much of a hurry to shed one's winter clothes at the first sign of fine weather: 'Ne'er cast a clout till May be out.' The sartorial conventions confirm a natural order behind which the notion of Providence is clearly visible. 'God gives cold according to the cloth.' To behave circumspectly was a way of expressing the harmony between man and the universe, as well as recognition of the strong opposition between being well dressed and well fed, since it was still too often necessary to choose one or the other. This is why linen occurs more often than outer clothes in proverbs relating to propriety. To look after it properly was an economic necessity: 'She who neither sews nor patches needs a large income.' But this should not be carried to extremes, since such labour might be a waste of time ('Those who patch, spend time but save nothing') or of linen and clothes ('For every wash, a tear'). What mattered was to observe order and moderation in the tasks of upkeep: 'When the vines begin to sprout, it's too late for a great wash', and so remain loyal to the ethic of the domestic economy and the conventions.

But proverbial sartorial propriety was relative. On the one hand, it emphasised a conception of the body based on visible appearances, that of 'good manners'. On the other, it permitted a greater laxity, and a different propriety. The rural society of the nineteenth century (which one might suppose was no different previously) was less shocked than the town by the smells, stains, filth and parasites which were a fact of life, and which folk wisdom frequently associated with wealth and plenty.

This disparity demonstrates our point: the culture of appearances changed during the course of the modern period between town and country, between 'rich' and 'poor', between 'educated' and 'uneducated', for all sorts of reasons. These changes had been made possible not only by the propagation of the new norms of 'good manners', upheld by the churches and parish schools, but also by the general diffusion of the objects, means and aids of the new sartorial economy, in towns thanks to the second-hand clothes trade and itinerant mercers, in the country thanks to peddlars. These transformations necessitated a reinterpretation of habits and behaviour, and so constructed new representations which obeyed the same cultural coherences as the general practices, to which we will now return.

## CARE IN THE COUNTRY

Rural customs reveal both the indefiniteness and the separation of activities: specialisation between the sexes (weaving and making clothes were predominantly male, spinning and caring for clothes almost entirely female); specificity of tasks (dress was very early the monopoly of professionals such as tailors, linen weavers, cobblers and shoemakers), while day-to-day upkeep was the province of every woman who had been taught to wash and sew. The appearance of true female technicians, who took over tasks which had hitherto been general, and assumed a place in the hierarchy of village activities, enhanced by their role as 'ferrywomen' in women's lives (the laundress and the dressmaker demonstrated and manipulated rites and symbols at the essential periods of initiation), coincided with the late consolidation, say between the end of the eighteenth and the end of the nineteenth centuries according to region, of what ethnologists call 'traditional society'.[26] The constitu-

---

[26] Fabre, 'Passeuses au gués du destin', pp. 1078–9.

tion in the modern period of the domestic economy, that is, a stronger link between household and family life, could accommodate both greater indefiniteness – each woman doing everything for all women, and the beginning of a specialisation with age – the matrons and midwives instructing mothers who transmitted their knowledge and culture to their daughters.

At the same time, there could appear a division of labour according to the requirements of the economic and social hierarchy of rural communities. Running the households not only of the very rich but of prosperous farmers required the labour of the mistress of the house and a permanent staff of female servants of all ages with temporary women workers, paid by the day or the job, for the more labour-intensive tasks: sewing for festivities or mourning, laundering the household linen. In humbler farm houses and the cottages of smallholders, labourers and the unfortunate, the family had to shift for itself, which did not preclude solidarity among women. Mending, washing and cleaning were, like cooking, the chief occupation of them all.

Confirmation comes in inventories. In Brie in the seventeenth and eighteenth centuries, and in the Mâconnais in the eighteenth and nineteenth centuries, as in Poitou,[27] the necessary household equipment was listed in notarial deeds, which sometimes makes it possible to reconstruct activities: how to 'make new out of old', creature of necessity, and a reminder of practices usually ignored since performed by the poor and leaving no trace. The sewing material is largely unsurprising, though pins and needles, manufactured by what was often a largely unmechanised rural industry, were coarser and stronger than today, able to pierce thick and solid fabrics or rude and heavy linens. In villages, they were sold by peddlars in cases of a dozen or a gross, and their manufacture fascinated the founder of liberal political economy, Adam Smith. Thimbles were also common, as were the scissors carried in both town and country in pockets or on the belt, and found in the Parisian inventories compiled by the clerks at the morgue.[28]

Knitting-needles and crochet hooks for wool, to make or darn

[27] Baulant and Vari, 'Du fil à l'armoire', pp. 273–80; Tardieu, *La Vie domestique dans le Mâconnais*, pp. 147–51; Pellegrin, 'Chemises et chiffons', pp. 283–98.
[28] Roche, *Peuple de Paris*, chapter 6.

thick woollens, stockings and hose, complete this humble domestic armoury which both made it possible to mend and care for linen and clothes and shaped the personalities of the young girls sent out to watch the flocks whilst spinning or knitting. Pins and needles soon found a role in their amorous games and love affairs. Molière, in *Don Juan*, refers to the country boys who bought them as gifts 'from every passing mercer'. They were everywhere part of the life of young girls, used in guessing games – pricks foretold the future – and magical rites for the casting of spells. Their sexual symbolism, the '*chat*' (cunt) and the '*chas*' (eye of the needle) was commonplace, and training in their use was central to the education of family and school.[29]

While boys ran, girls sewed. A lesson in sewing and knitting was a lesson in deportment and morality. Rousseau saw it as the natural bent of the weaker sex and, like Fénelon, as the cure for boredom and day-dreams:

Almost all little girls are reluctant to learn to read and write; but they are always willing to learn how to hold a needle. They already see themselves as grown-up and think with pleasure of how these talents will one day be useful for adorning themselves. Once this first path is opened, the rest is easy: sewing, embroidery and lace-making come of their own accord.[30]

Even the church played an active role in constructing this culture of ordinary work; its embroidered linen was given by pious and devout women, rich and poor, its growing cult of the Virgin and the Holy Mother Saint Anne exalted maternal pedagogy, its confraternities of the Rosary, proliferating in the wake of the Catholic Reformation, glorified a cult in which the image of the young girl protected by her pins, like a rose by its thorns, could play a role in the symbolism of modern love affairs.[31]

In daily life, the good housewife was revealed by the way she looked after her family's appearance. For the poor and deprived, the care of linen and clothing meant a daily struggle: cleanliness

---

[29] Verdier, *Façons de dire*, pp. 236–58; Fabre, 'Passeuses au gués du destin', pp. 1081–2.

[30] J.-J. Rousseau, *Emile, Oeuvres complètes*, vol. IV, p. 479 (p. 368 of Penguin Classics edn of 1991)

[31] Fabre, 'Passeuses au gués du destin', p. 1082; L. Châtellier, *L'Europe des dévots* (Paris, 1986), translated by Jean Birrell as *The Europe of the Devout* (Cambridge, 1989).

was the treasure of the poor. The shirt, for example, was not an external sign of wealth; owning enough shirts to be able to change frequently did not mean that they need not be cared for. The speed with which they wore out and the way they were looked after were as revealing as the number and quality of the articles.[32] New shirts were rarely in a majority: in peasant inventories, they were more often 'worn-out' or 'nearly worn-out', 'bad' or 'very bad', 'in holes' or 'unwearable'. The age of their owners, and that of the clothes themselves, the damage inflicted by vermin or rats in poorly protected wardrobes and the wear and tear of work all help to explain why old clothes were always more common than new, the more so as peasants also increasingly bought clothes second-hand and cheaply from old-clothes men.[33]

These assorted garments had to last, and were patched and mended as long as possible; they were worn till they were threadbare, when, though they lost their market value, they found other uses. Old linen worn to rags could serve many purposes. It was used to make children's clothes or layettes or small articles of linen or improvised sheets to wrap round babies. It was made into bandages, whose medical qualities were enhanced by magical properties. Linen which had been in contact with the body substituted for it in the practices of white or black magic. The rites at springs or therapeutic statues required the use of the linen of the sick person.

Major repairs to the clothes of both sexes were often performed by tailors, which may explain the small quantity and modest value of the necessary materials in peasant inventories, though lesser repairs and mending were probably very early undertaken by rural housewives. However, it was not until the nineteenth century that needlework as a whole was definitively feminised. The balancing of the need for new and rates of wear and tear involved another form of technical intelligence, in which the old new and the new old were constantly manipulated and re-employed. Nothing was wasted and anything could be created in the transmutation of textiles.

---

[32] Pellegrin, 'Chemises et chiffons', pp. 283–6.
[33] Morineau, 'Budgets populaires', pp. 226–8.

## SMALL OR GREAT WASHES

The struggle to maintain an appearance which conformed to social requirements was a stimulus to accumulation. In general, people wore outer clothes which were more or less patched and mended according to their means. Constant mending was compatible with propriety and respect for the forms. But linen was another matter; how often it was washed depended on how much you owned. If you had only a few shirts, and not many petticoats and stockings, they needed constant attention: six shirts, changed every two or three days, in good weather, when linen dried easily out of doors, meant that a household in the Limousin had to wash at least once a fortnight; once a week, according to season, was more likely for a Poitevin family. This was in accord with those proverbs which advised: 'Only wash clothes which are lousy' and 'A wise housewife washes when the sun shines.'

These two phrases succinctly summarise the reasons for large-scale and communal washing.[34] For the majority of the rural population, it was necessary to wash thoroughly a minimum change of linen; a minority owned enough linen to allow summary washes which made it possible to preserve dirty linen, which would otherwise have rotted, followed by the great washes of spring and autumn. One process was familial and domestic, alchemical and silent; it involved filling the wash-tub with ashes and the linen which had been given a preliminary rinse, then pouring and repouring over it big buckets of hot water. The other was collective, noisy and jolly: the linen was rinsed and soaped, beaten on the river bank or at the wash-house, wrung out, then laid out in the meadows or hedgerows to dry.

The two techniques could be adapted to a greater or lesser accumulation of linen, and to more or less frequent washing. But only the great wash made it possible to deploy the enormous trousseaus so important to the social hierarchy. It evoked representations of the rural female world which associated the virtuous wives and mistresses of great houses with accumulation, even wealth. In the nineteenth century, it was a stage in the cycle of labour and days felt as propitious to renewal and new departures. Between two

[34] S. Tardieu, 'Le Trousseau et la grande lessive', *Ethnologie française* (1986), pp. 281–2; Verdier, *Façons de dire*, pp. 108–32.

seasons, the transition from dirty to clean was like the victory of life over death, eternally recurring, and a festival which brought women together. Once or twice a year, the female collectivity of the wash-house participated in social control; assembled around its matrons, often old and sometimes ugly, it read in its linen the whole history of the village, discussed it and committed it to memory.

For Burgundy and Languedoc, Yvonne Verdier and Daniel Fabre have reconstructed this spectacular, but perhaps last and only short-lived, avatar in the rural existence of linen. This close union between the function of customs and the global symbolism of acts supposes a triple conjunction: that of an increased consumption of linen, that of the religious and moral significance of the frontiers of the clean and the dirty and that of a minimal diffusion of domestic and collective equipment, in particular the provision of water to houses and the construction of wash-houses.

CHANGE IN THE TOWN

It seems likely that the accumulation of more linen by more people, for show, from the seventeenth to the nineteenth centuries, was important in strengthening beliefs and symbolic significances and in establishing new practices, although technical changes and equipment remained rudimentary; rural communities had other preoccupations before the Revolution than the supply of water or making it universally available by means of the dense network of pumps, fountains and wash-houses in existence by the third quarter of the nineteenth century.[35] Till then, the care of linen was dependent on the labour of the men and women who drew and carried scarce water. This was the responsibility of servants at all levels of society, only poor labouring households needing occasionally to fend for themselves. The history of washing before running water, when the use of water was inevitably parsimonious – in sum, before the nineteenth century, that great century of linen – remains to be written. Happy the villages and small towns built beside a river!

By the eighteenth century, the principal elements of a new system, the need for it and the beliefs which underpinned it, were all in place. The revolution of appearances could not but, in the end, lead to a revolution in clothing care. This decisive change

---

[35] Corbin, 'Le Grand Siècle', pp. 301–2.

happened first within the urban aristocratic families. But it was above all the coincidence of need and means among the urban population that led to professional laundering and washing, thus, for a while, to another relationship to linen.

From this point of view, early modern Paris was little different from early industrial Paris. The real rupture came later, in the late nineteenth and twentieth centuries, with the return to domestic washing and laundering made possible by running water 'on all floors', the relatively inexpensive galvanised sheet-metal boiler and, much later, though already contemplated by inventors in the century of Enlightenment, the washing machine; nor should we forget the new detergents.[36] These activities were then de-collectivised and de-professionalised.

We should not see the earlier changes too schematically. Different attitudes co-existed within the Paris of Louis XIV, as in that of Louis XVI, and family labour continued alongside the new trades; it was a matter of means, social milieu, the presence or absence of servants, the organisation of labour within the family and perhaps also the degree of acculturation of manners. Though developed in response to growing needs, the new practices also increased them, since they speeded up wear and tear; they thus helped to create the world of obsolescence.

### HOW THE SCHOMBERG FAMILY KEPT CLEAN

Within the noble urban family, the upkeep of clothes became an important element in domestic expenditure.[37] In October 1771, the baron de Schomberg started a new account book for personal expenses, which included practically all his household's costs up to 1777, so making it possible for us to calculate how much was devoted to the care of linen and clothes. This is what was spent on laundry alone in six years:

| | |
|---|---|
| 1771: 18.1 *livres* | 1775: 60.15 *livres* |
| 1772: 53.8 *livres* | 1776: 65.6 *livres* |
| 1773: 61.14 *livres* | 1777: 74.16 *livres* |
| 1774: 69.12 *livres* | |

---

[36] M.-C. Riffaul, 'De Chaptal à la mère Denis, histoire de l'entretien du linge domestique', *Culture technique*, 3 (1980).

[37] Dusart, 'La Consommation vestimentaire d'une famille', pp. 137–46, 171–9.

Laundry cost an average of 5 *livres* a month, rather more if we exclude 1771, probably an underestimate or for only three months. Compared with expenditure on clothes, which was at this period of the order of 3,500 *livres* a year, that is, just under 300 *livres* per month, the figures do not seem particularly high, but the cost of cleaning clothes, the repair of gowns and the care of lace and trimmings, carried out by a tailor and an embroiderer, should be added. Between 1782 and 1788, when other books enable us to calculate expenditure on washing and laundry, the costs were rather higher:

July 1782 to May 1783: 171 *livres*

September 1784 to February 1785: 77 *livres*

May 1786 to September 1787: 151 *livres*

October 1787 to August 1788: 158 *livres*

The cost of the Schomberg family's laundry doubled, exceeding 12 *livres* a month, whilst spending on new linen and clothes fell to less than 1,000 *livres* a year. This change could result from under-recording prior to 1780, which seems unlikely, given the detail of the entries, or certain tasks might have been performed by the household servants, in which case it is not clear why the practice ceased after 1780. In fact, the explanation is to be found in a closer analysis of the system as a whole, which reveals the division of tasks within a family which regulated its behaviour so as to reconcile the need for distinction with good housekeeping.

Care of the wardrobe was almost entirely entrusted to tailors, who undertook to clean and restore as good as new outer garments and gowns, at a cost of between fifteen and twenty *livres*. This was an expensive and fairly rare operation, as cleaning had not yet supplanted changing. More important was mending, and the whole household's clothes were sent on average once a year to a skilled practitioner; in the case of the servants, who wore out their clothes more quickly, the interval was shorter. The process was often accompanied by alterations, which enabled garments to be passed from one person to another, from the baron to his valets or from the baronne to her maidservants. The cost of these repairs, included in the general bills from the tailors, was not negligible; perhaps between 5 and 10 per cent of the monthly expenditure on clothing.

The linen was looked after quite differently. When baron

Schomberg was a bachelor, he employed a linen-draper, Mme Guénault, who both made and cared for his linen. It was washed weekly: in one week in 1759, five shirts, three handkerchiefs, one pair of half-hose, six of thick socks (it was winter), one pair of sleeve ruffles and more irregularly caps, sheets, a pair of stockings and some drawers. Here we have a model of noble behaviour costing between 2 and 3 *livres* a week, and for a bachelor soldier who changed his shirt and collar – the most visible items – daily, his handkerchief every two days, but his drawers only every twenty-seven days! This was perfectly acceptable behaviour. It was not until after 1762 that baron Schomberg began to change his drawers weekly. His personal hygiene improved with his marriage, but was still a long way from the daily changing suggested by Fernand Braudel.[38] The linen was darned and mended at the same time that it was washed and bleached.

In this family, three methods were adopted for the care of linen: some tasks were performed outside – bills for this are few after 1761; some were done by servants, 'maids of all work' or chambermaids; there was some reliance on specialists – washerwomen and laundresses – who came to their house in the country rather than those in Paris or Versailles. Whatever the method, the work was done by women and it was closely supervised by the mistress of the house. A sound knowledge of the basics of upkeep was a criterion in the recruitment of domestics: 'I would rather have a local girl than some wonder-woman who will be bored in the country, unless someone tells you of a good girl who is a good needlewoman and, above all, laundress', wrote Mme de Schomberg gaily to her husband in 1770. To say of a chambermaid that 'she is a fairy with the linen' was a great compliment,[39] found in other noble correspondence which reveals similar concerns.[40] At Corbeville, for example, one or more washerwomen and a woman to do the ironing came regularly to see to the family's linen. This seems to have happened almost every week or every fortnight; it was paid for by the day *en bloc* every month, or even every two months. This is a frequency which reveals town habits and the changing made

[38] Braudel, *Civilisation matérielle*, vol. II, p. 287.

[39] Arch. dép., Versailles, E 3146, 19 April 1780; Dusart, 'La Consommation vestimentaire d'une famille', p. 178.

[40] Sabatier, *Figaro et son maître*, p. 177. The Berthier de Sauvigny washed at their château, in the moat or in the Orge.

possible by an abundant wardrobe. The linen was repaired by the servants, except for delicate items such as lace, which were sent out.

Three aspects of these practices, suggestive of a nobility both careful and thrifty, merit our attention. First, the baronne was a model aristocratic housewife, that is, she tolerated luxury but not extravagance. Second, the expenses show the continued close interdependence of all the elements in the clothing economy: the suppliers, producers and tradesmen saw to the care of clothes; the tailor looked after the outer garments, for which he employed *fripiers* or dyers who were menders and cleaners, the linen-draper saw to the undergarments, using washerwomen and dressmakers, the hatter cleaned the hats and the shoemaker had the shoes repaired by cobblers. The aristocratic family economy thus regularly mobilised all the different elements composing the total system. It was a strength, in that the division of labour supported consumption, but it was also a weakness, if the credit which kept the whole system going collapsed.

Lastly, we see that conspicuous consumption was not an inevitable concomitant of wealth. The Schomberg neither accumulated linen nor undertook a great wash, but rather divided their cleaning between household servants and specialists, in village or town. The way clothes were cared for is particularly revealing, since it combines materiality and representations, practices and social images: in this case, the pursuit of simplicity within opulence – and still a matter of the proprieties. 'I am so loved by my family and friends although simply dressed that I have no reason to change my costume', confessed Mme de Schomberg in 1787. This was one response to the diffusion of the urban values of cleanliness on the eve of the Revolution. We will see what options were open to the majority of the Parisian population when we look at the practices and practitioners of laundering.[41]

LAUNDRY AND LAUNDRESSES IN PARIS

Both social convention and hygienic precepts imposed on everyone the obligation to change their linen with increasing frequency.

---

[41] I draw here on the thesis by C. Ungerer, 'Le Blanchissage à Paris au XVIIe siècle', Paris 1, whom I would like to thank.

However, for an agglomeration of between 600,000 and 700,000 persons, this presented huge material and economic problems; medical opinion might regard it as reasonable to change the shirt every two or three days (and even more often in summer), but this meant a total of at least 250,000 shirts to be cleaned everyday, not to speak of other items such as stockings, sheets and whatever underwear the frivolous or the chilly might choose to wear. As we have seen, the majority of the stable population possessed a wardrobe sufficient to permit them to change with this, or in some cases an even greater, frequency. But how did this happen? In practice, laundering encompassed a range of activities and also one major division of tasks according to the type of linen; fine and coarse linen was separated, and silk stockings, bands, lace and lawn dealt with separately. This distinction implies different processes and different locations; however, the profession, which never managed to become a corporation, was also to some degree united by common operations, using similar equipment and the same locations, and by observance of the regulations and the social and economic constraints which dictated their different and complex relations with clients who had different means and requirements.

Iconography and the observations of a few practitioners anxious to modernise the craft give us some idea of the work performed by laundresses.[42] It could be done at home, in hovels or courtyards which often still contained communal pumps, but it was mostly carried out on the banks of the Seine or the Bièvre. They resounded to the din of beetles and brushes, the culmination of a series of operations taking place in shops more or less well equipped with wash-tubs, coppers, clothes-lines, soap-boards and baskets, not to speak of the various washing aids: soaps, starches and sulphur. Until the eighteenth century, washing was dependent on 'soaps, ashes from new wood, soda and pearl ash', which was still the case in country districts in the nineteenth century.[43]

However, changes were appearing in Paris; soap had become

[42] J.-J. Lequeux, 'Lettre sur le beau savonnage'. Paris, Year XI, B. N., Esiampe Lb 34 4.

[43] Chaptal, 'Notice sur un nouveau moyen de blanchir le linge de nos ménages', *Annales de chimie*, Paris, Year IX, pp. 291–6; Cadet de Vaux, *Instruction populaire sur le blanchissage domestique à la vapeur* (Paris 1880).

common, though ashes were still used, before being thrown into the Seine. The use of black or white soaps according to the wash, which both simplified the work and did less damage to the linen, accompanied the first linen revolution before the nineteenth century. Savary tells us that the dry, hard soaps came from the Mediterranean, from Toulon and especially Marseilles, and that the black or green liquid soaps came from the north, from England and Holland, from Calais and Amiens. Above all, he shows that a greater use of soaps was a feature of many crafts, from dyers to perfumers. The fact that he makes no mention of laundresses shows that his information about Paris was out of date. The Revolution saw veritable 'soap riots' involving laundresses and women of the people.[44] However, soap notwithstanding, the linen of Parisians still had a yellowish tinge, and it was fashionable to send it to be bleached in England or Holland, even the West Indies, to achieve a snowy white.

It was this which inspired technicians and chemists to search for ways of achieving whiter linen more rapidly and more cheaply. On the eve of the Revolution, the queen's laundry at Epinay, Gillet d'Angers, who washed for the hospitals, and Moret and his associates learned from the Batavian and English experience and established model establishments at moderate prices: 3 *sols* for a shirt, 8 *sols* for a pair of sheets. Two innovations resulted from this inventive research: the steam laundry promoted by Chaptal and Cadet de Vaux, which 'whitened the dirtiest sheets from the Hôtel-Dieu', and 'Javelle water'; they did not immediately transform common practice but, in the longer term, steam and chlorine cleansed linen as they helped to cleanse towns.[45] Between the end of the eighteenth and the beginning of the nineteenth centuries, the ideal of 'whiter than white' inspired the researches of more or less philanthropical scholars, industrialists and economists who wanted to make a purified linen available to all. Laundry joined food as a basic requirement of workers; the two were already guaranteed in contracts of apprenticeship and agreements with journeymen.

This growing demand had long been of concern to the urban

[44] A. Mathiex, 'Les enragés et les troubles du savon' (June 1795), *Annales révolutionnaires* (1921), pp. 355–65.
[45] Corbin, *Le Miasme*, pp. 143–50; Pellegrin, 'Contrats d'apprentissage en haut Poitou au XVIIIe siècle', *Bulletin de la Société des antiquaires de l'ouest* (1987), pp. 259–309.

authorities. The town *Bureau* and the police collaborated in the supervision of washing, and the contradiction between the desire for a salubrious town and the needs of the population and the profession is evident. The aim was to drive outwards an activity which was polluting and unhealthy and which hindered navigation and the provisioning of the water-carriers at the embankment. By the seventeenth century, ordinances forbade laundresses from washing in the town centre (between the Pont Saint-Michel and the Pont-Neuf), originally in summer from fear of infection and the refuse which accumulated. The town and royal architects observed, inspected, denounced and periodically posted their prohibitions; but to no avail, the laundresses ignored them and remained mistresses of the Seine, low water and stench notwithstanding. Economic interest and the norms of bodily hygiene were more powerful than fear of sanctions.

Despite prosecutions, the number of infractions by washerwomen and water-carriers was huge. It was as if the triumphant civilisation of good manners mocked the civilisation of putrefaction.[46] For centuries, urban prosperity had implied humidity and ferment, which had allowed the industries dependent on water, the tanners, dyers, tawers and laundresses of canvas and linen, to grow and support a large and industrious population. Neither the fears of the urban authorities nor those of the doctors and hygienists could topple a centuries-old equilibrium.[47] Nothing changed, the confusion was unabated, indeed the population of washerwomen grew, the professionals having to make room for the activities of those too poor to afford their services. The town taxed the laundresses (2 or 3 *sols* per site, per day), sold washing-boat concessions and supervised the quays and ports, for whose security it assumed responsibility; it regulated the tipping of used ashes, relations between the trades, drying in the streets and even the exhibitionism of bathers which constituted a threat to morals. These efforts were only partially successful against the facts of real life.[48]

---

[46] A. Guillerme, *Les Temps de l'eau, la Cité, l'eau et les techniques, Nord de la France, fin III, début XIXe siècle* (Paris, 1983), pp. 150–229.

[47] C. Ungerer, 'Les valeurs urbaines du propre', *Ethnologie française* (1986), pp. 295–7.

[48] A. Farge, 'L'espace parisien au XVIIIe siècle, d'après l'ordonnance de police', *Ethnologie française* (1982), p. 125.

The creation of a laundry system accompanied the civilisation of manners, and the appearance of organised laundresses on the river banks was late. From the fifteenth to the eighteenth century, their number grew and with it the need for control. Of course, many Parisians, bourgeoisie, masters and merchants, wage-earners of every type, not to speak of the innumerable religious institutions, continued to wash at home; it was one of the principal tasks of servants of both sexes, and professionals were used only in emergencies. The wash-houses of the hospitals and convents were thus the laboratories of another type of collective wash, the laundry of the confined sick and poor the stimulus for technical and economic research. Nevertheless, the facilities established in towns in the modern period made possible the transformation of washing from a private into a public activity.

The way the system functioned is revealed by contracts and regulations for the washing-boats, and by leases and adjudications. Substantial 'farmers', three between 1723 and 1780, took up the general leases for between 4,000 and 7,000 *livres* annually and administered sub-leases agreed for between 300 and 400 *livres* a year with the lessees of boats with stools; they, in their turn, leased the wash-tubs to washerwomen. In the seventeenth and eighteenth centuries, the number of boats ranged from seventy-seven to ninety-four, that is, an average of some 2,000 places, mostly on the Right Bank (59 per cent of places in 1723, 50 per cent in 1780); the banks opposite the Cité were less densely occupied. They were a distinctive feature of the river landscape, frequently painted, and greatly added to its animation, especially between the Pont Marie and the Pont Royal. On the Left Bank, the laundresses concentrated on the Bièvre so as to avoid paying the tax of 3 *sols*, and there established their tubs. The town tolerated them 'to avoid the total ruin of more than four hundred families entirely dependent on the income from washing'. They were also increasingly found between the Ile des Cygnes, the Gros-Caillou and La Grenouillère, where the washerwomen refused to use the washing-boats for which a charge was made. This geography corresponds to a technical specialisation which was refined over time. Private washing was ubiquitous, especially where it cost least; however, the profession fixed on the centre for the laundering of fine linen and on the periphery, where there was more space, in particular for hanging out, and a readily available female labour force, for coarser

linen. This was the speciality of the washerwomen of La Grenouillère. Throughout the capital, amateurs and professionals
co-existed, as did laundering and the other water trades; the
tripe-dealers only removed their boats from the quays of the Right
Bank around 1770; the Bièvre was a cesspool of insalubrious
industries, as Doctor Hallé reminded the Academy of Sciences in
1789.

With 2,000 places in the boats and several hundred wash-tubs, in
spite of the poor quality of the water, Paris could more or less cope
with its laundry, but the rich, as we have observed in the case of
the Schomberg, found other solutions; they had their linen bleached
in the country or even, sometimes, abroad. The ideal of whiteness
confirmed, even strengthened, the hierarchy of appearances: for
some, the majority, linen yellowed by repeated washing, for others,
immaculate white *à la hollandaise*.

The work of the laundresses thus became central to the economy
as well as the culture of clothing. It is one further example of the
role of women in the major transformations. They are to be found
in small family enterprises or toiling alone in tiny workshops. They
came together in the washing-boats which developed a life of their
own, often punctuated by quarrels and disputes. The washerwomen
were rather too ready with their tongues, or so it was claimed in
judicial proceedings and soon in literature.[49] We can surely see
here the permanence in towns of beliefs and reputations which
survived more openly in villages. Here as elsewhere, they laboured
hard but enjoyed the privilege of working in a group and of
acquiring the ambiguous status of amphibious creatures; in Paris,
as in the countryside, they ruled the quarter and street where they
lived in a form of social control. The Parisian washerwomen had
the gift of the gab, which their work encouraged, and they exercised
over the river a rather aggressive linguistic sovereignty, displayed
at the expense of the police, the port security, sailors, bathers,
washing-boat lessees, indeed of men in general.

The records of the police, the hospitals and the notaries convey
the practices and the perception of this diverse, turbulent and
canny milieu. 'Anyone who has only a couple of shirts washes
them himself; if you don't believe me, go one Sunday to the Pont-

---

[49] Verdier, *Façons de dire*, pp. 132–5; P. Sébillot, 'Lavandières et blanchisseuses', in
*Légende et curiosité des métiers* (Paris, 1895), pp. 2–3.

Neuf at four in the morning, and you will see, on the edge of the river, numerous persons half-naked under a redingote washing their only shirt or kerchief',[50] observed Louis Sébastien Mercier, always interested in linen. The thrifty and the poorer workers did the same. But the majority of the population opted for the laundresses' shop, since neither the inadequate supply of water nor the conditions of lower-class housing made washing easy.[51] In their cramped lodgings, the less well-off found it a tiny economy which failed to compensate for the lost hours of work.

All classes of society appear in the archives of laundering, from the marquise to the water-carrier, from the minor abbé at court to the maid in a great house, who often sent her clothes to the wash alongside those of her employers. The debts recorded in inventories after death show clearly that in Paris, 'people mostly sent their linen to be washed by laundresses'.[52] The laundry became a sign of integration into urban life, and not to use one was an indication of failure and marginalisation. For the launderers, contracts with institutions, hospitals and convents or with great families could be very profitable, but the trade was principally dependent on ordinary people and the bourgeoisie. The latter, according to the account book of the wine-merchant, Beuvert, of the rue Saint-Jacques, kept track of their expenses and their trivial contacts with the artisans of their street or quarter. It was common to share one's laundress with one's landlord, lodger or 'governor', who had chosen her for her honesty, skill and proximity; the relationship was here part of ordinary sociability. It made possible the credit which was once again indispensable to the functioning of the clothing economy. Legal disputes reveal another aspect, the distrust of a profession which might steal or maltreat the linen entrusted to its care. Rétif de La Bretonne tells the story of two young women who, by more or less extended loans, constantly renewed their outfits at the expense of their clients.[53] For some, the laundress 'circulates too much, sees too much, knows too many people and handles too much dirt to be honest'. The trade both attracted and repelled; it was at the heart of the ordinary life of the people of Paris. This is why Alxiore in the *Lettre sur le beau savonnage qu'on pourrait*

[50] Mercier, *Tableaux de Paris*, vol. V, p. 117.
[51] Roche, *Peuple de Paris*.
[52] Ungerer, 'Les valeurs urbaines du propre', p. 296.
[53] Roche, *Peuple de Paris*.

*appeler savonnement de Paris*, addressed by the architect, Lequeux, to mothers of families, can appear as the emblematic figure of an 'art useful to all and now indispensable'.

Goyon de La Plombanie, a writer whose importance as an economist is recognised today thanks to J.-C. Perrot,[54] revealed in *L'homme en société*[55] how the Enlightenment pondered laundering and its importance to the economy of appearances.

> There are very few people who are not in a position to know from experience that the amount they spend on linen for their own use in proportion to their estate and means is not very much; but it is greater as a result of the dreadful way in which linen is laundered. The laundry usually does more damage than normal wear, unless one takes great pains to watch it through all the operations to which it is subjected every time it is washed. Those who are in the happy position of being able to have this sort of work done at home and under their own eyes can easily see what a difference there is between laundering the linen at home oneself, as is the practice almost everywhere in Flanders, and entrusting it to people who practise the trade publicly.

The way Paris washed, soaped and ironed meant that the sumptuary expense which it was intended to contain was rather increased, and should be limited, since:

> Laundry has become a requirement of indispensable necessity [*sic*]. Because in Paris, the very poorest people put on clean linen at least once a week: at the minimum, a shirt, a collar and a kerchief, and it costs 3 *sols* to be done cheaply. Every month at least, a pair of sheets has to be done. That is another 4 or 5 *sols*, or 1 *sol* extra a week.

Here we have a real-life calculation of the cost of a minimal upkeep, where part of the wash – stockings and caps – was done at home. The prices at the model laundry of la Briche were similar: 1 *sol* for a collar, half a *sol* for a kerchief and 3 *sols* for a plain shirt (5 *sols* if it was trimmed), whilst a sheet cost on average between 6 and 8 *sols*. In sum, the calculations of the economist and the entrepreneur agree that the weekly wash cost the ordinary man some 5 or 6 *sols* a week – with a wife, the cost was double, with

[54] J.-C. Perrot, 'Despotische Vernunft und Okonomische Utopie, H. Goyon de La Plombanie, la France agricole et marchande, Avignon-Paris, 1762', in *Utopiefor-schung*, 3 vols. (Stuttgart, 1985), vol. II, pp. 336–57.

[55] Published in 2 vols. in Amsterdam in 1768; see in particular vol. II, pp. 47–57.

two children, at least quadruple – making no allowance for all the washable accessories (aprons, pockets, table and household linen, coats or gowns of washable linen). For a family with only one wage, where the father brought home from six working days 25 *sols* a day, the washing represented a weekly expenditure of between 15 and 20 *sols*, that is, between 10 and 13 per cent of the budget. The accounts of a bourgeois family of six reveal a weekly wash costing in the region of 10 *livres*, that is, ten times more.[56]

Among the rich and the less rich, shirts, collars and stockings were washed most frequently, but it was impossible to keep up with the advice of the manuals of good manners and the hygienists. The culture of appearances was caught between the past and the future, the visible and the invisible, the clean and the dirty. Material necessity overruled the precepts, which tell only part of the story.

La Plombanie tells us the cost for the town as a whole. He assumed three *livres* a week in the case of the rich and the very rich,[57] half as much for craftsmen and shopkeepers, that is, an average of 12 *sols* per Parisian, or 30 *livres* a year. For a population which he estimated – Paris, its suburbs and satellites, including Versailles – at 1,000,000 persons, that meant an annual expenditure of 30,000,000 *livres*: no small sum within the budget of old urban France! This was why it was necessary to find new methods to make economies, reduce the cost to Paris and organise cheap washing for all by means of wash-houses and better techniques.

The washing utopia contributed to the general good and to financial equilibrium. Its deep meaning seems to me to be its demonstration of the link between practices and representations within the clothing culture. Its economy rested on an unstable equilibrium between demand and the response of the trades, the capacity of the majority of consumers and the supply of the proliferating professions united by the chain of production, commercialisation and credit, the new and the second-hand, more rapid replacement and upkeep. In the imagination, it emphasised the union of the conventions and cleanliness, the strength and the weakness of the precepts of the triumphant good manners or of the hygiene which went unheeded.

[56] Ungerer, 'Les valeurs urbaines du propre', p. 297.
[57] The cost was about four *livres* in the case of the Schomberg, for a household of five or six.

# Part 4

## Truth and the mask

Le masque! Le masque! Je donnerais un de mes doigts pour
avoir trouvé le masque.

Diderot, *Le Neveu de Rameau*

# 14. *Clothes in the novel*

C'est parce que j'ai le courage de me dévêtir devant vous que
je mérite votre reconnaissance et votre amitié.

Rétif de La Bretonne, *Monsieur Nicolas*

Our study of the consumption, care, production and commercialisation of clothes has shown the role within the clothing economy of
norms and codes which were profoundly imbricated in the ordinary
and extraordinary manifestations of dress. Here, individuals could
play on appearance and reality, while society pondered the dilemma
of truth and disguise. By revealing the power of sartorial signs, the
requirements of social life showed the importance and the permanence of the two essential functions of costume: to reveal a personage conforming to a recognised hierarchy; to suggest the possibility
of an intrinsic liberty and to permit a victory over the self, measurable by reference to the moral imperatives of the Christian society
which remained fundamental, whatever else had changed.

The constitutive principle of the material civilisation of good
manners was challenged by the clothing revolution among the
lower classes of eighteenth-century towns. Whilst a feeling for dress
and the means to a new sensibility became general, the contrasts
between the sexes diminished, though they did not disappear, the
frontiers between social groups were blurred and the prospect of
greater mobility seemed to promise. Louis Sébastien Mercier feared
that the people were losing their simple ways and compromising
both their authenticity and their health in exchange for the fragile
and frivolous dominion of appearances.[1]

'The Parisian is generally of necessity sober and eats badly in
order to pay his tailor or his cap-seller.'[2] The consumption of
clothes was one of the mechanisms which animated the town-

[1] Roche, *Peuple de Paris*, pp. 178–9.
[2] Mercier, *Tableaux de Paris*, vol. VIII, pp. 120–4.

theatre dear to the disciples of Jean-Jacques Rousseau and denounced by all moral observers as corrupting of persons and social
relations alike. The life-style of the idle classes, given over to
masked games, ostentatious frivolity and a non-transparency of
being,[3] became the norm for more people, which is why styles of
dress were so much debated during the Revolution. Urban modernity was already infiltrating the countryside by numerous channels,
which the moralists deplored as an unnatural contamination. In so
doing, they give us the opportunity to assess the importance of
artifice in the models and practices of society as a whole.

## THE TRUTH OF DISGUISE

It is a commonplace of moral philosophy and literature to speak of
the opposition and the sham of being and seeming.[4] In eighteenth-
century texts, however, the idea is reiterated in order to emphasise
the difference between the true self and the role invented in response
to the demands of the dominant sociability, wholly devoted to
forms, where one's true or natural feelings could not be revealed,
where one existed only in the eyes of others. 'The man of the world
is wholly his mask', wrote Rousseau, 'what he is, is nothing, what
he appears to be, is everything.'[5] The code of the worldly imposed,
in a sense, the truth of the mask. Paris was a town where people
judged by appearances above all, where it was easy to impress by
one's manners because everyone was an actor, and no-one was
duped.

A description of the social world of the Enlightenment in theatrical terms is not impossible, if we accept that reality and representation are not wholly antagonistic and that the players are not
always conscious of the difference; here I perhaps differ from
Philip Stewart.[6] The frontier between the private and the public
changed between the seventeenth and the nineteenth centuries, and
clothing helped to trace the new boundaries inasmuch as the

---

[3] J. Starobinski, *Jean-Jacques Rousseau, la transparence et l'obstacle* (Paris, 1957),
and *Le Remède dans le mal critique et légitimation de l'artifice à l'âge des
Lumières* (Paris, 1985).

[4] P. Stewart, *Le Masque et la parole. Le langage de l'amour au XVIIIe siècle* (Paris,
1973), pp. 79–89.

[5] Rousseau, *Emile*, in *Oeuvres complètes*, vol. IV, p. 515.

[6] Goffman, *Presentation of the Self*; Stewart, *Le Masque et la parole*, p. 85.

principles of court society, the failure of modern states to control appearance, the transformation of the moral and material culture of both townspeople and country dwellers, the greater role of numerous urban intermediaries and the mobility of commerce governed in turn, or even simultaneously, the definition of private space and that of a world ruled by the publicity of reason.[7] In the short run, in daily life and concrete situations, before the actors' eyes, sartorial habits changed and both made visible and helped to confuse the hierarchies. One appreciates how, for the philosopher Diderot, the social world could be read as pantomime, a tragic farce for some, a happy show for others,[8] where each dressed how he ought, as he wished and above all how he could.

The taste for literary and theatrical disguise was only the expression of an exoticism favourable to the depiction of the artificiality of behaviour. It remains to be studied, from *L'Astrée* to the *Francion*, from baroque spectacle to the dramatic representation of the Enlightenment.[9] 'Just as our bodies are clothed, so now in their way are our souls; the time for baring souls will come like the time for baring bodies, when we die', wrote Marivaux, an acute observer of the contradictions between the invented and the real self.[10] A reading of novels should reveal the specific reality of a set of mental images.[11]

## THE AMBIGUITY OF THE MASK

The social artifices of the age allowed the wearing of masks.[12] In the disguise of the theatre or the festival, in public or private masquerades, the practice is attested throughout eighteenth-century Europe, in private houses and out of doors, during the day and at night. The ubiquity of masks shows the influence of the practices

[7] Ariès, *Histoire de la vie privée*, vol. III, pp. 7–10.

[8] D. Diderot, *Le Neveu de Rameau*, ed. J. Fabre (Paris/Geneva, 1954).

[9] A. Cali and C. Ferrandes, 'L'Infrazione al codice, Il *Déguisement* nell' *Astrée* di Honoré d'Urfé, Il Romanzo al tempo di Luigi XIII', *Quaderni del Seicento francese*, 2 (Bari/Paris, 1976). See also Pellegrin, 'L'être et le paraître'.

[10] *Journaux et Oeuvres diverses*, ed. F. Deloffre and M. Gillot (Paris, 1969), p. 390; Stewart, *Le Masque et la parole*, p. 80.

[11] Pellegrin, 'L'être et le paraître', p. 528; B. Baczko, *Les Imaginaires sociaux. Mémoires et espoirs collectifs* (Paris, 1984), pp. 11–62.

[12] Stewart, *Le Masque et la parole*, pp. 86–7; G. Bertrand, 'La Fête princière et le masque, 1715–1789', mémoire de DEA, EHESS (1980).

of the theatre, of the *commedia dell'arte* on its progress through
Europe and in the festive rituals of princely courts, but it also
reveals the wide social diffusion of the carnivalesque transgression
of charivaris and Shrove Tuesday processions. The mask connoted
both the liberating licence of the upper ranks of society and the
contravention of norms by the lower classes. For society as a
whole, it showed that one could realise a desire for anonymity by
the manipulation of open forms. More than an additional stratagem
in the paraphernalia of festivals, it was a liberating instrument
which perfectly demonstrated the representative function of appearances and clothing. 'Parisian women', wrote the anonymous author
of the *Agreeable Criticism* published in London in 1708, 'are all
allowed to go everywhere masked, concealing and revealing themselves as they chose. With an eye-shade of black velvet, they go to
church as if to a masked ball, unknown to God or to their
husbands.'[13]

These conventions, strange only in our eyes, reveal the potential
of play on equality, since singular and contrasted identities were
rendered ordinary and uniform by means of artifice. Like make-up,
which was intended to give both sexes a visible conformity decreed
by fashion, the masquerade reveals the ethos of a world where
sociability imposed respect for the rules of conversation and the
conventions. We can here perceive the profound genius connecting
material transformations and intellectual practices. We see the
intelligence and the purpose of the philosophic salons, where
polite conversation could at the same time inhibit originality of
thought, create a conformism and encourage paradox rather than
sincerity.[14] Freedom could then find expression under the disguise
of manners and in the exaggeration of ideas, as it could enjoy the
protection of the mask and the sartorial incognito of gallant or
popular festivals. We see this more clearly, paradoxically, in the
diatribes of the denouncers of masks, such as Rousseau and Diderot, and in general among all who despised worldly conventions

---

[13] *An Agreeable Criticism of the City of Paris and the French, giving an Account of
their Present State and Condition . . . A Translation of an Italian Letter written
Lately from Paris by a Sicilian to a friend of his at Amsterdam* (London, 1708), p.
16.

[14] D. Roche, *Les Républicains des Lettres, gens de culture et Lumières au XVIIIe
siècle* (Paris, 1988), pp. 242–53; A. C. Kors, *D'Holbach's Coterie, an Enlightenment in Paris* (Princeton, 1977).

and wished society to recover the transparency of a mythical past, even to generalise the abolition of differences. It is another way of understanding the role played in the transformation of habits by a clothing which was neither wholly imaginary nor wholly real. 'The mask makes it possible to oppose the law, without wishing to abolish it or deny its power.'[15] Similarly, every clothing fact gives a text a degree of realism which conforms to the conventions of a period and reveals their transitory nature. It is this interaction of norms and practices which we must now examine.

## NOVELS, DICTIONARIES AND FASHION MAGAZINES AS EVIDENCE OF THE CULTURE OF CLOTHING

Clothes in the novel offer a first model, easy of access thanks to the triumph of this new form in the eighteenth century, but difficult to use given the sheer number of texts to be studied, the difficulty of establishing boundaries to the genre and the lack of any simple and straightforward way of interpreting the clothes themselves. We will try to establish how images of society are revealed through the manipulation of clothing symbolics in the practices described and transformed by the literarity of the novel, in sum in the link which is established between social realities and the realities of the collective imagination.[16] The clothing system thus takes its place among the mechanisms which provided *ancien régime* society as a whole with a collective schema for interpreting individual experiences, its horizon of diffusion and reproduction.[17] For a certain public and under certain conditions, linked to the modes of production and of reading, the novel illustrates the formula of Mirabeau: '[it is not enough] to show man the truth, the point is to impassion him for it; it is of little account to serve his basic needs if you fail to capture his imagination'.[18]

We need also to observe how the forms of adhesion to the models offered for general consumption changed. We can attempt

---

[15] G. Lascault, *Figurées, défigurées. Petit vocabulaire de la féminité représentée* (Paris, 1977), pp. 119–21.

[16] Baczko, *Les Imaginaires sociaux*, pp. 29–30; Pellegrin, 'L'être et le paraître', pp. 519, 528.

[17] R. Koselleck, 'Historie Fortschrift', in *Historisches Lexicon zur politischsozialen Sprache in Deutschland* (Stuttgart, 1974).

[18] Quoted in Baczko, *Les Imaginaires sociaux*, p. 53.

this through a study of the clothing system developed by the *Encyclopédie* of Diderot and d'Alembert.[19] Three themes can be detected in the treatment by the encyclopedists of the facts of dressing and clothes.[20] The first and most obvious emphasises, within the general perspective of the dictionary, all the technical aspects linked to labour and manufacture; we find a technological and economic analysis of fashion and its influence on productive and commercial organisation, especially in the relations forged between France and the rest of Europe. The second reveals the organic vision of clothing found among the social elites, especially in reforming circles. We find an opposition, widely accepted if not unchallenged, between 'natural clothes', which conformed to nature and were analysed from a functional point of view, and 'artificial clothes', where what mattered most was what they signified. The reforming logic, in particular that developed by the medical doctors, many of whom collaborated in producing the entries on clothing in the *Dictionnaire raisonné*, here came up against customs and habits;[21] they reveal the utopian character of the medical discussion of clothes and its impact on the formation of revolutionary thinking about dress.[22] The 'healthy uniform' foreshadowed the reforms which had such symbolic, if not real, importance during the Revolution.

This leads on to the third theme, which brings together the moral and political vision of fashion and conduct, of their influence on the way of life of societies and of the proper role in the world of the man of science and the man of letters. The sartorial semantics reveal both the incoherence of appearances, torn between social and technical imperatives, even the choice of words, and the coherence of a clothing system which reveals the economic and productive bases of Enlightenment society. They are combined with a triumphant cultural vision sustained by the transformation of manners but determined not to surrender to the futile seductions of intellectual fashions.

---

[19] See J. Proust, *Diderot et les Encyclopédists* (Paris, 1962); R. Darnton, *L'Aventure de l'Encyclopédie, un best-seller au siècle des Lumières* (Paris, 1982).

[20] 'La Moda e l'abbigliamento', ed. Carlo Roccella, *Collezione dell'Encyclopedia* (Milan, 1981), pp. 9–22.

[21] P. Didier, 'Le Système du vêtement dans le *Dictionnaire raisonné des arts et sciences*', mémoire de maîtrise, Paris 1 (1983); Perez, 'Le Vêtement dans les logiques médicales'.

[22] Pellegrin, 'L'Uniforme de la santé'.

So it is to fashion and its problems that we eventually return. Can we imagine the frivolity of a period, and what conditions are necessary to the emergence of such a phenomenon in a world whose profound legitimacy remained that of tradition and history? A study of the birth of the fashion press in the context of a journalism aimed at both men and women will help us to answer this question. To the 'natural' and functional culture proposed by the *Encyclopédie* and popularised by the doctors, there was opposed a culture of frivolity and femininity which presented itself as the expression of a moral aesthetic of 'good taste' and 'good form'. These French (and European) creations partially marked a rupture which is still influential today. The major change, in my view, was the fact that a new image of female roles and a lauding of the creativity of the second sex coincided with the elaboration and generalisation of a new model of consumption. At the same time, the popularisation of a discipline of the body, an organisation of time, of proper rhythms obedient to the shifts of fashion, together questioned the relationship of individuals to society.

Novels, the *Dictionnaire raisonné*, medical texts and fashion magazines will allow us to examine the culture of appearances in its relation to the real and in its imaginary realities.

FICTION AND CLOTHES[23]

Like elaborate dress, the novel attracted the criticism of the moralists of the seventeenth and eighteenth centuries. It was not until the end of the century that the success of the genre was assured, with the help of English influence.[24] This history explains the two principal problems for any thematic reading of works of fiction. Their very large number, in France and in Europe, makes it impossible to analyse the total output of a period, so makes it difficult to measure change in a victorious aesthetic form. The

---

[23] J. Debouzy, 'L'esprit du roman, Réflexion sur le roman anglais du XVIIe et du XVIIIe siècle', *Revue d'histoire moderne et contemporaine* (1989); I have found P. Fauchery, *La Destinée féminine dans le roman européen du XVIIIe siècle* (Paris, 1972) particularly helpful methodologically; see also G. Benrekassa, 'Le typique et le fabuleux: histoire et roman dans *La Vie de mon père*', *Revue des sciences humaines* (1978), pp. 31–56; J.-M. Goulemot, *Mémoires de Valentin Jamerey Duval*, preface (Paris, 1981).

[24] G. May, *Le Dilemme du roman au XVIIIe siècle* (Paris, 1963); H. Coulet, *Le Roman jusqu'à la Révolution* (Paris, 1967).

formal anarchy of the genre and the constant controversy dogging its history are hardly conducive to the study of a theme so diffuse as that of clothing habits, in any case less easily perceptible than the introspective analysis of the passions or the study of human situations through narrative choices designed to emphasise 'the imperative nature of the needs underlying behaviour in the prolongation of an economy of social existence expressing the conditions of the age'.[25] Let us learn from the analyses produced by historians of literature that what matters is to perceive the typical response which the novelist seeks to produce in the reader, and so understand the gulfs created between actual practices and fictional acts, that is, how an unreal object can have a far from imaginary projection on reality.[26]

There is no need, therefore, to claim for the novel an illusory unity. Let us accept that the eighteenth-century novel offers both a moral landscape and the possibility of perceiving a relationship to the collection of institutions, practices and utensils which define the ordinary life of a society, and which the Enlightenment called *moeurs*: clothing is among them.[27] Nor do we need to specify precise margins to our enquiry; if the novel drew its strength and evocative power from the climate of general introspection which emerged at the beginning of the eighteenth century, we may be permitted to annex to the genre stories which claim to be autobiographies but which contain elements drawn in part from the fictional epic; one thinks of the *Memoirs* of Casanova. The link between the reflection of lived events and their formulation in fictional or biographical form is not perceptibly different in either case; only the common culture which, in the domain of habits, linked the writer and his readers matters to us. Novels consistently demonstrate it.

### CLOTHES IN UTOPIA AND IN RÉTIF DE LA BRETONNE

A reading may benefit from a degree of concentration, so we will focus our attention on two characteristic models: that of the fictional utopias produced after 1750,[28] and that of Rétif de La

[25] Debouzy, 'L'esprit du roman', p. 3.
[26] Fauchery, *La Destinée féminine*, pp. 19–21.
[27] Ibid., pp. 35–9.
[28] Michel, 'Les Répresentations vestimentaires'.

Bretonne's *Les Contemporaines*.[29] This choice emphasises the importance for the novel of the fifty years preceding the Revolution, a
period prolific in utopias, when the creative process flourished in
the rich context of modifications to its social and cultural surroundings,[30] and when the critique of urban life provided Rétif with a
repertoire of observations and ideas conducive to the posing of
moral questions.[31] On the one hand, we read a mixture of anticipa-
tion and assertion, 'the features which are guessed and prophesied
for tomorrow's world or the day after tomorrow's', in the words of
Lucien Febvre writing about the *Utopia* of Thomas More.[32] The
genre offers types of social situation and, as it forecasts the future,
tries to impose guiding images which are found in the most diverse
forms of intellectual activity. It offers a dream of the future on the
basis of the life-styles of the present. On the other hand, the
novelist is able to present many situations, often repetitive (Rétif's
obsession with women permeates all his work) and where his
vision of reality is influenced either by the need to criticise (he was
an observer eager to reform morals) or make positive proposals (he
was anxious to present effective didactic models). Both utopias and
novel conceal an ideology; to interrogate it permits us to interpret
the texts as knowledge.[33]

The aesthetic of the Enlightenment novel is, happily for us,
inseparable from a conception of the body, though many texts are
silent with regard to the material details of clothing. A more
detailed study of the theme in works produced across Europe
would reveal, despite the universality of the fiction, contrasts in
behaviour and the diffusion of values and images. An analysis of
the sartorial connotations, which do not entirely coincide with
production, would reveal itineraries of exoticism, refuges of primitive nature, the expression of national characteristics and the presentation in a variety of ways of the relationship which links clothing
and passion and fluctuations of the psychology. The introduction
of clothes, even of linen, into fictional situations, and the anecdotes designed to illustrate the picturesque dimension of clothing,
more particularly for the lower classes, can reveal the meaning of

[29] Desmangeot, 'Le Système du vêtement'.
[30] B. Baczko, *Lumières de l'utopie* (Paris, 1978), pp. 18–20.
[31] Roche, *Peuple de Paris*, pp. 38–63, 177–84.
[32] *Pour une Histoire à part entière* (Paris, 1962), pp. 736–42.
[33] Benrekassa, 'Le typique et le fabuleux', pp. 31–56.

customs, reflect changes to sensibility and permit a sociology of the relationship between fictional manners and historical practices. However, it is clear that we have not yet reached the point when the description of costume makes its entry into literature, an original irruption, since detailed and meaningful, and an essential innovation, since it caused the novel to use clothing less as an accessory or mask, or to express a role or a condition, than as a powerful revelation of interiority, an obligatory means to decipher the other.[34] The relatively rare sartorial signs in the eighteenth-century novel are a clearer expression of man in society than the complex and teeming references in the novels of the nineteenth century, where they reveal the private man and feminine intimacy.[35]

## A SOCIOLOGY OF CLOTHING IN FICTION

By the seventeenth century, every foray into fiction confirms the social roles of clothing. Thus Sorel and Furetière provide good examples of social marking, where the costume corresponds to the personage, and ways of wearing colours, shapes and fabrics reveal first and foremost the socio-political hierarchies of dress. In the *Francion*, the gown and the shimmer of fabrics help to differentiate sexes and ages, and exalt social adherence, or mock it as with the gowns of magistrates. Colours serve to commend distinction and nobility: 'Here, it is all a question of shades, those which denote good form.' As in real life, a person can be precisely recognised for what he is, even for what he claims to be. The fictional alchemy makes it possible to castigate social turncoats and defend the need for reality and appearance to conform. The sartorial metamorphoses serve to illustrate both the autonomy of the culture of appearances and the appropriateness of the person to the personage expressed by successive changes of clothes and disguises. For an aristocratic culture, the affirmation of origins and personal liberty were what mattered above all.[36]

This early fictional tradition persisted throughout the century of the Enlightenment. Its vision of society hardly ventured beyond the

---

[34] Philippe Perrot, *Le Travail des apparences* (Paris, 1984).
[35] Ariès, *Histoire de la vie privée*, pp. 15–20.
[36] Pellegrin, 'L'être et le paraître'.

horizon of the rich and the idle. The other social groups appear only for form's sake, except for valets, maidservants and inn-keepers. The urban proletariat and marginals are introduced for their exoticism, as in the novel of low life. Peasants are decorative or illustrate the myths of the natural. As a result, subject to a more exhaustive inventory, the sartorial sociological realities seem deliberately biased, though novels can still yield a harvest of ordinary detail. We know how Rétif de La Bretonne stylised his peasants in order to exalt a patriarchal ideal and human nature; he turned their dislocation to educational purpose.[37] 'The social range of the quality extends from the nobility to the bourgeoisie, taking in a few refugees from the people.'[38] This was the social sphere of reference of potential readers, in sum the impact of the imagined clothes. Thus the diffusion of the images followed that of the progress of literacy and of the collective and private commercialisation of the book.[39]

If the world of the novelists remained that of the quality, that is, of a confused community with barely measurable values, it was also a milieu in the process of change, where the frontier passed less between the bourgeoisie, 'monkeys of the nobility' as in the seventeenth century, than between those integrated by the culture of leisure and the world of the acculturated petit bourgeoisie, prosperous peasants and small farmers, enriched urban shopkeepers and artisans. Their ascent towards the lofty spheres of refined spirits was then associated by the authors with the acquisition of the material signs of their adherence and the conquest of new sartorial styles, in sum with their entry into the civilisation of good manners, avatar of court society, domain of the proprieties and their constraints.

Whereas the seventeenth century mocked sartorial superfluity as a scandalous sign of the suspect acquisition of rank and fortune, evident proof of a vainglorious change of social class contrary to social order, eighteenth-century fiction illustrated the metamorphosis of manners allowed by learning new ways and adopting the

---

[37] Roche, *Peuple de Paris*, pp. 41–7.
[38] Fauchery, *La Destinée féminine*, p. 37.
[39] D. Roche, 'Sociétés et culture' in P. Goubert and D. Roche, *Les Français et l'Ancien Régime*, 2 vols. (Paris, 1985), vol. II; R. Chartier and H.-J. Martin, *Histoire de l'édition française* (Paris, 1982–4), vol. II, under the direction of D. Roche, *Le Livre triomphant*.

habits of people of quality.[40] In *Le Diable boiteux*, Lesage still described a 'knight of plebeian race', endowed with every satirical attribute which could be bestowed on him by a society as rigid in its hierarchies as in its formal and sumptuous outfits.[41] Clothing retained its place in the list of indicators of usurpation, alongside luxurious accommodation, extravagant spending on equipages and servants and an overloaded table. The social preoccupations were no different from those in the *Caquets de l'accouchée* of the reign of Louis XIII. As in *Le Bourgeois gentilhomme*, clothes were still presented in such a way as to show that the bourgeois and his wife longed to copy noble manners. The desire for social promotion was infectious. Thus, in Boursault:

> Foolish vanity puffs them all up,
> The sergeant's wife, if she could afford,
> Would wear clothes just like a bawd;
> The pimp's wife wants, in order to impress,
> To equal the wife of the lawyer in her dress;
> The lawyer's wife even dares
> To copy the wife of the counsellor's airs;
> The counsellor's wife is then not hesitant
> Even to vie with the wife of the president.[42]

The values expressed by the authors of the classical period conformed to the logic of the society of orders: the clothes ought to make the monk.

In contrast, sooner or later, and more or less overtly, the values authenticated by the novelists of the eighteenth century became those of a world which was gradually acquiring, if not a greater social mobility, which remains to be proved, at least some relaxation of the social hierarchies and probably, in consequence, less restricting conventions. A new style of life triumphed in which the bourgeois could become noble and the noble be 'bourgeoisified'. In the literary tradition, especially when it described the town and urban themes, appearance demonstrated the possibility of an osmosis of the classes. It no longer denounced parvenus so much as urban corruption.

[40] J.-V. Alter, *L'Esprit antibourgeois sous l'Ancien Régime, Littérature et tensions sociales aux XVIIe et XVIIIe siècles* (Geneva, 1970), pp. 106–13.

[41] *Le Diable boiteux* (Paris, 1894), p. 332.

[42] *Oeuvres complètes*, 10 vol. (Amsterdam, 1721), vol. I, *Les Fables d'Esope*, p. 81; Alter, *L'Esprit antibourgeois*, pp. 118–20.

It showed a society which was changing its character, opening up to contradictory influences, 'transferring to the plane of myth the interests and tensions which govern the social body'.[43]

MODESTY AND THE CLOTHING ECONOMY

If the novel remained restrained in its inventory of clothing, it was because more pertinent signs were available: the language of conversation and of passion, the convention of less rigid human relations. P. Fauchery has shown the three ways in which female dress was presented in the novel.[44] First, costume was superposed on the body which it repeated and protected. Its significance lay in valorisation and hyperbole. Glorifying the female body, it yet conferred on it a greater erotic value;[45] it was a shackle which impeded female mobility. The expressive power of the novel here emphasised the habitual roles of women ruled by the virtues of indoors and the home. Second, clothes were always associated with modesty. Bernardin de Saint-Pierre, in the death of Virginie ('Virginie, seeing that death was inevitable, placed one hand on her clothes, the other on her heart'),[46] hallowed the ultimate value of dress, integral part of the person. Lastly, dress had a role in the portrayal of seduction and various forms of amorous expression.

In these different acceptations, clothing always conveyed a moral and social meaning which served to indicate differences of origin and psychological contrasts. The Julie of *La nouvelle Héloïse* was less of a coquette as a young girl than when married and a mother; she needed less to please her lover than later to captivate her husband. For Jean-Jacques Rousseau, women's dress and clothes in general served to contrast two types of social behaviour, two moral economies. In Paris, Saint-Preux described Parisian women: 'Let us begin with the outside, which is what strikes most observers. [The women are] slight rather than well-built, they lack a fine figure, so they willingly adopt fashions which conceal the fact; I find it rather foolish of women in other countries to choose to copy fashions concocted to hide faults from which they do not suffer.'[47]

[43] Fauchery, *La Destinée féminine*, p. 39.
[44] Ibid., pp. 204–12.
[45] J.-J. Rousseau, *La Nouvelle Héloïse*, in *Oeuvres complètes*, vol. II, p. 147.
[46] *Paul et Virginie*, p. 203 of Paris edn of 1958.
[47] *Oeuvres complètes*, vol. II, pp. 265–8, see also pp. 234–5, 242.

The clothing of Parisian women concealed more than it revealed; it was that of a society ruled by fashion, though this precluded neither cleanliness nor delicacy, qualities indispensable to Rousseauist dress: 'You see the same fabrics at all levels and one could scarcely distinguish a duchess from a woman of the bourgeoisie were it not for the fact that the former possessed the art of finding distinctions which the latter would not dare to imitate.'[48] The novelist revealed himself a shrewd observer of the pursuit of distinction in an urban society in which, in his eyes, the confusion of appearances expressed the corruption of manners.

At Clarens, in contrast, clothing reflected the simplicity and authenticity which accorded with the principles of an economy closer to nature. It was simple and well chosen, 'the local materials provide almost all our furniture and clothes ... [dress] is not neglected but elegance is all, wealth never shows itself, still less fashion'. Here, the 'abundance of the necessary' reigned and dress conformed to need, rank and means. In the Rousseauist economic utopia, clothes and ornament retained an educative role,[49] and signified the symbolic opposition between town and country.

## THE SARTORIAL METAMORPHOSIS OF THE CORRUPTED PEASANT

This is clearly expressed in the popular fictional theme of the new-rich or corrupted peasant, notably in Marivaux and Rétif.[50] For the peasant, to enter a town was like 'landing on the moon', since the rules of the social game were no longer clear. Jacob, neither rich nor poor, son of a village nob, set off 'to seek fame and fortune' in Paris. An *arriviste* sprig, with a glib tongue, a certain style and a few manners, 'a good-looking lad', he must, if he was to succeed, abandon his rustic ways and country clothes. His metamorphosis, which the novelist compresses into a few hyperbolic days, takes place in the *hôtel* of a great lord, under the instruction of the maidservants, watched over by the mistress, who supervises and advises. 'Two days later, they brought me my clothes and linen and a hat and all the rest of the outfit.'[51] Powdered, curled and

[48] Ibid., vol. II, p. 267.
[49] Ibid., vol. II, pp. 550–3, see also pp. 609, 760.
[50] Roche, *Peuple de Paris*, pp. 177–80.
[51] Marivaux, *Le Paysan parvenu*, in *Romans*, pp. 568–76 of Paris edn of 1949.

generally licked into shape, the young rustic had been cleaned, whitened, dressed and transformed! Marivaux vividly expressed the necessity of a change of manners, the symbolic and real role played in this by dress and the influence of the novel on manners.

Rétif, too, forty years later, believed in this triple pedagogy. Returning to the theme, he described the same acts. But the failure of Edmond, despite all his efforts, expresses not so much a loss of sartorial conviction as the author's desire to persuade his readers to deplore the lure of the city and convince them of the dangers of urban immorality.[52] Fictional women were no different. The new urban existence of Marivaux's Marianne was punctuated by similar incidents.[53] Her clothes were stolen, and she was offered new. Clothing evokes dissolute seduction, sexual display and the dangers of city life for virtuous girls, but it also drives home the importance of social masks, since the fascination of clothes, fashion and the circulation of objects promoted the confusion of ranks.

## SEDUCTION IN CASANOVA, EDUCATIVE RIGOUR IN ROUSSEAU

The novelists put great emphasis on change – which their dreams may even have promoted. The attractions of a system of consumption based on the transitoriness and fascination of clothes were in any case programmed. You could accept the inevitable and exploit its possibilities, as did Casanova in his *Memoirs*[54] and Rousseau in the education of Emile and Sophie.[55]

For Casanova, clothing was primarily a language since he liked to dress up as much as to talk.[56] A chronological survey of incidents in which clothes occur shows the persistence of the theme and its textual applications; it flagged only towards the end, as if its power was exhausted by force of repetition, even by age. Casanova feared and detested old age, which he saw as the final cessation of the power of the appearances and fashions necessary to his pleasure: witness the portraits of the duchesse de Grammont

[52] Rétif de La Bretonne, *Le Paysan perverti ou les dangers de la ville*, 4 vols. (The Hague/Paris, 1776), vol. I, pp. iv–v, 30–60.

[53] Marivaux, *La Vie de Marianne*, in *Romans*, pp. 94–109.

[54] Ed. R. Abichared, 3 vols. (Paris, 1960).

[55] *Oeuvres complètes*, vol. IV.

[56] C. Thomas, *Casanova, un voyage libertin* (Paris, 1985), pp. 194–207.

and the maréchal de Villars.[57] For the rest, we find some half-dozen stock situations, not without some overlap; thus the theme of linen often complements that of hygiene and plays a part in licentious manoeuvres or worldly acts. The relatively equal importance accorded to the various sartorial themes may, as in the novel, reflect real life or question it by a mythological exaggeration in its imaginative horizon.

Casanova reveals the ubiquity of the clothing system which prevailed in the middle of the Enlightenment. He describes a dress which accorded to rank and fortune,[58] and portrays the world of people of quality, where costume, linen and jewels were inseparable from acts and habits. Thus the son of Mrs Cornelis, a pupil at the *pension* Viard, rue Saint-Victor, in Paris, learned 'to play the flute, ride, handle weapons, dance the minuet nicely, change his linen daily, reply politely, behave graciously, talk pleasantly about nothing and dress elegantly'.[59] Clothing is once again a sign of 'good form' and belonging to 'society'. But it is inseparable from other acquisitions, hygiene, a little washing and the practice of changing daily, or even more frequently, the linen, shirt and drawers which Casanova so enjoyed.[60] Having nothing to change into meant staying in bed; a trip to the laundry was a necessary preliminary to any important move; replenishing one's stock of fine linen – coarse shirts were for the peasantry or suspect nuns – was expensive, but essential.

The linen and clothing economy is also present, with its personnel of tailors, second-hand clothes dealers, jewellers, mercers and innumerable female fashion merchants.[61] They signified the diffusion of Paris fashions as much as the desire to look good or seduce.[62]

---

[57] *Mémoires*, vol. II, pp. 118–19, of the chevalier d'Arginy: 'His clothes were decorated with flowers and pompoms as in the time of Madame de Sévigné'; pp. 507–8, of the maréchal de Villars: 'I thought I was looking at a seventy-year old woman'; vol. I p. 508, of the duchesse de Grammont: 'I saw a decrepit old crone quite amazingly dolled up'.

[58] Thomas, *Casanova*, pp. 195–6.

[59] *Mémoires*, vol. II, pp. 157–8.

[60] Casanova hated women in drawers, especially black; see vol. III, pp. 125–6: 'Adèle allowed me to see her black panties ... I have always had a horror of women in panties, but especially black ... those black panties put black into my soul.' Needless to say, she removed them before her seduction.

[61] *Mémoires*, vol. I, p. 539: 'What makes Lyons rich is its good taste and good market, and the divinity to which the town owes its prosperity is fashion.'

[62] Female fashion merchants, linen-drapers and linen merchants mostly appear as secondary characters, or as principal players in scenes of seduction; see also

Table 37 *The occurrence of clothes as a theme in the* Memoirs of Casanova[a]

| | Clothes and conditions (economic, social and com- mercial) | Cleanli- ness, hygiene and water | Linen | Make one's toilet, dress and shine | Seduc- tion, gift and dressing someone | Masks, novelties and disguises |
|---|---|---|---|---|---|---|
| Before 1757 | 20 | 15 | 9 | 4 | 26 | 7 |
| 1757–63 | 18 | 9 | 6 | 14 | 25 | 10 |
| 1764–74 | 10 | 3 | 8 | 7 | 6 | 7 |
| Total | 48 | 27 | 23 | 25 | 57 | 24 |

[a] See *Mémoires*, ed. R. Abichared, 3 vols. (Paris, 1960)

Casanova was for a while a maker and producer of painted silk fabrics and indiennes. He was not notably successful; he preferred seducing his female employees to maximising his profits.[63] As with its other themes, *L'Histoire de ma vie* makes these habitual roles metaphors, but they never contradict the norms and practices known from other sources.

### THE PASSION FOR CLOTHES AND PYGMALIONISM

The biography constantly emphasises the imaginative function of clothes. Though all the time dealing with sex and seduction, thanks to an erotic writing which was neither dangerous nor shocking ('Say it, but don't call a spade a spade, that's what matters'), Casanova shows that the descriptive luxury of clothing, which contrasts with the banality of the images of love and formalistic simplicity of the amorous dialogue, 'should be read for itself not as the displaced excess of a forbidden nudity, but as the true prop of the story of a life and its immemorial record'.[64]

*Mémoires*, vol. II, pp. 249–60 for the Baret episode, where Casanova was at the same time client, publiciser and seducer.

[63] *Mémoires*, vol. II, pp. 235–7, 260–1.

[64] Thomas, *Casanova*, p. 198.

Two expressions convey the sense of an approach which, as in fiction, eventually confers on clothing an autonomous and metonymical life: 'to make one's toilet' and 'to adorn oneself', for imposing himself and them; 'to dress', for to undress his conquests. The two activities ruined him financially but were symbolically complementary. The point was to acquire in the eyes of others, by the prestige and splendour of his attire, a social and personal identity which was seriously compromised by his life-style as an adventurer. He needed to add to the never-failing pleasure of dressing and displaying himself that of transforming and exposing the women whom he loved and seduced. His frivolity was the ultimate result of a belief in the sartorial expression of social roles: elegance remained, in a world of supreme refinement, the best passport to good society, as it remained also for simple souls; Casanova could escape from his Venetian prison because sumptuously clothed,[65] whilst the splendour of his appearance guaranteed him entry to aristocratic society, and consequently resources, even a share in economic redistribution through games of chance.[66] Further, by decking a woman out, Casanova could deploy his artistic talents, and show that the fascination of dressing her in whatever displayed her best was more sexually provocative and powerful than undressing her. 'Stripping only reveals what is there', and it made a poorer spectacle – a few episodes of quite explicit voyeurism apart –[67] than the voluptuous pleasures of a demiurgic prelude which in a way authenticated the power of the gift economy in aristocratic societies. In sum, clothes in Casanova express the power of social propriety, a respect for fashion – expression of adherence to court society, the ultimate model – and the dream of never-ending seduction, in which elegance and finery were already desire.

[65] *Mémoires*, vol. I, pp. 1061–2.

[66] Ibid., vol. III, p. 104: 'For my part, wishing to shine in the eyes of my proud oligarchs, I dressed myself splendidly: I had a suit of ash-grey nap velvet embroidered with gold and silver spangles, a shirt trimmed with needlepoint, [sleeve ruffles] which cost at least 50 *louis*, plus my diamonds, my watches on a diamond chain, my sword of the best English steel, my snuff-box embellished with fine brilliants, and my knight's cross, also of brilliants with my buckles of the same stone.'

[67] *Mémoires*, vol. II, p. 822, Lia, a young Jewess, performs a veritable strip-tease.

## CLOTHES IN *EMILE*: CONFORMISM AND REFORM

Casanova was free with information about how he had acquired his habits. He had learned cleanliness in his childhood in Venice, in the shady and artificial theatrical circles where his mother held sway; he had acquired elegance during the course of the adventures which took him, via numerous occupations and many vicissitudes, to the liberty and libertinage of smart society. Rousseau, on the other hand, offered his readers a sartorial utopia inasmuch as his didactic novel offered a total picture of a different society, and appealed to their imagination by means of concrete images of daily life. Consequently, *Emile* is interesting for its examples of fictional figures of the Enlightenment, but also because it influenced writers of very different ideologies, including Mme de Genlis, Sophie de La Roche and Rétif, and because it reached a cultivated and wealthy public which conducted various experiments on the basis of its advice, as is shown by the letters of his correspondents and admirers.[68]

In Rousseau, the culture of appearances was taught and learned by a rational process rather than in the haphazard manner described by Casanova. This apprenticeship was inseparable from an overall education which reveals the new ideas about the sanctity of childhood and the love which it should be shown. The new autonomy resulted, in the long term, in a debate on special clothes for children (something Rousseau hardly discussed), but more specifically, in the short term, in the application to costume of the reforming principles of the culture of the body. Clothing ought to contribute to the present and above all the future health of children of both sexes; Emile and Sophie would no longer be clothed according to the old bad habits everywhere predominant, but in accord with the norms of a more natural and less confined education.

The clothes of little French boys were unhealthy; they would be better off in clothes which freed the limbs, allowed the humours to circulate, facilitated exercise and accustomed them to a more active life.[69] The body should be toughened, for which nature and the

---

[68] D. Roche, 'Les primitifs du rousseauisme', *Annales: ESC* (1971), pp. 151–72; Darnton, *The Great Cat Massacre* (pp. 201–38 of French translation).

[69] *Emile*, pp. 371–2.

people, supposedly closer to their roots, or at any rate less decultured by civilisation, provided the models: 'I would counsel both not to change costume according to the seasons, and that will be the constant practice of my Emile. By this I do not mean that he will wear his winter clothes in the summer, as do sedentary people, but that he will wear his summer clothes in the winter, as do working people.'[70]

Girls should be treated in the same way, since the first culture should be that of the body, even if the purpose was different for each sex; for one, the development of charm and grace, for the other, that of strength and skill. Sophie should be liberated from her 'Gothic shackles', that is, she should no longer wear 'whalebone corset'; she would then discover freedom of movement and robustness, the manners and beauty of the ancients.[71] But here, the similarity of methods between little girls and little boys ceased, since the former must learn the actions appropriate to their role. 'Observe a little girl spending the day around her doll, constantly changing its clothes, dressing and undressing it hundreds and hundreds of times, continuously seeking new combinations of ornaments, well- or ill-matched, it makes no difference ... she awaits the moment when she will be her own doll. This is a very definite primary taste. You have only to follow and regulate it.'[72] Sophie must learn to be a woman according to the conception of female nature held by Rousseau, without breaking with the dominant mentality.

In fact, underlying Rousseau's reform was an image of a society where the language of signs ought to be clearly legible, so that clothing would recover its eloquence in proportion to each person's estate. It had a political function which should be copied from the Romans: 'Different clothing according to ages and according to stations – togas, sagums, praetexts, bullas, laticlaves; thrones, lictors, fasces, axes, crowns of gold; ovations, triumphs. Everything with them was display, show, ceremony, and everything made an impression on the hearts of the citizens.'[73] The way one dressed was a rhetoric; it took on the civic reason of a body. It was also a moral economy, and ought to renounce the wastefulness of luxury,

[70] Ibid., p. 373 (p. 127 of Penguin Classic edition of 1991).
[71] Ibid., pp. 705–7.
[72] Ibid., pp. 706–7 (p. 367 of Penguin edition).
[73] Ibid., pp. 646–7 (p. 322 of Penguin edition).

reject the slavery of gilded clothes and the sham of opulence and allow more transparent social and personal relationships, uniting people despite their differences.

Thus the conformism of Rousseau, though he might employ the hackneyed themes of Christian clothing morality and the economy of good manners,[74] and though he denounced ostentatious extravagance and superfluous consumption,[75] was compatible with other perspectives which broke with the principles to be discerned in dress à la Casanova, but limited to the register of worldly relations. In *Emile*, too, one should appear what one was, but the social person was not all: one might dazzle by one's appearance but one could only truly please by one's personality.[76] The true citizen, in tune with his times but open to the future, could not be content with the pleasures of the toilet. To dress and undress women, as Casanova liked to do, was in a sense to play with dolls like little girls, to refuse the political roles of male, Roman, even Spartan, society. The seductive exchange fundamental in Casanova was only a by-way in the gift economy,[77] which rejected the equality of relations between men dreamt of by Rousseau, and despite the inequality of conditions and sexes: a man is not made by his clothes, whereas he was altogether made by them and enslaved by his prejudices. If a person is all in his attire, the new distribution of roles imposed by the real Revolution could not but inspire terror in Casanova;[78] we know that Rousseau to some extent inspired him with transitory equality and the transparency of appearances. But *Emile* did not necessarily lead to changes in dress; a sort of new conformism, a 'pre-dandyism' in which clothes were the passport to a frivolous equality, is discernible:

> I would want my fortune to provide ease everywhere and never to create a feeling of inequality. Garishness of dress is inconvenient in countless respects. In order to retain all possible liberty, when I am among other men, I would want to be dressed in such a way that in every rank I appeared to be in my place, and that I did not stand out in any – so that without affectation and without changing my appearance, I could be one of the people at

[74] Ibid., pp. 713–15, 745–6.
[75] Ibid., pp. 572–4.
[76] Ibid., pp. 713–14, 779.
[77] Ibid., p. 683, 'one buys neither one's husband, nor one's mistress'.
[78] Thomas, *Casanova*, pp. 116–22, 194–5.

the *guingette* and good company at the Palais-Royal. In this way I would be more the master of my conduct, and I would put the pleasures of all stations always within my reach. It is said that there are women who close their doors on embroidered cuffs and receive no-one who does not wear lace. I would go and spend my day elsewhere. But if these women were young and pretty. I could sometimes put on lace in order to spend – at the very most – the night there.[79]

The ease and sociability of mutual attachment permit a variety of experiences. But is the equality of appearances perhaps only possible to those exceptional beings united in the community of the sensitive, if not the distinction of good taste? In his own life, Rousseau began his personal reform by a sartorial revolution, exchanging his fashionable clothes for more modest outfits and the 'Armenian coat' which provoked laughter in the salons. The *Confessions* and *Emile* reveal the contradictions of reality and the imaginary in the wisdom of appearances. This same tension would permeate utopian writings and Rétif.

## CLOTHES IN THE UTOPIAS AND *LES CONTEMPORAINES*: THE CORPUS

Like the novel, the utopia as a genre lacks clear boundaries. But a treatment of clothing is essential to its definition; Jean Servier makes it one of the nine criteria he uses to define the genre, and according to Pierre Versins: 'In sum, clothes make the utopian.'[80] Their value for us is that we are able to compare real and fictional clothing more easily inasmuch as literary studies have shown how the codification of utopian models only works from concrete bases.[81] We find a fabulous representation, a quasi-mythology of the clothing culture, where the forms, functions and uses of dressing and costume are organised into a textual system in order to produce the visible within the readable,[82] and reveal the hidden

---

[79] *Emile*, p. 683 (p. 348 of Penguin edition).

[80] Michel, 'Les Répresentations vestimentaires', pp. 1–30; J. Servier, *L'Utopie* (Paris, 1979), pp. 93–4; P. Versins, *Encyclopédie des utopies* (Lausanne, 1972), pp. 596–7.

[81] C.-G. Dubois, *Problèmes de l'utopie* (Paris, 1918), p. 14; A. Cioranescu, *L'Avenir du passé: utopie et littérature* (Paris, 1972), p. 25; E. Bloch, *L'Esprit de l'utopie* (Paris, 1977), pp. 50–5.

[82] L. Marin, *Utopiques: jeux d'espace* (Paris, 1973), p. 92.

meaning of diffuse practices. Utopias achieve their effect through a compromise between principle and reality; an anthropological truth of clothing can be discerned as they steer their course between lived and dreamed cultures.

A hundred texts have been analysed from this perspective, covering the years from 1750 to 1789; they constitute, hardly surprisingly, a disparate corpus, a true reflection of utopias since their origins with Thomas More.[83] Inhibited by the rational, dominated by the ideological and fictional discourse, more or less strongly attracted in the direction of the novel, the authors might choose from many formulas: the imaginary voyage in space or time, the fictional dialogue, the rediscovered correspondence, the constitutional construction or the political, even didactic programme. Certainly, the novel is superior for organised reflection and with it the cultural unity consistent with the social limits of the world of the authors, united by the desire to show themselve free thinkers.[84] No precise frontiers separate the playful from the global social project, and we find not so much a community of the imagination as the coherence of an approach which articulates permanent unease through images of otherness.[85] We will look first at utopian clothing, then at its functions.

Rétif's *Les Contemporaines* gives us an opportunity to use the novel in a different way, to compare an example of the transformation of the clothing context in the language, and how it was imagined from a more specific perspective. Whereas the utopias modulate individual and collective social dreams by materialising diverse societies, Rétif's novel makes clearer the impact of recollection and the distortions of a personal vision torn between obsession and didacticism.[86] Behind the text describing a fictitious clothing system, we see the ideology of urban acculturation and the town/

[83] Marin, *Utopiques*, pp. 81–2; M. Winter, *Compendium utopiarum typologiae und Bibliographie literarischer Utopien* (Stuttgart, 1978).

[84] Baczko, *Lumières*, pp. 31–3, 60–4. The authors share three characteristics: they are from the scholarly and cultural elite, often in conflict with the established order and unstable, always travellers and mostly preoccupied with political reform; they include both some great names of the Enlightenment (Prévost before 1750, Sade, Diderot and Rousseau in his way) and some second rankers (Mercier, Grivel, Poncelin de La Roche, Casanova, Brissot); the utopia was both a game and a means to other ends.

[85] Baczko, *Lumières*, p. 61.

[86] Desmangeot, 'Le Système du vêtement', pp. 5–30.

country opposition in a still predominantly peasant society. The work is largely autobiographical and influenced by the personal journey of the novelist who, after *Le Paysan perverti*, *L'Ecole des pères* and the first fifteen volumes of *Les Contemporaines*, moved from depicting middling and exalted conditions to describing the ordinary lot, a progress which Pierre Testud called 'naturalism on the move'.[87] The successive editions and reprints added to the size of the corpus and the range of its field of observation; sixteen volumes before 1780, forty-two in the so-called Leipzig edition printed between 1780 and 1785; this is the basic text used by Marie-Christine Desmangeot, on whose work we draw here.[88]

## CLOTHING IN UTOPIAS: A SIGN OF MATERIALITY

No utopia, if we except two rather marginal works,[89] places the clothing system at the centre of its plan. However, few texts disregard the theme, which appears everywhere in a more or less developed form: 38, that is, a fifth, of the 160 works listed by Alain Michel ignore it completely. The extent to which they describe garments, discuss clothing or simply refer indirectly to the costume of the utopians is a matter not so much of a more rational vision or imaginative approach as of the desire of the authors to make their work more complete, more vivid and more specific: clothing is always one among other signs within a narrative or a more global political design. It is a useful excuse for constructing another history or another geography which diverged from the immediate social situation. It may be developed at length or only mentioned in passing. Like other utopian features, it obeyed both the rule of contingency and the logic which made a certain materiality indispensable to a convincing imaginary society. In its production and

---

[87] P. Testud, *Rétif de La Bretonne et la création littéraire* (Geneva/Paris, 1977), p. 101.

[88] The complete edition in 42 volumes in-12 consists of 272 short stories and 444 anecdotes (B.N., Rés. 23098A*QQ**); part 1, 1780–1, 17 vols. of the *Contemporaines* or the *Contemporaines mêlées*; part 2, 1782–3, 13 vols., *Les Contemporaines du commun*; part 3, 12 vols., *Les Contemporaines par graduation*; see also J. Rives-Childs, *Rétif de La Bretonne, témoignages et jugements, bibliographie* (Paris, n.d.).

[89] Marquis de Caraccioli, *La Critique des dames et des messieurs à leur toilette* (Paris, 1770); Beffoy de Reigny, 'Les anecdotes du vaisseau chargé de modes', in *Les Lunes du cousin Jacques* (Paris, 1785).

consumption, and in the description of its components, utopian clothing expresses a distance: it was the tangible symbol of an often successful formalism.

The clothes in utopias were not necessarily utopian, and were less often alternatives to than consistent with actual habits and practices. Their authors were not particularly imaginative when it came to inventing new raw materials or technical processes. In fact, in a discourse which was constantly torn between the need to praise the marvels of nature and that to criticise culture, the descriptions of clothing made apparent the relativity of European behaviour compared with a fictional exoticism where dress had to correspond to a state of civilisation; it was, in the words of Condorcet, 'the sign which separates man from the animals'. The physical context was important in revealing these contingencies, whether it was fantastic (as in *Le Monde de Mercure*)[90] or naturist, extending to every latitude, from hot to cold, from tropical islands (as in *L'Elève de la Nature*)[91] to temperate climes (as in the *Histoire des Calligènes*),[92] or even simply analogous to Europe, and more or less free of climatic determinism (as in *L'an 2440*, the look forward in time of Louis Sébastien Mercier, which was really Paris).[93] In accord with the imaginary geography of the Enlightenment, which was primarily spiritual and philosophic, the climate influenced behaviour and permitted types of development, helped to make visible cultural contrasts and allowed endless discussion of the opposition between necessity and superfluity. The space of utopian clothing was never wholly neutral since it allowed authors to criticise or extol the behaviour of the 'Europe of the ancient parapets', and combine poetry and reason.

## CULTURAL CLOTHING AND NATURAL CLOTHING

The vocabulary, language and images of clothing reveal the all-pervasive influence of ideology. On the one hand, culture ruled, and the clothes remained those of civilised cities. Often a subterfuge, modelled on Robinson Crusoe, solved the problem: a washed-up

[90] Béthune, *Relation du Monde de Mercure* (Geneva, 1750).
[91] Beaurieu, *L'Elève de la Nature*, 3 vols. (Amsterdam/Paris, 1771).
[92] Thiphaine de La Roche, *Histoire des Calligènes où Mémoires de Duncan* (Amsterdam/Paris, 1765).
[93] 1786 (n.p.).

trunk or shipwrecked vessel yielded their cargoes, and their clothes, fabrics, shoes and headgear became rational models for the indigenous populations. A colonialism of dress imposed the superiority of western manners and discovered the raw materials, techniques and even the forms suitable to a bodily and cultural metamorphosis.[94] Victorin, in Rétif's *Le Mont inaccessible*,[95] brought 'all the discoveries and facilities of his age', since he lacked the time to let history begin all over again; he wanted no longer to depend on anyone, so he transposed his universe and dressed as Frenchmen the natives he civilised. The French adventurer invented by Lesuire was another Robinson Crusoe, but more severely handicapped:[96] having arrived naked on his island, he invented felt and reinvented spinning, weaving and tanning. He covered his nudity with leaves, stuffs and skins, and contrived stockings, shoes and caps which were those of an ordinary European. Necessity and reflection taught him every trade and, at the end of the day, we are back with convenience and elegance.[97] Too often, however, the trunk of Robinson Crusoe and the ingenuity of the travellers drew utopia into the sphere of trade and the economy of luxury. Artificiality threatened manners in spite of warnings, instability gained on all sides. The utopian discourse became simply the echo of that of the clothing reformers.

Where nature ruled, we find all the fantasies of the illuminist imagination in love with primitivism; the principal device was to imagine a situation where the external conditions of human existence guaranteed social transformation. Human happiness lay at the end of a road which might take every conceivable route, from radical challenge to moderate reform.[98] To begin with, the clothes were those of savages or, less often, non-existent. 'When we emerged from the hands of nature, we were naked', wrote André, author of *Le Tartare à Paris*,[99] and for Morelly, 'nudity is an ornament of nature, abandoned by all the peoples of the earth who

---

[94] M. Duchet, *Anthropologie et histoire au siècle des Lumières* (Paris, 1971), pp. 60–1.

[95] *La Découverte australe*, 4 vols. (Paris, 1787), vol. I, and preface to the 1977 edition by J. Lacarrière, pp. 15–17.

[96] Paris, 1782, pp. 2–18.

[97] As in *L'Elève de la Nature*, where Ariste in turn climbs back up, history passes from the state of nature to society.

[98] Baczko, *Lumières*, pp. 60–1, 124–5.

[99] Paris, 1788, p. 82.

are clothed'.[100] In the history of utopian peoples, initial nakedness equated to the beginning of the personal adventures of the Robinson Crusoes, all eager to restore their sartorial humanity and so rediscover the familiar context of the proprieties. The most metaphysical and the most challenging utopias, those proposing a new moral and social condition, *Le vrai Système* of Dom Deschamps,[101] or *Le Voyage à Tamoé* in the marquis de Sade's *Aline et Valcour*,[102] included nudity among the means to denounce lying, hypocrisy, guile and the artificial passions. Other conventions reigned for the young Tahitians of Diderot or of Bricaire de la Dixmerie.[103] With the help of exoticism, the utopias drew sustenance from travel stories, and their success was assured by the same public;[104] we see the triumph of another relationship to the body.

A MORAL AND INITIATORY CLOTHING

Clothing as a mask had been denounced since Thomas More, whether it served to conceal a bodily deformity (the theme then figured in utopian marriage rites: the Ajoïens of *La République des philosophes* wore special clothes,[105] and in *Le Monde de Mercure* the two nights preceding the wedding served to decode the enigmas of dress)[106] or spiritual faults (*L'Elève de la nature* saw this as a trait of human nature, since 'men are probably badly made and use these draperies to conceal their faults').[107] Utopian naturalism strove to show the features which would restore to dress the moral ingenuousness it had lost in civilised countries. To this end, it made many inventions; imaginary materials created wardrobes which were both aesthetic and functional: a protective sun lotion in *Le Monde de Mercure*, salamander skin in Villeneuve's *Le Voyageur philosophe*, cloth of asbestos, butterfly wings or crystal or down of

---

[100] *La Basiliade* (Messina/Paris, 1753), p. 27.
[101] *Le vrai Système* (ed. Paris/Geneva, 1959), p. 177; Baczko, *Lumières*, pp. 123, 130–2.
[102] Paris, 1785, p. 103 (Tamoé).
[103] *Supplément au voyage de Bougainville* (Paris, 1773), p. 150 of 1972 edn; *Le Sauvage de Tahiti* (London/Paris, 1770), p. 46.
[104] Duchet, *Anthropologie*, pp. 10–69.
[105] P. Poivre, *Voyage d'un philosophe* (Yverdon, 1708), p. 114.
[106] *Monde de Mercure*, p. 254.
[107] *Elève de nature*, vol. I, p. 60, vol. II, p. 190.

humming-birds in Voltaire's *L'Eldorado*, cork in the underground abodes of gnomes.

On the island of the Calligènes, the inhabitants were threatened with a general nakedness: 'with regard to clothing, everything was lacking'; the population increased, but there were no usable plants and no animals, hence neither wool nor skins. The original population had been refugees fleeing Europe and religious persecution; once shipwrecked, they quickly exhausted the stock of materials they had got from the ship and sparingly distributed. Almont, founder of the city, father of a family and creator of a moral civilisation, then discovered 'aerial flax'.

The episode reveals the many symbolic and initiatory values invested in the clothing of the Calligènes. The chosen plant was born of the sea, like the island society which had escaped from and been purified by the waters. 'It was an aerial flax. It rose in the air and floated in the wind. As if beneath the sea, these plants adorned with different colours and composed of almost imperceptible filaments, with no strength in their stem, no stiffness in their parts, are supported by the water and sway in the waves.' Once discovered, cultivated and transformed, the aerial plant produced clothes which, 'thanks to the materials ... were of such great beauty that, despite the little skill, the fabrics had a brilliance and a quality which rendered them equal, and perhaps superior, to those which the Europeans most admired of this type'.[108] In its physical qualities, the utopian wardrobe surpassed anything civilisation could produce.[109] This was because it had a moral value and originally only met a need; it resisted time, and its beauty and the brilliance of its colours were only improved by wear; it made social relations easy since the fabrics enjoyed the extraordinary property of imparting a sweet scent 'exactly as needed', so that everyone was informed by smell as much as by colour and shape. 'To say that a gown

---

[108] *Histoire des Calligènes*, pp. 71–9.

[109] The point is underlined by the scatalogical origins of the material in *La Lune du cousin Jacques* (pp. 122–3): 'You ask why we spin dung and you cannot imagine that such a dirty material could be of the slightest use ... it is no more surprising to transform a fibrous mud into a coat or a garment than to transform clay into transparent crystal ... your hemps and your flaxes need much more preparation than our droppings to become shirts or kerchiefs.' A primary raw material guaranteed the virtue of the lunar clothes, the moral alchemy of the utopia used a sign of gross materiality for an ultimate purpose which was all the more elevated.

smells good is to say that it is beautiful and in good taste', 'to have a good nose' was to possess good judgement in the true sense, and in society the scent of clothes, the shimmer of fabrics and the brilliance of conversation intermingled. Nature and culture were reconciled as the categories of the perceptible. Visibility was all.

One could continue indefinitely the catalogue of sartorial inventions dreamed up to give greater transparency to fictitious societies, and so once again discover, by other routes, condemnation of social confusion and all the ethical furore provoked by the transformation of appearances and the widespread revolution in the consumption of linen and clothes. However, to leave it there would probably be to take too literally the social substitutions in literature; the process was subtler, even if its prime meaning suited the profound didacticism and desire to predict the future of the authors of the utopias. Should we rank them on the side of rupture or of conservatism? Do they represent a consciousness of change or the ideology of immobilism?[110]

## CLOTHES FOR THE PAST AND CLOTHES FOR THE FUTURE

Let us accept that the political and literary novels and the utopian texts were intended to challenge in the sphere of clothing as in other spheres, because their discourses are such as to bring together phenomena which are scattered, although a product of the same imaginative structures.[111] The sartorial theme is then a sign of a global project for moral reform. It spontaneously adapted to the language then being employed for similar questions by philosophers and politicians. Rousseau can here be read as a utopian or not, as one wishes, since *Emilie* and *La nouvelle Héloïse* discuss analogous questions and offer comparable solutions; a change of society was inconceivable without a reform of behaviour, for which models could be found in the past, a golden age, or in the future, an eschatalogical progress. Thus the very different ideas of the authors of utopias came together in their criticism and their formulation of new norms.

This is a familiar theme. To emphasise the critique of morals, every aspect of the economy of dress was questioned; the rejection

[110] Baczko, *Les Imaginaires sociaux*, pp. 87–92.
[111] Ibid., pp. 94–5.

428 _Truth and the mask_

of buying and credit;[112] a rational and regulated organisation of production;[113] distrust of circulation;[114] the desire to limit costs and fix levels of consumption; denunciation of a poorly understood luxury; the eulogy of parsimony in adornment and, of course, an attack on fashion, which might be coupled with a more general discussion of the power of public opinion, as in Rousseau's _Emile_.[115] The desire for reform is visible in the discussions of a more convenient and simpler clothing, and one that was healthier; in utopia more than elsewhere, clothes were the sign of a society's health.[116]

---

[112] The ideal of barter appears in Sade, _Tamoé_, p. 452, and in Caraccioli, _Critique des dames_, p. 113; in _L'An 2440_ (pp. 29–31), Mercier criticises 'the art of making debts'.

[113] The abbé Coyer, in _Chinki, Histoire cochinchinoise_ (Paris/London, 1768), offers a critique of the corporations aimed at a more rational organisation of production, and in _L'Ile frivole_ (Paris/The Hague, 1751), he invented the 'controller of fashion' (p. 12); M. A. Roumier, in _Le Voyage de Milord Ceton_ (Paris/The Hague, 1765), gives this responsibility to an academy of women (pp. 250–7); in _Le Prince_ (Amsterdam/Paris, 1751), Morelly develops the idea of commercial control (pp. 106–10).

[114] _Sauvage de Tahiti_, pp. 44–5.

[115] The polemic about harmful or useful luxury permeates the utopias: Villeneuve in _Le Voyageur philosophe_ (p. 33), Roumier (p. 11 of vol. II of _Voyage dans la planète Mercure_), Morelly in _Le Code de la Nature_ and Dom Deschamps in _Le Système_ all despise luxury and superfluity; Mercier in _L'An 2440_ defends a useful luxury.

[116] Mercier, _L'An 2440_, pp. 25–8, gives a good example of model reformed clothing: 'The way in which he was dressed ... in no way displeased me. His hat was no longer of that sad and gloomy colour, nor encumbered with horns, all that was left was the crown which was deep enough to keep on the head and which was also surrounded with a brim. This neatly rolled brim remained folded over as long as it was not needed, and could be lowered or brought forward as its wearer wished, to provide protection from the sun or bad weather. His neatly pleated hair formed a knot behind the head and a light sprinkling of powder let its natural colour show. This simple arrangement meant no pyramid plastered with pomade and pride, nor those dreary wings which make people look for ever startled, nor those rigid curls which, far from recalling flowing hair, are only expressionlessly and gracelessly stiff. His neck was not strangled by a narrow muslin band, but surrounded by a cravat which was more or less warm according to the season. His arms enjoyed complete freedom in sleeves of medium width; and his body, lightly clad in a sort of sober waistcoat, was covered with a mantle in the form of a gown which was extremely useful in wet or cold weather. A large scarf nobly encircled his kidneys and was equally warm. He had no garters cutting into his shins and impeding his circulation. His long stockings covered him from his feet to his belt, and comfortable shoes in the form of ankle-boots enclosed his feet.' Free circulation, convenience, cleanliness, adaptability to the seasons, all the imperatives of a reformed clothing are present.

We need to look more carefully at the interaction, even the opposition, between the desire to differentiate, in accord with a belief in the social efficacy of signs, and the determination to standardise. The variety of territories and spaces in utopia often required the former, whilst imagining the future suggested a complex interplay between the collective dimension – which demanded that appearances be controlled and regulated, above all when greater equality was desired – and the need to articulate individuality and the social, and maintain the functional differences between the ages and sexes, between holiday and work, between political roles, even between social groups.[117] In sum, the theatre of the utopias saw enacted the basic conflict of the culture of appearances, in which egalitarianism confronted the sense of hierarchy, and individualism confronted social, religious and political regulation. In utopia, difference should be a reminder of duties, and uniformity warn all utopians that they were only human. The reign of variety without differentiation was possible.[118]

## *LES CONTEMPORAINES*, CLOTHED AND UNCLOTHED

In its own way, *Les Contemporaines* returns to all these questions. Rétif gives us, as well as a penetrating view of the clothing question in Parisian society, a lesson, which is inseparable from the fictional strategies. He affirms a desire to encompass and describe all conditions of society but with a moral purpose, and employs effective literary techniques to this end: a hotch-potch of descriptions with endless variations; the use of short stories and narratives, only tenuously linked, which allow his imagination free play.[119] This is what differentiates him from the great novelists of the nineteenth century, such as Balzac and Zola, who convey a more mythical vision of dress, whilst Rétif remains more prosaically fictional. However, his importance lies in the play he reveals between idealism

---

[117] Morelly, *Le Prince*, p. 40; Sade, *Tamoé*, p. 215; Morelly, *La Basiliade*, p. 37; Villeneuve, *Le Voyageur philosophe*, p. 37; in the *Aprilis* of Duplessis (Paris/London, 1787), p. 60, women wore hats and men wore caps; Morelly, in *Le Code de la Nature*, pp. 205–6, lists the possible categories; Mercier, *L'An 2440*, pp. 38, 65.

[118] M. Ozouf, *La Fête révolutionnaire* (Paris, 1976), p. 134.

[119] Desmangeot, 'Le Système du vêtement', pp. 29–31, 48–53; Roche, *Peuple de Paris*, p. 179.

and realism, and the way he seeks to use his profound sensibility to portray the life of the mass of the population in their most undesirable as well as their most desirable aspects.[120]

The society which Rétif observed and recorded can be read in different ways: it lay at the point of intersection of the novelist's choices and real life. Its topography was essentially urban; Rétif used the Parisian street scene for exotic effect, he localised without too great a concern for accuracy and he consistently idealised the peasant world in order to point the contrast with the corruption and deculturation of the population of Paris (see tables 38 and 39): in the country, attitudes to clothing were healthy, in the town, they were baleful and must be corrected by a new aesthetic morality of appearances. Urban clothing was therefore a constant preoccupation, coupled with a heavy concentration on women and girls: their beauty was necessary to the novel's theme, and the comparison of their virtues with those of men was part of the rhetoric familiar to the characters in short stories.[121] The pretty sempstress, the lovely milkmaid, the graceful shopkeeper, the sturdy young woman, shame-faced women, ugly women, virtuous women, glorious wives thus composed a gallery of female sartorial habits, but like the thousand facets of one story, which Rétif was telling primarily to himself.

Society according to Rétif was dominated by the intermediate classes, those mixed and mobile groups unified by the sociability of shop, street and work, merchants, craftsmen, artists.[122] If we add domestic servants, we have the group responsible for the clothing revolution and Rétif emphasises the role of women producers and consumers. 'Among all the merchants, women remain important, and the reason is clear: in a certain type of company she is all since she has the title, as with the linen-drapers and the dressmakers, in others without having a title, she can do everything as with the mercer fashion merchants'; women were initiators in production,

---

[120] Mercier, *Le Journal des dames* (1776): 'All the same, everybody wanted to read him and most people found striking portraits, vividly drawn characters, a profound knowledge of the manners of the capital . . . an astonishing energy in many pictures of corruption and crime, and details which testify to the author's vivid imagination. He possessed both truth and genius', quoted by Desmangeot, 'Le Système du vêtement', p. 53.

[121] Fauchery, *La Destinée féminine*, p. 308.

[122] See the postscript to vol. XIX of the first edition of *Les Contemporaines* and the story *La Jolie Pelletière*; see also *Le Ménage parisien*.

Table 38 *The society of* Les Contemporaines (I)[a]

|  | Town | Country | Men | Women | Young girls |
|---|---|---|---|---|---|
| Contemporaines mêlées | 82 | 1 | 25 | 37 | 21 |
| Contemporaines du commun | 66 | 1 | 18 | 12 | 37 |
| Contemporaines graduées | 11 | 1 | 4 | 7 | 1 |
| Total | 159(98%) | 3(2%) | 47(29%) | 56(35%) | 59(36%) |

[a] See M.-C. Desmangeot, 'Le Système du vêtement dans *Les Contemporaines*', mémoire de maîtrise, University of Paris 1 (1982), pp. 31–40; the tables are based on a systematic listing of situations in which clothing occurs

as in the standardisation of behaviour and a new elegance was apparent in the manners of the people.[123]

RÉTIF'S CLOTHING IN PLACE

In the 162 situations in which clothing figures, Rétif's description proceeds from the physique to dress. The body was first described on the basis of a topology of highly symbolic elements; the hair connoted behaviour,[124] the colour of a face moral health, the delicacy of the limbs and the figure erotic promise, the arch of a foot a fetishistic fascination.[125] Nudity was rare in an author who was satisfied with fleeting perceptions; 'the air which gives life to her charms' was for him sufficient; he expressed an essential femininity, 'of nature', which the artifice of dress ought to emphasise rather than conceal. There was no need to describe male or female wardrobes; they were those of their age, and only of interest when they were needed to add realism, or when they revealed significant associations, for example, fabrics and colours: simple white linens announced unsullied purity, luxurious and shimmering fabrics revealed complex feelings, even depravity. Clothing could mark every

[123] Rétif de La Bretonne, *Les Nuits de Paris*, 7 vols. (Paris/London, 1788), pp. 182–3, 580, 887–92.

[124] *Les Contemporaines*, story 64, *La Petite Coureuse*, declaration of M. Bouteille; Desmangeot, 'Le Système du vêtement', pp. 61–3.

[125] Brunettes were honourable, lively, alert, tender and proud; blondes were more ambivalent and always more delicate; for fetishism, see Dr Louis, *La Revue médicale* (1904).

Table 39 *The society of* Les Contemporaines (II)

| | Merchants and artisans | Liberal professions and army | Intellectuals and artists | Miscellaneous crafts | Nobility | Bourgeoisie | Miscellaneous[a] |
|---|---|---|---|---|---|---|---|
| Contemporaines mêlées | 38 | 8 | 1 | 3 | 13 | 2 | 18 |
| Contemporaines du common | 48 | — | 5 | — | 2 | 2 | 6 |
| Contemporaines graduées | — | 6 | — | 1 | — | — | 1 |
| Total | 86 | 14 | 6 | 4 | 15 | 4 | 25 |

[a] Those defined by a qualitative sociology; poor, modest, fairly rich, rich, orphans, small masters, scholars, etc.

step in the progress of a seduction; it could emphasise the body, a sign of provocation and coquetry, or frustrate desire, a last means of defence. Certain intermediate clothes attracted particular attention; the déshabillé, the garment for an erotic and intimate interlude, combining fluidity, transparency, suppleness and softness; the formal corseted robe, on the other hand, expressed the values of the society of external appearances, the temptations of coquetry and fashion.

Rétif's fundamental 'Pygmalionism' conferred a special significance on clothing as a gift. Lace, fabrics, trimmings, gauzes, silk stockings, gowns, stays, shoes, hats and caps, buckles and brilliants acquired a double virtue: they made it possible both to transform a 'silly working girl' into a swan, and to denounce the dangers of corruption and describe all its mechanisms. It was not powerful enough wholly to destroy the ideal of a clothing hierarchy which revealed social distinctions, and Rétif often used the nature of a garment or a detail of costume to identify a character's social status: 'dressed like a bourgeois', 'wearing a sword' (that is, a nobleman), 'like a doctor', 'like a working girl', 'like a peasant' were key expressions which show the power of the threat looming over a real life where to change one's costume was to change one's situation. The business of M. Robin, hero of *La belle Ferronnière* failed: 'He was unprepared by the cultivation of his natural talents to supply the deficiency of luck; but he possessed courage and religion ... he went out, sold his coat, which was clean, donned coarse cloth, bought some pails and, for the rest of the day, exercised a painful profession.' On the other hand, there could be no social ascent without a sartorial metamorphosis, but it was always because the person was prepared; the moral identity was safe.[126] Rétif here joins the utopians and reformers in exalting the values of cleanliness, exorcising the dirty and the unhealthy and advocating the new hygienic practices. The lesson of the *civilités* was not far off, but it was reinforced by the teachings of a philosophy wholly devoted to reconciling collective transparency and the opacity of individual consciousnesses.

The dress of the heroes of novels, clothing in the utopias and the costume of *Les Contemporaines* were brought together by one same

---

[126] Many examples: *Le Nouveau Pygmalion, La Petite Coureuse, La Nouvelle Halle, La Jardinière et la bouquetière, La Poudrière-pommadière.*

imaginative structure. They neither wholly reflected reality nor were wholly autonomous: they promoted certain values which in no way departed from the naturist and progressive references of a rational thinking in love with progress, but without wholly abandoning the norms and codes of the Christian moral economy. On the plane of fiction, the normalising intention resolved the contradiction generated by the contemporary clothing revolution, and sought to combine the clarity of the hierarchies, the visibility of characters and morals and sensibility to the formal change which accompanied the transformation of social relations, in particular in towns. Less charged with fabulous and mythological power than the characters themselves, the imagined clothes followed their development and helped show their changed nature. It was a sign of materiality for a society which was seeking its identity between the simulacrum and authenticity.

# 15. *Rational and healthy clothes*

Il n'y a pas une seule brochure sur l'art de faire des chemises, des bas, des souliers, du pain; l'*Encyclopédie* est le premier et unique ouvrage qui décrive ces arts utiles aux hommes.

Chevalier de Jaucourt, 'Héraldique', in *Encyclopédie*

The critical reading proposed by Jacques Proust, the greatest living specialist in the *Encyclopédie*, for the plates which illustrate it, and still form part of its attraction, at once locates it 'on the margins of Utopia'.[1] This supports my thesis; the *Dictionnaire raisonné des sciences, des arts et des métiers* is in my view one of the principal keys to an understanding of both gap and correspondence between the image of the clothing system in the modern period and the realities which informed it, and which it informed. The words and plates of the *Encyclopédie* are harnessed in the service of the grand design of a rational account of the totality of what is observable: 'The human spirit can make itself a representation of the things which are wholly appropriate to it and which are at the same time wholly comprehensible to it.'[2]

The processes and consequences systematised by the necessities of dress were an important part of this project, as a count of entries shows. So we should be able to find here the stylisation imposed by the needs of a social pedagogy: a dream of a clothing which corresponded to the demands and codes of society as seen by and described in the illustrations and written entries of the *Encyclopédie*:[3] the complementarity of the two mediums was a key element in the demonstrative power so clearly sought by Diderot. Once again, we find not so much a realistic picture as the possibility

---

[1] J. Proust, *Marges d'une utopie, pour une lecture critique des planches de l'Encyclopédie* (n.p., 1985).

[2] Proust, *Marges d'une utopie*, p. 1.

[3] Proust, 'L'Image du peuple au travail', pp. 65–85.

of interrogating a convergence of meanings. The *Dictionnaire raisonné* was read throughout Europe and the obsession of the cultural elites with their dress is laid bare.[4] It was inseparable from a desire to escape the immediacy of a spontaneous and external world, a concrete reality, without abandoning it, and to use it as a barrier. The philosophy of the encyclopedists, though it cannot be reduced to a single interpretation, proceeds from this great exercise in exposition which presents 'naturalness maintained, though transformed and apparently distanced'.[5]

The idealisation of the vision can accommodate an essential materialisation illustrating the textile and clothing symbiosis, a reality then changing and growing immeasurably richer. In sum, we would appear to have a means of access to an organisation of things in which technology and the changes caused by trade and fashion are discussed in a way that emphasises the organic vision of a milieu in love with reform. The clothes themselves and their symbolics are mobilised for social transfigurations; ultimately, a representation of nature and artifice, and a new image of the body incorporating the medical logics of the age, imposed the voluntarist idea that to a new man there should correspond a new costume, to the reason for the needs the need for reason.

### THE ENCYCLOPEDISTS AND CLOTHING

Produced, assembled, sold and worn, their social implications and their aesthetic and moral significance disputed, clothes occupy an important place in the *Encyclopédie*: 3,036 entries in the whole corpus, not counting the references scattered throughout the vast compilation assembled by Diderot and his collaborators,[6] for example, in the chevalier de Jaucourt's article 'Heraldry' and, more generally, in the articles on grammar and language, which are studded with anecdotes and historical details about clothing customs. It is a constant theme throughout the publication: at the least, 2.2 per cent of the material listed in volume III, published in 1765, and at most, 7.6 per cent in volume XII, published in the

---

[4] Darnton, *L'Aventure de l'Encyclopédie*.
[5] Dagognet, *Rematérialiser*, p. 51.
[6] Didier, 'Le Système du vêtement', pp. 12–13, 31–49 and table, pp. 45, 46; the quantitative list and attribution of articles by author is based on R. N. Schwab *et al.*, *Inventory of Diderot's Encyclopédie, Studies on Voltaire* (1971).

same year. To put these figures into context would involve a comparison with other themes, material or conceptual, by means of the cross-referencing. The pervasiveness of this theme, which we are able to trace, makes plain that the clothing system was for the *Encyclopédie* a fruitful area for debate, evidence of a sensibility which was more than mere archaism or modernism. Of the 3,000 entries, a good third (1,032) are articles which are more specifically cultural, sociological, historical, literary or more properly moral and normative, concerning etiquette and fashion, ancient and modern, with some dabbling in exoticism. The remaining two-thirds deal more directly with the technical and economic aspects of the contexts and processes of manufacture and sale. With regard to clothing, the emphasis of the *Encyclopédie* was overwhelmingly on providing information about the arts and crafts and the organisation of production.

The influence of these two orientations can be seen in the choice of words. There is a large number of apparently minor terms, essentially drawn from the vocabulary of the crafts, which acquired a new status through being enshrined in print; they also made available to a wider world a mass of detail about the apprenticeship practices, equipment and skills involved in the manufacture and sale of clothes. The degree of detail was made necessary not only by the complexity of the old manufacturing processes but by the desire to provide a complete classification of the principal words, often with their synonyms. The discourse was directly organised round the plates, which convey information, and make it possible to combine static and dynamic description.[7] At the same time, the illustrations are a sort of publicity; they offer an accurate and attractive picture of their subject as if to promote it, displaying it in an ambience free of conflict, appealing and calm, in effect exalting a way of life; more subtly, they provoke desire.[8] If we accept this interpretation, suggested by J. Proust, it is easier to understand how the *Dictionnaire* could serve so many purposes; from reasoned and clear information to fantasy, from conscious instruction to the revelation of a social ideology, the *Encyclopédie* reveals both the lessons of a material history of reading and those of an intellectual analysis of the triumphant consumption.

[7] Proust, *Diderot et les encyclopédistes*, pp. 171–7.
[8] Proust, *Marges d'une utopie*, pp. 6–7.

Table 40    *The principal clothing themes in the* Encyclopédie[a]

| Rank | Rubrics | Total number of articles | % |
|------|---------|--------------------------|---|
| 1 | Silks, silk | 241 | 8 |
| 2 | Trade in 'exotic' and foreign clothes | 192 | 6·3 |
| 3 | Ribbon-weaving, braid, trimmings | 161 | 5·1 |
| 4 | Trade, geography, regulation of trade | 134 | 4·4 |
| 5 | Dyeing, dyers | 95 | 3·1 |
| 6 | Ancient history, Graeco-Roman antiquity | 106 | 3·5 |
| 7 | Drapery, broadcloth | 95 | 3·7 |
| 8 | Box-maker, pinner | 88 | 2·9 |
| 9 | Hat-making, hat | 81 | 2·7 |
| 10 | Buttoner | 78 | 2·6 |
| 11 | Wool (manufacture) | 74 | 2·4 |
| 12 | Shoemaking, shoe | 71 | 2·4 |
| 13 | Wool, woollen | 70 | 2·3 |
| 14 | Grammar, French language | 70 | 2·3 |
| 15 | Manufacture | 66 | 2·2 |
| 16 | Leather (currier, flesher) | 65 | 2·1 |
| 17 | Fashion, fashion merchant | 63 | 2·1 |
| 18 | Embroidery, embroiderer | 62 | 2 |
| 19 | Mounter, jewels | 61 | 2 |
| 20 | Ecclesiastical history and affairs | 60 | 2 |
| 21 | Modern history | 58 | 1·9 |
| 22 | Leather (chamois leather dresser, tawer) | 56 | 1·8 |
| 23 | Tailor, dressmaker | 56 | 1·8 |
| 24 | Arts, merchanical arts | 54 | 1·8 |

[a]See P. Didier, 'Le Système du vêtement dans le *Dictionnaire raisonné des arts et sciences*', mémoire de maîtrise, University of Paris 1 (1983)

FROM *ABATS* (WOOL) TO *ZINZOLIN* (DYEING): 3,036 ENTRIES

A quantitative approach to the main rubrics emphasises exteriority (see table 40). Purely technical concerns dominate: thirteen out of twenty-four rubrics, including three-quarters of the articles on clothing, are devoted to description of the technical processes of manufacture or the skills of a craft, such as dyeing, ribbon-weaving, drapery and hat-making. It is the apotheosis of the technical system dominant in the seventeenth and eighteenth centuries, accompanied to a lesser degree by description of the improved processes, for example, in the articles 'Silk-weaving loom' and 'Stocking loom'. The trade in raw materials was by no means neglected, either as such – commerce, geography, regulation (4.5 per cent of articles) – or in the sub-headings of each entry, to illustrate prov-

enances and destinations. Silk and silks and the trade in exotic products reveal the critical points of the system of consumption, whilst
the more traditional manufacture was relatively neglected: respectively 15 per cent for the first two, compared with 1.8 per cent for
tailoring and 0.8 per cent for the linen-draper. The lexical system
could offer only an imperfect reflection of the reality of the global
clothing system; it conformed to the dominant economic vision of
the time: production primed trade, and the regulatory function of
the economic machinery was more central to the debate than the
mechanisms for the diffusion of consumer habits. The articles which
are heavy with economic import are those crammed with facts about
the processes of production, the types of raw material and the methods
of commercial control, for example, 'Broadcloth' and 'Silk'.

Each rubric is organised into a system by the use of cross-references
which make it possible to get a complete view of the subject. Thus the
series 'Hat', 'Hatter' and 'Hat-making' (volume III, p. 175) covers a
vast constellation of sub-headings – *castor, feutre* and *peau de lapin*
for the raw materials; *arçon, chaudière, fouloir, fourneau, frottoir,
goupillon, rond de plomb* and *tamis* for the tools; *abattage, affûtage,
appareiller, arçonner, arrondir, arroser, battir, coupeur, coupeur de
poils, dorage, dresser, eau, égouter, éficeler, éplucher, étouper* and
*marcher* (the fabric of a hat); *rafraîchir, raffûter, repasser, teinture,
tondre, tirer*, etc., for the techniques; trade was described under 'Hat-
making', the uses of the hat in 'Christian clothing', 'Biretta',
'Capuchon', 'Mitre' and 'Toque', all articles of 'Ecclesiastical
history'. Readers start wherever they want or are able, according
to their requirements; they need to have a good appetite.

ERUDITE AND DIVERSE CONTRIBUTORS

To meet a huge need, Diderot called on a small nucleus of specialists, who formed a team of authorities and experts in the clothing
field. He himself and the chevalier de Jaucourt wrote most of the
entries, probably more than 80 per cent (subject to the precise
identification of the articles). The attribution of an article probably
meant less to the eighteenth-century reader than to the historian of
ideas and manners,[9] but it is not entirely without interest to know

---

[9] Proust, *Diderot et les encyclopédistes*, pp. 118, 550ff., and *Tableau sur l'identification sociale et culturelle*; see also J. Lough, *The Contributors of Encyclopédie*

that Diderot wrote, among others, the articles 'Appearance', 'Belt', 'Capuchon', 'Coquetry', 'Cover', 'Pannier' and 'Wig'. His interest in the complexities of materiality and behaviour is not belied, and his desire for direct technical information is well known. It led him to pick the brains of the stocking-weaver Barrat, Laurent and Bonnet, both silk workers, the gauze maker Doucet, the haberdasher La Bassée, the tawer controller of farms la Sallette, Magimel, a goldsmith who lived on the Quai Pelletier in Paris, and several anonymous technicians. Jaucourt, 'Master Jacques', probably compiled a number of articles as yet unidentified; he drew on a vast range of works in various genres, and in connection with clothing, on the great dictionaries of Richelet, Furetière, Trévoux and Savary des Bruslons.

A smaller number of specialist articles were written by some twenty others, who provided copy as commissioned and in fields in which they were authorities. Belin, a naval engineer, wrote the articles 'Hood' and 'Sewing'; Boucher d'Argis, *avocat* and counsellor to the *parlement* of les Dombes, wrote the articles on sartorial jurisprudence – 'Mourning', 'Frock', 'Vestment' and 'Lieutenant de robe courte'; the engineer Eidous provided 'Boot' and 'Button' for military equipment; Durival wrote on uniform ('Clothing', 'Cartridge-pouch' etc), as also did Le Blond, instructor in tactics at the Ecole Militaire; Le Romain, another engineer, who had been in the West Indies, revealed the secrets of the 'Cotton-worker'; the doctors Barthès, Venel, Vandeness and Villiers wrote on hygiene and health, though the latter wrote the article 'Felt'; the great surgeon Antoine wrote thirteen articles, including 'Bandage', 'Mask', 'Needle', 'Headgear' and 'Slipper'. Deleyre produced the important article 'Pin', Lenglet du Fresnoy the historical articles, including 'Mourning', the abbé Mallet the ancient words (forty-three), M. de Saint-Lambert the articles 'Luxury' and 'Manner', and Suzanne Marie de Vivens, marquise de Jaucourt, sister-in-law of the chevalier, wrote 'Furbelow' and 'Fontange'. We have here a microcosm of the team responsible for the *Encyclopédie*.[10]

---

(London, 1973); D. Roche, 'Encyclopédistes et académiciens', in *Livre et société dans la France du XVIIIe siècle*, 2 (Paris, 1975).

[10] One could also cite Landois, an artist Charles Leroy, the mechanic Jean-Baptiste Leroy (*arbre de métier à tisser*), Duclos (*étiquette*), Brisson, inspector of manufactures (*toilerie*), the engraver Papillon (*chapes*), and the apothecary Montet (*vert-de-gris*).

Members of the Academy (a third), technicians, scholars, engineers, men of power and economic control, doctors who legislated for health, all participated in this popularising Enlightenment venture. They believed the study of the production of appearances to be of interest to a wide public.

## THE CLOTHES OF A CHANGING SOCIETY

The *Dictionnaire* first provides basic lexical and etymological information; it is thus an inventory of language useful in the past, and still today, to understand words and their changing meanings. Obvious though it may be, this is a by no means negligible function, and with regard to clothing, it is invaluable for the exotic or the archaic. Who immediately knows the meaning of *zinzolin* or the sartorial use of a *paumelle* or a *carreau*? Who can identify the provenance of a *chembalis* leather or a *boutanes*, a *tang* of mousseline or a *sparagon* of wool? Who can say without its help what were a *calyptre*, a *chlène*, the *omophos* or the *syrna*? In addition, the *Encyclopédie* explains functions and practices on the basis of detailed classifications, whether of uses or materials. The methods and processes of manufacture receive pride of place.

Readers also find a social presentation and an ideological vision of clothing questions. They are introduced to the issues underlying the most inoffensive definitions and can follow the fundamental argument about luxury which was aired at length within the *Encyclopédie*, as elsewhere, after 1750. The definitions of clothing also insidiously raise philosophical and religious issues. Let us look at 'Hair-shirt': it is first defined as 'a small garment of cloth of horsehair for the use of penitent persons who wear it next to the skin and thus experience constant discomfort . . . there is sometimes more to be lost in the way of goodness in a moment of ill humour, than to be gained by ten years of hair shirts and discipline'. Having begun objectively, the article ends by criticising a religious practice. The article 'Capuchon' also attacks the monks with a cross-reference to the article 'Cordelier'. 'Furbelow' introduces a wider discussion of the fickleness of fashion and its metaphysical significance, and ponders the progress of the human spirit: 'This great wheel of the world which brings back every event, brings back every fashion, and makes furbelows reappear.' So etymology and history are invoked to explain various meanings, but the latter question the guiding notion of the encyclopedists concerning human progress and the perfectibility of man.[11] Whether they are grammatical, historical, technical or economic, by the use of nuance, allusion and implication, the words chosen to trace the contours of the clothing system can, at the end of the day, lead to a political reading.[12]

### A CLOTHING SEEN AND READ EVERYWHERE?

This brings us to the question of the readership of the *Encyclopédie* and the nature of the social image of appearances that it helped to propagate. The idealised reality of a rich and idle society shines through both articles and plates; its way of life and its clothes were those of the *sanior pars* of the privileged of rank and fortune. They were certainly among the *Encyclopédie*'s chief readers. However, its success, and its appearance in successive cheaper and lighter editions, from in-folio to octavo,[13] disseminated the model of the habits and needs of the world of good form and good taste, which was also that of the novel, to ever wider circles, especially among the various urban bourgeoisies which also provided the masonic and academic elites.[14]

The vast majority of the population, peasants, urban workers, marginals, a few exceptions apart, remained excluded both from its description of habits and from reading, at least directly. The bourgeoisies of talents and technicians and the better-off producers, the principal economic players in the clothing system, dominated the republic of the encyclopedists, where their role in the elaboration and reception of the images of dress is made plain. However, the *Encyclopédie* does not portray a transparent universe, united under the aegis of the ascendant classes;[15] it was not, as is sometimes claimed, a monument erected to the triumph of the new ideas and new capitalist manners. I see it rather as a contradictory and open model, which relates the needs, actions and practices of the

---

[11] Roccella, 'La Moda', p. 11.

[12] Proust, *Diderot et les encyclopédistes*, pp. 202–4.

[13] Darnton, *L'Aventure de l'Encyclopédie*; also his *The Great Cat Massacre* (pp. 201–38 of French edition).

[14] Roche, 'Encyclopédistes et académiciens', pp. 73–89; *Siècle des Lumières* vol I, *La Société académique*.

[15] A. Soboul, *Textes choisis de l'Encyclopédie* (Paris, 1962).

dominant, idle classes to the creative activities of the producers, the reception by the growing body of consumers and the role of the many social intermediaries who, by their creativity and their appropriations, sometimes dynamic, sometimes merely imitative, helped to disseminate the clothing revolution. Thus it played a part in the changes in social behaviour, now more mobile and less stable.

The *Encyclopédie*, lexical invention taken to extremes – witness the list of extraordinary, often incomprehensible and not easily decipherable words – corresponded to a desire to restore social communication at a time when it had been confused by the frenetic proliferation of fashion signs, and above all by their percolation from the front to the back of the world stage. The complexity reached by the system of dress, and its level of refinement and elaboration, were such as to render the language of clothes almost impenetrable.[16] In ordinary society, where one needed to read and be read, where tiny signs revealed social position and personal intention, it was important not only to be able to confirm that one belonged to an order, more or less noble or more or less wealthy, but to inform and be informed how close one was to court society and its satellites, the setters of fashion, and so affirm one's good taste. It was also necessary to know how to proclaim one's singularity or conformity in the publicity of appearances.

The material vocabulary of clothing thus raises all the basic questions concerning the encyclopedic project. It served not only to decode the manners of a narrow social group, but valorised the wide diffusion of its manners from top to bottom of society; it expounded a new culture of dress where, for perhaps the first time in history, the wind of change penetrated to the lower ranks, even to the most immobile and unproductive. The instability of things, of words and of men progressed alongside that of ideas. Clothing contributed to a new organisation of human relations, where the links between economic and material, and moral and political, analysis were employed in the description of techniques, in history and erudition and in the cause of reform, and where, as in the utopias, the gulf between knowledge and action was reduced.

---

[16] Roccella, 'La Moda', p. 10.

## THE TECHNOLOGIES AND ECONOMIES OF CLOTHING

The technological and economic dimension of the clothing system took pride of place: 192 articles deal with the circulation of foreign fabrics, 134 with trade and its regulation, whereas over 2,000 entries are purely technical. If we look at the number of plates, despite a certain autonomy dictated by the practicalities and requirements of illustration, the emphasis on methods and craft structures is amply confirmed: 250 plates out of nearly 1,250. We become aware of a bias in the view of clothing presented to the public, though rather tempered by the fact that the definitions of tools and techniques are shorter than the discussions of trade and the items of trade (see 'Silk', 'Indienne', 'Wool' and 'Broadcloth'), and that a dictionary is rarely read consecutively. Its principal feature was to locate the elements of textile production and clothes manufacture within a clearly ordered circuit.[17]

On the one hand, behind every object lay the workers and employers in workshops, assistants and lads in shops and wage-earners in the more modern 'factories', though proto-industrial structures still predominated; here we find the complex processes of manufacture and the employment of equipment, especially in the traditional industries. On the other, every product involved trade networks and circuits, the routes for the supply and distribution of raw materials and the clothes offered for sale, a market, consumers, a vast system of national and international exchange. The *Encyclopédie* makes it possible to trace the clothing circuit in its entirety. It was aware of the urban growth created by the emergence of new social outlets and modes of distribution, for example the entries 'Marchandes de modes' (volume X, p. 598) and 'Revendeuses à la toilette' (volume XIV, pp. 226–7). The epiphany of dress and adornment was made possible by many changes which brought production and consumption closer together. As in other domains, the *Encyclopédie* asserted and exalted the conquest of manners.

[17] Ibid., pp. 12–14; Didier, 'Le Système du vêtement', pp. 98–151.

SARTORIAL CONTROL AND LIBERTY: HOW THINGS WERE
USED

However, the *Encyclopédie* also identified the hot spots in the
network and analysed conflicts and debates. The principal problem
remained to understand how the textile and clothing sector, highly
regulated and controlled by the craft guilds, could constantly
respond and adapt to fluctuations in demand.[18] In other words,
how could creative initiatives reach the consumer and assuage his
unquenchable thirst for novelty?

The mechanisms of adaptation are revealed in the article 'Printers
(with stencils)': as the taste for printed fabrics spread, a small
number of masters split off from the corporations to which they
belonged and formed a new group of producers, privileged, regulated in its turn, well protected from competition, but also controlled and stabilised within its own sphere of activity. If tastes
changed, the new corporation was left high and dry, and obliged to
reduce its numbers. The sector as a whole was dependent on the
initiative of a tiny group of creative entrepreneurs who had links
with fashionable society, supplied the court and the wealthy and
benefited from many contacts; rather than randomly manipulating
styles, they acted only after careful consideration of potential
profits, aided by their highly developed ability to anticipate changes
in taste. This micro-milieu played in the material sphere of clothing
a role analogous to that of the little groups of entrepreneurs of
ideas who operated in the world of books: for example, Lebreton
who gave work to Diderot and Panckoucke,[19] or Favart and
Beaumarchais in theatrical circles. The launching of a new fashion
required different raw materials and the establishment of good
relations and profitable contracts with the merchants who imported
exotic or foreign cloths or with the entrepreneurs who controlled
the manufacture of new fabrics, the diffusion of the new manufacturing processes and even the introduction of new machinery. It was
changes in consumption which forced the creation of new equilibriums and compelled the corporations and proto-industrial manufacture to adapt.

The *Encyclopédie* upheld the order of trade in the domain of

[18] Roccella, 'La Moda', p. 13; *Imprimeurs*, vol. VIII, pp. 624–30,
[19] Darnton, *L'Aventure de l'Encyclopédie*, pp. 177–200, 239–45.

Table 41 *The geography of textile provenances in the* Encyclopédie

---

Asia: 131 entries (East Indies 66; Surat 12; Persia 7; the Levant 31; China, Japan and Siam 13, etc.)

Africa: 2

The Americas: 2

Europe, not including France: 26 (Holland 8; Spain 6; Italy 5; England 4; the Empire 3)

France: 37 (Flanders 8; Normandy 8; Beauvaisis-Picardy 7; Burgundy 5; Brittany 3; Languedoc 2; Lyons 1; Paris 1; Orléans 1; Poitiers 1)

---

clothing, since it best expressed the encounter between the system of needs and the measure of values, a general principle of utility. The lexical predominance of an exotic textile geography mixed the sensitivity of the market and the reality of prevailing tastes, as table 41 shows. We see three zones – France, Europe and Asia – all differently affected by modernity and tradition. The two poles of the East Indies and the Levant highlight the increase in the import of lighter fabrics – cottons, printed muslins and linens – and their triumph in spite of hostile regulation.[20] The *Encyclopédie* here repeated the familiar critique of interventionism and panegyric of the individual economic agent, the debate between the defenders of economic regulation by public law or by private right:[21] to defend trade, the natural order and the liberty incarnated by the triumph of consumption was also to defend cultural entrepreneurs. In mid-century, economic management itself was no longer confident of its doctrine, the pressure of demand had not only assured the success of the new textiles but allowed industrial initiatives rich in future promise, such as that of Oberkampf, to get off the ground. 'Indiennage' and its vocabulary highlighted innovation and the *Encyclopédie* ratified the new trends in the sartorial spectacle, the taste for cottons (75 mentions), silks (26), muslins (12) and taffetas (5), at the expense of wool (18 entries).

---

[20] S. Chassagne, *Oberkampf, un entrepreneur capitaliste au siècle des Lumières* (Paris, 1981), pp. 9–17.

[21] F. Markovits, *L'Ordre des échanges. Philosophie de l'économie et économie du discours au XVIIIe siècle en France* (Paris, 1986), pp. 161–3.

EXOTIC AND TRADITIONAL TEXTILES

Table 41 reveals other changes. They hardly affected Europe, where we still see evidence of the traditional commerce in the heavy broadcloths and lighter serges of Holland, the wool of Spanish merino sheep and the beautiful and rich fabrics produced by the clothiers and silk manufacturers of Italy. We do not yet see the triumph of England, on which France came to depend for cotton, which would cause problems for the silk industry of Lyons, hit by the decline of figured materials and rich fabrics,[22] though its decay should not be exaggerated. The fashion industries could find ways of defending themselves; the vogue for the hooped gown showed that, to compensate for the fall in the price of fabrics, it was possible to increase the amount used, and so maintain the value, by covering the hoops and whalebone of the formal robe or elegant gown with metre after metre of taffeta, cotton and muslin.[23] The French textiles mentioned in the *Encyclopédie* reflect the traditional geography of production, but the new areas also appear; the importance accorded to silk, an article of thirty-six pages in volume XV, with many plates, shows the economic stakes at issue in a changing market.

In the case of the indiennes, consumer fancy and description of long-distance international trade predominate; in the case of the traditional textiles and French silk manufacture, discussion of their problems and the host of minor facts which demonstrated the baleful effects of regulation are to the fore: see, for example, *bouille* and *bouiller* (volume II, p. 357), the mark put on pieces of cloth by the agents of the farms, *plomb* (volume XII, pp. 778–80), *marquer* (volume X, p. 137), *empointer* (volume V, p. 592), *ponce* (volume XIII, p. 14), *timbre* (volume XVI, p. 33), all terms symbolic of the outdated values of control. The *Encyclopédie* had come off the fence. The clothing system it expounded was strongly influenced by its concern to penetrate to the heart of things and reveal the improved appearance within everyone's reach. This dictated its pioneering stance, but its economic doctrine lacked overall coherence.

[22] P. Cayez, *Métiers jacquard et hauts fourneaux. Aux origines de l'industrie lyonnaise* (Lyons, 1981), pp. 71–7.
[23] Roccella, 'La Moda', p. 13.

The clothing economy of the encyclopedists, like their technology, was perhaps composed of contradictory, even conflicting,
elements.[24] In its polemic on mercantilism, for example, the profits
procured by the re-export of fashionable articles justified the export
of currency to pay for the costly raw materials. Their processing
made the difference: French luxury dominated Europe. It was
economically profitable according to the chevalier de Jaucourt,
who quoted Montaigne in praise of the industry of a people which
managed to 'make others pay for its own costumes and ornaments'
('Fashion', volume X, p. 590). But there was a risk; it was moral
since one shut one's eyes to the need for practices which sustained
profits and one sank into the obscurity of the mechanisms of luxury.

### THE MATERIALITY OF CLOTHES AND LABOUR EXALTED

Two influences operated on the taxonomy of clothes and costume
and the description of their manufacture and sale: a shop-window
effect, lauding the skills and the products, inspired and assembled
by the inventive genius of men and women, especially French; a
mirror effect, which subjected the whole to a philosophical, moral
and political critique and made it more or less converge or diverge
in relation to the rational coherence of the whole.

The plates, too, were influenced by these two perspectives. They
demonstrated processes, identifying tools and the uses of materials;
they presented labour in its context, the workshop or shop, always
emphasising the artistic quality of the crafts: 'Stylish shops and
workshops like living-rooms were traversed by a gracious farandole
of lace-makers, spinners, fan-makers, furriers, furbishers and
feather-dressers.'[25] We have already discussed the illustrations of
the trades of the tailor and the linen-draper. At the same time, the
text accompanying the plates, or the references to articles, or even
anodyne details which intrigued attentive readers, could reintroduce
more visible signs of existence and emphasise the difficulty of a
purely transparent reading.[26] As an encyclopedia, priority had to
be given to information and its illustration for successful popularisation; the critical philosophy questioned the levels of reality and

---

[24] Markovits, *L'Ordre des échanges*, pp. 15–19.
[25] Proust, *Marges d'une utopie*, pp. 4–5.
[26] Ibid., pp. 10–11.

representation, proposed a more analytical discussion which reflected the economic changes taking place within the clothing system, presented technical improvements and challenged guild organisation. In its discussion of clothing habits, the *Encyclopédie* did not go all the way with the utopias and the dreams of reason; it retained a firm base in the reality of the babel of fashion which was then Paris.[27] Pictures and text described and illustrated the clothes of the seriously rich, and revealed some of their tangible impact on the world of the only comfortably off and even on the workers and the poor.

But in the programme which the omnipresent chevalier de Jaucourt recapitulated in the article 'Dress' (volume VIII, pp. 11–17), the enthusiasm and pride of the encyclopedists shines through. The text describes the operations and the illustrations portray the objects, both bequeathing to posterity the secrets of the transformation of things and the world, something never previously attempted on such a scale. Behind the finished products, their perfection and their elegance, human agency was now visible, the role of human beings in the mastery of materials and their processing; clothing was an instrument in the domination of nature.

However, the elegant dress of the Parisian women it portrayed was characteristically designed to cause its origins to be forgotten and to conceal all traces of the labour which had been necessary to achieve such perfection. The readers were conducted on a journey which led from the workshops where clothes were assembled to the factories where raw materials were processed, from France to distant countries where nature had been generous. The elegant woman turned out by the fashion merchant might be wearing ostrich feathers from Africa, perfumed leathers from Spain, artificial flowers from Italy, cottons imported from the Indies, muslins and shawls transported by the slow caravans of Persia, laces from Holland, baleen from whales fished in the icy waters of the Arctic, tranquil linens woven in the workshops of remote provinces and precious silks worked and decorated by the designers and embroiderers of Lyons. She was a sort of monument erected to the glory of human labour and the appropriation of the known world.

The constant insistence on the manual dexterity of the workers, their good taste, their creative fantasy, their technical imagination

[27] Roccella, 'La Moda', pp. 14–15.

and their capacity to invent new forms and combine decoration and colours in a constantly changing and subtle manner, conferred on the artisanate the function of repository of the 'proofs of the sagacity of the human spirit', to quote d'Alembert. It restored to the activities and products of the thousands of men and women whose labours were necessary to achieve this absolute quality a creative capacity, which combined materiality and intelligence.[28] We are a long way from the fulminations of Rousseau against the civilisation which turned people away from true knowledge, though very close to the appeals of *Emile* who would exchange 'the whole Academy of Sciences for the least confectioner of the rue des Lombards'. The encyclopedists, among them the indefatigable chevalier de Jaucourt, were able to perceive the emblematic value of textiles and clothing in the culture of the Enlightenment: it was the symbol of its capacity to unite words and things, the aesthetic of the visible world and the dream of human progress in and by labour. The matter and the manner of textiles, their transformation into garments, the metaphor of appearances, permeated not only industry but the whole culture.[29]

### DIDEROT'S MORAL AESTHETIC OF CLOTHING

Let us pause, for a moment, at a text too famous to ignore. Its interest is sufficient justification, quite apart from the personal affection I feel for Denis Diderot, as for an old friend, and the shared habits which mean I can never part with an old garment without distress. Mme Geoffrin, a Parisian *salonnière*, had, it will be remembered, presented Diderot with a magnificent new dressing-gown.[30]

> Why did I not keep it! [his old gown] It was made for me; I was made for it. It fitted every fold of my body without chafing; I was picturesque, I was handsome. The other, stiff and starchy, makes me look like a mannequin. There was no demand to which it would not respond; poverty is almost always obliging. If a book was covered with dust, one of its flaps volunteered to wipe it. If the ink dried and refused to run from my pen, it

[28] Dagognet, *Rematérialiser*, pp. 48–50, 101–9.
[29] Ibid., pp. 155, 159–63.
[30] D. Diderot, in *Correspondance littéraire*, 15 February 1769, *Oeuvres complètes*, ed. R. Levinter (Paris, 1967), vol. VIII, pp. 7–13.

presented its flank. You could see traced on it in long black streaks the many services it had rendered. Those long streaks announced the man of letters, the worker, the writer. Now, I look like a rich idler; no-one knows who I am.

At one level, we see here evidence of the material and the intellectual coming together through the shaping of appearances and the choice of clothes. It was not by chance that the dress of the writer, which emphasised his intellectual creative ability, was that of work done in private and of daily life. The dressing-gown was a garment of the rich and well-to-do, and for women an adornment; for Diderot, it was a symbol of his trials and labours. In 1772, when the piece was written, he was free of the *Encyclopédie*, but not of the need to write for a living. The old indoor garment had adapted to his habits, as it had travelled with him on the journey which had taken the son of a master cutler of somewhat plebeian origins to success, embourgeoisement and the status of a famous writer. He expressed regret that one could not remain what one had been, deep conviction that clothes communicated clearly and fear that one's moral significance might not be appreciated as a result of a new outfit: 'No-one knows who I am!' The sartorial aesthetic was always a moral of the union of the person and the personage.

But in Diderot's badinage, we can discern another register:

I do not weep, I do not sigh; but all the time I say: Cursed be he who invented the art of adding value to common cloth by dyeing it scarlet! Cursed be the precious garment that I revere! Where is my old, my humble, my comfortable scrap of homespun? My friends, hang on to your old friends. My friends, fear the onset of riches. Let my example be a lesson to you. Poverty has its freedoms, wealth has its constraints ... That is not all, my friend. Hear the ravages of luxury, the consequences of a consequent luxury. My old dressing-gown was at one with the other tatters which surround me. A straw-bottomed chair, a wooden table, a Bergamo tapestry, a deal shelf which held a few smoke-stained, unframed prints, nailed at the corners onto this tapestry, and three or four busts hanging between them, used to form, with my old dressing gown, a most harmonious indigence. Now, everything is out of tune. No more cohesion, no more unity, no more beauty.

The need for a unity of material culture and moral aesthetic is proclaimed, and its rupture by the discoveries of art, the growing gap between need and necessity, indeed the ravages of luxury, are denounced.

The humour of Diderot, who compared himself with Diogenes, emblematic figure of the cynical philosopher, detached from social contingencies, free and steadfast, was far-sighted. He suddenly questions the whole process of the clothing revolution and, with it, the dream of a way of life organised by art and thought, by an everyday materialism inspired by the sensitive soul and critical reflection. In sum, we see the contradictions of the civilisation of appearances, the analytic fissure running through the whole *Encyclopédie*. How could one be the 'disciple of the rainbow without being its slave'?[31] Or, to put it less colourfully, how could one reconcile need and necessity, artifice and nature, reason and sensibility?

### NATURAL CLOTHES AND ARTIFICIAL CLOTHES

Much space in the *Dictionnaire* was devoted to the attempt to resolve this problem. As Carlo Roccella so justly observed, the dichotomy which opposed natural clothes and artificial clothes survived every critique: that of the anthropologists, who knew that decoration could precede dress, that of the psychologists, who revealed the sexual symbolism of garments, that of the linguists, who relentlessly tracked down their significations, and that of the sociologists, who had demonstrated the power of social conservatism beneath transgressions of sartorial norms. This convenient separation was fully operative in the discourse of Diderot and his collaborators.

Let us look first at history and erudition for signs of the omnipresence, absence or progress of artificiality:[32] a good hundred entries are devoted to the historical explanation of clothes.[33] Of course, this springs partly from the culture of the authors, the abbé Mallet, Lenglet du Fresnoy and above all Jaucourt, pupils of the colleges and educated in the humanities. This explains the direct or more recherché references to great authors such as Horace, Pliny, Juvenal, Virgil, Suetonius and Martial. Readers were made familiar

---

[31] D. Diderot, *Pensées sur la peinture* (Paris, 1781).
[32] Didier, 'Le Système du vêtement', pp. 51–67.
[33] Erudite historical and literary terms account for almost 13% of the total number devoted to clothing.

with the clothes of the ancient Greeks and Romans; the articles 'Pendant' (volume XII, p. 292), 'Toga' (volume XVI, p. 318), 'Tunic' (volume XVI, p. 746), 'Purple' (volume XIII, pp. 245–6) and 'The shoe of the ancients' (volume XV, pp. 404–6) illustrate a conception of life perceived through a relationship to costume, and a costume which was always significant. Ancient clothes enjoyed the advantage of greater proximity to fabulous origins, or at least to the expressive qualities of a dress fitting to social institutions, public life and religious structures. The article 'The shoe of the ancients', filling two pages of four columns, is presented as a complete synthesis of knowledge on the subject: 'If the reader would like to combine this article with that on footwear and also glance at the treatise of Balduinus *De Calceo antiquo*, he will have almost all he needs on this subject.' The entry 'Toga' lists fifteen types of toga distinguished according to social rank, age, season and function and could be completed by all the appropriate male and female satellites, with *robes, tuniques, trechedima, symara* and *ricinium*.

One wonders whether the compilation and dissemination of so much erudition helped to familiarise the reading public with forms and styles, at a time when other representations were appearing in painting inspired by archaeology and antiquity. The neo-classical fashion enamoured of simplicity, in the antique style, may in part have been inspired by it. However, I have found no plate illustrating the formal aspects of ancient clothing, with the exception of shoes and jewelry ('Antiquity', first volume of plates and volume XII). The visualisation of historical clothing lagged well behind the learned discourse; the artificial and the natural were opposed almost incidentally.

HISTORY OF CLOTHES, RELATIVISM OF HABITS

In contrast, modern, civil and ecclesiastical history provide many of the expected examples of sartorial obsolescence proving the vanity of fashion or the superfluity of ostentatious consumption. The list contains a random mix of reminders of venerable habits, evocation of the sumptuary laws and analysis of frivolous excess, as in 'Amorous women' (volume VI, p. 467) or 'Miniver' (volume X, p. 357). The article 'Dress' (volume VIII, pp. 11–14) analysed at length the fluctuations in the length of clothes, their complexity and, more generally, the extreme fickleness of sartorial habits; the author, the chevalier de Jaucourt, was ultimately led to conclude that explanation, even rational description, of these immeasurable facts was impossible: 'Since Henri IV, our clothes have so often changed their appearance that it would be ridiculous to go into tedious detail.' However, this scepticism did not stand in the way of a mass of suggestive details which give an idea of the evolution of sartorial styles and, above all, condemn artificiality and its mechanisms: read 'Hennin' (volume VIII, pp. 131–2) and 'Fontanges' (volume VII, pp. 105–6), 'Liveries' (volume IX, p. 621) and 'Wardrobe' (volume VII, p. 512). Here, fashion and the distinctive contrivances of court society were described and ridiculed.

Artifice was further attacked in the various entries dealing with ecclesiastical clothing. Their author, the abbé Mallet, devoted a good third to sacred history and the rest to the vestimentary monuments of the modern period: 'Stole' (volume VI, p. 68), 'Sacred clothes' (volume VIII, pp. 15–16), 'Tonsure' (volume XVI, pp. 413–14) and 'Veils' (volume XVII, p. 423) are prominent; they serve to link the development of clerical costumes to ecclesiastical customs, thus to the institutional history and genealogy of the church.

The progress from the lay clothes of primitive Christianity – those of everyone – to the clothes of the modern clergy was implicitly presented as the history of a widening gap which increasingly separated ecclesiastics from everybody else. The role of the councils, especially Trent, was emphasised in order to express both the trend towards differentiation, accentuated in the seventeenth century, and the desire for control on the part of the clerical authorities, constantly challenged by the imperatives of fashion, to which the clergy were not immune: read 'Biretta' (volume II, p. 94), 'Calotte' (volume II, p. 564), 'Beard' (volume II, pp. 70–6), 'Soutane' (volume XV, p. 222), 'Tonsure' (volume XVI, pp. 413–14) and 'Veils' (volume XVII, p. 423).

History might turn into satire, see again 'Capuchon', where hostility to monasticism emerges more clearly. The abiding impression is that of a clergy different from other men, and this particularism, expressed in a plethora of detail – the various colours of the monastic orders, the diversity of liturgical costumes which were more or less remote from their primitive forms, the multiplicity of ecclesiastical head-dresses – revealed a different society, whose sartorial customs defied the coherence of universalism and reason.

Civil society also lent itself to such a treatment. If nature appointed the clothes which were most functional and best adapted to customs and bodies, the encyclopedists could enjoy contrasting their immutability with the instability of contemporary costume. The article on 'Clothing' (volume XVII, p. 22) accepted the three principal functions which remain those of any anthropology of dress, modesty, protection and decoration: 'We understand by this everything which serves to cover the body, decorate it, or protect it from harm from the atmosphere.' The terminology of the *Encyclopédie* here indicates fairly successfully what is arbitrary and what is not. The definition of the natural makes dress an extension of the corporeal and is expressed in the articles as a whole both by the concise style and the limited number of entries. This consensual character was valorised by the contrast with the superabundance and exuberance of anything to do with finery or ornamentation. The article '*Civilité*' (volume III, p. 497) equates the individual and his social image ('good manners (*civilités*) make a man appear on the outside what he should be on the inside') and reveals a certain conformism in the overall conception of clothes, difficult to discern in the natural manifestations alone, by no means easy to reconcile with the relativism of customs imposed by history. The abbé Mallet, in the article 'Mourning' (volume IV, p. 910), having given the usual justifications for the required colours and their symbolism, wryly concluded: 'These are surely explanations which should be regarded in the same light as those offered for allegorical dreams. One could provide many others, equally unconvincing, if red was worn for mourning. Everything depends on national customs, which make different colours into signs of joy, or tears, or sorrow.'

## THE ARBITRARINESS OF TASTE, THE POWER OF CONSTRAINTS

The fact of costume thus expressed the social, existing between the stability of constraints (or permissions) and the arbitrariness of 'taste' (volume VII, pp. 761–70), 'arbiter in many things such as fabrics, adornments and equipages'. The geography of manners then revealed the immutability of modesty: the *langoutit* (volume IX, p. 244) 'is a piece of linen cloth used by Indians to hide those parts which distinguish the sexes'; similarly, the 'pagne' (volume

VI, p. 745), the *ou-cavou* of the Caribbean (volume XI, p. 700) and the *kutkras* of Hottentot women (volume IX, p. 140). Respect for social hierarchies was discovered in the exotic customs of orientals: the 'turban' (volume XVI, p. 749) was all of green for the emirs, decorated with three plumes for the great lord, but only two for the grand vizier, made of white linen for some, of red wool or striped taffeta for others. A similar respect could be found in France in the 'gown' (volume XIV, p. 309), which varied according to function and rank within the church, the university and *parlement*, in the 'toque' (volume XVI, p. 420), which distinguished graduates, and in the 'coiffure' (volume III, p. 390), which differentiated young girls, unmarried women, married women and widows. The society of the *Encyclopédie* did not escape sartorial constraints; they were recorded in all their variety, shedding light on the codes and habits of all.[34]

The article 'Mourning' (volume VI, p. 910) consists of a summary of the traditions and practices of the etiquette of court society and its imitators. It lists the recent ordinances regulating it: 25 June 1716, court and family mourning reduced to six months; 8 October 1730, limited to three months 'with the exception of mourning for husband or wife, father or mother, grandfather or grandmother, or others of whom one was the heir or legatee, for whom alone one could wear mourning and which remained fixed'. Similarly, 'uniform' (volume XVII, p. 381) was shown as essentially linked to the need for distinctive recognition since, like the gown of the *lieutenant de robe courte*, military clothing expressed a social function rather than responding to natural need. The historical development of costume thus always taught, whatever was at issue, a distancing from origins and very often the triumph of fashion.

FASHION CRITICISED OR FASHION ADMIRED?

Fashion was a constant preoccupation of the editors, despite their relativist and sceptical claims. The plethora of articles dealing with the variety of worldly practices, the large number which describe ornaments, jewels and arrangements, and the many entries devoted to the forms and styles of clothing reveal a fundamental contradiction.

[34] Didier, 'Le Système du vêtement', pp. 76–8, 92–6.

On the one hand, the *Encyclopédie* set out to exalt the progressive achievement of artisans in the mechanical trades, a rehabilitation which, in the sphere of clothes at least, involved eulogising the creativity of frivolous crafts such as ribbon-weaving (161 articles), button-making (78), the wig-maker (42), silk and silks (241) and fashion (63). The clothes trades were clearly ranked among 'the most important branch of philosophy', and included among the activities of those 'occupied not in making us think we are happy but in actually making us so', to quote Diderot. It was perhaps necessary to admit a measure of frivolity in a dynamic of progress acceptable to the wider world of well-to-do readers touched by the clothing revolution.

On the other hand, the philosophical critique of manners, and the lessons of naturising nature, imposed a morality of dress diametrically opposed to the excesses of Paris fashions and the practices of high aristocratic society. The article 'Fashion' denounced its caprice and excess (volume X, p. 598):

Fashions constantly come and go, sometimes without the slightest appearance of reason, the bizarre usually being preferred to the beautiful, solely because it is new. If a monstrous animal appears among us, women transfer it from its stable to their heads. Every part of their finery takes its name, and no proper woman fails to wear three or four rhinoceros; another time, they scour the shops to find a cap *au lapin, aux zéphyrs, aux amours* or *à la comète*. Whatever they say about the speed with which fashions change, this latest one has lasted almost a whole spring; and I have heard it said by some of those who pontificate about everything that this is hardly very extraordinary given the dominant taste of which, they continue, this fashion reminds us. An inventory of all past and reigning fashions in France alone would fill, without much exaggeration, half the volumes we have announced, were we to go back only seven or eight centuries to our ancestors, albeit they were people much more serious than us in all respects.

Here we have the critique of the superfluity of appearances and the folly of changes imposed by a mistaken regard for public opinion. It is barely distinguishable from the routine fulminations of preachers and moralists. It has the same basic premises: the indecipherability of appearances is the sign of a sick society. The exaggerated hunger for novelty destroys the material vocabulary of habits and, as it spreads, it generalises the culture of artifice to the detriment of that of nature and a sobriety which had been traced in universal history and geography. Ultimately, as Montesquieu observed in the *Lettres persanes*, the generalisation of the phenomenon of fashion passed from the tangible to ideas and was impossible to account for. A society sick in its sartorial signs, when there is runaway consumption and transgression, initially by the rich and then by almost everybody else, is a society which 'burdens itself with forces so complicated and so indirect, with memories so confused, and markers so numerous that one gets lost in a web of inextricable prescriptions and relations ... No-one any longer knows the route or can follow the signs', as Valéry so justly wrote apropos the *Persanes*. The social world seemed as natural as nature, but it survived only by magic and enchantment.[35]

The satirical depiction of error and the anthropology of clothing combine to interrogate this period, poised between order and disorder, where the question 'how can one be what one is?' was not only a matter of appearances. How could one be a Persian? The skills of the tailor made Ricca invisible when he abandoned his Persian clothes for European dress, and thereby lost public attention and esteem. How could one record the multiplicity of sartorial conventions, the disposition of panniers (volume XI, p. 819), the intricacies of fontanges, the variety of trimmings, how reconcile praise for their conception and execution with the need to propose, by means of criticism and history, etymology, technology and practices, a new edifice of manners and social relations?

It is hardly necessary to recapitulate the *Encyclopédie*'s familiar enumeration of excesses; it is well known. The inventory of fashions and finery is full and accords with a description of the mechanisms of consumption already observed. Two principles are at work in the diffusion of fashion: simplification, which extends usage and diversifies presentations – as with the 'mantelet', which gives way to the lighter mantilla, and the 'fontange', which is reduced to a simple ribbon; and sophistication, which causes decorative details and extravagances to proliferate – as with buttons and the innumerable varieties of trimmings. We may note also the dimorphism introduced by the greater attention paid to female than male garments: 'a coquettish man, and they exist, suffers from the most

[35]  Paul Valéry, *Variétés II* (Paris, 1930), pp. 55–7, 59–65.

contemptible failing of women' ('Coquetry', volume IV, p. 183): this is still conformist, but it also reflects the acceleration of the demands and possibilities of the second sex in the society of urban consumption. At a deeper level, the economy and another conception of the body and of appearances were at issue. The *Encyclopédie* drew its readers into logics assembled by the medical discourse on clothes of the Enlightenment. The former has often been studied in and out of the *Encyclopédie*,[36] and it will be useful to devote some time to it.

## CLOTHING AND THE PROBLEM OF LUXURY

We have noted the importance of luxury to locating the notion of the clothing economy in relation to the principles of the Christian economy: Bossuet and Fénelon defended these principles strongly; La Villethierry was still popularising them at the dawn of the eighteenth century. The norms of production were related to those of morality, wealth being acceptable only if the system of redistribution transformed it into charity: the economy functioned for gift and not for profit; the values of dress were those of conformity to one's social estate. The Enlightenment, to put it briefly, justified promotion by wealth and its expression in appearances: the values of dress were those of the sociability of appearances. Voltaire's *Le Mondain* exalted to the level of myth the champions of luxury and defenders of a refined enjoyment. On the one hand, frugality, asceticism and condemnation of excessive earthly riches, the desire to limit sumptuary expenditure – the *Télémaque* of Fénelon can be read this way; on the other, the pursuit of pleasure, the worldly life and the triumph of the courtier, social utility and the right to ostentatious consumption.[37] 'If private vices make public gains', to adopt the formula of Mandeville in *The Fable of the Bees*,[38] the clothing morality of classical society totters, which is enough to bring norms and practices into opposition.

---

[36] C. Borghero, ed., *La Polemica sul lusso nel settecento francese* (Turin, 1974), which includes a basic bibliography; the two classic texts for the history of luxury are A. Morize, *L'Apologie du luxe et le mondain de Voltaire* (Paris, 1909) and W. Sombart, *Luxus und Kapitalismus* (Munich, 1913).

[37] Borghero, ed., *La Polemica*, introduction, pp. xii–xvii.

[38] B. Mandeville, *The Fable of the Bees* (pp. x–xii of Italian edition, Rome/Bari, 1987).

In other words, ethics, which inspire not so much a paradox as a new principle for understanding the economic relationship between private and public interest, took note of the attitudes to clothing revealed by the actual conduct against which preachers fulminated in vain: praise of luxurious dress complemented the glorification of the accumulation of wealth and its various external manifestations. Circulation and the town were its locales and means, luxury expenditure and ostentatious consumption its manifestations, transferred from the world of the court to the financial and industrial bourgeoisie. Werner Sombart saw this as the very cause of capitalism.[39]

From the reign of Louis XIV to that of Louis XV, from the publication of Bayle's *Dictionnaire* to that of the *Encyclopédie*, historians of ideas have traced the twists in the debate and the stages in the triumph of the defence of luxury and fashion. The penetration of the money economy, which was not only a matter of specie, but involved all types of negotiable instruments, hence all the possibilities of credit (whose importance for the predominant social groups, in particular the rural and urban intermediate classes, has perhaps been underestimated) considerably accelerated the process. The debate was certainly much sharpened by the expansion of the urban economy. The *Encyclopédie* here recorded changing habits and echoes of the debate.

The article 'Luxury', long attributed to Diderot,[40] was in fact the work of the marquis de Saint-Lambert, author of a pamphlet published a little earlier, *Essai sur le luxe* (1764). It summarised a position which was acceptable to authors such as Condillac, Holbach, Helvetius and, of course, Diderot.

Luxury is the way one uses wealth and industry to procure an agreeable existence. The first cause of luxury is discontent with one's estate; the desire to better oneself, which is and ought to be in all men. It is the cause of their passions, their virtues and their vices. This desire must necessarily make them love wealth; so the desire to enrich oneself enters and ought to enter into the armoury of every government not based on equality and the community of goods; the principal object of this desire must be luxury; there is therefore luxury in all estates and all societies; the savage has his hammock, bought for animal skins; the

---

[39] Sombart, *Luxus* (p. 215 of Italian translation, Parma, 1982).
[40] Vol. IX, pp. 763–4.

European has his sofa and his bed; our women wear rouge and diamonds, the women of Florida paint themselves blue and wear glass balls.

Saint-Lambert accepted the universal necessity of the luxury which stimulated economic activity (it played the role of the profit motive in the liberal analysis) and its logic in the political regulation of unequal societies. He linked it directly to appearances – especially women's – and the comforts of life. It was a beneficial factor for development: 'It is in the nature of men and things that States in time grow rich, the arts attain perfection and luxury increases.' But, and here Saint-Lambert differed from Mandeville and the first apologists of luxury and the civilisation of appearances, all these elements could be taken to excess, too far removed from the natural and the necessary; they corresponded only to the artificial needs of a society of the rich and idle. For Diderot himself, luxury could be desirable if it was kept within reasonable bounds, and if it corresponded to a general prosperity and a more equal distribution of wealth.[41]

The *Encyclopédie* was here the propagandist for a luxury born of economic health and for the wealth of the largest number.[42] It differed from the disciples of Voltaire and the apotheosis of ostentation, without accepting the ideas of the partisans of the sumptuary laws, unable to control the luxury of clothes and a source of inequality by their imposition of distinctive signs according to estate.[43] On the contrary, the intervention of the state should be confined to encouraging manufactures and supervising the movement of the population of workers and technicians, especially foreign. The clothing economy of the encyclopedists lay at the confluence of the reasonable pursuit of a moderate luxury, stimulus to industry and production, and the consumption increased by the new needs of a wider society, increasingly concerned with comfort and the pursuit of happiness. It did not follow Voltaire, and even less the physiocrats, who condemned dress and fashion as sterile as part of their denunciation of urban waste and praise of landed wealth.[44]

The *Encyclopédie*, inasmuch as one can discern in it a single

---

[41] In *Mémoires pour Catherine II*, ed. P. Vernières (Paris, 1966), chapter 26, pp. 144–60.

[42] Borghero, ed., *La Polemica*, pp. xxxii–xxxvi.

[43] Vol. IX, pp. 672–3.

[44] See, for example, N. Baudeau, *Principes de la science politique et morale, sur le luxe et les lois somptuaires* (Paris, 1912), ed. A. Dubois, pp. v–vi, 24–5.

coherent guiding notion, seems to me here to range itself on the side of trade and commercial values, as its general rehabilitation of the arts and sciences required. It thus expressed less the economic and ideological apogee of the triumphant commercial bourgeoisie than the variety introduced into life by the rise of the middle classes, the greater role of the many intermediaries, the creation of a way of life in which sociability required acceptance of the culture of appearances, the decline of religious values within these milieus and, lastly, the increased pace of clothing consumption. It here registered the more fevered pulse of the urban metropolis.

However, the editors, Diderot certainly and Jaucourt probably, were aware of the contradiction between the artificial naturalness of needs created by the expansion of fashion – 'the vital form of fashion being natural to man as a social being', to use the expression of Georg Simmel[45] – and the values appropriate to their dream of a more reasonable and less unequal society, reconciling unity and difference. The arbitrary changes and sartorial excesses of fashion unbalanced a social organism threatened by degeneration and a profound deformation, of which the evolution of dress and its distance from nature were sure signs. By finding these more or less everywhere in the material lexicography, the encyclopedists joined the ever larger cohort of the would-be reformers of costume. This viewpoint was well expressed by M. de Jaucourt:

> The variety in the way we dress is as great, says M. Buffon, as the diversity of nations. And strangest of all is that out of all the types of clothes, we have chosen one of the most inconvenient, and that our way, albeit generally imitated by all the peoples of Europe, is at the same time, of all the ways of dressing, that which takes up most time, and that which seems to be least suited to Nature.[46]

## CLOTHING IN THE MEDICAL LOGICS OF THE ENLIGHTENMENT

The little group of doctors who collaborated in the description of dress was not, contrary to expectations, that most strongly motivated by a desire for reform. They provided mainly technical articles. Venel wrote 'Silks' and 'Toadstone', Villiers 'Felt', the surgeon, Louis, 'Bandage' and 'Needle', but also 'Slipper' and

---

[45] G. Simmel, 'La Mode', in *Tragédie de la culture et autres essais* (Paris, 1988), pp. 88–126.
[46] Vol. VIII, p. 12.

'Headgear', whilst the apothecary, Montet, compiled the entry 'Verdigris', important in dyeing. It was probably Diderot himself, in his articles 'Pannier' and 'Wig', and the chevalier de Jaucourt, with 'Dress', 'Fashion' and 'Footwear', who went furthest in analysing the relationship between types of dress and the harm done to the body by the clothing transformation. This both reveals a major preoccupation and reflects the medical culture of the two chief movers of the *Dictionnaire raisonné*. The question was central to the debate within a medical body undergoing change and compelling attention by its desire for action.[47] Clothing became an important way of expressing the new, less traditional, medical vision of the body.[48]

This emerged in a profuse and dispersed discourse, which included major treatises and slim volumes, dictionary entries (we know that Diderot had translated Robert James' *Medical Dictionary*), articles in specialised journals and communications to the academies or to the Royal Society of Medicine. The theme came into its own after 1770, with at least twenty works on the subject published during the next two decades, and its emergence as an obligatory argument in all treatises on social medicine, as is shown by the works of Tissot[49] and the *Medical Topographies* jointly initiated by the Royal Society and the provincial academies.[50] Further, it was adopted by philosophy and education, Rousseau giving a lead. All the friends of the people, all the demographers before the name, who sought ammunition against the alleged causes of the depopulation and 'degeneration of the human species', joined the fray. Vicq-d'Azir himself discussed it in several articles

---

[47] Pellegrin, 'L'Uniforme de la santé'; Pérez, 'Le Vêtement dans les logiques médicales'.

[48] F. Lebrun, *Se soigner autrefois. Médecins saints et sorciers au XVIIe et XVIIIe siècles* (Paris, 1983); J.-P. Goubert, dir., 'La médicalisation de la société française 1770–1830', *Historical Reflections*, 9, 1–2 (Waterloo, Ontario, 1982), and 'Santé, médecine et politique de santé' in *Histoire, économie et société*, 4 (Paris, 1984).

[49] Tissot, *Avis aux gens de lettres et aux personnes sédentaires sur leur santé* (Paris, 1767), and *Avis au peuple sur sa santé* (Paris, 1767); Bienville, *Traité des erreurs populaires sur la santé* (Paris, 1775); there is a bibliography of printed works in Pellegrin, 'L'Uniforme de la santé'.

[50] J.-P. Peter, 'Entre femmes et médecins. Violence et singularité dans le discours du corps', *Ethnologie française*, 3–4 (1976); 'Les médecins, les morts et les objets de la maladie', *Revue historique* (1971), pp. 13–38; 'Une enquête de la Société royale de médecine, malades et maladies à la fin du XVIIIe siècle', *Annales: ESC* (1967), pp. 711–51; Roche, *Le Siècle des Lumières*.

in the *Encyclopédie méthodique*, last stage in the Enlightenment's popularisation of all areas of knowledge, thus extending its influence into the first quarter of the nineteenth century.[51] Published in 1792, the article 'Collar' boldly proclaimed 'that we ought to make to this part of our manners, our customs and our costumes, the same changes that we are now making to our Constitution and our laws'.[52] By the end of a great movement which had denounced scholarly errors and popular prejudice alike, and which dreamed of a new costume for new citizens, clothing reform was the order of the day.

A NEW BODY AND NEW CLOTHES

Three main strands dominated the debate, which engaged a vast public of specialists, amateurs and the growing number of people anxious to learn more about the new principles of health and hygiene.[53] A greater medicalisation, medical intervention in more sectors of social life and the pedagogy of expertise contributed to this collective craving. It was, first, a way of asserting a new vision of the corporeal, and thus of rediscovering in dress the imperatives of nature; second, the new principles must be applied: for the liberated body, liberating clothes, and vice versa! Lastly, the impetus achieved generalised the clothing debate and encouraged medical thought to relocate it in a better-understood and better-controlled environment; moral reform and the social utopia are again visible in the ideas and in the variously realistic and successful initiatives they provoked. Clothes and dress were proper subjects for legislation in the public interest.[54]

At the end of the eighteenth century, it was the aim of the doctors to restore its freedom to the body. The latter had won its autonomy to the extent that medical thought no longer confined sickness within a system of analogies or saw it as an entity distinct from the organism; the sick organ was perceived at the intersection

---

[51] Darnton, *L'Aventure de l'Encyclopédie*, pp. 21–88, 342–86; S. Tucoochala, CHJ, *Panckoucke et la librairie française 1736–1780* (Pau/Paris, 1977).

[52] See *Médecine*, directed by Vicq-d'Azir, 13 vols. (Paris, 1790–1820), article *Col.* vol. IV.

[53] Roche, *Les Républicains des lettres*, 'Talents, raison, sacrifice (Les Eloges de la Société royale de médecine)', pp. 308–30.

[54] Pérez, 'Le Vêtement dans les logiques médicales', pp. 6–7.

of two systems of questions; it was part of a whole (the individual organism) and it was the manifestation of a socially thought ensemble. The clinic, whose birth has been described by Michel Foucault,[55] could then resort to the old precepts of Hippocratic medicine; it changed their meaning: clothing was no longer only a guarantee of health, but could, like the society which produced it, cause sickness.[56] Clothing, like society, must recover its freedom in accord with the precepts of nature. It thus joined the group of norms which defined a better and more comfortable life.[57] Throughout the century, a stream of works continued to instruct according to the ancient principles of the manuals of good living.[58] Clothing was included among the inconveniences, causes of discomfort and illness. For lassitude, apoplectic fits and the various accidents which threatened life, it was necessary to loosen clothes which were too tight.

Some of this advice found its way into the numerous dictionaries and, above all, the articles in the *Gazette de santé* devoted to medical matters – a treasure-house of routine, common-sense practices.[59] It was repeated and developed in treatises or in the more utilitarian and systematic analyses scattered through reviews in journals,[60] which aimed to channel this self-medication: the instructions about clothes were not simply recipes. Nevertheless, the vogue for ancient texts revealed a loyalty to traditional ideas which were close to proverbial wisdom, and not always far removed from the instruction of the manuals of 'good manners': sartorial wisdom

---

[55] M. Foucault, *Naissance de la Clinique* (Paris, 1963), pp. v–vi (translated by A. M. Sheridan as *The Birth of the Clinic* (London, 1973)).

[56] Pellegrin, 'L'Uniforme de la santé'.

[57] Pérez, 'Le Vêtement dans les logiques médicales', pp. 10–28.

[58] For example: *L'Ecole de Salerne ou principes généraux pour conserver la santé* (Paris, 1736); L. Cornaro, *Conseils pour vivre longtemps*, translated 1701, 1784, 1807; *L'Art de jouir d'une parfaite santé et de vivre heureux jusqu'à une grande vieillesse*, new translation of the treatises of Lessius and Cornaro (Paris, 1785) going back to texts of the sixteenth century and even, with the Salerno school, to an earlier tradition.

[59] *Gazette médicale*, 209, 11 October 1811; 'when it rains cover yourself up, avoid humidity, protect yourself against fog by wearing good wool next to your skin, and from the mire of the streets by solid shoes'.

[60] Itard, *L'Hygiene domestique ou l'art de conserver la santé et de prolonger la vie, mis à la portée des gens du monde* (Paris, Year II); and *Journal de médecine préservatrice* (Pluviose, Year II), *Journal universel des sciences médicales* (1816); the *Gazette de santé* of July 1777 warns the public against 'the murderous epidemic of recipe books'.

was above all respect for tradition and moderation.[61] Advice was also to be found in the *Res non naturales* of scholarly works,[62] which mix climatic theories, the anthropological observations of travellers and criticism of customs. Clothing was often a sign of moral disorder, and medicine thus found itself condemning fashion and its excesses. A comparable lesson was to be found in Diderot and Jaucourt; clothing, a sign of moral degeneration, was also a symptom of physical deformity: read again the article 'Pannier'.[63] The harmony of human equilibrium and an imagined nature was broken in practice,[64] the body being threatened by sartorial excess.

What was needed was a return to nature, mistress of life and of moderation.[65] The civilised man, whose health was imperilled, should renounce unnatural clothes. The medicine of the Enlightenment was wholly Rousseauist in its principles and readily turned to the illustrious citizen of Geneva for the most pertinent explanation: 'Our clothes are fetters!'[66] A historical mythology mobilised medical erudition to prove it, and confirm the dangers which threatened a human race spoiled by manners and clothes which were artificial and harmful.[67] There was only one cure: let nature prevail! This was above all the case with procreation and childhood. Clairian wanted to liberate men from their breeches, which threatened precociously to corrupt their semen, and put them in kilts, since trouserless peoples 'had more developed organs of procreation' than those of the 'little masters'; as did the Parisian bakers who laboured half naked at their kneading-troughs and ovens. Faust

---

[61] See De La Framboisière, *Avis utile pour la conservation de la santé* (Paris, 1639); this text, contemporary with the *civilités*, demonstrates how important was the appeal to tradition to justify hostility to the new habits.

[62] *La Médecine éclairée par les sciences physiques* (Paris, 1791); *La Médecine statique de Sanctoris* (Paris, 1772).

[63] Vol. IX, p. 819; see also *Encyclopédie méthodique*, '*Manche*'; *Gazette de santé. Constitution médicale*, no. 1, 1 Thermidor, Year XII; also no. 36, 21 December 1809, and 11 July 1809.

[64] L.-J. Clairian, *Recherches et considérations médicales sur les vêtements des hommes, particulièrement sur les culottes*, 2nd edn, Paris, Year IX, p. 20.

[65] A. Leroy, *Recherches sur les habillements des femmes et des enfants* (Paris, 1777), chapter 2.

[66] Leroy, *Recherches sur les habillements*, chapter 5; B. C. Faust, *Hommage fait à l'Assemblée nationale de quelques idées sur un vêtement uniforme*, Strasburg, Year II; article '*Corset*' in *Gazette de santé*, 5, 11 February 1811.

[67] Clairian, *Recherches et considérations médicales*, p. 18; Leroy, *Recherches sur les habillements*, chapter 4.

denounced stiff bodices, stays, all tight clothes which 'oppressed the breasts', the girdles which ruined nurses and the children's clothing which compromised the future.[68] A utilitarian and functionalist thought aimed to make the clothing of the people revert to natural principles and a moral aesthetic in accord with the ethos of the age: happiness lay at the end of the road.[69]

## CLOTHING AND THE BODY'S HUMOURS

The sartorial liberation had first a medical significance, since it took into account all the obstacles which made sense within the ancient conception of the medicine of the humours, now reformulated in the prevailing Rousseauist vocabulary.[70] Galen and Hippocrates continued to influence medical theories, which saw the body as a mass in which fluids permanently circulated, their stagnation a cause of illness and death.[71] 'Our tight clothes restrict all the essential parts of our bodies ... they compress our lymphatic vessels ... they divide the body into two and the circulation between these two parts is prevented', wrote B. C. Faust.[72]

These principles encouraged the search for strategic points which could be freed from the barriers and obstacles which prevented the easy flow of the humours: the neck to be liberated from cravats, shirt collars, band-bearers, ribbons and necklaces;[73] the bust and waist to be freed from boned bodices, stays, cords, girdles and laces, which caused difficulty in breathing and deformity; the wrist to be released from constricting sleeves and cuffs; the testicles to escape from tight-fitting breeches; the legs to be relieved of garters. In sum, sartorial medicine waged war on the rigours of tight buttoning and lacing, all the ligatures prejudicial to the fluidity of the phlegms, or cause of a heat which stunted normal growth, a major risk in the eyes of those haunted by the degeneration of the race and the danger of depopulation.[74] But one can also detect in

---

[68] *Encyclopédie méthodique*, '*Habillement*'; Clairian, *Recherches et considérations médicales*, pp. 8–9, 18–20; Faust, *Sur un vêtement uniforme*, pp. 19–20, 30–5.

[69] R. Mauzel, *L'Idée du bonheur au XVIIIe siècle* (Paris, 1960), pp. 319–20.

[70] Pérez, 'Le Vêtement dans les logiques médicales', p. 60–75; see also Vigarello, *Le Corps redressé* (Paris, 1978).

[71] Tissot, *Avis aux gens de lettres*, p. viii.

[72] Faust, *Sur un vêtement uniforme*, pp. 9–10.

[73] *Encyclopédie méthodique*, vol. IV, '*Col*'.

[74] Pellegrin, 'L'Uniforme de la santé', p. 8.

this concern with free circulation the great metonym of water which marked all Enlightenment thinking, from physics to economics, from medicine to political analysis, whose workings were vividly pictured in hydraulic terms.[75]

The values of normal perspiration formed part of the sartorial therapy. Linen and clothes ought to encourage the production of excretions, free the organism of an excess of humours,[76] and so permit a freer expression of the accord between the physical and the moral. To the religious image of the body as prison of the soul, dedicated to ascetic fasting, succeeded a conception both determinist, where the body influenced the spirit, and somato-physiological, where the action of the spirit on the body permitted the rehabilitation of the passions. Sartorial hygiene contributed to the knowledge of the reciprocal influences of the spiritual and the corporeal: well-designed clothing would dispel sadness and restore to the civilised man his 'grandeur of soul'.[77]

Always liable to be treated intemperately, the question of dress inflated all the debates about sex and women, pleasure and eroticism, already to be found in the novel or the *Memoirs*.[78] Under the cloak of reason, the medical discourse reflected the fantasies and preoccupations which structured the imagination of the age: clothing was only a pretext for the expression of a morality, where the fascination with women or childhood was put at the service of the regeneration of the species, or where the quest for natural values might help to fill the growing gap between the being and his profound truth.[79]

## SOCIAL TRUTH OF CLOTHING, TRUTH OF BEINGS

The liberation of the body and the medical clothing revolution culminated in an analysis of the milieu and in political and social reform. They were 'objects of the public weal', whose artificial constraints must be assessed and whose regeneration must be activated. A physics of societies brought clothing into the realm of

---

[75] Markovits, *L'Ordre des échanges*, pp. 171–80.
[76] *Encyclopédie méthodique*, vol. IV, *'Boules'*, *'Brosser'*; vol. VIII, *'Manche'*; vol. XIII, *'Vêtements'*.
[77] *Encyclopédie méthodique*, vol. VII, *'Habillement'*.
[78] Hoffmann, *La Femme*, pp. 559–65.
[79] Ibid., p. 562.

two major references, the atmosphere and the climate.[80] Prevailing beliefs about air permeated all the connections established between clothes and health; they protected from the 'direct impact of the air';[81] they allowed through 'an air whose balsamic and salutary influence acts so powerfully on animals and plants'.[82] Dress helped to create around men an 'artificial climate'; it was thus called on to fight against the fatalities of social determinism. To strive for the reform of clothing habits was now to promote a moral revival. Dress contributed to the malaise of urban civilisation, which was infiltrating the rural refuges of nature, where, in any case, too many prejudices already constituted a threat to the species. Alphonse Leroy entitled one of his chapters 'How clothes have combined with other causes to promote degeneration'; to remedy this, new legislation was necessary: 'We need also wise laws to prevent physical and moral corruption. We generally attribute too much to the influence of the climate, and political institutions have a more tangible impact on the population, health and morals.' Leroy's book ended with an appeal for government initiative and a profession of faith in 'the most advantageous of revolutions'.

In the last decade of the century, medical projects attempted to establish a new sartorial order, less artificial, or at least more in accord with the doctors' conception of nature and the relationship between the physical and the moral. They carried on the aims of the encyclopedists; they adapted, though they largely accepted, the positions of Rousseau and they added all the concerns of the populationists anxious to preserve the state, and then the nation, whose power would be guaranteed by the number of its citizens. The sartorial medical utopia ended in political morality. In the difference between the ideas underlying the projects and the possibilities of a concrete reform which was never achieved, we see the distortion produced between the progress of the clothing revolution and the moral imperatives of the aesthetic of adornment. Fashion had not disappeared, nor, with it, questions about the links between social and individual appearance and the truth of beings.

---

[80] *Encyclopédie méthodique*, vol. IV, *La Médecine éclairée par les sciences physiques, exposition d'un plan complet d'hygiène.*
[81] Clairian, *Recherches et considérations médicales*, p. 50.
[82] Faust, *Sur un vêtement uniforme*, pp. 8–9.

# 16. *Fashions in reason and reasons for fashion: the birth of the fashion press in France*

S'il m'était permis de choisir dans le fatras des livres qui
seront publiés cent ans après ma mort, savez-vous celui que je
prendrais . . . Non, ce n'est point un roman que je prendrais
dans cette future bibliothèque, ni un livre d'historique . . . je
prendrais tout bonnement, mon ami, un journal de mode
pour voir comment les femmes s'habilleront un siècle après
mon trépas. Et ces chiffons m'en diraient plus sur l'humanité
future que tous les philosophes, les romanciers, les
prédicateurs, les savants.

A. France

So utopias and the novel could not escape fashion, and nor could
the *Encyclopédie* or the medical discourse. This encounter was
crucial, since the period, especially after 1750, saw the development
of a fashion press which, though essentially French, was read far
beyond the boundaries of France. It helped to reshape the dress of
the European elites who were its readers, in line with French
worldly sensibilities, just as their conduct and culture had previously been influenced by the luminaries of French philosophy,
whose ideas had circulated through the increasingly numerous
channels provided by books and the press.

The analogy merits our attention, and not only out of idle
curiosity; it deserves better than the habitual contempt of the
historian of ideas for minor subjects or the facts of everyday life,
and greater objectivity than tends to accompany the desire to
rehabilitate at all costs the female culture of the past, from the
perspective of a more or less authentic feminism. What I wish to
show is how, and in what intellectual and editorial, logical and
moral, context, the transformation of the clothing system allowed
the irruption of another culture and, with it, the entry of our
civilisation into another world. The reign of diversity and change

could then begin, if not unchallenged, since new means of communication allowed a new universe of symbols to be propagated and a new ideology to be spread, by projecting them in the materiality of things.

## THE ENLIGHTENMENT, FASHION AND JOURNALISM

This role devolved on the fashion press,[1] that is to say, on those periodicals which set out to present, on a regular basis, collections of fashion, in the event primarily clothes, and which combined text and illustration.[2] *Le Cabinet des modes*, first published by the Parisian bookseller, François Buisson, on 15 November 1785, continued its career after 1786 under the title of *Magasin des modes nouvelles françaises et anglaises*, and then as *Le Journal de la mode et du goût* from 1790 to 1793; it was the unchallenged leader of a genre which had started well before 1750 and which played a crucial role in the history of culture.[3] It was a press which catered for men as well as for women, and was written by women as well as by men. It directly questioned public opinion and its fluctuations, and it promoted change in other ways than did the ideas of the philosophers, and this in spite of their profound contempt for journalism, whether in the service of the great literary, philosophical, learned and political journals – such as the *Mémoires de Trévous*, the *Journal des savants*, the *Gazette* and the *Mercure* – or that of lesser publications such as the *Affiches* or *Le Journal de Paris*, the first daily paper to be published in France.[4] Very occasionally, the battle of ideas and the controversy attracted the attention of the prima donnas of philosophy, who could not resist

[1] For the wider history of journalism, see C. Bellanger *et al.*, eds., *Histoire générale de la presse française* (Paris, 1969), vol. I (L. Trénard and J. Godechot); E. Hatin, *Histoire politique et littéraire de la presse française*, 8 vols. (Paris, 1859–64); ibid., *Bibliographie historique et critique de la presse périodique*. There has been a recent revival of interest in the history of periodicals, largely thanks to J. Sgard and a team of French and other scholars; see *Dictionnaire des journalismes* (Grenoble, 1976); *Bibliographie de la presse classique 1600–1789* (Geneva, 1984); Martin and Chartier, *Histoire de l'édition française*, vol. II, *Le Livre triomphant*, pp. 198–205.

[2] A. M. Kleinert, *Die Frühen Mode Journal in Frankreich, Studien zur Literatur der Mode von den Anfängenbis, 1848* (Berlin, 1980), pp. 14–16.

[3] Kleinert, *Die Frühen Mode Journal*, pp. 11–12.

[4] P. Rétat, ed., *Etudes sur la presse au XVIIIe siècle* (Lyons, 1978); *Le Journalisme au XVIIIe siècle* (Lyons, 1982); *L'Instrument périodique* (Lyons, 1985); *La Presse en 1989* (Lyons, 1989).

engaging in polemics with the vulgar popularisers; however, they generally kept their distance from a mode of expression reserved to trivial matters and, above all, a deceptive topicality, conveyor of criticism, which it was easier to accept for others than for oneself, and seen, in the last analysis, as a minor literary genre, more powerless than creative.

The entry of women into journalism,[5] the permanent and central presence of fashion in the periodicals and its regular actualisation in texts and images undermined many prejudices and raised many questions at a decisive moment, when the functioning of *ancien régime* society was beginning to change both profoundly and superficially. The new press reveals if not the new place of the second sex in society, at least the new role it saw for itself in the world, at all events new relations between the sexes. Like the clothing revolution, the fashion periodicals had a double function: that of a mirror in which society saw itself and was seen; that of a precipitating factor hastening an evolution which produced and reproduced, if indeed the image of something does not repeat so much as modify and renew it.[6]

The educated and scholarly milieus, at least as they are revealed in the *Encyclopédie* or the socialised world of the academies, both observed and debated modes of dress; their fascination with manners did not prevent them from being taken as seriously as other branches of the tree of knowledge; indeed, they gave birth to anthropology.[7] It was also the case that these men of letters and artists, amateurs and scholars, united 'by the common good of the human race and a reciprocal sentiment of benevolence', could not but be influenced in their ordinary way of life and choice of clothes by the milieu with which they lived in symbiosis: good Parisian society, the customers of the craftsmen responsible for the principal transformations of fashion. Their external image had to express this *aggiornamento*. As Carlo Roccella justly observed, most of the social and intellectual groups involved in the turbulent diffusion of the Enlightenment did not draw the ultimate conclusions, though

[5] Rimbault, 'La Presse féminine'; S. Van Dijk, *Traces de femmes, Présence féminine dans le journalisme français au XVIIIe siècle* (Amsterdam, 1988), Etudes de l'Institut P. Bayle, Nijmegen, no. 18; N. R. Gelbart, *Feminine Opposition Journalism in Old Regime France, 'Le Journal des dames'* (Berkeley, 1987).

[6] F. Dagognet, *Pour une théorie générale des formes* (Paris, 1975), pp. 7–8.

[7] Roccella, 'La Moda', pp. 9–22.

the wind of change still, in the long run, altered their mentality, their ideas and their behaviour.[8]

The question then becomes how, in actual practice, the contradiction between the criticism of fashion and its increasingly obvious manifestations was resolved for milieus which were also those of journalism, and which could not escape the ambience in which the clothing and consumer revolutions were taking place. It is not so much a question of what type of wig or hoops were worn by these men or women, though such questions are not without interest, as of how the original and reforming milieus which questioned the dominant social and political system were, or were not, able to be detached from the external appearances which were its most eloquent expression. It is also a question of how there could come about more insidious changes, in the long run more challenging than the sort of sudden abandonment of habitual costume attempted by Jean-Jacques Rousseau in his quest for greater transparency.[9] The search for originality in dress could easily appear as a further manifestation of the artificial instability of fashion, so that the finer spirits might conclude that it was better to follow fashion in their choice of clothes, but not in their modes of thought.[10] In so doing, they made possible a new means of communication, which combined an informative text and visualisation in pictures, the actualisation and popularisation of a moral and philosophical culture and the formation of new sartorial as well as intellectual practices, such as reading.[11]

The genre included more literary journals, aimed at a wider public but with a specifically female bias, and periodicals devoted primarily to fashion. Its originality lay less in the subjects it dealt with than in its new journalistic practices.[12] It gradually emerged from the ruck of periodicals, few of which failed to devote at least some space to fashion and costume. It differed from, though was inspired by, the many collections of engravings and prints, the 'true children of fashion', which aimed to show how clothes evolved,

---

[8] Ibid., p. 14.

[9] J. Starobinski, *La Transparence et l'obstacle* (Paris, 1967); B. Mely, *Jean-Jacques Rousseau, un intellectuel en rupture* (Paris, 1985).

[10] *Encyclopédie*: 'Affectation', 'Beaux', 'Galanterie', 'Efféminé', 'Mode', 'Savoir-vivre' and 'Singularité'.

[11] R. Chartier, *Lectures et lecteurs dans la France d'Ancien Régime* (Paris, 1987).

[12] Rimbault, 'La Presse féminine', p. 3; Kleinert, *Die Frühen Mode Journal*, pp. 15–17.

and whose history can be traced back to the seventeenth century and the *Monument du costume* of the reign of Louis XVI. It diverged from a whole range of ways of providing information about clothing, probably born with fashion itself, and accelerated by the growth of towns.[13] Gradually, a clearer sense of purpose led to more standardised practices, oriented towards a specifically female public. Innovation flourished, since the magazines included literary and moral criticism and debate (as in *Le Journal des dames*),[14] demands by women, often expressed in correspondence solicited by the editors, and above all models of conduct, 'ways of doing things', recipes, cures, advertisements, all destined to shape a new culture of femininity. 'Reason will be admitted to our journal', wrote M. de Beaumer in the prospectus for *Le Journal des dames*, in October 1761, 'as long as it wears a gracious smile. We will not be afraid to associate the Arts with the most frivolous of fashions. If one ought to find Montesquieu and Racine alongside pom-poms and ribbons on a well-equipped toilet table, a women's library has to admit the lightest of booklets.' To instruct and to amuse, to please but also to reason were the guiding notions of the new journalism.

## FASHION DOLLS, TRUE CHILDREN OF FASHION

The exchange of fashion news quickly assumed two principal forms: innumerable ambassadors involuntarily spread far and wide the practices of external worlds; information was consciously sought from the centres of production and manipulation, the great commercial fairs and above all the network of princely courts. Princes and princesses listened to the descriptions of observers and began to have sent to them models of foreign clothes worn by 'fashion dolls'.

The dolls were eagerly discussed at the Italian, English and French courts, offered as wedding presents and adorned the collections of curiosities made by the European nobilities. In France, the hôtel de Rambouillet and les Précieuses devoted exhibitions to these fragile mannequins, made of wax, wood or porcelain, their

---

[13] Kleinert, *Die Frühen Mode Journal*, p. 21; F. Kiener, *Kleidung, Mode und Mensch* (Munich, 1956), pp. 135–8.

[14] M. Hillier, *Puppen und Pupenmacher* (Frankfurt, 1968).

clothes changing with the season. The shops of the rue Saint-Honoré were quick to organise the manufacture and adornment of these emissaries of French fashion which, in the eighteenth century, were despatched monthly to the four corners of Europe and the world. In time of war, miniscule Pandoras dressed in déshabillés or négligés and life-sized Pandoras in full court dress enjoyed diplomatic immunity, and were even given cavalry escorts to ensure their safe arrival. Wives of the great sultan in his seraglio, tsarinas and princesses in St Petersburg and Moscow, German margravines and English grand duchesses speculated about their dispatch and impatiently awaited their arrival. Even the elegant ladies of the New World sent for them in order to keep up-to-date. Spies used them to conceal their messages. In sum, the Europe of good form and court society was dependent on these Parisian merchants' dolls; they were displayed in shop windows and admired beyond the beau monde; they were an aspect of the Enlightenment.

From the beginning, the publication of the fashion journals could be presented as an alternative, almost guaranteed success, for these expensive, delicate and, in the last analysis, not very convenient artificial figures, periodically presented to an admiring world. Their fall from favour, by a fascinating displacement, helped to create the literary and pictorial mythology of the mannikin, of which our contemporary imagination still bears trace, witness André Breton in *Nadia*: 'Adorable temptress in the musée Grévin; this woman pretending to hide in the shadows to fasten her suspender, who, in her timeless pose, is the only status I know to have eyes: those of provocation.'[15]

Engravings of fashion, whether offered in collections or separately, quickly became an essential source of information.[16] Text and illustration were effectively combined to make the changes, if not the newest styles, widely known. They helped to drive the fashion dolls out of the information market because they were cheaper and more mobile, and because the capacity of the typographic presses to adapt and print in large numbers enabled them to convey their images well beyond aristocratic circles. The fashion plate gave substance to evanescent and ever-changing combina-

---

[15] G. Lascault, *Figurées, défigurées. Petit vocabulaire de la féminité représentée* (Paris, 1977), pp. 90–1.

[16] J. L. Nevinson, 'L'origine de la gravure de modes', *Actes* of First International Congress on the History of Costume, Venice, 1952, pp. 252ff.

tions. It associated ideas, those of traditions of the body and those of the male and female roles, thanks to pictorial representations. They helped to make fashion accessible to the rising bourgeoisie, those most determined and impatient to acquire aristocratic clothing distinction. But they can also be read as the apogee of a civilisation of the visual, where empirical and sensitive combinations served to express the social situation, and formal arrangements helped to indicate distance or proximity with regard to the courts, centres of power. The fashion plate thus enjoyed some of the power of collections of emblems and arms, of figurations of seals and devices. It was still part of the Catholic and holistic world. It reinforced the éclat of the social.[17]

### DESCRIPTIONS OF MANNERS, ENGRAVINGS OF FASHION

Depictions of costume and of fashion then diverged, the former to portray the diversity of past customs or national dress, the latter to present the clothes of the present day. Since the sixteenth century, such collections had been highly successful, disseminating 'portraits' in which the costume was only one among many marvels in the spectacle of creation, 'reflection of a chaos introduced into the world by man'. The transition from isolated picture to unified collections was encouraged by the needs of ornamenters and professionals in dress and also responded to the taste of collectors and the interest of the *philosophes*. The text began to prevail over the image, the sense over the visual. The aim was now to please and to instruct, and curiosity, leitmotiv of sixteenth-century authors, and a chaotic profusion of images, gave way to the analysis and utility which predominated in the collections of the eighteenth century.[18]

Table 42 gives some impression of how the genre progressed between 1600 and 1800.[19] The number of engravers remained

[17] Dagognet, *Pour une théorie générale*, pp. 98–104; A. Planche, 'Le blason des couleurs en armes, livrées et devise de Sicelle, héraut d'Alphonse V d'Aragon, codage et corrélation', *L'Ethnographie* (1984), pp. 255–68.

[18] N. Pellegrin, 'A propos des représentations des costumes régionaux français d'Ancien Régime', *L'Ethnographie* (1984), pp. 387–400.

[19] Based on the inventory by R. Gaudriault, *Répertoire de la gravure de mode française des origines à 1815* (Paris, 1988). It records author-engravers, so ignores numerous anonymous ventures. The chronology is that proposed by Gaudriault, who aimed to give only an overall view.

Table 42 *Production of fashion plates*

|          | Engravers | Number of plates |
|----------|-----------|------------------|
| 1600–49  | 7         | 102              |
| 1650–99  | 19        | 290              |
| 1700–49  | 11        | 229              |
| 1750–99  | 20        | 1,275            |

relatively stable throughout the period, a consequence of the spe-cialisation of the artists and above all the editors, even though engravers of quality such as Callot and Watteau were able to produce only a small number of series, although these were of high aesthetic quality from the beginning. The figures do not reveal the volume of production or diffusion. Loose or in collections, the pictures might reach a varied public, not necessarily able to read, in search of precise information about clothes or simply pleasure for the eye. Artists of high repute, such as J. Le Pautre, S. Le Clerc and B. Picart, were actively involved. In the years 1670–1700, the editors of the rue Saint-Jacques, the Bonnart, Dieu de Saint-Jean, Arnoult and Trouvain published hundreds of collections. Finally, the eighteenth century culminated in a massive explosion: the years after 1770 saw the appearance of the great series of the *Galeries de mode* produced by Esnaults and Rapilly between 1778 and 1787,[20] the *Monuments du costume*[21] and, in a way returning to the spirit of the first collections, the *Costumes civils de tous les peuples connus* of Grasset de Saint-Sauveur. Together they developed a graphic art and familiarised a public with the still irregular periodisation of presentations of fashion.

Their success was increased by the many copies and pirated editions. The plates were often reproduced by the *almanachs de mode* which aimed at a fashionable clientele, and enjoyed great success thanks to a conveniently small format and a considerably

---

[20] F. Tétat-Vittu, 'La Galerie des modes et costumes français chez Esnaults et Rapilly rue Saint-Jacques à la Ville de Coutances (1778–1787)', *Les Nouvelles de l'Estampe*, 9 March 1987, pp. 16–20.

[21] Bertrand, 'Les monuments du costume'; Cophornic, 'Recherches sur les monuments du costume du XVIIIe siècle', mémoire de maîtrise, Paris 1 (1984); Desmangeot, 'Le Système du vêtement'.

increased print run.[22] With his *Almanach nouveau ou recueil des jolies coiffures à la mode de Paris*, the hairdresser Davault was hugely successful in mixing engravings, information and advertisements; he launched a genre which was imitated, between 1774 and the Revolution, by the *Almanachs de la toilette*, *Le Bijou des dames*, *Le Manuel des toilettes*, *Les Etrennes les plus utiles aux dames*, *Le Manuel des grâces*, *Les Fantaisies aimables* and, as late as 1789, *Les Lacets de Vénus*! By this stage, the principal characteristics of a feminine press had become part of the stock-in-trade of printer-publishers, authors and engravers: the association of pictures and text, advice about clothes to copy, information on a wide range of topics and the regular repetition of these ephemeral lessons. The fashion press developed and combined these features, as, for example, from 1785 to 1793, in *Le Cabinet des modes*, whose changes of title should not conceal a fundamental unity. It was a periodical, it mixed discourse and illustration, and during its lifetime printed over 400 plates. In 1794, it was transformed into the *Almanach des modes françaises et anglaises*.[23] It was in a way the culmination of the creative labour and sympathetic and inventive imagination of those responsible for a women's press.

## FROM THE LITERARY AND GALLANT JOURNAL TO THE FASHION MAGAZINE

The fashion magazine also inherited practices bequeathed by the authors of the gallant, satirical and literary press,[24] a natural consequence of including information about court and town festivities. *Le Courrier français* and *La Muse historique* already devoted a few marginal pages to fashion, which figured more regularly in *Le Mercure galant* of Doneau de Visé after 1672, without ever being wholly systematic or autonomous. The information was scattered and disorganised, reflecting the debates of the moralists and caricaturists who attacked the dangers of the spread of luxury and condemned expensive materials and exaggerated shapes.[25] One can

---

[22] Kleinert, *Die Frühen Mode Journal*, pp. 22–39, 43–8. Mercier estimated the print-run of the most famous of the almanachs, that of Mathieu Laensberg, at 60,000.

[23] Kleinert, *Die Frühen Mode Journal*, pp. 46–8.

[24] Ibid., pp. 49–59.

[25] Godard de Donville, *Signification de la mode*; 'Les mécanismes de la mode sous

also detect echoes of the last debates on the sumptuary laws which, like satires and sermons, gave such happy publicity to the habits and products they denounced that their attempt to prevent their circulation and diffusion were inevitably doomed. The gallant press already encouraged consumption and, like the ordinances, ensured the triumph of the manners of court society and the political eloquence of clothing. Courtiers and coquettes of Paris, 'the little darlings of the day', cared only for fashion, which was now expected of provincials and foreigners, and which had passed from Versailles to Paris, 'from the ladies of the town to rich bourgeois women, and from them to milliners', according to *Le Mercure galant* in 1672.

Gallant journalism often used the device of the letter; it allowed a well-bred tone, which promoted a feeling of sympathy between reader and writer. The latter made confidences and observations, repeated the gossip of the salons and used various means to make his fictions sound like facts so as to win his readers' confidence, give an air of authenticity to his information and provoke imitation. Cautiously, and only enhancing the appeal of the objects described or the manners discussed by appearing to distance himself from them, the writer revealed his discoveries, not without frequent repetition, a mass of detail and picturesque description. The gallant gentleman journalist only referred to fashion by reason of an external and wholly social legitimation, since it had not yet achieved recognition and totally autonomous expression. The overiding impression is of an almost existential dialogue and the employment of the procedures which would later ensure the success of advertising: presenting an attractive picture of the object put into circulation, locating it in the most distinguished possible context, selling not so much a product as a life-style and, by all these means, whetting the appetites of the consumers.[26] This was how Diderot and the encyclopedists used plates, and it was by adopting similar textual and illustrative strategies that the editors of the fashion magazines set about winning a public.

However, the literary and gallant journals still made little use of illustrations; *Le Mercure* reproduced only a dozen in all, at the end of the seventeenth century; they disappeared after 1730, but the

l'Ancien Régime: l'exemple de la botte (époque Henri IV–Louis XIII)', *L'Ethnographie* (1984), pp. 115–24.
[26] Proust, *Marges d'une utopie*, pp. 6–7.

first essays of the feminine press had by then shown the potential of the genre and confirmed the existence of a huge public. They would illustrate the conjuncture of a milieu of authors – men and women, men sometimes disguised as women, women often passing as men, their sex determined by their pseudonym – and the milieus caught up in the transformation of clothing habits, and as a result experiencing a growing need for more precise and more regular information.[27]

## FASHION PRESS, FEMININE PRESS (1710–93): A PRECARIOUS ENTERPRISE

The years 1710 to 1785 saw the launching of some twenty journals, at the rate of one every four or five years.[28] Most were ephemeral creations which lasted only as long as an initial prospectus and a few numbers, a few months or a few years: for example, *Le Nouveau Mercure galant* directed by Mme Dunoyer in 1710, *Les Saisons littéraires* of Mlle Barbier in 1713, *La Spectatrice* published by the widowed Mme Pissot and Jean de Nully in Paris between March 1728 and March 1729, *Les Amusements du beau sexe et des dames, Le Nouveau Magasin français, Les Amusements de la toilette* and *Les Amusements périodiques* between 1740 and 1760, *La Bibliothèque des femmes, Le Courrier de la mode, Le Journal du goût* and the monthly fashion publications from 1755 to 1780.

Five or six periodicals were fortunate enough to escape this fate: *La Quintessence des nouvelles*, also published by Mme Dunoyer, in Amsterdam, lasted some twenty years; this was a *lardon*, that is, a racy production printed on the long, narrow paper characteristic of Dutch gazettes, using a small in-folio;[29] another was *Le Nouveau Magasin français* of Mme Le Prince de Beaumont, which lasted two years, with a brief revival in 1758. *Le Journal des dames* was the best example of this highly original formula, combining a critical view of the Parisian world and a female discourse, maintained despite a succession of editors, Campigneulle, La Louptière, Mme de Baumer and Mme de Maisonneuve, Mercier and Dorat, to name only the best known. It survived difficulties and censure

---

[27] Rimbault, 'La Presse féminine', pp. 13–46; Kleinert, *Die Frühen Mode Journal*, pp. 55–62.
[28] Rimbault, 'La Presse féminine', pp. 15–16, 23.
[29] Van Dijk, *Traces de femmes*, pp. 85–133.

for nearly twenty years.[30] *Le Journal de monsieur* and *Le Courrier lyrique* also deserve mention; less ephemeral, they also lasted for over five years. In comparison, *Le Cabinet des modes*, though with three different titles between 1785 and 1793, remained throughout under the fairly advanced direction of Jean Antoine Lebrun, and was a runaway success. It enjoyed a great vogue and adapted to the times. Its cessation was symbolic of the temporary rupture during the Terror between fashion journals and their public.

The fragility of the earlier enterprises seems to me to underline that of the old journalism. It was a risky venture in the society of privilege, where the editors were dependent on those possessing capital or a monopoly of production, that is, the milieu of the rich Parisian booksellers. It was a type of publication which had to struggle to win a public which it was difficult to reach in the technical context of limited print runs and a restricted circulation which depended on subscriptions and bookshop sales. The women's press was also dependent on the post; when it improved after 1770, the journals fared better and initiatives were less short-lived.[31] However, it was a long time before the journal was able to escape the modes of production and distribution of the book, the usual product of the bookseller-printer.[32]

The Revolution made possible a veritable liberation, and pamphlets and periodicals proliferated; 'public opinion ruled', and the fashion press and women's journalism enjoyed a final success. It was now based on a solid national and European market: in 1761, *Le Journal des dames* was distributed in thirty-nine French towns and forty-one abroad; it reached the elites from Cadiz to Saint Petersburg, from Stockholm to Naples; its circulation was comparable to that of *Le Mercure de France* or *L'Année littéraire*. But this achievement was dependent on constant attention and unceasing labour. The quest for subscriptions could only be successful if delivery delays were reduced and interruptions eliminated. Quarrels with bookshops, squabbles between editors and contributors, the interference of the censor and the failure of effective protection explain mistakes, difficulties and failures.[33] 'The bookshops have

[30] Gelbart, *Feminine Opposition Journalism*, pp. 290–303.
[31] B. Lepetit and G. Arbellot, *Atlas de la Révolution française*, vol. I: *Routes, canaux, transports et communications* (Paris, 1988).
[32] Sgard, *Dictionnaire des journalismes*, pp. 198–205.
[33] Rimbault, 'La Presse féminine', pp. 62–81.

always been the tyrants of authors, they grow rich at their expense; to have a journal's list kept by these moneygrubbers, you have to pay dearly; what has to be given to the bookshop swallows up the profit from the journal', wrote Mme de Baumer to M. de Malesherbes when she abandoned *Le Journal des dames*.[34] She had put her finger on the problem; to surmount these difficulties, the new journalists must acquire a new public.

## MALE AND FEMALE JOURNALISTS, FEMALE AND MALE READERS

The fashion press also needed to find a formula to suit its market. One is struck by the ambiguity of its origins. This was first a consequence of the function of the old journalism: 'Let who will become a journalist and the most disgraced of writers may tomorrow disgrace his fellows', wrote Louis Sébastien Mercier, who spoke from experience, having edited *Le Journal des dames* for many years.[35] The press was still essentially a press of reviews, criticism and extracts; journalism was more compilation than a true labour of information. The genre was disparaged even by those who benefited from it and were sometimes, like Mercier, aware of the need to strike a proper balance: to justify a valuable role in the popularisation of knowledge, 'to analyse and instruct without succumbing to the prejudices of the day', to let the public pronounce as arbiters of opinion.

The new press had to progress on three fronts: it had to discover men and women capable of achieving recognition and continued success among the powerful personages in possession of the literary field; it had to seek out its public; it had to widen its appeal by offering both a new type of subject and new methods. 'To please', wrote La Louptière, 'is the first duty of journalism for women.' According to Mme de Maisonneuve, in 1765, shortly after, it was 'to preserve true taste'.[36] Who ought to please, and whom, and how, were the principal problems facing a genre whose uncertainties and difficulties are revealed by the curve of creations. At its height, *Le Cabinet des modes*, among others, found a formula whose

---

[34] B. N., MS. ff. 22135, f. 91, 30 May 1763.
[35] Gelbart, *Feminine Opposition Journalism*, pp. 207–48; Mercier, *Tableaux de Paris*, vol. VI, pp. 137–8.
[36] Advertisement in the *Journal des dames*, April 1761 and January 1765.

immediate success justified both its policy and its investment: it accepted the role of intermediary between those who received and those who created the consumer revolution, in clothes as in other things, and thus placed the press in the slipstream of fashion.

The group of journalists who developed this new formula was typical of literary circles: socially diverse and open, it included both first- and second-rate writers, who also worked on journals other than those for women. Two specific features deserve particular attention: it was a testing ground for as yet unrecognised talents, often from the provinces; the participation of both men and women was crucial, the latter playing a new and original role, which expressed an undeniable cultural enlargement and their entry – disputed – into literature. The low status of the press worked in favour of this promotion since male competition was less fierce than at more elevated levels. The journal could thus play the same role as the novel, women journalists developing analogous tactics for using fiction and journalism to achieve their literary advancement in a world totally dominated by men. This strongly accentuated their ability as popularisers, assiduous courtiers between the literatures.[37]

The first women journalists were thus particularly exposed to criticism. At all events, they emerged from the anonymity which still remained the rule for Mme Dunoyer, more famous in her own day for her adventurous life and her relations with the young Voltaire,[38] better known for her moral and fictional oeuvre than for her work as a journalist. Mme Le Prince de Beaumont, Mme de Beaumer, Mme de Prinzen, Mme de Maisonneuve, Mme de Montanclos, Mme Dufresnoy and Mme d'Ormoy all wanted to win recognition and justify their role.[39] In society, they were able to occupy marginal positions: Mme Dunoyer was an adventuress, a Protestant, an émigré and talented; Mme de Beaumont was a governess in London, and probably an actress, before achieving success in feminist education. Some of them occupied more central positions: Mme de Saint-Aubin married twice within the high nobility, Mme de Maisonneuve had connections in the General Farm and at court, like Mme de Prinzen and Mme de Montanclos,

[37] Fauchery, *La Destinée féminine*, pp. 93–107.
[38] Van Dijk, *Traces de femmes*, pp. 85–133.
[39] Ibid., pp. 135–81; Rimbault, 'La Presse féminine', pp. 85–8, 107–26; Gelbart, *Feminine Opposition Journalism*, pp. 38–66.

who were both protected by Marie-Antoinette. Mme Dufresnoy's rise was astonishing: daughter of a goldsmith and wife of a Parisian *procureur*, she broke into literary circles by her amazing prolificity. They all found in journalism an identity which accorded with their moral philosophy and their desire to write as women and for women. They were neither rebels nor marginals nor victims, but, like the novelists, they fought for an authentic mode of expression.

## MASCULINE WRITING AND FEMININE WRITING

'There would be no point in my concealing my sex, the carelessness of my style, and the lack of order you will find in my work would have told you . . . No more is needed to reveal a female author and a Frenchwoman to boot. So it is with a woman that you are invited to consort once a month.'[40] In so introducing herself, Mme Le Prince de Beaumont let slip the mask to parody the masculine conception of the feminine style, in accord with the stereotypes operative since the seventeenth century; Mme Dunoyer made a similar point.[41] On the other hand, there were many male journalists who, in order to conquer the new public, disguised their writing under the mask of feminine frivolity. This explains the common treatment meted out to both by Rivarol in his *Almanach des grands hommes* and *des grandes femmes*:[42] his aim was to trace the frontiers of the recognised talent in the Republic of Letters, and the satirist pierced with the same dart the 'bluestockings' and the 'gutter Rousseaus' who prospered in the 'new-look' journalism.

The men were mostly clever young tiros fresh from the provinces where they had first sought fame in the academies.[43] The chevalier de Bastide was from Provence, Boudier de Villeneuve had left a respectable Norman noble family for a legal career in Paris, César de Missy was a pastor who had lived in Holland and England. Journalism was a stage in their careers. In the team of writers

---

[40] In the *Journal des dames*, January 1764, Mme de Maisonneuve wrote, 'As a women's journalist I have an obligation to speak to all women, and this is an obligation I accept for my journal'; Mme de Beaumont, in *Le Nouveau Magasin français* of January 1750, made a similar statement.

[41] Van Dijk, *Traces de femmes*, pp. 132–3.

[42] Paris 1789; R. Darnton, 'The Fact of Literary Life in 18th Century France', in K. M. Baker, ed., *The Political Culture of the Old Regime* (Chicago/Oxford, 1987), pp. 261–91.

[43] Roche, *Le Siècle des Lumières*.

working for *Le Journal des dames*, eight out of twenty were nobles, half of them Parisians of good birth, the rest provincials: the latter had taken the initiative for the launch in the persons of Thorel de Campigneulles, a rich Lyonnais not yet twenty-five years old, Relongue de La Louptière, from Champagne, Saint-Péravi and Billardon de Sauvigny, Mathon de la Cour, another Lyonnais, member of the local academy, and lastly François de Neufchâteau, fifteen years an academician, and making a career in the magistrature, freemasonry and journalism. The others were Parisians or provincials of an older generation, the former including Mercier, Du Rozoy, Sautreau de Marcy, Lemierre and Dorat, the latter La Harpe, Thomassin de Juilly, Sacy and Meuniers de Querlon. Most supported the Enlightenment, all had grasped the literary and publicity value of the women's and fashion press. They made little money but they won fame; though they did not all participate with equal vigour in the political and literary insurrection of *Le Journal des dames*, they contributed to the critical ferment of old society, principally by encouraging women to think and dare to be.[44] This they did in two ways: by persuading them to be what they had been, dispensers of pleasure and consumers, catalysts of the worldly life; but also to become politically and intellectually different. Lebrun Tossa, successful editor of *Le Cabinet des modes*, clearly perceived the strength of these aspirations.[45]

Dromois de Pierrelatte, son of an artisan hatter, a seminarist without a vocation and a teacher without a class, went to Paris hoping to follow in the footsteps of Rousseau and others; protected by the comtesse de La Mark, he founded a journal with the bookseller Buisson; a small and active team of contributors included Tillet, Desmarets, Montigny and the marquis de Condorcet – all of the Academy of Sciences – alongside Billardon de Sauvigny, formerly of the Stanislas Bodyguard, a cavalry lieutenant and royal censor, German, a publicist who had tried to launch *Le Courrier des nouveautés* in 1758, and another censor, Thiroux de Crosne. Their roles were not clearly differentiated and Buisson seems to have been the effective director, Lebrun only acquiring the title of

---

[44] Gelbart, *Feminine Opposition Journalism*, pp. 298–303; Van Dijk, *Traces de femmes*, pp. 8–10, 120–5, 180–6.

[45] Levu, 'Le Journal de la mode'; Kleinert, *Die Frühen Mode Journal*, pp. 42–120; F. Vitu, 'La Révolution et le premier journal illustré paru en France, 1785–1793', *XVIIIe siècle* (1989).

editor in 1790, when the team and the context of publication changed. He would be its prime mover to the end, and fashion journalism finally paid off.[46]

## FEMALE READERS AND MALE READERS

The major unknown remains the public. The journalists cast their nets wide; they aimed to reach 'scholars and those who aspired to scholarship', 'sensitive souls', the ladies who 'polish our manners', 'ladies, above all' for the *Le Journal des dames*, but also 'young ladies'. Mme de Montanclos addressed 'learned women', 'pious women', women 'less concerned with study', 'mothers of families' and lastly 'all classes of citizen'. In 1785, *Le Cabinet des modes* wanted to reach 'the two sexes who always and everywhere have sought to adorn themselves in order to please each other', though the less inventive men's fashions would receive less attention than those for women. In the last analysis, the target was 'good society', and the potential consumer and luxury market would dominate its columns, the Parisians and provincials who were part of good society or aspired to belong.

A qualitative definition throws some light on the social composition of the readers. They were fewer towards the bottom of society, where reading habits were different, but they included the public much enlarged in the eighteenth century by the spread of literacy and schooling:[47] *petit bourgeois*, men and women, producers and consumers, and all the many intermediaries, domestic servants, whose intellectual appetite was constantly stressed by Mercier, and typographic workers and journeymen glaziers, as Ménétra and Rétif show. This social openness is difficult to demonstrate from the usual sources, but seems incontestable, and much enhanced by the inclusion of women; as with the novel, it facilitated and legitimised a new cultural fusion. Thus the readers of the women's magazines and the fashion magazines were the readers of all

---

[46] Levu, 'Le Journal de la mode', pp. 19–21: AN, V¹. 552, letter from Buisson to the *garde des Sceaux*; he estimated the costs at 22,600 *livres*, income at 25,700, providing a profit of the order of 3,000 *livres* to be distributed; with an annual subscription in 1785 of 30 *livres*, there must have been 856 subscribers.

[47] R. Chartier, M.-M. Compère and D. Julia, *L'Education en France du XVIe au XVIIIe siècle* (Paris, 1976), pp. 45–85; D. Roche, 'Sociétés et cultures', in *Les Français et l'Ancien Régime* (Paris, 1985); *Peuple de Paris*, pp. 204–41; F. Furet and J. Ozouf, *Lire et écrire*, 2 vols. (Paris, 1977).

periodicals, *Le Mercure*, *Le Journal de Paris* and the *Affiches*, as is shown by the surviving lists of subscribers, by correspondence and by the literary evidence.[48] They included both sexes; a certain level of wealth was necessary given the price (*Le Journal des dames* cost 12 *livres* in Paris, 16 in the provinces and 18 abroad, which was half as much as *Le Mercure de France*; the more expensive and better-illustrated *Journal des dames* cost 30 *livres*);[49] a degree of curiosity was also essential.

Whilst the new press reached primarily the social elites and society women, it went some way beyond this narrow group because the fever of consumption and the lure of fashion had spread so far. The process of diffusion was accelerated by the development of the press as a whole, also compelled to reflect these new preoccupations, to which both *Le Journal de Paris* and the *Affiches* accorded more space. Pirated editions and foreign copies also contributed. *Le Cabinet des modes* was imitated, revived, translated and adapted in England, Italy and Germany.[50] The competition was stimulating, though it sometimes made success elusive in an overcrowded market. The *philosophe* and his partner could find material for reflection on fashion, 'favourite goddess of the French': this was in itself a triumph for the new culture. In the new journalism, one informed oneself and was formed.

## WOMEN AND THE ENLIGHTENMENT AND FEMININE CULTURE

Titles, slogans, prefaces, forewords, advertisements and introductory prospectuses show how editors and editresses chose to instruct whilst also diverting their leisured female readers. Symbolic in this

---

[48] For a comparison with literary and scholarly circles, see Roche, *Le Siècle des Lumières*, chapter 2.

[49] Rimbault, 'La Presse féminine', pp. 32–3; Van Dijk, *Traces de femmes*, pp. 9–11. In the year 1775–89, a highly specialised worker earned between 4 and 5 *livres* a day, and a Parisian mason on average slightly more than 2 *livres* a day; thus it cost between 3 and 6 days' pay to subscribe to the *Journal des dames*, between 6 and 15 for *Le Cabinet des modes*.

[50] Rimbault, 'La Presse féminine', pp. 40–1. *Le Cabinet des modes*, copied in London, was in its turn imitated by *The Fashionable Magazine*, 1 November 1786. It was pirated in Germany and Liège, copied without ceremony in Milan and Venice. The precise history of these interconnections remains to be traced, M. A. Guering Van Herlan, 'Copies des gravures françaises et anglaises dans les périodiques de modes italiens, 1785–1895', in *Rassegna di Studi e di Notizie*, 13, Castello Sforzesco (Milan, 1986), pp. 335–57.

regard was the choice of the time of making one's toilet as most appropriate for this education in the agreeable and the useful,[51] this rational instruction in fashion and the Muses: 'The toilet seems to us the only favourable time', wrote the anonymous author of *Les Amusements de la toilette*; '*Le Journal des dames* is suitable reading whilst making one's toilet', reiterated M. de La Louptière. So the contents should be appropriate for privacy, for an expressive moment in female life,[52] when, in the flowery language of the age, the Muses could chatter without dismaying the Graces.

The idea was in itself hardly new – it was the aim of the whole classical literary programme in the Enlightenment – but its orientation towards private space and a hitherto largely uninstructed public was a major cultural shift, source of the permanent tension in the new journalism, torn between 'the pompoms and the sciences': 'pleasing' implied novelty and frivolity, 'instruction' entailed the serious, the education of the heart and the soul; the one was fascinated by appearances, the other sought the being.[53] The women's press was at the heart of the major debates sparked off by the growth of luxury and the consumption of clothing.[54] It had grasped what was at issue and it tried to give to the Enlightenment a proper place in the culture of femininity.

READING FOR WOMEN AND EDUCATING THROUGH CURRENT AFFAIRS

The feminine culture which evolved in the pages of the women's magazines was probably less innovative in its means than in its aims. It was largely dependent on reading, of magazines, books and printed matter, and it is significant that the periodicals devoted almost exclusively to fashion did not at first give space to announce-

---

[51] Rimbault, 'La Presse féminine', pp. 121–6; *La Spectatrice*, 1728, 10th week, p. 226; *Amusements de la toilette*, 1755, p. 4; *Nouveau Prospectus du Journal des dames*, May 1763; foreword to the *Journal des dames*, April 1761; 'Epître dédicatoire au beau sexe', *Amusements de la toilette*, 1755, p. 8.

[52] R. Chartier in Ariès, *Histoire de la vie privée*, vol. III, pp. 76–117.

[53] 'Advertisement of Mme de Maisonneuve', *Journal des dames*, January 1765, p. 7; slogan of *Le Cabinet des modes*: 'boredom was born one day of uniformity' (Le Motte Houdar); in twenty-one titles analysed by Rimbault, the words 'amusing' and 'amusement' occur seven times, 'comic' twice, 'novelty' and 'new' nine times.

[54] Mme de Beaumer, who at first paid insufficient attention to the toilet was subsequently obliged to allocate it more space to achieve the balance her public expected; 'Avis', *Journal des dames*, 1771 and 1775.

ments of new books,[55] which were noticed elsewhere in the form of reviews or advertisements. The new items had a practical purpose, giving the name of the bookshop, place of publication and price. They convey some idea of the ideal library proposed to the woman reader. It is hardly surprising that it was dominated by books produced in Paris, which accounted for more than 80 per cent of the total. For the rest, a timid cosmopolitanism allowed reference to books from Holland, Switzerland, Italy and above all England. Anglomania was, as we know, a paying proposition, despite the uneasy relations existing between France and her rival.

Intellectually, the selections of the editresses displayed some originality. Whereas overall the period saw an increase in the number of books devoted to the sciences and the arts, and to philosophy, and whilst the provincial presses were still largely churning out editions of religious works, the women's press concentrated on *belles-lettres*, on poetry and the theatre, on the novel and the short story, in sum on books to while away the leisure hours.[56] This no doubt reflected a way of life, but perhaps also a desire to promote those genres in which women were predominant.[57] Philosophy appeared indirectly, the gallery of great men being a convenient way of airing issues of current concern in an accessible way, and the sciences and the arts a way of introducing education and medicine. The women's magazines were worldly, modern in their desire to adapt to the needs of their readers and above all wholly secular. This may have been a form of self-censorship (Mme Le Prince de Beaumont implied as much when she determined to publish only pieces which did not offend 'religion, good order, charity or morals'),[58] but it also suggests the emergence and success of a new, utilitarian and profane conformism, which was that of the academic elites.[59]

[55] See the *Cabinet du nouvelliste, Courrier de la nouveauté, Courrier de la mode, Publication des modes* and, of course, *Cabinet des modes*.

[56] F. Furet, ed., *Livres et société dans la France du XVIIIe siècle*, 2 vols. (Paris/The Hague, 1965–70), vols. I and II; Roche, 'Sociétés et cultures', pp. 222–44.

[57] Van Dijk, *Traces de femmes*, pp. 158–60; table 9 analyses the choice of books written by women or female issues in *Le Journal des dames*; in 817 articles and 308 announcements, the proportions were 10% and 4.5% respectively.

[58] *Le Nouveau Magasin français*, 'Advertisement' January 1750; the 'Epître dédicatoire' of the *Amusements de la toilette* for 1755 makes a profession of faith in conformity.

[59] Roche, *Le Siècle des Lumières*, pp. 284–5.

They were no more innovatory in the realm of current affairs. The female press devoted a large amount of space to the miscellaneous news which had long been successful with the vast public who enjoyed being astonished by the *Canards* and *Avis divers*. However, the *nouvelles, anecdotes* and *faits divers* are hardly evidence of the social taste of the female readers of the fashion press, since they appealed to everyone, on the margins of the scholarly and the popular. This curiosity tells us nothing new about the division of roles in society, since men and women were equally interested, but it certainly propagated a way of looking at current events and of apprehending the world.[60] Sensational crimes, flamboyant frauds, acts of heroism, major catastrophes, natural phenomena, suicides, deaths and monsters gave a new perspective on a new space: it was socially wider, and it was no longer only Parisian, but geographically resolutely national, even cosmopolitan. The topical pages, which indiscriminately mixed society items, human-interest stories, politics, military news and morals, offered not so much a female view of the world as a means of access to information intended to instruct, to deliver a practical and moral lesson, usually conformist. It is only by straining interpretation that one can see it as a manifestation of feminism; this existed, but is to be found elsewhere.

Female culture is not always written in the feminine. It first found its voice by frequenting works edited mainly by men, and by paying attention to events lived largely by them. In so doing, it detached itself from the habitual views which journalism in general still held of the role of women in society, and from the prejudices which conditioned it.[61] The judgements passed on works by women, even by journalists writing for women, show that the latter could not venture too far in the creative domain without risking finding themselves reproaching an excessive fidelity to the stereotypes of their sex and their writing, or without provoking more violent reactions than those reserved for their male homologues.[62] It was from within ambiguity that the feminine press gradually constructed the new identity of women, both by prescribing norms and stock themes by works of male critics (where an idea of

[60] Rimbault, 'La Presse féminine', pp. 140–55.
[61] Van Dijk, *Traces de femmes*, pp. 258–78.
[62] Ibid., pp. 79–80, 245–54.

woman triumphed with the eulogy of modesty) and by a distance which was measured by a prudent giving of ground or rejection.[63]

## THE FEMININE PERCEPTION OF THE WORLD: AN APPROPRIATION

Let it no longer be said that according to the dictates of nature, we ought to stay at home, confine ourselves to the education of our infant children, and supervise the activities of our servants; that we have neither sufficient spirit nor strength to manage the affairs of the Republic, make war or peace, render justice, cross the immensity of the oceans. Reason and experience make it plain that we could do all of this, that the unequal division of dignities, which, by giving all to some, reduces us to the most stultifying idleness, is the fruit of the ambition of the one sex always envious of the other.[64]

The tone of the article published in April 1764 in *La Bibliothèque des dames* does not mislead. Demands were being articulated, and they can be read between the lines of very different contributions. Difficult though it may be to define the feminism of the Enlightenment without lapsing into anachronism, or to rank authors for or against, since they lend themselves to differing interpretations, what is important is to be able to trace in fashion journalism the formation of a consciousness,[65] the emergence of a cluster of preoccupations which linked women more closely to each other.[66]

The diversity of the works produced and the opinions expressed by both male and female journalists cannot altogether disguise the formation of female strategies of appropriation, in particular in *Le Journal des dames*. They effectively pointed the contrast between women's abilities and their social inutility in the world of idleness and privilege. Female journalists and male editors placed the achievement of equality between the sexes in the wider perspective of equality. In revealing tones, on occasion throwing caution and the dominant conformism to the winds, they contributed to the

---

[63] Ibid. pp. 285–6.
[64] Rimbault, 'La Presse féminine', p. 161; *Bibliothèque des dames*, April 1764, p. 211.
[65] Van Dijk, *Traces de femmes*, pp. 259–60; Gelbart, *Feminine Opposition Journalism*, pp. 30–7.
[66] Ibid. p. 263.

erosion of values which threatened the *ancien régime*:[67] they appealed not only to the lessons of history (they demonstrated the importance of female heroism) but to those of theatrical criticism (they attacked the citadels of good taste, the Academy and the Comédie-Française, for example, with Mercier in *Le Journal des dames*) and lastly to those of a whole moral, medical and pedagogic discourse and political philosophy, echoing the debates of the age, torn between tradition and change.[68] There is nowhere a wholly rational and coherent image of the second sex, since it varied according to the types and intentions of the writing, but we find the alliteration and amphibology of a common language, the new journalism organising the dialogue between the republic of scholars and the opinions of its readers, eager for the fray.

A whole strand in this debate was barely distinguishable from the arguments of preachers and moralists: wives, mothers and women were reminded of their duty, which was to adorn society by their virtues rather than by their talents and graces; the corruption of the worldly life-style was denounced; it was once again asserted that clothes should be such as to make appearance coincide with reality. But the banality of the conservative model contrasted with other, more resolutely innovatory, claims: Christian marriage and matrimonial customs were discussed, the radical *Spectatrice* seeing them as an intolerable and useless servitude;[69] the more measured *Journal des dames* was hardly less severe. A juster conjugal morality and less authoritarian relations between the sexes seemed to be within reach. The discussions of education and training tended in the same liberating direction: women should have them by right, since their inequality in this domain was more culturally determined than decreed by nature. Rousseau, Sophie, Emile, houses of religious education, family life and the roles of mothers and fathers were all dragged into the debate. An egalitarian breeze was blowing. It whispered new lessons about the happiness and morality of societies, one of whose principal aims was to show how the same awareness inspired the feminine ideas which contested the prevail-

---

[67] Gelbart, *Feminine Opposition Journalism*, pp. 286–7.
[68] Hoffman, *La Femme*; 'L'héritage des Lumières. Mythes et modèles de la féminité au XVIIIe siècle', in *Mythes et représentations de la femme au XIXe siècle* (Paris, 1976), pp. 7–21.
[69] *La Spectatrice*, 1728, 2, p. 34; 1728, 12, p. 267; 1729, 15, pp. 327–41; Rimbault, 'La Presse féminine', pp. 168–77.

ing order, and which achieved political eloquence (for example, with the call for more citizen births),[70] and the new dimensions of the body, part of the transformation of appearances and the consumer revolution led by people of quality. A similar movement challenged ways of life, the low priority accorded the body and the conquest of individuality, in a word, the logics of the social.

## FEMININE CULTURE, TRIUMPH OF THE BEING OR OF APPEARANCES

Two themes were crucial: that of the superiority of mind over body and that of fashion versus good taste. The new press adopted all the elements of the philosophical critique and medical observation – questions about luxury, moral problems. Like the philosophers and the men of letters, it was divided as to the social lessons to be drawn, and paradoxically, we see fashion refuted in a discourse which consecrated its triumph. In proposing a feminine reading of the worldly Enlightenment, the editors and editresses aimed to legislate in this domain as they pleased. In a world where the values of court society now compounded those of a public domain ruled by reason and a new emphasis on human relations, women could claim the right to manage part of the public sphere. The issue of appearances was essentially ideological, since it exposed the fundamental tension between being and seeming. This emerged in the conflicts over roles expressed in terms of the opposition of genres or in debates about feminine nature or culture. To denounce the excesses of fashion was thus to go beyond the habitual satire of morals; it was to try to measure the perverse effects of an instrument of liberty.

In pleading for the values of the mind, in proposing a sociability based less on coquetry and artifice (the mask) than on a return to nature and the empire of the virtues (the truth), in equating the development of the body and the instruction of the soul, the feminine press revealed the moral dangers of fashion whilst also exalting its power and efficacy. In promoting material novelties, in proclaiming the facilities of the arts, it defended happiness, glorified the feminine identified with the human in civilisation and

---

[70] Gelbart, *Feminine Opposition Journalism*, pp. 301–2; Kleinert, *Die Frühen Mode Journal*, pp. 90–2, traces the evolution of the *Cabinet des modes*.

contributed to the victory of individualism. The relaxation of the moral conventions and the retreat of religious rigorism coincided with this liberation. Fashion was born in the midst of privilege and hierarchy, where it developed despite the norms of the Christian economy and the holistic society. Towards the end of the eighteenth century, it seriously undermined them, since it associated the pleasure ethic with a new vision of life devoted to the minor arts, joint instruments of the liberation of beings and of their domination, as the permanence of distinction bears witness.

## LIBERTY, EQUALITY AND FRIVOLITY!

The feminine press raised the status of objects and practices designed to bring happiness, conferred on the phenomena of the clothing revolution a dignity they were denied by religious morality and accepted the turbulence and social confusion which was contested by the aristocratic logic of court society. This explains the success of *Le Cabinet des modes* before and during the Revolution. It was a way of materialising a discourse of independence and pioneered a type of journal which actualised for ever the culture of appearances. It wove round men and women alike a web of objects, garments and practices which both disciplined and liberated bodies and souls: frivolity could be subversive!

*Le Cabinet des modes*, hero of the new formula, succeeded where *Le Cabinet des nouvellistes*, *Le Courrier de la mode* and *Le Courrier de la nouveauté* had failed. This was partly for technical reasons: convenient format, affordable price, high-quality typography, beautiful pictures and regular appearance. But above all it had as its potential readership a world transformed by the lessons of the encyclopedists and materially altered by the clothing revolution, and this up to 1794, well into the Terror! It accepted the role of intermediary between the milieus of creators and producers and those of consumers.

Feminine journalism served fashion and presided over the birth of publicity, which guaranteed the quality of its information and enlarged its readership. It utilised the material and intellectual power of images, true writing of the new sensibility.[71] Its illustra-

[71]    Kleinert, *Die Frühen Mode Journal*, pp. 71–90.

tions were always accompanied by a commentary,[72] at first a simple legend, then a more composed and composite text combining on a regular basis information about fashion, aesthetic comment, moral and philosophical debate, historical references, and theatrical, poetical, musical and soon political, news.[73] This mix taught the social eloquence of the body and the ideology of the wise use of fashion. Between 1785 and 1792, the length of the captions increased, as if carried away by the heady excitement of liberty and the explosion of debate which flourished with the Revolution. Three principal functions emerged and provide the final lesson of the feminine journalism: to emphasise a different culture of the body; to describe the mechanisms and means of a system of consumption, essentially sartorial, which underpinned it; to paraphrase it in a discourse of social morality placed under the aegis of triumphant fashion.

## THE PRESENTATION OF THE BODY

It was primarily the female body which was presented through the record of all the ordinary objects which composed the domain of the intimate, in three successive circles, of varying importance, those of the body, the clothes and the home, zone of naturalness and privacy, which now intruded into public life.[74] By learning to manage their proper domain, women helped to invert the old significance attributed by 'good manners' to the relationship between body and clothing.[75] The latter lost its ceremonial meaning, the former, liberated by finery and fashion, signalling a hidden sexuality,[76] expressed the values of the personal and the natural. As in the novel, the body itself was scarcely described, rather there was reference to a masculine–feminine image in writing which expressed an aesthetic and a way of life, another visibility of the being. A regard for hygiene, an orderly way of life and fashion also contributed. Baths expressed the power of the mythology of the

---

[72] Levu, 'Le Journal de la mode', pp. 31–4.
[73] Kleinert (*Die Frühen Mode Journal*, pp. 86–7) estimates that fashion accounted for between 20% and 30% of the texts.
[74] R. Sennett, *Les Tyrannies de l'intimité* (Paris, 1979), pp. 60–7; A. Pardailhé-Galabrun, *La Naissance de l'intimité. 3,000 foyers parisiens au XVIIIe siècle* (Paris, 1988).
[75] Rimbault, 'La Presse féminine', pp. 200–1.
[76] J. Baudrillard, *L'Echange symbolique et la mort* (Paris, 1976), pp. 141–8.

clean and were a sign of virtue. Perfumes and make-up lost their negative moral connotations[77] and their pure function as social mask, and now helped to define not so much the personage as the person, by emphasising the particularity of the face or the body; they expressed the naturalness of artifice in the common sociability.

The fashion press made a major contribution to the transition from the ritual functionality of the body and clothing, dominated by ornament, decor and display, to the liberation of appearances. The body was no longer a mannequin for the clothes but the secret reference in the various signs of fashion to its new reality. Advertisements for cures and advice about clothes indicated by turns the zones where moderation and modesty defined a rational beauty in accord with nature, an aesthetic of grace: 'Everybody is in a position to satisfy that passion which they carry from birth for the objects which will present them to the best advantage and effect.'[78] The being must submit to appearances.

## PUBLICITY AND THE SYSTEM OF CONSUMPTION

It was publicity which assured the success of both practices and objects and changed the role of clothing. Fashion was no longer the preserve of the privileged of court society and the rich bourgeoisie, but a commercial necessity and a mirror of the personality. Fashion and advertising progressed hand in hand, informing and transforming. The feminine press generalised the few publicity techniques which were as old as journalism itself. Inventions, processes and new products which produced new behaviour also found a place in the *Affiches* and *Le Journal de Paris*. *Le Cabinet des modes* here followed *Le Journal des dames* and *Le Courrier de la mode* and allocated much of its space to advertisers.[79] The triumph of the sartorial economy was fully reflected there, as were

---

[77] Rimbault, 'La Presse féminine', pp. 210–18; the danger of cosmetics was a theme of medical literature: see Lecamus, *L'Art de conserver sa beauté* (Paris, 1754) or Deshays-Gendron, *Lettre à Monsieur XXX sur plusieurs maladies des yeux causées par l'usage du rouge et du blanc* (Paris, 1760). Use in moderation was recommended for the teeth, the hair and the face, less often for other parts of the body. The 'admirable vinegar' of Maille was presented as a general cure-all.

[78] G. Lipovetski, *L'Empire de l'éphémère* (Paris, 1987), pp. 102–3, quoting *Le Magasin des modes*.

[79] Rimbault, 'La Presse féminine', pp. 218–50. This advertising deserves a study in itself. In *Le Cabinet des modes*, the amount of book advertising increases whilst

the new cosmetics and the vogue for perfumers, glovers, jewellers and artists of every type. The press became the theatre for clashes between competitors and for the display of all the concoctions dreamed up by fashion merchants. '[They] have an infinite capacity to vary the taste for ornament: a journal [*Le Cabinet des modes*] created expressly records all these various arrangements which change not only for the court, the town or the country, but also for the salon, the study, the boudoir and the *chaise longue*', observed Mercier, ever a shrewd observer.[80]

On the economic plane, customers and producers were now brought together in a new way. Announcements and models created a three-way circulation, in which the commercial relation flourished: from the journal to the persuaded reader who bought from a vendor; from the producer to the journalist, who was helped to publish by the advertisements; from the journalists to the creators who were encouraged to promote their products, and the relations between merchant and consumer and between customer, reader and journalist were revealed in the flow of correspondence and the number of subscriptions.[81] The market, vehicle of a transgressive force which combined the tendency to social levelling and that to variety and individual distinction, took shape.

This strong socialising impulse is revealed by the efforts of the journals to reach a wider public, which also benefited the advertisers. All ages were affected: the accent placed on youth was an attempt to persuade, children appearing rarely but in accord with their new status; all social milieus might recognise themselves in the euphemistic allusions to the nobility, to wealth, to gallantry, to sexual grace and to the good taste of the little masters.[82] The Revolution checked these mechanisms for a while, but time was on their side. By playing on words and forms, the editors of *Le Cabinet des modes* proved the persistence of the search for distinction through taste, even if in the guise of republican simplicity. ' "Luxury is finished" cry the merchants, already gold and silver

that for fashion diminishes between 1785 and 1793; 1786–7 books 10%, fashion 90%; 1789 books 40%, fashion 60%; 1783 books 100% (a reflection of the political turbulence).

[80] L. S. Mercier, 'Tableau de Paris' in *Journal des modes*, vol. XI, pp. 217–19.

[81] Kleinert, *Die Frühen Mode Journal*, pp. 112–14; 'La mode, miroir de la Révolution française', *Francia* (1989).

[82] P. Bourdieu, 'Le couturier et sa griffe, contribution à une théorie de la magie', *Actes de la recherche en sciences sociales*, 1 (1975), pp. 7–36.

are no longer used in dress, only plain clothes are worn. So much the better for everybody, say I', wrote Lebrun Tossa, on 25 June 1790:

> and you merchants, who fear you will lose, will gain. If the barbarous practice of covering one's clothes with metal has disappeared, taste, in France, has not, and it will find a new vigour. Luxury, in any case, whatever one thinks of it, exists only through superfluity [which] instead of being concentrated in the hands of a small number will be spread over the generality of citizens. Then luxury will consist only of comfort, cleanliness and elegance of form.[83]

The advertisements, the correspondence, the services offered and the defence of quality gave birth to the models of modern consumption: hire, postal sales, the despatch of samples, indications of the measurements of garments, procedures for delayed payment, post-and-packing charges; in sum, the eulogy of fashion proceeded by direct sales.[84] It materialised its effects in a new way.

FASHION TAMED

Fashion was a motor of the urban economy and instrumental in an effective transformation of social relations. It was a global social fact where every element contributed to the balance of the whole, and the feminine press, for the first time in history, put this system on display. Simultaneously appealing to the values of morality and of economic utilitarianism, it promoted the necessity of consumption as an essential category of existence: 'A scientific point interests scarcely 500 citizens, an attractive fashion affects 4,000,000 subjects, a maker of trifles can enrich 10,000 workers by a single stroke of genius', wrote Lebrun Tossa.[85] The retreat of the Christian economy is apparent in the notion that greater spending by the rich restored a little equality to the poor. Not without reticence, since the debate had gone on for half a century, reading *Le Journal des dames* provided proof. Between reality and the imagination, the

---

[83] *Journal de la mode et du goût*, 5 July 1790.

[84] Rimbault, 'La Presse féminine', pp. 238–41; these services were offered when fashion advertising was diminishing, novelties becoming fewer and high society was dispersed. The journal participated in the trend towards commercialisation even in the crisis.

[85] *Magasin des modes*, January 1787, p. 53.

discourse of fashion imposed the efficacy of the commercial order and the power of the new.

That clothes should have been the instruments of this change is hardly surprising; they carried in themselves this power, the new coat bending us to its shape before adapting to ours. Even more, in the texts which described them and the images which represented them, clothes generalised the association of the material, the sensible and ideas. *Le Cabinet des modes* offered an infinite variety of such marriages, where the political or more generally cultural symbolism – the 'Figaro cap', the 'housewife apron' – encountered the materiality of new fabrics or the affective attractions of expressive colours. These changes were made possible by a range of appropriations, social and personal, of the use of forms.

One gets some idea of this by glancing through the series of plates offered by Lebrun to his female readers, as well as appreciating their beauty and quality. They convey the impression of an everyday life organised according to new drives and principles. Time is controlled by changes of costume and no longer wasted, since it was possible to combine making one's toilet with instructive reading; space is better regulated, as Mercier perceived, by a succession of customs and costumes according to social necessity, whether of court or boudoir, private or public. In sum, there was a general order, all the more effective in that it enjoyed all the appeal of play and caprice. Further, in the theatre of fashion, women played the leading roles, as they did in real clothing consumption. By these means, they acquired a new dimension, less oppressive than liberating. Certainly, the accepted metaphors attributed to femininity and to fashion a similar inconstancy, coquetry and frivolity. But at the same time, in the collective consciousness, women were accorded the role of universal instructors in the attraction of objects and in the social organisation of appearances. Women had undeniably achieved an autonomy – this was an aspect of the feminism of the Enlightenment – but this emancipation was limited: the principle of the equality of persons ceded to the inegalitarian celebration of female beauty.[86] The clothing revolution could hardly achieve what the political Revolution could only briefly envisage!

[86] Baudrillard, *L'Echange symbolique*, p. 149; Lipovetski, *L'Empire de l'éphémère*, pp. 163–5.

The importance of feminine journalism lies principally in the Europe-wide experience, for more than fifty years, of an association conceived to bring together the intellectual interests of women and the profound transformation of manners. From a feminine perspective, the Enlightenment meant working to alter the equilibrium established between roles and between public and private life and accepting the egalitarian creativity of the self. The feminism of the age could there find an authentic expression despite the contradictions. But at the same time, the press for women became a fashion press, materialising in a new way the culture of the second sex, even though it never excluded either male models or readers. It thus had the power to be at the same time an instrument of liberation or of oppression, according to whether, when read or acted upon, it was the object of a passive or an active appropriation. Fashion then appears in its multiple guises, stimulus to change, impresario of distinction, creator of social equality and revealer of the inequality of appearances.

# Conclusion
# The culture of appearances:
# consumption and morality

> Il est peu utile de philosophiser de sociologie générale quand
> on a d'abord tant à connaître et à savoir et qu'on a ensuite
> tant à faire pour comprendre.
>
> Marcel Mauss, *Oeuvres*, volume III, p. 354

My starting-points were problems and facts. The problems were
those posed for historians of my generation by the possibilities and
expansion of cultural history, and by the questions of a social
history anxious to understand the interdependence of social facts
and of a history of material culture free of techno-economic imperi-
alism. The history of clothing in traditional French society, from
the seventeenth to the early nineteenth centuries, lent itself to such
a venture both by the relative absence of discussion in a domain
preoccupied from the beginning with the history of forms and
fashions, and by the character as global social fact of clothing
practices. My aim was not another study of the evolution of upper-
class dress (attractive though that might be), but to understand
how it fitted into what it is convenient to call a cultural whole,
along with that of the rest of the population.

## THE HISTORY OF CLOTHING: THE HISTORY OF A CULTURAL CONSUMPTION

This new perspective, this hypothesis that another history of costumes and customs was possible, presupposes the notion that we
can discover the tenuous but decisive link which mobilised the
consumption of all and that of individuals within the ordinary
context of their family life. Whilst historians and economists have
tended to concentrate on production, consumption and its social
mechanisms have suffered relative neglect. This lack of interest,
and the priority given to production, may be explained both by the

indifference of historians to the real world of objects without high aesthetic value, and by the notion that consumption is a late phenomenon, contemporary with the major economic and social transformations of the nineteenth and twentieth centuries, something which had scarcely begun at the end of the eighteenth century. New developments in European and American historiography[1] have had, it must be said, little impact on French research, whether it has asked different questions of analogous objects and spaces (as with the *Histoire de la vie privée* or *La Naissance de l'intime*),[2] or whether it has not yet connected the world of producers and manufactures to that of the market and demand, a few exceptions apart.[3] Micro-economic studies analysing the relations between manufacturer-sellers and consumers, and macro-economic studies of the expansion and specific character of the market in traditional society, are better able to reveal, even change our conception of, the original features of the ways in which pre-industrial economy and society functioned.[4]

The history of clothing makes such a shift possible because it asks questions of the inventory of consumption and things. The acquisition and ownership of objects relate to the functioning of the social mechanisms, revealing essential changes in economic behaviour, but they also question a society's norms, religious and moral as much as political. The totality of the conventions which determine the acquisition and ownership of clothes, their use and their demonstrative power, have the advantage of revealing the imbrication of material culture and moral and philosophical imperatives, and even their juridical expression, as the history of restrictions on clothing and the sumptuary laws shows. The problems of luxury and of ostentatious consumption, the social representation of the hierarchies of wealth and status in the order of appearances,

---

[1] J. Brewer, 'Commercialisation and Politics', in McKendrick, Brewer and Plumb, *Birth of a Consumer Society*, pp. 197–263; S. Schama, *The Embarrassment of Riches, an Interpretation of Dutch Culture in the Golden Age* (London, 1987); J. C. Agnew, *Worlds Apart: the Market and the Theatre in Anglo-American Thought, 1550–1750* (London, 1986).

[2] Ariès, *Histoire de la vie privée*; Pardailhé-Galabrun, *Naissance de l'intime*.

[3] J.-C. Perrot, *Caen au XVIIIe siècle, Genèse d'une ville moderne*, 2 vols. (Paris, 1976); B. Lepetit, *Armature urbaine et organisation de l'espace dans la France pré-industrielle (1740–1850)*, 2 vols. (Paris, 1987).

[4] N. McKendrick, 'The Commercialisation of Fashion' in McKendrick, Brewer and Plumb, *Birth of a Consumer Society*, pp. 34–99.

the role of distinctive emulation in the redistribution of the signs of adherence, then reappear substantially in the cultural equilibriums, the different distributions and the changing moral significances which coincide with the displacement of these categories over time. The history of clothing helps to challenge the modes of classification which are habitually employed: the popular and the scholarly, the dominated and the dominant, rich and poor, town and country, creation and consumption, the real and the imaginary. In so doing, it presents the researcher with the major problems of any cultural analysis, 'culture being at the same time system and process, institutions and individual acts, expressive reserve and signifying order'.[5]

Because clothing is a cultural fact produced by history and which resists history, to study it in other ways than by anecdotal and repetitive popularisation makes it possible to see the social role of the natural and functional constraints, internal or external to the system of which it is at the same time object and subject. This makes possible a historical anthropology of things.[6] Clothing is a global social fact in the sense in which Mauss used the term, and it may be that the analysis of global social facts goes some way to resolve the conflicts between opponents or partisans of serial and macroscopic studies and the defenders of *microstoria* or case studies.

### THE CLOTHING REVOLUTION AND THE CONQUEST OF LINEN

Consumption is the sole end of all production, as Adam Smith observed. In the case of dress, it is measurable, if at all, by the inventory of belongings and the cost of their care. These developed differently in town and country. In the cities, the eighteenth century was a major turning-point; in Paris, everyone spent more on clothes whilst the difference between the dress of the poor and that of the rich also increased. Most people had already by the end of the seventeenth century crossed the frontier of necessity, leaving behind the beggars, vagabonds and unintegrated poor still dressed in rags; for them, the hospital was also a refuge where they might be clothed. At this level, people went short, and the values of

[5] R. Barthès, 'Histoire et sociologie du vêtement', *Annales: ESC* (1957), p. 441.
[6] M. Douglas, ed., *The World of Goods. Towards an Anthropology of Consumption* (New York/London, 1979).

protection were all. But for a larger number, to present an appearance was possible, and this is what all the intermediaries, merchants, artisans, officials and men of talents, chose to do. Their clothing culture was that of the apogee of the *civilités* – appearance should reveal status and the being – but at the same time it showed signs of an openness to change which was favourable to the spread of habits copied from court society. Lastly, a few individuals and small groups vied with each other, their wealth allowing them to accumulate a considerable capital in the form of ostentatious clothing. The point is, however, that such choices never wholly coincided with either wealth or status. By the beginning of the eighteenth century, a general change was beginning. Women were its architects in every milieu, but the sexual dimorphism of dress was not yet fundamental. The logics of status, chance and need interacted at the different levels of urban society, whilst remaining more autonomous in the country.

By the eve of the Revolution, the pace of change had speeded up. The greater standardisation of behaviour in towns was notorious; in villages, it was beginning, thanks to markets and fairs and to the network of peddlars: maestros of dressing-up and purveyors of illusions, distributors of cheap reading-matter and creators, on credit, of new needs. The needs were those of the many urban intermediaries, whose spending on clothes had grown to such a degree that one can speak of a clothing revolution. In all social categories, it was women who were chiefly responsible for circulating the new objects and the new values of a commercialised fashion and superfluous consumption. Leaders in sensibility, they were already the shop windows of men, except perhaps among the nobility. The increase in consumption corresponded to changes in behaviour. The hierarchical society, encased in the heavy and durable broadcloths and costly silks which were the mark of court elegance and its urban imitators, was succeeded by a more open, less stiff and more frivolous world. Both colours and fabrics grew lighter, the perception of social presentation changed profoundly.[7] Fashion affected everyone, as the success of indiennes reveals.

The wind of change also blew in provincial towns. Though its

---

[7] The study of the culture of appearances in painting remains to be tackled; it would need the skills of both an art historian and a historian; see L. A. Stone-Ferrier, *Images of Textiles, the Weave of Seventeenth Century Dutch Art and Society* (Ann Arbor, 1978).

strength, chronology and diversity remain to be studied, it is apparent that it everywhere helped to change habits of consumption and alter behaviour. A splendid text from Montpellier shows how luxury and finery had triumphed; it is by no means unique and brings out the social importance of appearance:

> Great finery is the rule in this town. The women and girls of the first and second estate have gone overboard for it. The most beautiful silk fabrics, made up in the best of taste, are used for their clothes. Fashion or taste require that they have several for the seasons of winter, spring and summer, so that they can change for each season. They must also have elegant déshabillés and mantillas of every type and colour. This is matched by fine linen and lace. Footwear generally consists of shoes of white damask. Hairstyles are at the moment small, since they curl their hair, which they pull back and up to the top of their heads, a style which is most becoming: in particular, it gives an air of youthfulness which enhances the beauty and the softness of the face. To this are added plumes, ear-rings, necklaces, bracelets, rings, diamond buckles, a gold watch hanging from a clasp weighed down by a hundred trinkets, a gold snuff-box, the flask and the case also of gold, a muff and a fan; this is on the outside and is the rule for women with rich husbands ... The men are no less enamoured of finery. Coats of velvet in winter and silk in summer, and waistcoats of cloth of gold and silver are very common, to the point where they now make a sort of large surtout or redingote of velvet to be worn over coats of broadcloth. Bag-wigs are the most common. Lace cuffs and fine linen are becoming general: they are changed everyday, which means you need a lot of them. It is hardly necessary to add that men too have a watch, a gold snuff-box and rings. Canes with gold apple heads are very common.[8]

There were now two ways one could behave: as required by traditional relationships or as dictated by personal choice, that is to say, the public, where appearance ought to reveal estate and the moral being, or the private, where the values of the intimate might

[8] See J. Berthélé, ed., *Inventaire et documents des archives municipales de Montpellier* (Montpellier, 1920), vol. IV, pp. 1–163; C. Pascal, 'Société et urbanisme à Montpellier aux XVIIe et XVIIIe siècles, le sixain de Sainte-Croix (1665–1788)', mémoire de maîtrise, Paris (1988), pp. 112–113. (I would like to thank Jean Jacquard for having drawn my attention to this text.)

correspond to the person.[9] But the two perceptions were tending to merge. Clothing codes were in turmoil: the ladies of the court dreamed of dressing in town as among their family – witness Mme de Schomberg – and their servants imitated them. Everywhere, social nuances were disappearing.

Appearance no longer revealed the real being and even less status, which once again shifted the frontier of distinction. When the Revolution arrived and luxury went out, one could proclaim the advent of uniformity without adopting the means to achieve it: at the top, those striving for elegance accommodated to the simplicity which was now all the rage; at the bottom, the poor expressed their distance from the most symbolic manifestations by proclaiming, for a brief moment, a specific sensibility and the counter-values of the 'fragile life'. This was another language, denounced by political grammarians of all hues since it broke, wholly or partially, with the moral values of that great conquest of the Enlightenment, linen. The latter proclaimed in another way both the standardisation necessary to all socialisation and the difference favourable to distinction and imitation. The civilisation of manners prevailed for the majority of the population, where appearances needed to distinguish, but the conquest of linen further increased the confusion of signs, even if it was now necessary for poverty to be seen to be clean. The new ways of caring for clothes contributed.

Poverty and parsimony were no doubt still the rule for a large part of the urban population and amongst the peasantry, but their culture of appearances was not therefore necessarily underdeveloped. Social and individual rivalry was possible even with coarse materials and limited means, and with fewer accessories and details. In its diversity, dress created a common language from top to bottom of society. Both desired and needed, it was an agent of social change since it carried within it an incitement to change. Sartorial signs were no simpler to decipher in the past than today.

## THE PRODUCTION AND COMMERCIALISATION OF APPEARANCES

A study of the system of production reveals who created, and by what means, these transformations and their circuits of diffusion.

[9] Sennet, *Tyrannies de l'intimité*, pp. 80–98.

The textile culture took shape, within the proto-industrial context, on the one hand for a large-scale and rapid production, on the other for high quality products, in one case by and for factories, in the other by and for the guilds. These two poles were not irrevocably separated: the increased sale of fabrics mobilised clothes manufacturers and linen merchants.

In the village, the cloth trade was everywhere, even though basic items were already made by specialists and trade had eroded the self-sufficient family economy. Further research is needed to show how domestic roles were modified and above all how the new habits were spread. In its first manifestations, regional costume was probably emblematic of this transitory stage. It was far from uniform but extremely varied, and expressed local and individual rivalries before it came to characterise larger groupings by a process of triumphant folklorisation in the nineteenth century. The village tailor and the labour of women testify to the persistence of a conception of clothing dominated by its protective function (as proverbs show), by ritual socialisation (clothes had a role in every social event from birth to adolescence, from marriage to death) and by the constraints of good manners and propriety. The old rural clothing moulded the body, and working and holiday clothes were clearly differentiated: in the one case, flexibility and functionality, in the other, ritualisation and status, everyday modesty and festive finery. The revolution of appearances in the village exploited all these contrasts. The universal adoption of linen standardised in its turn the system of consumption, modes of production and methods of upkeep, which probably reached their apogee only in the nineteenth century. For the earlier period, further work is needed to put flesh on the bare bones of the hypotheses formulated here.

In the towns, a very wide range of producers responded to the changes in consumption. The Parisian corporations, organised both to meet urban demand and supply a profitable export trade, set an example in the commercialisation of skills and knowledge. The Revolution revealed their importance as a sector, their vulnerability to external events and the continuing importance of the role of women and girls; this was a specific feature of production, which we have already observed in consumption. There were some extremely able and successful businesswomen. Their dynamism was apparent within the guild structure, among the dressmakers, the linen-drapers and the fashion merchants.

Whilst the sexual specialisation of the crafts tended to persist, inter-guild rivalries helped to standardise trade and ensure the triumph of Paris fashions. Their striking elegance probably influenced the nature of the changes, and diffused sartorial models and models of behaviour together. The theatricalisation of appearance, linked to the success of the French dress glorified by Garsault, and the ability of its creators to adapt to social needs, all played a part. Elegance both responded to and sustained the dynamic of change, and thus the confusion of signs.

Theft and the second-hand trade were the other face of the Parisian system; together, they created illusions and effectively diffused practices to the margins, both equally reprehensible in the eyes of good society. Thefts of clothing and linen provide a good illustration of fluctuating attitudes to crime and, ultimately, the symbolic importance of a means of exchange which also made it possible to appropriate the appearance of another. These were crimes firmly rooted in the new habits of consumption; they emphasised social disparities and speeded up the confrontation of manners.

The second-hand clothes trade had similar effects, but it should not be seen as a purely marginal practice. It shows how different clienteles helped to structure the clothing economy, revealing the essential frontiers between the new and the used, the ready-made and made-to-measure, manufacture and repair. The persistent aura of suspicion with which literature surrounded the second-hand trade, identifying it with theft, receiving, illicit trading and fraud, or at least dubious sales talk, has to be compared with a different reality and practices; bargaining over transactions, actively seeking out customers and selling ready-made clothes – which changed the relationship to garments by breaking with the custom of wholly individualised labour – were not incompatible with honest commerce and were designed to reach a new consumer market: the masses.

The processes which finally triumphed in the nineteenth century had been in place since the eighteenth, well before the definitive transformation introduced by the big stores.[10] The clothing revolution could not have happened without the beginnings of the empire of distribution. The latter grew in parallel with practices of upkeep and cleaning. In the country, these were domestic, fully integrated

---

[10] P. Perrot, 'Splendeur et déclin du marché du Temple', *L'Histoire*, 33 (1981), pp. 6–15.

into the traditional conception of the body and the standardising social processes of village relations; in towns, in contrast, cleaning was already highly commercialised. By the end of the eighteenth century, laundering was an integral part of the production of urban appearances, the collective consciousness emphasising both the connection between propriety and cleanliness and the contrast between the demands of hygiene and the practicalities of real life. This opposition shows both the inadequacy of a reading confined to the texts, and how the norms which inform the discourse are constitutive of a reality.[11]

## THE COLLECTIVE CONSCIOUSNESS, MASK AND TRUTH OF APPEARANCES

Our analysis of the fictional discourse – the utopias, the romanticised life story of Giacomo Casanova, *Les Contemporaines* of Rétif, the *Encyclopédie* of Diderot and the medical logics, part of the varied output of a milieu preoccupied both with stability and reform – leads to the same conclusions. All these documents faithfully reflect the material signs of the new culture, revealing where it progressed rapidly, where people held back.

The clothing of novels and utopias, the rational dress of the *philosophes* and the hygienic costume of the medical devotees of fresh air transcend the strict actuality of the social evidence to reveal the cultural disjunctions produced by the new consumption. They established a fictional world whose unifying solidity was based on the permanent communication between authors and public, united by the essential references to contemporary debates: the fable of luxury and scarcity, the contrast of readability and social transparency, the aspiration to express the being through appearances; in sum, truth and the mask were their principal themes. There can be no doubt that they express the aspirations and debates of a society torn between the values of ritualised exchange and the proprieties and those of the individual identity, as between privilege and the egalitarian virtues. However, I am less sure than Philippe Perrot that it is either necessary or possible to describe this major social caesura as a 'drama of the bourgeois

---

[11] I here differ from the interpretations of, among others, Corbin, *Le Miasme* and Vigarello, *Concepts of Cleanliness*.

body': it was first the rupture visible in the urbanity of manners, it then spread to all social groups. The 'play' then became more complicated and, in the nineteenth century, can be read as farce or tragedy. For historians, this is precisely the problem of mentalities and culture, and of representation.

The feminine press offers another example. It provided an experience of social education, combining intellectual interests and material culture. It gave a feminine perspective to the Enlightenment, and raised all the debates glimpsed elsewhere. But it also proposed an ordering of time and space, a vision of the body concealed and the sexuality contained by clothing, which helped to overthrow – certainly on the surface, how deep is more difficult to assess – the traditional equilibrium of the social and sexual roles. Appearance could determine the being without damage; it liberated as much as it oppressed.

## MATERIAL CULTURE AND INTELLECTUAL CULTURE

The history of needs can certainly only be written systematically; starting from his regrets for his old dressing-gown, Denis Diderot shows how one can proceed from one element to the whole: 'Everything is out of tune. No more cohesion, no more unity, no more beauty.' With this incursion into the fragile destiny of clothing culture, I have tried to illustrate this thesis. Today as in the past, clothing relates to our profound conception of the sacred, the social and the individual. It has enabled me to trace the shift in frontiers which changes the ground.

Everyone knows that the map is not to be confused with the ground. The historian proposes a route, marked out by the fragmentary evidence of the archives, the fictional images of literature and the rational arguments of philosophers. In the eighteenth century, he can trace the transition between two worlds, one where the social being must correspond to the representation he gives of himself and which is given of him by others,[12] and one where the changing social configuration allowed a little confusion of being and seeming. We see here how porous is the boundary between reality and the imagined since what is visible is the erosion of the discriminatory function of signs. The accumulation

---

[12]  R. Chartier, 'Avant-Propos' to Elias, *Société de Cour*, pp. xv–xxvi.

of clothes had the effect of reducing the degree of difference towards the top of society, where a radical transfer of the function of appearances onto the female body expressed a new way of marking social distances, whilst lower down, the distinctive virtues would long be maintained. Order and rank could still be read in innumerable nuances, confusion might reign, but did it really deceive? That depended on each person's social attention, hence on a position which was inherited, acquired or sought in a field of interdependent and never wholly clear relations: that of life itself.

The importance here of the age of Enlightenment is to show how the signs of adherence are perceptibly acquired at the same rate and according to what are, in effect, comparable processes in the domains of intellectual and material culture. Social attitudes are produced through identical stages of apprenticeship and diffusion, but with the sexual roles reversed: in the domain of reading, men triumphed before women; in that of dress, women were the first victors in terms of real gains, those of sensibility and an effective frivolity. At the same time, we need to recognise the power of the intermediary groups, and the active role of key micro-milieus, where the material and cultural transformations march in step. The study of uniform supports this claim.

## ORDER OF APPEARANCES, POLITICS OF LANGUAGE

The culture of appearances is first an 'order'. To understand it, it is necessary to learn the language which allows communication in a country which is foreign, and consequently stirring to the imagination, where the spiritual and the material intermingle with particular force. There, the mental becomes corporeal, the individualised body displaying the fleeting traces of the person and clothing revealing the hidden correspondences between substance and spirit.[13] The unity of the culture established amidst the ruins of classicism, the challenge to court society and the critique of the unequal world can be read in the clothing system. Clothes, like books, demand mastery of a body of information, which increases in both volume and complexity.

---

[13] Dagognet, *Pour une théorie générale*, pp. 13–15, *Rematérialiser*, pp. 8–16, 101–9.

Clothing seems to me to be a way of thinking the perceptible. We are justified in applying to its analysis the models which are employed to understand social change. Its economy reveals an organisation of the social strategies of exchange which is in accord with the power of signs.[14] Languages were a major preoccupation of the eighteenth century. The président de Brosses, Rousseau, Condillac, Diderot and many others sought a common explanation of the articulation of words and things, a way to understand the effects of the calculations which ruled relationships between men, in sum an ordering of information which posed the question of the interpenetration of social facts as a language.

The social and cultural function of clothing can only be understood in terms of communicability. We need therefore to analyse the effect produced by what is seen on whoever sees it, as for any order of discourse where who comes first is not the speaker but the hearer.[15] Diderot did this, so discovering the very order of a society where each moral was a code, a way of speaking, or of presenting oneself, and because each of these codes would only be a transcription of the civil laws.[16] The question of the power of signs leads to the political; mastery of them was at issue in all the discussion of the clothing transformation. Rousseau saw as wholly identical the two principal registers of the debate – the being only acquires his identity through the power of appearances, the political style has its equivalent in the domain of dress – since they both responded to the organisation of language. A return to a 'natural costume', where 'the sign says everything before one speaks', where the recipient of the message discovered the code for himself, was the wish of all those who denounced masks: it would permit a society without representation, reconcile the individual and the social, appearances and politics. In due course, the Revolution would live out this dream of the uniform of liberty, in which transparency and difference would be combined.[17]

---

[14] Markovits, *L'Ordre des échanges*, pp. 19–20.
[15] Ibid., pp. 41–3, 67–95.
[16] As, for example, in the *Supplément au Voyage de Bougainville*.
[17] Ozouf, *Fête révolutionnaire* (Paris, 1976); M. Vovelle, *Les Métamorphoses de la fête en Provence de 1750 à 1820* (Paris, 1976). The subject of clothes for and in the festival deserves to be examined for the period as a whole, since it is a chief point of articulation of the clothing culture in traditional and new society.

The century was also influenced by its liberation from the dominion of need. It saw the introduction of metaphor, and luxury expenditure far in excess of what was necessary, 'exchange took place in words as in other goods, their mutual import gradually winning, extending from the individual to the nation and even in the long run from people to people'.[18] All else being equal, the analysis of président de Brosses applies to the clothing system, where luxury and fashion wielded their power and their language erupted, contributing to the confusion of codes, the erosion of significance and the difficulty of defining distinction. That their effects were so much disputed shows that they were at the centre of the debate in its economic dimension as well as its moral profundity.

Two logics were active here from the beginning: that of the Christian economy and the appearances which conformed to status; that of the new economy which made economic development and the political hierarchy of urban life coincide, where appearances were ruled by the laws of consumption and confusion.[19] Cantillon and Boisguilbert, each in his own way, established this liaison, where the economic and the social were driven by the stimulus of demand.[20] The clothing transformation, the commercialisation of fashion and the linen revolution helped to place the collective sensibilities far from the horizons of Christian asceticism, on the side of earthly happiness.

CONDILLAC AND CLOTHES

Theoretician of perception, economist of language and linguist of the economy, Condillac developed this argument, bequeathing us a vision which was unified but in accord with the aporetic developments of the philosopher's thought.

His premises are revealed in his *Essai sur l'origine des connaissances*: 'All our needs are interconnected and perception can be seen as a series of fundamental ideas to which we relate everything

---

[18] *Traité de la formation mécanique des langues*, 2 vols. (Paris, 1765), vol. I, pp. 53–65.

[19] Lepetit, *Armature urbaine*, vol. I, pp. 163–75.

[20] A Sauvy, 'La Stimulation de la demande de Law à Mirabeau', in *Religion, société, politique, mélanges en hommage à Jacques Ellul* (Paris, 1983), pp. 655–65.

which forms part of our knowledge.' And, in particular: 'To a need is linked the idea of the thing to satisfy it.'[21] Once the powers of perception and of imagination were established, the metaphors of clothing consumption could dominate the code of social relations. Among the Ancients, gestures communicated thought, among the Moderns, clothes informed. Their history could be read like that of the writing whose ornaments were universally understood: the abstract and the sensible were closely interconnected, and the natural and the artificial indivisible.

In the economic order, utility would be the essence of the social and the basic of value. Natural needs and artificial needs would then distinguish the degrees of civilisation. 'There will even come a time when artificial needs, by dint of diverging from nature, will eventually change it completely and corrupt it.'[22] In economic development, Condillac put clothing at the centre of a system of material culture based on needs: 'When a society begins to enjoy things of secondary necessity, and allows choice in its food, its clothing, its lodging and its weapons, it has more needs, and more wealth.'[23] Tailors take their place as a constituent element in an open social classification, organised into four classes symbolic of the satisfaction of primordial needs: tillers of the soil, architects, armourers and tailors; the circulation of wealth begins by increased consumption, the arts crown the edifice which is based on urban wealth. In the isolated and stationary state, needs equal means, the imagination is limited, 'everyone will wear clothes according to their estate'.[24] In the developed and urbanised state, the order of exchange is established, and with it the dynamic of clothing consumption.

Luxury is blameworthy because it corresponds to the excess which ought universally to be recognised as such and threatens the equilibrium: 'Linen is no longer a luxury ... and silk began to be less of a luxury when it began to be a product of our clime: and it will be less so, in proportion as it becomes more common.'[25] Though it was necessary to distinguish the magnificence, the com-

[21] *Oeuvres complètes*, 18 vols. (Paris, 1821–2), vol. III, pp. 49–50.
[22] Ibid., vol. IV, *Le Commerce et le gouvernement considérés relativement l'un à l'autre*, pp. 6–7.
[23] *Oeuvres complètes*, vol. IV, pp. 31–50, especially p. 48.
[24] Ibid., vol. IV, pp. 264–72.
[25] Ibid., vol. IV, pp. 208–9.

fort and the frivolity of luxury, their consequences still threaten any equilibrium: 'It is only too true that the luxury of a great capital is a principle of misery and devastation.'[26] The logics of the consumer economy, which were articulated on the concentration of labour, power and consumer goods, spending by the citizens and luxury, and the theatrical display of sartorial appearances, come into conflict with the political and moral necessities of the city: wealth is necessary, but not the rich.

## FASHION IN FASHION

The debate about fashion was thus one of the major themes of Enlightenment thinking and its heritage. It is far from futile, and we have seen how, at every step, we come back to it in one form or another. No-one escaped its influence.

In town and village alike, its invigorating influence was felt in trifles and in essentials. Pictures and print, the patter of the peddlar and the humble contents of his pack, with the assistance of credit, made it possible for rural society at least to begin to change, if not to become as passionately engaged as the urban elites: fashion was probably an effective instrument of standardisation, like language, in the sense not so much of the adoption of Parisian extravagances in the depths of the countryside but the general acceptance in the bodily and sartorial sphere of a reference to a central point, situated elsewhere, which radiated with the full power of the imagination. The role of those groups obliged by their position in society to set the tone – parish notables, farmers' wives, rich marriageable girls, women of the lesser nobility and their servants – should be studied in this light, their cohesion only able to operate through their singularity.

In the towns, and for the producers and the intermediaries, the century of the Enlightenment saw the widespread internalisation of these new attitudes; the fashion press offered its small world of women readers a materialisation of their attractions, which still fascinates today. Women, on whom depended the education of future generations, learned to master this language between words and things. This wide diffusion, or at least the threat of it, explains why fashion, its moral power apparent to all, was criticised and

[26] Ibid., vol. IV, pp. 350–87.

condemned by the most diverse philosophies. The superfluity of fashion in relation to need, its fickleness, its caprice and above all the link it established between personal vanity, consumption and the prestige of appearances, united critics on all sides. As in the baroque age, but on a larger scale thanks to the transformation of manners, clothing was at the heart of a debate about the meaning of civilisation. Christian economists, mercantilists, liberalists, physiocrats, Rousseauists, preachers and *philosophes* were all agreed, if not without qualification or contradiction, on the analysis and the remedy, though they disagreed over essentials. Moral apologists for fashion were rare, perhaps because it questioned the very notion of progress by its patent circularity, just as it questioned the notion of tradition in the name of an evolution with no other purpose than itself, ephemeral princess of unreality. It was perhaps still within the economic and moral theme of luxury that fashion, like its economy, was drawn by the fashion of the economy.

## THE HOLISM AND INDIVIDUALISM OF FASHION

Can we, then, think fashion? The men of the Enlightenment tried to do so, by treating it as a sort of *enfant terrible* of the triumphant arts and the frivolous mistress of a progress disseminated for the happiness of all by the new culture of manners. They had perceived the elements of a dispute which is still with us, inasmuch as fashion was effectively the result of a double historical movement, accelerated in western civilisation, which is not to say that the others have altogether escaped, as Georg Simmel and Leroi-Gourhan confirm.[27]

Fashion perfectly incarnated the social mechanisms of the display of court society.[28] It was an instrument in the distinctive hierarchisation of groups: it announced differences in status and value, even class positions; its visualisation of practices indicated distance from

---

[27] G. Simmel, *La Tragédie de la culture, et autres essais* (Paris, 1988), pp. 94–8; A. Leroi-Gourhan, *Milieu et technique* (Paris, 1975), pp. 198–241.

[28] The very interesting work of Norbert Elias needs to be revised on the basis of further archival study. See P. Merlin, 'Il Tema della Corte nella storiografia italiana ed europa', *Studi Storici* (1986), pp. 203–42, also the forthcoming thesis of Marcello Fantoni comparing court and town in Florence, Padua, Milan and Turin in the sixteenth and seventeenth centuries.

the centre of worldly decisions, which was also that of political power. The king, even more the queen, animated the court by their choice of fashion, and were copied by the town. This is perhaps why the fulminations of the church were in vain; the abbé Pluquet[29] echoed Bossuet and Fénelon, encouraged by archbishop Christophe de Beaumont after he had unsuccessfully condemned Helvetius and Rousseau in a famous mandate of 1770. Fashion, royal teacher of 'distinction',[30] established the triumph of the 'exchange value of the sign' in the kingdom of consumption.

The rule of fashion was based on other forces which emphasised the logics of individuality, and the power of the new in the combination of the fantasy of costume, the inflated concern for and personalising of appearances and the dynamism of change.[31] Fashion was stimulated by class competition, but also sustained by the social ratification of individualism. Between the seventeenth and the end of the eighteenth centuries, it materialised these two trends – singularising and standardising, privatising and collective. By these decisions it gave form to clothes and manners, and we need to ask how; if novelty proceeds more quickly than popularisation, the need for change can prevail over the imitative confrontation of classes.

The accusations of the Christian economists derived from their awareness of the destructive forces which fashion, frivolous teacher of liberty and equality, introduced into the unequal society. The *philosophes* attacked it in the name of an earthly morality, a utilitarianism in which the values of transparency were indispensable. Fashion vulgarised the message, the means of communication impoverished communication, the economic excesses threatened the equilibrium to be achieved before progress could be made.

---

[29] *Traité philosophique et politique sur le luxe*, 2 vols. (Paris, 1786); see also abbé Gauthier, *Traité contre l'amour des parures et le luxe des habits*, by the author of the *Traité contre les danses et les mauvaises chansons* (Paris, 1780).

[30] J. Baudrillard, *La Société de consommation* (Paris, 1970), pp. 170–5; *Pour une critique de l'économie politique du signe* (Paris, 1972); Bourdieu, *La Distinction*, pp. 255–60; G. de Tarde, *Les Lois de l'imitation* (Paris, 1890), pp. 265–7.

[31] G. de Lipovetski questions the existence of fashion in 'savage' and ancient societies, placing its emergence in the thirteenth and fourteenth centuries in the West; he connects fashion to Christianity and egalitarianism and denies the determining influence of class divisions (*L'Empire de l'éphémère, la mode et son destin dans les sociétés modernes* (Paris, 1987), pp. 29–79, 51–107, 188–214); see also P. Yonnet, *Jeux, modes et masses* (Paris, 1987).

518     *Conclusion*

Fashion as daughter of luxury was a major theme in economic thought.

It is significant that Adam Smith pays it little attention in *The Wealth of Nations* (1776) and that, to find it, we need rather to turn to his *Theory of Moral Sentiments* (1759). Another model of society and economy makes no reference to the old debates of moral economy: bourgeois and liberal man has no problems with luxury and fashion. But it is also interesting to see that Karl Marx, in Book I of *Capital*, resorts to a clothing metaphor to decipher the hieroglyph of value and analyse the importance of qualitative appearances in its constitution.[32] The exchange of glances between the man who sells his linen and the man who wants to get rid of his coat are economic fable,[33] but by serving to demonstrate the fetishism of the commodity, it throws light on the role of fashion, luxury and the textile culture in the mercantile relation and the organisation of the world. The dialectic of use and exchange, the link and the opposition between the concrete and the abstract, the role of need and of desire which, in the culture of appearances, in turn take strength and life are all there: 'The linen expresses its value in the coat; the coat serves as the material in which that value is expressed.' Let us not forget this illustration of the coherence of the material, the power of textiles to initiate and mobilise and their ability to distinguish.

Between these interpretations, it is better not to choose, not out of the desire for theoretical eclecticism but because to give priority to one or the other would prevent our measuring the changes in knowledge and practices. The questions posed in the eighteenth century can remain today unanswered; they still orient our social choices. Did fashion in the age of Enlightenment change its role? Did it, having cemented the theatrical appearances of the holist society, and been one of the visible manifestations of the coherence of the old world, serve to undermine its bases in order to proclaim the rule of individualism and the triumph of the private? Did it, from the beginning and in its social specificity, by its nature, unite the instinct for equalisation within the distinctive hierarchies and that for the individualisation of persons, the appeal of egalitarian imitation?

[32] K. Marx, *Capital* (Penguin Books, 1976), p. 139.
[33] B. Guibert, *L'Ordre marchand, réflexions sur les structures élémentaires de la vénalité* (Paris, 1986), pp. 29–36.

The reality of knowledge and the representation of practices do not provide a simple answer, but rather invite us to question the texts and the images differently, to discover how expressive conflicts can smooth and modify the relations between the collective and the individual. When the individualism of manners coincides with new social spaces regulated by the public use of reason, another art of living has commenced its trajectory. The triumph of the culture of appearances then rediscovers the virtues of the monads of Leibniz: it unites the whole and the part.[34]

Paris, Florence, Paris, 1984–9

---

[34] L. Dumont, *Essais sur l'individualisme, une perspective anthropologique sur l'idéologie moderne* (Paris, 1983), pp. 80–114; see also *Homo aequalis*, Vol. I (Paris, 1977).

# Index

# Past and Present Publications

General Editor: PAUL SLACK, *Exeter College, Oxford*

* Published also in paperback

† Co-Published with the Maison des Sciences de L'Homme, Paris